Certified Ethical Hacker (CEH) v12 312-50 Exam Guide

Keep up to date with ethical hacking trends and hone your skills with hands-on activities

Dale Meredith

BIRMINGHAM—MUMBAI

Certified Ethical Hacker (CEH) v12 312-50 Exam Guide

Group Product Manager: Vijin Boricha
Publishing Product Manager: Meeta Rajani
Senior Editor: Athikho Sapuni Rishana
Content Development Editor: Sayali Pingale
Technical Editor: Nithik Cheruvakodan
Copy Editor: Safis Editing
Book Project Manager: Neil Dmello
Proofreader: Safis Editing
Indexer: Pratik Shirodkar
Production Designer: Prashant Ghare
Marketing Coordinator: Hemangi Lotlikar

First published: June 2022
Production reference: 2170123

Published by Packt Publishing Ltd.
Livery Place
35 Livery Street
Birmingham
B3 2PB, UK.

978-1-80181-309-9

www.packt.com

This book is dedicated to all my students over the years. Those who have sat in on one of my live classes, watched my courses on Pluralsight, or listened to me speak at conferences. Thank you for putting up with my jokes. I know some were rough, some were good, and some I need to retire. Thank you all for allowing me to be a part of your learning journey. If you learn something from this book, do me a favor and reach out to me on social media and let me know. Some of my best days are the ones that start with folks letting me know I did something to help them.

Foreword

Continually learning, evolving, and growing is a skill everyone should master. Being able to facilitate that growth and transfer that knowledge to others is an absolute gift. I have been an IT leader and author for over 20 years, having published over 40 courses on cybersecurity, networking, business continuity/disaster recovery, security leadership, and governance. I've always looked up to people who are great presenters and have the unique ability to transfer their knowledge effectively, break down complex topics into digestible chunks, and, most importantly, have fun in the process.

I have been very fortunate to personally know Dale Meredith for the better part of a decade, for he has that unique gift of teaching while making it fun. I call it *edutainment*, and every time I watch one of his courses or read an article he has published, I learn something. It could be a piece of technical detail I was not aware of (or had forgotten about) or something about the way he delivers material. Keeping a listener engaged while delivering training is no easy task, and in this Dale excels.

Cybersecurity is a vast and complex topic, with new threats emerging every day. The goalpost is constantly moving, and the need for certified, competent cybersecurity professionals gets bigger every day. Hundreds of thousands of cybersecurity jobs go unfilled globally each year as companies of all sizes and all industries face increased threats daily. It is no longer a matter of *if* a company will be targeted, but rather *when*. Being able to think like a hacker and solidify a company's defenses has never been more critical.

Dale has helped hundreds of thousands of people around the world to learn everything from hardware and networking to cybersecurity and ethical hacking. I am excited to see the impact this book will have on people's careers, and ultimately their lives. This book will provide the knowledge necessary to develop critical cybersecurity skills and will empower you to take action, all while having fun in the process.

– *Christopher Rees*

Enterprise IT Leader and Author

Contributors

About the author

Dale Meredith is an EC-Council Certified Ethical Hacker/Instructor and a Microsoft Certified Trainer. Dale has over 10 years of senior IT management experience and was a CTO for an ISP. Dale's skill as an IT trainer lies in clarifying complicated concepts and ensuring students understand the theories. Dale's teaching style is memorable and entertaining. His expertise has led to many opportunities, including teaching teams in Fortune 500 firms, universities globally, the Department of Homeland Security, and many US military branches. Along with authoring video courses, consulting, and classroom training, you can catch Dale on stage speaking at IT conferences around the world, helping teams keep their companies safe, relevant, and *breach*-aware.

To my wife, Alice Meredith, the strongest woman I've ever met (she has to be, to be married to me!). Thanks for supporting me in my love of technology and building me up when things got rough.

To my kids and grandkids, thanks for letting me be your Batman. "Everything's impossible until somebody does it" – Bruce Wayne

Thanks to the team at Packt (Neil, Sayali, and I'm sure countless others behind the scenes) for being patient with me. Thanks for giving me this opportunity.

Thanks also to Scott Merritt, the man who took so much off my plate to allow me to focus. Your work ethic and knowledge allowed my dream of being published to take place...Thank you, my friend.

About the reviewers

Vinod Babu Bollikonda is a cybersecurity speaker, trainer, and technopreneur with two decades of experience in information technology and cybersecurity. He is a certified trainer for CompTIA, Microsoft, EC-Council, and ISACA courses, and a research scholar (PhD) on a niche topic in cybersecurity. He has worked at iGATE and Franklin Templeton and delivered training across 14 countries on 35 customized course curricula in cybersecurity. Vinod has also delivered expert-level training in a number of niche areas, including embedded, IoT, automotive, and industrial control system security testing. He has served as a security consultant on cybercrimes related to the dark web and cryptocurrencies and is the cofounder of VSVS Technologies. Vinod's hobbies include undertaking research on extra-terrestrial sounds and experiments with **software-defined radio (SDR)**.

– Thanks would be a small word to my beautiful wife, Swapna, the cofounder of VSVS Technologies, who helped me throughout this journey.

Sai Praveen Kumar Jalasutram is a certified and experienced cybersecurity professional with expertise in security operations, incident response, threat intelligence, threat hunting, forensic investigations, malware analysis, and detection engineering. He has worked for various global organizations across multiple industries, including government, technology, and education as a security consultant expert for enhancing cyber threat detection. Sai is one of the key developers of the Certified Ethical Hacker (CEHv10) and **Certified Threat Intelligence Analyst (CTIA)** certifications for EC-Council. In addition, he has also authored articles for multiple cybersecurity magazines and has always endeavored to contribute to the cybersecurity community.

– I'd like to thank my family and friends who understand and support me in every aspect of my life. I would also like to thank my mother for her unconditional love and affection for me and for making me the person I am, and my bosses and peers for supporting me during my journey in cybersecurity. Finally, I would like to thank the cybersecurity community for everything they do to keep the world secure and a better place to live!

Table of Contents

2
Introduction to Reconnaissance

3
Reconnaissance – A Deeper Dive

4
Scanning Networks

5
Enumeration

8
Social Engineering

Section 2: A Plethora of Attack Vectors

9
Malware and Other Digital Attacks

10

Sniffing and Evading IDS, Firewalls, and Honeypots

11
Hacking Wireless Networks

12
Hacking Mobile Platforms

Section 3: Cloud, Apps, and IoT Attacks

13
Hacking Web Servers and Web Apps

14
Hacking IoT and OT

15
Cloud Computing

16
Using Cryptography

Preface

Ethical hacking is a special type of cybersecurity that aims to diagnose and find security flaws before malicious actors can. This guide will give you an overview of these threats as well as advice on how to prevent them, so you can start securing your network today!

As the use of and dependence on technology grows, so do the risks associated with it. While there are many challenges in maintaining a secure network environment, one of the biggest problems cyber attackers face is finding vulnerabilities to exploit. This is where ethical hacking comes in. Ethical hackers use the tools and techniques developed by malicious actors to find security weaknesses before they can be taken advantage of.

One of the most popular and well-known ethical hacking certifications is the **Certified Ethical Hacker (CEH)** credential offered by the **International Council of Electronic Commerce Consultants (EC-Council)**. To become a CEH, individuals must pass an exam that covers a range of ethical hacking topics, including reconnaissance, footprinting, scanning, and enumeration, gaining access to systems (including Trojans and viruses), stealing data, hiding tracks, and social engineering.

This guide will give you the preparation for the CEH 312-50 exam. We'll cover the topics listed on the exam blueprint, as well as additional resources you can use to study for the test. By the end of this guide, you should have a good understanding of what ethical hacking is and how to perform it effectively.

Let's get started!

Who this book is for

This guide is for anyone who wants to learn more about ethical hacking and how to protect their organization from cyber attacks. This could include security professionals, IT administrators, and anyone else who wants to learn more about the basics of ethical hacking and how to become a more effective cybersecurity professional.

What this book covers

Chapter 1, Understanding Ethical Hacking, covers the elements of InfoSec, the cyber kill chain methodology, different hacking concepts, types, and phrases, as well as the concepts of ethical hacking.

Chapter 2, Introduction to Reconnaissance, is all about reconnaissance. Everything has a starting point, and the starting point for attackers when they target an organization is through the process of reconnaissance/footprinting.

Chapter 3, Reconnaissance – a Deeper Dive, delves into reconnaissance in more depth. Now that you've got a basic understanding of the information we're trying to gather during the reconnaissance stage, let's dive deeper by looking at OSINT and at publicly available data such as social media services, job sites, and even going back in time to view previous versions of a company's web page.

Chapter 4, Scanning Networks, tells us that scanning the network is the process of discovering this type of information. In some cases, we can remain undiscovered, while other techniques might alert a security team.

Chapter 5, Enumeration, explores how enumeration can expose things such as usernames and groups on systems, routing tables, system names, and network shares.

Chapter 6, Vulnerability Analysis, demonstrates how vulnerability analysis is key in providing security to any company's infrastructure from external as well as internal threats.

Chapter 7, System Hacking, focuses on the tools and techniques that can be used by attackers to hack the systems identified in our first four steps. This is the ultimate goal of attackers, and it will show you just how vulnerable you might be.

Chapter 8, Social Engineering, describes an easier method that attackers are discovering and actively using to avoid steps 2 to 5. Humans. We are the weakest link. There is no defense against social engineering; only constant vigilance and training of employees can help to circumvent these techniques.

Chapter 9, Malware and Other Digital Attacks, describes some of the most common attack vectors that hackers will exploit, including malware, viruses, ransomware, and **denial-of-service (DoS)**.

Chapter 10, Sniffing and Evading IDS, Firewalls, and Honeypots, examines how sniffing can provide insights into the possibilities of different types of poisoning attacks taking place on a network. These types of attacks and information can help an attacker avoid honeypots and even get around firewalls and **intrusion detection systems (IDSs)**.

Chapter 11, Hacking Wireless Networks, explains how wireless networks present a completely new attack vector that can be challenging to secure. Attackers will go after these networks as many times, lower encryption technologies are often used as well as the vulnerabilities associated with devices and software that are involved.

Chapter 12, Hacking Mobile Platforms, talks about how mobile devices are quickly replacing desktops and laptops as they allow users to not only do the same productivity tasks, but also store critical information such as contact lists, calendars, and credentials. This chapter will show the threats to mobile platforms that attract attackers to these targets.

Chapter 13, Hacking Web Servers and Web Apps, covers how the growth of the internet and web technologies, combined with rapidly increasing internet connectivity, has led to the emergence of a new business landscape. The interconnectivity of services, plugins, operating systems, APIs, and web shells creates an environment ripe for misconfigurations and missed patches.

Chapter 14, Hacking IoT and OT, explains why organizations using IoT or OT devices as part of their network need to protect both the devices and the information from attackers. All security professionals need to understand the landscape of cyber threats, industrial infrastructure, and business.

Chapter 15, Cloud Computing, examines how the push to cloud-based computing has been fast and advantageous for organizations; however, just like any technology, cloud environments also pose several threats and risks. Attackers are targeting vulnerabilities in the cloud software to gain unauthorized access to networks

Chapter 16, Using Cryptography, describes how cryptography and **cryptographic (crypto)** systems help in securing data from being compromised during online transmissions, but they are not unhackable. Careful deployment and maintaining a healthy environment will help keeps attackers out.

Chapter 17, CEH Exam Practice Questions, lets you see what you have learned!

To get the most out of this book

You should have an understanding of basic network functions and technologies. TCP/IP and the OSI model are key concepts. You should also be familiar with firewall types and functions and have a basic understanding of web servers, web applications, and the security vulnerabilities they present. Familiarity with cryptography basics should also be established before attempting the CEH exam.

OS requirements
Windows, Kali Linux, macOS, and Android

The only software you might want to consider would be some type of virtualization solution such as VMware, VirtualBox, or Hyper-V to create a network to practice some of the techniques discussed, but it's not required.

Download the color images

We also provide a PDF file that has color images of the screenshots/diagrams used in this book. You can download it here: `https://static.packt-cdn.com/downloads/9781801813099_ColorImages.pdf`.

Conventions used

There are a number of text conventions used throughout this book.

`Code in text`: Indicates code words in text, database table names, folder names, filenames, file extensions, pathnames, dummy URLs, user input, and Twitter handles. Here is an example: "An attacker could exploit the application with the `setuid` or `setgid` flags to execute malicious code with elevated privileges."

Bold: Indicates a new term, an important word, or words that you see on screen. For example, words in menus or dialog boxes appear in the text like this. Here is an example: "Under the **Research** category, you can go to **Threat Analysis** and see what's currently going on in that area."

> **Tips or Important Notes**
> Appear like this.

Get in touch

Feedback from our readers is always welcome.

General feedback: If you have questions about any aspect of this book, mention the book title in the subject of your message and email us at `customercare@packtpub.com`.

Errata: Although we have taken every care to ensure the accuracy of our content, mistakes do happen. If you have found a mistake in this book, we would be grateful if you would report this to us. Please visit `www.packtpub.com/support/errata`, selecting your book, clicking on the Errata Submission Form link, and entering the details.

Piracy: If you come across any illegal copies of our works in any form on the internet, we would be grateful if you would provide us with the location address or website name. Please contact us at `copyright@packt.com` with a link to the material.

If you are interested in becoming an author: If there is a topic that you have expertise in and you are interested in either writing or contributing to a book, please visit `authors.packtpub.com`.

Share Your Thoughts

Once you've read *Certified Ethical Hacker (CEH) v12 312-50 Exam Guide*, we'd love to hear your thoughts! Scan the QR code below to go straight to the Amazon review page for this book and share your feedback.

`https://packt.link/r/1801813094`

Your review is important to us and the tech community and will help us make sure we're delivering excellent quality content.

Section 1:
Where Every
Hacker Starts

In this section, you will get insights into the different elements of InfoSec as well as an understanding of ethical hacking terms and concepts.

This part of the book comprises the following chapters:

- *Chapter 1, Understanding Ethical Hacking*
- *Chapter 2, Introduction to Reconnaissance*
- *Chapter 3, Reconnaissance – a Deeper Dive*
- *Chapter 4, Scanning Networks*
- *Chapter 5, Enumeration*
- *Chapter 6, Vulnerability Analysis*
- *Chapter 7, System Hacking*
- *Chapter 8, Social Engineering*

1
Understanding Ethical Hacking

The **Certified Ethical Hacker (CEH)** certification exam is neither easy nor designed to be easy. If it was not hard, everyone would do it – its difficulty is what makes it great. Ethical hackers are the essential workers of the IT, cybersecurity, and software development world, and the CEH certification is one of their baseline requirements. This guide covers the basics of ethical hacking. It's useful to CEH exam candidates and people who are concerned about the vulnerabilities in their environments.

This comprehensive overview will help you to do the following:

- Cover the basics of the CEH certification.
- Gain a strong and practical understanding of ethical hacking.
- Know the requirements and the skills you need to become a CEH.
- Evaluate yourself against ethical hacking standards.
- Decide whether the CEH certification is right for you.

This chapter will meet these goals through the following topics:

- The benefits of the CEH certification
- Information security

- The Cyber Kill Chain
- The behavioral identification of attackers
- Information security controls
- Information security laws and standards

The benefits of the CEH certification

The US **Department of Defense (DoD)** issued the directive *8570.1* in 2005 instructing everybody that handles US government IT to have baseline IT certifications, including ethical hacking. This is one of the most important reasons cybersecurity professionals pursue the CEH certification.

Besides being an industry standard, the CEH certification is internationally recognized, making it valid and valuable in IT industries across the world.

It is also a valuable certification on any IT résumé. It means a candidate understands how hackers think, and with everything that's been going on recently as far as hacking and technology are concerned, IT experts with this certification are, and will remain, in high demand.

Is the CEH certification right for you?

You will get the most out of this certification if you are a cybersecurity officer within your company or if you are a penetration tester, internal or external auditor, security professional-standard administrator or consultant site administrator, or a techie home user who wants to know how secure your environment is.

The requirements and the skills you need to become a CEH

There are standards to maintain as a CEH. This includes skills, values, and ethics from the International Council of E-Commerce Consultants (EC-Council) Code of Ethics, which you can find at `https://www.eccouncil.org/code-of-ethics`. The most critical of these requirements include the following:

- Privacy
- Disclosure
- Area of expertise
- Unauthorized usage

- Authorization
- Disclosure
- Project management
- Knowledge sharing
- Confidence
- Legal limits
- Underground communities

Let's look at them in detail.

Privacy

Ethical hackers come across information they are not allowed to use, steal, share, modify, change, or destroy. From security numbers to customer databases and intellectual property, their access is unlimited. It is their responsibility to guard that information at all times.

Disclosure

It is not uncommon for ethical hackers to uncover things that are uncomfortable to see, watch, or talk about. If they stumble upon such information or content, their duty is to report it. They owe it to the authorities or the concerned people to disclose everything they discover, however unsettling, gross, grave, or discomforting.

Area of expertise

An ethical hacker should not misrepresent themselves, feigning to know more than they do. Ethical hacking demands honesty about what an ethical hacker can and cannot do and openness about their level of knowledge, skill sets, and limitations. If you lack the necessary experience or training to handle something that's outside your realm, it is ethical to ask the company or employer to get an expert to handle it.

Unauthorized usage

An ethical hacker is to avoid using illegal or unethically obtained software and hardware. Also, if they uncover evidence of unauthorized usage in a company, they should not accept bribes to keep their lips sealed or join in for personal gain.

Authorization

An ethical hacker needs to limit themselves to using resources, data, and/or information in authorized ways. Also, when working, an ethical hacker lets the company know how they intend to use data or information. They should also ensure that they get consent where necessary and avoid cutting corners.

Disclosure

When an ethical hacker discovers an issue in hardware or software, they verify with or notify the hardware manufacturer that their product is faulty before going public with information about the vulnerability. If the manufacturer does nothing about it, they blow the whistle to save users and share the solution if possible. Some folks would refer to this as a *zero-day* vulnerability, meaning that the vulnerability has been discovered before the vendor has any idea that it exists.

Project management

Ethical hackers need great management skills to be efficient and to manage their projects effectively. They need to set clear goals, have a reasonable project timeline, and communicate.

Knowledge sharing

Ethical hackers commit to learning, keeping abreast with new developments, sharing new discoveries, engaging fellow EC-Council members, and creating public awareness. They do this by teaching or giving free lectures, spreading information on social media platforms, and enlightening the people they know on securing hardware and software and how to use this knowledge.

Confidence

Confidence, as an ethical hacker, means you should always present yourself in a professional, honest, and competent manner. This means even when you're competing with someone else for a particular project. In layman's terms, no backstabbing, folks. Now, as we go through the chapters in this book, we're going to be introducing some tools that can be extremely dangerous to networks. As an ethical hacker, you need to make sure that you have experience with any software, tricks, or tools you utilize against a network. An engagement is not the time or place to learn a new tool or technique. You need to be extremely careful. Do not fix issues you discover that are not within the scope of your project. Even if you think you know what's best for your company or their company, you always get guidance and permission for any action. There is no compromise. What we mean by this is that you are in no way going to purposely compromise or cause a company or organization's system to become compromised through the process of your professional dealings with them.

Legal limits

Whatever project an ethical hacker accepts needs to be approved, authorized, and legal. The code of ethics informs all their decisions. They always know what they are doing and what's expected of them; they are aware of their limitations, know what they can and cannot do, and know what's considered fair play and what's malicious.

Underground communities

Ethical hackers commit to not engaging in black-hat activities or associating with communities of black-hat hackers. They don't aid or help black-hat hackers advance their mission; they only engage them to find out what's new, what they know, what they do, and how they think.

Ethical hacking

Ethical hacking is a proactive cybersecurity approach that involves the use of hacking methods, concepts, and tools to uncover weaknesses in a system before a potential attacker exploits them.

An ethical hacker thinks like an attacker or a criminal profiler. They know how to steal passwords and usernames, and how to find and exploit vulnerabilities and get away with it. Ethical hackers use the same tactics that the bad guys use. The only difference is that they have permission to do it. Also, ethical hackers bring more to the table. Here are some of the most important skills, ideal behaviors, and principles ethical hackers use:

- **Expertise in architectures, programs, and networks** – You need to know the ins and outs of how **Transmission Control Protocol/Internet Protocol (TCP/IP)** works. You need to understand networking structures and functions. You don't necessarily need to be an expert in all programs, but you do need to know how programs are installed, the modifications they make, and the possible security threats they pose.

- **Proficiency in vulnerability research** – Ethical hackers need to keep up with the bad guys. So, find out as much as you can about new vulnerabilities. Additionally, ensure that you are good at the hacking techniques that attackers use because you might need to try them out on a particular target.

- **A good understanding of the hacking techniques attackers use** – Ethical hackers are not vendor-specific; they understand the techniques attackers use across the board – the hacks that can be used against routers, **Intrusion Detection Systems (IDSes)**, and so on.

- **Follow the code of conduct** – Ethical hackers adhere to a strict code of conduct as required by the EC-Council.

- **Disclose to the appropriate people** – Ethical hackers owe it to their employers and clients to disclose what they ought to. They have a duty to disclose to authorities what they uncover if it is illegal. Ethical hackers also come across vulnerabilities in their clients' systems or infrastructures when evaluating them. The code bars them from exposing such information. They know what is off limits.

- **They are good at the tactics and strategies attackers use** – They know the tactics and the strategies. They don't just make stuff up or take shortcuts.

- **They understand no means no** – If a client or employer gives specific guidelines of what's allowed and what's not, an ethical hacker will draw a line between the two and respect that decision. They will not try to cross it, and if there is a change of scope, they ensure it is done in writing.

- **They never target a system or network they don't own or are not allowed into** – It's not a skill per se, but if during the test a good ethical hacker is told to *stop*, they do so. Failure to do so has turned the lives of some ethical hackers upside down.

- **They note and report results** – They report *all* results, even if it might hurt someone whose good books they want to be in, such as the manager who recommended them for that penetration testing job.

- **They report their findings to legal authorities** – They know they have a duty to report illegal activities or plans to the authorities and, as such, they ensure that the contract allows that. However, some jurisdictions place a legal responsibility on ethical hackers, even if the contract forbids such disclosures. Failure to report to legal authorities makes the ethical hacker an accessory to the crime. There are other ways out of such situations, including laws such as the Whistleblower Protection Act, which safeguards ethical hackers in specific types of disclosures.

- **Confidentiality** – When an ethical hacker encounters information that is deemed confidential, they know who to share their findings with, unless it goes against the laws of the land.

Honing important skills, embracing the principles of ethical hacking, and knowing the ways of attackers are key. I wrote this chapter to give you the information you need to pass your CEH exam and know what you need to navigate the cybersecurity world. We've also covered different types of attacks and how attackers exploit vulnerabilities. Our next step is information security controls – our weapon against attackers.

What is information security?

For a proper foundation in information security, this section covers the following topics:

- Information security – a general overview
- The **Confidentiality, Integrity, and Availability (CIA)** triad
- Types of cyberattacks
- The hacking phases
- The types of hackers

You'll be able to broadly define information security, as well as understanding the CIA triad, knowing various types of cyberattacks and the stages of hacking, understanding the types of attackers and their motivations, and knowing the steps of the **Cyber Kill Chain (CKC)** methodology.

An overview of information security

Information security is the process of securing data and information systems that process, store, and transmit data against illegal access. Organizations must protect their information, as it is a key asset.

Behind most breaches, attackers have motivations and objectives. A motive arises from the belief that a target has something important. The goal of the attack could be to interrupt the target organization's day-to-day activities, or to steal important information for fun, or even payback. As a result, the attacker's goals are determined by their emotional state. Once the hacker/attacker has defined their objective, they might use a variety of tools, strategies, and methodologies to take advantage of flaws in a system.

Information security is part of information risk management. It refers to the processes and measures designed to protect and maintain the **confidentiality**, **integrity**, and **availability** of information. This goal of information security is commonly known as the CIA triad; these three components guard against **cyberattacks** that lead to unauthorized or unlawful access, use, sharing, modification, scanning, stealing, and/or destruction of information.

The CIA triad

The CIA triad is a security model that informs the policies and efforts an organization puts in place to secure its data from unauthorized access. Let's look at its components in detail.

Confidentiality

Confidentiality is guarding against theft or unauthorized or unintentional access of data. The first step toward achieving this is **authenticity**, which is the verification process that requires the user to prove their identity or their claim to the rightful ownership of an account before access is allowed. Big companies whose databases attackers have compromised are increasingly hitting the headlines. Attackers target them for highly prized customer information. Attackers also go after governments for military, political, criminal, and other similar reasons.

An example of the damage a breach of confidentiality can cause happened in Utah. A hospital backed up their records and sent them through a courier service. The driver changed his mind along the way and headed home for the weekend, instead of dropping the tapes off at the Granite Mountain Records Vault (a vault system that is dug out of a granite mountain in Utah). Someone with itchy fingers saw the well-wrapped package and broke into the car. In an instant, the aluminum metal case bearing patients' vital medical records and confidential information was gone.

The hospital ended up spending thousands of dollars seeking identity protection services for patients whose personal and vital information landed in the wrong hands. Besides this kind of loss of data, there's the risk of data modification without authorization and accountability, which is known as non-repudiation. If John Doe modifies a document under a secure system, there needs to be a way to tell whether or when that happened.

Integrity

After you have proved your authenticity, you expect to find your data safe, not altered. You want to be sure you can trust the source and the keeper of this data. For example, when trying to access your bank account, you want to be certain you are accessing your account on your bank's app or site and that the data you will find on there is valid and protected.

Availability

People have a right to access their data whenever they want, but sometimes attackers stand in the way of this by launching a **Denial-of-Service** (**DoS**) attack. DoS refuses users access to accounts or resources. How does this benefit attackers? This is a common malicious attack against businesses. It stops users from transacting or accessing a service or resource. This denial of availability costs companies millions of dollars and, sometimes, users.

Types of cyberattacks

Cyberattacks happen when attackers – people with different goals and motivations – spot and take advantage of vulnerabilities in a system. They do this to gain access to a network or to get valuable or confidential data without authorization.

Attackers violate systems or processes to disrupt operations, steal crucial or confidential information, or seek retribution. They can cause chaos within an organization, instill fear, create financial losses, and ruin the reputation of an organization or business by publicizing their political stands, propaganda, religious beliefs, and so on, using the target's mediums of communication.

Cyberattacks fall under different categories. These include the following:

- Passive attacks
- Active attacks
- Close-in attacks
- Insider attacks

- Distribution attacks
- Phishing attacks

Let's look at these in detail.

Passive attacks

A passive attack is also known as a sniffing attack or an eavesdropping attack. Attackers monitor traffic and then intercept data before it reaches recipients.

Active attacks

Unlike passive attacks, active attacks are disruptive. Active attackers are usually out to exploit a vulnerability and cause harm. Most systems detect them. An active attacker will try to disrupt the communication or services between systems, throw things into disarray or cause hiccups within the network's security, and attempt to gain access. Some tricks include a DoS attack, a man-in-the-middle attack, session hijacking, and SQL injection.

Close-in attacks

In close-in attacks, the attacker is usually physically close to the target or the network. Their motive is to gather, change, or disrupt flowing information. Examples of close-in attacks are eavesdropping, shoulder surfing, and dumpster diving. Social engineering also falls under this category. An attacker deceives the target into sharing personal or confidential information and then uses it fraudulently.

Insider attacks

As the name suggests, insider attacks come from the inside. Attackers use their privilege and access to violate policies from within to compromise information systems. They do this by stealing physical devices, planting malware, backdoors, or keyloggers.

Distribution attacks

In these attacks, the attacker will either tamper with or modify hardware or software before installation. The attack begins soon after installation. To accomplish this, an attacker tampers with the hardware or software at its source or during transmission. A perfect example of a distribution attack is SolarWinds' attack in 2020. After accessing and adding malicious code to SolarWinds' software systems, attackers produced and sent Trojanized updates to the software program users. Victims of this attack included 425 Fortune 100 and 500 companies, including titans such as Cisco, Intel, and Microsoft, leading telecommunication companies, top US government agencies – including the Department of State, the Department of Homeland Security, and the Department of Energy – and reputable learning institutions.

Phishing attack

A phishing attack is also a popular form of cyberattacking. Cyberattackers use a trick, where they create a fake website that looks exactly like the original one. Once the cyberattackers are done with the development of the fake website, they send an email to the customers with the link to the fake website. When the customers try to log in using the username and password, the cyberattackers record it, and they use the same information on the real website to access the customer's account.

The technology triangle

The technology triangle, like the Bermuda Triangle, is mysterious, just not as big. It is a pain in the neck for everyone involved with technology – hardware developers, the coffee-loving IT person, and that software developer who sits in the corner looking at their screen all day.

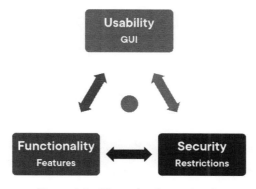

Figure 1.1 – The technology triangle

One concept that makes their heads hurt is usability (the GUI environment) versus functionality (the features) versus security (the restrictions), as seen in *Figure 1.1*.

Usually, the dilemma is striking a good balance between these. It's hard because sometimes moving from usability means losing security and functionality, while inclining toward security makes you lose functionality and usability.

Finding this balance is tricky, and that's why some operating systems lean more toward one area. An example is the Windows 2000 server when the internet was brand new and everybody wanted a piece of it. Trying to be nice, Microsoft set up servers for their users and whenever a user deployed the operating system, it would automatically install the **Internet Information Services (IIS)**, which is a web server environment. This web server environment had every feature turned on and had more holes than Swiss cheese. While it was helpful to users who were not tech-savvy, Microsoft compromised on security.

Microsoft then introduced Windows Vista with the annoying UAC popup that's always asking whether you are sure you want to do something. Do you want to allow this app to make changes to your device? Do you want to allow this app from an unknown publisher to make changes to your device?

Typing in a username and password irks most users, so, while Microsoft moved a bit toward security, they lost usability and functionality.

Microsoft is a perfect example of this dilemma. Their user-friendly interface has in many situations actually created vulnerabilities for their platform. Reports show a 181% increase in the number of reported vulnerabilities between 2016 and 2020.

Most people are always wondering why they have to jump through IT hoops to use software or hardware. They want a plug-and-play IT world where all they need to do is head to the local technical store, grab what they need, plug it in, push a few buttons, and voilà! It's ready. Some companies understand this need and strive to make their products as easy to use as possible. While it is easy to achieve usability, most easy-to-use hardware and software is vulnerable to attacks.

Types of hackers

Hacking is gaining unauthorized access to information or data in a computer or system, or configuring a different mechanism that makes a device or the target of the hack operate differently to how it was intended.

There are different types of hackers and they are differentiated by the activities they carry out and their motives.

Black-hat hackers

A black-hat hacker carries out the type of attacks where they don't have permission or authorization to be on the target network or to be doing what they're doing. They're lawbreakers.

White-hat hackers

Unlike black-hat hackers, white-hat hackers are authorized to be on a system and to be doing what they are doing. They are the good guys. They don't use or misuse the information they have access to as professional security – they only share exploits about the bad guys with the white-hat community for the good of everyone.

> **Important Note**
>
> The hat color terms come from Hollywood. Back in the early days of film, the bad guy was identifiable from the black hat that he wore, while the hero would wear a white hat. This actually continues today in film, as I'm sure we've all seen a villain dressed in black while the hero is dressed in white (you know, a long time ago in a galaxy far, far away…).

Gray-hat hackers

Gray-hat hackers are reformed black-hat hackers. However, it's still hard to trust them because they can always relapse in a moment of weakness. They can be white-hat today, but if they get a deal that's too good to turn down, their ethical hacking principles may go out the window and they will name their price.

Suicide hackers

As the name suggests, a suicide hacker is carefree. They don't bother to cover their tracks after an attack. Their mission is the only thing that matters.

Script kiddies

Script kiddies are as clueless as they come. They are ambitious but lack real training and experience. They rely on YouTube videos and other free online resources and tools to hack and perform unauthorized activities. Most script kiddies work inside our network infrastructures.

Spy hackers, cyberterrorists, and state-sponsored hackers

These are high-profile, malicious hackers. They do the dirty work for governments, government agencies, organized groups, and big corporations fighting for the lion's share in the market. They are mostly driven by religious beliefs, political affiliation or agenda, business opportunity, and so on. Like suicide hackers, they stop at nothing. They focus on executing their mission; everything else, including repercussions, is secondary.

The difference between a spy hacker and a state-sponsored hacker is that a spy hacker gets their paycheck from a rival business to steal intellectual property, while the state-sponsored hacker gets paid by a government or government agency. State-sponsored hacking makes it possible for states to get hold of secrets from other countries, military organizations, and multinational companies or organizations.

Hacktivist

A hacktivist is an attacker who gains unauthorized access to a network or files to further economic ideologies or political or social agenda.

Hacktivists' motivations vary, from vandalism to protest, humiliating and/or calling out an individual, a group, a company, or a government. Their attacks often include defacing or disabling their target's website.

Other major targets of hacktivism are big corporations, such as Apple and Microsoft, and the big pharmaceutical industry. Tons of vegan animal rights activists and eco-activists also use hackers to push their beliefs or to go after certain companies.

Hacking phases

What comes to your mind when someone talks about the most secure system? Most people think of Linux and other operating systems. But attackers can attack or hack these technologies because they all have loopholes and vulnerabilities.

A *friend* (I cannot confirm whether I was involved with this or not) who was involved with a penetration test at a bank showed up at the branch with a new blade server and announced that he was running late, and needed to install a new server to make things work faster.

He feigned it was very heavy to make them hurry up. To his surprise, they did and let him in the server room unaccompanied. He rummaged through a shelf of tape backups and put some in his bag. He also grabbed a couple of hard drives that had important data and then deployed the server through a backdoor.

As a security professional, you need to anticipate any form of attack and avert it. If there is no digital hack, look out for a physical one or a social engineering hack. Your job is to discourage, deter, misdirect, and slow attackers in every way possible.

Hackers have time on their hands and are always looking for any opportunity or vulnerability to gain access to your system or information.

Having a good grasp on how hackers think helps security professionals look in the right places. This is especially important because attackers don't carry out their mission in one go. It's a process with phases. With each step or phase, the attacker inches closer to the target's environment. Let's look at each of these phases a little closer.

Reconnaissance/footprinting

This is the first phase of hacking. It involves looking at a target and trying to figure out who they are and what they have to offer. It is the most time-consuming phase for attackers, but it comes with a big payoff. The attacker gathers as much information about your company as possible and then prepares the attack based on it.

There are two ways to do this:

- Passive reconnaissance
- Active reconnaissance

Passive reconnaissance

There is no direct interaction with the target in a passive reconnaissance, so the target does not know that an attacker is looking at them. Passive reconnaissance also involves researching a target on common and public platforms.

In a passive hack, the attacker goes through the company's web page like a typical visitor, except that he or she is there to gather information. For example, a hacker can head to a company's website to look at job openings. It's neither wrong nor illegal.

Social engineering is another passive reconnaissance technique. Usually, it exploits human psychology to gain access to systems, locations, data, and information. Attackers use social engineering to manipulate people to share personal or critical information about themselves that is useful in advancing the attack.

Marketers are masters of social engineering. They will set a table at your local grocery store or mall and offer you free samples – small tasty pieces of beef or a mouthwatering bite-sized burrito. You will not know what hit you – even if you don't buy whatever they are promoting, you will listen to what they have to say about their products, and that could be the whole point of their being at the store.

Attackers use the same technique to harvest information.

Active reconnaissance

In an active reconnaissance, the attacker has direct interaction with the target. The attacker will engage with the target's system, scan the network from an internal or external perspective, and also conduct a port scan, seeking open ports.

An example of an active reconnaissance technique is when an attacker pings the target's server. That's touching the target's server, right? It's a bold move. Attackers use active reconnaissance when they discover or have every reason to believe it is unlikely that their activities will be noticed.

Dumpster diving

Old credit cards, water bills, receipts, lost IDs, companies' internal memos, forms, financial statements, lists, and so on carry valuable information that can be used by attackers. Like detectives, attackers search through trashcans, dustbins, and the like, looking for items that will help them complete target profiles.

A classic example of dumpster diving happened in the '90s, when the Department of Justice was investigating Microsoft for their practices. The Oracle Corporation hired a detective agency that went dumpster diving on the Microsoft campus and came up with information that pointed to Microsoft having some under-the-table deals.

The New York Times reported, *"The Oracle Corporation acknowledged today that it had hired a prominent Washington detective firm to investigate groups sympathetic to its archrival, the Microsoft Corporation, an effort that yielded documents embarrassing to Microsoft in the midst of its antitrust battle with the government."*

Scanning

Scanning is the phase where an attacker tries to gather as much information as they can. They do this using active techniques such as ping sweeps and passive techniques such as passive scanning. An attacker sniffs the traffic and identifies the target's machines and operating systems, looking for a *way in*, or what we call an attack vector or attack surface.

Gaining access

An attacker can also map out systems, other hardware devices, attempt to detect where a target's firewalls are, where the routers are, find out whether they can discover the IP address scheme, and so on. It tells them which targets to stay clear of and the targets they need not waste time on. Security professionals counter these attacks by gaining as much knowledge as possible about the latest attack tools and the system vulnerabilities that attackers have figured out a new way to exploit.

The next thing you'll want to do is shield your system from tools such as a port scanner that looks for ports that may be opened up by services. To protect your system, ensure that services are not running on machines that they shouldn't be running on. Properly audit the systems.

Another useful tool is a vulnerability scanner, which attackers also use – except, of course, they use the pirated versions. This tool will tell you, *"Man, your default machines don't have the latest service pack installed for Windows 7 or Windows 8.1!"*. The thing with scanning is, if you're not scanning for vulnerabilities, somebody else who shouldn't be doing it will do it in an attempt to get into your network.

Maintaining access

After making their way in, attackers want to maintain access. An attacker can decide to pull the system out and use it as a launch pad for what they want to do with it. They can use the system to carry out attacks, and finish scanning out or footprinting the target's environment to install Wireshark to sniff the network and send results back to their location. They can also decide to install a Trojan that steals usernames and passwords, or scans for documents with certain number sequences.

Experienced attackers wind up hardening the target's machine. If they pwn (take control of) your machine completely, they want to make sure they maintain total control of it. They inject their own backdoors or Trojans, effectively clearing the vulnerabilities they exploited. It might stop other attackers but not them, because they will use a different mechanism next time.

The Term pwned

No, we did not misspell this word. It is slang spelling of the word "owned." It came from the game *Warcraft*, where a programmer misspelled "owned" within the game text. If you beat another player, the message was supposed to say, *"Dale has been owned,"* but instead we were given, *"Dale has been pwned."* It means that you've been dominated by another player or, in the world of hacking, I have total control of your system.

To stop this, install a honeypot or a honeynet (fake systems and fake networks). It will attract attackers, but they will only end up wasting their time and energy on the fake target. You will have distracted or slowed them down.

Clearing tracks

This is the fifth and the last stage of an attack. After getting into the system, getting or doing what they wanted, the next smart move is covering their tracks – leaving the place as neat and clean as they found it, or *better*.

Most attackers get rid of their own entries in the log files to ensure you don't suspect they were there, because they know if the first entry in a log file was deleted, the target or security professional will want to know who deleted the file.

After that, they install a rootkit to hide their tools. Alternatively, they use steganography and hide their secret data inside the target's MP3s, or even images, to avoid detection in the white space (the unused bits in a TCP header).

This is known as a cyber blind, as an analogy to a duck blind, which is used by hunters to hide where ducks frequent, waiting to lay an ambush.

The purpose/goal of cyberattacks

So, where do these cyberattackers come from? Generally, people call them hackers or cybercriminals, but we are going to call them attackers. There is a huge difference between a hacker and an attacker. Let me explain: if we talk about a hacker, it is simply someone who exploits a target to work outside its intended purpose. A great example of this is back when I purchased my first Xbox; I modified it so that I could put a bigger hard drive inside and store all my games on it. I never needed to grab a DVD! Or how about *rooting* your Android device? Typically, these actions are not illegal but rather modifying systems/targets to do something different.

On the other hand, an attacker is someone who has a different motive/goal/objective to gain unauthorized access to a target. Normally, they use the same techniques, but they are looking for different outcomes (mostly illegal ones). Attackers can be internal or external to an organization and a threat to known or unknown vulnerabilities in an IT infrastructure.

We can summarize their goals by highlighting most of the objectives that attackers have:

- To disrupt an organization or the operations of a business
- To grab/steal information that is either important or private

- To take an act of revenge after losing out to an organization
- To create a financial issue
- To hurt the reputation of an organization

The Cyber Kill Chain – understanding attackers and their methods

The **Cyber Kill Chain** (**CKC**) are steps that trace stages of an attack, right from reconnaissance through to exfiltration of data. There are several models for describing the general process of an attack on system security. This model was first developed by Lockheed Martin.

Phases of the CKC

Here are the phases of the CKC.

Reconnaissance

In the reconnaissance phase, attackers gather general knowledge about the system or network. It can be a passive or active attack.

Weaponization

The attacker is going to couple the payload code – which is going to enable access remotely – with exploit code that will exploit the software and/or the security flaw.

Delivery

Here, the attacker identifies a vector to transmit the weaponized code to the target environment. They can use a website, an email attachment, or a USB drive.

Exploitation

This step is the weaponization of the code. The malware gets triggered when the target clicks on the link in the malicious email or runs the code off of a USB drive they found lying in the parking lot.

Installation

This mechanism, also known as the backdoor, enables the weaponized code (malware) to run a remote access tool for the intruder and to achieve persistence on the target system.

Command and Control (CNC)

This is when the weaponized code gives the attacker access to the target's network or system. The weaponized code establishes an outbound channel to a remote server that can be used to control the remote access tool and possibly download more tools to expand the attack.

Actions and objectives

In this phase, the intruder uses the access they've achieved to collect information from the target system and begins to transfer it through the remote system. The intention could be data exfiltration, encryption for ransom, data destruction, and so on.

Tactics, techniques, and procedures

The term **Tactics, Techniques, and Procedures** (**TTPs**) relates to the activity and method patterns associated with specific threat actors or groups of threat actors. TTPs are useful for assessing threats and characterizing threat actors, and security professionals can also utilize them to bolster an organization's security architecture. The term *tactics* refers to a set of rules that specify how an attacker performs. The term *techniques* refers to an attacker's technical approaches to achieving intermediate results during an attack.

TTPs should be understood by organizations in order to secure their networks from threat actors and prospective attacks. TTPs allow enterprises to block assaults at the outset, protecting the network from catastrophic harm. They help you understand the mindset of an attacker and predict what an attacker might try to do next.

Adversary behavior identification

The process of identifying the common tactics or strategies used by an adversary to conduct attacks on an organization's network is known as adversary behavioral identification. It provides security professionals with information on upcoming threats and exploits. It aids in the planning of network security architecture and the adaptation of a variety of security procedures as a defense against various cyberattacks. Common behaviors to watch out for include the following.

Internal reconnaissance

At this stage, the attacker collects internal information about a target network to be able to move through the network. The attacker will do reconnaissance internally – enumeration of systems and hosts, and looking out for different types of commands that are being issued on the target's network, including activities such as attempting to resolve hostnames or IP addresses. Activating remote systems is beneficial for averting this.

PowerShell

PowerShell is a great automation tool for users, but attackers exploit it as an automation tool to transfer data from the target network (data exfiltration) and to launch further attacks. Monitoring PowerShell transcript logs and Windows event logs can help identify the presence of an attacker.

The command-line interface processes

Attackers use command-line tools to gain access to target systems – to read files or their contents, modify files, create accounts, and so on. They're very easy to do from a command-line interface. Security professionals detect this behavior by looking for logs with process IDs that bear unfamiliar numbers and letters. Malicious files getting downloaded is also a pointer to this type of attack.

Suspicious proxy events

The adversary tries to create and configure multiple domains pointing to the same host to allow fast switches between domains. In this kind of attack, speed is of the essence for attackers. They have to switch quickly to elude security professionals. To catch them, check the data feeds that are generated by those domains to find unspecified domains.

HTTP user agent

In HTTP-based communication, the server identifies the connecting HTTP client using a user agent field. Attackers modify the content of the HTTP user field to communicate with any system that may be compromised or have a vulnerability to carry out attacks against it.

CNC servers

Attackers use CNC servers to communicate remotely to the systems that they've compromised. They do this through an encrypted session. To stop them in their tracks, a security professional needs to be on the lookout for unwanted open ports, encrypted traffic – especially outbound connection attempts – and so on.

DNS tunneling

Intruders use DNS tunneling to hide malicious traffic. An intruder can communicate with a CNC, bypassing security controls to grab data off of the target systems, and so on. Unfortunately, because it's in a DNS tunnel, it just looks like normal DNS traffic going through the network.

Web shell

Here, attackers use web shells to change the web server by creating a shell within the website itself, allowing them remote access to the functionality of the target server. A security professional can identify web shells running in a network by analyzing server logs, error logs, and suspicious streams that might pop up on this, such as user agent strings.

Data staging

Once intruders gain access to a target network, they stage or create different data-staging techniques to collect and combine as much information or data as they can. They can collect financial information, data about customers, employees, business models, tactics, and so on.

Most IT professionals deploy or create network infrastructure layouts to track their networks. Once intruders gather this information, they exfiltrate data or destroy it. To prevent this, security professionals look at event logs, and for data-staging areas by monitoring network traffic for malicious files.

Historically, security tools have depended on the identification of malware signatures, but there's little chance of this type of detection beating an experienced attacker. They know better than to use outdated tactics. It's very unlikely they will use tools that can be found in a database of known file-based malware, which explains why threat research has moved beyond the identification of static malware signatures.

Indicators of compromise

An **Indicator of Compromise** (**IoC**) is a residual sign that an asset or network has successfully been attacked or is being attacked. Often, an IoC can be identifiable because intruders are using some type of tool that leaves behind an ID, such as a malware signature.

Most IoCs require subjective judgment calls based on the security professional's experience and knowledge of the target system, because these IoCs are mostly identified through suspicious activities – not obvious incidences. It's also important to note that there are multiple targets and vectors of an attack, and potential IoCs will be different too. Correlating multiple IoCs to produce a complete and accurate narrative of events is key.

Common IoCs

Let's look at some common IoCs:

- Unauthorized software or unauthorized files
- Suspicious emails
- Suspicious registry or filesystem changes
- Unknown ports and protocol usage
- Excessive bandwidth usage – especially on the outbound side
- Rogue hardware devices
- Service disruption and defacement, maybe of a web page
- Suspicious or unauthorized account usage

Multiple IoCs can be linked to identify a pattern of an attacker's behavior. This behavioral analysis can then be used to model threats and perform proactive threat hunting.

One way of identifying a threat is associating indicators you discover in your logs with reputation data. A reputation threat research source will identify IP address ranges to a DNS domain that's associated with malicious activities, such as sending spam or a particular **Dynamic Denial-of-Service (DDoS)** attack.

Information security controls

"I don't even call it violence when it's self-defense. I call it intelligence," Malcolm X said.

These words capture the essence of information security controls – designed to help us protect networks.

Enter ethical hacking

So, what is the necessity of ethical hacking? Why do we need to do this? Well, we hear – almost daily – about how fast technology is moving. Because it's moving and growing so fast, it adds complexity. And because of rapid growth, and complexity, it creates issues for us.

So, with ethical hacking, we are going to try to accomplish the following:

1. First of all, you need to review systems and infrastructure, such as hardware, copy machines, switches, and Wi-Fi access points.

2. The next step is to test the current security, and you can do that via a *pentest*. After testing the current security, you will know how bad your system is, and by looking into that, you will be able to create solutions to cover the loopholes when it comes to the security of your system/computer.

> **Pen Test**
>
> A pen test is also known as a penetration test. It is a simulated cyberattack on your computer system to monitor for exploitable vulnerabilities.

3. The next thing you need to do is retest the solutions to ensure that the created solutions are helpful.

4. Now, when we're looking at this, we typically also need to be aware of both scope and limitation. The scope of ethical hacking is part of the risk assessment, auditing, as well as fraud. There are also best practices and a really good look at governance.

> **Ethical Hacking**
>
> Ethical hacking is commonly used as a penetration test to identify vulnerabilities and risk, identify the loopholes in a security system, and take corrective measures against those attacks.

The importance of ethical hacking

Ethical hacking is practiced to guard sensitive data from attackers. It works to protect your resources from attackers who want to exploit the vulnerability. Using ethical hacking, a company or organization can discover security vulnerabilities and risks.

Attackers keep themselves updated, figure out new mechanisms, and take advantage of new technologies to steal your data by gaining unauthorized access to your system/data.

In this scenario, you need somebody who can help to counteract these types of attacks, that is, an ethical hacker.

> **Ethical Hackers**
>
> They are security specialists who conduct these assessments. The proactive work that they do supports improving the security posture of an organization.

Understanding defense-in-depth strategies

Earlier on, we mentioned that information security controls work as self-defense or a safeguard for the cybersecurity of your computer. One of the baselines for securing your networks is using a defense-in-depth strategy (*Figure 1.2*). This means deploying different protections at different levels.

Layered protection

To understand the layer protection strategy, we'll take a look at banks and how bank robbers look at them. So, how does a skilled bank robber look at the bank they are planning to rob? They plan the robbery following these steps:

1. First, they'll case the joint. In this step, they look at things such as the parking lot area to ensure successful entry and exit, marking where the doors are, how to access which section of the bank, and where the safe is.

2. The robber then looks at the bank's security measures, such as CCTV cameras, the security alarm, security guards, and so on.

3. Lastly, they go inside and interact with the bank staff. This presents them with the opportunity to familiarize themselves with the bank's processes and procedures.

Banks invest in the best security equipment and personnel, but we still read about robberies. Banks improve their security by putting in place various security measures. In our world, we call that layered protection. We come up with different security layers for separate components.

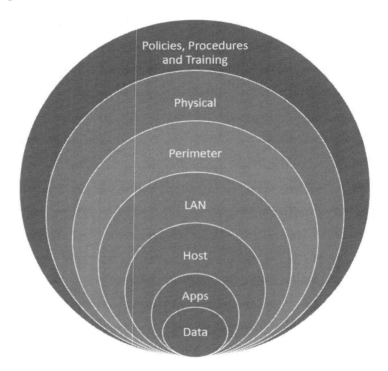

Figure 1.2 – A defense-in-depth strategy is designed to put "roadblocks" at each level to slow attackers

Layered protection is used in the protection of data that travels between various servers and components in the enterprise. Most organizations will deploy a corporate firewall in order to keep attackers out. The companies think that the firewall is good enough, but they let their application server talk to their database server without any security measures between them. While this approach is a good start, encrypting the data streaming between the two servers would be better in case an attacker penetrates the firewall. We can protect the resource by isolating the application server behind another firewall, effectively adding another layer to our defenses.

A single layer of protection can never adequately safeguard any company. Even if one door is closed, hackers will immediately locate another wide open, and they will exploit any weaknesses. On the other hand, you may fix the gaps in your security by using a variety of defenses simultaneously, such as firewalls, malware scanners, IDSes, data encryption, and integrity auditing solutions.

> **Important Note**
>
> We can't stop attackers. Our job is to slow them down or at least discourage them.

Information security laws and standards

There's a difference between a law and a standard or guideline. A standard is a document created through consensus and approved by a body that governs a particular industry. It is a foundation upon which common rules, guidelines, and activities for that particular environment stand.

Let's start with the basics.

Payment Card Industry Data Security Standard

Almost everybody that is involved with the credit card-processing process, including processors, merchants, issuers, and others, have to adhere to these standards in order to accept credit cards. These standards include the following:

- **Payment Card Industry Data Security Standard (PCI DSS) audits** – to ensure they have built and are maintaining a secure network. They confirm you have your firewall configurations in place.

- **Protecting the cardholder data** – to ensure that you're not using defaults for system passwords, and so on. It also includes protecting the cardholder data itself – meaning you need to encrypt it while it's in motion or in storage.

- **A Vulnerability Management Program** (VMP) – this shows that you are able to maintain a VMP – that you use and regularly update your antivirus or anti-malware software solutions, as well as the programs involved in every system that is used in the credit card process.

- **Strong access controls** – to ensure that we restrict access to cardholder information so that the business doesn't get everything; they only get what they need at any given time and it's on a need-to-know basis. This ensures that only the data that's needed is transmitted or received by that business.

- Going through and assigning unique IDs to each person with computer access.

- Restricting physical access to any of the cardholder information that the company is storing.

- We also have to prove that we regularly monitor and test our networks, and of course, we're going to update those in time.

- **Information security policy** – you have to prove you have a policy in place and that you're going to maintain it and update it for anybody that's involved in the process of handling any type of credit card information.

ISO, IEC 2701 2013

This standard specifies the requirements for implementing, maintaining, establishing, and continually improving information security management systems within an organization. So, we're going to make sure that we establish security requirements and goals for the organization as far as security is concerned, and then we're going to make sure that we do so in a cost-effective manner. We are going to make sure that it also helps us with any type of compliance – whether it's regulations or laws – and we're going to make sure that we define a new information security management process as we evolve.

It also helps us to check the status of information security activities within the organization. It's also used by organizations to help us provide information security information to customers if need be.

Health Insurance Portability and Accountability Act

If you are based in the US, you have probably had interaction with the **Health Insurance Portability and Accountability Act (HIPAA)**. When you go to the doctor, or any type of medical professional, they always have a signed HIPAA form.

HIPAA provides federal protections for any individual's health information that's maintained or stored by any type of health company, medical professional, or hospital.

They have also laid out several rules for administrative, physical, and technical safeguards. This includes things such as electronic transactions and code set standards. Any transaction, including health claims, payment, remittance, claim status, authorizations, and payments, has to be secured – whether it's in motion, in storage, or at rest.

Privacy rules

This establishes another standard to protect people's medical records and other personal health information, including who the health care provider is, what the health plan is, and so on – all this information has to be secure. It also gives us (the patients) the right to control our health information, including the right to look at, and actually get, a copy of our health records.

Security rule

This rule requires appropriate physical, technical, and administrative safeguards to make sure that we have CIA of electronically protected health information.

National identifier

This is basically ensuring that each employer has a national number that identifies them on all of the different transactions that may take place.

Enforcement rule

This contains provisions related to any type of compliance and investigation, as well as the possibility of imposing penalties for violations of any HIPAA rules.

The Sarbanes-Oxley (SOX) Act

This was created in 2002 to help protect the public and investors by adding additional accuracy and reliability when it comes to corporate disclosures. Now, unfortunately, this act actually doesn't go through and tell the organization how they must store their records. Instead, it describes the records that the organization must store and how long they must store them for.

The key requirements for SOX are organized into several titles, including the following:

- **Public Company Accounting Oversight Board**: This creates a central oversight board tasked with going through and making sure that audits are performed, as well as helping to handle quality control.

- **The auditor independence**: This helps to specify that new auditors are required to be rotated. It also restricts auditing companies from providing consulting services to their clients.

- **Corporate responsibility**: This looks at the interaction between auditors that may be external, as well as corporate auditors, or committees, and their responsibilities. It also goes through and helps to specify the behaviors of corporate officers, and issues penalties for noncompliance.

- **Reporting requirements**: This covers all applicable laws, rules and regulations, orders, directives, and other requirements of a supervisory body that mandates retention of financial transactions or similar information.

- **The analyst's conflict of interest**: This one provides a code of conduct for security analysts and makes sure they disclose any knowledgeable conflicts of interest that they may have.

- **Commission resources and authority**: This goes through and helps to define the **Security Exchange Commission's (SEC's)** authority to censor or bar security professionals from working if they've violated any of these other titles.

- **The studies and reports**: This goes through and specifies the different types of studies that the SEC can conduct and how they report their findings.

- **The corporate and criminal fraud accountability**: This was created in 2002 and it has seven sections, describing the different criminal penalties for going through and altering financial records or manipulating them – fudging the numbers or interfering with investigations.

- **The white-collar crime penalty enhancement**: This sounds pretty serious, doesn't it? This actually goes through and increases the criminal penalties associated with white-collar crimes, whereby it recommends stronger sentencing guidelines.

- **The corporate tax returns**: This basically tells us that the CEO should sign the company tax return… which is almost a given, right?

- **Corporate fraud accountability**: This goes through and identifies any type of tampering or fraud as criminal offenses and then connects those offenses to specific penalties.

The Digital Millennium Copyright Act

The **Digital Millennium Copyright Act** (**DMCA**) incorporates two different treaties that were signed back in 1996 by the World Intellectual Property Organization. It helps to define the legal prohibition against circumventing any technical protection measures that are out there for copyright holders. You are not supposed to be able to rip a DVD because a given film company has rights to it. That's where the DMCA comes into play. It guards against copyright infringement.

Federal Information Security Management Act

The **Federal Information Security Management Act (FISMA)** was passed in 2002 and creates several different standards and guidelines that are required by congressional legislation. FISMA is a framework that's effective for information security controls that are out there. It includes things such as standards for categorizing information and information systems by the impact that that system or information would have on the business if it were breached. There's also a standard for minimizing security requirements for information and information systems, as well as some suggestions for us, because selecting security controls and assessing those security controls also gives us some suggestions for security authorization systems.

General Data Protection Regulation

General Data Protection Regulation (GDPR) is at a global level and went into effect in 2018. It's very stringent when it comes to privacy and security laws globally and carries some very hefty fines for anybody who violates it. While it is an EU-specific law, it has implications for services based all over the world that service geographies in the EU.

GDPR includes various protections and accountability principles:

- **Lawfulness transparency and fairness**: This means that the processing of data has to be lawful, transparent, and fair to the data subject.

- **The purpose limitation**: This basically tells you, *"You better have a reason for handling this type of data!"*.

- **Storage limitation**: Normally, this identifies that you can only store personal information for a specific period of time and for a specific purpose.

- **Data minimization**: This ensures that we're only collecting and processing the information that's necessary for the particular purpose of getting that information.

- **Accuracy**: This states that you have to keep personal data accurate and up to date.

- **Accountability**: In this case here, the data controller is responsible for making sure that they adhere to GDPR compliance with all these different principles.

- **Integrity and confidentiality**: This means that when it comes to this data, we're typically going to make sure that it's encrypted with good encryption, not something that's outdated just because our app only works with this particular type of encryption. So yeah, you've got to keep up to date.

The Data Protection Act 2018

The **Data Protection Act (DPA)** 2018 is a framework for data protection that came out of the UK, and it's designed to protect individuals when it comes to personal data – making sure that personal data is processed lawfully. It also talks about the rights that an organization may or may not have to different personal information. It also sets out different protection rules for law enforcement and how to handle data protection when it comes to other areas, such as national security or even defense.

> **Important Note**
> With this said, every country has its own laws and standards. Find out which laws and acts apply to you based on your location.

Summary

This chapter laid a solid foundation for certified ethical hackers. It covered the fundamentals of ethical hacking, including why we do what we do, the strategies we use, and the information security laws and standards that security professionals need to have at their fingertips.

To cover all the basics, it introduced you to cyberattacks, attackers, ethical hackers, hacking techniques, and strategies, and what happens in both the good guys' and the bad guys' camps.

After listing the benefits of having a CEH certification, the chapter covered the fundamentals of CEH.

It gave you a pretty good grasp on information security, the tenets of the CIA triad, types of cyberattacks, the hacking phases cybersecurity professionals watch out for, the technology triangle, types of hackers and how to identify them by the way they behave and the attacks they carry out, the hacking phases and what happens at each stage, why cyberattacks happen, and what motivates attackers.

It also covered the behavioral identification of attackers, the methods attackers use to execute attacks, and the strategies and techniques cybersecurity professionals use to discourage, deter, misdirect, or slow them.

It also got you to study the world's best hacker framework, the CKC, as you went through the steps that trace the stages of an attack, right from reconnaissance through to exfiltration of data.

Now that we've got a good understanding of information security, let's next dive deeper into how attackers begin to target organizations by performing reconnaissance and footprinting. The next chapter will show you how easy it is to discover intelligence, such as systems being used, names of employees, infrastructure layouts, and even data on social media that could help attackers breach a network.

Questions

As we conclude, here is a list of questions for you to test your knowledge regarding this chapter's material. You will find the answers in the *Assessments* section of the *Appendix*:

1.   What is the goal of ethical hacking?

     A. To detect security flaws before they are exploited by attackers

     B. To search for updates and patches

     C. To get a competitive advantage over your rivals

     D. To put your security skills to the test

2.   What does *covering your tracks* mean?

     A. Determining the extent of the investigation

     B. Concealing activity

     C. Cleaning up following a pentest

     D. Using a rootkit to hide tools

3.   What is the name of a set of software tools that allows an attacker to access a target remotely and remain hidden for long durations without detection?

     A. GDRP

     B. A rootkit

     C. A social engineering kit

     D. SIEM

4. Which of the following attacks is considered *hard to detect*?

    A. Distribution

    B. Insider

    C. Close-in

    D. Active

    E. Passive

2
Introduction to Reconnaissance

Reconnaissance is fundamental during the hacking process. Through reconnaissance, hackers will gather information about their target to use against them or to access a vulnerability that they can exploit. The more information hackers have on their targets before beginning any type of attack, the more likely it is for them to succeed and not get caught.

So, let me ask you a question – when you're shopping for a car, do you buy the first one you come across with a **For Sale** sign? You probably don't. At least I know I don't.

I do a lot of research before making a big purchase. I go through consumer reports and reviews to dig out as much information as I can about that specific car.

Today, I have access to multiple online services to assist me in finding out everything about a car, including its history, previous owners, quality reviews, and so on. That's precisely what **reconnaissance** and **footprinting** are all about.

So, what is reconnaissance and what does it have to do with hacking?

Reconnaissance is the process of gathering as much information about our intended target as we can to make our attacks easier.

This book covers different types of recons and the information we need to collect. There is a plethora of information we can gather from the target without their knowledge.

You will notice that I will flip back and forth between the points of view of a hacker and an ethical hacker. That's the job of an ethical hacker – to first think like a hacker and profile a target. Then, at other times, I must think like an ethical hacker who could perform reconnaissance as part of a penetration test to help an organization protect itself.

I will mention penetration testing, or pen testing, frequently throughout this book. That's what we do as ethical hackers! We try out different attacks on systems to see how secure they are. Then, we can (sometimes) help our targets mitigate those vulnerabilities.

In this chapter, we'll cover the following topics:

- Overview of reconnaissance
- Search engines
- Google hacking
- Using WHOIS
- Using ping and DNS

Now, it's never a good geek session without playing around with some tools. So, you're going to see a lot of tools, especially in the upcoming chapters. So, get your ball cap, put it on sideways, and let's get busy!

Overview of reconnaissance

In a battle, a successful attack depends on how much you know about your enemy. Knowledge of where and how many troops, their supply chain, and their equipment is vital to a strategic approach to engaging the enemy. It's very similar to why we recon before our attack.

Recon is the first and most convenient way an attacker gathers information about a target. The purpose of recon is to learn as much as you can about a target. For example, does it have remote access capabilities? What ports and services are being used? What does an organization's security profile look like?

Attackers spend at least 70% of their time in this phase because it's a way to get a ton of information about the target (without being discovered).

First, we will collect as much **elementary intel** as we can about the target – and when I say elementary, I mean basic, foundational stuff, including things such as what the website looks like, where the organization's physical location is, when it was founded, who the officers of the organization are, whether they operate from one location, and whether they have any branch offices. It is even useful to review press releases and news clips about the organization. How did they start?

The next step is trying to discover what **operating system** is running on their machines. Luckily, it's almost impossible for them to track everybody hitting their publicly visible systems. Are they running Windows? Are they running Linux? What web servers are they using? Are they using IIS, perhaps Apache? If they're running FreeBSD, can I figure out what version they're using? Are they using an older version of IIS on an old 2003 server? All this information will help me plan my attack.

Next, we'll perform some queries, which entails using tools to discover things – for instance, all the DNS names out there. We might use WHOIS for this. Our goal is to discover information about the underlying network infrastructure. For example, we might find out that a particular online company is hosting our target's resources. Maybe that company has had some security issues in the past, so we will probably want to look at any other companies that are partners with our target. You don't think that's important? Go Google search `Target Breach`, and you'll see that attackers used a **heating, ventilation, and air conditioning** (**HVAC**) partner company that maintains Target's refrigeration systems to pivot into their credit card systems.

Next, we must find what **vulnerabilities** might be available to us for our attack. We already know what to target since we know the operating system version, and we might even know the web server version. Using that information, we will start our research (or *reconnaissance*) on potential vulnerabilities. Again, our goal at this stage is to find any information that provides us with any insight into the potential target. Sometimes, even one little piece of information can come back to help you in the end.

Figuring out the **network architecture** that's being used is crucial. During the reconnaissance stage, you should look at the systems, routers, or switches they're using because they can also be potential entry points. We also need to map out the network to know what is in the **demilitarized zone** (**DMZ**). What IP address ranges are being used? What's behind the firewalls? What IP address ranges are used internally? What type of desktop clients are they running? If we can see that visually, we will have a better idea of where we are as we get into the environment.

The more we learn about the target, the more we'll understand what they're doing. We might even discover how often they look at their security. Also, when it comes to looking for information on employees, the weakest link in any computer system sits between the chair and the keyboard. Social engineering is an essential tool for ethical hackers.

Show Your Work!

Reconnaissance is a systematic and methodical process. We go through the same steps, looking for the same information. This process gives us a complete profile of the target's security environment, which helps reduce the attack area. Instead of wondering which machine to go after, we will be able to use our understanding of the target's security posture to get very specific regarding which domains, child domains, network blocks, or IP address ranges to go after. But we don't want to go after all of them. We want to focus the attack as much as possible so that we have a clear target in mind.

To keep track of all this reconnaissance, you need to build up a **Target Information Profile** (**TIP**). The focus of the profile will be to note possible vulnerabilities to prioritize your attacks better. It's also crucial to keep track of where you've tried attacks. Naturally, we'll try the path of least resistance first; afterward, we'll start the footprinting phase of reconnaissance, which is mapping out the target's network.

Types of reconnaissance

There are several types of recon available to us – passive, active, anonymous, and pseudonymous.

Passive reconnaissance

Passive reconnaissance is especially relevant when we talk about scanning. It requires no direct contact with the target. The type of information we gather with passive reconnaissance could include IP addresses available on the internet, operating systems, and web server software that's being utilized.

We can also find out whether any services are open on those systems, UDP- or TCP-based, whether they have any access control mechanisms, whether they have an **Intrusion Detection System** (**IDS**) appliance, and so on.

There's passive scanning and active scanning. Passive scanning uses publicly available sources to gather as much information as possible about a target without being detected by anyone. In contrast, active scanning is aggressive and can be traced back to a source.

Passive scanning is synonymous with *internet reconnaissance*, which refers to gathering information about your target on the internet, often using an online search engine. The only difference between the two is that passive scanning could refer to information gathering from physical sources, such as newspaper or magazine articles.

Active reconnaissance

On the other hand, active reconnaissance includes touching the target by going for a job interview, asking questions about the employees, or even walking through the environment to see what you can discover. When you're gathering information on a large organization, in a large building, it's crazy how freely you can walk around and even use your social engineering skills (a method for hacking humans). For example, just walking in and acting like you're in charge is one way of testing how vulnerable the employees are to social engineering attacks.

Anonymous reconnaissance

Anonymous reconnaissance is about gathering information from sources that can't identify you, so everything you're doing can't be traced to you. This includes using a proxy or VPN solution to hide your location and identity as you access public content.

Organizational or private recon

Another type of recon is **organizational** or **private recon**. This entails going through and getting information from the organizational event calendar, email service, and more.

Finally, we have **pseudonymous reconnaissance**. Pseudonymous recon is like **anonymous reconnaissance**, except the sources may not be directly published by employees or the organization (information is posted anonymously or under a false name). It could be an employee who wants to remain anonymous, such as a whistleblower, or a corporate employee or government official who doesn't want anything posted online under their name. Regardless of their reason for remaining anonymous, collecting information from those sources is referred to as being pseudonymous.

Goals of recon

What are we trying to get out of this reconnaissance phase? The answer is as much as possible. We are trying to find the type of information that will help us focus our attacks.

This information can be divided into system and network information, standard technical practices (source code and naming conventions), and organizational information (location, policies, and employee information).

This section will review what you should be looking for. Then, I'll show you how to find it.

System and network information

System and network information includes things such as domain names (and not just whatever `.com`, we also want to know the child domains they're using). Do they have a child domain? (*Here's where my Batman addiction comes out.*) `partners.wayneenterprises.com` or `extranet.wayneenterprises.com`? This means we're going to be looking for all external-facing domains. It's helpful to find any internal domains they may be using. What did they register? Did they register both `wayneenterprises.com` and `wayneenterprises.net`? Are they both exposed? This might tell us that `.com` is their external domain, and that they may be using `.net` internally.

We also want to discover addresses that are being utilized more broadly at the organization, not just for their website. They might have VPN activity, which would beg the question – who are they getting their IP addresses from? What range? What IP address block are they using?

Next, we'll look at unmonitored and private websites. I don't know how many times I've come across companies that have websites a developer just put up for testing purposes. No one's monitoring them. Likewise, maybe an employee has posted a website on their internet-facing server.

It's also necessary to try to discover TCP and UDP services that are open and exposed. Do they have an IDS? What access control systems are they utilizing? Are they supporting a VPN, and if so, can we discover what their VPN endpoint is? Is it a Windows box? Is it a Cisco VPN solution? Phone numbers are also important – both analog phone numbers and VoIP.

We also want to gather information regarding the operating systems. We want to discover as much information as possible about users and groups. What name structure are they using for their user accounts? Is it *first initial, last name*? Is it *FirstName.LastName*?

Banner grabbing is another useful technique we will review later. It's a way of identifying a system; when I throw certain commands at operating systems, a Windows box will respond one way, while a Linux box will respond another way.

We also want to try to gain access to any of their routing tables to see how packets are being routed.

Standard technical practices

System names can also be an important clue for us. I love when IT guys name their servers `Thor` or `Zeus` or `Gandalf`; it makes it easy to figure out what the other server names are. Better yet, sometimes, they name them after the computer's name – for example, `Win 2012` – and then they also include its purpose – `Exchange 1`, `SharePoint 2`, `VPN 7`, and so on. The same is true of desktop machines (we're not necessarily going after the server right away). They name them all something such as `Desktop 57` or `Marketing 05`.

One of the more secure ways of handling system names is to use serial numbers, although that will not stop us. If we can see the computer name and recognize it as a serial number, we will go to Dell's website, type in the serial number, and find out what's in that machine. It's a hard realization to come to, but you cannot stop hackers. Your job is to slow them down.

The other essential thing we need to find is passwords. It's especially fun when people have documents or spreadsheets where they save passwords to keep track of them.

We'll also go through their access control systems to find out the requirements for password length. What are their complexity requirements? (Do they require uppercase, lowercase, special characters, and numbers?)

Organizational information

Never forget to dig into organizational information. Websites can expose quite a bit of crucial information. The company directory is one of the biggest resources for hackers because end users are the weakest links in any environment. You should try to pull employee details. Pick an employee, maybe somebody in the marketing department, and try to find them on social networking sites such as LinkedIn, Facebook, Twitter, and Instagram. See what their likes and dislikes are; see whether they're complaining about something being unfair at work, their cat's name, their first-grade teacher's name, or their best friend's name. All that information can be utilized. (You can see where I'm going, right? Passwords.)

Location details can also tell us quite a bit about the organization. For example, what's their physical security like? Would I feel comfortable walking into that building and casing out the joint? Did they just recently move? You may not think this information comes in handy, but trust me, there are many times I've seen passwords based on street addresses, so location details are essential. Make sure you record the addresses of the main office and any branch offices.

Phone numbers will come in handy if we decide to conduct a social engineering attack. For example, I might call a target up and act as if I'm looking for a job. Job sites are another treasure trove of information for us. If they have a job posting listed for an admin, I can find out what servers they're using or the technology solutions they have deployed.

Look at the source code for your target's web pages. Are there any comments the developers have accidentally left in? Can we discover the security policies they've deployed? Have they had any training on how to lock down their systems? Have they trained their employees on handling social engineering attacks?

Pay close attention to any links they have on their website or between servers. How are people coming into their server from other websites? This could help us determine whether they have a partner relationship with another company. That partnering company could become our target because they will likely have an established trust relationship or some type of connectivity back to our original target. Get a background on that organization, as well. Here, you'd go through the same process as we did previously with our target organization. How and when did they get started? Who are their founding members? What were the struggles of the company when they first started? Look at news articles about that company. Find press releases that the company has issued. Anything that we can find out about the organization will help us out.

Overview of the tools of recon

There are hundreds of tools out there that will help you recon your target. They fall into one of the following three categories: search engines, websites, and applications. We will start with the low-hanging fruit – search engines.

Most of the time, people only look at the first couple of pages on a search engine. Studies show they don't go beyond three pages of results. Do yourself a favor – don't just stick to those three pages. Look on page 10 or even page 15 of those results; there's a good chance you'll see historical information pop up. You can even try a variety of search engines because they give different results.

After doing your preliminary searching on search engines, start looking at websites. Start with the target's website. Again, look for information such as contact information or other domains or subdomains (if your target is `wayneenterprises.com`, do they have a subdomain called `mail.wayneenterprises.com`?). There are also some web-based recon tools out there that have nothing to do with the organization. They're just tools that we can access via the internet to show us more information. We'll review these, particularly in *Chapter 4, Scanning Networks*.

Finally, we have applications. You'll find hundreds of tools to gather information about your target. Some of them are designed for good; some for evil (yes, I'm rubbing my hands together now). There are also some built-in commands that we normally wouldn't suspect, such as command-line interfaces for nslookup.

There are also hundreds of PowerShell commands out there that could be of benefit to you, as well as scripting languages, and I'm not just speaking from the Windows world. There could also be commands such as `dig` in Linux that we can use to recon our target.

We'll go over more of these tools throughout this book – keep in mind that it's important to grasp the basics so that you know exactly what you want to get out of these tools.

When you go through an organization's systems, ask yourself questions such as the following:

- Is SNMP being utilized?
- What system architecture are they using throughout their environment?
- What are their standard naming practices?
- Are they using all the latest and greatest by Microsoft?
- Do they have a little bit of Novell still out there?
- 32-bit or 64-bit?
- Are they supporting remote systems and not just VPNs? Are they using Microsoft's DirectAccess (pseudo-VPN solution)?
- What is the physical security of the building like?
- Do they have a kiosk machine in the hallway?
- Do they have users that travel around with laptops or tablets?
- How are passwords stored?
- Are the employees on social media?
- What kind of security policies have they deployed? Are the users trained?
- Do they support **Bring Your Own Device (BYOD)**?

> **Note**
>
> I have a love-hate relationship with BYOD because, as an administrator, it's a nightmare for me sometimes. I get why companies do it. They don't have to go off and buy the tablet for their employee. They get to use their tablet – they're already used to it – but what happens if they lose that tablet?

As we discussed earlier, all this information will be stored in your TIP. This is critical because if we are targeting multiple companies, we need to keep our information straight.

Once we've gathered that information, we should start drawing out a blueprint or map of the network. We may not have a complete picture yet, but we'll at least have various potential entry points. As we get into other phases of hacking (such as scanning), we want to be able to pull up a full diagram of their environment. When dealing with such a wide range of information, it's best to create a visual – and that's the footprinting part of reconnaissance.

Search engines

Typically, you will start gathering information slowly. So, first, you'd start with a Google search, then you'd check out the target's website, and then you'd go deeper. For the sake of organization, I will show you what you can find out through four major categories: search engines, the organization's website, what companies give away (which is not necessarily on their website), and, finally, employees.

I will show you the tools and methods you need to gather data for your TIP. We'll even use some tools you're familiar with, but we'll leverage them a little differently. Fire up your computer. Let's get going!

Let's start with the basics

Here is a website that you can practice attacks on. It's called **HackThisSite.org** (`https://hackthissite.org/`), and it's a free site that hackers use as a training ground to test some stuff out. It also has some stuff on it – blogs, news releases, and so on.

Start by pulling up your favorite search engine; in my case, it's Google. We'll start with a simple search on the target – so, type in `hackthissite.org`. The first thing it shows is the actual website, and it gives some additional information about pages on that website that we might not be aware of.

Again, don't limit yourself to the first page; scroll down further. Take note of the results that come up. For example, Reddit has some reviews on it, and it appears to have a Facebook page (although that could be an impersonator).

Some other companies have referenced **HackThisSite.org** – this can be important because some of these third-party links and reviews could give you some vital information, such as partnerships or clients that might have a trust relationship with the target.

Now, let's look at a different target – my old wireless ISP service (from back in the day) called `UtahWISP.com`.

Even though this company doesn't exist anymore, you will find several articles about it. Yahoo Local shows me some information, including the street address and a map to show its location (that will be important for us). It's also on Google Plus.

Let's switch to Yahoo. This time, type in `hackthissite.org`. Sometimes, search engines can even help you determine the URL structure of an organization. For example, in the **HackThisSite.org** site search result, there's also a login directory, an information page, and a registration page.

A simple search will often lead to important information because people don't always have control over what the search engines display. There are some ways around this; you can tell Google to not index your environment, but even that information can be exposed.

Now that you know what to look for in your initial searches, I'll show you how you can get even more information out of Google.

Google hacking

Note that when I say Google hacking, I'm not referring to trying to hack the Google servers.

First and foremost, you need to understand how Google works. Normally, what happens is you type in something such as `how to raise baby ducks`. Google quickly responds with sites telling you how to raise baby ducks.

Now, how does Google do this? Their servers are designed to go out and look at every single website that's out there, even if it's a little blog site. Their servers crawl through the entire internet and index what it finds. **Crawling** is the process of going through and making a note of every page and word on that page; all those words are then indexed, which is how Google can pull up random websites about ducks.

There are some limits to Google. I know you're saying, *Dale, say it's not so. Google has no limits.* Well, it does. The limit is 32 words in a Google query.

We're going to be taking advantage of the **Advanced Search** section of Google. You probably have experience using this interface (you big Google nerd), but this time, we'll be using some interesting operators and their syntax to discover all kinds of fun stuff that companies don't realize is accessible. Please note that this isn't usually done when you first begin to recon a target. Start with a basic search. Then, once you have more detailed information, you can move on to Google hacking.

We can tweak our search results in **Advanced Search**. We'll review the syntax you need to know about in the next section:

Advanced Search

Find pages with...

all these words:	water heaters
this exact word or phrase:	
any of these words:	
none of these words:	-solar
numbers ranging from:	to

Then narrow your results by...

Figure 2.1 – Google – Advanced Search

If you're looking for heaters within a specific price range, you can simply type $300 and $400 in the **numbers ranging from** field.

Google operators

Google operators are the different ways that we can use syntax to refine search results within the **Search** bar. All of this is also possible in the **Advanced Search** section. It is up to you and your comfort level whether you use the symbols or the **Advanced Search** page to configure your Google operators.

Before we start, there are a couple of rules for using Google operators:

- There should be no space between the operator and the search term itself. If you're searching for water heaters and you don't want a solar one, you can search for `water heaters -solar`. The important part to note is that there is no space between the – operator and `solar`.

- Searches are not case sensitive, so it doesn't matter if you type `BaTmAn`. It will return the same results as searching for Batman.

The following are the three most basic methods of tailoring your Google search results:

- **Combining terms**: Most of us, when we're searching for something, type in something along the lines of `Batman Dark Knight`. Unfortunately, by not specifying how those words should be grouped, we'll get everything about Batman, the dark, and maybe some medieval knights. One of the things we can do is to use quotation marks to associate the words. Instead of `batman dark knight`, we can type `"Dark Knight" Batman`, with `Dark Knight` in quotations. The other option is to type `Dark.Knight`, with a period in between the two terms that have a space.

  Note that the space indicates `AND`, but we are also able to change that to `OR`.

- **Boolean operators**: The `AND` operator is assumed when you type in a string of words with only a space, but you can also indicate the `AND` operator with a plus sign (+) or with the word `AND`. If you'd like to use the `OR` function, you can type in `OR` or use the pipe symbol (|).

- **Excluding terms**: If you only want to know about Batman and not the Joker, you can subtract him by typing in `Batman -joker`. The results that appear will all be pages that don't contain any normal text (there may be a link) that references the Joker.

Now, we can get into the more sophisticated Google operators:

- `cache`: By using the `cache` operator, we can specify that we want to see Google's cached version of that page. This comes in handy because a page may go offline either temporarily or permanently, yet you'd be able to see the last cached page that Google has on their servers.

- `link`: The `link` specification shows a list of web pages that have links to your target site.

- `related`: The `related` operator goes through and shows us pages that are similar to the target page. It shows us pages that have the same type of wording by doing a basic text comparison.

- `info:`: By typing `info:`, followed by the page or the URL, we can view what information Google has on our target website.

- `site:`: To find results only within a particular site, type your search terms, then `site:` and the URL of a particular site. For example, if I want to look for water heaters at Home Depot, I could type in `water heaters site: Home Depot`.

- `allintitle::` This limits the results to those websites that contain all the search words in the title. To find sites that have `Batman` in the title, I would type `allintitle:Batman`, and Google would find all those websites. This is commonly used in penetration testing.

- `inTitle::` This operator looks at documents that contain that search word in their title. You could use this to look for documents that are titled `Passwords`, for example.

- `allinURL::` This limits Google's results to only the pages with all your search words in the URL.

- `inURL::` This operator limits our results to just documents that contain the search word in the URL.

Next, let's look at examples of using Google operators.

Using Google operators

Let's go over a few useful scenarios for how to use Google operators.

First, let's search for `intitle:"index of"`. This will give us a list of web pages that support directory browsing. **Directory browsing** (or **traversal**) is a hacking method that allows attackers to access restricted directories and files within the website and executes a command outside the web server's root directory:

Figure 2.2 – Google search using operators

The first link that comes up shows us a directory structure for Linux. We could just go through this structure and find Ubuntu. This is probably where they're going to have a download of Ubuntu, as well as different projects that they're working on. You never know what you might find because some people may not know this information is being exposed.

By using `inTitle:`, we're telling Google the words we're looking for, but we aren't saying that it absolutely must have `of` in the title. `allintitle:`, on the other hand, means that all the words in our search must be present in the title.

As an example, let's try `inurl:admin`. This search will return sites that have `admin` or `administrator` in the URL itself; sometimes, there are associated login pages:

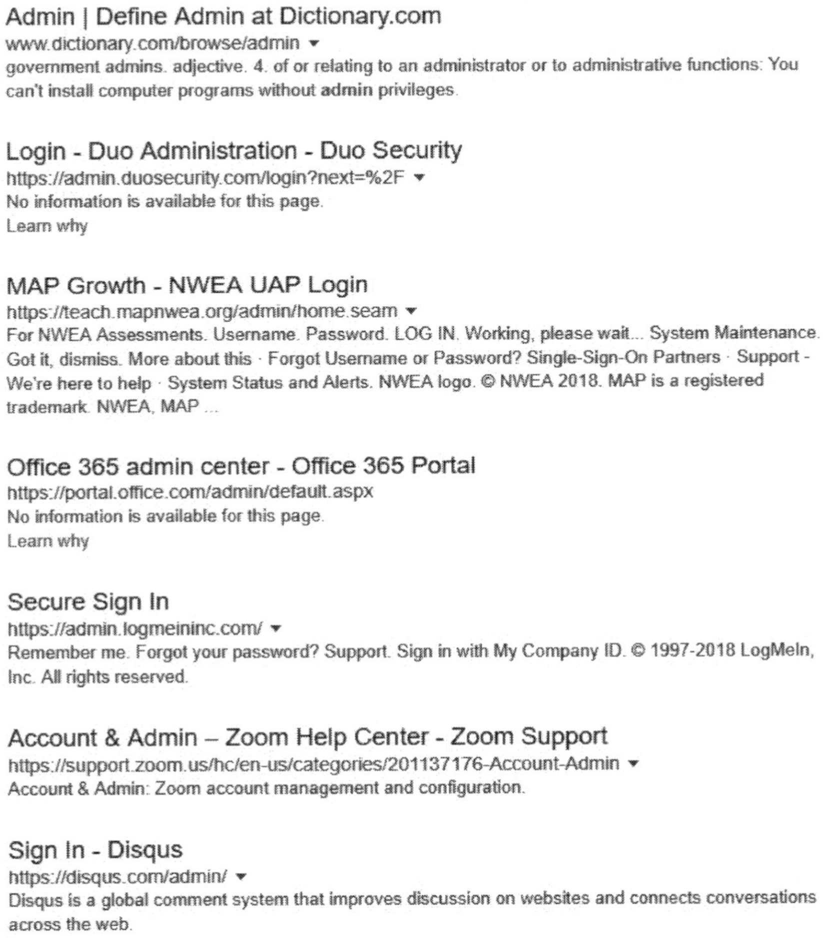

Admin | Define Admin at Dictionary.com
www.dictionary.com/browse/admin ▾
government admins. adjective. 4. of or relating to an administrator or to administrative functions: You can't install computer programs without admin privileges.

Login - Duo Administration - Duo Security
https://admin.duosecurity.com/login?next=%2F ▾
No information is available for this page.
Learn why

MAP Growth - NWEA UAP Login
https://teach.mapnwea.org/admin/home.seam ▾
For NWEA Assessments. Username. Password. LOG IN. Working, please wait... System Maintenance. Got it, dismiss. More about this · Forgot Username or Password? Single-Sign-On Partners · Support - We're here to help · System Status and Alerts. NWEA logo. © NWEA 2018. MAP is a registered trademark. NWEA, MAP ...

Office 365 admin center - Office 365 Portal
https://portal.office.com/admin/default.aspx
No information is available for this page.
Learn why

Secure Sign In
https://admin.logmeininc.com/ ▾
Remember me. Forgot your password? Support. Sign in with My Company ID. © 1997-2018 LogMeIn, Inc. All rights reserved.

Account & Admin – Zoom Help Center - Zoom Support
https://support.zoom.us/hc/en-us/categories/201137176-Account-Admin ▾
Account & Admin: Zoom account management and configuration.

Sign In - Disqus
https://disqus.com/admin/ ▾
Disqus is a global comment system that improves discussion on websites and connects conversations across the web.

Figure 2.3 – Google search using the inurl:admin operator

Now, let's try `allinURL:` and add another word, such as `index`. (Type `allinurl:admin index` into Google.) This search means that we will only get results that have both `admin` and `index` in the URL. Scared yet?

So, what can we find with Google operators? We can find the following:

Devices and appliances

- ❏ Default settings
- ❏ Accessible via browser
- ❏ Application defaults
- ❏ Internet printing
- ❏ Internet cameras
- ❏ Server defaults

Think outside the box

- ❏ Directories – intitle:index.of.
  Admin directories?
- ❏ Find specific files
  Logs / password files / by file extension
- ❏ Web servers
- ❏ Directory traversal
- ❏ Extension walking

Figure 2.4 – Search result of the allinurl: operator

We could use `intitle:` to look at specific types of files (maybe in an administrative directory). We could find log files specifically, or perhaps log files that help identify the server. We could identify which of the servers is an Apache server. We could even move around in a directory structure.

Another neat thing we can do with Google operators is extension walking. **Extension walking** allows us to go through and change file types. For example, once I've located HTM files, I could use a substitution technique to find files with the same filename and different extensions. So, if I found `/docs/index.htm`, I could modify the URL to `/docs/index.asp` to try and locate the `index.asp` file in the `docs` directory.

Speaking of which, one of my favorite things to do is use extension walking to find backup copies of web pages (because, and no offense to them, developers are lazy). They leave the backups of the old versions of the web page on the server and trust me, Google indexes those.

Let's think about what we've gone over in this section from an attacker's perspective (or a pen tester's perspective). As an example, let's say that you're trying to determine the operating system of a public-facing **Small Business Server** (**SBS**) 2003. When you install SBS, it has a frontend page that says, in the title, **Welcome to Windows Small Business Server**. `inTitle:` will show you links about Windows Server 2003. But if we scroll down further, we will find pages that unintentionally reveal what server they're hosted on.

Try a different one and search for `intitle:"open webmail"`. Google will show us some servers out there that are running Open WebMail. You can also try `intitle:"mvblog powered"` to find blogs or websites powered by MvBlog. MvBlog is prone to several different input validation vulnerabilities, so I could just quickly go and find several targets out there that are using that technology as part of my pen testing process.

Let's look at another way to use `inTitle:`. The title page of Microsoft's remote access servers contains the phrase **remote desktop web connection**. At the beginning of the results, most of the pages are going to be Microsoft's, but as we scroll down further, we'll find other sites that are using those servers. One time, I found a login page where you could type in your username and password, and then you could select which server you wanted to log into from a drop-down box. It listed all their servers, their email server, their SharePoint server, and so on. Sometimes, it's too easy.

Now, this one will be especially important to remember: `intitle:"root/etc/ passwd" intext:"home/*:"`.

Surprisingly enough, this can show you the password directory for a few Linux boxes. Again, you never know what people might leave exposed.

Error logs are yet another valuable source of reconnaissance information. Error logs might tell you what a server's running or their user behavior, or even the controls they've put in place.

For our first example, we'll try the `intext:"access denied for" intitle:"shopping cart"` query. This can show us exactly which sites are using MySQL in the backend of their shopping carts (or checkout pages). As ethical hackers, our next question to ask is whether MySQL has any vulnerabilities.

Let's take this a step further. You probably already know that you must be careful about which devices you're hooking up to the internet and with every device that has a web interface. That's because people like me, and now us, can probably find it.

I'll demonstrate this with an `inTitle:` search by typing `intitle:"bluenet video viewer"`. What I get back is a list of broadcast-quality videos that are on the internet – full 30-frame per second options based on an IP.

In some cases, I've been able to use this to take control of a camera on the beaches in the Caribbean, which was kind of fun. You can do this with several popular cameras; you just need to look up the specific name of the camera; for example, `snc-rz30 home`.

Let's try another one. Type in `Camera Live Image" inurl:"guestimage.html"` and we'll try to find live views using live cameras. These cameras have HTTP servers on them. Look at any of these listed in the search results as an IP address:

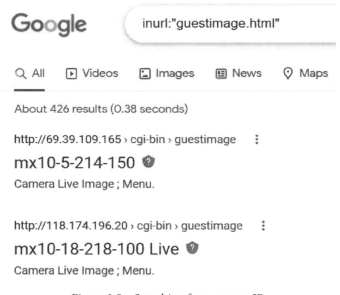

Figure 2.5 – Searching for a camera IP

If they still use the default username and passwords, we could even get into the setup of that camera:

Figure 2.6 – Live feedback of the camera

We can do the same thing with printers, for example. Printers are typically URL-based, so our search query will be `intitle:"Remote UI" intext:"Printer status"`:

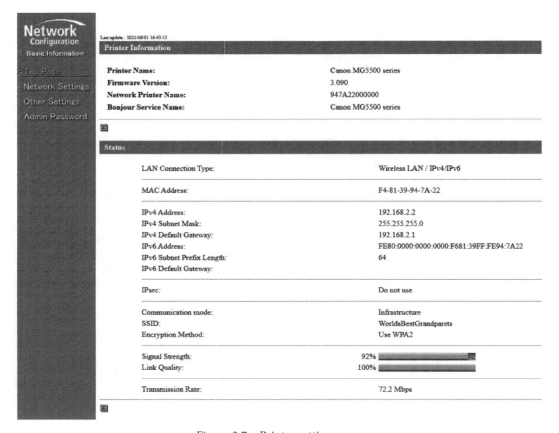

Figure 2.7 – Printer settings page

If you want to search even deeper, try the following:

- `inurl:root.asp?acs=anon`: These results would take us directly to the main page of Outlook access public folders and an Exchange address book.

- `ext:sql intext:"alter user" intext:"identified by"`: The extension you're looking for is SQL. This query would show me files that contain SQL instructions where the administrator set a password for the database user.

If I haven't said it enough, you must be aware of everything you are exposing to the internet. You don't think I can find out whether your router's a Cisco router or a Linksys router? Guess again.

Google Hacking Database

Now, you know how to use Google operators the hard way. Guess what, script kiddies! There's something out there called **Google Hacking Database (GHDB)** (`https://www.exploit-db.com/google-hacking-database/`). A man by the name of Johnny Long created this Google database and, luckily for us, it expands daily because of the multitude of vulnerabilities that continue to pop up:

Figure 2.8 – The Google Hacking Database page

At the top is a list of new entries, such as a search for WordPress Flash plugins, for example:

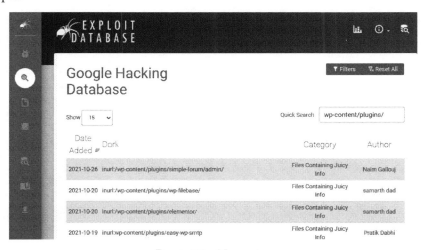

Figure 2.9 – New entry

But you could also scroll down and find tailormade lists showing common things such as web server detection, files that contain passwords, sensitive online shopping information, and pages that contain login portals, error messages, printers, video cameras, and more. In this section, I'll provide some examples of the detailed information that you can find using this resource – and there is a lot. How about getting a list of database backups that are exposed? I know, you're using the *palm to forehead* gesture right about now.

Exploit Database is available for download, which will be especially useful for those who plan to do penetration testing. There is a section dedicated to exploits – remote exploits, web application exploits, and so on:

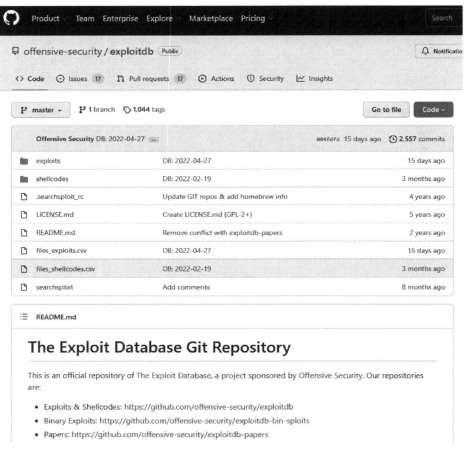

Figure 2.10 – exploitdb GitHub repository page

This was created by just using Google to aggregate all the found vulnerabilities out there. Now, it doesn't tell you how to fix them, but at least you'll know they exist. You can also find a list of web application exploits on the same page.

In addition to this site, which reviews best practices (for example, privilege escalation via client management software), Johnny Long, the mastermind of GHDB, has several white papers available. His work is a fantastic resource for everyone in this field. He has written several books and runs a charity called **Hackers for Charity**, which takes hardware and office equipment that some companies may deem outdated and installs them in third-world countries to help set up networks in more remote areas.

Other Google hacking tools

There are some other Google hacking tools that you can use to make things even easier:

- **Google Hack Honeypot**: This tool is designed to go out and provide reconnaissance against hackers or attackers that would use these search engine techniques on you. It creates a type of honeypot for you. In other words, it's a fake Google result.

- **SearchDiggity**: This is a web GUI interface for Windows that provides a framework for using Google hacking tools. You can add additional components to it such as GoogleDiggity, BingDiggity, PortScanDiggity, and MalwareDiggity.

- **Metagoofil**: This tool is quite powerful. It goes out and grabs metadata on any document that's publicly exposed, whether it's a DOCX, a PPTX, a DOC, or a PDF. Then, it downloads those files from the target and extracts the metadata so that you can see what's being exposed (especially usernames and passwords).

- **SiteDigger**: SiteDigger searches Google's cache for any types of errors or misconfiguration issues present on your target organization's website.

Now, if you're starting to get concerned about your network, don't worry too much. That's the natural reaction you feel after going through some of this information. Toward the end of this book, I'll show you some reconnaissance countermeasures and what to look for during penetration testing to prevent giving away so much information to potential hackers.

Using WHOIS

WHOIS is a huge database that contains information regarding every website on the internet. It contains common information such as who owns the website, their email address, and some other information. A website called `domaintools.com` offers a nice WHOIS interface, but all the data comes from ICANN's service.

> **Note**
>
> The **Internet Assigned Numbers Association (IANA)** delegates the registration of domains and assignment of IP addresses to five different **Regional Internet Registries (RIRs)** around the world. These provide information to WHOIS about your target websites.
>
> ARIN represents the United States, Canada, the Caribbean Islands, and North Atlantic Islands.
>
> LACNIC is used for Latin America, as well as some portions of the Caribbean.
>
> RIPE is for Europe, the Middle East, and Central Asian registration.
>
> AFRINIC is the registrar for Africa and parts of the Indian Ocean.
>
> APNIC is the registrar for portions of Asia, as well as the Oceanic rim.

We can use WHOIS either in the command line or through a web interface, such as the one available at `whois.domaintools.com`.

Linux has this capability built into it (the `whois` command), but you may not always have access to a Linux box, so using a website is often more convenient.

Type in either a domain name or an IP address of any site out there. I'm going to review the WHOIS results for `HackThisSite.org` here:

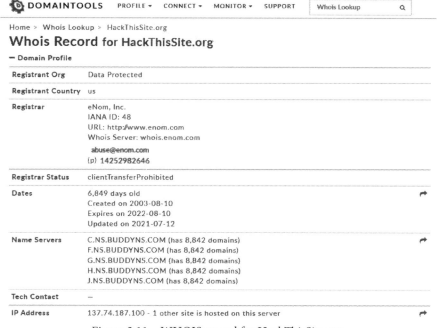

Figure 2.11 – WHOIS record for HackThisSite.org

At the top, you can see that they have protected their email. But we can still see the IP address of the dedicated server, that the IP address is based out of Las Vegas, Nevada, they've maintained this site since 2003, the number of images on the page, and the number of links – both internal and external.

This website also gives us the physical WHOIS record. This is what you would see from a Linux machine if you were to run the whois command on a **command-line interface (CLI)**.

Let's review the interesting information we obtained from WHOIS in the preceding screenshot:

- Where it was registered (Enom, Inc.).

- They're protecting themselves with the WHOIS privacy protection service. Many people won't use this service; HackThisSite.org did because they're expecting to get hacked (boy, that's weird – I wonder why they'd think that?). Sometimes you can use this tool to see the person that registered the domain name, as well as the admin, their email address, and possibly their cell phone number. You can also see the following:

  - Technical contact information (this is supposed to be who you'd contact if a technical issue has occurred).

  - The name servers or the DNS servers that are hosting the name to IP address resolution. In this case, they're using BUDDYNS. It looks like they have their own name servers (NS1 and NS2.)

  - DNSSEC is unsigned. DNSSEC is a protocol that's used for encrypting DNS transfers. Since this is not encrypted, this could be a possible point for us to look at.

Pay very close attention to the contacts listed here if they're visible. Typically, when someone registers a domain, they use their home address. (Phone numbers and email addresses are very useful for social engineering attacks.) It's also important to note any anomalies. For example, if the website is `widgets.com` but the registrant's email is `brucewayne@gotham.com`, I know that the person who registered it is most likely not working for the target organization. They may have a third party helping them out. Usually, this is someone's nephew's, brother's, sister's, or uncle's third cousin who happens to know something about computers, who helped them out with registering their domain name.

Keep track of when their domain name expires. It's very common to see someone else take someone's or an organization's domain after it has expired. Some even extort the original organization by threatening to use the domain for a different purpose that would confuse (or horrify) current customers. Their goal is to get the organization to buy the domain name back at a profit. We call these folks cyber-squatters or trolls.

> **Important**
>
> Note which servers are hosting the DNS information in your TIP. In the future, you'll learn how to compromise every website on that same server by using **Simulink bypassing**. You can look forward to that book. To do that, you need to know the names of the servers you'll be attacking.

Command-line interface

If you want to collect a little more information than what you would get from a website, fire up a Linux box. Using WHOIS on the command line is slightly different from the web interface; you should be able to use both.

Open a standard Terminal session. Type in `whois` and then whatever website you like. In this example, I'll be using `HackThisSite.org` again. Notice that it kicks back a lot of similar information that we saw through the web interface, but we have some other tools available on the command line:

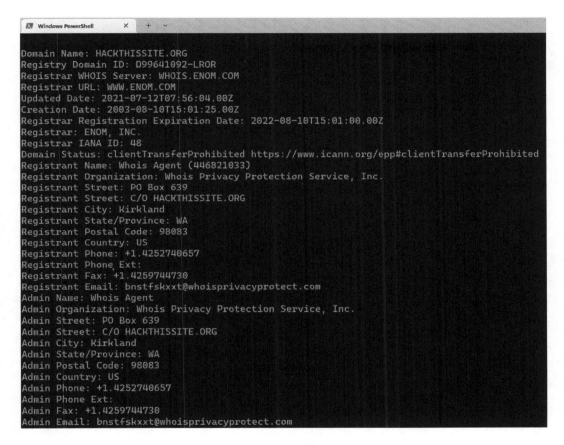

Figure 2.12 – WHOIS through a Terminal session

Here, we'll often see an IP address block that shows the IP address range that it belongs to. Again, you won't see that with this website because they've protected themselves rather thoroughly. We can also select a specific registrar to search with, and we may find even more information. Using the `whois -h whois.arin.net [IP or 198.148.81.136]` command, we can find a network range, actual phone numbers, some contact information, and even an address:

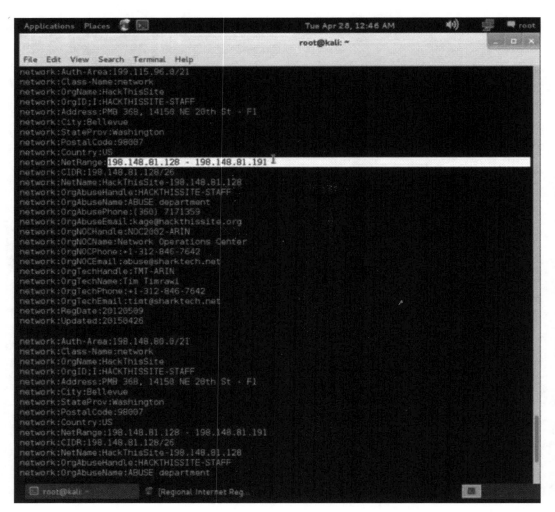

Figure 2.13 – Finding the network range in Terminal

In the next section, we will learn how to use ping and DNS.

Using ping and DNS

To gather even more information about our target website, we're going to use some common tools – **ping** and a DNS tool called **nslookup**.

First, open a command prompt (on a machine with internet connectivity). Start with a simple *ping* of the website we're trying to target. In this case, we're using www. hackthissite.org. Notice that it first resolves the IP address as 198.148.81.137. Then, we can see the typical ping results – the round-trip time that it took to hit that box and come back:

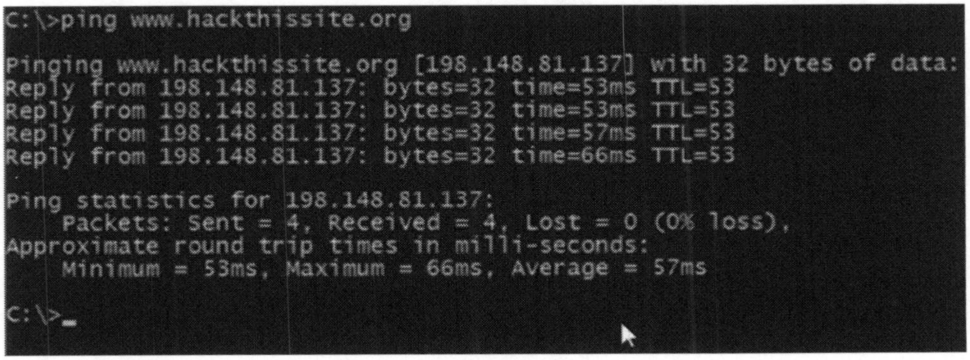

```
C:\>ping www.hackthissite.org

Pinging www.hackthissite.org [198.148.81.137] with 32 bytes of data:
Reply from 198.148.81.137: bytes=32 time=53ms TTL=53
Reply from 198.148.81.137: bytes=32 time=53ms TTL=53
Reply from 198.148.81.137: bytes=32 time=57ms TTL=53
Reply from 198.148.81.137: bytes=32 time=66ms TTL=53

Ping statistics for 198.148.81.137:
    Packets: Sent = 4, Received = 4, Lost = 0 (0% loss),
Approximate round trip times in milli-seconds:
    Minimum = 53ms, Maximum = 66ms, Average = 57ms

C:\>
```

Figure 2.14 – Using ping

Now, we can start playing around with this by increasing the size of the packet that's going across. Right now, it's just 32 bytes. This will allow us to determine which routers allow for bigger packet sizes, which will be helpful when we start to attack the target. Change the original ping command so that it reads ping hackthissite.org -f -l 1300:

```
C:\>ping www.hackthissite.org -f -l 1300

Pinging www.hackthissite.org [198.148.81.136] with 1300 bytes of data:
Reply from 198.148.81.136: bytes=1300 time=70ms TTL=53
Reply from 198.148.81.136: bytes=1300 time=69ms TTL=53
Reply from 198.148.81.136: bytes=1300 time=69ms TTL=53
Reply from 198.148.81.136: bytes=1300 time=70ms TTL=53

Ping statistics for 198.148.81.136:
    Packets: Sent = 4, Received = 4, Lost = 0 (0% loss),
Approximate round trip times in milli-seconds:
    Minimum = 69ms, Maximum = 70ms, Average = 69ms

C:\>
```

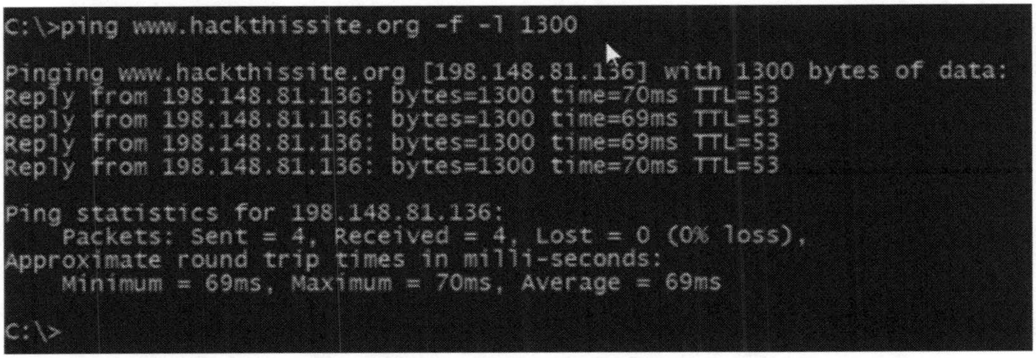

Figure 2.15 – Reading ping hackthissite.org -f -l 1300

> **Note**
>
> Use the up arrow to reload a previously entered command. The letter before
> 1300 is a lowercase L.

-f indicates that you don't want to fragment the packet as it goes across. -l lets you specify the buffer size you want to use. Increase the packet size incrementally until you're notified that the packet can't be sent without being fragmented:

```
C:\>ping www.hackthissite.org -f -l 1500

Pinging www.hackthissite.org [198.148.81.136] with 1500 bytes of data:
Packet needs to be fragmented but DF set.
Packet needs to be fragmented but DF set.
Packet needs to be fragmented but DF set.
Packet needs to be fragmented but DF set.

Ping statistics for 198.148.81.136:
    Packets: Sent = 4, Received = 0, Lost = 4 (100% loss),

C:\>_
```

Figure 2.16 – Reading ping hackthissite.org -f -l 1500

When it says the packet needs to be fragmented, this means that 1500 bytes is too big to be passed through some of the routers; the packet will be dropped. Our next step is to try to decrease the increments to find out what the maximum acceptable packet size is. Find the threshold and make a note of it. Here, you'll see that this router's threshold is for packets that are smaller than 1464, as 1465 won't pass through:

```
C:\>ping www.hackthissite.org -f -l 1464

Pinging www.hackthissite.org [198.148.81.136] with 1464 bytes of data:
Reply from 198.148.81.136: bytes=1464 time=70ms TTL=53
Reply from 198.148.81.136: bytes=1464 time=70ms TTL=53
Reply from 198.148.81.136: bytes=1464 time=70ms TTL=53
Reply from 198.148.81.136: bytes=1464 time=71ms TTL=53

Ping statistics for 198.148.81.136:
    Packets: Sent = 4, Received = 4, Lost = 0 (0% loss),
Approximate round trip times in milli-seconds:
    Minimum = 70ms, Maximum = 71ms, Average = 70ms

C:\>

C:\>ping www.hackthissite.org -f -l 1465

Pinging www.hackthissite.org [198.148.81.136] with 1465 bytes of data:
Packet needs to be fragmented but DF set.
Packet needs to be fragmented but DF set.
Packet needs to be fragmented but DF set.
Packet needs to be fragmented but DF set.

Ping statistics for 198.148.81.136:
    Packets: Sent = 4, Received = 0, Lost = 4 (100% loss),

C:\>
```

Figure 2.17 – Reading ping hackthissite.org -f -l 1464

Next, we want to see the path that the packet took to get to the target IP address. To do so, we'll use another command, `traceroute` or `tracert`, with the IP address:

```
C:\Users\dmeredith>tracert 198.148.81.136

Tracing route to hackthissite.org [198.148.81.136]
over a maximum of 30 hops:

  1    <1 ms    <1 ms    <1 ms  10.10.10.1
  2     5 ms    <1 ms     1 ms  192.168.0.1
  3    12 ms    20 ms    15 ms  207-108-176-13.slkc.qwest.net [207.108.176.13]
  4    12 ms    12 ms    11 ms  slcy-agw1.inet.qwest.net [207.108.177.97]
  5    21 ms    21 ms    21 ms  dvr3-brdr-01.inet.qwest.net [208.168.152.134]
  6    22 ms    22 ms    22 ms  72.164.247.150
  7    22 ms    23 ms    22 ms  edge01.xe5-4.comcast.sharktech.net [70.39.96.225]
  8     *         *        *    Request timed out.
  9    23 ms    22 ms    23 ms  hackthissite.org [198.148.81.136]

Trace complete.

C:\Users\dmeredith>
```

Figure 2.18 – Using the tracert command

As you can see, traceroute displays the different hops the packet goes through (`hops` represents different routers). Note any increased response times and the address of the router that may have dropped the packet. This could be due to a router that just went down. It could also be that this router doesn't respond to **Internet Control Message Protocol** (**ICMP**) requests, which is what ping utilizes (typically, it's the latter).

Finally, you could use those same ping commands to increase the packet size until it fails on each of the addresses in the list; this would tell you where the limitations are located on each device along our path.

The next step is to find other IP addresses that could be associated with this domain name using another CLI tool called **nslookup**. nslookup compares a domain name with an IP address. It has two different modes – interactive and non-interactive.

> **nslookup Modes – Interactive and Non-Interactive**
>
> **Interactive** mode allows you to issue multiple requests without leaving the nslookup interface, while **non-interactive** exits the nslookup interface and returns you to your command prompt as soon as it finishes resolving the IP.

If you were to use nslookup for yahoo.com, as I did here, you would be using non-interactive mode. In this mode, it returns a couple of different IP addresses that are linked to Yahoo. It's a non-authoritative answer, which means that the DNS server I used (Google) is not authoritative for Yahoo. That makes sense, right? They're not in charge of Yahoo:

```
C:\>nslookup yahoo.com
Server:  google-public-dns-a.google.com
Address:  8.8.8.8

Non-authoritative answer:
Name:     yahoo.com
Addresses:  206.190.36.45
          98.139.183.24
          98.138.253.109
```

Figure 2.19 – Using nslookup

To enter interactive mode, simply type in nslookup and hit *Enter* without specifying a domain name. In response, we'll get the server that we'll be using to issue queries against. Then, we can type in a URL (let's go with yahoo.com again). It will show you the IP addresses you would normally resolve to when browsing with your computer or phone:

```
C:\>nslookup
Default Server:  google-public-dns-a.google.com
Address:  8.8.8.8

> yahoo.com
Server:  google-public-dns-a.google.com
Address:  8.8.8.8

Non-authoritative answer:
Name:     yahoo.com
Addresses:  98.139.183.24
          98.138.253.109
          206.190.36.45
>
```

Figure 2.20 – Interactive mode

Let's try to find A records now (an A record simply links a computer name to its IP address). This time, we'll try HackThisSite.org. nslookup provides us with several different IPs, including some IPv6 addresses (the entries that start with 2610:):

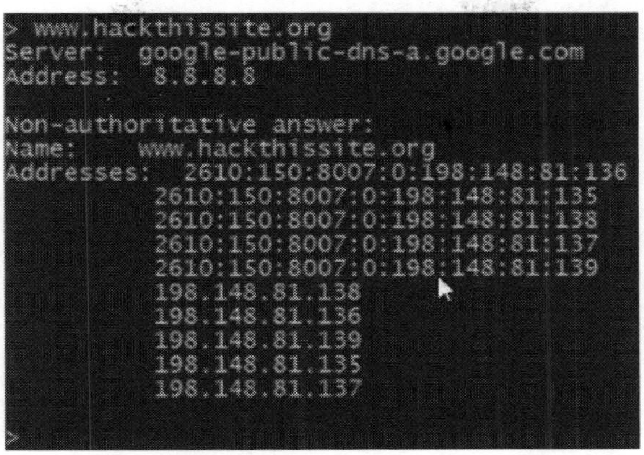

```
> www.hackthissite.org
Server:    google-public-dns-a.google.com
Address:   8.8.8.8

Non-authoritative answer:
Name:      www.hackthissite.org
Addresses:  2610:150:8007:0:198:148:81:136
            2610:150:8007:0:198:148:81:135
            2610:150:8007:0:198:148:81:138
            2610:150:8007:0:198:148:81:137
            2610:150:8007:0:198:148:81:139
            198.148.81.138
            198.148.81.136
            198.148.81.139
            198.148.81.135
            198.148.81.137
>
```

Figure 2.21 – Performing nslookup on HackThisSite.org

We can use nslookup to resolve back specific name records using interactive mode. For example, we can find out what a mail server IP address is by typing in set type=mx, which directs nslookup to search based on a specific attribute, which is designed to identify email servers. Then, type in your target site (I used HackThisSite.org):

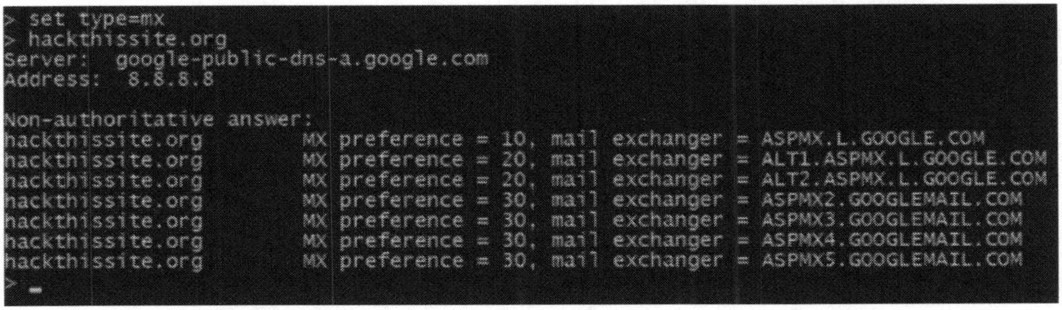

```
> set type=mx
> hackthissite.org
Server:  google-public-dns-a.google.com
Address:  8.8.8.8

Non-authoritative answer:
hackthissite.org        MX preference = 10, mail exchanger = ASPMX.L.GOOGLE.COM
hackthissite.org        MX preference = 20, mail exchanger = ALT1.ASPMX.L.GOOGLE.COM
hackthissite.org        MX preference = 20, mail exchanger = ALT2.ASPMX.L.GOOGLE.COM
hackthissite.org        MX preference = 30, mail exchanger = ASPMX2.GOOGLEMAIL.COM
hackthissite.org        MX preference = 30, mail exchanger = ASPMX3.GOOGLEMAIL.COM
hackthissite.org        MX preference = 30, mail exchanger = ASPMX4.GOOGLEMAIL.COM
hackthissite.org        MX preference = 30, mail exchanger = ASPMX5.GOOGLEMAIL.COM
> _
```

Figure 2.22 – Resolving specific name records using interactive mode

BAM! Now, we know which machines oversee answering emails, or at least their A record names. Based on these results, we can tell right away that Google maintains the mail servers through Google Mail. As an attacker, the next step is to find out the IP address of this mail server. Return to the A record results by typing `set type=a`. Then, enter a mail server's name – for example, `alt1.aspmx.1.google.com` – to view the IP address for that box:

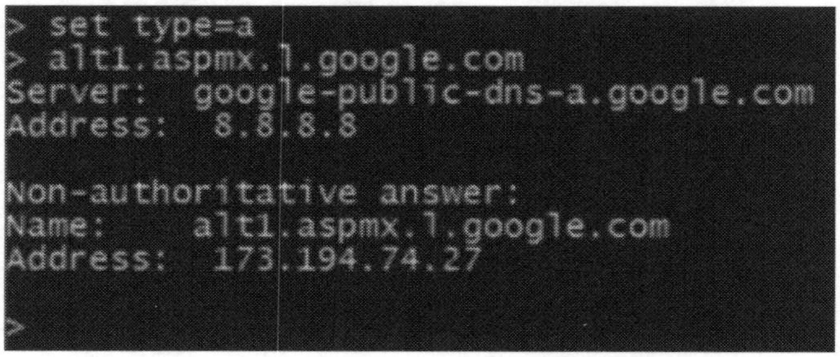

```
> set type=a
> alt1.aspmx.1.google.com
Server:  google-public-dns-a.google.com
Address: 8.8.8.8

Non-authoritative answer:
Name:    alt1.aspmx.1.google.com
Address: 173.194.74.27

>
```

Figure 2.23 – Finding the IP address of a mail server

We also want to figure out what the name of the server is. So, once again, change the type using `set type=cname`. A cname attribute is an alias for an A record name. Then, type in the target URL. In the results, we will see the name of the primary name server and the associated email address, which is `admin.hackthissite.org`. (I know, you're thinking that's not an email address. Where's the @ at? Well, in nslookup land, the first dot replaces the @ symbol, so the email address is, in fact, `admin@hackthissite.org`.) We will also see the serial number, how often it refreshes, and the default TTL:

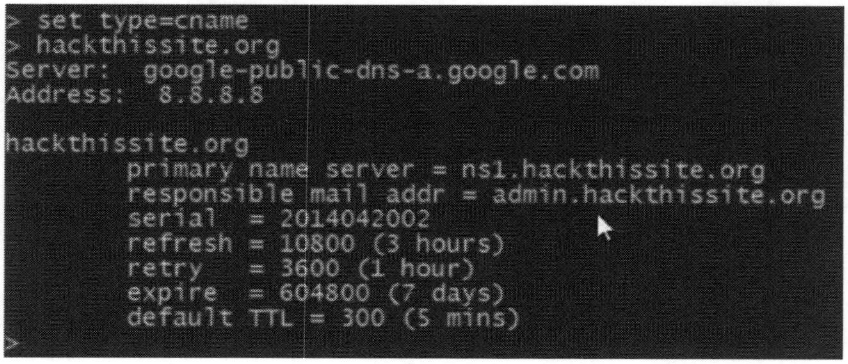

```
> set type=cname
> hackthissite.org
Server:  google-public-dns-a.google.com
Address: 8.8.8.8

hackthissite.org
        primary name server = ns1.hackthissite.org
        responsible mail addr = admin.hackthissite.org
        serial  = 2014042002
        refresh = 10800 (3 hours)
        retry   = 3600 (1 hour)
        expire  = 604800 (7 days)
        default TTL = 300 (5 mins)
>
```

Figure 2.24 – Finding out the name of the server

Sometimes, we're not able to resolve an IP address, particularly when it's an internal IP address. In those cases, set the type back to a, and then type `server [IP address of the DNS server]`. The IP address here is of the DNS server you want to use (for example, in my case, my internal DNS server is `10.10.10.254`). The returned IP addresses are non-authoritative because my DNS server is not in charge of the target site:

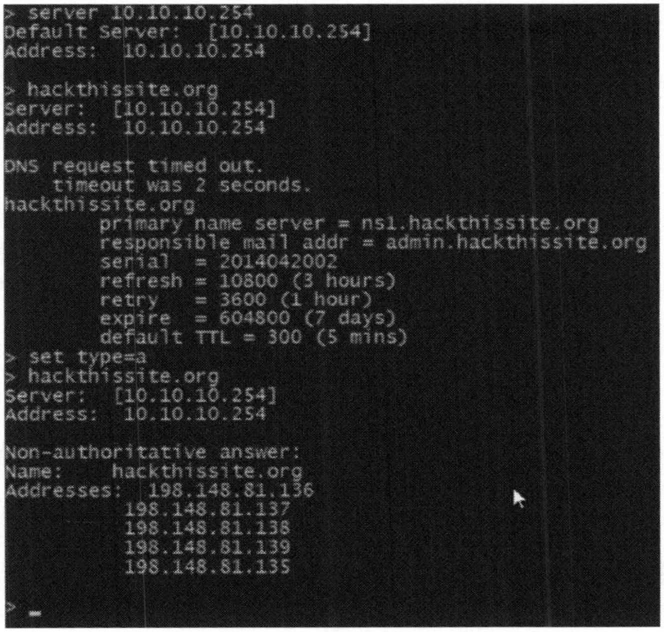

```
> server 10.10.10.254
Default Server:  [10.10.10.254]
Address:  10.10.10.254

> hackthissite.org
Server:  [10.10.10.254]
Address:  10.10.10.254

DNS request timed out.
    timeout was 2 seconds.
hackthissite.org
        primary name server = ns1.hackthissite.org
        responsible mail addr = admin.hackthissite.org
        serial  = 2014042002
        refresh = 10800 (3 hours)
        retry   = 3600 (1 hour)
        expire  = 604800 (7 days)
        default TTL = 300 (5 mins)
> set type=a
> hackthissite.org
Server:  [10.10.10.254]
Address:  10.10.10.254

Non-authoritative answer:
Name:      hackthissite.org
Addresses:  198.148.81.136
        198.148.81.137
        198.148.81.138
        198.148.81.139
        198.148.81.135

>
```

Figure 2.25 – Resolving an IP address

This information can be extremely beneficial for finding targets that are exposed on the internet. After learning about this, a lot of people want to know how to stop this kind of information gathering. There isn't a countermeasure; to send an email, two email servers must communicate with each other. For example, if I try to send an email from `HackThisSite.org` to `Google.com`, my `HackThisSite.org` server needs to be able to *WHOIS* Google and find the mx record for Google to send my email messages.

Once again, as you go through each of the steps here, document them in your TIP so that you have it as a reference when you move onto the more active stages of hacking.

Summary

In this chapter, we started with an overview of reconnaissance, learning how attackers gather information about a target to know when and how to strike. From identifying the machine, they need to target the domains in use, the network blocks in place, and the IP addresses to go after. We looked at passive reconnaissance, active reconnaissance, anonymous reconnaissance, and pseudonymous reconnaissance.

We also covered the goals of reconnaissance – to find out what attackers are looking for (system and network information, the target's standard technical practices, and their organizational information).

Then, we delved into search engines as one of the four ways attackers gather information. A simple search often displays loads of information people have no control over. We discussed how the target's website, free giveaways, and what employees say help attackers during the initial search. After that, we turned our attention to Google hacking, Google operators, the Google database, and other Google hacking tools.

Now, this is just the beginning. In the next chapter, we'll dive a little deeper and see what we can discover about our targets using publicly available intel and social media services.

Questions

As we conclude, here is a list of questions for you to test your knowledge regarding this chapter's material. You will find the answers in the *Assessments* section of the *Appendix*:

1. What is the purpose of reconnaissance?

    A. To discover a target

    B. To map out the target network

    C. Scanning a network

    D. To avoid detection while gathering data on a target for potential vulnerabilities

2. When trying to obtain employee names and addresses, what is the best source to use?

    A. WHOIS

    B. Tracert

    C. Traceroute

    D. Netcraft

3. What information gathering tool will provide you with information about a web server's operating system?

    A. DNSlookuptHE

    B. nslookup

    C. Netcraft

    D. tracert

4. Following reconnaissance, what's the next step to be accomplished?

    A. Enumeration

    B. Scanning

    C. System hijacking

    D. SQL injection

3
Reconnaissance – A Deeper Dive

Did you know that most organizations give away *intel* for free! I know, right?! During the *reconnaissance* stage, it's important to know that by virtue of the internet *being the internet*, there's so much data freely available online that it makes the job of an attack extremely easy. This type of intel is often referred to as **open source intelligence**, or, if you want to sound like the cool kids, you say **OSINT**.

In this chapter, we'll cover the following topics:

- Investigating the target's website
- The Wayback Machine
- What organizations give away for free
- Employees – the weakest link
- Reconnaissance countermeasures

Investigating the target's website

Let's look at how to conduct reconnaissance on a target's website and how we can make use of other research sites. When you're doing reconnaissance, the target website is often where you'll land after a quick online search. That's where you'll learn the business's exact functions, location, contact information, clients, who the leadership team is, and sometimes, way more than that. You'll want to pay close attention to everything on the website.

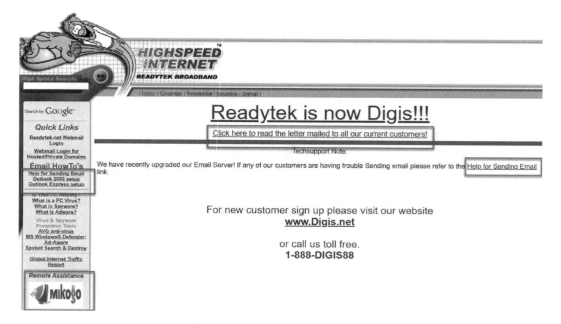

Figure 3.1 – Investigating a website

In *Figure 3.1*, we can see a couple of pieces of information on this main page. First, on the left side, they've provided information on how to set up **Microsoft Outlook** with their particular email product. I already clicked through and saw how to set up via **Microsoft Exchange 2003**, where they also gave me the **Simple Mail Transfer Protocol (SMTP)** servers they utilize. Later, I'll describe how we can use that information to do banner grabs to identify the email server.

We can also see that they use remote assistance software. When you see that an organization utilizes third-party software, it's a good idea to do some vulnerability research to find out whether there are any issues with that product that could get you into the target's system. There are also links everywhere on the page – for example, the **Help for Sending Email** link highlighted in *Figure 3.1*. Explore all the links. They may have helpful information.

This company got bought out by another company (you can see that they've linked to the letter they mailed to all their current customers). Read that letter – it may discuss any new platforms they're utilizing.

Let's look at another target site in *Figure 3.2*. First, look at all the posts they've linked to – for example, **Business Connectivity: Big Data is Everywhere**. Some of their additional posts might be valuable to us; they might discuss details about the history of the company and other information we want to know. Even if it's historical, it may give us a clue for how we approach the phases after reconnaissance.

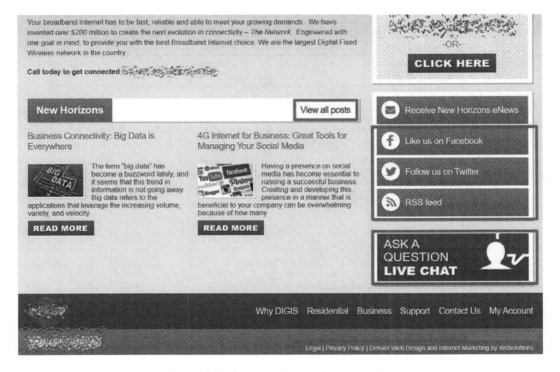

Figure 3.2 – Investigating another target site

This company has given us a lot of valuable information. They provided direct links to their **Facebook** and **Twitter** accounts. They have a chat service listed here. If you see something like that, find out what chat service they're utilizing and do vulnerability research on it.

Check the bottom of the page – and I mean the *very bottom*. People tend to overlook the legal imprint and privacy policy, but you should take note of it if it's there. Websites also typically name their web designer at the bottom, as we see in *Figure 3.2*. Do some research on that company because they could be hosting multiple targets we may want to exploit.

Look at links to form-based pages, like a *contact* or *support* page. In *Figure 3.3*, since this is an email-based form, it could show the information they don't intend for anyone to see. View the page's source information/code to see the HTML, ASPX, or whatever it is they're using:

Figure 3.3 – Email-based page

Inside that code, we might see some identifying comments that developers typically insert for their own memory. You'd be amazed at what we find inside of the page source code, as you don't see it in the web page itself. It's hidden – at least, hidden to the average user.

Many companies post things they think are completely innocuous, but a hacker looks at information differently from how a consumer does. For example, most companies have a page titled *About our staff*. Sometimes, they have links to their employees' emails, or they have photos of them and links to their social media accounts. Social media accounts will be particularly important because sometimes people share too much when they think no one is looking. They might even share details about their work projects. Therefore, it is important to do your due diligence when looking into employees (I'll show you how to do that later).

Some sites have dedicated forums or even **internet relay chat** (**IRC**) (especially if we're looking at an organization with a lot of nerds, as you see on `HackThisSite.org`). Look at what people are talking about. If they have IRC statistics or quotes, look at those. We could start a social engineering attack by contacting somebody in this company and saying something like, "*Hey, what's it like working there? I'm thinking about applying.*"

To really dig into the website, ethical hackers often use a program called **HTTrack** (`https://www.httrack.com/`). It downloads a copy of any given website to your hard drive, including some of the backend code. Just think about the possibilities there. Using HTTrack, we can see exactly how this page is laid out, which might give us more information, such as whether they're saving their images to a different location. This is a very easy program to run. Simply create a project, categorize it, and assign a folder on your hard drive for it to download to.

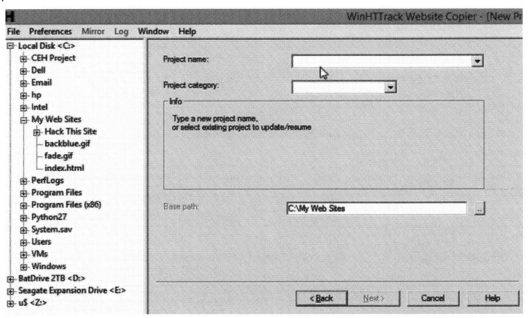

Figure 3.4 – HTTrack website copier

As you can see in *Figure 3.5*, you have the option to **Download web site(s)**, as well as the option to **Download web site(s) + questions**, which means you get to decide whether to download its associated links. Or, you could download the site into separate files. There is even an option that finds and downloads all ZIP files on a site:

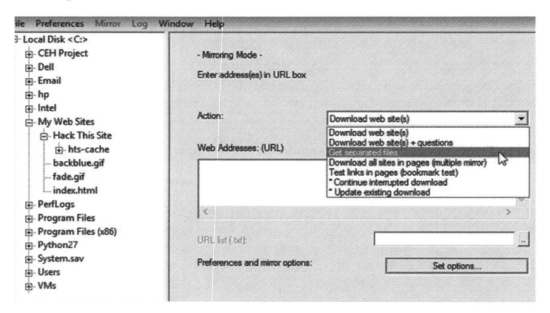

Figure 3.5 – HTTrack, downloading the site

There are plenty of options that we can configure to get exactly the information we need (just click **Set options…**). For example, what do we want to scan for? By default, the program looks for images and CSS pages. Note that we're probably not interested in advertisements, so we can exclude them from the download.

Another thing that's important to remember is to change your browser ID and accept cookies.

Make them think a different browser is hitting their server (this option is under **Browser ID**). Throw them off the trail. Make it seem like you're using a **Linux** box even though you're running a **Microsoft** box. If you're going through this with me, download the site (HackThisSite.org).

In the past, I've found **Microsoft Excel** spreadsheets on a site. I have even found password files. Regardless of whether you find those kinds of files, it's important to have a good understanding of how the target's site is laid out.

Another tool we can use to map out this system and possibly even expose things is a **link extractor** utility. This utility usually goes through a given website and tries to extract both internal and external URLs for it. To find one that works for you, you can just search **Google** for link extractor. In *Figure 3.6*, I'm using the one at **Webmaster-Toolkit** (https://webmasterstoolkit.com/). All you have to do is type in the web address of the site you're targeting and hit **Extract the Links**. Seeing all the different links used on this website could help us figure out the server infrastructure. Some of the links could even provide other ways into the environment.

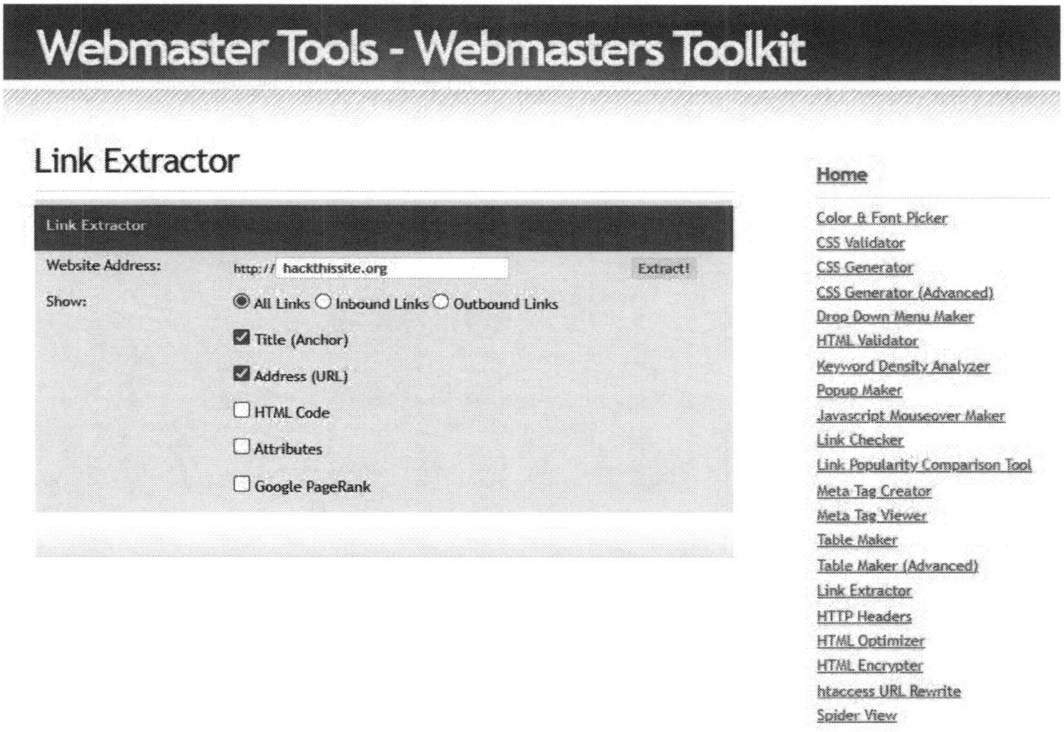

Figure 3.6 – Using the Link Extractor tool from the webmaster toolkit

After extracting the links, the result is as follows:

Webmaster Tools - Webmasters Toolkit

Link Extractor

Link Extractor	
1	HackThisSite **https://www.hackthissite.org**
2	TOR .onion URL **http://hackthisjogneh42n5o7gbzrewxee3vyu6ex37ukyvdw6jm66npakiyd.onion**
3	IRC **https://www.irc.hackthissite.org/chat**
4	Discord **/discord**
5	Forums **https://www.hackthissite.org/forums**
6	Store **https://www.cafepress.com/htsstore**
7	URL Shortener **https://hts.io**
8	CryptoPaste **https://cryptopaste.org**
9	Like Us **https://www.facebook.com/HackThisSite.org**
10	Follow Us **https://twitter.com/hackthissite**
11	Fork Us **https://github.com/HackThisSite**

Figure 3.7 – Result of the link search

When looking at these results, make sure to check whether they expose anything, for example, `extranet.wayneenterprises.com` or maybe `mail.wayneenterprises.com`. The famous keywords to look for are `email` or `restricted`. I'm sure you can think of
a few others on your own as well.

Advanced DNS tricks

Let's go a little deeper into **nslookup.io**. One type of DNS record is called an **SOA**, or **Start of Authority**. An SOA stores a record or information that's important about a domain or a zone containing adminstrative information that could be helpful to you.

Follow these steps:

1. Just like before, type `set type=soa`. This type looks for the authoritative server.

2. Enter the target URL (in our example, this will be `hackthissite.org`).

3. Exit nslookup. The screen should look like the following:

```
> set type=soa
> hackthissite.org
Server:  google-public-dns-a.google.com
Address:  8.8.8.8

Non-authoritative answer:
hackthissite.org
        primary name server = ns1.hackthissite.org
        responsible mail addr = admin.hackthissite.org
        serial  = 2014042002
        refresh = 10800 (3 hours)
        retry   = 3600 (1 hour)
        expire  = 604800 (7 days)
        default TTL = 300 (5 mins)
> exit
```

Figure 3.8 – nslookup, looking for the authoritative server

4. Ping the URL that was identified as the SOA to get the IP address (ns1. hackthissite.org).

5. Once you've got the IP address, go back into nslookup and change the DNS server you're using with the server [IP address of SOA] command. That means that nslookup will use this DNS server to do the resolution.

6. Next, change the type to find any address by typing set type=any.

7. Type ls -d [target site or hackthissite.org].

```
C:\>ping ns1.hackthissite.org

Pinging ns1.hackthissite.org [198.148.81.188] with 32 bytes of data:
Reply from 198.148.81.188: bytes=32 time=159ms TTL=55
Reply from 198.148.81.188: bytes=32 time=169ms TTL=55

Ping statistics for 198.148.81.188:
    Packets: Sent = 2, Received = 2, Lost = 0 (0% loss),
Approximate round trip times in milli-seconds:
    Minimum = 159ms, Maximum = 169ms, Average = 164ms
Control-C
^C
C:\>nslookup
Default Server:  google-public-dns-a.google.com
Address:  8.8.8.8

> server 198.148.81.188
Default Server:  dns.hackthissite.org
Address:  198.148.81.188

> set type=any
> ls -d hackthissite.org
```

Figure 3.9 – nslookup, finding any site by type

8.   That final step will execute what is referred to as a **zone transfer**, which will tell the authoritative DNS server to send us a list of every single computer name or DNS name linked to an IP address. It shows the MX records and the A records. It shows whether there's a www or an FTP (maybe it's FTP1 or FTP2). This is a very easy way to pull all the server names out. Again, all we're doing is executing a normal, expected command against their own DNS server. Most secured DNS servers today only allow zone transfers to take place between specific IP addresses or computer names. However, don't think that will totally protect you – I could easily spoof the IP or computer name.

9.   Let's set the type back to return the mail server information (set type=mx). Take a look at the MX preference number. This number represents the order in which the server responds (the lower the number, the higher the priority).

```
> set type=mx
> hackthissite.org
Server:  dns.hackthissite.org
Address:  198.148.81.188

hackthissite.org          MX preference = 10, mail exchanger = ASPMX.L.GOOGLE.COM
hackthissite.org          MX preference = 20, mail exchanger = ALT1.ASPMX.L.GOOGLE.COM
hackthissite.org          MX preference = 20, mail exchanger = ALT2.ASPMX.L.GOOGLE.COM
hackthissite.org          MX preference = 30, mail exchanger = ASPMX2.GOOGLEMAIL.COM
hackthissite.org          MX preference = 30, mail exchanger = ASPMX3.GOOGLEMAIL.COM
hackthissite.org          MX preference = 30, mail exchanger = ASPMX4.GOOGLEMAIL.COM
hackthissite.org          MX preference = 30, mail exchanger = ASPMX5.GOOGLEMAIL.COM
hackthissite.org          nameserver = ns2.hackthissite.org
hackthissite.org          nameserver = b.ns.buddyns.com
hackthissite.org          nameserver = c.ns.buddyns.com
hackthissite.org          nameserver = d.ns.buddyns.com
hackthissite.org          nameserver = e.ns.buddyns.com
hackthissite.org          nameserver = f.ns.buddyns.com
hackthissite.org          nameserver = ns1.hackthissite.org
ns1.hackthissite.org      internet address = 198.148.81.188
ns1.hackthissite.org      AAAA IPv6 address = 2610:150:8007:0:198:148:81:188
ns2.hackthissite.org      internet address = 198.148.81.189
ns2.hackthissite.org      AAAA IPv6 address = 2610:150:8007:0:198:148:81:189
>
```

Figure 3.10 – nslookup, looking for mail server information

In the preceding example, I am looking at MX records for HackThisSite.org again. From this results list, we can see that their primary mail server is ASPMX.L.GOOGLE. COM. We can also see that they've got a couple of redundant servers here (the lower priority GOOGLEMAIL servers). Often, when you perform a zone transfer, you're able to see the **TTL (time to live)**. If the TTL is set too long, such as 3600 (which is 1 hour), we could poison their DNS.

What does it mean to *poison* their DNS? It means that I change the IP address (or hostname) to direct you away from legitimate servers and toward fake ones.

Let me demonstrate with an example. The equivalent in an attack scenario would be to do this to their server to infect their DNS. First, I'll play with a file on my system.

Let's go into my Windows directory, System32\drivers\etc, and open in **Windows Notepad** a file in there called HOSTS. All computers look at this file (HOSTS) before they move on to sending a request to their DNS servers. I'm going to emulate a DNS poison attack using this file (technically, this is a DNS poison attack, but most of the later Windows operating systems set this file as read only, so it's only the administrator who can do modifications). I'm going to take the IP address of yahoo.com and make it equal to google.com. If I saved this file, every time I tried to go to google.com, my computer would go to this IP address (Yahoo's):

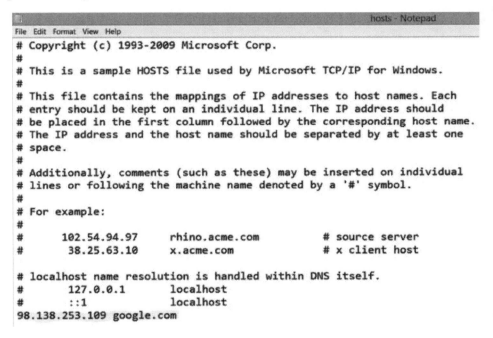

```
                                                    hosts - Notepad
File  Edit  Format  View  Help
# Copyright (c) 1993-2009 Microsoft Corp.
#
# This is a sample HOSTS file used by Microsoft TCP/IP for Windows.
#
# This file contains the mappings of IP addresses to host names. Each
# entry should be kept on an individual line. The IP address should
# be placed in the first column followed by the corresponding host name.
# The IP address and the host name should be separated by at least one
# space.
#
# Additionally, comments (such as these) may be inserted on individual
# lines or following the machine name denoted by a '#' symbol.
#
# For example:
#
#      102.54.94.97     rhino.acme.com          # source server
#       38.25.63.10     x.acme.com              # x client host

# localhost name resolution is handled within DNS itself.
#       127.0.0.1       localhost
#       ::1             localhost
98.138.253.109 google.com
```

Figure 3.11 – Changing the IP address of Yahoo to Google's

The concept of poisoning a DNS is to redirect any traffic to an alternate IP address (at least for a little while). For example, I would make it so that every time an employee tries to access **Citibank**, they go to my IP address, where I would have a website very similar to Citibank's that prompts the user to enter their username and password. Then I would forward the user to the real Citibank site after capturing their login information (insert evil laugh).

All this research will be vital when you're working on a penetration test for an organization. Remember that for each of these sources, you need to look at them from a hacker's perspective – not from the perspective of a normal end user.

Netcraft

There are several tools out there that can help you with reconnaissance and footprinting. **Sam Spade** is one that's talked about a lot:

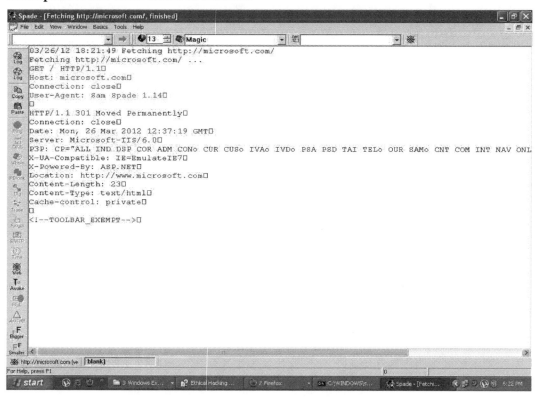

Figure 3.12 – Sam Spade

It's an application that adds a **graphical user interface** (**GUI**) to a lot of the reconnaissance tools we've been talking about thus far. While people use it as a vulnerability scanner to help secure their systems, attackers also frequently use it to find vulnerabilities.

While Sam Spade is an application that can be traced back to you (by IP), **Netcraft** is an online tool that looks at public-facing sites and helps to discover external servers. In some cases, it also looks at operating systems and even applications that are running on those servers via a banner grab. This last part is what usually scares people the most when they learn about NetCraft. Try it out for yourself at `https://www.netcraft.com/`.

A **banner grab** is simply identifying a system by looking at what ports are open and how the system responds to a request to said ports. A Windows server responds to a request on port `80` a little differently than a Linux box. Those differences are what help services (and some tools) to identify the target system.

Netcraft is intended to secure an environment by exposing any problems or vulnerabilities and then fixing them. As an attacker, this is something I will make use of. Netcraft has a variety of services that are focused on helping you secure your environment, but its primary use for us is in finding out the web server a site is using.

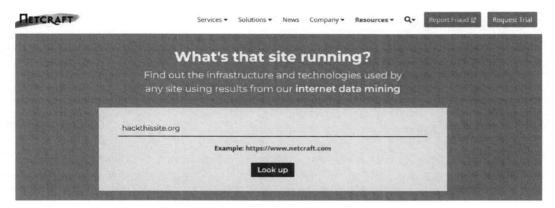

Figure 3.13 – Finding out the web server of a site using Netcraft

Let's pull up Netcraft and try it on our favorite – `HackThisSite.org`. You can see they give us quite a bit of background information here:

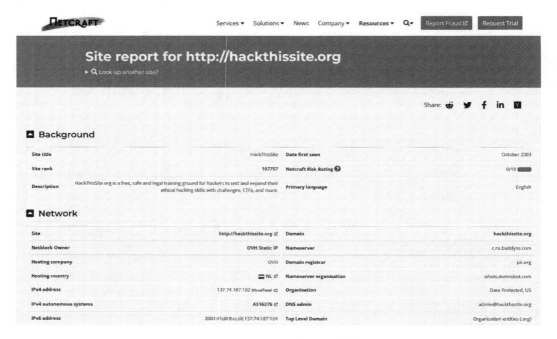

Figure 3.14 – Trying Netcraft on HackThisSite.org

It has extracted some keywords that they utilize. It's given us the site's IP address, including its IPv6 address and the domain registrar. We can also see the hosting history, which shows us that they are using a load balancer based off FreeBSD, which (if not patched properly) could be a great target. Netcraft also shows us their web tracks and the server-side technologies they're using, such as PHP, SSL, JavaScript, and CSS.

Site Technology (fetched 24 days ago)

Server-Side

Includes all the main technologies that Netcraft detects as running on the server such as PHP.

Technology	Description	Popular sites using this technology
PHP	PHP is supported and/or running	www.mediafire.com, www.tutorialspoint.com, www.washingtonpost.com
SSL	A cryptographic protocol providing communication security over the Internet	

Client-Side

Includes all the main technologies that run on the browser (such as JavaScript and Adobe Flash).

Technology	Description	Popular sites using this technology
JavaScript	Widely-supported programming language commonly used to power client-side dynamic content on websites	

Client-Side Scripting Frameworks

Frameworks or libraries allow for easier development of applications by providing an Application Program Interface (API) or a methodology to follow whilst developing.

Technology	Description	Popular sites using this technology
jQuery	A JavaScript library used to simplify the client-side scripting of HTML	www.xnxx.com, www.cnblogs.com, www.msn.com

Figure 3.15 – Web tracks shown by Netcraft

More information is shown in the following screenshot:

Web Browser Targeting

Web browser targeting enables software applications to make use of specific functions of the browser as well as optimizing the application for specific browser versions.

Technology	Description	Popular sites using this technology
Content Public Key Pins Report Only	Report MITM attacks	rapid7ipimseu.okta-emea.com, adobe.okta.com, arco.okta.com
Strict Transport Security	Web security policy mechanism whereby a web server declares that complying user agents are to interact with it using only secure HTTP connections	www.instagram.com, web.whatsapp.com, mail-redir.mention.com
Strict-Transport-Security (preload)	No description	www.canva.com, www.w3schools.com, opensea.io
X-XSS-Protection Disabled	Cross-site scripting protection is disabled	www.google.com, l.facebook.com, t.co
Referrer Policy	Restrict referrer information included in subsequent requests	www.mozilla.org, www.ecosia.org, www.xvideos.com
Strict-Transport-Security (including subdomains)	No description	support.microsoft.com, mail.protonmail.com, docs.microsoft.com
Content Security Policy Report	Detect, mitigate and report attacks in the browser	www.roblox.com, yandex.ru, mail.google.com
Content Security Policy	Detect and mitigate attacks in the browser	discord.com, accounts.google.com, twitter.com

Doctype

A Document Type Declaration, or DOCTYPE, is an instruction that associates a particular SGML or XML document (for example, a webpage) with a Document Type Definition (DTD).

Technology	Description	Popular sites using this technology
XHTML	Extended version of the Hypertext Markup Language	www.ghanaweb.com, www.majorgeeks.com, www.sigmalive.com

HTML 5

Figure 3.16 – More information

What are they using to see which web browser their users are utilizing to access their website? As you can see, we can learn a lot of information with this tool.

When I test it with my old site (`utahwisp.com`), it gives us the site's hosting history, including the IP address, web server, and operating system. If you are conducting a penetration test on your organization's infrastructure, this will be quite useful because it's great at pulling up what server and web server service you're using:

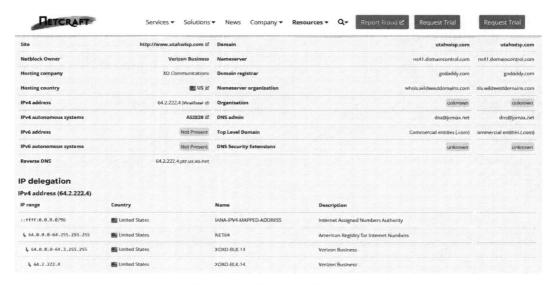

Figure 3.17 – Testing utahwisp.com

One other nice thing about Netcraft is that it shows you a *Netcraft risk rating*. Zero out of 10 is a great rating for security, but that doesn't mean it's not hackable. Obviously, them revealing this information exposes quite a bit to an attacker. There are a lot of tools created for legitimate purposes, such as Netcraft, that attackers can capitalize on just by shifting their perspective.

The Wayback Machine

At this point, the internet has been around for quite some time, and there are a number of retired web pages and websites. **The Wayback Machine** (`https://archive.org/web/web.php`) allows us to view previous versions of websites that may not even exist anymore. Think of it as *the* archive of the internet. Once we find the older version of our target site, we can scan for *historical data* that people didn't mean to expose. Now, before I got my start in security, I had no idea this tool was out there, but it's really interesting to use for fun as well (you know, like showing your kids what **Amazon** used to look like):

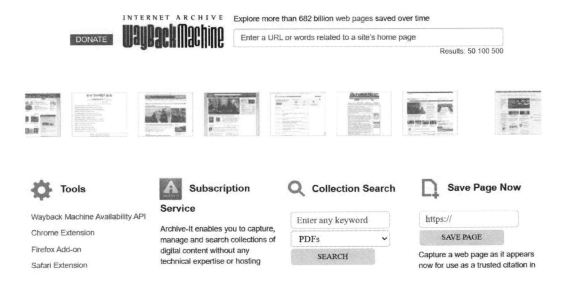

Figure 3.18 – The Wayback Machine home page

You can see here that they have saved over *456 billion* web pages. The Wayback Machine goes through websites and detects any changes – if it detects a change, it makes a note and caches that information. As an example, I'll use my old company's website. The site is no longer being maintained, but you can see there was some activity in 2003. There is one snapshot of my site from January 10, 2003:

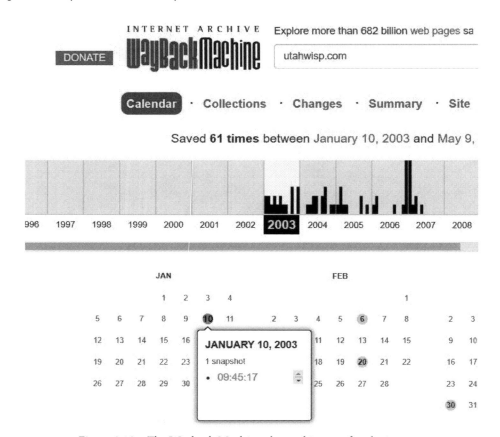

Figure 3.19 – The Wayback Machine change history of utahwisp.com

In the snapshot, you can see my web development skills. My prowess was considerable. This is back in the days when we used Notepad. I think by then I'd moved up to **HotDog**, which was one of the first WYSIWYG environments for web design.

What can we find here that would be useful for our purposes? We can find the purpose and messaging of the organization, where it's located, contact information, such as a cell phone number, and information about the email options available, including a login page. Note that this is just an example – your target will still be operational, so a lot of the infrastructure is probably still in place:

Figure 3.20 – More information from Wayback Machine

When companies first built their web pages (especially back in the day), they listed all kinds of information. They didn't think it was a security risk. That means, if we go back and look at previous versions of their website, it could expose quite a bit, for example, employee or leadership personal information. There may even be a press release section where they announced that they're moving to **Microsoft Server 2000** and looking toward moving to **2008**. Even when people think they've removed historical information from a website, there's always a record of it somewhere.

What organizations give away for free

When I was about 25 years old, there was a radio station, *The Q*, in the city where I lived that was holding a big contest that included giving away a big prize package. They would hide this big wooden Q every day, which was about a foot by a foot in depth and in height (30 x 30 cm) and about 2 inches (5 cm) thick, and give out clues for where to find it. If you found the Q, you won a prize package that could include a couple of four-wheelers, a trip to Hawaii, TVs, tons of stuff.

I was tracking the clues that they gave out each day, and I thought I knew where it was, so I looked around for hours in this huge park. After about three or four hours, I gave up. It turned out that I was about 25 feet (8 meters) away from it when I gave up. I still regret that today. It's the same thing here with reconnaissance – you've got to look *everywhere*, despite the massive amounts of information that become available to you.

The more you try to find out about your target, the more you're going to find. Victor Hugo, the famous author of *Les Miserables*, once said, "*Perseverance, secret of all triumphs*" – this is especially true for reconnaissance.

In this section, we'll look at what else you can find out about your target. We'll look into the information they're publishing that can be useful for us as ethical hackers. That includes job sites, promotional materials, social media, and email.

Job sites

Job sites give us so much information. I'm not just talking about standard job sites – we'll also get information from company-run job sites, including the career pages included on the corporate website.

When we start looking at a well-known job site, we start searching by job title or technologies. Companies might inadvertently expose the different technologies they're using when they advertise for specific jobs, even if it's for a temporary project. I'll be doing these very specific searches since I'm not actually going to target a company, but you will also want to look at all the job vacancies that your target organization has advertised online.

Remember that you are not looking at this as a potential employee or the employer. Look at it through the eyes of an attacker.

I'll use **Monster** (`https://www.monster.com/`) as an example. Start by looking for some technical positions, such as **systems engineer**. In the following example, based on the qualifications they're looking for, we can see that they're using **Microsoft Active Directory**, **Windows Server 2008**, **VMware**, and **Hyper-V**.

They're also looking for someone with knowledge of **Cisco,** which means we can infer what kind of routers and switches they're probably utilizing. They also mention the **SolarWinds** and **Spotlight** monitoring tools, so now we know what type of monitoring tools they're using internally. Once you get this information, you'll want to investigate the architecture of each component and see whether there are any vulnerabilities, or better yet, you might see any security systems that you'll need to avoid.

Job Requirements:

- 5+ years of experience supporting an *enterprise IT environment*
- 3+ years of experience Active Directory and general domain service administration and design
- 3+ years of enterprise Windows server 2008 administration
- 2+ years supporting enterprise virtualization technologies (VMWare and Hyper-V).
- Outstanding customer service skills as well as strong verbal and written communication.
- Knowledge of network topologies.
- General knowledge of Data Center practices.
- Experienced problem solver with the ability to resolve issues while retaining a strong customer service focus and a positive attitude and excellent communication skills.
- Collaborative team player with the ability to multitask while providing clear documentation of production processes as necessary.
- Process driven with a strong attention to detail.

Additional Assets:

- MCSE Certification.
- Knowledge of the Cisco UCS platform.
- Knowledge of SaaS environments.
- Experience with large server farms.
- Knowledge of Solarwinds and Spotlight monitoring tools helpful.

Figure 3.21 – Job requirement for a systems engineer

Let's try searching a different way – by keyword. Find people who are looking for someone who knows something about some outdated servers. Let's go with `server 2003`, for example.

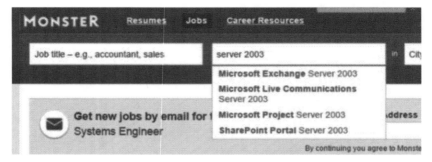

Figure 3.22 – Searching with the "server 2003" keyword on Monster

Once again, we'll look at a recruiting agency's job posting. They request experience working with **Microsoft SharePoint 2010** authentication and permissions models, as well as administering SQL. So, there we have information about the backend. They are also looking for someone with experience with **Visual Studio .NET**, and it looks like they have both intranet and internet portals that are being hosted by SharePoint. All these systems are way outdated, and it would surprise you how many organizations out there are still running systems this old. If they weren't, I wouldn't be so busy!

Figure 3.23 – Job requirements of a SharePoint administrator

The same thing can be done by looking at other job sites, such as **DICE** (`https://www.dice.com/`), **Indeed** (`https://www.indeed.com/`), and more. Pay special attention to the jobs that your target advertises, as these will give you valuable insight into the systems they're running and their overall network architecture. You might even get a sense of what security controls they have in place. For example, what type of **intrusion detection system** (**IDS**) do they have installed?

Can you see now why job sites make me all giddy inside? They can give us a plethora of information, and this makes our job so easy.

Marketing and customer support

We can learn so much just by looking at the organization's social networking profile. As demonstrated in the previous section, recruiters and job sites can provide valuable information, such as the platforms or systems the target is using. We can also take note of how they support their users because that can be important for a social engineering attack. For example, I could call a random employee: "*Hey Jim, this is Fred in the IT department. I just reset your account, and I need to make sure that your password is going to work correctly and log you in. What's your password, really quick?*"

If the user support is done via email, I can spoof an email and make it look like it's coming from their IT department. Or better yet, a **CEO fraud email attack**, where an attacker (after reconning a company) poses as an executive, creates an emergency issue, and requests money from someone in accounting or their assistant to be transferred to a specific account. We can also look at the user surveys the target puts out to collect feedback, as the questions they ask might give us an insight into their business strategies.

If we start looking at the products they're promoting, that should also give us some information about their product specifications. To use this in practice, if I notice a particular target uses a given piece of software, I will backtrack and find out all I can about that software.

In our culture, we are sharing way too much information, both personally and from a business perspective. Social networking environments such as **Twitter**, **Facebook**, **LinkedIn**, and even **Google+** are now used for marketing and personal purposes. This combination can expose information with very tangible consequences. Hopefully, if you're reading this, you understand that if you post something, you can't take it back, and it doesn't matter if you delete it immediately. We've seen thousands of people lose their jobs because of the things that they've posted online. Likewise, we've also seen a lot of companies lose money because of this.

Let's look at some of the different methods we can use to mine these social sites for our target's data. Obviously, start by looking around (from an attacker's perspective) and see what you can find. Look at their previous posts. Look at photos being uploaded or posted. Check out employees' personal sites. It's shocking how few people put controls on their websites.

Financial and competitive analysis data

Businesses often conduct competitive analyses to assess their competitors or to figure out their market strategy. As attackers, we can use services that are intended for business analysis for somewhat more nefarious purposes.

There are many sites out there we could use, but I'm going to focus on some of the more popular ones, such as **Yahoo Finance**, **Google Finance**, **CNN**, **MSNBC**, **MarketWatch**, **The Wall Street Transcript**, and more. Several of them provide information such as the market value of a company's shares, the company profile, and its major competitors. All this information may be helpful in future penetration testing, especially for social engineering attacks.

You can get this information through tools that allow for competitor analysis, or by setting up email alerts for updates to a specific company's profile. For example, if Microsoft posts something about the new **HoloLens**, or if Google posts something about ending **Gmail**, you obviously want to be notified about this kind of information. You'll have to register for those services, but it's a good way of monitoring what's going on with the company.

Competitive analysis tools allow businesses to discover information about *competitors*.

Attackers utilize these services to find out basic company information, such as when and how it was founded, or its leadership, location, and products. Many of these tools don't just provide analysis of competitors; they might also provide analyses of their products, their customer base, their suppliers, and more. They use the same techniques that we've already gone over to gather that information. They then charge money for it and give you a nice formatted report with patents, trademarks, catalogs, customers, vendor interviews, press releases, annual reports, and more. They basically go out and do all the spying for you, and there's nothing illegal about that.

Employees – the weakest link

Have you ever lost something and it ended up being right in front of you? This usually happens with my glasses. I'll be looking everywhere for them and running around the house saying, "*Anybody seen my glasses?*" And my wife will turn to me and say, "*They're on top of your head.*"

It's the same concept with different reconnaissance techniques. Some of the data that we gather in the reconnaissance phase is incredibly easy to find. In fact, a lot of the information can be found through online services that we're probably already using:

Employees: What Can Be Learned

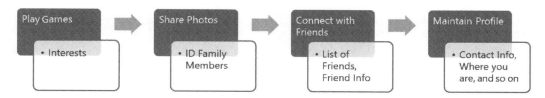

Figure 3.24 – Online services where information can be gathered

The employee side is where things get scary. For example, if an employee plays games, that may show us their interests and hobbies (not that I think that somebody sits at home with a hammer and crushes candy). This information provides us with a good sense of what people are familiar with, which could help us out with passwords in the future.

To take it to the next level, you can create a fake persona and start interacting with the target. For example, if you're a big fan of a particular gaming console, you could try to get into the forums where they're talking about doing repairs. You could even ask your target a few questions to start and build a relationship. This is a small taste of what *social engineering* is – another method for us to gather information.

What photos are they sharing? From these photos, we could find out some things: who their family members are; where the picture was taken; if they go to that place frequently. Today, smartphones even tag photos with **GPS** (**Global Positioning System**) coordinates, making it much easier to find out where someone is. We can glean even more information from the backgrounds of the photos – this could be their street address, a sports league they're in, or the school their kids attend. I know that's a little family-related, but it can be dangerous. I'm very protective about families and I hope you guys can recognize the problem with posting seemingly harmless information about your kids.

Employees might post pictures of them at the local bar on the weekends, revealing where they go to hang out with friends. Now, we know where to go to meet people that work for that organization.

Who are they connected to in their friend list? This could give us some potential additional targets. But more often, it's important for answering security questions. One of the security questions we get all the time when trying to reset a password is, *Who was your childhood best friend?* We might be able to figure that out just from interactions on social media. If that doesn't work, we could deploy a minor social engineering attack. For example, if I see that Bruce Wayne is friends with Clark Kent, I could send Bruce Wayne a spoofed email from Clark Kent asking about additional information that I might need for an attack.

Does the target often post their location or what they're doing? For example, Bruce Wayne says he's going to Metropolis this week. For us, the attackers, that means he's out of Gotham City, and the banks are wide open for me to rob because he's not there to protect them. Did the target post their phone number on their profile? Do they have strict privacy settings in place?

Think of security this way: I could be the safest driver in the world, but a drunk driver could still crash into me. Likewise, I can do everything I can to block people from getting to my information, but my best friend might have a profile that's wide open. If we've interacted online, that could expose some additional information about me, like my friends or hometown.

Facebook

According to **Tech Crunch**, approximately 2 billion users log in to Facebook every month. That's around 1.3 billion logins daily:

`https://techcrunch.com/2017/06/27/facebook-2-billion-users/`

Over 300 million photos are uploaded daily. And when people go to Facebook, they spend 20 minutes per visit, on average. Facebook is an inextricable part of daily life. This means this site is not only valuable for reconnaissance, but is also useful for the *attack* stage. There are as many as 85 million fake profiles.

Let's look at some of the information we can extrapolate out of a Facebook page – John Wayne's to be precise. I've found his Facebook page, and he's been doing some posting, which is kind of bizarre:

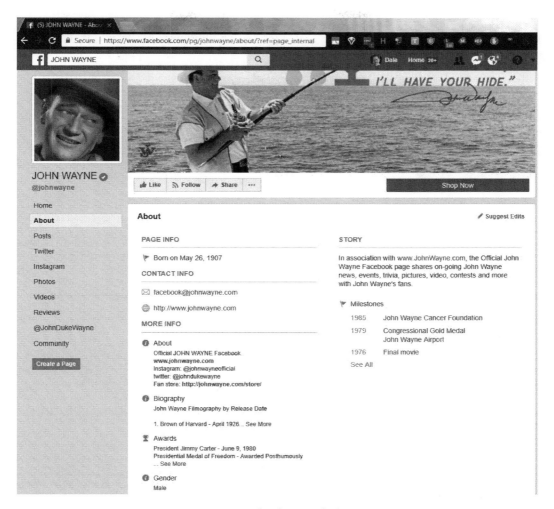

Figure 3.25 – Facebook page of John Wayne

People will put all kinds of personal information on their Facebook pages because we're often unaware that seemingly trivial data can be very revealing in the wrong hands. From these pages, and specifically from John Wayne's page, we know his personal website, when he went on a business trip, what airline he likes, his birthday, his personal achievements, his parents' names, where he's lived, his pets' names, his high school, hobbies, and more. We can find out who his friends are based on who posts comments on his photos. When he's tagged in a photo, we can look at the buildings in the background to see whether we can identify where he is. Is his car in the picture? Can you see a license plate number? He posted a picture of him and his daughter, so now we know her name and roughly when she was born.

As you can see, people tend to put a lot of information online – even for deceased celebrities. What does that say about their interest in sharing personal data on the internet?

LinkedIn

LinkedIn, designed for business relationships, is also a popular social media platform. It has approximately 13 million companies currently listed and a total of 467 million users. Let's go over what we could discover with LinkedIn.

The key information you should record in your **Target Information Profile** (**TIP**) from LinkedIn is as follows:

- Current and past employment data

- Educational information, certifications, and skills

- Personal interests, contact information, and location

- Notable connections and groups they may be a part of

For example, you can look at the technical skills listed, see where the target got their education, and investigate that particular program for more details about their abilities. As mentioned before in the *Job sites* section, we're able to see what type of platforms the target is used to working with, which may give us a sense of what their current employer is using (if that's what we're going after). Don't ignore the groups that people join – we're often able to see what someone is struggling with because people tend to join groups to help them with specific projects or issues they've encountered.

We will also be able to gather more information if we are connected to the person. In some cases, people will accept LinkedIn connection requests just to build their professional network. Because this is a professional platform where people don't generally share very personal thoughts, even fewer are concerned about the information they may expose through this site.

Let me show you an example using my own profile:

Experience

 Author
Pluralsight

Dec 2014 - Present · 6 years 7 months

Worldwide

Dale is also a PluralSight Author, having published several courses on Cyber-Security, Ethical Hacking, CSA+, GCIH and ECIH.

 Speaker / Trainer / Consultant
My Mentored Learning, Inc.

Oct 2011 - Present · 9 years 9 months

Worldwide

Working with end-users and IT professionals to help increase their learning with SharePoint, Exchange, Active Directory, System Center, Powershell, and others. Creating and publishing video training materials for online learning.

 Microsoft Certified Trainer/Certified Ethical Instructor
New Horizons Salt Lake City

Oct 2006 - Oct 2011 · 5 years 1 month

United States

Microsoft Trainer: Specializing in Server Deployment, Network Infrastructure, Exchange 2003-2010, SharePoint 2003-2010, SCCM, SCOM, Active Directory, Certified Ethical Hacker/Certified EC-Council Instructor

 Manager of Information Systems
UtahWISP

Dec 2001 - Oct 2006 · 4 years 11 months

 Microsoft Trainer
Advanced Technical Training

May 1997 - Oct 2001 · 4 years 6 months

Salt Lake City, Utah

 Manager of Information Systems
MicroSupply, Inc.

Feb 1992 - May 1997 · 5 years 4 months

Salt Lake City, Utah

Figure 3.26 – A LinkedIn page showing the Experience section

In some cases, you can estimate the network infrastructure of a person's current employer based on their past experiences. As we go through this profile, you can see here that I worked for *My Mentored Learning, Inc.* That's my existing company that I use when I go out and teach. We also have *New Horizons* out of Salt Lake City. There's *UtahWISP* and *Advanced Technical Training* (another training center). Look especially at the certifications that I've listed in *Figure 3.27*. I'd say right away that this person knows something about Microsoft Servers, Exchange, SharePoint, and Systems Center. In a real-life scenario, you could infer that I'm also using that experience (and potentially those specific technologies) in my current job.

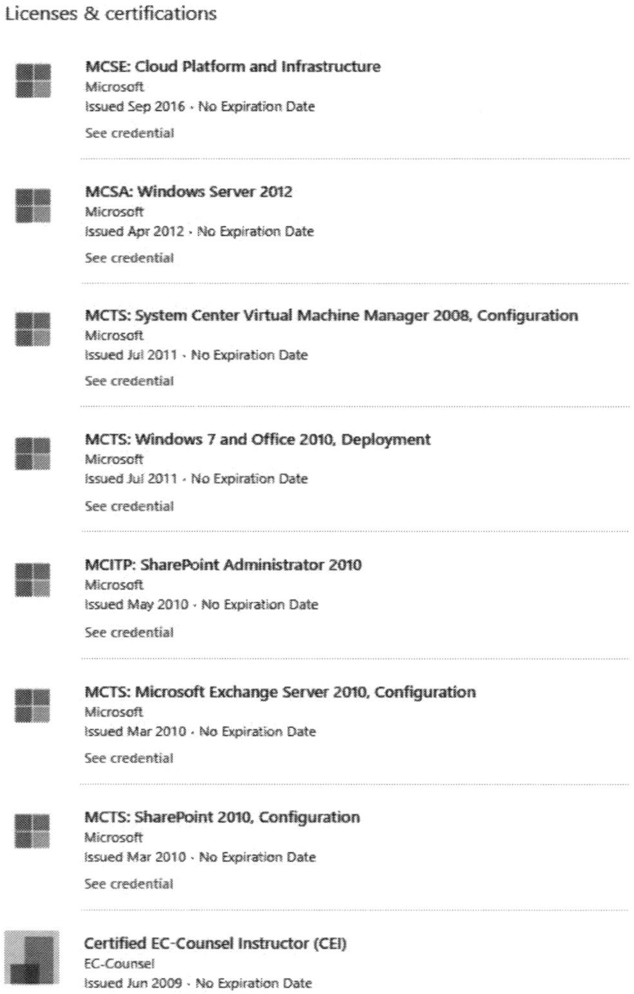

Licenses & certifications

MCSE: Cloud Platform and Infrastructure
Microsoft
Issued Sep 2016 · No Expiration Date
See credential

MCSA: Windows Server 2012
Microsoft
Issued Apr 2012 · No Expiration Date
See credential

MCTS: System Center Virtual Machine Manager 2008, Configuration
Microsoft
Issued Jul 2011 · No Expiration Date
See credential

MCTS: Windows 7 and Office 2010, Deployment
Microsoft
Issued Jul 2011 · No Expiration Date
See credential

MCITP: SharePoint Administrator 2010
Microsoft
Issued May 2010 · No Expiration Date
See credential

MCTS: Microsoft Exchange Server 2010, Configuration
Microsoft
Issued Mar 2010 · No Expiration Date
See credential

MCTS: SharePoint 2010, Configuration
Microsoft
Issued Mar 2010 · No Expiration Date
See credential

Certified EC-Counsel Instructor (CEI)
EC-Counsel
Issued Jun 2009 · No Expiration Date

Figure 3.27 – Licenses & certifications section

Researching people

By now, you know how employees might provide valuable information for our reconnaissance. That could be because they share too much on social media, their skills, and past employment history, or maybe one of them *is the vulnerability* we want to target with a social engineering attack.

Overall, we are trying to create a profile of each person. Even seemingly innocuous information may be helpful because people often base their passwords on things that they reveal online. Look for information such as job title, hobbies, whether they're involved in any type of charitable work, or anything that may be of interest. We also want to try to collect things such as phone numbers, home addresses, email addresses, and possibly bank or credit card details.

To find those things, most people will use third-party products. There are obvious sources, such as personal blogs or social media, but there are also dedicated online search products for finding this type of information. These include sites such as **PeopleLookup** (https://www.peoplelookup.com/), **AnyWho** (https://www.anywho.com/whitepages), and **CheckPeople** (https://www.checkpeople.com/).

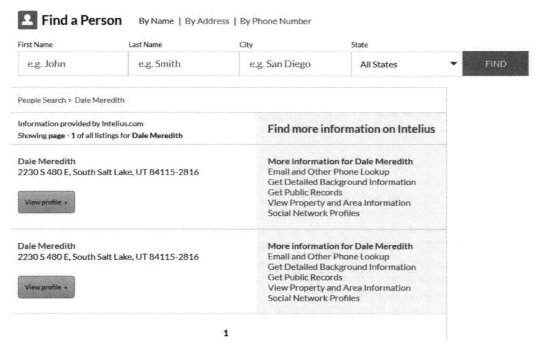

Figure 3.28 – Looking up people on PeopleSmart

I used myself as an example and searched with **PeopleSmart**. All I had to do was enter my name and the city of Salt Lake City, Utah, and hit **Search**. These types of websites search public records, as well as court records, and make them accessible to the average person. It's all already out there, but they've made it easy for us to get a hold of it. Note that most of these are paid services and require a little more information. But even with the free version, I can see my old phone number and address. You may want to take this to the next level by finding the addresses on **Google Maps** so you understand where this person lives. Again, the purpose of this is to give you some hints and details that you will add to your database of information or your TIP.

> **Pro-Tip**
>
> Many of these search engines, such as Google and Yahoo, will provide notifications on updates. If someone changes something on that website, you could be notified of those updates. Trust me – attackers are already doing that to see when you post a new job.

Social engineering

I define *hacking* as getting a device to do something outside of what it was designed to do. That's exactly what social engineering attacks accomplish, or, as I like to call it, *human hacking*.

By default, humans are not designed to give up personal information. We know it's wrong, but we continue exposing information about ourselves because people or services convince us that we should somehow trust them (this is called *gaining the target's confidence*).

> **Information**
>
> A **McAfee** documentary (`https://www.youtube.com/watch?v=yzU82U196pU`) from a few years ago perfectly illustrates the power of social engineering. It describes one of the most famous social engineering attacks that targeted a woman based solely on the fact that she visited a genealogy website. A group of people pretended to be related to her and preyed on her emotions (a hallmark of social engineering). They claimed that they were trying to escape a bad situation and needed money to do so. She ended up giving them over $500,000. Ultimately, this was revealed by a gray hat hacker who investigated the extent of the damage by hacking her again to see how the attackers had targeted her (`https://www.youtube.com/watch?v=F9GylhWsVc8`).

So, how is this typically done? One of the most basic methods is **dumpster diving**. Surprisingly, this is what it sounds like. You can find a lot of information about someone in their trash can. A great example of this was back in the days when Microsoft was under investigation by the US Department of Justice about how they were implementing **Internet Explorer**. You can read about it at `http://www.newsweek.com/diving-bills-trash-161599`. **Sun Microsystems** hired people to go and dumpster dive at Microsoft's location. Because trash is not considered company property, they pulled out some reports showing some of Microsoft's questionable behavior.

We can also **eavesdrop** on a target. Eavesdropping could include **physical listening** (like when you listen to the person in the cubicle next to you), **digital eavesdropping** (via email, for example), or so-called **shoulder surfing** (secretly watching what people are doing).

I try to protect against the latter as much as I can. In fact, my wife thinks I'm crazy because whenever I'm out and about and have to swipe my debit card, before I type in my PIN code, I physically turn around and make sure no one is trying to shoulder surf. There are also digital methods of shoulder surfing – where people use their cell phones to capture images. I'm very suspicious of people who are on their cell phones that are right behind me in a checkout line because, even if they have the phone up to their ear, their camera could be recording my PIN. The same principle can apply to passwords, so be mindful of typing your password into your phone in a public place.

Eavesdropping can also be dangerous because it may allow people to more convincingly impersonate an employee of an organization that you are legitimately involved with. Perhaps you take a phone call in your local grocery store, and you're complaining about your bank, Citibank. A scammer might hear you and then call you up and say that Citibank has an issue and is calling people up asking them to confirm their identities. In that way, they're using minor details about you to get you to reveal potentially valuable information about yourself or someone you know.

You've got mail = I've got you!

Another great tool for gathering intelligence is *email*. We can track when an email has been read, if it has been forwarded, the time spent reading it, any links visited, the types of servers being used, the OS the recipient is using, and more. There's a lot of information embedded in emails.

Let me give you an example:

Figure 3.29 – Information embedded in an email

This is an email header I got from *Thrifty Car Rental* – a typical email advertisement about some upcoming car rental stuff. Look at this header information – it's available for every email. Back in the old days when we didn't have Outlook, a lot of this technical information was listed at the beginning of all your emails. Now it's hidden, but you can still expose it by looking at advanced headings (typically).

From the header alone, we can see who the email was sent to, the date and time that it was sent, the server it came from, the sender's IP address, and even the authentication system being used by the sender. That means if we want to obtain the name of one of Thrifty's email servers, all we have to do is sign up for emails from them.

There are several tools that we can use to gather information from emails that are completely invisible to email recipients. **Email Lookup** (https://www.ipaddresslocation.org/) by IPAddresslocation.org scans the headers for you. If you want to track what's going on with a particular piece of email, you can use **eMailTrackerPro** (http://www.emailtrackerpro.com/). It will show you a map of the likely location of the sender and some WHOIS information. **PoliteMail** (https://www.politemail.com/) is a tool you can use with Outlook. It creates a map that shows all the different email servers that a particular email hopped through.

DidTheyReadIt (`http://www.didtheyreadit.com/`) is another application or tool that you can use to find out whether an email recipient read an email or whether they just deleted it right away. **ReadNotify** (`https://www.readnotify.com/`) can tell you when your email is opened, if it was reopened, if the recipient forwarded it to somebody else, and if so, who it was forwarded to. This one also has a nice GUI.

These kinds of services are especially popular in the sales and marketing sector – they want to know when you've opened a message, clicked a link in it, and even how long you spent reading it. If you're working for a company, the marketing team may already have access to these tools.

Today, based on reverse lookup, most email servers drop an email if they believe a header has been forged. When an email comes in, the server asks, *What's the name of the email server this came from, and what's the IP address in the header*. Then it does a reverse lookup to see whether those are still true statements because most of the time, when someone is forging a header or spoofing the email address, that information won't match up and your email server will drop it. Using these types of tools helps security professionals to see whether their email systems are susceptible to different types of reconnaissance.

A great example of this is, as I mentioned previously, countless corporations falling victim to CEO fraud emails. Attackers spoofed corporate email accounts and impersonated executives to fool employees in accounting or HR into executing unauthorized wire transfers or sending out confidential tax information, as seen in this article:

```
https://krebsonsecurity.com/2016/04/fbi-2-3-billion-lost-to-
ceo-email-scams/
```

Reconnaissance countermeasures

One of my favorite movies is *The Hunt for Red October*. When the torpedoes are coming in, Sean Connery yells, "*Release the countermeasures!*" And this is exactly what we need to do here. We need to understand the *countermeasures for reconnaissance* and what we need to be looking for when performing penetration tests (pen tests). You might know GI Joe's famous quote, "*Knowing is half the battle.*" This also applies to us. Knowing what you are exposing and knowing what the attacker is capable of is half the battle.

In this section, I'll show you how to put your shields up and implement those countermeasures, as well as some best practices for reconnaissance. I'll also show you how to set up for a pen test and the actual workflow of what you should be tracking when doing reconnaissance.

Countermeasures

So, how do you defend yourself against the kind of reconnaissance techniques we reviewed earlier?

The first thing you need to do is make sure you have configured your routers to not respond to certain types of traffic. In other words, ensure they don't identify themselves.

Here's a fun exercise. What's the default **SSID (Service Set Identifier)** on the **Linksys** router? Oh, that's right, it's `Linksys`. What I like to do is take that Linksys router and change the SSID to **D-Link** – because that's the default broadcast for a D-Link router. That's misdirection. When an attacker comes, they're going to try to launch D-Link attacks at my router and not ones for Linksys. So, please, configure your routers to not give out information they shouldn't be.

Here are a few tips for protecting yourself:

- Make sure that you use some kind of IDS.

- When you deploy your web servers, don't leave them with the default configurations/settings.

- Get rid of *powered by...* because it can give away too much information (you saw that earlier when we went through Google hacking techniques).

- Enforce security policies. That includes training employees to adhere to the policies so they don't respond to someone calling them up and saying, "*Hey, this is Billy Bob down at the IT department, I need to reset your password – can you tell me what it is currently?*"

- Implement (and enforce) security policies on servers. Just having them and not enforcing them is like a parent threatening to ground a kid and not following through.

- Do some reconnaissance on yourself.

- Close unused ports, and if you do have open ports, whitelist them.

- Disable unnecessary services on web servers. Microsoft has a **Best Practice Analyzer (BPA)** tool that will go through and tell you what services aren't needed that you have turned on based on the role of that server.

- Prevent search engines from caching. There's a file you can create called a `robot.txt` file. This file tells Google which folders and files not to crawl or index. The only downside to this is that (you're going to laugh at this one) I can use Google to find websites that have `robot.txt` files in them.

- Disable directory listings in order to prevent people from learning the OS or doing directory traversal.

- Configure the internal and external DNS (separately):

  - For example, if your public-facing site is `gotham.com`, make sure your internal DNS environment is not also `gotham.com`.

- Restrict input types (such as pipes, commas, and colons). This will be even clearer if you watch videos on SQL injection, as restricting your input types is what's going to save your bacon.

- Avoid cross-linking on your site (linking to other pages within your website). That just helps Google.

- Always remember – humans are the weakest link. In fact, my favorite quote is, "*There is no patch for human stupidity.*" There was a report that the IRS started a big push to train all their employees on how to avoid social engineering attacks. Within 30 days, they pen tested them, and 65% of their employees gave up their information. Train your employees and help them set up encryption or stronger passwords. Send out updates through an organizational newsletter if you've got one. It pays off.

Now, I know that reconnaissance can be overwhelming as far as remembering what to look for, so I've got a great solution for you. Wander over to the **OSINT Framework** (`https://osintframework.com/`). As its name implies (*Open Source Intel*), this site will help you cover all your bases during your research by using open source (or publicly available) intel. Plus, it might give you some other ideas of where to find more intel on your target:

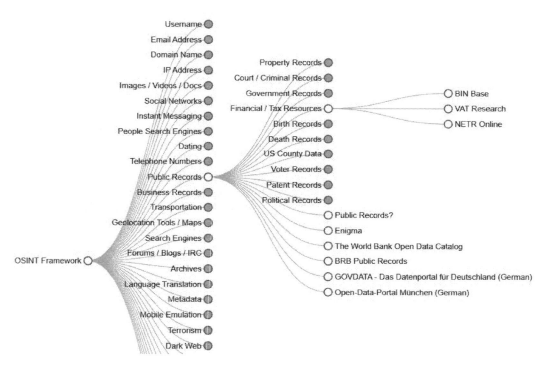

Figure 3.30 – OSINT Framework

With that, we have come to the end of this chapter. Congratulations on completing it successfully.

Summary

Our quest led us to investigate how attackers gather information from their target's website to know the target's exact business functions, important contact information, clients and partners, the management team, and so on. We learned how to use WHOIS, the command-line interface, ping and DNS, and SOA to gather information. We learned about more tools that help with reconnaissance and footprinting, such as Sam Spade, Netcraft, and the Wayback Machine.

We saw how what the information organizations give away for free can reveal a ton of vulnerabilities. So do job sites, marketing materials, customer support, social networking profiles, and financial and competitive analysis data.

We also discussed employees as the weakest link. Their hobbies, the things they share or post online, the places they go to after work, what they buy, and more all give attackers the clues they need. We then discussed how attackers use these clues to join the groups their targets frequent, befriend them or their friends on Facebook, connect on LinkedIn, and/or find a way to socially engineer them.

In the *People search* section, we learned how to profile people using third-party products such as PeopleLookUp, Anywho, and CheckPeople.

Now that we've done some reconnaissance, our next step is to start scanning the networks we've discovered. We'll do this to find live targets and understand the infrastructure of the target organization. Scanning is done via various techniques – some passive, and others active.

Questions

As we conclude, here is a list of questions for you to test your knowledge regarding this chapter's material. You will find the answers in the *Assessments* section of the *Appendix*:

1. Which information may be gathered using nslookup?

    A. A DNS server location

    B. Hostnames and IP addresses

    C. WHOIS intel

    D. A nameserver and operating systems

2. Which of the following is the most accurate description of footprinting?

    A. Investigating a target

    B. Enumeration of services

    C. Discovery of services

    D. Dialogue with people

3. Which record will disclose details about a domain's mail server?

    A. Q

    B. MS

    C. MX

    D. A

4. What alternative options do you have if you can't collect enough information from a target directly?

    A. Social engineering

    B. EDGAR

    C. Competitive analysis

    D. Scanning

4
Scanning Networks

As an ethical hacker, or possibly the attacker ourselves, we've gone through and completed some of the first steps of attacking networks and systems. The first step we did was our reconnaissance in the previous chapter. If you're not familiar with that phrase, or what those steps involve, you need to go back to that chapter. Reconnaissance gave us a perfect view of the network. Now, it's time to get specific. In this chapter, we're going to get a little more active and involved.

In the initial stages of looking at our target, we did our footprinting and reconnaissance. Now, it's time to scan. This chapter will ensure you understand what you're doing and what scanning is.

You may be thinking, *Wait, I thought we achieved everything we needed to achieve during the reconnaissance stage!* Well, we didn't get as much information as we needed. And that's the whole goal here. Again, if the attacker can find out as much information as they can before they go after the system, it makes their time getting into the system a breeze, and there's a good chance they won't get caught.

In this chapter, we'll discuss the different techniques for scanning. We'll also look at some common scanning tools. However, we don't necessarily focus on the tools since there's going to be even more tools out there in no time. The goal here is to understand the concepts of what these tools can do. So, let's jump in.

We will cover the following topics in this chapter:

- Grasping scanning

- Understanding the three-way handshake

- Checking for live systems and their ports

- Scanning by thinking outside the box

- Banner grabbing and OS fingerprinting

- Vulnerability scanning and drawing out the network

- Preparing proxies and other anonymizing techniques

Grasping scanning

In this section, we will discuss the various types of scanning techniques and the goals, techniques, and tools that are used for scanning.

Types of scanning

So, what are the different types of scans an attacker can use? To start, let's categorize these into three different sections. We'll discuss network scans, port scans, and vulnerability scans.

Network scans

During a network scan, the attacker simply puts a packet out onto the network to look at every device on the network and goes through them, trying to identify them. During this process, it provides us with information to help us to see which hosts are currently live. This can be done with something as simple as a ping. Unfortunately, using a ping won't give us much besides revealing if the system is up or not. We'll also be able to see what type of operating system is running on those devices. This is not just about revealing what's on the operating system for a desktop or a server, but what operating systems are currently running on the router, on a switch, or a printer.

We'll also want to go through and be sure we pick up all the IP addresses. We know we have a range from the reconnaissance side, but we want to make sure we go through and look at individual IP addresses and see if we can group them in a specific order.

Now, what I mean by this is that, as an attacker, I might be able to go through and see you're using an IP address of 192.168, the first 10 IP addresses for servers, and maybe 250 through 255 for printers, or network services. This information will help me when I see a node. I can go through and say, *Oh wow, that particular server happens to have this IP address. I wonder if the server sitting next to it has the next IP.* So, this helps me go through and figure out more. If you want to think of it as adding more to your reconnaissance steps, then do.

Port scans

Now, as we hit those machines, what we want to do is discover what a port is. Typically, a port is an IP address with an attached protocol. Let's take an IP address of, for example, 192. 168. 0. 15. We know that this is the IP address or target address, but when we add to it a protocol, such as HTTP, it becomes a port. If you want to look at it differently, here's what it would look like from a port perspective: you have the IP address followed by 80. Port 80 is a very typical port that's associated with an IP address that displays web pages. Sometimes, you might see 443. That's a secure port on that device.

There are more than 65,535 ports out there that we can run on each machine. As we do the port scan, we want to see which ones are open and which ones are closed. We normally focus on the first 1,023 ports. We must go through and see which ones are responding and correlate that with what services use those ports, which will give us an exact footprint (an exact representation of that machine). No, you don't need to go through and memorize all 1,023 ports. Just know that there are some very common ones. We already mentioned port 80 and port 443. We also have port 25 for email, port 53 for DNS, ports 20 and 21 for FTP, and so on. We want to scan and see which of those ports are open. In some cases, ports are specific to certain services.

Vulnerability scans

As IT professionals, we do this to identify what possible threats there are to operating systems and/or applications that have been installed in the environment. You'll also want to make sure you can identify the vulnerabilities of the OSes and their applications. In some cases, we can install a Service Pack or do an update of some sort, and this will create new vulnerabilities. This should be something every IT person does almost monthly, or at least any time there's any type of update. Why? Because an attacker will do this same type of vulnerability scan – we'll look at some vulnerability scanning software later.

As we mentioned earlier, most of the software we see and think, *Oh, it's designed for good!* is anything but. Think of what an attacker can do with a particular piece of software. If an attacker can make it into your network, they'll want to do a vulnerability scan to see which systems can be compromised.

What's the goal?

Scanning can have a couple of different objectives. We've talked about some of these already, but I want to make sure you grasp this, especially for your immediate future – that is, if you plan on taking the Ethical Hacking exam!

The first objective is to identify live hosts. More importantly, I want to know when a host comes online. Again, if you're going to introduce a new idea system, I want to be aware, so I know I've got to be a little trickier and sneakier with you. I also want to go through and make sure I gather all the IP addresses. If an IP address changes, I want to be notified. Networks are consistently evolving and we're always changing up our IP addresses. Now, we may not be changing them from the server's perspective, but trust me – desktops are always changing IP addresses. If I've compromised a particular box and its IP addresses change, I want to be able to track that somehow. Scanning is going to help me with that.

Again, once I've got the IP address, the next thing I want to do is ensure I know which ports are still open and which ones are closed. This can expose information such as the operating system or even the architecture. Again, I'm going to make a notation of the results I get from my scans.

As I've mentioned previously, certain Windows boxes respond in a specific way to an open or closed port that's different than a Linux box or a UNIX box. So, looking at how it responds to us can help us identify our architecture as well. Most of those functions are built into the scanning software you'll see demonstrated later. I'll also go through and check for vulnerabilities and threats. Again, if I can identify the target, its OS, and the services that are running on it – *Hey, it's an Apache server! What version of Apache? Version 2. 6* – I want to go off and find out what vulnerabilities existed for that version of Apache.

I'm typically talking about web servers because they get attacked quite a bit, but there are vulnerabilities for specific machines – one that's running Adobe Acrobat Reader, another for iTunes, and so on. I'm going to try to compromise a box, if not multiple boxes, within your environment. It doesn't have to be a server – again, my main target may not be the server, it could just be your desktop systems. I'm also going to go through and look at the security risks and services running on those machines.

From the attacker's perspective, the security risk is going to involve thinking, *What is my risk of exposure when I attack this machine?* It's easy to think it's just the Windows boxes that always get attacked because they're easy to attack, but guess what? I can attack a Mac or even a Linux box – nothing is foolproof. Of course, some may be more difficult than others to go after, and some will end up exposing me.

Scanning can be extremely *noisy* or *chatty* on the network, depending on the type of scanning you're doing. So, I'm going to make sure my security risks are low. I'm going to do some scans that could be very stealthy.

I'll also go through and look at the services that are running – all kinds of services. Is SNMP running? Is NNTP for time running on that box? Are the file and print services running on a particular box? Again, what applications (server-based applications)? Is it an exchange box? Is it a SharePoint box? Is it a SQL box? What services are running that could give me some type of access to this system as a whole?

What techniques are used?

There are different techniques for scanning different technologies. Some of the different techniques we use will include techniques for either internal or external networks. Typically, these are almost the same type of technique. Because of those pieces of software or scans that we do, they don't care if they're internal or external; it's just a different way of looking at it – if I'm attacking a public IP address range versus an internal IP address range.

We'll also have a different technique for not just looking at computers – I want to be looking for printers, switches, routers, and any other devices on your network. I mean, nothing is more fun than compromising one of the network devices you have no idea someone is monitoring – your printer's OS, the OS on the switch, or the OS on the router. If I can compromise and issue my commands to my zombies on your network via one of these devices, it will be extremely hard to track because nobody ever suspects them.

Another technique is Wi-Fi, which is such an open book force. As we take more and more advantage of wireless technology, I can just jump into the network. If I am visiting a location and I can hit the Wi-Fi, I'm good to go. Well, guess what? There are some specific techniques I can use on a Wi-Fi network that are different than what I would use on an internal or external network to do my scans.

If I'm able to hit a server, one of the first things I'm going to do is banner grabbing. This is a very interesting technique known as operating system fingerprinting, or OS fingerprinting. Banner grabbing will help me take advantage of the way servers respond to identify themselves – a Windows box, a Linux box, and so on.

What you saw in our previous course on reconnaissance was that when we used Netcraft, this entailed using banner grabbing techniques to identify those public-facing servers. We can do that internally to identify the different targets on the network.

Tools used for scanning

So, what tools are used for scanning? Well, where do you want to start? I could use a standard command line to do a ping to see if there is an active or a live host or node on the network. I can also go through and use Nmap, which is probably one of the more popular scanning tools out there. It's more than just a scanning tool. We can also use an angry IP scanner, a nifty little tool that I used when I had my wireless ISP service. We assigned IP addresses to each of the antennas we'd put on our customers' homes.

Initially, we went through and had them all organized, saying, *Here is this antenna and it has an IP address of 1, and here's the next one, which has an IP address of 2.* This works perfectly until you have an antenna go out. In that situation, you'd have to go through and change the IP address. We would quickly jump onto the wireless network, do a quick angry IP scan, and see which IP address we could utilize next because a host or IP address wasn't live, meaning it was usable. Interestingly, most antivirus products pick up angry IP scanners as malicious software, yet they're just ping sweepers.

Luckily, SolarWinds have a plethora of utilities, especially the engineering set, which you can utilize. Some of the things it scans include Ethernet and Bluetooth. They've got all kinds of tools –and not just scanning tools – their solution is amazing. We also have Colasoft ping, Ping Scanner Pro, and Visual Ping Tester, which, after it pings, helps map out the network. There are a ton out there. You may have a favorite, but there are a couple of them you may want to pay attention to. I will not tell you which ones they are, because I shouldn't as an ethical hacker, but some are going to be focused on your immediate future if you plan on taking the Ethical Hacking exam.

Understanding the three-way handshake

Let's talk about how polite computers are when it comes to communicating with each other, shall we? So, part of the scanning concept is understanding what they refer to as the three-way handshake. Again, it's very polite.

Mike O'Cain, who is an American football coach and former player, once said *I don't remember who came up with the handshake idea, but it was a great one.*

This is true because there are some advantages when it comes to the three-way handshake and computers.

To understand the three-way handshake, you must get your geek on. You need to understand what's going on in the background. To cover this in a way that makes sense, we'll look at TCP and UDP communications. We'll also look at the different flags that a TCP header has. After that, we'll look at the extremely normal three-way handshake and ensure you understand the communication that goes on between computers as they're about to *talk to each other*. I'll whip out some Wireshark for you, and we'll discuss how it takes place.

We'll start by looking at some what-ifs… what if something else happens differently than what the computer is expecting? Get your pocket protector ready, whip out your pin, and let's get learning.

TCP and UDP communications

When computers want to talk to each other, they need to set up ways of communicating. There are two different ways computers can do this to make the initial connection: TCP and UDP.

TCP communications

TCP has a huge advantage over UDP because when one computer talks to another via TCP, it tries to negotiate a connection between the two computers. Again, this is very polite – *Hello, I would like to communicate with you, is that all right?* – as they communicate with each other and send data back and forth. Another advantage of TCP is that it has what's referred to as delivery acknowledgments. *Thank you, sir! I did receive that packet, you may continue.* It's very similar to when UPS delivers a package to you – you sign for it. Again, you're acknowledging you received that packet or package. It also has a little fault tolerance built into it because of error detection, which means it can retransmit packets it sees did not get delivered. *Oh, I see you didn't get that! Well, let me send it to you again. Once you get it, please send me back a delivery acknowledgment.*

As the packets get delivered to the destination, it does what's referred to as in-order delivery. If we need to send over five boxes via UPS, we can mark them as boxes 1 of 5, 2 of 5, 3 of 5, 4 of 5, and 5 of 5 for easy identification. The same helps a computer reassemble data as it's received. TCP also goes through and does congestion control. If it sees that too many packets are coming to it, it'll try to slow things down.

If there is a downside to TCP, it's that TCP is slower than UDP because of all this retransmission, in-order delivery, congestion control, and delivery acknowledgments going back and forth all the time.

The other reason it's a little slower is because of the header size. It's about 2 0 bytes. In UDP, it's around 8 bytes; a little smaller. Besides having bigger headers, it also has a bigger overhead. Some of the fields that are required by TCP when it's communicated are sequence number fields in the packet. There's also an acknowledgment number, data offset, a reserved field, a checksum field, a source port, a destination port, and about 12 different fields compared to UDP, which only has four.

TCP is also stream-oriented, which means data is read as a byte stream, whereas in UDP, the packets are just sent individually and are only checked for integrity if they arrive. Part of that is handled by data flow control. So, TCP does flow control, which, again – remember our three-way handshake – requires three packets to set up a socket connection before the user data can be sent, so TCP handles reliable transmissions.

Again, as we mentioned previously, it has all these features. Some of the applications we see use TCP include Simple Message Transfer Protocol, File Transfer Protocol, Telnet, Hypertext Transfer Protocol, and even HTTPS.

UDP communications

The evil twin of TCP is called UDP. Now, it's not that we hate it, UDP just has some differences. For example, UDP is connectionless-based, which means that when two computers want to send data and they're going to do it via UDP, *I'm just going to send you the data, I don't care if you get it or not*, is how they communicate.

A great example of seeing this is if you like streaming music. Sometimes, while streaming music, suddenly, the music will stop and then kick up again. That's because it's UDP and unlike TCP, there's no guaranteed delivery. Another analogy you could use is TCP is FedEx, where they guarantee overnight delivery, and UDP is the ordinary US mail system, not priority mail – you just put the letter in there and hope for the best.

It also uses smaller packets. At just 8 bytes, it's extremely small.

Again, part of this is because the header itself only has a source port, a destination port, and a checksum value associated with it. When data is transmitted, only one packet goes across at a time, and with UDP, there is no guarantee that the packet is going to hit the destination. It's extremely fast, though, and because of that, there is no error checking involved. With TCP, we were very polite; *Did you get it? Was it correct?*

With UDP, packets are also delivered out of sequence. When the packets are sent, they're sent individually. They're only checked for integrity if they arrive because we don't have that in-order delivery mechanism that TCP has. Again, the packets arrive out of order. Packet 5 may arrive before packet 4. So, there's no form of ordering messages or tracking connections.

One of UDP's biggest advantages over TCP is that UDP is extremely fast. There's no congestion control either, which is a possible advantage. I only look at it as a disadvantage because if the network gets saturated, there's no way of stopping the packet from going across or the network adjusting on the fly, yet with TCP, we have flow control. Technically, UDP is message-oriented, meaning it's a protocol we use in message transport or transfers. However, because it's not connection-based, this means that one program can send a ton of packets to another and that it would be the end of the relationship.

Some of the applications that are used by UDP include DNS, DHCP, TFTP, and SNMP. VoIP utilizes it too. All types of video conferencing tools, such as Skype, use UDP. I'm sure you've been in a video conference where, suddenly, the video stream locked up and looked as if the participants were in an old 1930s movie that was choppy. This happens because some of the packets are missing or there was no guaranteed delivery, but it eventually catches up.

Now that I have described and explained how computers talk to each other and love each other, we will discuss how TCP sets up that three-way handshake.

TCP header flags

TCP uses what we refer to as flags to represent different types of communications and connections we'd like to establish. For example, one of the flags you might see is SYN, which is short for synchronization. The synchronization flag includes a sequence number. Now, sequence numbers themselves don't increase sequentially; they are linked to the source machine and the destination machine.

Technically, the numbers are randomized when they're created, and they're based on the payload. That number can be anywhere from zero to over four billion. Most sniffing products out there, such as Wireshark, will display the relative sequence and acknowledgment numbers in place of the actual numbers, which makes it a little easier for us to see.

Another type of flag we might see is ACK, short for acknowledgment, which simply means that I got your request, where you stated that you'd like to do something. We also have FIN, short for finish, meaning jobs done.

The other flags we might see are PSH, which means I need to push data to you. There's also URG – short for urgent – *Excuse me, I need to send this packet to you immediately, please.* Finally, there's RST, which is just saying: *I need to reset the connection (Figures 4.1 and 4.2).*

Now that we know about the different flags TCP uses to create, establish, and leave connections with other computers, let's look at them in a normal three-way handshake:

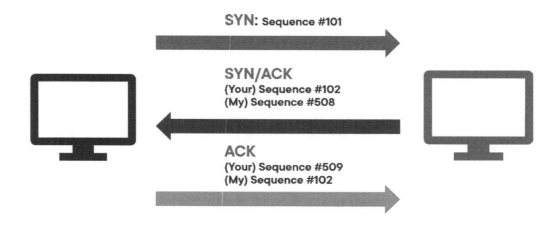

Figure 4.1 – Two-way handshake diagram

Let's say we've got two computers (*Figure 4.1*). The source computer on the left needs to set up a connection with the destination computer on the right. It does this by sending a SYN with a sequence number. *My sequence number is 101.* The destination computer sends back and responds to a SYN, with a SYN/ACK. *I got your acknowledgment and your sequence, so your next sequence number will be 102, and here is my SYN or my sequence, which is 508.* The source computer responds with an ACK saying, *You're right, my sequence number was 102 and your next sequence number will be 509.* See how the sequence numbers synced? This is done to help you identify that we have established a communication channel between the two systems:

Figure 4.2 – Three-way handshake after transfer

Now, when the source computer has finished transferring the information (*Figure 4.2*), it starts with a FIN – *I'm finished. I'd like to stop now. This relationship just isn't working out.* The source computer responds with *Okay, I acknowledge that; I'm going to tell the application to stop SYN information, and when it's done, I'm done.* In response, the source computer sends, *Oh, hey, it was nice talking to you. I'll call you sometime. Maybe we could do this again!*

Checking for live systems and their ports

Scanning for live systems can be very loud or noisy on the network, but if you can do it strategically, the target might never see we're going through their network looking for targets.

Now, let's look at different ways to check for live systems.

ICMP sweep/ping sweep

This is the most common way to check for live systems. Like a sonar ping in a submarine, we ping and hope we get a return, which tells us how far away the target is or where the target is located. A standard ping uses the ICMP protocol, which is not only well known but also very noisy on the network – so much so that most IT professionals will block ICMP traffic as a deterrent.

Port scanning

Just because a machine does not respond to a ping sweep or an ICMP sweep doesn't mean it's not there. So, we can perform port scans in various ways and specify IP addresses. We can still try to check if it responds. We'll show you how to do that next. So, let's get pinging!

Nmap

Now, in your immediate future (my way of saying in the exam), you will need to know the syntax for some Nmap commands. There are many, but I'll highlight the most important ones as we move along. When we get into some of the additional scans that we can accomplish with Nmap, I'll ensure that you see all the different options:

Switch	Example	Description
-sS	nmap 192.168.1.1 -sS	TCP SYN port scan (Default).
-sT	nmap 192.168.1.1 -sT	TCP connect port scan (Default without root privilege).
-sU	nmap 192.168.1.1 -sU	UDP port scan.
-sA	nmap 192.168.1.1 -sA	TCP ACK port scan.
-sW	nmap 192.168.1.1 -sW	TCP Window port scan.
-sL	nmap 192.168.1.1-3 -sL	No Scan. List targets only.
-sn	nmap 192.168.1.1/24 -sn	Disable port scanning. Host discovery only.
-Pn	nmap 192.168.1.1-5 -Pn	Disable host discovery. Port scan only.
-PS	nmap 192.168.1.1-5 -PS22-25,80	TCP SYN discovery on port x. Port 80 by default.
-PA	nmap 192.168.1.1-5 -PA22-25,80	TCP ACK discovery on port x. Port 80 by default.
-PU	nmap 192.168.1.1-5 -PU53	UDP discovery on port x. Port 40125 by default.
-PR	nmap 192.168.1.1-1/24 -PR	ARP discovery on the local network.
-n	nmap 192.168.1.1 -n	You should avoid DNS resolution.
-p	nmap 192.168.1.1 -p 21	Port scan for port x.

Next, let's look at the hping tool.

hping3

I know what you're thinking: *That's cool, but what happens if a machine doesn't respond to an ICMP request or a ping sweep?* Oh, young Padawan, follow me now.

First, you need to understand that tools such as hping3 can craft packets to work around security measures.

Packet crafting is the process of adding customized data payloads to application layer protocol packets. A customized data payload refers to any arbitrary content that cannot be identified as part of the protocol.

Installed by default on Kali Linux is a nifty tool that's called hping3. Using hping3, I can utilize TCP, UDP, ICMP, and even RAW protocols. The hping3 utility is a network packet generator and analyzer that can be run from the command line. hping3 can be used for TCP/IP and security testing, such as port scanning, firewall rule testing, and network performance testing, thanks to its ability to create bespoke network packets.

hping3 switches can cause the tool to scan in the following ways:

- -0 (Raw IP mode)
- -1 (ICMP mode)
- -2 (UDP mode)
- -8 (Scan mode)
- -9 (Listen mode)

What's firewalking?

The concept behind firewalking is that we can try to determine what layer 4 protocols an IP address, such as a router, will pass by. Even though we can't ping it, it may allow port 80 through.

Firewalking is designed to help us get around IDS systems, firewalls, and routers. It's very similar to traceroute, but instead, it tries to determine if a particular packet via a port can pass from the attacker's system to your target through the packet filtering device.

We use firewalking to help define the firewall's access control list or determine what's allowed to pass through. The firewall may not be allowing other ports to pass through, but maybe it allows port 80 to pass through – which it does by using **time to live** (**TTL**). Now, what I mean by that is that traceroute – a networking utility that allows you to see the routers a packet passes through to get to its destination – gets a list of the IP addresses of each of the routers along the way. To determine this information, traceroute uses a TTL.

A TTL is implemented with an IP to prevent packets from looping indefinitely on your network. Now, as each device receives a packet, the TTL counter decreases by one. If the counter is less than or equal to 0, then the packet is dropped, and you get an ICMP error message that says that the TTL exceeded in transit. Now, this error message will typically hold the IP address of the router that dropped the packet as the originator. So, what happens to the packet when you're firewalking? It gets forwarded if the port is open and gets dropped off if the port is closed.

Let's say that we have two systems, and as we do a simple ping, our packets get passed from one router to the next and then to their eventual destination. We may not see all the different routers or hops that it passes through on a ping command, but if I do a traceroute, I'll go through and start to see the IP addresses, but then I'll start seeing packets being dropped off.

Mobile apps that help

We often talk about tools we can use on our laptops, but because mobile devices are becoming so influential in our lives, there's a ton of apps out there that can help us as far as network discovery is concerned. If you open your app store and type in network scanning, scanner, or network scan, you will see a plethora of different utilities.

One I use quite a bit is Fing. Fing is designed to keep track of all the different devices that are currently on your network. It provides cool tools, including showing the current location. It has vulnerability tests built into it and Wi-Fi intrusion protection. You can also check your internet speed and look at your Wi-Fi's performance. Additionally, you can go through and set up different people and assign devices to them.

It's also great at finding devices. It found my TP-Link switch (*Figure 4.3*), it can get my MAC address, it shows me my vendor, and I can also go through and have it notify me when it changes status, which is kind of interesting:

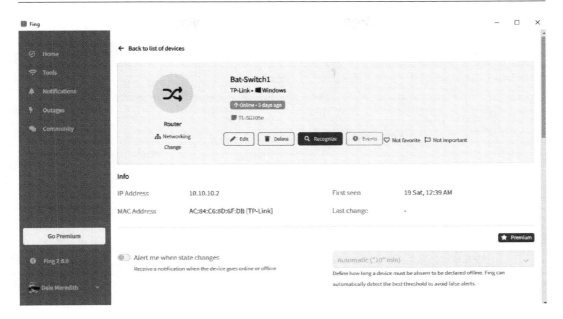

Figure 4.3 – Finding devices using Fing

You can also go through and block a device. I have most of mine set up so that if a device hits my network by default, it gets blocked.

There are other products out there as well – both on Android devices and iOS devices.

Scanning by thinking outside the box

So, when we scan a network, we have some tricks that can be used to get a system to respond without being detected. Now, the normal three-way handshake we know about involves a SYN followed by a SYN/ACK and then an ACK. What if we change up the order of the handshake and craft packets so that we send a SYN/ACK first? Or a FIN? Using these types of methods, we can pick up targets on the network that normally wouldn't respond to an ICMP scan. Let's talk about some of these scans.

Full scans

A full scan is simply the same process that we talked about previously – the three-way handshake. It's just that here, while a computer is talking to another, an attacker is going after a target. What they'll do is send a standard SYN. Attached to that SYN, we'll have a port number.

As you may remember from the three-way handshake, it'll simply respond with a SYN/ACK. And now that we've seen the acknowledgment, we can finish that off by just doing an ACK and then a reset, which means that, okay, I didn't want to talk to you. Now, if it responds this way again, using a full three-way handshake, we know that the port is, at that point, open. Contrary to that, if we have the same environment and we send a SYN and we get a reset option, then we know that the port is closed.

The disadvantage of a full scan is it's very noisy. Most IDS systems will pick this up and it'll be logged somewhere. But you can use it as a last resort, especially if you're a hacktivist and/or you're being hit by a hacktivist. They don't care if they're getting caught, or maybe they're just taking it on the assumption that you won't be looking heavily at your logs.

Half-open scan

A half-open scan is also known as a stealth scan. Now, remember how the three-way handshake worked? What if we modified this a bit? Let's say that we have the target and the attacker, and normally we send a SYN, right? Well, if we send a SYN, its normal response is to send a SYN/ACK. Remember what the third step of the three-way handshake was? It was to do an ACK that I got your acknowledgment and your SYNC? Well, what if I set an RST instead? By sending an RST, the scan partially opens a connection but stops halfway through. Now, because it stops without having done a full connection, it stops the service of ever notifying it of an incoming connection, so, it typically doesn't get recorded anywhere. Now, if I get the SYN/ACK from my target, I know that the port is open. If I do the same thing, where I send a SYN and it responds with an RST, well, guess what – the port's closed.

Xmas scans

A Xmas tree scan uses a technique that uses our ACK, RST, SYN, URG, PSH, and FIN flags to see if a particular port is open. Unfortunately, these flags only work against systems that are compliant with what is referred to as RFC 793, which means this does not work on Windows boxes because Microsoft followed their own RFC when it came to TCP/IP, so they left some of their stuff out.

So, how does a Xmas tree scan work? Well, we have our attacker and our target, and the first thing that we're going to send is a combination of a FIN, an URG, and a PUSH.

In response, the target machine is going to come back with nothing. If it comes back with nothing, that's because I said, *I'm finished*, and the computer goes, *finished*? We didn't even start talking, dude! So, if it comes back with nothing, then we know the port is open. Now, if I go through the same environment and I do the same FIN, URG, and PUSH and I get an RST, you guessed it – it means that the port is closed.

So, as far as your immediate future is concerned, remember that Xmas (or Christmas) tree scans don't work against Windows or Microsoft products.

FIN scans

Let's go back to our attacker and target again. Do you remember the three-way handshake? What do we start with? A SYN? No, let's hit them with a FIN, meaning, *I'm done talking to you!* The target machine will go, *Well, I don't even know how to respond to that because we haven't even started talking yet.* So, no response tells me that the port is open. Again, if I want to see if the port is closed, I send my FIN, and if I just get an RST/ACK, then the port is closed.

NULL scans

A NULL scan is kind of unique because it typically works on UNIX and Linux systems. Again, it does not work on the Microsoft platform.

Instead of sending anything, when we send the packet, it's going to go through TCP, but guess what? There's going to be no flag. It's not going to be a SYN, an ACK, or a FIN – it's just going to be nothing; the flag is empty. When the target receives that packet, it responds with nothing, which means that you're sending me information I have no idea how to handle. And because it doesn't respond, we know that the port is open.

The opposite of that is true, just like we saw with the Xmas tree scan. If I send a TCP packet with no flag implemented, the kernel will drop it if it's open, or it'll send an RST/ACK back to the attacker's machine, which tells me that the port is closed.

UDP scans

Do you remember the advantages and disadvantages of UDP? There's always a catch 22, right? The three-way handshake is caused by TCP and when it comes to UDP, there's no three-way handshake, there's no overhead of TCP, and that creates some advantages for us. One of the advantages is that it's a lot harder to monitor because there is no initial handshake. UDP itself is less informal as far as regarding it in an open port. The frames can be overloaded or be larger, so we can exceed the limitations of TCP frames. Again, Microsoft-based operating systems don't have any type of ICMP rate limiting built into them, so the scan is extremely efficient against Windows-based targets. The disadvantage of UDP is that we get port data only; we're unable to take advantage of some of the other options that are available to us, especially when it comes to Nmap, such as being able to identify the operating system. To see those things, we're going to have to include some additional parameters.

So, let's take our target and attacking machine. If the attacking machine sends a UDP packet that says, *Hey, is port 31 open?*, and the target machine says, *Hi, I'm not going to talk to you*, that's a no response and means the port is open.

The same concept applies if we go through and implement our attacking and target machine to do the same thing; is port 31 open? In this case, we will get an ICMP port unreachable error message. In that case, we know that the port is closed.

I know you're thinking, *Let's take a look at this!* Well, the big challenge with UDP scanning is doing it quickly. Both ports that are filtered and open rarely send any type of response, and this leaves Nmap to time out quite often. Closed ports are an even bigger problem. They usually send back an ICMP port unreachable error. Sometimes, you do get some false positives pop up. The cool thing is that Nmap will detect rate limiting and slow down to make sure the network doesn't get flooded with a ton of useless packets. Unfortunately, the Linux style limit of 1 packet per second makes scanning 65,000 ports take about 18 hours.

Now that we've gone through and looked at the different scanning techniques we can use, we'll move to those we can utilize to evade the **Intrusion Detection Systems** (**IDSes**) that are looking for the types of scans we have looked at.

Idle scans

An idle scan is where you're sitting in your car on Main Street on Friday night checking out the people next to you in the car while you're idling. Just kidding... This scan is tricky and very hard to detect because of how everything works inside of the three-way handshake and how computers are designed to respond.

We'll use the TCP port scanning mechanism and the regular three-way handshake, but instead, we're going to spoof the source address to the target. We're going to make the target think, it's not me scanning you, it's somebody else – *Look over here!* Now, there are some advantages to this because we get to blame somebody else. *It wasn't me; it was this computer over here creating the problems for us.* The disadvantage of this scanning mechanism is that it does require you to have a zombie – a system that I've already penetrated, compromised, or know about. I don't even need to own or pwn it. It's just going to be an IP address I know that's out there behind your existing firewall or your IDS system. It requires this because I'm going to use that zombie as the source address.

Listing scanning

A list scan is fast, and it goes through and enumerates every IP address range that you give in a specific target or a block on each. Then, it does a quick reverse DNS lookup on each of those IPs. One of the advantages of a list scan is that a lot of times, the name of the system could give you a hint about what it's doing.

SSDP scanning

Simple Service Discovery Protocol (SSDP) is an interesting and tricky scan. It's a network protocol that generally communicates with other machines. So, when a system comes up and says, *Hey, I'm looking for printers or I have an available printer*, this service goes through and helps with universal plug and play. It generally works when the machine is not firewalled. However, there can be times where we'll work through a firewall. So, an attacker could use SSDP scanning to detect universal plug-and-play vulnerabilities that could allow them to launch a buffer flow or even a denial-of-service attack against the target.

Countermeasures

So, how do we release countermeasures and what are the different countermeasures that we can implement? First, firewalls need to be configured to look for SYN scans. This is because most of the firewalls today – if they aren't updated – will have each manufacturer using different mechanisms or ways of scanning for SYN attacks.

Another thing you'll want is your IDS systems to be able to detect Snort or Nmap. Snort is a product that looks at traffic and helps evaluate and determine what's going on. It's almost like a silent sniffer, hence the name Snort. Again, you'll want to check with your IDS systems to make sure they support those features.

We'll also want to go through and only open the ports that are required to be open. So, if I'm doing a scan on a system and I see that no ports are open on the machine, that tells me something's up. Why is the machine on at all? It must be giving some type. I mean, a DNS server has a port open. A domain controller has certain ports open. So, you want to limit the number of ports that are opened. That's one of the things you should be doing. But going back and talking about those different scans, I would detect if I did a scan on an IP address and I had 0 ports open. At this point, I know that between me and the target, I've got some type of device that's blocking that. So, again, we only want to open the ports that are required for the services of that server.

We also want to go through and make sure that we filter ICMP messages, making sure that we don't allow ICMP traffic to pass through unnecessarily. I know that takes away the ability to do some pinging, but we want to filter and record that.

We'll also need to go through and test our network using the techniques I've just shown you. Again, part of our job as ethical hackers is going through and making sure we can withstand what can be discovered from the attacker using these same techniques and tools.

Finally, we're going to go through and keep our firewalls and IDS systems up to date and patched. Now, I know this doesn't look like a lot as far as some people go, but that's all I can do. Again, I will go back to the analogy I use all the time: that I know I have a higher risk of getting in a car accident driving on the freeway and getting injured or killed versus flying, but I'm still a little paranoid about flying. It may be a control issue for me, but I know those risks, and I'm willing to take them just to be able to drive and live in an area where I live – outside of the big city.

One of the most interesting conversations I've had was with a friend who is a white hat for Microsoft. When I was trying to open my ISP service out in my area, he said, *Do you really want to do this?* After asking what he meant by that, he said getting on the internet and becoming an ISP service will make me a target. I said, *Dude, but I live in this little bitty town. I mean, a population of 2,000.* He said, *It doesn't matter because on the internet you're strictly a number. They don't care about where you're located.* But I took that risk, and we have that risk today. We all know we can go shopping on the internet. It's convenient. However, we know that there is a chance that our identities can be stolen. Still, it's a chance we're willing to take.

More IDS evasion methods

There are other ways that we can get around IDS systems. One of them is to spoof your IP, but we're going to sniff the responses out there. We can also use a proxy or a pwned machine. So, a zombie is kind of a combination of the two.

Another way that we can do this is to fragment the IP packets, which I'll show you in a second. Then, if you're able to, you can use something called source routing – a method or a technique that you can use to specify the route a packet should take through the network. So, when you have a packet that has source routing specified on it, going through the network, the device that makes the routing decision, such as your router, will look at the path specified inside the network packet to determine where to forward the packet. So, we can force packets to bypass some of our IDS systems.

Now, as far as IP fragmentation is concerned, or IP fragments, the concept is to get past these IDS systems. Typically, they're looking for normal-sized packets going through, and they monitor them. Anything else that's small is typically ignored. So, when a big packet goes through, it gets blocked based on its packet size and its protocol. Maybe your IDS system is blocking FTP or a specific port. Well, instead, let's break that packet into smaller packets, which will pass right through and be reassembled at the target machine.

Banner grabbing and OS fingerprinting

We've gone through and found our live targets and we've scanned them to see which ports were open. Our next step is to try to identify the systems. How are we going to do that? When I say identify, I'm talking about finding what operating systems and what applications are possibly running on that machine. We're going to do that with banner grabbing and OS fingerprinting.

The best way to sum up what this module is about was best phrased by the famous scholar Joey Tribbiani, who said, *How you doin?* That's exactly what we're doing here! We're trying to get to know the system. We're trying to identify the target. So, we'll go through and look at OS fingerprinting, which is the process of going through and identifying the operating system by the way that it responds to certain types of packets we're going to send to it.

Now, there's something else we can do called **banner grabbing**. This is a very direct way of identifying the system, and it's something you can't stop as an IT professional. It's just the way operating systems are designed to work; they respond in a specific way to different requests. Eventually, we'll go through and look at our countermeasures. Again, there are some things you can't stop, but I can slow the attacker down. I can't stop them; you're going to give yourself a heart attack thinking that you can stop them, but you can't.

OS fingerprinting

The reason why we do this when we're doing pen tests today is because the tester usually starts by gathering as much information about the target as possible. One of the things we want to make sure we get hold of is the operating system or trying to identify the operating system itself. We typically do this by sending specific types of packets to the target machine. Now, if we can hide this information, then we are making it more difficult for the attacker to decide what type of attacks to throw. Often, you'll discourage the attacker; not that they can't get in, but they may want to try to find something else that's a little bit easier. Therefore, the focus on the initial information you're gathering is trying to discover what OS is being used. This makes us extremely, extremely active on the network.

There are several different approaches we can use to find the operating system of an unknown host without having an account or any other way of logging directly onto the machine.

There are two types of fingerprinting. The first is known as **active fingerprinting**. Now, in active fingerprinting, I'm going to use some packets that I'm going to go through and design to help me identify the operating system. Depending on the application you're using – and I'll be using Nmap since it's one of my favorite tools – as well as the responses or the way the target machine responds to my packets, I'm going to compare it to a database of known responses, and that's going to help me identify the operating systems. Unfortunately, there's a downside to this: because it's so active, there's a high probability I'm going to be detected on the network.

There's also **passive fingerprinting**, which involves sniffing the network and looking at the packets to see what the source IP is. You or your application will record over a certain period, and you'll gather enough information that will help you ID the target.

The upside, at least from the attacker's perspective, is that it's very, very quiet in that it's very hard to detect they're doing this on your network because they're just sniffing packets. Now, granted, it would take the attacker a while to do this, which is something you don't have – time.

Countermeasures

So, what are my countermeasures? How do you stop people from fingerprinting and possibly banner grabbing your servers? Well, there are a couple of things you can do. First, you can go through and misdirect by using fake banners. For example, in IIS, we can go through and change what the banner reports back as. There's a tool Microsoft has for this. It's called the **IIS lockdown tool** and it will help lock down an IIS box, especially the older versions of IIS.

I'm a big fan of misdirection. If I buy a Linksys wireless router, what would be its default wireless SSID? It's Linksys, right? An attacker driving by who sees my Wi-Fi will throw Linksys attacks at it. To avoid that, I will take my Linksys router and change its SSID to Belkin or Netgear, to have them throw the wrong attacks. The same concept applies here. Go and fake the banners.

There's also a nifty little tool out there, called ServerMask, that you can run to make the server look like it's something it's not, such as an older version of IIS, or an older version of Apache.

You can also turn off services that aren't needed because these services and ports can be used to identify the operating system. If you have some Linux boxes, you also need to go through and change the `ServerSignature` entry inside the `httpd.conf` file.

If you are dealing with Apache servers, you can go in and turn the `ServerSignature` line to `ServerSignature` off in the `httpd. conf` file.

You can also go into the same file (the `httpd. conf` file) and look for a section called **mod headers**. There, you can go through and change the server's name. So, I could type in IIS version 6.0 and leave the attacker scratching their head, wondering why their attacks aren't working.

Vulnerability scanning and drawing out the network

Now that we've gone out, found our live machines, footprinted the OS, or done a banner grab to identify the OS, our next step is to go through and look for vulnerabilities.

Remember, our goal is discovering those targets – hopefully to find out what type of operating system and possibly what applications were running. That's exactly what vulnerability scanning and drawing out the network does for us.

Some IT guys wonder if vulnerability scans are important and my answer – my favorite line from a famous character – is, *A man's got to know his limitations.*

You must understand what your limitations are, what your vulnerabilities are.

Now that we agree, we'll go ahead and look at some of our greatest weaknesses. We'll do that by understanding what vulnerability scanning is. After that, we'll look at how it works, the different mechanisms we can use, and how various software programs may look at your network infrastructure.

We'll also look at some vulnerability scanning tools and do a little vulnerability scanning.

We will then talk about drawing out the network, which we partly do to remember – as attackers – the network we were just on when we revisit it.

And, of course, we'll learn about some tools associated with how we draw out the networks.

As we get to this step, which is extremely active, we'll draw the line between being a black hat and a white hat because you will actively go out and try to find out what's wrong with the systems that you've identified. So, before you do this on a network, you better make sure you have permission. Okay? Now that you've gotten your permission slip signed by your parents or guardians, let's get going.

What is vulnerability scanning?

A vulnerability scanner is used to go through and look at a variety of vulnerabilities across a network, and we'll go through and use a piece of software that does that.

There are several vendors out there that create vulnerability scanners. Most of the tools we use are designed for good but are sometimes used for evil. So, this software is going to go through and look at information such as your network systems, switches, routers, and computers – which it'll try to identify based on the operating systems that are running and what vulnerabilities they are not patched for, including applications.

When we talk about applications, we're not necessarily talking about Word or Excel. It could be a server-based application, such as SQL, Exchange, or any other type of email server. These are applications that run on a server platform. However, this can include applications at the desktop level because, again, I'm going to try to break into any target I can find. So, if you have Adobe Acrobat and it hasn't been properly patched and it's on a desktop machine, I'm going to go after that machine because I can use its resources later to maybe attack or daisy chain into other systems in your network.

A commonly asked question is, *How are these vulnerabilities created?* Well, they're created as several different mechanisms and in several different ways. Some of them are done because of a user-initiated task. For example, a user goes through and shares directories to folks they shouldn't be sharing them to, fails to run an antivirus solution, or fails to keep up to date with that antivirus solution. In some cases, you may have a *weekend geek*, as I like to call people who brag *I build computers*, who know everything but deliberately load back doors on their systems while trying to hack into the system, only to open the systems for real attackers.

Vendor-created vulnerabilities can sometimes be caused by software bugs, operating system patches, and services that have been turned on without any notification – and some of those services might be unnecessary, insecure default configurations, web application vulnerabilities, and even system admins.

Some of these vulnerabilities are caused by lazy admins who go ahead and install an application that needs a service account. Lazily, they use the default built-in domain administrator account to run the service. Sometimes, they make configuration changes to solve a temporary situation and forget to switch it back. Some also lack password protection policies. This means they allow small password links to be used (seven or eight characters) instead of longer passwords.

Types of scanners

First, we have networked-based scanners. These are designed to go out and do things such as assess possible vulnerabilities on remote web servers or even perform port scans to determine which ports may be open.

You can't avoid having open ports if you're doing anything with that server to provide access to resources, but we need to make sure only the ports that are needed are open.

We'll look at web app scanners here. These will go through and assess the security aspects of a web application by looking at SQL injection. Web app scanners also look for things such as cross-site scripting.

Tech Tip

Web application scanners don't necessarily provide a comprehensive security check on every aspect of the target web application. There may be a need for doing additional manual checking, such as looking at a login account if it's locked out after so many invalid attempts. You may need to go through and look at those types of things when you're testing a web application.

We also have host-based scanners, which are installed on the host that's going to be scanned. It has direct access to what's referred to as low-level data, such as services or configuration details that may be on a host operating system. Because of this level of access, it provides better insight into user activities that could be considered risky, such as using easily guessed passwords or even no password at all.

It also detects signs that an attacker has already compromised the system, which would include going through and looking at suspicious filenames or unexpected system files that are showing up, or even device files. In some cases, we might see unexpected privileges being given to programs.

A host-based scanner can also perform baselines or filesystem checks. Typically, network-based scanners don't do this level of security check because they don't have direct access to the filesystem on the target. A great example of a host-based scanner would be a database scanner that goes through and performs detailed security analysis of authorization, which accounts have been given authorization, the authentication mechanisms being utilized, the integrity of the database, and possibly any security loopholes that may be in the database system (weak passwords, misconfigurations, and so on).

How does vulnerability scanning work?

What are the limitations? Because there are some definite drawbacks. The first is that human judgment is required. Vulnerability scanners can only report the vulnerabilities it finds according to the plugins that are installed inside the database. They are not designed to determine whether the result is a false negative or a false positive, so we always need someone to look at the data and analyze it after scanning.

You should also note that it's strictly a snapshot. A vulnerability scanner only looks at a specific system at a specific time. Therefore, you can't just do one vulnerability scan and assume you're safe. You must do this continually. As new vulnerabilities emerge, or if people are making changes to configuration settings, we might introduce new security holes.

Another limitation is that it only knows what it knows. A vulnerability scanner is designed to discover the specific vulnerabilities it's aware of. It's not designed to identify other security threats. So, you must keep this bad boy updated.

There's one more limitation. I call it *parts as parts*, or plugins. Most vulnerability scanners rely on these plugins to determine possible issues or possible vulnerabilities. Plugins become part of the scanning database, which expands the vulnerabilities that are known by the scanner. Now, some vulnerability scanning software programs may refer to them as scanning profiles, but the term plugin is normally what most all vendors refer to them as.

Again, the scanner only checks for those vulnerabilities it knows about. It can't identify what it doesn't know about. However, not all scanners need plugins. For example, a port scanner doesn't need a plugin; it'll hit a range of ports.

So, what are the benefits? Well, first, a vulnerability scanner allows you to detect and handle known security issues early. As a security expert, by doing ongoing security assessments all the time using these scanners, it would be very easy to identify vulnerabilities that may be present on your network. And these vulnerabilities could be either external or internal.

Another benefit is detecting new devices on the network, or rogue systems, that connect without any type of authorization or permission. This is typically what we find when we perform pen tests. I'll try to find a port that's not being utilized, and I've got a nifty little Raspberry Pi device – a tiny mini-computer that is about the size of a standard cell phone. I can hook that up to a port, walk away, and come back a couple of days later after it will be done sniffing your network. A vulnerability scanner will pick those things up.

A vulnerability scanner can also help you with inventory, verifying all the devices that are supposed to be on the network are on the network. It can also help with inventory things such as operating system versions, what OSes have been patched, what software has been patched, and what hardware configurations have been used. My favorite is: *Hey, Billy, why does your machine only have 8 GB of RAM when we put 16 GB in it, and how's that machine running at home now?* Again, this type of information is extremely useful when it comes to tracking and managing your environment. One of the things you'll hear me say over and over is that your first line of defense when it comes to securing your network is understanding what's on your systems, especially when it comes to software. Well, guess what? A vulnerability scanner can help you do this.

Vulnerability scanning tools

So, how do you choose a vulnerability scanner? Well, there are hundreds and hundreds out there. There are so many choices, so little time. Everyone has a preference, but if you're looking for your first vulnerability scanner, here are some things that you may want to take into consideration.

How often do they update their database and plugins? Again, we will go back to the statement that vulnerability scanners only know what they know. So, it can't identify a vulnerability if its plugin isn't available or hasn't been updated for a new vulnerability. So, a reputable vendor can produce updates and new plugins daily, weekly – you choose. How safe do you feel? I'd also be looking for scanners with an auto-update feature to ensure I don't have to worry about downloading them every day. It can be a scheduled task.

We'll also want to look at quality versus accuracy. If a vulnerability scanner finds a vulnerability, the question is, *now that I have found 300 vulnerabilities, how many of those were accurate (were not false positives)?* The accuracy that critical vulnerabilities are identified with is much more important than the number of vulnerabilities that have been checked. This is because the same vulnerability could be counted more than once by the same scanner.

We also need to look at the quality of the reporting options that are available to us. A good vulnerability scanner should have a reporting mechanism that gives very clear and concise information about how to fix some of the problems you've discovered. A scanner that has a great reporting option or feature with a nice backend database can make an administrator's life a lot easier when they need to perform follow-up scans after doing the initial scan, if there have been configuration changes, or they a need to make comparisons between the results of a previous scan and the current one.

Another thing to consider is the deployment process. Whether you put the scanner in front of the firewall or behind the firewall, it's going to influence the results you get. Scanning the internal network from outside the firewall is only going to detect the services that are available to the outside user or attacker. It will not look at the vulnerabilities from within the internal side of the network. That won't be visible to you because of the protection the firewall provides.

On the other hand, scanning the machines in your DMZ from inside may not provide a complete picture of your security. So, to get a complete picture of your security, make sure you do your scans externally and internally.

Now, what about port ranges? We already know that open ports could imply we have a security weakness somewhere, and port scanning is one of those we looked at earlier. Knowing that's what the attackers will use, part of your vulnerability scanning should include port scanning.

Some vulnerability scanners only check the first 15,000 ports, yet there are over 65,000, so make sure that you find out how many ports are scanned in the default settings. Oftentimes, you can override these settings by changing the configuration options of the vulnerability scanner.

After scanning

Now, let's talk about the post-scanning practices. What do we do afterward? When you get your reports, it's important to interpret the scanning results correctly to avoid identifying vulnerabilities that are not there.

It's also important to go through and set priorities on the different vulnerabilities you're discovering. A vulnerability on a server that's exposed to the internet would have a higher priority than, for example, Billy Bob's machine down in the mailroom.

Also, note that when you get service packs, or Patch Tuesday from Microsoft, or any other software vendors, any time you apply new patches, you should immediately run new scans. Make sure that your database has been updated but rescan once those patches have been applied.

Again, if you make any configuration changes, you need to run a vulnerability scan once you're done. You should also do this if you plan to deploy any new software, even if that includes your desktop platforms.

The cons of vulnerability scanners

Dun-dun-dun! Beware! Vulnerability scanners create some issues. You will need to be aware of some of those issues as, well, the most important ones will be potential threats. I know I just said it's a vulnerability scanner, but yes, it's a potential threat. You can end up crashing an already vulnerable server if all the plugins, such as one that tests for a denial-of-service scan, are enabled. So, when you go through and configure your scans, initially, you need to pinpoint which portions of the scans are necessary.

Normally, for preproduction systems, it's probably okay to enable all the plugins, including high-risk ones, but when it comes to the ongoing continual scans on a production system, you should be very wary. Alternatively, consider disabling certain high-risk plugins.

When you're handling the results, do yourself a favor – don't post them on a website in your organization, upload them to Dropbox, or put them somewhere a hacker could find them by doing a Google hack. If you do, you can name the document something like `howtobreakintomynetwork.pdf`. Otherwise, safeguard this information and keep it in a safe place. I would recommend encrypting it because the last thing you want to do is hand a treasure map over to an attacker.

We've talked about some of the cool things vulnerability scanners offer and we know that they were created for good. You also need to have some policies and actions in place in case somebody uses one of these tools against you, such as an employee, not necessarily somebody outside your company. You will find, especially in larger enterprise environments, weekend geeks who bring in a piece of software to scan because they saw something cool on YouTube.

You need to make sure you have policies and procedures to specify whom, how, and when vulnerability assessment tools can be used. These policies can include notifications of when the scan is going to be done, management approval, and possibly legal clearance. No one should be allowed to conduct a vulnerability scan without prior permission!

More tools for scanning

So, what are some of the tools out there? Oh, man. I'm only going to be able to give you some highlighted tools here because there are a plethora of these tools out there for us. These tools include looking at something called Nessus, which is among the more popular ones out there. We also have tools such as Core Impact Pro, which has some cool features built into it, including an Android agent and Windows domain information gathering modules. They also have support for WMI.

We also have Microsoft Baseline Security Analyzer, which goes through and provides baseline security for particular servers. Microsoft's built these features into a lot of and some of their newest server platforms where they have some best practice analyzer tools. So, if you've got some Windows servers out there, especially those that are running Server 2012, you may want to pop one of those bad boys off and see what it kicks out and says about the best practices for that server.

GFI LanGuard is another great product, and it has been out there for ages.

There's also Retina. I had an opportunity to play around with Retina when I had my ISP service. We used it to look at vulnerabilities. I had a friend who had an ISP service but didn't know much about the legality of security. He ran Retina on his network and would send out emails to his customers saying, *Hi, your machine is missing these patches*. At the time, his customers were grateful and would buy his service pack. That's kind of borderline because he never had any permission to hit their systems. Yes, they were on his network, and he had contracts that said he does scans on the network, but that was probably aggressive.

We also have Saint (**https://www.carson-saint.com/**). One of the things Saint likes to advertise is that their product helps you comply with government and industry regulations such as PCI, HIPAA, SOX, NERC, FISMA, and COPPA.

Why draw out the network?

Now that we've gone through and scanned for vulnerabilities, our next phase is to draw out the network. A lot of people wonder why they need to draw out the network. Well, take it from an attacker's perspective. First, you're not the only network he's tracking. He must have some way of visualizing your environment, so when he revisits it, he goes, *I remember they have a server box here, a Linux box; they're running XP on this machine, they're still running server 2000.*

He may also want to see if he can figure out the missing pieces because maybe he's not picking something up, such as a skip in an IP address range.

Now, these pieces of software are designed to help IT personnel go through and manage their networks. Some of them will give you a live map and start showing you important things such as when a node goes down.

It will also help show both the physical and logical paths.

So, let me ask you, what do you see on this map? (*Figure 4.4*)

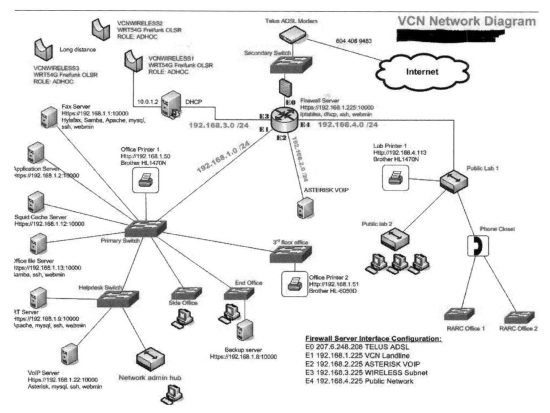

Figure 4.4 – VCN network diagram

Can you see operating systems? What else? I can see the devices— a Dell station, a Brother printer, and available apps. I might be able to track architecture, too.

Some mapping programs will help you store additional information notes. So, here is my warning for you: you may be using something like this already in your environment, and typically, these programs save the layout as a file extension.

As an attacker, one of the things I'm going to be looking for are those extensions because if I can download a map, you've already created it for me, thank you! I will store those types of files somewhere secure and, preferably, encrypt them.

So, what are the tools that help us visualize? There are many of them, but one of the most used is WhatsUp Gold, which I liked using back in my old ISP days. It would tell us when an antenna went down so that we could notify the customer or dispatch somebody out to their house before they even knew that they were having an issue.

There's also The Dude, which got its name from the The Big Lebowski movie. The main character is The Dude. We also have NetworkView as another great little product, as well as OpManager. Microsoft also makes a great little product called System Center Operations Manager, but it does require us to load an agent, yet others can just be done via ping and port scans. We also have LANsurveyors and FriendlyPinger – which is quick and dirty.

Preparing proxies and other anonymizing techniques

Before we start attacking systems or launching our attack at a company, we need to prepare our proxies and discuss another technique called **HTTP tunneling**.

There are other ways that we can use different anonymizing techniques to hide who we are and where we're coming from. We want to create an environment where it's almost like a magician's misdirection – look over here while I attack you from here.

So, first, we'll go through and look at placing the blame on someone else. In this world, where we have hundreds of thousands of devices hooked up, why not utilize them (systems) to go through and create proxies? So, we'll look at what a proxy is, why we use a proxy, and how to use a proxy. Then, we will look at a scary technique that's being utilized today that should have you very concerned: HTTP tunneling. *Wait a minute, my users can do what?* will be your reaction when you see it. We will then close this chapter by looking at some other types of anonymizers that are out there. Let's go look at those droids, shall we?

What is a proxy?

A proxy can do several things. A lot of companies will use a proxy. They'll use it to hide the identities of their systems behind their firewall, although sometimes, the firewall is their only proxy.

A good example is the ISIS server by Microsoft, which acts as a proxy. It goes out and gathers the websites for you. People only see the IP address of the one machine; they don't have a clue that you have multiple machines behind it.

It can also be used to filter undesirable content. A lot of companies also use this feature to keep employees focused on what they're supposed to be working on.

Sometimes, it also provides anonymous IDs to websites because websites track all kinds of information. One of the things they track is what IP address you are coming from and in this case, it's going to see the IP address of your proxy. We can also utilize it to NAT the IP address from the outside world. Again, it's just acting as a frontend for us.

It provides us with a little bit of protection. It's not going to fool a good hacker, but for most uses, there's not a ton of IP addresses being registered from your business going to websites.

In fact, because of some of the IP addresses, and some of the ways web browsers are utilized today, some website owners can detect what operating system you're utilizing. This can be determined based on the web browser that you're using. The big thing here – for us too – is that it saves on bandwidth. Back in my day, when I had my ISP service, we implemented a proxy server to help reduce bandwidth because everyone's default page back then for Internet Explorer was to pull up msn.com.

Instead of me having 600 employees firing up msn.com, eschewing the same information over and over, why not have the first request go out and have the proxy cache up that web page? And so, the second request comes to hit the proxy server, and the proxy server just quickly checks with msn.com, sees that there are no changes, and immediately returns across the network. Instead of doing so across our internet bandwidth, it just transfers to the page. It was very fast. It saved us almost 40% of our bandwidth.

One of the biggest shockers for me was getting a list of the most popular websites that were being cached up. It was a big eye-opener for me. So, you can see there are some great benefits to using a proxy for a corporation. Now, the question is: *Why do attackers use proxies?* Well, they do it kind of for the same thing – to hide their IP address from you and place blame somewhere else. They get to mask the actual source if they want. You can even set up a proxy and still spoof the address beyond this proxy.

If I was an attacker, and I wanted to, I could access internal data that's behind a firewall. If I can get someone to load up a piece of malware I've distributed and they're behind a nice firewall they fired up, it reports back to me, sets up a proxy for me, and I will be inside your environment without lifting a finger to get past your firewall.

We also use them for misdirection. *Look over here while I'm doing this over here.* I can have you believe that the attack is coming from the mailroom server, or Dick Grayson's computer down in the Marketing Department, when it's actually coming from me.

We also use it to help create what we refer to as a proxy chain – where multiple proxies are involved.

How to use a proxy

So, how do we use a proxy? Well, as an attacker, there are several different ways I can make communications or connections to your servers and your machines. First, I can be very blunt and hit you directly. The downside of this is that any IT person worth their weight in salt would find it easy to backtrack and find out where the attack is coming from.

Some attackers will go through and compromise a machine or use a machine they've compromised and be able to issue the attack. Alternatively, they will spoof the address. Again, when we look at log files and see somebody's attacking our servers, we relate it to, in this case, the server in the middle, which the attacker has control of. Now, that's a decent attacker, and this is what common attackers do. The great attackers we see in movies are difficult to trace because a simple call to their cell phone goes through a bazillion links, making it impossible for detectives to get to them in time.

A proxy chain is where an attacker is going to pwn several machines to route their traffic through. You might be able to discover the first proxy IP address they are attacking you with, but just when you think you have figured out who it is, you realize that it's been hopped through from another IP address so that you can get to the second proxy server. And you could keep backtracking to the third and maybe to the fourth.

A good attacker might use multiple machines within your network, but that's easy for you to go and backtrack. For even better cover, some want to have the first two machines in your network, and then outside of that (a completely different network), and then have those machines attack you because you don't have the rights to go in and look at those machines' log files. It would make it harder and harder to figure out what's going on as you back up the chain.

Usually, by the time you find them, the next time they connect to you, they may take a completely different route. It is very easy to detect an attacker utilizing a proxy daisy chain because it's easy to see that source IP, but it's extremely hard to discover where the attack is coming from.

Proxy o'plenty

There are several tools out there that can help with proxying or making yourself somewhat anonymous. One of them is proxifier, which allows network applications that don't normally support working through proxy servers to operate through an HTTPS proxy or chain. This allows people to surf websites that are typically restricted, especially by government or corporate organizations. It gets you past their firewall and hides your IP address. It can even use different protocols through the chain as it makes its way through your proxy chain.

We also have SocksChain, a product that goes through and functions as a Sock server that transmits queries through a chain of proxies. Again, we can use this for client programs that don't support Socks but work with a TCP connection such as Telnet, HTTP, or IRC. It is designed to hide your IP address from being displayed on the targets' logs or even mail headers.

Fiddler, an HTTP debugging proxy server application, also operates as a proxy server. It captures HTTP and HTTPS traffic and logs it for the user to review that information. It's a way that we can implement a man-in-the-middle attack using signed certificates.

Fiddler can also be used to modify HTTP traffic for troubleshooting. Again, these tools are created for good, but they can end up in a user's hands to be used for evil.

We also have **The Onion Router** (**TOR**). TOR is a combination of software and an open network that stops websites from tracking you. Because we can utilize the TOR network, I could set up some proxies – there are some programs out there that'll set up proxies in the TOR network for me – so that I can connect to new sites and instant messaging services if my company blocks those. It also encrypts and decrypts packets using public key encryption.

We also have Proxy Switcher, which, as its name suggests, allows you to surf anonymously on the internet without showing your IP, allows you to go through several different proxies (you could get a list of available proxies) and IPs, and go through and select which ones you want to be routed through. So, it hides your IP, allowing you to access restricted sites.

The Proxy Workbench program is also a handy product. With it, you can go through and get a list of free proxy servers out there and create a proxy chain. Plus, it's very graphical and has a nice GUI.

So, again, I reiterate that this course, or all these courses, are not necessarily about learning about the different pieces of software. It's understanding what they can do because when you do your software inventory, your first line of defense is always knowing what's installed on people's machines. So, do a software inventory. Are they running TOR or are they running Proxy Workbench? Do they have Fiddler installed? Do they have Nmap installed? Those are going to be red flags for you.

HTTP tunneling

Now, let me tell you about something that kind of scares me today regarding people getting around the security environments we set up or even our security appliances. It's called **HTTP tunneling**.

HTTP tunneling is designed to create a tunnel with HTTP. This means that if a user can install this on their system, they fire up their system, and they normally go through our standard network. They hit our firewall, which then sends them out to the internet, and they're able to go out to the websites they want to go to. However, any type of restricted sites or services the security team has said we don't allow in our network infrastructure get blocked.

That's the way things are supposed to work. It's not your network – it is the company's network. As an employee, you are getting paid to do a job, not things they deem unacceptable during company time.

Well, we have all heard of a **virtual private network** (**VPN**) before, where we create a VPN between us and another machine. Some VPNs use certain ports, but the in-thing is creating a VPN tunnel using ports 80 and 443 and that's what scares me. Users fire up their machines, install a piece of software that does HTTP tunneling, and then make a connection to the firewall. The packets they pass to the internet that are trying to get to restricted websites go across via port 443 if they want to be secure while doing so. The problem is that your router will not block it because that's the port that we use to browse the internet. But as an attacker, I can encapsulate another protocol inside that HTTP packet because it's in a tunnel. I can submit that to an HTTP tunneling server, which then goes out as a proxy for me to that restricted site.

As far as the IDS system and router are concerned, it's just passing port 80 but encapsulating it in FTP, and maybe you're not allowing FTP. Or it looks like it is using port 80 to go to your HTTP tunnel server website, which could be Billy Bob's site, yet they are being redirected so that they can go to some hacker's site or some inappropriate website.

This is extremely hard to track. So, again, the best way you're going to detect these types of activities going on in your network is, I repeat, knowing what software is installed on each of your machines, and what it's designed to do. Why? Because for this to work, they must download some type of software that sets up this VPN solution for them.

Anonymizers

We also have anonymizers, which is a way of hiding ourselves. Instead of being identified as Bruce Wayne, we get identified as John Smith. There are several tools or mechanisms we can use as anonymizers. We can circumvent our IDS systems and firewall rules and use an anonymizer to get to restricted content that may be either on the network or outside of our network. We can also use an anonymizer for protection against online attacks. If attackers don't know who we are, aren't we just using the same tools against the attackers? Absolutely! And finally, we can use it to afford us a little bit of privacy.

One of the tools that we can use is **Ultra Surf** (**U-Surf**), which allows you to set up a proxy. It re-identifies you and allows you to route through a proxy to hide your identity.

We also have G-Zapper. If you are a little paranoid about Google and how they're tracking you, you can use G-Zapper. It goes through and zaps the Google cookie that's on your machine so that when you go to Google, it doesn't automatically log you in, and you're able to do your searches without logging in and therefore not be tracked by Google.

However, just because it's not tracking your search history doesn't mean you're completely anonymous. Other things are tracking your IP address unless you're using something such as a VPN.

There's also one named Hide My IP. Its name tells you what it's going to do.

Not to be outdone, another company came out with a similar tool. It's a Chrome extension you can install on your browser. I apologize for the name, but it's called Hide Your Ass. It's a plugin for your Chrome browser. You can go to a website but before you hit *Enter*, you can select the Hide Your Ass icon and it'll go through and make it look like your IP or request is coming from a different location, giving you some protection.

Summary

In this chapter, we talked about various methods of scanning a target network. We talked about using both passive and active techniques. We also took the time to look at various scan types. You will want to make sure you've reviewed these types while studying for your exam. Remember, some are not viable on Windows-based systems. We also looked at how systems can end up identifying the operating systems they are running on by implementing a Banner Grab. Using vulnerability scanners can also generate a ton of intel on target systems. Finally, we discussed why it's important to map the network and how to hide by using proxies and proxy chains.

In the next chapter, we'll focus on enumerating targets, which will expose things such as users, services, and other goodies.

Questions

As we conclude, here is a list of questions for you to test your knowledge regarding this chapter's material. You will find the answers in the *Assessments* section of the *Appendix*:

1. Which of the following is an example of banner grabbing?

    A. Application research

    B. Passive OS fingerprinting

    C. Footprinting

    D. Active OS fingerprinting

2. What are the three types of scanning?

    A. Gray, black, and white

    B. Server, client, and network

    C. Active, passive, and hybrid

    D. Port, network, and vulnerability

3. What is the primary goal of performing port scans?

    A. Checking to see whether any routers have been patched

    B. Finding system names

    C. To determine where a ship may dock

    D. Detecting services/applications that are listening

4. Your system has been hacked. The IP address indicated in your logs is from France, yet the originating IP address is from Brazil. Which of the following options did the attacker use?

    A. Hide My IP

    B. TOR network

    C. Proxy chain

    D. WarpProxy

5
Enumeration

Enumeration is interesting. It does something that we typically don't want to happen. It makes systems behave abnormally or in a way that we wouldn't expect them to. *Steve Wozniak*, one of Apple's founders, said that *a lot of hacking is playing with other people, you know, getting them to do strange things*, and that's exactly what enumeration does for us. Enumerating is a core part of evaluating any target. An enumeration can be as simple as running a reverse DNS lookup on an IP address, or as complex as the entire OSINT process being run on a target. Enumerating a target is one of the most important steps in penetration testing. The goal of performing enumeration on a network is to gather as much information about the network as possible. This process typically looks at hosts and the services that they provide. With this information, an ethical hacker can identify and exploit vulnerabilities in the network.

Before enumerating a network, it is important to understand exactly what an *enumeration* is and why it's useful.

In this chapter, we'll cover the following main topics:

- What is enumeration?
- Ports and services to know about
- Enumerating via defaults
- NetBIOS enumeration

- Enumerating using SNMP

- Enumerating via LDAP

- Network time protocol

- Enumerating using SMTP

- The golden ticket – DNS

- Oh wait, there's more!

- The countermeasures

Let's get started!

What is enumeration?

This technique is usually conducted internally. While it can be done through reconnaissance, it is a slightly higher risk because we need an active connection to the target machine, which means what we're doing could be detected by a security team. When a user makes a connection to a network share, they must provide credentials. Those credentials are associated with what we refer to as an **access control list** (**ACL**). This ACL contains usernames and groups that have access and the permissions for those who access them. So, maybe we can trick the target machine into giving us that information without presenting our credentials.

We'll also look at some services. If we know of a specific service from looking at our reconnaissance and scanning techniques, we can enumerate those services to give us information that is about more than just the operating system. It's called a **null session**. A lot of the newer operating systems have blocked this capability. The issue is not everybody is up to date, and there's always one little machine out there nobody is tracking. Also, maybe you can't afford the latest and greatest, so creating these null sessions is a way to make an active connection and then query the services and/or shares.

When we hit a target, we extract information such as usernames and possible groups. In some cases, we also pull the groups and the users who are members of that group. If we can't do this yet, we should be able to pull the machine's name and network resources and services that may be running on that system.

Again, some of the information we might be able to pull could also include routing tables – especially if it's like a switch or a router of some sort, along with auditing services. We will also try to expose some applications. Again, we should have been able to discover applications via our scanning and reconnaissance phases, but often, the application itself can give up a lot of data. Additionally, if I can get ahold of some DNS and **Simple Network Management Protocol** (**SNMP**) information, it can make your life a living nightmare.

Now, let's discuss enumeration weak points.

Some of my favorite enumeration weak points

When it comes to enumeration, an attacker will typically look for what we call *the low-hanging fruit*. This means we'll look for the easiest weak points first. Here are some of the lowest fruits that attackers will target initially.

Business card

How can a business card provide a weakness? Well, think about it. What's on your business card? Your name, address, and company name. That doesn't seem to give up too much information, right? How about your email address? They might not spam you, but guess what? Most companies – because of the way Active Directory works, or any directory services – go through and create usernames (what's referred to as distinguished names), which would be a way of logging into the network. We typically think of logging in as being domain\username (gotham\bwayne). Most directory services technologies will also accept bwayne@gotham.com. It uses the same naming syntax that is associated with email.

As an attacker or hacker, I need at least two pieces of information to come for you: a login name and a password. If you hand me a business card and you were able to log into your system using that same email address, I just got 50% of your information. I probably don't need a business card, because I can get your email address off your company's website. Scared yet?

Windows groups

As we mentioned previously, these groups are created and maintained by your IT department and have been given **security identifiers** (**SIDS**). They contain other objects such as the user accounts themselves, or SIDS.

When a user tries to gain access to a resource, they present their credential. This credential is then looked at by the file server, which says, *Let me check if you're a member of a group that has access or have been given explicit access. In this case, let me look and see if the group "marketing folks" have access to this file or resource.* I can, therefore, enumerate a Windows group and say, *Okay, which user accounts are a member of this "marketing folks" group?* Again, I can end up enumerating everybody in every department at your organization.

Default passwords

Default passwords are one of my biggest pet peeves. I get it – technology is moving extremely fast, and a lot of times, we just don't think things through. This is one of those things I wish I could get across to everyone, including home users. We go and purchase the latest and greatest router and, according to their instructions, we hit one button and it auto-configures. With one click, we're on the internet, and we're *safe*. Well, probably not. So many devices today come with default passwords. It's very easy to log into the system to enumerate it just by using those passwords if no one's changed them.

There are websites dedicated to storing default passwords. It's nothing nefarious, it's just very convenient, especially for an IT guy who walks in and goes, *Well, SMC switch, I wonder what the default admin password is on this one because I need to log in.*

Next, let's discuss the ports and services you'll need to know about.

Ports and services to know about

Let's consider the ports and services you will want to be familiar with:

- Most of the DNS information that goes across the network is going to be using port 53.

- **Simple Mail Transfer Protocol** (**SMTP**) typically uses port 25.

- Microsoft RPC endpoints use TCP 135.

- The global catalog service, which is a stripped-down version of Active Directory that users and applications take advantage of all the time, queries port 3286.

- The NetBIOS naming service, which is typically the computer name to an IP address, uses port 137, both TCP and UDP.

- LDAP or LDP is the protocol used by Active Directory, Open Directory, and all the different directory services out there. It uses TCP and UDP port 389.

- SMB, which is our server message block over NetBIOS, is what creates shared resources or shared folders, and it uses TCP 139 to make connections.

- We also have SNMP, which uses UDP 161. The other SMB technology that it can use is TCP, which is going to be associated with port 445 on TCP.

> **Note**
>
> It's important to know about these services and the ports they operate on. You need to understand or memorize some of the ports and services that different technologies utilize for your exam.

All these services are utilized in day-to-day operations on the network. You could go through and block all these ports if you'd like, but that system isn't doing much online. A good analogy for this is saying, *I understand the risks of driving on the freeway; I have a higher chance of getting in a car accident. However, I accept those risks, knowing the flaws and possible situations that can take place. I'm going to prepare myself for that – I'm going to be more aware of the road around me, how fast I'm going, how far ahead the car is in front of me, which exits are coming up, and avoid distractions.* If you think in terms of normal network traffic, the issue with these ports is that you need to be monitoring the traffic on them. This is because anything you're not expecting is going to throw a flag in the air, stating that something may be going on in your network.

Enumerating via defaults

This subject drives me bonkers; it makes me want to pull out my hair, thinking about how naive people are out there. In 2015, CNN released a study showing 90% of the credit card readers out there use the same password. It's the default one – it's either 166816 or z 66816. Now… don't rush to your bank or ATM to see if that password works. That's not our purpose. The point is, there are these types of vulnerabilities.

This is our biggest security issue because defaults exist everywhere. I love the phrase *complacency will be your downfall*. I know we have tons of devices and technology out there being thrown at us – servers, desktops, routers, tablets, phones, switches, Wi-Fi, and so on. The demand is always there in getting it set up and getting it done fast. Sometimes, we have the issue where devices get deployed with our default passwords or default user accounts. Every device out there has them because you must go through and set it up.

Never leave the default user accounts or passwords in place! *Never!* Don't assume or say it's just a small device, it's just my cell phone, it's just a tablet my kid plays on, or it's just my home router.

A *friend* of mine (ok, maybe it was me or maybe it wasn't) was doing a lot of traveling and while visiting a small town where some family lived, they went to the local convenience store to withdraw some cash. Once they were in front of the ATM, they noticed that instead of a normal ATM screen, it was asking for a password, and they hadn't put their debit card in yet.

They tried some known default codes, first typing in 1234. They got an error and then typed in 0000 and got another error. They tried 1212 and to their surprise, they were presented with the administrative screen of the ATM. They could get into the setup and do config testing. Out of curiosity, they selected tests. They were presented with another menu that invited them to test a receipt, meaning print a receipt. They could also test a cash distribution. Yeah, that would have issued cash to my *friend*. Being an ethical hacker who just likes to see how things work, they went over to the front counter person and told them about it. They disconnected the plug and powered it back up, and the ATM started running correctly.

So, either somebody had just serviced the ATM and didn't completely exit out or there was a glitch. But again, think about the defaults being used here and the vulnerabilities that can be presented.

NetBIOS enumeration

What is NetBIOS? Well, let's put our memory caps on and take a trip down memory lane. NetBIOS has been around for some time and is often mistaken as a protocol. It stands for **Network Basic Input Output System**, and it's technically a program that allows applications on different systems to talk to each other over LAN.

> **Warning**
> Some of the things you see, especially when it comes to NetBIOS, might be a little outdated. We'll talk about why we still cover it, why we still talk about it, and why it's relevant today.

It was created by IBM back in the old days. IBM kind of left it behind and Microsoft adopted it. Since then, NetBIOS has become an industry standard. It's used on Ethernet, and if you're old school, it's also used in Token Ring. If you are familiar with Token Ring, I'm not referencing anything about hobbits… NetBIOS is used inside of the options when we are inside Windows. If we go into the network settings for a network interface, it's under the clients for Microsoft networks. In there, you'll see an option that says *file and print services*, which is where we can turn things off and on.

> **Note**
>
> Remember, not only is it important to know what applications are on your machines, but also what users can run from even a thumb drive.

Some of these things won't work on newer operating systems, such as Windows 7 and higher. However, from my experience, there's always a system on the network that's not up to date, or one they had no reason to update.

Some of the commands you can use to enumerate NetBIOS include using the built-in utility in every single Windows system, called `nbtstat.exe`, using the `nbtstat -A <target-ip-address>` command. This will display the services running on the target, as well as group memberships and domain information.

> **Note**
>
> For the detailed functions of nbtstat, simply type `nbtstat` into Command Prompt:

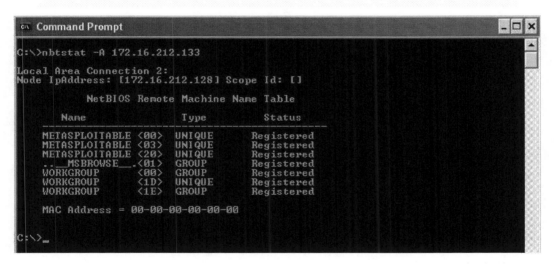

Figure 5.1 – Results of the nbtstat command

Next, we'll learn how to enumerate with SNMP.

Enumerating using SNMP

What could go wrong? Well, quite a bit. Little things make big things happen.

SNMP has been around for a long time and has gone through several version changes. We'll go through and look at what SNMP is and why administrators enable it. While it makes our lives easier, any time we talk about ease of use, remember the technology triangle. Once we implement heavier in terms of ease of use, or from the GUI perspective, we lose security.

What is **SNMP**? It stands for **Simple Network Management Protocol**. It's exactly what it sounds like – a protocol that runs the application layer and allows us to manage different devices. Now, whether they're routers, switches, firewalls, wireless access points, or even servers, they report back to a centralized location so that we can, as its name implies, manage devices:

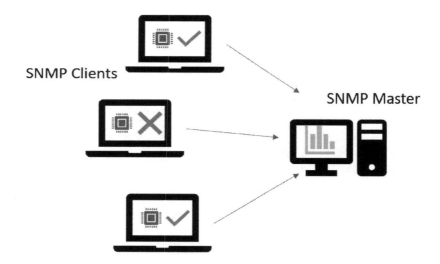

Figure 5.2 – SNMP clients gather performance intel and report back to a centralized reporting point

So, again, an administrator can see what's going on. If a CPU is overloaded on a particular router, if server memory is being over-utilized, and so on, the administrator needs to be warned about these things. Besides devices, a lot of operating systems, including both Windows and Linux, support the SNMP protocol. Typically, we install an agent on these devices, and they report back to a management console. The Management Console, or management station, will then send out requests to the agents to retrieve certain information you've plugged in and are trying to monitor.

The agents we install on our components and the management software program are going to talk to each other, but we don't want them to just talk arbitrarily. There's a little bit of security that's implemented with SNMP, but not enough as far as the security is concerned, or the lack thereof. It all depends on the version of SNMP you're running. Version one is very simple, basic, and extremely vulnerable to SNMP enumeration. They then released version two, which was the same as version one, except they added some additional components and enhancements to it. Still, it is not very secure.

The reason SNMP has a bad rap about not being secure is because the two communication channels that are used between the agent and the management software use two different types of passwords. One of them has read access, while the other one has read and write access. Now, here's where the issue comes into play. For the public, which has read access, meaning my software can go out and read information and pull CPU information and whole memory information, the default password is public. Now, that was slick, wasn't it? And you'll never guess what the private password is. Sometimes, we refer to these passwords as just community strings.

For most of the devices we're monitoring, IT guys have come up with an administrative username and password or possibly even, say, a switch, a router, or a wireless access point. They must link it up and say, *Only these users are allowed through, or these computers are allowed through,* which means information is being stored somewhere on that box and SNMP is designed to extrapolate that.

They then came out with version three, which is the latest version of the protocol. There's a lot of emphasis being placed on the area of authentication and privacy. So, we can select or specify restricted user access. We can also encrypt data on the fly. This does require more complexity because we must configure it to do these things, which is the other issue we have to kind of fight here. After all, some security holes can be created.

A very common issue I see out there is many IT guys going off and purchasing the device that supports SNMP. What they don't realize is that, by default, versions one and two have backward compatibility enabled. If you must do this, disable versions one and two unless you don't mind somebody pulling off information. Now, you may be thinking, what type of information could they pull off a device like this? Well, they can pull off quite a bit. They can look at enough information that puts your network at risk. They could very easily use it to grab the routing tables of routers; they can change your configurations if the defaults are in place because the private community string gives it the right permissions. If it's a host machine, they could also look at file shares, ARP tables, and traffic statistics.

We can use **Management Information Base (MIB)** here, a virtualized database that provides descriptions of the network objects that can be managed through SNMP. It's done hierarchically and each of the objects in the MIBs is dressed in what they refer to as OIDs. **OID** is short for **object identifier**. It is a numeric name that's given to objects inside of the MIB so that it can uniquely identify the objects that are present within the hierarchy. It's used by SNMP to convert the OIDs into plain human language.

Microsoft has a list of MIBs they include on the server platform. The most utilized is for DHCP. It monitors traffic between a DHCP server and the clients. There's one for WINS, which is being deprecated at the time of writing. There's one for hosts, which helps you monitor the resources, CPU, network cards, memory, and hard drives on host resources. We also have the LNMIB, which contains the different types of objects for workstation and server services.

Enumerating via LDAP

So, what is LDAP? The reason why it sounds familiar to us is because we use it as a database to store user account information and object information about our network. Microsoft utilizes it in Active Directory. Novell e-directory also utilizes it and, of course, Apple uses Open Directory. Now, this is the technology that contains or stores our user accounts and our computer accounts. From an Active Directory perspective, it contains/stores everything that's involved in our Microsoft platform.

Some people think Microsoft stole this technology from Novell, but LDAP is an open standard. Novell followed it first with e-directory. Microsoft then followed up behind them by using their implementation, called Active Directory. Because these are open standards, there's a lot of similarity between the names and the syntax being utilized.

Now, full disclosure here... I'm not a big fan of Apple, but Apple's Open Directory is also another implementation of LDAP. They're using LDAP there, which includes an Apple password server, and they also use Kerberos 5. Technically, it's a form of what we refer to as open LDAP, an open source implementation of LDAP. It's platform-independent. Linux, Solaris, Microsoft, HP, HP UX, and Android use LDAP.

Understanding LDAP

Let's look at what's behind LDAP. There are what's referred to as **Directory System Attendant (DSA)** ports. It's what the client uses to start an LDAP session by connecting to an LDAP server. By default, this port is on TCP and UDP 389. If by chance, they're using SSL, they are technically using LDAP, which is utilized on port 636.

There's another service called the global catalog, which is simply a smaller or a stripped-down version of the full database. When you open an email client such as Outlook and hit **I'd like to create a new email** and you hit the **To** box, Outlook queries – via exchange – the global catalog server and extrapolates some of the basic information, such as the username and email address.

By default, those ports are set to communicate on TCP and UDP 3268. Again, if you're using any type of encryption, it's done on port 3269.

The structure is technically based on what's referred to as the X 500 model, which has been around for ages. What we mean here is that this database, since it's based on this model, has what's referred to as classes.

Classes

Classes are a way of looking at objects. For example, I can have a class that represents users, have another class that represents groups, and another class that represents computers. See where I'm going here? Classes represent objects. Each of those classes has its own set of attributes. For example, in the user class, the attributes would include first name, last name, city, state, and ZIP code. These classes, attributes, and objects can be found inside of an LDAP environment by using what we refer to as a unique identifier or distinguished name.

A distinguished name is very distinctive; every object must be its own entity; you can't have duplicating objects. So, in the case of a user whose name is Bruce Wayne, who belongs to a Gotham.com domain, his distinguished name or unique identifier would be listed as cn=Bruce Wayne,dc=gotham,dc=com. Within the distinguished name, cn stands for Common Name, and dc stands for Domain Component. You'll often see ou as well in here, which stands for **Organizational Unit**. So, that would be represented as gotham.com or Gotham City, if the last dc was equal to city. You must understand distinguished names, especially if you start enumerating to find out where they're located.

What can we learn from LDAP?

There's a lot because you can mostly query an LDAP server anonymously.

> **Note**
> Good IT guys ensure you can't anonymously hit the domain controller, but when you think about the domain controllers, they are there to ask for authentication. So, typically, anonymity is allowed.

Some of the things we can find out would include group names. When we see these group names, we could extrapolate users that are a member of that group. I can even pull up individual users. Now, because I can pull up these names, I should also be able to check the account information, such as the other attributes that are associated with these objects, the city's state, ZIP code, login hours, and password reset thresholds. Again, most attributes can be looked at very easily.

We can also look at system names, which is where I come back to naming your systems – making sure you don't give away what they are. I know I've shown you my environment where I have Batcave DC1; you can tell it's a domain controller. However, if mine was an actual production environment for a company, I would never do something like that. However, still enumerating through LDAP, I can easily determine which box is a domain controller.

With tools such as JXplore and Hyena (*Figure 5.3*), I can pull up the Active Directory schema (the layout, though you can think of it as an Excel spreadsheet that lays out attributes and classes). I should not only see the schema, but also the classes. Therefore, I should be able to drill into user accounts, group accounts, server names, and more:

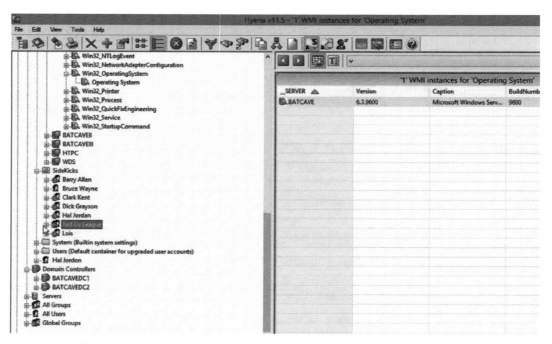

Figure 5.3 – Results from Hyena regarding an Active Directory infrastructure

We'll discuss Network Time Protocol next.

Network Time Protocol

Okay; guess what? We can enumerate using time! There's a protocol out there that our computers use to synchronize the time between each other. It's called **Network Time Protocol** (**NTP**). Now, you may be thinking, Dale, you cannot possibly have a quote about this. Well, guess again. Cindy Lauper said, *If you're lost, you can look and you will find me, time after time.* When it comes to hacking, the things that you don't expect end up giving up information.

NTP is a protocol that we use for synchronizing our clocks between all the systems in a LAN network. This has been around for decades, having been developed in 1981 by David Mills. In a domain, one of the most important settings will be time, and all the computers in the domain need to be within a certain timeframe. For example, in the Microsoft world, the computers or the desktops themselves can't be more than 5 minutes out of sync. Now, technically, domain controllers use NTP with what they refer to as **UTC**, which is Coordinated Universal Time.

UTC is independent of time zones and enables NTP to be used anywhere in the world, regardless of time zone settings. That's why they're able to keep up, whether you're in Mountain Standard Time or Eastern Time and so on. In a typical Microsoft environment, there's going to be one computer that is flagged as the NTP server for the entire domain. It's referred to as a PDC emulator, which is also known as one of the most **flexible single master operations** (**FSMO**) roles. This is the machine that oversees time, and it gets its time from the BIOS clock, which is the default. A best practice of Microsoft is to get the PDC emulator server to synchronize with an atomic clock on the internet. Now, all this communication is taking place on a specific port, and that is port UDP number 123. This port needs to make sure that it's open so that all the domain controllers will synchronize themselves with the PDC emulator and that all the domain member's servers and domain workstations are synchronized with one of the domain controllers.

You need to ensure that port 123 on UDP is accessible. In a domain, time synchronization takes place when the Windows time server turns on during system startup and, every now and then, as the system is running. NTP itself is extremely accurate. And when I say extremely accurate, it depends on the network that it's synchronizing across. If it's a private network, it can synchronize the machines to be within 200 microseconds of each other. And in a public network, it does slow down a bit to under 10 milliseconds.

Now, these computers, which are talking to each other to synchronize their time, open them up for enumeration. So, what can we learn from NTP? Well, we can do a lot of things, including pulling a list of hosts off an NTP server because they're all reporting into the NTP server to make sure they're synchronized. There will be some residual information listing hostnames and with those, we should also be able to get IP addresses listed. We may even be able to pull off system names and we will even see operating systems being displayed.

With basic NTP commands, we should be able to trace the chain of NTP servers, as well as query the NTP daemon and its current state, and monitor the NTP daemon. NTP attacks are primarily **Denial of Service** (**DoS**) based to wreak havoc on an organization.

Enumerating using SMTP

Who would think a simple protocol that we use in day-to-day life, such as SMTP, could reveal so much about a network? A famous T-shirt went around at Blackhat several years ago. Most people didn't understand the meaning. It simply said **I read your email.**:

Figure 5.4 – I read your email T-shirt from Blackhat

That's so true. Normally, email is transmitted in clear text, meaning that messages are readable. As email servers communicate with each other, they also transmit information via the SMTP protocol, which can be used to further enumerate your network.

The purpose of this is not necessarily to read people's emails, even though that could give up a lot of information. It's more about looking at what we refer to as the headers of the email, which is the information that gets attached to the beginning of the email during transit, which exposes quite a bit.

So, what is SMTP? It's simply a protocol we use for delivering emails between email servers and across the internet. It utilizes a process referred to as store and forward, which means that the SMTP protocol moves your email on and across the networks. It uses DNS to look up a specific type of record, called an MX record, to identify the server it needs to forward or store the email in. It also works closely with **Mail Transfer Agents** (**MTAs**) to ensure it sends the email to the right computer and email inbox. SMTP directs how your email moves from your computer's MTA to an MTA of another computer or even several computers.

I know this is a bit confusing but because all of this happens in the background, we don't have to worry about it. Once the email gets inside our network infrastructure, we typically use other types of protocols. For example, we might use POP, IMAP, or MAPI to deliver the emails internally. However, externally, out on the internet, SMTP is the big bad boy of the block. SMTP uses a couple of ports, including port 25 and port 587 for submission.

Some commands take place between the servers to communicate and deliver emails. There is a set of codes that help simplify those communications. When you send an email message out, it gets converted into strings of text that are separated by these code words (their numbers), which identify the purpose of each of the sections being transmitted.

Typically, only other SMTP servers understand what those commands are as the message travels toward its destination. Sometimes, it passes through several computers, as well as their individual MTAs. It may also be stored briefly before moving on to the next computer within that path.

Some of those commands include specifying the email address of the sender. This command also tells the SMTP server that a new email is starting and makes these SMTP servers reset all their states and buffers. There's also a receipt to the recipient of the email. There's also the command data, which starts transferring the email message itself. It will typically receive the attachments and the body text. Once the SMTP server sends the email across, it waits for a specific code to verify that the destination server received it. This verification is typically done with an acceptance code called a 250 reply code, which means everything is okay. There's also a verifier, which asks the server to confirm or verify that a specific username or mailbox exists.

If you're starting to think like I've been trying to teach you to think, think about how that command can be useful to you. One of these commands can be used to probe for login names on servers, as well as possible groups.

Servers that ignore the `verify` command will usually send some type of reply, but they will not send information the client is looking or asking for. The fact remains that either a yes or a no gives me quite a bit of data.

We also have the `expanded` command, which is like the `verify` command, except for in the case of a mailing list, it shows the members of that mailing list. The SMTP `expand` command causes a sent mail to expand to all the recipients and makes sure each of those recipients gets one of those email messages that were initially in the data section.

Knowing that, what could we possibly learn from SMTP? Well, we can download a list of names off the internet. This list could have been utilized to verify what users are valid within the network and which ones are not. This is how a lot of spammers clean up their spam lists. It can also help me expose a possible target, making sure that it's a valid login name.

Next, we'll discuss DNS enumeration.

The golden ticket – DNS

When it comes to enumeration, one of the most revealing things you can do is get a hold of all the computer names and IP addresses on the network in one shot. We can do that with DNS enumeration. DNS is responsible for turning names into IP addresses. *What's in a name?*, William Shakespeare would ask. Well, in this case, everything, because what DNS holds for me can reveal a ton of information. I can see server names, what services are being offered up, and I can identify domain controllers if I need to, as well as websites or SQL servers.

Most of the network connectivity that takes place there, as far as computers figuring out where things are located goes, is handled by DNS. If I can enumerate that, I can pull a plethora of information:

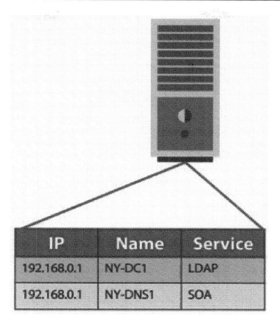

Figure 5.5 – DNS records associated with the services that are installed

As you can see, we have **192.168.0.1**, which is resolved to the computer name of **NYC-DC1**. It happens to be running LDAP. What that tells me is that when I'm trying to log into a domain environment, I need to find an LDAP server. It also tells me that the LDAP server is equal to NY-DC1, which is equal to an IP address, and I can make the connection. In the case of the bottom entry, **192.168.0.2**, this tells me that's a server whose name is NY-DNS1, which is my **Start of Authority (SoA)**.

With enumeration, we can go through and look up the records and identify what records are registered with which computers. We can also do something called **cache snooping**. Cache snooping is where the DNS server resolves names to IP addresses for client machines. For example, if I say I'd like to go to www.yahoo.com, I can submit that entry to my DNS server and it will go and resolve that, get an IP address, and submit it back to me. That information is stored inside the cache memory of my computer. If I can snoop that cache, especially for an internal DNS server, I can see what computer names have been resolved by this box. We can also use a Google lookup. If I can enumerate via Google's DNS servers, I might be able to find out a lot about your infrastructure, especially if you have subdomains.

Reverse lookups

We also have reverse lookup capabilities. When normal name resolution takes place, we have a name. I'm trying to go to `yahoo.com`, and in return, I get an IP address from the DNS server. Reverse lookup is the opposite, where we have an IP and I want to know what name is associated with that IP address. I have an IP address of `192.168.0.1`, but I have no idea what the computer name is. This reverse lookup is done with what's referred to as a pointer record, and we can do this against either IPv4 or IPv6 addresses. We can also do zone walking. Zone walking isn't difficult to understand. This is a technique that helps us reveal internal records if the zone is not properly configured. We can ask, what subdomains do you have behind you? This can help us map network hosts by enumerating the contents of the zone.

Zone transfers

This is the big bad boy. If I can do this with your DNS servers, look out – I'm going to be in heaven. When I teach the Microsoft Server platform, I talk about how to set up a DNS server. One of the things that we do is set up the one DNS server to replicate only with a secondary DNS server. We want to make sure that it only replicates with *that* second DNS server. The reason behind this is that, if it's not set up correctly, an attacker will attempt to contact your DNS server and say, *Hey, would you please replicate with me and tell me who you've got because I don't have anybody in my database?* Now, I have a complete record and map of your environment, including MX records, hostnames, and all kinds of other records. This can help me do something later called **DNS poisoning**, where I'm going to put invalid records into your DNS zone.

DNS records

So, what's behind DNS? Well, we know that it's a database itself that contains computer names and their IP addresses. It operates on port UDP 53, as well as TCP 53. Typically, we use UDP port 53 for doing standard lookups such as *Hey, I need yahoo.com's IP address*, where zone transfers are typically done through TCP port 53. The reason why we use UDP is because it's a much faster resolution. We'll look at some of the records in detail next.

A records

So far, we have mentioned that the database itself consists of multiple records that point to IP addresses, the names these records help identify, and, in some cases, the services that are running. One of those records is an A record, or as the Canadians would say, *a record, eh?* This is simply just a hostname being resolved to an IP address.

AAAA records

These are the same things as A records, except instead of pointing to IPv4 addresses, they point to IPv6 records.

> **Side Note**
>
> The Fonz is a big fan of AAAA records. AAAAAAAY! Okay, for you young ones out there, if you don't know what that reference was, go Google it – Happy Days, The Fonz.

CNAME records

A CNAME record is an alias that points to another A record. So, for example, my A record or AAAA record could be batcave and pointing to an IP address, but maybe I have another name for that same computer, which I'm going to call www. So, whether somebody types in www or batcave, they will go to the same IP address/location. So, a CNAME record points to the A record reference.

MX records

Then, we have MX records. No, not motocross. These are mail exchange records. This helps us identify the server/servers that oversee sending and receiving emails.

NS records

We also have NS, which are name servers. Hey, name servers! If an attacker can find those records, they would be the IPs of the DNS servers that I'd want to try to enumerate with. This is a major score here.

SOA records

We also have SOA, which is the primary DNS server. This would be another record I would want to get a hold of and see if I could do a zone transfer with.

PTR records

We also have PTR records, also known as pointer records. Again, this is the reverse lookup, so if we only have an IP address and we don't know the computer name, or we don't know what the hostname is, if I can do a reverse lookup, I'll be able to extrapolate that information.

SRV records

Then, we have something called SRV records, or service records. These service records record what services are running on which machines. For example, in a Microsoft Exchange environment, if I open Outlook, create a new email, and hit my little **To** button, I will see the big list of email addresses for my company:

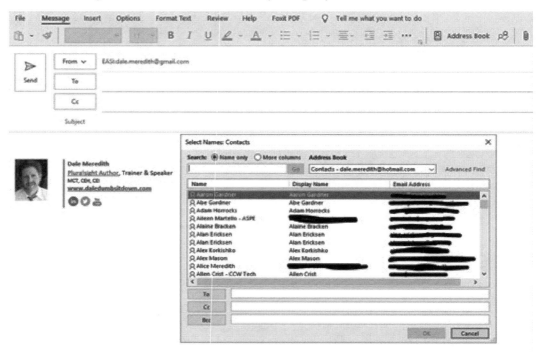

Figure 5.6 – Global Address Book populated by a Global Catalog Server

Well, what happened is that my computer went and looked at the DNS to find a computer on the network that offers the global catalog service. It identifies, contacts, resolves, and gives me back email address information.

Sum it up

So, what can we learn from DNS? Folks, it's the mother lode – it's the secret treasure of enumeration. This is because, in one fell swoop, I can find out every single computer name on your network, their IP addresses, and the services they're running, which all help me determine which vulnerabilities might be out there that I could use as a point of entry. Now, we can also pick up, as I mentioned previously, the server names and workstations. Believe it or not, sometimes, IT guys use their workstations to, for example, monitor network traffic. I want to know what that box is, hopefully so that I can avoid it. I should also be able to see which services are running on which servers. Again, I can find an LDAP server, which would be my domain controller, so I can find a global catalog server or a Kerberos server. Once I have a list of all your domain controllers, I'm going to go back (remember when we talked about doing NetBIOS enumeration?), where maybe I can discover what OS is being used. If it's a 2012 server, I'm going to get giddy inside because that's an older OS that's probably not patched or Microsoft stopped supporting it.

Oh wait, there's more!

There are more ways we can enumerate; it's not limited to just the Windows platform. They work on almost all devices; none are safe. It cracks me up when friends and family members tell me how they feel safe because they don't run Windows, and that they're running Linux or a version of Unix. But here's the dirty secret; if it deals with a protocol, you are not secure! You are dead wrong if you think any operating system or device is safe. There are different ways to attack all types of boxes, whether it's a Linux box, a Unix box, a Cisco router, and so on. In one of their old marketing campaigns, Apple bragged that they were virus-free—they don't get malware. Today, they know better. In Golden Eye, a 1995 spy film, a hacker named Boris Grishenko would scream, *I'm invincible!* whenever he was onto something. Toward the end of the movie – spoiler alert – something unpleasant happens to him. The same applies to some of these operating systems today, giving us a sense of invincibility.

IPsec

IPsec is a commonly implemented technology for gateway-to-gateway, LAN-to-LAN, and even VPN-based enterprises. Most of the IPsec-based VPNs use the **Internet Security Association Key Management Protocol (ISAKMP)**. It's used to establish, negotiate, modify, and delete SAs, as well as the cryptographic keys in a VPN environment.

So, what does it need from a hacking perspective? Well, this is simple. An attacker can perform a simple direct scan for the ISAKMP protocol, which uses UDP port 500. We could use tools such as Nmap here.

VoIP enumeration

This is an interesting enumeration. VoIP is replacing most of the traditional telephone services in both corporate and home environments. The overall concept here is that VoIP is utilizing your network or internet access, and it does so through **Session Initiation Protocol** (**SIP**), one of the protocols that VoIP uses to perform voice calls, video calls, and so on.

SIP uses UDP or TCP ports 2000, 2001, 5050, and 5061. There are several tools out there that you can use to enumerate VoIP. Metasploit has some built-in tools. There are also tools such as SIPvicious, an auditing tool that can be used to scan phone systems by performing an invite scan. And, of course, the attacker could then combine this *invite scan* with a *call command* to determine the weak passwords that are used to connect to a particular phone host or a PBX network. Another popular tool out there is svmap, a free, open source scanner we use to identify different SIP devices and PBX servers on a particular network.

If you think outside the box and think about these different VoIP solutions and the information they may communicate across the internet, you might look at doing some Google hacking.

Enumerating with Remote Procedure Call (RPC)

RPC is a technology we use to create distributed client-server programs. It allows the client and the server to communicate via these programs.

You can fire up Kali if you want and use Nmap. The command that you would use would be nmap -p 135. Then, you would specify the target machine. In our case, it would be 192.168.01-254. If you suspect a particular target machine, you could just type in the full IP address of the target machine.

The countermeasures

Countermeasures are designed to protect a network or system from an attack by either preventing the attack from happening or detecting when it has happened. This enables security professionals to take corrective action to ensure their systems remain secure. Countermeasures must be taken seriously because once an attacker has enumerated a network, penetrating the system becomes significantly easier.

Defaults and NetBIOS

When it comes to defaults, we're talking about default settings – whether it's the default settings for NetBIOS, your wireless access point, or SQL database defaults. The rule is: do not create a security hole by leaving default username and passwords or default settings in place. Change them. For example, I get into my servers via remote desktop all the time, but I don't use the default ports. I've changed them up. Likewise, be aware of your ports. Of course, you can't change some of them. I can't change the DNS port unless I implement something such as a socket pool, a feature of the Windows Server platform that randomizes the ports, but that's another book.

Also, if you don't want shares to be accessible to users on a particular box, then turn off your **Server Message Block (SMB)**. Now, you wouldn't want to do that to a file server.

SNMP

As far as countermeasures go for SNMP, remember that this is the protocol that allows us to monitor and manage network devices as well as servers. If you don't need it, turn it off. If you're going to have it turned on, make sure that you at least start using version 3 because it has better security associated with it.

Another thing you can do from the Windows Server platform is use a group policy, which allows us to control settings on servers. I would also look at the additional restrictions for anonymous connections. If you have any older servers, have them locked down (for the love of Pete, update them). Also, block port 161, both TCP and UDP.

Alternatively, if you still need to use SNMP, go to your firewall rules and allow 161 to be opened, but only to specific machines, which would maybe be your monitoring server. This also goes back to the aspect of when it comes to SNMP, don't install the agent on a device you will not use it on. You don't necessarily need to monitor every single device. If you are going to turn it on, one of the things you may want to look at is implementing IPsec filtering, which encrypts the traffic going back and forth between the agent and the server monitor. And of course, be very careful about any quick-fix solutions by vendors saying that you need to open a null session because null sessions can be extremely dangerous.

LDAP

LDAP is the protocol that we use to authenticate users and store user accounts and objects in Active Directory, at least from Microsoft's perspective. Other LDAP services include open LDAP and several others, but they all use the same protocol.

One of the things you want to do is separate the email address from login names. While you're at it, don't use the default, which is typically the login name, which is their email address. Why? Because, as an attacker, I will go to your website and see if you list email addresses for some of your company officers or employees. I will then go through and try those as login names within your network. It's shocking how many companies still use an email address schema for logins.

> **Note**
>
> If you're not sure about this one, throw your three-finger salute on your computer (*Ctrl + Alt + Delete*) and log off. Now, if my login name is normally Bwayne and my domain is gotham.com, odds are that if I use bwayne@gotham.com instead for my login in and it works, you might want to rethink your Active Directory environment!

Now, you may also need to remember that LDAP traffic is unsecured when it goes across the wire. So, we may want to look at using SSL to encrypt our traffic. Another thing that I'm a big fan of is encrypted drives that store the LDAP database using BitLocker, which is a great solution. Full disk encryption, or another drive encryption technology, is a great idea to ensure that if somebody does get physical access to it, they cannot access the information. And hey, BitLocker is free! #BonusPoints.

Network Time Protocol (NTP)

All the computers on the network get their time from a centralized location. This depends on whether you're using a Windows product or possibly a Cisco router as your NTP server or Juniper device because Windows doesn't use the NTP protocol. This means it's not susceptible to the NTP vulnerabilities that are out there, but it has its own problems.

When it comes to NTP, make sure you watch your ports. Remember that the default port is 123, which is easy to remember. You also need to understand what software is installed or what patches have been applied, especially to these hardware devices. Sometimes, we install software, and it opens ports without our knowledge because maybe they need to use an NTP protocol. And of course, use those commands that we talked about to check your own NTP Master so that you understand what information is being exposed.

Simple Mail Transfer Protocol (SMTP)

One of the things we want to do is ensure we have disabled open relays. For most of the email servers out there, the open relays are already turned off. It's kind of funny because back in the old days, they were turned on, to make it easy for you. But if you are familiar with the technology triangle, when we make things easier, we end up opening more security holes. Also, drop unknown recipients. Again, most of the products out there that handle email will do reverse lookups. They will look at the header of the email, which always states the IP address of where it came from, and it'll do a reverse lookup to DNS. And if it doesn't match up, it'll drop it out of there.

DNS

DNS is our name server – it's what resolves a computer name to an IP address. So, first, we want to configure DNS zone transfers to be sent to specific or explicit servers. Also, make sure the hostnames of computers you don't want to be visible to the outside world are not referenced to an IP address in your DNS zone files.

When you check the DNS zone files – that is, you know what names are listed within the database – make sure that you check both internal and external DNS servers. I've seen situations where IT guys have taken the internal database and just simply copied it into the external DNS server to make things easy for themselves.

For the love of Pete, there's a DNS record out there called a HINFO record that specifies the server's type of CPU and operating system. It was designed initially so that applications such as FTP could use special processes when they were communicating with the servers of a known CPU or operating system. But think about that one for a second. If it's a file that's accessible from the outside telling you the server's name and operating system, you're not going to have a very good day.

Summary

In this chapter, we covered a lot of ways to enumerate a targeted network. Some of these methods are caused just by the way networks and the internet are designed to work. From protocols such as LDAP and NTP to services such as NetBIOS and DNS, there's a lot to watch out for. Again, remember what I taught you earlier: you can't stop attackers – you can only slow them down. Don't get discouraged by not being able to stop some of these issues. Instead, be aware of them and monitor them closely.

In the next chapter, we'll look at how attackers find vulnerabilities on our infrastructure and how we can be one step ahead of them by using the same techniques to keep our systems up and secure.

Questions

As we conclude, here is a list of questions for you to test your knowledge regarding this chapter's material. You will find the answers in the *Assessments* section of the *Appendix*:

1. Which of the following best describes enumeration?

    A. User and machine name identification

    B. Cracking passwords

    C. Recognizing routers and firewalls

    D. Active network system recognition

2. Which function is performed by SMTP?

    A. Transmitting status information

    B. Network equipment monitoring

    C. File transfer

    D. Sending email messages

3. To view NetBIOS information, what command should you use?

    A. Nmap

    B. netstat

    C. nbtstat

    D. telnet

4. _____ is used to synchronize clocks on a network.

    A. SAM

    B. NTP

    C. NetBIOS

    D. FTP

6
Vulnerability Analysis

Vulnerability management is the process of using tools, processes, and knowledge to reduce risk related to IT systems. This includes the entire life cycle, from initially discovering vulnerabilities through reporting them, prioritizing them according to business needs, remediating them through software or procedural changes, verifying that they have been fixed, and documenting lessons learned for the future.

Note that vulnerability management is not a one-time event. It's an ongoing process that needs to be revisited regularly. New vulnerabilities are discovered all the time, and old ones are fixed or become irrelevant. You need to make sure your systems are always up-to-date and that your patches are current.

In this chapter, we'll cover the following topics:

- Vulnerability analysis – where to start
- Vulnerability classifications
- The life cycle
- Ongoing scanning and monitoring

Let's dive in!

Vulnerability analysis – where to start

A vulnerability assessment is a systematic review of security weaknesses in an information system. Specifically, it looks for vulnerabilities in computer systems, applications, and network infrastructures. It evaluates if the system is susceptible to any known vulnerabilities, assigns severity levels to those vulnerabilities, and recommends remediation, if and whenever it's needed.

Vulnerability assessments also provide an organization with the necessary knowledge, awareness, and risk backgrounds to understand and react to threats to its environment.

Vulnerability classifications

Vulnerabilities can be classified into the following categories:

- **Misconfiguration**: You'll hear me preach about this all the time because it's one of the most common vulnerabilities. Misconfiguration is caused by human error. It allows attackers to gain unauthorized access to your systems. There are different types of misconfigurations because they could happen on application platforms, databases, the network itself, and even web servers. As misconfiguration could occur because someone may have forgotten to update the application or the database. They may have disabled the security settings or some features that are needed, or they may have gone set up permissions incorrectly or misconfigured SSL certificates.

- **Default installation vulnerabilities**: These are typically done when we hit the *Next* options during installation. I get it. Sometimes, this happens. Installing an application where the attackers and everybody else are expecting it to be and using the same directory structure can create a vulnerability.

- **Buffer overflows**: These are common software vulnerabilities, and they happen because of coding errors. What typically happens here is the attacker undermines the functionality of the program and tries to take control of the system by writing content beyond the allocated buffer size. If you overload the buffer, you end up creating a vulnerability, which could be anything from a system crash, the system becoming unstable, or even allowing some programs to do things they normally wouldn't do.

- **The server's operating system**: Not patching the server's **operating system (OS)** appropriately may cause a vulnerability. Attackers are always looking or scanning for servers to see if they have them in a patch with the latest and greatest OS.

- **Design flaws**: These are caused by either incorrect encryption or junky data validation processes; either the communication or the backend of an app or even a bad design flaw within the network infrastructure itself.

- **OS flaws**: I know what you're thinking, and the answer is no, it's not just limited to Windows. Linux probably has more patches than Microsoft does. But it's because of these types of flaws that attackers can use Trojans, worms, and even viruses to attack those machines. So again, it comes back to patching.

- **Application flaws**: Research your applications or any mainstream product regarding what flaws are associated with your applications. You also need to be notified of when those flaws take place, or when they've been discovered. So, update and keep your applications current.

- **Open services and ports**: Often, we install stuff, and it opens ports or starts up services or features we may not use on that product or from that application. So, why have it open? Security professionals need to be on a constant lookout and scan the networks or systems for any unnecessary or insecure services or ports.

- **Default passwords**: It cracks me up how many times people continue to use default passwords on devices, software, or the OS itself. The reason these are vulnerabilities is that if somebody just wants to get the application installed, they just hit next and take the defaults, and then in those defaults is the default password. They think, "*Oh, I'll change it later*" and then they forget, move on from the project, get fired, or someone else takes over. Whatever the case, these default passwords are going to be the bane of our existence. So, please do me a favor – make sure that you keep your passwords secret as you are installing the applications.

Now that we've identified potential areas for vulnerabilities to take place, let's look at what vulnerability assessments you should use.

The benefits of a vulnerability management program (VMP)

One of the reasons some companies skip using a **vulnerability management program** (**VMP**) is that they often think that the devices or services they are currently using are already protecting them. However, we must remember that a firewall strictly does what a firewall is supposed to do, which is to accept or allow connections through, based on the ports or the protocols they are using. The same applies to an antivirus program. It will scan documents or files within our systems to make sure they haven't been infected. We may also have an intrusion detection system in place, but again, that's only looking for active connections.

However, a VMP looks at the network devices, servers, workstations, and mobile devices and pinpoints weaknesses that need to be fixed or patched. Hopefully, they do this before they get breached. With close to 100 vulnerabilities being announced each week, your organization's network is only as secure as its last vulnerability assessment.

One of the problems preventing organizations from using a VMP is that the vulnerability scans and the reports they get, as well as the remediation process, can be extremely overwhelming. However, if you look at this from a different perspective, if your team is on top of the remediation process and the scans, those reports will become less intimidating because you're going to be more on top of things.

An ongoing VMP process, in combination with a proper remediation process, will help you ensure your network is extremely secure and can withstand the latest attacks.

Here are some of the benefits of a VMP:

- A VMP can help identify which risks need to be repaired or fixed. If we thoroughly monitor activity, we will get more information about the systems on our network. This allows us to contextualize all the different nodes or systems listed within the scan report itself. They can make better assessments about what needs to be fixed, when, and how. They also get to know which risks are extremely pressing versus those that aren't as important.

- Time is money. Some argue it takes too much time to perform vulnerability scans and the remediation process. They forget to compare it to the amount of time they spend remediating huge risks that are detected too late or, worse, having to deal with bad press right from the fallout of some type of breach in their environment. By looking at these reports and monitoring what's going on, it becomes clear that this is a huge time saver. It saves you from working every night and weekend because a breach is taking place and you're trying to fix things.

  If a company or organization is managing its vulnerabilities effectively, it will spend little time monitoring its systems. When a risk is detected, it can usually be fixed quickly and easily. It also saves you from doing a ton of work in a short time since your systems and network are secure and up to date.

- It improves security. Organizations that manage vulnerabilities are looking at it as a process, not just a one-time activity. Organizations that consistently and continually monitor their environment, to ensure they're one step ahead of attackers and the threats that are out there, maintain a more secure and safer environment.

- It saves money. This is probably the number one benefit of implementing VMP. It will save you from a costly breach. It's commonplace to see companies hit the news for being breached, and they end up facing huge costs from several different areas. Not only do they need to pay somebody to come in to get things under control, but they may also suddenly have to upgrade their systems or replace different components. And, of course, we can't forget the ominous lawsuits that they may acquire because of the breach.

As I traveled around the world in the early 2000s doing different workshops for government agencies and training classes with corporate 500 companies, this conversation would take place. I would hear the IT staff saying that they couldn't get the budget to upgrade their OSs or their systems because nobody thought it was important, or that they could get by. Well, that's not the case anymore. And a lot of my customers (and hopefully, you) will change their thought processes.

Please have your CFO or CTO know that you have two choices: pay for the upgrades now when it's not a mission-critical issue or a breach issue or pay a lot more down the road when that breach takes place. I think that's the mindset or the new norm we need to embrace. It's not a matter of if you get breached, but when.

Instead of being reactive to issues that come up, you should look at being proactive. If you know me or have taken any of my courses before, you will know that I'm a big fan of being proactive.

Now, let's talk about vulnerability assessment types.

Vulnerability assessments

Vulnerability assessments let you examine the ability of an application or a system – which includes current security procedures and controls – to withstand any type of attack.

The following are some advantages of having a good vulnerability assessment process:

- It should identify, measure, and then classify the vulnerabilities. And then, based on the reports, you, as a security professional, will understand how to lock things down.

- During a vulnerability assessment, you should be able to identify weaknesses and classify them based on their importance and severity. You'll also want to classify them based on the type of device they are and/or the communication channels they use.

- It should give you additional security measures or identify those things you need to do to fix some of these weaknesses.

- It should be able to scan for vulnerabilities based on the network.

- It should be able to identify open ports. You will see a lot of crossovers here because the assessment should be able to identify the services that are running, the unnecessary ones, and any application weaknesses. Vulnerability management products will help you identify applications that have not been updated or need to be updated.

- It should be able to identify any service weaknesses. If it's running, we need to make sure the service itself is secure. And typically, it's going to identify services that haven't been patched or faulty because of their design.

- It should help us identify configuration errors and show us accounts that have weak passwords, no passwords, or haven't changed their passwords in umpteen years.

Now, let's look at the different types of vulnerability assessments that are available to us.

Types of vulnerability assessments

There are different kinds of vulnerability assessments you can run, including the following:

- **Active assessments**: These are typically where we use network scanners to scan the network to identify the hosts, any vulnerabilities on those hosts, all the different nodes, and the services – anything that's on the network. Active network scanners can reduce the intrusiveness of the checks that they perform. So, you can make them extremely loud, or extremely quiet, or stealthy, if you will.

- **Passive assessments**: This is where we sniff the traffic. So, we're not going after a specific target – we're just looking at the traffic to see if we can identify active systems, services, or applications, and then try to determine the vulnerabilities present. Now, because we're sniffing the traffic, we should also be able to get a list of users who are currently on the network.

- **External assessments**: External assessments are one of the many methods that are used in ethical hacking. An external assessment means that the assessment is conducted over the internet, generally beginning with a port scan or some other form of network mapping.

The main goal of an external assessment is to locate vulnerabilities in the organization's public web pages and services (if any exist). Once these vulnerabilities have been located, an internal assessment must be performed to exploit them.

A common misconception when it comes to external assessments is that they are designed to assess the security of private networks, such as DMZs and internal networks. The vulnerability scan will not reveal vulnerabilities on your internal network if your public web pages are directly connected to your private network. Internal hosts (such as file servers) aren't visible over the internet unless you've opened specific ports and services.

- **Internal assessments**: This type of assessment looks at everything from an internal perspective. Internal assessments are typically designed to reveal vulnerabilities on the private network. For this reason, internal assessments typically reveal more risks than external assessments because an attacker would much rather hack into a file server or mail server than try to hack your public web pages.

There is usually more to the story than simply whether or not a vulnerability was found. For example, an internal assessment may reveal that a web application on your company's website has been identified as having several vulnerabilities. However, this does not give you the whole picture. Perhaps one of those vulnerabilities could be mitigated by changing the default credentials for a database on your website. Since this is a common area of vulnerability, it would be difficult to assess the risk of not changing those default credentials from a vulnerability standpoint alone.

This is just one example of the nuanced reality of vulnerability assessments. Your organization must assess the risks surrounding each vulnerability to assess their true impact. This is part of what makes an internal assessment so valuable.

- **Host-based assessments**: You can probably guess what this means, right? Here, we're going to do a configuration-level check at each of the host machines, whether they're a server or a desktop. The type of thing I want to look at includes whether I can get a hold of a registry and see if it has been incorrectly configured, as well as any file permissions and software configuration issues.

- **Network assessments**: This shows you vulnerabilities such as unnecessary services, weak authentication, and missing patches on your desktops, laptops, servers, and the network devices themselves. Is the interface for your switch through HTTP? Is it open? What's authentication mechanism is used? Is there weak encryption?

- **Application assessments**: Here, we're looking at apps that are installed everywhere. When I say apps, I'm not just referencing apps on workstations. SQL, Exchange, SharePoint, and WordPress are all examples of apps. Anything that loads up on the servers is an app and we must make sure it has been patched and configured correctly and is up to date. I've seen something happen a couple of times where a company claims all their systems are up to date, they're strictly running the latest and greatest in Windows, and that they do network scan only to discover they have a host machine running an older version of either an application or an OS. Their reason? "*You see, we don't want to have to pay for the upgrade*" or "*The company isn't around anymore.*" Guess what? It's time to find a different solution unless you want to trend on Twitter for a day or two because you've been breached.

- **Wireless network assessments**: We use this assessment to test our wireless networks and try to identify any rogue wireless networks that could be somewhere within your company. These audit client-specific sites with a wireless network. They do this by sniffing the wireless network traffic and trying to crack the encryption keys. And if I'm able to get in through wireless, then the whole network assessment comes into play, right?

Now, let's discuss the life cycle of a vulnerability assessment process.

The vulnerability life cycle

Every time I see the words *life cycle*, I think I need to go out and exercise, but the purpose of the life cycle here is to make sure we follow every step to find solutions and remediate them. In this case, these steps will help us find security weaknesses and remediate them before they become exploits:

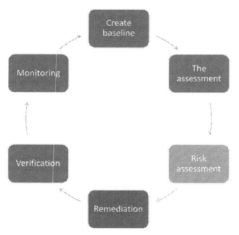

Figure 6.1 – Vulnerability assessment life cycle

Here are the steps of the vulnerability life cycle process:

- **Creating a baseline**: In this phase, we look at critical assets, identify them, and prioritize them to create a good baseline for vulnerability management.

- **The assessment**: This is a critical phase of vulnerability management. What we do, as security professionals, is identify and know the vulnerabilities within our infrastructure.

- **Risk assessment**: All we're doing here is measuring or summarizing the vulnerability and the risk level – some systems may be at a higher risk level than others. Again, it depends on what their function is and who is operating them.

- **Remediation**: Remediation is the process of fixing those vulnerabilities based on the risk assessment. We need to know which ones are the most important and then tackle them accordingly.

- **Verification**: We take this step to make sure we've fixed the issue. It allows the security team to check whether all the phases we've done previously have been followed and if the identified vulnerabilities have been fixed.

- **Monitoring**: Regular monitoring needs to be performed to help you maintain and always have the lastest updates. This is because a new update will have you create a new baseline where new threats will come out daily. So, we're going to continue monitoring.

Now, let's discuss some of the vulnerability assessment solutions that are available.

Types of vulnerability assessment solutions

There are four types of vulnerability assessment solutions you can look at. They are as follows:

- **Product-based solutions**: These are installed somewhere within your network. They could be installed in the private or non-routable space, as well as the internet addressable portion of your company's network. The only downside to installing these within your network is that they're going to be behind a firewall, and they can't always detect vulnerabilities on the outside.

- **Service-based solutions**: These are typically offered by third parties or the consultants you are using. Some of the solutions are hosted within your organization, such as a cloud-based solution.

- **Tree-based solutions**: This is a hybrid-type solution. A security professional will select a particular scanner for scanning services on Windows products, databases, or web servers but then use a different scanner for the Linux boxes.

- **Inference-based solutions**: Here, we start our scans by building up an inventory or identifying all the protocols that have been found on a particular machine. Once we've discovered or identified those protocols, the scanning process starts to detect which ports are attached to the services, such as an email server, a database server, or a web server. After it finds these services, it selects the vulnerabilities on each machine and starts to execute the relevant tests.

The importance of corporate policies cannot be understated, so let's talk about that next.

Corporate policies and regulations

With corporate policies, our goal is to obtain support for security awareness within the organization and outline, in general terms, the risks, guidelines, and responsibilities in our environment. Creating and enforcing security policies can help legally because it shows due diligence. The policy needs to stress its goals and responsibilities. Some parts may require technical details, while others may be accessible to everybody within the company. As we create these policies, the guidelines need to be backed up by a detailed technical implementation policy at a departmental or managerial level.

For example, a network manager can implement a policy to protect data that's passing through the organization's network. Someone in HR could make sure security training is taking place, as well as an awareness program. A firewall administrator could implement a policy to help protect data that's passing through certain ports.

> **Important Note**
> Some parts of the security policy, such as its standards, procedures, and guidelines, should be confidential. It would not be smart to make details of your security system or your DR plan accessible to the public or even to all employees. This information could assist somebody in a malicious attack.

When it comes to regulatory environments, some companies and organizations are bound by laws and regulations that govern the way they store, transmit, and process information, especially if the organization handles sensitive personal information or data from the government.

Organizations operating with industries such as healthcare or payment card processing must comply with industry regulations. The issue is that a lot of these laws don't prescribe or give any specific information about using a VMP.

Some examples are as follows:

- **Health Insurance Portability and Accountability Act (HIPAA):** This regulates how healthcare providers and anybody who interacts with a health care provider insurance company, as well as any business partners that they deal with, store information.

- **Gramm-Leach-Bliley Act (GLBA):** This controls how financial institutions handle customer financial records. None of these laws tell us what type of vulnerability scanning we need to implement.

- **Payment Card Industry Data Security Standard (PCIDSS):** This specifies security controls over transactions for retailers who handle credit cards and service providers partnering in those transactions. The interesting thing is that the majority of people think PCIDSS is a law. Well, it's not. It's simply a standard; you can choose to follow it or not. The ramification of not following it is that the credit card company or your merchant providers could say "*We'll no longer support your transactions.*"

- **Federal Information Security Management Act (FISMA):** This regulation requires government agencies and anybody who operates or interacts with the government, or on behalf of the government, to comply with a series of security standards. In the case of PCIDSS, it lists the following as part of the requirements when it comes to a VMP:

  - First, you need to implement VMP. They don't care which one; they don't say you have to use a specific one – they just say you must use one.

  - Another requirement PCI specifies is that internal scans must be conducted by a qualified person – somebody who has been trained to do internal and external stuff. The external stuff must be done by someone outside your organization.

  - They also specify that organizations must run their scans at least every quarter. Also, anytime you make any major changes to your network, such as adding a new firewall rule or upgrading some networking components in their firmware, you need to make sure everything is still safe. And, between the internal and external scans, these must be done by a qualified person or a vendor – a vendor for the external scans and personnel for the internals. They become qualified by going through a series of steps, including filling in an application and training and enrolling with the PCI Security Standards Council.

  - Organizations are also required to remediate any high-risk vulnerabilities as fast as possible. They need to repeat the scan to make sure they've resolved or have a clean system to ensure the fix that was implemented applied the appropriate settings.

A lot of organizations conduct scans to ensure nothing embarrassing shows up before they have an outside vendor come in. As I mentioned previously, FISMA is another regulation out there for government agencies, and they have a list of requirements for organizations that are subject to FISMA. I haven't seen any detailed information about this regulation, except for the fact it applies to government agencies, but some of their requirements are very similar to PCIDSS.

The scope of scanning

When it comes to scopes, we're referencing what the scan looks like regarding the range of hosts or subnets included within the scan. If you have a large network, it will probably make sense to schedule scans of different portions of the network at different times. This is going to help you reduce the impact of the network's performance and make it easier to analyze the results of each of the scans.

You may want to devise scans of limited scopes to identify issues or meet a particular compliance goal. Now, I would say there are a few questions you should ask yourself when it comes to scoping out vulnerability scans.

First, ask, "*What systems and what networks should I include in the vulnerability scan?*" Remember, we don't have to scan every system.

Second, ask, "*What tests will be performed against the systems that are discovered by the vulnerability scan?*" This could create some issues for you if you're unprepared for or don't understand what tests are being done within the VMP.

Third, ask, "*Are the systems online?*" That sounds basic, but remember, the information you know about the system is only as good as the last scan you achieved.

Scanning frequency

Defining our scan frequencies can be limited by several factors, including the following:

- **Technical constraints**: This is the primary factor. Scanning a Windows workstation for vulnerabilities is typically very low and it can be performed each time the host connects to the network. When it comes to something such as a code review or vulnerability analysis, for customized applications, this must be handled a bit more delicately and it can be a little bit more expensive. So, again, the technical constraints could limit the frequency of scanning.

- **Scanning the system**: You may only be capable of performing a certain number of scans each day. Your organization may need to adjust the scan frequency to make sure all the scans can complete successfully and within a given time.

- **Risk appetite**: It's like rolling the dice. For each scan activity, there is a cost that's associated with it. Again, if we look at that customized application, there might be a policy that dictates a scan or review but only if the overall threat intelligence changes. For example, let's say there's some new code exploit that's been discovered. So, again, the organization's risk appetite is its willingness to tolerate risks within your environment. Let's say, for example, that your company or organization is extremely risk-averse. Well, you may choose to conduct your scans more often to help minimize the amount of time between when the vulnerability becomes something that's of importance or comes into existence.

- **Regulatory requirements**: Regulations may make it impossible for you to increase your risk appetite. If your company must adhere to certain regulations, especially using scanning controls at predetermined intervals or according to a formal change management process that can affect that schedule because it must be followed.

- **Workflow**: As an organization develops and improves its security policies and controls, it adopts a more mature security model. As your security capabilities increase, vulnerability management and information security assurance need to be baked into your network management and software development workflows.

- **Business constraints**: Business constraints may limit your organization because vulnerability scans can be resource-intensive. For example, it may not be in your best interest to scan during periods of high business activity; you want to make sure you try to avoid critical processes from being disrupted. We want to make sure we schedule them to run at the appropriate time.

- **Licensing**: This can curtail the bandwidth that's consumed by the scanner or even the number of scans that you conduct at the same time.

As a security professional, you must learn to balance each of these considerations when planning a vulnerability scanning program. It's best to start small and slowly expand the scope and the frequency over time so that you learn by doing along the way.

Types of scans

There are different types of scans that our vulnerability scanners or VMPs can do, as follows:

- **Active scan/non-credentialed scans**: This scan proceeds by directing test packets at a host without being able to log onto the OS or application. What we get out of this is a specific view that allows us to see what the host exposes to the network. These are also referred to as remote scans. Now, even though you're doing a non-credential scan, you could put include things such as default passwords for service accounts in devices. Active scanning also consumes more network bandwidth and runs the risk of crashing a target of the scan, causing some weird results, or even an outage.

- **Passive scans**: A passive scanner watches network traffic, usually through a mirrored port, and tries to identify the policy definition or the CVEs. This type of scanning has the least amount of impact on the network because it's simply sitting there listening, as opposed to a credential scan. This is where you give a user an account with login rights to various hosts. You can specify a username and password. This gives you in-depth analysis, especially when you're detecting when an application or security settings could be misconfigured. It also helps demonstrate if an attacker has compromised one of your user accounts.

- **Agent scans**: This type of scan is where we install an agent on the different stations or targets that we plan on scanning. The agent is simply a piece of software that reports back to a specific server or service and is managed by an administration server. It runs the scans locally and then sends the report at a set schedule to the administrative server. Nessus is a VMP that has an agent that you can install on a Windows host. The biggest advantage here is that agent-based scans help reduce the impact on your network since everything is being done by the agent on the local machine and only the results are reported back. However, one of the drawbacks is that the range of agents could be limited to a particular OS, but most of them today support all the major OSs. The other disadvantage would be that this is now another application that you, as a security professional, need to make sure the agents are up to date with so that an attacker can't compromise it and use it to get into your environment.

    We must also worry about scanning levels, which focus more on the sensitivity level. We can do a discovery scan, which is used to create and update your inventory of assets. This is typically done to identify the hosts in the services they're running.

- **Assessment scans**: This will only contain options for analyzing hosts for vulnerabilities and/or malware.

> **Important Note**
>
> A vulnerability can include misconfiguration, as well as software exploits. Typically, an assessment scan will present options for comparing the OS and application settings against a policy template. Another option would be to test for weak passwords or recycled passwords. Note that an assessment scan can create a ton of network traffic, so be very careful.

Now, let's talk about scanner maintenance.

Scanner maintenance

Scanner maintenance is a piece of software. As with any technology product, we need to make sure the VMPs are healthy and strong. We do that by implementing proper care and feeding for that application. Administrators should conduct regular maintenance of their VMP to make sure the scanning software and the vulnerability feeds are up to date. The process of regularly patching and upgrading your VMPs will help protect the organization against scanner-specific vulnerabilities.

The other thing you need to be worried about is the plugins. A lot of these products allow you to place additional plugins to help you tweak the environment. However, some of these plugins are written by individuals who may not keep them up to date, which, based on future vulnerabilities, could make your system susceptible to an attack. So, administrators should configure their scanners to retrieve the new plugins or their updates. It's even better if you do this daily.

Classifying data

You must recognize what pieces of information are important when you're considering data assets in your environment and this is going to depend on your situation. For example, blueprints for a jet ski may not be that important if you're a company that rents jet skis out, but if you're the jet ski manufacturer, that is probably a little bit more important and may need to be kept confidential.

Sometimes, if an attacker gets a hold of your company's organization chart, it not only shows who works for whom but also the more sensitive information.

So, how do you classify data? Well, that's easy.

There are four different things you should be looking at, as follows:

- **Product development, production, and maintenance**: This information could be quite vital to a company. What we often see with breaches is customer contact information being released. Sometimes, this includes financial operations and controls – the collection and payment of debit cards and payroll taxes.

- **Legal obligations**: Legal obligations help maintain accurate records for a given period and also contractual obligations to third parties via **service-level agreements** (**SLAs**).

Next, let's look at document management.

Document management

Also known as data handling, this is the process of managing information over its life cycle, all the way from the creation process to its destruction. At each stage of this life cycle, security considerations are extremely important. Most documents will go through one or more different draft stages before they're published. But as a draft, the document will be subject to a workflow, which helps describe how editorial changes are made or approved. We see a lot of these workflows being created in a Microsoft product called SharePoint.

The workflow goes through and specifies – and this could be paper-based – who the authors, editors, and reviewers are.

As part of the creation process, the document must be classified based on how sensitive it is. Now, typically, those classifications are given labels, as follows:

- **Unclassified**: There are no restrictions on viewing this document.

- **Classified**: This is also known as restricted, private, or for official use only. Viewing is restricted to the owner, organization, or third parties under a non-disclosure agreement.

- **Confidential**: This is one of the lower ends of the classifications when we're dealing with some of the higher-end ones, but it's set up so that the information is sensitive and can only be viewed by approved personnel within the organization. We may also want to include an **non-disclosure agreement** (**NDA**) here.

- **Secret**: This is also called medium. Viewing is restricted because this information is too valuable to permit any risk of it being viewed. Think of it as top-secret information, just like you see in spy movies.

- **Double secret probation**: This one is even higher than top secret.

Let's talk next about the why it's important to have an ongoing scanning and monitoring process.

Ongoing scanning and monitoring

When it comes to ongoing scanning and continuous monitoring through the cycle – procurement, as well as replacing, and the issue of new tactics or new threats and techniques being utilized – it's not enough to perform a vulnerability assessment only once. You need to have some type of plan for an ongoing scan. As we mentioned earlier, you need to come up with a schedule and stick to it.

Continuous security monitor refers to the process of continual risk assessment. This means we maintain a high level of awareness of the threats that are coming out or have been released into the wild. It also refers to performing routine audits of rights and privileges in real time.

To truly have a good understanding of monitoring, you need to create an initial baseline to help identify any variations. You need to compare them. It's kind of like when someone says my system seems to be slow. Well, compared to what? We must have something to compare it to. Having the ability to compare to an initial baseline helps you identify any type of variations that could represent an incident that's taking place and needs to be investigated.

Understanding which scanner you should use

There is a difference between what you may see in the exam and what may be acceptable in the real world. You must do in-depth research to decide on the best product for you. This is why it's important to understand different vulnerability scanners.

Again, my goal here is not to tell you exactly which one to use, but to look at the different features and different options you have available to you. Now, typically, a vulnerability scanner is just a type of network mapper that aims to detect whether the network is exposed to any threats.

There are numerous tools out there that may do other things, such as footprinting and fingerprinting tools, and to some extent, maybe even some password cracking. But when it comes to vulnerability scanners, you want to look for one that is kind of the answer or the suite or the Swiss Army knife to your solution. You're going to want to make sure they do things such as not only mapping out hosts but maybe even detecting the services that are running.

Now, let's get back to what the core features of a vulnerability scanner or VMP does. It should not only be able to map the network for hosts and detect the services that are running, but they should use techniques such as banner grabbing to scan for things, such as what level the system or the target has been patched, the security configuration, as well as the policies or network shares, unused user accounts, weak passwords, rogue access points, whether antivirus software has been configured on it, and so on.

A vulnerability scanner can be implemented in two different ways – either as software that's installed or as a security appliance. It can either be a VM or actual appliances you can purchase that are rack-mounted.

There are other types of scanners out there too, including web application vulnerability scanners that look at specific vulnerabilities in applications, such as SQL injection or **cross-site scripting** (**XSS**) software attacks.

The difference between open source and commercial scanners

Most people believe open source is the best because it doesn't cost any money, but we have some products out there that got their start as open source and then turned into commercial. Some continue to offer both features. Open source scanners are typically open to anyone who wants to use them, and they are free. Since open source scanning tools are open source, you can also integrate with other open source tools for a more integrated solution.

Commercial vulnerability scanners offer end-to-end testing that ensures compliance with security standards. This is a good feature for companies that need to make sure their environment is secure and not open to vulnerabilities. Commercial scanners typically provide 24/7 support, while smaller open source scanner companies may only be available during certain hours of the day.

To decide whether you should use commercial or open source scanners, you need to look at your environment and see what works best for your organization.

When you're deciding which type of scanner is right for your company, consider these factors:

- How many resources do you have?
- Do you need help with custom scanning features?
- Will you need support (learning or troubleshooting)?
- What types of compliance standards do you need to be able to validate?

As you can see, there are several reasons why companies may want to consider using either an open source or commercial product when choosing a vulnerability scanner.

One of these products is Nessus, produced by Tenable Network Security. It's one of the better-known commercial vulnerability scanners out there. It's available on-premises via Nessus Manager, as well as in the cloud (the tenable cloud). They also have a professional version that you can run on smaller networks. The product also has a home edition that can be used for free in addition to a paid subscription.

Nessus started as an open source product. It provides the source code for many other scanners that are out there. The default scans that you can perform with Nessus use plugins from the Nessus subscription feeds.

On-premises versus the cloud

It's important to understand that not every solution is going to be the best one for your environment.

On-premises is something you install and manage yourself.

When it comes to the cloud, this is where we still manage but we don't have to worry about keeping things up to date. Most of the time, these products will update themselves as soon as they become aware of certain vulnerabilities.

We also have to consider databases and where we store them.

In the case of one vendor, where they install a client on your machine that scans that machine and then uploads it to the database, it's located within the cloud itself.

Others will keep them on the database in the local machine, and report back. It just depends on which way you want the communication channel to go and how often you want it to go.

My only problem with relying on the cloud – and this is just a personal thing – is that things can break. For example, a **denial-of-service** (**DoS**) attack can affect your ability to contact your vulnerability scanning cloud provider. So, make sure that you have some backups there.

Now, when I say everybody's involved, I mean that a lot of people are getting involved in this environment. Google has a cloud security scanner that's available to you. It's called the Amazon inspector. There's also Retina, which is owned by Beyond Trust. They have a cloud vulnerability assessment. I've used an on-premises version of Retina and I enjoyed it. Nessus had something called tenable I/O, which is their cloud solution. McAfee also has a **security as a service** (**SaaS**) concept.

We also have Secure Works, which has a nice interface to it. Alien Vault is another product that's out there as well. We also have Koalas, a cloud-based service that is probably one of the most popular and it's a great solution. Users install sensor agents on various points in their network, and the sensors upload data to the cloud platform for analysis.

Security Content Automation Protocol (SCAP)

A developing area of security analysis and threat intelligence is the correlation of information that's produced by different security tools, such as vulnerability scanners and IDS systems.

SCAP allows compatible scanners to determine whether the computer meets a particular configuration baseline. To learn more about the specifications for SCAP, you can visit `scap.nist.gov`. Yes, it's a government thing.

The MITRE corporation helped develop some of the key components of SCAP, which can be used on multiple scanning or vulnerability devices. It developed dictionaries of identifiers that are used in the NIST vulnerability database. These identifiers give us a standard means for identifying products to refer to in a vulnerability or a platform very consistently.

Some of these identifiers are as follows:

- **Common Vulnerability Exposures (CVEs)**: This identifier helps identify cyber security vulnerabilities in published OSs and application software.

- **The Common Platform Enumeration (CPE)**: This is also maintained by the **National Institute of Standards and Technology (NIST)** and deals with OSs, applications, and hardware devices. If you need some common best practices statements, that's where the **Society of Corporate Compliance & Ethics (SCCE)** comes into play. It's the common configuration enumeration.

- **Common Weakness Enumeration (CWE)**: In addition to these identifiers, SCAP uses several other components.

- **Open Vulnerability and Assessment Language (OLA)**: This is good If you're looking for flaws in the designs and development of software that could potentially lead to vulnerabilities. This is an XML schema that is used to describe a system's security states and query vulnerability reports and other information that is too detailed for now.

- **Extensible Configuration Checklist Description Format**: This is also an XML schema, but it's for developing and auditing best practice configuration checklists and rules. In the old days, best practices guides were written for administrators to apply manually. This component provides a machine-readable format that can be applied and validated using compatible software. If you're asking yourself, "*How do these vulnerability scanners know how to fix themselves?*" it's because of these components and identifiers.

- **Common Vulnerability Scoring System** (**CVSS**): This is now maintained by the Forum of Incident Response and Security Teams. CDSS is a means of linking vulnerabilities to a standard metric. So, we understand how important certain vulnerabilities are. The metrics generate a score from 0-10 based on the inherent characteristics of the vulnerability, as well as the environment where the exposure occurs and the changing characteristics of the vulnerability over time. The higher the score, the more critical the issue is.

Exploit scanners

When it comes to exploits scanners, most of our vulnerability scanning software uses non-intrusive scanning techniques. Non-intrusive scans use network fingerprinting and banner grabbing or allow the agent to read the system configuration as files pass through or even from log files. These normally don't cause any performance problems for the server or the host, but they can return a high number of false positives.

We also have intrusive scanning techniques, which usually involve an attempt to exploit a detected vulnerability. One of the most well-known exploit frameworks out there is Metasploit, an open source platform that's maintained by Rapid7.

The free edition is a Community Edition that comes as a package for both Linux and Windows. Being a framework, it has a ton of tools that allow us to discover hosts and their vulnerabilities, and then identify or create exploit modules to target those vulnerabilities. Metasploit can use Nmap or its tools. Again, since it's a framework, it can connect to vulnerability scanners such as OpenVAS, Nessus, or Nexpose. We can also have and implement a key scanner to help us open a reverse shell so that we gain full access to the directory structure of the target system that's using those vulnerabilities.

A common technique a lot of these exploit frameworks use is fuzzing, which involves sending invalid or random data to the application to test its ability to handle unexpected data. That application is then monitored to see if it crashes, fails, or responds incorrectly. One of the most advanced commercial fuzzers out there is Peach Fuzzer. It has a free-to-use community edition, plus a professional and enterprise edition with different licensing models. The platform is supplemented with what they call peach pits, which are different packs (add-ins). Microsoft used to have fuzzers too, but they no longer make those available for download. Instead, Microsoft is moving to a cloud-based fuzzing service that is codenamed project Springfield.

So, you have your scan report, and it has a big list of vulnerabilities that it's detected. Normally, these vulnerabilities will be associated with a **Common Vulnerability Scoring System** (**CVSS**) score. It's designed to give you a very basic way of prioritizing the response actions. You should review the whole report and try to identify – from your own experience and knowledge – whether the vulnerability has been overrated or underrated.

The results of most of the vulnerability reports will be relatively straightforward for us. Perhaps the system hasn't been receiving updates, or you investigate it by looking at the event logs. The job of an analyst is to spot something that's out of place or a bit odd and then investigate the cause. Part of your job is to try to see if you can make things less confusing by looking at the following tips:

- **Reconcile the results**: Vulnerability scanners can misinterpret the information they get back from the different probes they've sent out. If you can't reconcile a particular issue that you've found, you may want to consider running a scan using a different software product to try to confirm the results. You should also review logs, as well as any other data sources. If you're having trouble linking a vulnerability report to a particular host, or even a software application, use the logs on the host that's associated with that IP to correlate the results – perhaps an application was present during the scan and since then, it has been uninstalled.

- **Compare the best practices**: Some of the scanners that you may use will measure systems and configuration settings against best practice frameworks. This might be necessary for regulatory compliance, or you may want to conform to your own external agreed standards of a best practice.

The only issue might be that some compliance scans may return results that are not high priority or might be considered low risk. For example, maybe you've scanned a Windows 8 machine and there are some .NET Framework versions or browsers that are no longer supported. To remediate this type of problem, you would run the Windows update and ensure that the Windows update has been scheduled for future updates. You'd also want to investigate upgrading the Windows 8 machine to a more current version, then run the scan again, and work off any of the items that you find on your list.

Common Vulnerability Scoring System (CVSS)

The concept here is that the analyst must identify and assess vulnerabilities across several different types of hardware and software platforms that may be inside their network. They must also prioritize these vulnerabilities and remediate those that pose the greatest risk first.

However, when there's a ton of things to fix, each being scored using different scales, how does an analyst then convert this mountain of information into actionable information? Well, that's where CVSS comes into play. It's an open framework that addresses this issue and offers many benefits.

Let's discuss some of those benefits.

Ranking

Think of this as a system that rates your environment, which it does through a standard vulnerability score. When an organization normalizes vulnerability scores across its software and hardware platforms, it can leverage a single vulnerability management policy. This policy is like a SLA in that it tells us how quickly a particular vulnerability must be validated and fixed.

It's also important to note that when an environmental score is computed, the vulnerability becomes contextual, meaning that the vulnerability score is now representative of its risk to an organization. The scoring schema is based on several different things.

The base metrics

Base metrics include things such as exploitability. This metric measures the current state of an exploit technique. If the exploit code itself is publicly available and easy to use, the number of potential attackers also increases.

When you think of exploitability, you need to think about the attack vector, the complexity of the attack itself, the privileges and the type of user interaction required, and if the user has to click on an email for this attack to take place.

The scope metrics

This refers to a collection of privileges that's been defined by a computing authority, such as your application or the OS itself, when granting access to computer resources, such as memory or CPU. These permissions are assigned based on a method of identification and authorization. In some cases, you may find that authorization is easy or nonexistent. For example, if you have Ethernet traffic that's sent to a network switch, the switch accepts the traffic that arrives at its ports, and it's authorized to control the traffic flow to other switch ports.

Impact metrics

Impact metrics refer to the properties of the impacted component. Regardless, a successful exploit vulnerability affects one or more components. The impact metric is scored according to the components that suffer the worst or that are most directly and predictably impacted.

Analysts should constrain impacts to a reasonable outcome they can be confident an attacker can achieve.

Temporal metrics

This measures the current state of an exploit technique, the existence of any patches or workarounds, as well as the confidence that you have in describing the vulnerability. What we mean by this is that we look at the likelihood of a vulnerability being attacked. It's based on the current state of that exploit, regardless of updates.

Let's look at the WannaCry outbreak of 2017. What's interesting is that this vulnerability had low temporal metrics because Microsoft had patched it months before it became popular.

When it comes to the exploit code's maturity, I go back to that reference of real-world exploration to see that it may only be theoretical. Again, we may see a proof of concept come across. This doesn't necessarily mean that this vulnerability will be used against you.

Temporal metrics also include the remediation level of the vulnerability. You need to be able to prioritize that. Typically, the vulnerability is unpatched when it's initially published. The vendors may issue hotfixes or workarounds until an official patch on upgrades has been issued. This happens almost every day.

The report confidence

This metric measures the degree of confidence in the existence of a vulnerability and how credible the vulnerability is. A lot of times, we see these vulnerabilities come out, and people announce that they are present but nobody publishes specific details. So, its confidence is not very high. Later, the vulnerability may be confirmed and acknowledged by the author or the vendor, which would raise the urgency of that vulnerability to a higher level when it becomes known to exist with certainty.

The environmental metrics

This metric allows an analyst to customize their CVSS scoring based on how much the IT person feels it's important for their organization. They do that through things such as security requirements. Again, this is exactly what it sounds like: what security requirements do your company policies specify? What are the security requirements for a regulation that's out there? For example, if an IT asset supports a business function where availability is important, the analysts can assign a greater value to the availability relative to confidentiality and integrity. Each of these security requirements falls under one of three categories: low, medium, or high.

Modified base metrics

This enables the analyst to adjust the base matrix according to the modifications that exist within their environment. A great example of this is if an environment has made a general change for some software in the way that it would affect the exploitability, the scope, or the impact. Then, the environment can reflect this via the modification of the base matrix.

The cool thing about this is that the VMPs consider these CVSSs for us and will help you along the way.

False positives and exceptions

So, how do we identify false positives and exceptions? Many of the vulnerability reports that we get will contain numerous false positives or some *you're right, you're wrong* results. These are extremely time-consuming to investigate and eliminate. If there are substantial numbers of false positives, you probably need to tune and tweak your scan so that you can reduce the number of false positives that you're getting.

So, how do we do that? Well, we can start looking at validating applications that could be creating traffic that might be incorrectly matching a scanner signature for vulnerability. In this case, you can add it to your exception list so that you don't look at that particular result again.

Another issue is that the scanner could be using a heuristic analysis, which might be confused by a valid change in network usage. In other words, it might be necessary to establish new baselines to refer to.

Another issue that may pop up is that you might be running scans that aren't appropriate for your network – for example, running an application vulnerability scan when your network doesn't run that application. One of the things you should do is try adjusting the scope of the scan so that you are testing for the appropriate applications within your network infrastructure.

Finally, we have the issue that the scanner might be identifying vulnerabilities that could be exploited with administrative privileges, and not by end users. Now, one of the cool things you can do – especially with most of the VMPs out there – to reduce the incidence of false positives you get is identify the exception in the scan and configure it in a template. This may mean that you're going to exclude certain hosts from certain types of scans or continue to report the vulnerability but just assign it a lower priority. If you have systems that can't be patched or remediated, then you may want to watch those systems a little more closely.

Next, let's look at how, as a security professional, you can make sure you stay up to date with what's going on in the threat world.

Trends

One of the problems with security is doing things to create the illusion you have control. I do this all the time with my kids; they assume I know more than I do.

Normally, you're going to deploy controls that help identify infected or unpatched systems and give you a report that you can work off. This type of activity is good but in the back of your mind, you should be concerned that something else could be sneaking up on you without your knowledge. That's where trends come into play.

If you monitor the key matrix over a certain period, it should show you policies that aren't being applied or that an attacker is beginning to mount an extremely complex or multistage campaign against you.

The problem with trends is selecting which matrix to analyze and investigate, given the limited amount of time you have on your hands. Here, you should develop a metrics analysis program. You should also try to make sure it evaluates the effectiveness of each matrix you track.

Some of the possible areas for us to analyze are as follows:

- Looking at the number of incidences and detections, as well as the response time.

- Looking at hours lost or that were impacted in terms of costs.

- Looking at the network itself or its metrics – you can measure any number of issues here. You can look at the volume of internal and external traffic, the number of logins, the failure of logins, active ports, the number of authorized or unauthorized devices on your network, unauthorized software, and so on. These types of stats may only be interesting from a security perspective and that's because most networks will change – that is, they will get faster as they deploy new equipment and new cabling. You should focus on training as well as threat awareness education – how well is your staff informed about cyber threats? You can measure the number of programs or start grading your users based on their knowledge. We see a lot of this today with the companies that help you create emails that are designed for users to click on a link, and then a trunk monkey pops out and smacks them on the head.

- Looking at compliance. This is great – you've got all these rules and policies in place, but how many of them are being met? What is the percentage? Is it going up or down? Is it going down because the compliant targets are increasing? Or maybe the compliance is getting tougher to meet? Or maybe your policies are not being followed correctly?

- Looking at the external or outside threat levels – you need to ask yourself what your security looks like out on the internet in general terms. Are we seeing anything popping up and other companies or other competitors that are out there or anybody within our industry? Are there any major new threats for you to start looking for? When I get up in the morning and I start reviewing all my security websites, threads, and RSS feeds, I think to myself, does this apply to me? If it does, I need to include that in my scan so that I can make sure that I'm not vulnerable.

Now, because I love you all, I will mention some of those feeds I review all the time:

- **The SANS Institute**: They have a full training environment, but they also have tons of information about vulnerabilities that are out there and what's happening.

- **Dark Reading**: As their name suggests, their articles are about hacking, which is kind of cool. They cover everything, from the cloud to mobile, to the current breaches and attacks that are taking place.

- **Microsoft's Windows Defender Security Intelligence**: They mostly focus on Microsoft-based stuff, but they will also give you some updates concerning some other attack threats that are out there.

- **FireEye**: This is a great resource for you to use. One of their most popular resources is the recent zero-day exploits, which goes through and shows you some of the more popular ones. They also have a great resource of annual reports, as well as threat intelligence reports. You can also subscribe to their threat research blog if you'd like.

- **Alien Vault**: What you'll see with most of these is that most of the companies have ulterior motives because they have a product they're trying to sell. However, they still provide a lot of really cool information. When it comes to Alien Vault, they have a threat intelligence digest. All you have to do is sign up for it and you will start getting notifications as new breaches or security threats become available.

- **Symantec**: They also have a website for security intelligence that provides tons of information. Typically, what you'll find is that if one vendor knows about the breach or threat, most of them will also be aware of it too. So, sometimes, the information is just repetitive.

- **Secure Works**: While this company offers some services, they also provide a lot of information about threats for free under their insights. They have a knowledge center, as well as research and a blog that you can look at. For example, under the **Research** category, you can go to **Threat Analysis** and see what's currently going on in that area.

Summary

In this chapter, we discussed the benefits of a VMP. We looked at ongoing VMP processes and the importance of vulnerability research, which helps ensure the network is extremely secure and can withstand attacks.

Then, we discussed how to ID targets for scanning, how often, how deep, and what scope to scan targets with, as well as the different levels of configuration. We also covered classifying data so that when an incident occurs, you'll know what needs to take priority when it comes to fixing the issue. We reviewed which scanner to use based on your environment. We also reviewed ways we can remediate our network vulnerabilities. We also talked about SSL and TLS, making sure that our certificates are valid, and that we're using a strong enough cipher for this encryption. We also talked about the issues with virtualization.

In the next chapter, we'll dive into how to attack the targets that we've identified.

Questions

As we conclude, here is a list of questions for you to test your knowledge regarding this chapter's material. You will find the answers in the *Assessments* section of the *Appendix*:

1. To find a vulnerability, an attacker sends probes and fabricated requests to a target. What type of scanning is this?

    A. Passive scanning

    B. Active scanning

    C. Flooding

    D. Man-in-the-middle

2. To identify hosts and vulnerabilities, which type of assessment is used?

    A. Distributed

    B. Passive

    C. Active

    D. Automated

3. Which vulnerability assessment solution is said to be *placed in private or corporate resources*?

    A. Service-based

    B. Inference-based

    C. Product-based

    D. Tree-based

4. What kind of scanner is used when the location and data from a scan are stored on a single system?

    A. Cluster-based

    B. Proxy-based

    C. Network-based

    D. Agent-based

7
System Hacking

System hacking refers to the activities hackers use to gain access to, and compromise, digital devices such as computers, smartphones, tablets, and even entire networks. This course explains the main methods of system hacking—password cracking, privilege escalation, spyware installation, keylogging, and other tactics. We'll also learn the countermeasures **information technology (IT)** security professionals can use to fight different attacks.

Learning about system hacking will help you implement the strongest possible security practices and help you assess your current security protection and which possible vulnerabilities may be on your systems and networks. You'll learn which security features work the best for your environment, how to discover and fix security vulnerabilities, and how to anticipate them.

In this chapter, we will cover the following topics:

- Understanding our objectives
- Phase 1 – Gaining access and cracking passwords
- Phase 2 – Escalating privileges
- Phase 3 – Maintaining access and executing applications
- Phase 4 – Maintaining access and hiding your tools
- Phase 5 – Covering your tracks – Clearing logs and evidence

Understanding our objectives

We have three goals for this chapter, as follows:

- **Gain access to the target**: Identify the target, understanding the services available and which ports are open. Also, understand the user accounts that may be on the machine and, possibly, some vulnerabilities.

- **Maintain access**: Nothing's worse than getting into a machine only to be kicked out later because someone has made it more difficult for us to get in a second time.

- **Covering your tracks**: If you love watching animal or nature documentaries, as I do, you know dogs are genetically related to wolves, which explains why they have a lot in common. They particularly share one disgusting habit—eating their feces to cover their tracks, because their feces would announce their presence to other predators or prey in the area. As with wolves and dogs, we need to cover our tracks. If we don't, people will see that we're in the system. They will reimage the system or take it offline, fix all the problems we've created, and restrict our access. Covering your tracks is part of maintaining that access.

To accomplish these three goals, there are five phases we must pass through during the system hacking stage.

The five phases

Here is a brief overview of the five phases we will cover in this chapter:

- **Phase 1: Gaining access to the system**. Again, we've identified the system, we understand which services are running, and—possibly—know user account information. We need *two* pieces of information to gain access to the machine: username and password. There are several methods we can use for cracking passwords.

- **Phase 2: Escalating privileges**. We can either escalate the privilege of an account we create or take an account that already exists—such as Billy Bob in the mailroom—and give the account user administrative rights. Guess who will be in trouble if I get discovered. Poor Billy Bob. Now, we don't have to pick on a particular user account; we can use service accounts that are already active.

- **Phase 3: Maintaining access**. How do we do that? By launching applications or our tools. We have a toolset of things we like to work with, and there are specific tools I enjoy. I will launch those applications to continue my attack from the inside. If I have hit the initial target, or this is my intended or final target, I need to launch my application so that I can get back in more easily.

- **Phase 4: Hiding your tools**. Because we don't want people to see us on the system. You don't want somebody browsing around seeing a particular application installed on your machine. You need to hide that information. There are several ways to hide tools, including rootkits and steganography.

- **Phase 5: Covering your tracks**. How do we do that? Well, what's on a machine that typically tracks everything we do on a system? The **log files**. I sometimes refer to it as the big brother. This is where we separate the good hackers from the great hackers. To achieve our goal here, we will delete log files or modify them.

Let's discuss each of the five phases in more working detail.

Phase 1 – Gaining access and cracking passwords

If you know me, you know I have a big issue with passwords. I always jump on my soapbox whenever talking about passwords, because let's face it, we create online entities, and use accounts online all the time within our network or outside—on the internet. Everything about us is contained in these entities and we are to protect these with passwords. Now, here comes my soapbox…people are so stinking lazy when it comes to creating passwords—it drives me absolutely bonkers. As we move along, you'll understand why I'm so passionate about this subject.

Matt Mullenweg, who created WordPress, had this great quote: *Love is great…but not as a password.* Did you know that *love* is one of the top 20 passwords that people use, with a variation at the end of it? So, again, our whole goal here in this phase of gaining access is attempting to crack a password. We don't necessarily go after the big bad administrative password right away, because the second phase of gaining access is escalating privileges. So, we first need to see if we can find a password to gain access.

What's cracking?

Cracking is going through and looking for or discovering passwords that are stored on a machine locally or trying to do this during transmission. A great example of this is **File Transfer Protocol** (**FTP**). When you log your username and password, the default is to transmit both the username and password in clear text. Obviously, that's something I could pick up.

People ask me: "Is there a really good reason for cracking?" Yes, there is. Often, people forget their passwords, especially when it comes to standalone machines. I would never recommend trying to crack someone's password if you're in a domain environment because that's the purpose of the feature—being able to reset a password—but oftentimes, neighbors come over to me and say: "I forgot the password on my machine and I can't get in." Of course, I usually have a lot of red flags going up in my brain when they say: "All of a sudden, I can't get in." But we can reset local account passwords. Sometimes, a disgruntled person does something malicious in the domain environment, such as locking out everyone's password. This shows there are some good purposes for cracking.

When it comes to cracking, we have two different ways we can do it—we can automate or do it manually by using some interesting tools.

The problem we have when it comes to cracking passwords is that most users pick something they know because they must remember it, and that's what makes it easy to crack people's passwords. Most people will use a name of a family member, their pet's name, their favorite sports team, comic book heroes, swear words, favorite city, religious names, or a school they went to—college, elementary, or high school. These things might be easy to remember because they mean something to you as the user, but that's the reason why passwords are easily hacked.

Most people start off with these types of words and then add numbers at the end or the beginning of that password. Usually, those numbers also mean something to them. Most people use their birth year, graduation year, wedding anniversary, and so on.

However, while we require people to create difficult passwords, they still need to be easy to remember. Otherwise, we get help tickets being opened all day long: "Hey, I locked myself out. I don't remember my password." So, in my book, as far as a proper password policy is concerned, we typically rely on four different options: biometrics, thumbprint, **two-factor authentication** (**2FA**), and retinal scans, which is one of the exciting things about Windows 10: Microsoft is building biometrics into it, and it can't be tricked easily. If your laptop or tablet has a camera on it, it can use your face to log you in. And don't worry—they've done it with a **three-dimensional** (**3D**) aspect, something they learned from Xbox. Remember the Kinect? It does 3D recognition of your face and—sometimes—your body, which I find scary.

The geniuses behind this technology created it in such a way that if you hold up a picture of your face in front of the camera, it sees it as a flat structure. It realizes there's no depth. The demo they show you is of a gentleman holding a picture of himself up in front of his face and the laptop doesn't log him in. Once he removes the picture, exposing his face, the laptop immediately logs him in. With this, nobody can steal your biometrics, unless, of course, they cut your finger off.

We also have the option of using the **Common Access Cards** (**CACs**) you swipe. Unfortunately, somebody can steal them, which is why utilizing a password would provide additional security. I'm a big fan of **multi-factor authentication** (**MFA**), whereby you type in a password, then receive a text message with a code on your cell phone or to your email confirming you've registered. You verify with a code that the company has sent to you.

With the number of passwords that are getting cracked, I think we're going to see a huge change, and we're probably leaning toward biometrics.

Complexity

Complexity means as we create these passwords, we need to make them more difficult for attackers to guess. Typically, at least in Microsoft, we handle this by using three of the following four options—and they're good options as far as a rule of thumb is concerned:

- The first option is using uppercase characters in your password. Now, I wouldn't necessarily make all my characters uppercase—my computer might think I'm yelling at it.

- We can also use lowercase characters, and you can use these two in any order—you don't have to start off with an uppercase character then end with lowercase or vice versa.

- We can also inject numbers. So, at this point, we have what they refer to as an alphanumeric-based password.

- We can also use salting techniques (we'll talk about this later) to help randomize the password hashes.

However, if these four are the only ones you're using for your complexity, someone will eventually *pwn* you and, therefore, this is why we like special characters.

However, we need to be careful with special characters because there are some assumptions that both users and attackers make.

Any special characters will help you create complexity, but one of my favorite special characters—which drives attackers crazy—is the spacebar, but just because it's complex doesn't mean you're safe. You still must be careful.

First, you have to be careful about what we'll refer to as the **Fab Five**. This includes the @, $, 3, 0, and ! characters, which a lot of people think will trick attackers, assuming they'll never guess that the dollar sign represents *S*, the zero an *O*, and the 3 an *E*. Well, attackers have dictionaries and mechanisms to help them figure these out. Don't try 0penm3up, assuming attackers will not guess your 3 is *E* or L3tm3in is *Letmein*. My other favorite is op3ns3same. You don't think that's in a dictionary? I know this is a cool password, but it's not going to fool an attacker.

The reason why I always use Pa$$w0rd is that it's the default password for all Microsoft labs in the training environment. Microsoft requires that three of the four complexity requirements are fulfilled, and this one fulfills it. But complexity is not everything.

The strength of a password lies in its length. Never use real words because they're what we refer to as dictionaries out there. A dictionary contains a bunch of words, and there are tons of dictionaries for different subjects.

For example, assuming you know I like Batman, we'll put batmanrules in the password file shown here:

Figure 7.1 – Password security checker at https://security.org

If I try to brute-force attack this, it will take about 1 day to crack the password because it's made up of real words. In fact, if it wasn't as long as that (for example, batman), it would happen instantaneously because it will be in a dictionary somewhere.

I do a lot of community-based talks and seminars, and one thing I try to teach users (because this is such a pet peeve for me) is how to create complex passwords but still make them easy to remember for the end user.

One of the most effective ways to do this is by using a syntax we use daily. For example, I'm using a **Domain Name Service (DNS)** naming syntax, but because of the length and special characters of the periods, my password takes a little bit longer to brute-force attack. And hopefully, if my policy has me change my password before many years go by, it doesn't necessarily have to follow an actual DNS syntax. In fact, I'll do *M* because it's an upside-down *W*, or maybe I'll throw in a capital in there—MMM.ilovecrafstmantools. whatever. Yes, it doesn't have to be a real website—it can be anything you want.

Let's try to crack ilovecraftsman.tools. It's extremely long; we might have to go through the time-space continuum (or at least get our DeLorean up to 88 miles an hour to go forward in time before it gets cracked through brute force), as it would take almost 900 trillion years to brute-force this password. I just typed in one of my passwords: 9 sextillion years to crack. Game over—I win!

Password architecture

We can try to hack a password either while it's in storage or while it's in transmission, or what's referred to as in motion. So, where are passwords stored? Well, that depends on your operating system and the environment you're in. For example, when it comes to Windows, if this is just a machine that is not part of a domain, maybe a home PC or grandma's PC, or your laptop, there's a database on the hard drive referred to as the **Security Account Manager (SAM) database**.

The SAM database is located wherever you've installed Windows. The default is C:windows/system32/config/sam. In fact, let's look at it here. In the following screenshot, I've opened my File Explorer and I've gone to my C: drive where I installed Windows under System32. There's a directory called config—if you expand it, you'll notice there's this nifty little file called a SAM file inside. The passwords are stored in a *hash*, and this location or database is mounted up as a registry entry:

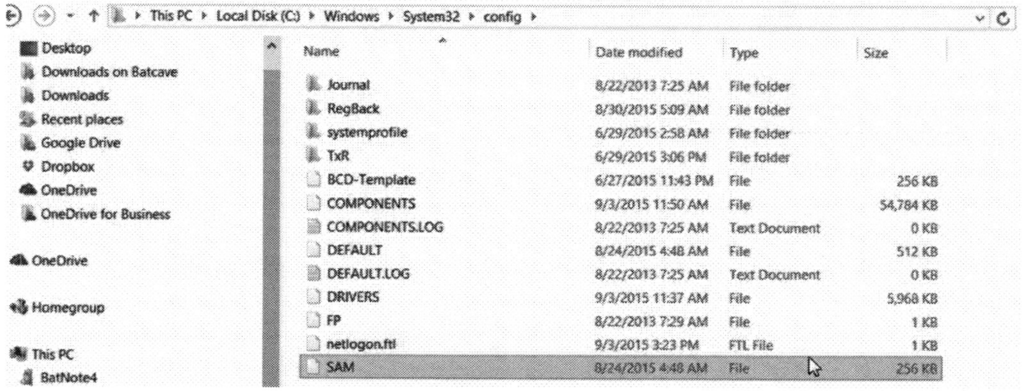

Figure 7.2 – Location of the SAM database

If you're in a domain environment, user accounts are not stored on the local drive of the client machine but in a file known as `ntds.dit`, which is located on every single domain controller in your environment. On your domain controllers, it's stored inside of a directory known as `C:\windows\ntds.dit`.

So, here I am on the `C:` drive of my domain controller and inside of my Windows directory. I have a subdirectory called `NTDS`, which is short for **New Technology Directory Services**:

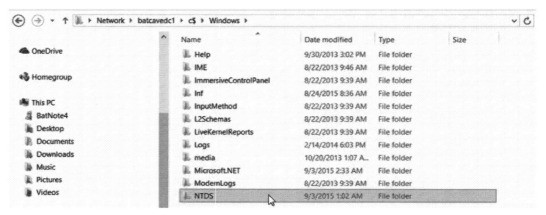

Figure 7.3 – Location of the NTDS subdirectory

Therein is the famous `ntds.dit` file, the database file that has all my accounts for my infrastructure, as we can see here:

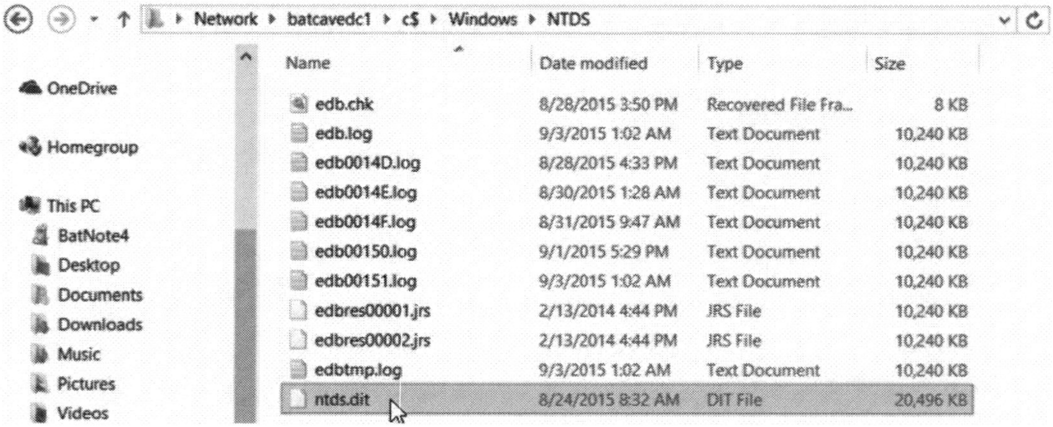

Figure 7.4 – Location of the ntds.dit Active Directory (AD) account database

Now, don't think Linux doesn't do the same thing, because guess what? It does! It stores its passwords inside of the `etc` directory in a file that's called `shadow` (`etc/shadow`).

For Apple, we store it in a file that's called a `plist` file, located in the `var` directory under `/var/db/dslocal/nods/default/users`.

With this file, the user is inside of the greater-than and less-than brackets (`<user>.plist`). `plist` has a shadow hash data property associated with it, and there are ways you can open this file up. Typically, you can't just grab these. If you're thinking you'll just go grab them, guess what? These files contain your authentication credentials, but they're stored as hash values. You can't just open it up. In fact, most of the files are going to be locked while the operating system is running. As far as it being hashed is concerned, you need to know that it's a one-way algorithm, which means I can't reverse the hash. "Okay, that's cool, then obviously I'm secure." Well—no, you're not, because as an attacker, I can steal it.

Methods for cracking/password hacking

There are several techniques used for cracking, as outlined here:

- Dictionary attacks (one of the most common ways we can go after passwords)
- Brute-force attacks
- Syllable attacks
- Hybrid attacks
- Rule-based attacks
- Good old reliable guessing

Let's look at them in detail.

Dictionary attacks

Dictionary attacks are exactly what they sound like. We have files that we can go and download off the internet (`https://zip-password-cracker.com` or `https://apasscracker.com`) and we can create our own because they are just text documents of words. When I say *words* in a dictionary attack, I mean I can find a dictionary based on different languages, whether that's English, French, German, Russian, or Klingon.

We also have dictionaries based on subjects. There's a dictionary out there that has medical terms in it, historical accounts, places, characters in books, their names, and even something specific to the book itself, such as a catchphrase.

Characters would also include movie characters—I have a dictionary that's filled with names from J.R.R. Tolkien's *Lord of the Rings* series. I also have a dictionary of famous people's names, movie stars, historical figures, locations, and events. Don't think you're getting tricky just because you're using a password that may not be a traditional password, because you're basing it on a real word. Please don't do that. And don't think for a second *I'll just put it in backward* because any password-cracking tool out there that's worth its weight in salt will do string manipulation. It'll take the word and try it in different combinations or reverse. So, no—you're not tricking me.

Brute-force attacks

Listen to me now, hear me later, understand me next week (using my Arnold Schwarzenegger voice). Brute-force attacks take longer to accomplish. What we mean by a brute-force attack is we try every combination of alphanumeric and specialized characters in a password. Now, obviously, if the password is only 6 characters long, brute-force attacks will go by relatively quickly, but when we get into passwords beyond 14 characters, it gets a lot more difficult. It requires more cycles to go through, and brute force has to try every variation. Tools such as John the Ripper, Cain & Abel, or Aircrack-ng are very useful.

There's an upshot to brute-force attacks, even though it does take longer and it tries every combination, which takes more cycles. Guess what? It takes time, but it's 100% effective. And who has time? The attackers do.

Syllable attacks

With a syllable attack, we take a password—in this case, we'll say the password is pass—and then do a combination of a dictionary and brute force and try every possible arrangement of every entry in the dictionary.

Hybrid attacks

A hybrid attack still uses a dictionary, but based on users being complacent, we're going to try different variations by including numbers and special characters at the beginning or end of the password. So, let's say I have Batman, and next month I must change my password, so I change it to Batman1, and next month I change it to Batman2. Well, a hybrid attack is going to eventually crack this one.

By the way, if you or your users just modify passwords each month by adding a character or two to at the very end of it, smack yourself on the forehead and promise you'll never do that again. But don't smack your users' foreheads—you might get called in by **Human Resources (HR)**!

Rule-based attacks

What do I mean by rule-based attacks? Remember enumeration? If you're not familiar with this, you can reference *Chapter 5* of this book, *Enumeration*. With enumeration, we can use the rules we've discovered, such as requiring users to have at least an 8-character password. I'm going to use those against you. And, knowing you use complexity, I'm able to discover you require two digits. So, I use a combination of brute-force, dictionary, and syllable attacks. Again, if I know that you only have 8 characters, it's all you require for your passwords, I won't try 9 or 10 characters. Or, if you don't require a digit, then why run through those digits?

Good old reliable guessing

There's also good old reliable guessing, which entails some reconnaissance and footprinting. This is where we try to figure out as much as we can about the target, whether it's a user or a company. Often, users base passwords on things they know. So, if I go on social media, there's a chance I will figure out their favorite sports team, what their pet dog was growing up, and their spouse's birth date. We share way too much information.

Types of attacks

Now that we know the different techniques used to do some cracking, let's talk about types of attacks.

Attacks are typically summed up in four different categories, as follows:

- Passive online attacks
- Active online attacks
- Offline attacks
- Non-electronic attacks

Let's discuss each category and the attacks that relate to each category.

Passive online attacks

These types of attacks are passive, which means we're not necessarily going to have direct communication with the machine or the target.

Sniffing

Passive online attacks include things such as sniffing the network to see if we can discover passwords going back and forth. An example of this is FTP, which uses clear text by default, so, just sitting there sniffing, we might be able to pick up some passwords.

Man-in-the-Middle (MitM) attacks

This type of attack occurs when an attacker places their machine or their hacking device between the source and the destination. They just handle all the traffic going back and forth. Again, I'm not modifying anything—it's so passive that it's hard for anyone to tell I'm doing anything. I'll just be capturing the data, making sure it all passes through me before it goes to a switch.

Sidejacking

This attack was made famous by a Firefox plugin that was called **firesheep**. It allowed an attacker to go to any Wi-Fi access point, such as at a Starbucks, some coffee shop, or internet café, and if they were on the same Wi-Fi access point as other users, they could steal their cookies in the middle of their transaction. They could then do things such as log on to their Facebook account or take over their Facebook session. Again, these are relatively passive—I'm not attacking a specific target.

Active online attacks

An active online attack is exactly that—it's a lot more active. We know the more active we are, the more chances we have of getting caught.

Hash injection

This is where we inject a compromised hash into a current session and then use the hash to authenticate to the network resources.

A hash is basically an encrypted password, and passwords are basically stored in the systems in the form of hashes. Now, if I had a file that stored usernames and passwords and it was completely clear text, there would be no use in having security, right? The reason is anybody could find that file. Remember that SAM database? Well, it stores user accounts and passwords in a hashed format.

Back in the day, Microsoft used something called a **LAN Manager (LM) hash**, which was a nightmare and still is a nightmare sometimes. I get this all the time whenever I teach about ethical hacking: "*Why talk about hash words and all this stuff with older operating systems? Why not be talking about the new stuff?*" Well, I'll be honest with you—it's almost like being a hunter. If I'm going to go out and hunt my prey, I'm not going to go out after the latest, newest target out there—I want to go after the oldest, because it's slower, and no one's paying attention to it. Who knows if it's been updated? The new stuff has newer technologies and sometimes makes it harder for me. I taught a class that had two IT people from a huge state organization, and as we were talking, they told me they still have some XP machines and some Server 2000 and 2003 systems.

You may be shaking your head, wondering why you need to upgrade a machine that maybe does one task. In my two students' case, the machine handled their imaging system for documentation. In another manufacturing facility was a robotic arm being controlled by a Windows machine. It just went back and forth all day long. Do these machines need to have Windows 10 on them if they work just fine with XP? If you created a password that was 14 characters or fewer, the LM hash would take all the letters—it wouldn't matter if you had upper- and lowercase characters—and convert them to all uppercase. After converting them to all uppercase, it would then pad any leftover fields to fill out all 14 characters. So, in this case here, I'd have three padded spaces. Then, things got kind of crazy. The LM hash then went through and split up the password into two 7-character strings. The two 7-character strings were then encrypted and combined back together.

For example, `BatmanR` would be hashed out to this value, and the leftover `ULES` with its padded spaces would be encrypted to this hash. Then, they would be combined, and that would be your LM hash, as illustrated here:

Figure 7.5 – How LM hashes are created

Microsoft then added NTLM, which is the NT LAN Manager hash. So, the result we would see inside of the SAM account database would include the user's name (in this case, `Bwayne`), a number listed after their name, followed by the next 32 characters, which was the LM hash, and then an NTLM hash appended. Now, the big difference between these two was in the password hash algorithm. LM used what they referred to as **diz**, which was very easy to crack.

Then, they came out with NTLM **version 1 (v1)**, which got us to using **Message Digest 4 (MD4)**, which was a better algorithm, but NTLM **version 2 (v2)** used MD5, which is even better, and technically, you should use it whenever possible. So, then you might see another account listed in there as administrator, followed by 500 for that number. 500's the **security identifier (SID)**—all administrative accounts in the Microsoft world end with 500 at the end of the SID. Again, I would see a combination of the LM hash and the NTLM hash.

> **Note**
>
> Anytime you see a hash that ends with a double AAD3B435B51404EE, this should mean something to you. This is a very common ending hash, and it describes the last 7 characters—remember that we must pad it to make sure we equal 14 characters? It tells me the password is 7 or fewer characters in length. Something similar happens if somebody types in a password that's over 14 characters. Remember that this happens with 14 characters. If it's over 14 characters, then the LM hash value is dumped and not utilized. Operating systems today, since Vista and higher, have the LM hash turned off.

Keyloggers

When it comes to keyloggers, we monitor every single key stroke going on a particular system or target. All those keystrokes, depending on the keylogger itself, could be transmitted back to the attacker.

Keyloggers are software programs that monitor and record keystrokes, mouse strokes, screenshots, who logged in, and at what time. It's amazing what some of these software programs do, but most of them will log keystrokes. There's a lot of software out there, and some have a legitimate purpose to them—for example, some parents or guardians want to monitor what their kids are doing on the computer.

We also have hardware-based keyloggers, which are extremely hard to detect. They will monitor every keystroke, and it doesn't look like it's a big bad device, but some of them have small applications built into them so that they either keep a log file and I just recover the device or they will simply email me the logs.

As a security expert, you need to know what's installed on your machines, both software and hardware. If you were to look on the back of a machine and saw one of the following devices plugged into the back of your system and the mouse was plugged into it, what would you assume?

Figure 7.6 – Keyloggers

The question is: *Is there a legitimate use for these devices?* It may be the company's business to know what people are typing—what information they're sharing. And it doesn't stop at devices that look like these.

There are keyboards you can modify—you can do this yourself and install a keylogger piece of hardware inside of the keyboard. You can also buy these new and deploy them out to your end users. Or, how about if I just send you a free one and it's connected to your system so that we're able to capture screenshots and record which websites you've visited? I can even read your email because as you type it in, it's going to be recorded. I could also capture login names. "*But hang on a second—when I type in my passwords, I get an asterisk.*" Well, guess what? Keyloggers don't log in asterisks—that's what you see visually.

If you are saying "*Those are physically connected devices*", I have bad news for you. There are Wi-Fi keyloggers out there. You are also in trouble if you have a Bluetooth keyboard (and most Microsoft keyboards are Bluetooth-based as far as connectivity from the keyboard to the system goes).

This looks like a **Universal Serial Bus (USB)** charger, but built inside of it is a Bluetooth keylogger:

Figure 7.7 – A keylogger hidden inside a USB charger

I don't have to be hooked up to your system. I can plug this in, and you'll just think: "*As a matter of fact, I could use it as a charger for my phone.*" In the meantime, it'll be picking up Bluetooth signals and detecting what people are typing on their Bluetooth keyboards.

Here's where it gets scary… they have acoustic keyloggers now. What does that mean? There are apps that are being experimented with right now. It takes time because it has to learn the sound of the keystrokes, but after a while, it'll be able to predict via sound waves which keys are being typed.

If that doesn't scare you enough, how about a rootkit logger? Yes—there are two that have been found in the wild already. One of them is called **Jellyfish**, a keylogger that runs inside the **graphics processing unit** (**GPU**) of the video card instead of through the processor or the **central processing unit** (**CPU**) of the system, and I don't know very many antivirus products that are looking at what's running on GPUs!

To raise the hair on the back of your neck, we also have hypervisor keyloggers. These are keyloggers that will reside in a piece of malware that is hypervised. It runs underneath the operating system, so it remains untouched, just like a **virtual machine** (**VM**).

We also have form-grabbing-based keyloggers. These are basically a piece of software that's going to record web form data and then send it across the internet to show the attacker which form data you're filling out. And no—it's not specific to PCs.

Offline attacks

These are interesting because. with offline attacks, we have all the time in the world. What's meant by an offline attack? If I can somehow get access to whatever is storing your passwords and user accounts and I get to play with it offline, I'm not going to hit that machine. I grab a database such as the SAM account database, or maybe I grab your `ntds.dit` file, and I can start throwing things such as a rainbow attack (which we'll discuss in more detail later).

We could also use one of the following.

Distributed network attacks

A **distributed network attack** (**DNA**) extends decryption capabilities beyond a single computer by using the distributed power of multiple computers across a network to decrypt files, find passphrases, and recover passwords.

Precomputed hashes

Here, an attacker can decrypt each word in a dictionary using a hash function and then compare it to the encrypted password. The downside to this is that it does require a lot of space, but the payoff is that it's extremely fast.

Non-electronic attacks

Non-electronic attacks are possible ways to gain access to valuable information without the use of technology. While these methods may be less common, they can still be very effective in obtaining the data or access you need.

Dumpster diving

This is where we look through trash. Now, that may seem beneath you, but trust me, it happens. Oracle caught Microsoft in a fib because they had done some dumpster diving in Microsoft trash bins.

Dumpster diving is a means for attackers to find information they could use to create trust. You can find medical records, resumes, personal photos, emails, bank statements, account details, information about software, tech support logs, government records, medical bills, resumes, and the like simply by exploring the intended victim's garbage. Once garbage is collected, the information is used to piece together identity profiles, making social engineering more likely to succeed.

Shoulder surfing

In this type of attack, somebody is obviously watching over your shoulder or using some type of mechanism. The latest and greatest now is, I have an electronic cell phone in my hand that does video. How about if I hold it up to my ear as if I'm talking to somebody, but I point my camera to where you're typing in a password? As a matter of fact, I'm paranoid about such things. When I'm out shopping, if I'm going to run my credit card somewhere, I always stop and look around and see if somebody's pretending to be on their cell phone and it happens to be pointing my way.

Social engineering

There's something we can do with social engineering that is a non-electronic attack, but kind of borderline. It's a very famous attack and it entails using a USB switch blade. Here, as an attacker, I configure a USB drive, and when you plug it in, it goes through and does some interesting things such as installing a keylogger for me, maybe a piece of malware, and it does it all silently. Maybe even the emails knew your logging credentials that I detected, and what I do is take that USB drive and just arbitrarily leave it some place where I know somebody will find it—for example, at the parking lot of a company, in the main lobby, in a hallway, near a bathroom: some place near the target company. If somebody picks it up, what's the first thing they're going to try to do? Plug in this bad boy and bing—they just got *pwned*!

Authentication methods designed to help

Included next are additional cracking concepts to assist you in the cracking process.

When NTLM authentication doesn't work for you

This authentication mechanism is proprietary to Microsoft and it's the default authentication that is used if some specific situations exist. I know you are saying: "They're using Kerberos." I know that, except if the following situations apply to you. It's only used when there is no Kerberos trust between two different forests and you're trying to share resources.

Another time NTLM gets utilized instead of Kerberos is if authentication is being attempted by an IP instead of by a DNS name because Kerberos requires DNS or a domain name environment. Also, if one or both systems are not a part of the same domain, don't think that you're not using NTLM, because you very well could be.

Another situation is if you have a firewall that's blocking Kerberos. Now that we know when it's used, how is it used? Well, it's based on a challenge-response algorithm.

The cool thing about this is passwords are never transmitted because you're just going to respond to a request or a challenge. As I mentioned before, NTLM came in v1 back with Windows NT. v2 was released with **Service Pack 4 (SP 4)**, so if by chance you come across an older NT system, odds are it will be running v2.

This is how it works: you have your client machine, and the user gets their login screen and types in their username and password. After this, Windows takes that password and runs it through a hash algorithm to generate a hash for the password that's been entered. The client then sends a login request to the domain controller, and since the computer has joined the domain, the domain controller is very much aware of that hash value associated with that login name. So, the domain controller then creates a random string and sends it and basically says: "If you are who you say you are, you should be able to answer this request." The client encrypts this request with the hash and sends it back to the domain controller. The domain controller then goes through, retrieves the password or the hash of the user's password, and compares it to see if it's the correct answer. If it's the same answer, then you're allowed to cross the bridge. If it's wrong, you don't get to pass. It reminds me of the famous *Monty Python and the Holy Grail* movie scene of the three questions and bridge of death.

Kerberos authentication

This is what we're using, pretty much up to date with the latest and greatest from Microsoft. Kerberos gets its name from the three-headed dog that guards the gates of Hell—or Fluffy, if you're a *Harry Potter* fan. It is ticket-based, so we issue tickets that are then used to represent the credentials. It's fast, because we don't have to keep re-authenticating the user over and over—or, possibly, the computer. Again, it avoids the transmission of passwords.

Now, there is one little kicker on this one and that is it's time-based. If you remember our chapter on enumeration, you should remember the **primary domain controller** (**PDC**). It's in charge of syncing everybody's clock to itself because when it comes to Kerberos, the default with Microsoft is you cannot have more than 5 minutes time difference between the PDC and your system clock. If you are, it won't authenticate you. So, let's look at how Fluffy is used.

First, we have a computer, a user, and a domain controller. The domain controllers have some special services running on them, and one of them is a **key distribution center** (**KDC**). If we have a file server that we're trying to gain access to, the user is going to make a request to the domain controller, saying: "I need to be authenticated, please." The domain controller responds back with: "Yes, what can I do for you? I can authenticate you.", to which the user's computer says: "I need to get a **ticket-granting ticket** (**TGT**)." Because the computer and the domain controller are members of the same domain, the domain controller can issue this TGT or ticket to the user or computer to be then utilized when they want to gain access to resources. When the user/computer wants to gain access to the file on the file server, they just simply present their TGT, the file server sees it's from a trusted source, and it will quickly check with the domain controller and say: "Is this account still valid?" The reason it does this is in case an administrator has locked the user out. Now, just because tickets are being utilized here doesn't mean that you're safe. We'll be looking at a tool later in another chapter called John the Ripper—a very famous tool, and probably one of the more powerful tools out there today. It's a Linux tool that can crack Unix, LM hash passwords, NTLM passwords, and Kerberos passwords.

Salting

Salting? Yes...my hash needs a little salt. So, what happens if you have two users with the exact same, identical, password? What is their hash going to look like? The solution? We can randomize the hashes by appending or prepending random strings—we call these salts—to the password before we hash. This helps us in having duplicate hashes and makes it hard for an attacker to find out what's going on.

Each salt needs to make sure it's unique for each password. Don't use the same string of characters for every password. If you do, all I must do as an attacker is figure out what your salting string is, and I'll then get everybody's password. For example, I have two accounts that are both using the same password, the hash values will be identical. If I use a salt, I can append some unique characters to the end of the password; therefore, two different accounts using the same password have different hash values. To check if the password is correct, we must be able to have access to the salt, so it's usually stored in a user account database along with the hash or as part of the hash string itself.

Now, I'll give you an unfortunate shout-out here because Microsoft won't use this. They kind of use it, in the aspect that the passwords in AD are hashed, but the ending hash is just the username itself. So, again, make sure that if you're going to salt your passwords, each salt is unique to each password. If you're a developer and you're creating your application and want to make it so that people have to log in, a common mistake is they'll hardcode in a salt into the program or generate a salt only once and then reuse it. If I'm using the same salt for every password, two users with the same password will have the same hash.

There's also the issue of your salts not being long enough—for example, 3 characters. 3 characters narrow down the limits of the number of possibilities the attacker needs to consider. Now, because I just told you the hash needs to be available, that creates a dilemma, right? If the key is kept on the system and the attacker gains full access to the system, they'll be able to steal the key no matter how long the salt is. The key needs to be stored in external systems such as a physically separated server dedicated to password validation. There is specialized hardware out there that also helps with storing salt keys.

Other cracking methods

Besides the methods we spoke about previously, there are a couple of other methods that deserve a mention.

Rainbow tables and other options

A rainbow table is a precomputed hash table, so I don't have to try every variation of the hash values—I precomputed them ahead of time. I just do comparisons. Unfortunately, these precomputed hashes take up a lot of storage space. There are, however, free rainbow tables you can download.

> **Note**
> You'd have to google them and be prepared for a HUGE file (**terabytes** (**TB**), in some cases). Go to `https://freerainbowtables.com` for examples.

You can also create your own rainbow tables if you have the storage space to handle these. What's interesting is, with new technology such as **solid-state drives** (**SSDs**) and cloud computing, attackers are utilizing these technologies to create rainbow tables at record speeds and utilizing the processing power of Amazon's cloud system or Azure. After they compile them, attackers will then go off and sell them.

Lookup tables

We can also utilize **lookup tables** (**LUTs**), which are just plain old tables. What this basically says is: "Does any hash out there equal this hash? Oh, look—I found one, and the password was password5," because that's what the hash equaled.

Here are some examples:

- Does any hash equal the following?

  `5f4dcc3b5aa765d61d8327deb882cf99: FOUND: password5`

  It then continues to go through those tables, saying: "Hey, what about this one?" Oh, not in the database, so nobody has that password or hash.

- What about the following?

  `6cbe615c106f422d23669b610b564800: not in database`

  Your cracking tool will then continue: "Hey, can I get a letMEin12? Any responses?"

- Can I get the following?

  `630bf032efe4507f2c57b280995925a9: FOUND: letMEin12`

  "Yes, here's another one—try this one." Here it is:

- `386f43fab5d096a7a66d67c8f213e5ec: FOUND: mcd0nalds`

And it will continue, depending on the size of the table you download.

Reverse LUTs

Similar to a LUT is a reverse LUT. These operate by saying: "I have a hash for the password of apple123—who on this list uses that hash? Oh, a couple of accounts... There's alice3, 0bob0, and charles8."

I love technology but sometimes, I look at new things and ask myself: "What's this going to do me security-wise?"

Let me show you something. The following screenshot depicts a computer system with multiple video cards. It was done as a project:

Figure 7.8 – GPU cracking system

Many of today's video cards have a GPU on them, and GPUs love cracking passwords. We typically think of a CPU as having multiple cores—for example, i7 might have 8 cores, or maybe you got a dual-core. Well, GPUs have hundreds of cores in them. In this research project, they set up five of these systems. They had 25 **Advanced Micro Devices (AMD)** GPUs and, between the five systems, they were connected at 10 gigabits per second (Gbps). Guess what? We don't have to do rainbow tables anymore. With this system and brute force, this cluster went through 348 billion NTLM passwords per second. What this means is a 14-character password took only 6 minutes to hack.

What about MD5? Well, I'll do 180 billion per second with this rig and, even if you think you're being secure and you're using **Secure Hash Algorithm 1 (SHA-1)**, you'll only slow me down to 63 billion passwords per second being brute-forced. Remember—a system such as this, I would use in an offline attack. I'll get your database and, probably, within a day or two, I'm going to have several login options for you.

Now that we have worked on gaining access and cracking passwords, let's discuss escalating privileges next.

Phase 2 – Escalating privileges

Wanting local administrative rights, even though you're not allowed them, is what escalating privileges is all about. So, the problem we have here is now we've gone through and hacked a password and figured out the user ID, we're stuck with the privilege of that user—or are we?

Kevin Mitnick, the world-famous hacker said the following:

> *It's true, I had hacked into a lot of companies and took copies of the source code to analyze it for security bugs. If I could locate security bugs, I could become better at hacking into their systems—it was all towards becoming a better hacker.*

When you think about it, what he was doing was elevating his privileges by getting to know the source code and seeing which bugs or vulnerabilities he had to escalate out of.

We've made it in. What now?

What do we do now? Remember how we made it in this far? We found a user account and cracked their password. Our goal now is to give ourselves adequate rights and permissions to do what we wish. So, never assume that just because you're not an administrator or don't have administrative rights, you can't accomplish your goal.

Once we make it in, our next step is to look around. If we make it in as a local administrator, I'm going to look at any configuration mistakes that have been made. I might also check out any design errors from the network infrastructure level. Again, there are many times you might find a target through a Google hack, and you make your way in just using a default username and password. You get in and think to yourself: "Well, I haven't fully reconned this environment yet", so, we may want to take another look at these design errors. Maybe they've been misconfigured or didn't change default passwords or default settings.

I also want to get a layout. This target I've hit, what is its purpose on the network? I'll also be looking at any programming flaws. I know—programmers *don't make mistakes*, right? They just come out with patches to enhance the application. That's kind of like IT people—they *don't make mistakes*. They just improve the performance.

Now, as far as our overall goals are concerned, we have four basic methods for escalation, as follows:

- **Pwning the admin/root account**

    One of the goals we're going to have is being able to *pwn* the `admin` or the `root` account.

- **Taking advantage of vulnerabilities**

    The second method is to take advantage of a vulnerability that may be in the application or in the operating system that's going to allow you access as a privileged user. There are many applications that raise the privilege of the currently logged-in user on the backend you may not have considered.

Try using `www.exploit-db.com`. It gives insights about vulnerabilities you could take advantage of. Some of them we will go through. We can do a privilege escalation with this one.

- **Using escalation tools**

  Another method of escalation is firing up a tool such as Metasploit, a complete framework and hacking suite designed to allow you to see if you have any exploits or any type of vulnerabilities in your network. But obviously, we know attackers are going to use these types of tools against us. The downside to Metasploit is it's extremely easy to use. You might find a YouTube video about it, which means that some 12-year-old is out there coming at your system.

  There are more tools such as these out there, including Canvas and Core Impact, which is a complete pentesting tool, and Armitage, which is basically a GUI frontend for Metasploit.

- **Social engineering**

  What if we just get somebody to do it for us? That's called social engineering. As an attacker, I can persuade people to run an application for me or maybe to look at a file for me. I must entice them somehow using one of the core emotions of social engineering. Typically, I'm going to do it either out of fear or greed, or I need some help—which is a very reliable social engineering aspect, because as humans, we like to help, right? All I can do is send you an email, attach a script or a program to it, and ask you to double-click on it because it's going to *patch your system for you*. I'll make it look as though the email came from IT staff. I could create a **Portable Document Format** (**PDF**) file that, when opened, executes a program for me.

Countermeasures

How do we stop this? Well, there are some countermeasures, but you need to remember your job is not to stop them – because you can't. You can only slow them down. And how do we do that? Here's how:

- The first way is using encryption, which helps you protect data that is considered sensitive. If I've encrypted data to a particular user, then regardless of what that user's permissions are or what my user permissions will be, I won't have access to that information.

- You could also consider giving least privilege when it comes to your users and applications. What we mean by this is don't overallocate your privileges. If somebody needs the ability to do something on a machine, take the time to figure out which rights and permissions they need and only give them those rights and permissions.

- You could also look at making sure your updates are done. It drives me bonkers because a lot of the privilege escalation issues can be avoided by making sure you are patching your systems.

- Another thing you can do is limit the interactive login. Interactive login is the right to throw a three-finger salute or the *Ctrl + Delete* keys on a box and log in. By default, regular users don't have the right to log in interactively on a server.

- You could also make sure that your service accounts are limited, using the same concept that applies to least privilege. I see this mistake done all the time where IT will go to install an application—a server application such as **Structured Query Language (SQL)** or SharePoint—and they need a service account that utilizes the machine. As far as the machine is concerned, a user is doing all the work, but it's being done by this account. Sometimes, IT will use the administrator account on the local box. Again, you need to evaluate what access these service accounts need because it could create a vulnerability or a hole for you.

- Another option is limiting the extent of the code if you're the developer and you are creating an application that runs at a high privilege level. Again, typically, it's when we take shortcuts that we create issues.

- You can also do privilege separation. With this type of approach, we limit the scope of programming errors and possible bugs.

- You can also test the operating system and your apps meticulously and review code if you're a developer. If you are an IT person and a developer says: "Here's a new app we're going to be using", there should be some type of documentation that says what was done where. You should question any type of code somebody wants you to place in your environment. And, if you are a developer, don't go off and download somebody's sample code and just copy and paste it. Make sure you understand what each line does.

- Using multi-factor is another countermeasure. This way, we place another safety-net layer for us.

- Do some stress tests. This is because many times when an application or an operating system gets overloaded, it creates vulnerabilities. You may even want to consider performing debugging using **BoundsChecker**. However, please realize none of these will stop everything from happening, but at least it'll make you feel as though you've got a handle on things.

Next, we'll discuss the types of escalation that will help us accomplish our purpose.

Types of escalations

Now that we know the different countermeasures used, let's talk about the different types of escalations.

Privilege escalation

This is any condition that allows an attacker to gain elevated access after the system has been compromised. So, we take a lower-end account and escalate its rights and permissions to a higher account, which allows us to pivot and have all kinds of fun. We also have what they refer to as **information disclosure**. This is basically any type of vulnerability that allows the attacker to gain access to data that is sensitive or protected. We also have what they refer to as **security feature bypass**. Now, this is typically caused by a software weakness that allows an attacker to bypass policies, validation, or even other safeguards such as bypassing **User Account Control** (**UAC**) or any type of filter. There are different types of escalation that you can perform. Determining which one you use will depend on what it is you're trying to accomplish. Privilege escalation can be accomplished by using **dynamic link library** (**DLL**) injection.

Horizontal escalation

In security terms, horizontal escalation is one of the most common methods used by attackers to achieve their objectives.

Attackers will often look for a way through the perimeter to get an initial foothold within a network. Often, they find a low-hanging fruit such as a user who has left their password blank or a web application that lacks proper security controls.

Once they have gained access to the network, the attackers will then look for ways to move laterally and spread their infection to as many systems as possible. By doing so, they can gather more valuable data or even take control of the entire network.

Offline access

Offline access is typically looking at machines that may not be always hooked up to the network. If a laptop gets stolen or if I'm able to compromise that laptop, I'm going to have all the time in the world because it's offline. And because of that, I can use some simple exploits to give myself total control of this machine, and then, hopefully, when you hook it back in, I'll be able to continue my total domination.

DLL and DYLIB hijacking

DLLs haunt us. It's something we must deal with. Most Windows applications don't use a fully qualified path when they load a DLL, so there's no structure. It basically says: *Run this DLL*. Instead, the default is that when an application launches, it first searches the directory from which it's been launched. Knowing most application developers and people take shortcuts—by not specifying a path—an attacker can load up a DLL inside of the application directory with malicious intent. An example of this is if an application needs the `library.dll` file (which is in the system directory) to install the application. If it can't find it, or if it finds it first in the path you're installing at, it'll never see the one in the system's directory of Windows. So, when the user goes through and loads up the application, it uses the DLL and the attacker will have full remote access to that box. Hmm—maybe this should make you wonder about downloading torrent files now, right?

Fortnite, a game that gets played by both children and adults, is extremely popular. Knowing this, attackers used to release *patches* to make players invincible or to give them extra guns. Well, sure it does, but it's mostly loaded with something else. In fact, security researchers discovered that flaw.

Don't think for a second Windows is alone in this. Apple is very much a target. But instead of using DLLs, Apple uses **DYnamically linked LIBraries (DYLIBs)**, which is basically the same concept. This is a dynamic library, hence the name, that an application may call, but DYLIBs are typically specific to a user. So, depending on how we want to deploy this, an attacker can just simply place a malicious DYLIB into a specific location. In a ton of cases, the loader in OS X is going to search for dynamic libraries in multiple paths. This is going to help the attacker inject a malicious DYLIB into one of the primary directories and then simply load the malicious DYLIB at runtime. This allows attackers to bypass security software, as well as even bypass Gatekeeper—a security feature of the macOS system that enforces code signing and verifies downloaded applications before allowing them to run. But again, I can bypass that all by doing a DYLIB hijack. Okay—let's stop picking on software. Let's talk about hardware!

Using CPU flaws

Let's talk about Spectre and Meltdown, shall we? Both these vulnerabilities are CPU-based and, unfortunately, the vulnerability goes back through all different types of chips over a long period. Each one of them takes advantage of either the memory's cache and the execution order, and/or takes advantage of branch prediction. Now, these are geeky terms but know that the vulnerability is there.

The other issue we have, especially when focusing on things such as Spectre, is that it has some interesting issues here because it affects CPUs from Apple, AMD, **Advanced RISC Machines** (**ARM**) CPUs, Intel, Samsung, and even Qualcomm. These are basically all the mobile phones on the planet, right? This vulnerability tricks the processor into exploiting a speculative execution to read restricted data. What that means is that if the chip identifies a program that includes multiple conditional statements, it'll start to execute and then conclude all possible outputs before the program does, which makes the system faster. This vulnerability allows the attacker to force the processor to accomplish a speculative execution of a read before bounds checking is performed. The result? The attacker can access and read **out-of-bounds** (**OOB**) memory locations. Those locations could include things such as confidential information—such as credentials that are stored in a browser—or even reading kernel memory or performing a web-based attack using JavaScript.

When it comes to Meltdown, this one's not as prevalent in all the CPUs, but it does affect any of the processors, whether Intel- or ARM-based, that Apple deployed. This vulnerability tricks a process to access OOB memory by exploiting CPU optimization mechanisms through speculative execution. The attacker can use either one of these vulnerabilities to execute or escalate their privileges by forcing an unprivileged process to read other adjacent memory locations, such as the kernel memory or physical memory.

One of the biggest problems with both these vulnerabilities is they're built into the chip, and the only fixes that they've been able to come out with to support the CPUs that were released that had this vulnerability, which goes back years, was a software fix that ended up slowing down the performance of the CPUs.

Access token manipulation

An attacker can gain escalated privileges through things such as access token manipulation. Windows itself uses access tokens to determine the owner of a running process. A user or an attacker can manipulate access tokens to make a running process appear as though it belongs to someone else other than the user that started the process. We refer to those as spoofed tokens.

Application shimming

This comes into play when the Windows operating system uses the **Windows Communication Framework** (**WCF**). We call it a **shim**, and it's what allows Windows 10 to execute or run older programs. For example, for programs that were created under XP and you've upgraded to Windows 10, you still want the application to run. These shims provide a buffer between the program and the operating system.

If you have ever done a compatibility wizard for Windows when trying to run an application, it'll ask you questions such as: "Does it need elevated privileges or did it run in previous versions of Windows?" That's helping you to build that shim. Now, the buffer, which the shim creates, is referenced when a program is launched. It needs to verify whether the program has access to the shim database. Some shims can be used to bypass the UAC, inject malicious DLLs, capture memory addresses, or even give the attacker the ability to install backdoors or escalate their privileges.

Other Windows issues

There are also a ton of processes within the Windows operating system that execute binaries automatically as part of their functionality or whatever it is they're trying to accomplish with this application. If the filesystem permissions on these binaries aren't set appropriately, the attacker can replace these with malicious files. We refer to this as a filesystem permission weakness. If the process that executes the binary has a higher-level permission, then the binary also executes under the higher-level permission, which may include the system account. Attackers can take advantage of this technique and replace the original binaries with their malicious ones to escalate or elevate their privileges.

We also have something called **path interception**. This is a method attackers use of placing an executable in a particular path so that it'll be executed by the application in place of the legitimate target application. Path interception helps the attacker maintain persistence on the system as well as escalate their privileges.

Scheduled tasks

The Windows operating system has this thing called task scheduler, which allows a user to configure to defragment their system every 3 days or so. A user with administrative privileges could use these utilities in conjunction with a task scheduler to schedule a script or a program that can be executed at a particular time and date. If a user provides proper authentication, they can schedule a task from a remote system using a **remote procedure call** (**RPC**). The attacker can use this technique to execute malicious programs at the system startup, during any type of maintenance, as well as performing remote execution and, of course, escalating our privileges.

Apple issues

For non-Windows folks, for macOS or OS X, during the boot process, `launchd` is executed to complete the system initialization process. Parameters for each of the launch-on-demand and system-level daemons are loaded using `launchd`. These daemons have a property list file (`plist`) that's linked to the executables that run at the time of booting. The attackers can create and install a whole different launch daemon that can be configured to execute at bootup time. These weak configurations allow the attackers to alter the existing launch daemons executable to maintain persistence within the system or to escalate their privileges.

I know—you're saying: "Please tell me that's all." No—there's even more. Remember that `plist` file I just told you about? Well, these files exist for any application or service. It includes the necessary information that's needed to configure them. The `plist` files themselves are technically just **Extensible Markup Language** (**XML**) files, and how easy is it to modify an XML file? Attackers can access and alter these `plist` files to execute malicious code on behalf of a legitimate user. They can also use them to maintain persistence, as well as escalate their privileges on that box.

Linux issues

If you are a Linux person, you're probably saying: "Man, we're safe!" Well, both in Linux and in macOS, if an application uses a `setuid` or a `setgid` flag, then the application will execute with the privileges of the owning user or the group. Typically, applications run under the current user's privilege, but there are some circumstances where the program must be executed with elevated privileges, but the user running the program doesn't have those elevated privileges. In this case, someone, maybe the developer, could set the `setuid` or the `setgid` flag for their application. An attacker could exploit the application with the `setuid` or the `setgid` flags to execute malicious code with elevated privileges. Do you see what's going on here? We're elevating our privileges all over the place.

Web shells

The last one is a web shell, which is just a script that can be uploaded to a web server—or maybe it becomes part of the server—that enables remote administration to a machine. This works well for things such as remote administration using PowerShell. The problem is, an attacker can create their own web shells and inject malicious scripts into the web server to maintain or escalate their privileges. They can also use them as a backdoor to gain access and control the server remotely. Typically, a web shell runs under the current user's privileges, but if that box has any type of vulnerabilities built into it, they can escalate their privilege and then install malicious software, change user permissions, add users and groups, steal credentials, read emails—almost anything.

Buffer overflows

Let's first back up and understand what the ultimate purpose of any program is that runs on a computer—it's to process data of some type. Usually, that data is going to be provided by a user, so the program needs to store the data somewhere, and the best place to put it into is memory. This is where our troubles begin. Many developers assume that user input will be reasonable to a certain extent. It would seem kind of unreasonable for, as an example, a URL address to be more than, say, 500 characters. And usually, developers will pad this by multiplying in either by 2 or even by 10. So, based on this assumption, the developer could reserve memory for a web page address that could hold up to 5,000 characters. Now this memory space that's reserved is called a **buffer**, and it's a buffer in **random-access memory (RAM)**. So, because the developer may never suspect that someone's going to use more than 5,000 characters, they usually don't apply any type of check. The data is just processed as it's applied. So, what happens if the user unintentionally—or possibly intentionally, with malicious motives—provides a web address that I don't know with 5,500 characters in it? Well, after writing that 5,000th character, anything else left over is bad, and it's placed in memory after the buffer, which results in a buffer overflow. Now, the purpose of these attacks is usually to allow the attacker to run their own code directly on this system. This is referred to as **arbitrary code execution**, or possibly they can execute their code and transmit it from one machine to another. This is sometimes referred to as **remote code execution**.

Denial of service

Then we have, obviously, our most famous one (probably): **denial of service (DoS)**. This includes conditions that allow attackers to consume all the resources of the CPU—the drive, connections, RAM—so that the process can no longer service legitimate requests.

Another type of vulnerability is another famous one, **cross-site scripting (XSS)**. This is a vulnerability whereby a malicious script is injected into a website, and then that script is downloaded and executed by the browser on an end user's system—or, should I say—a different user's system.

Another famous one is directory transversal. This is a vulnerability that allows the attacker to access restricted directories from where they've entered. For example, if I were to maybe go to my home directory on my production network that is assigned to a D. Meredith directory on a server somewhere, if I'm able to execute some malicious code and be able to move over to B. Wayne's directory to see their information, or C. Kent's, or even L. Lane's, we might have some fun there. We also have what they refer to as **cross-site request forgery (CSRF)**. These types of vulnerabilities allow unauthorized commands to be transmitted from the user to a web app.

So far, we have cracked a password, figured out our user account, got into the system, elevated our privileges—so, we're done, right? Well, we may have *pwned* the machine so far, but a total pwn is when we can maintain access via executing applications.

Phase 3 – Maintaining access and executing applications

Overall, the whole process in this phase is being able to make sure that we can always get back in. Again, from the attacker's perspective, you don't go through all the steps that we've gone through just to say: "Haha, I did it!" and walk away, right? We're also here to see what's going on and to get a clear picture of the system or the target machine. We are also detecting what other information could be available to us that might have been blocked to us before.

Let's say I'm an attacker who's created a piece of software, and I put it out into the wild and it phones home, and one day I see three systems have installed my piece of software. I'll use that software to get back in and then use some additional software to make sure I have an extremely clear understanding of the environment. One of the things I'll be looking for is if they have any type of **intrusion detection system** (IDS).

How do we execute applications?

Well, this is typically applied in one of the following three ways:

- **Spyware**: The most common and easiest way is via spyware. I know that's a hot word out in the industry and there are different levels of spyware—for example, there are legitimate spyware products out there. If I were to go in and install an application on my Android device, many times I'm saying: "Yes—go ahead and look at my contacts, or use my network connection."

  My father taught me something very valuable. He said: "There is no free lunch." If you are old enough to understand that phrase, you know he meant there's nothing for free out there. I know it says it's free—Gmail says: "Hey, it's free." But is it? We're paying a price for that. The price is Google going through and looking at your emails and looking for specific words so that they can sell marketing. That's how they make their money! Nobody's out there saying: "I'd like to be a Good Samaritan, spend countless hours creating an application, and just give it away for free." It doesn't work that way.

- **Backdoors**: We can execute applications via a backdoor, which allows a user or an attacker to come back in without being noticed. With a keylogger, I can say anytime a specific keystroke or combination of keystrokes are executed, please execute my program. Backdoors are great because they're stealthy and can also be used in **command and control** (**C2**) scenarios to bypass firewalls and IDS systems.

Spyware and backdoors

When we talk about spyware, we have this vision that comes up in our minds about uneducated users, such as grandmas (or, in my case, nieces and nephews), who install fake software or click on a link, and boom: "Bob's your uncle."

Spyware is normally installed by us when we download a file, app, or free product. Typically, the manufacturer wants to know how you're running that product, or maybe they are going to make money. In fact, I think it's funny that the last time I installed Java, if I hadn't hit the **Advanced** button during installation, I would have also installed some additional toolbars and software that I'm sure Oracle gets paid for.

Spyware is designed to capture our authentication credentials as we type them in. An attacker might even capture emails or fire up and record information when we type in something on a web form. Again, I'll use Google as an example since they're the big boy on the block and they give *everything away for free*. A lot of it is they're trying to capture habits. Well, think of that from the attacker's perspective. Could they not profile you a little better if they understood your habits? "What kind of habits?" That could be: "Hey, this target uses this password when it comes to banking sites", or "They use this password when it comes to their social networking sites", or "The target is just using a variation of a specific password." If I'm capturing both screenshots and keystrokes, I can start to capture habits. Even on your Android phone, if you download a free app from a torrent and sideload, it could be malicious, and these apps could start capturing your habits. Some legitimate apps track how long the user is using the app or even finger-swiping actions on your devices.

Also, when you go to install an application on your tablet, phone, computer, do you sit down and read the **user license agreement** (**ULA**)? No? I know—I sometimes don't either. But I understand the overall gist of it. That is—one: you don't own the software; and two: we are going to collect information about you, possibly access your contacts, see how long you use our app, and maybe see which app you open after using our app. If I deem the app to be that worthwhile, I'll accept that as a risk. However, I only accept it as a risk from legitimate software companies.

Types of spyware

Spyware is typically installed while installing an application. For example, if I download a copy of WinZip, and then during installation, I just hit **Next**, **Next**, **Next**, **Next**, **Next**, **Next**, **Next**, **Next**—which they're hoping I do—I might install a new toolbar, and that toolbar in **Internet Explorer** (**IE**) will track some of my activities.

Now, think of this from an attacker's perspective. Let's say a new version of Photoshop comes out, and as an attacker, I crack that product and put in my own piece of spyware so that when the user installs the app, my spyware gets installed. I'm going to make sure it's hidden so that they can't see it running. Yes, I can hide it from your Task Manager.

It's in videos

We also have spyware that comes across via video. I'm not talking about YouTube, although I'm pretty sure YouTube does monitor which videos you're watching on their channel. But that would be legitimate, right? Other video sources might tempt you with the latest blockbuster movie for free, but the truth is... it's not. I had a nephew who brought me his computer once and said: "Hey, it's running really slow and sluggish."

> **Important Note**
> Slow performance is one of the signs you have spyware installed.

As I'm going through and looking at it, I see all these programs that are firing up during startup, and as I'm talking to him, he tells me about finding this really cool website where he can stream movies that are still in the theater for free. Now, again, I'm sure Netflix spies on us; however, I'm more worried about someone coming to my house and making a mistake on my network or systems. My nephew tried to pull up the web page so that I could see it, and I jumped up: "Noooo", and quickly unplugged the network cable because I know what's out there.

Your printer is spying on you

There's also spyware for printing. How about if I load a piece of spyware and everything you print, I get a copy of it, please? Think about that for a second. What do you print? Are you sure you've never printed tax forms, medical records, or—better yet—let's say your doctor gets a piece of spyware on their machine because the doctor's receptionist thinks every time a popup comes up saying "You need to install this piece of software" Is this because they visit inappropriate or malicious websites? An attacker can install a piece of spyware and get a copy of every single document printed.

USB is guilty too

We also have USB-based spyware. Here, I have this piece of software that I show as kind of a **proof of concept** (**POC**). It's used quite often out there but I always have students come up to me and say: "Is there any way you can give me a copy of this whitepaper?" Or, they say: "Can you give me a copy of these VMs?" If I had malicious intentions, I could simply say: "Sure, just bring me a USB drive", and when they do, I would plug it in. I would have a little program whereby as I'm copying files to their USB drive, I'm also injecting spyware onto their USB drive so that when they plug it into their system, it injects everything silently, without their knowledge. It would also download everything on their USB drive to my machine as well.

Mic check – 1,2...1,2

We also have spyware that's injected into audio. There is no such thing as free MP3s! Again, let's think about both sides—legitimate reasons for spyware and the dark side of spyware.

Let's say you have an account with Spotify, Google, or Google Music. I guarantee those companies are monitoring and seeing what you're doing with their audio files: how many machines you've installed it on, how many times you've listened to it, and so on. Some of this is done with cookies, but if you're installing any type of application or plugin in your web browsers, I guarantee you're getting some type of tracking software.

If I want to get spyware on your machine, I'll go for a new album coming out by a popular musician or band, rip it, add my spyware, and post it on torrent sites. Whenever somebody downloads it and starts to play music, my spyware would kick in.

Email and phishing

We also have spyware that's distributed via email and the internet. We've talked about malicious websites, and I've seen them. People get emails saying: "Hey, this is the IRS. We're going to start filing charges against you because of your tax forms… click here." And you or the user clicks on the link, goes to a site, or executes a script that's malicious in nature.

Don't think for a second that attacks are limited to PCs/laptops. This is exploding on the mobile platform. One of the things I do before installing an application on my phone—because I know there could be something there to track what I'm doing—is look at the permissions to see what it is they need access to. If it's a game, I don't care how cool the game is. If it wants access to my contacts, there's no way it's going on my device. Likewise, review the permissions of applications. Most of the big vendors require you to do this, whether you're getting it from the iTunes Store, the App Store, Google, or Amazon—those I would consider somewhat trusted sources. History shows us that there have been many bad apps sneaking into their stores.

Be very careful about downloading software or applications from different repositories out there, even if it's the coolest thing ever. In fact, that's part of the social engineering aspect of hacking. I'm counting on the fact that you want this so stinking bad, you're willing to justify and jump through some hoops and maybe install a piece of software that's going to help me *pwn* you.

Next, we'll discuss the use of backdoors to further our ability to access our targets.

More about backdoors

When it comes to backdoors, we want to make sure we understand what they are.

Backdoors consist of two components—one of them is on the client side, while the other is on the server side.

The client is what I want to hopefully install on my targets, while the server is the box that all the clients will report into.

Many backdoors will also have automation built into them. Some of that automation could include things such as a **connect-back technique**. This is where I can get the client side installed on a target (maybe because they've downloaded my free evil copy of Photoshop), and, to bypass the security of most firewalls (most firewalls block all inbound connections unless they've been initiated by an outbound connection), I have the client connect back through the firewall to my server side.

We might also use what's referred to as the first-line backdoor, which is sending the initial malware. The primary backdoor acts as a downloader for other malware that we then get to install. Normally, when somebody is infected, there's going to be multiple backdoors created, not just one. So, if I get the first-line backdoor installed, then the second-line backdoor is what goes out and steals the information I'm looking for.

You may be thinking "I'll just delete it if I detect it" or "I have antivirus installed". Well, the issue here is that part of the automation of most of these backdoors and spyware programs includes the ability to make it impossible to update Windows. They disable your antivirus product, infect your host file, make sure you can't open it, and lock down the system to stop you from fixing it. Or, at least, it's going to take somebody with some computer knowledge, which typically isn't the standard user, to repair it.

Common backdoors

Some of the more common backdoors are the most popular ones out there. Back Orifice was a popular one. This was created by an organization that was called *Cult of the Dead Cow*. They got the name *Back Orifice* from the fact that Microsoft had a product line for all their server platform products. Not only Server 2000, but also SQL and Exchange, were all part of the BackOffice product line, so, making fun of it, they called it Back Orifice.

Sercomm manufactures most routers and parts that go on the router, and routers are sold by Netgear, Cisco, Linux and so on. Well, there was a backdoor in these devices, and it's funny that they came out with a patch that was supposed to fix the backdoor but didn't—all it did was hide the backdoor. Their backdoor worked across a particular port so that an attacker could open up a remote shell, reset the router, or even make modifications to the configuration.

When we talk about backdoors, I can't go very far without talking about some government agencies. Some of these backdoors were included in hardware being sold to other countries. The **National Security Agency (NSA)** has been working hard to come up with backdoors for encryption technologies. In fact, in early 2015, Microsoft issued a security advisory where they admitted they were aware of a security feature bypass vulnerability, which was known as **FREAK**. FREAK is short for **Factoring Attack on RSA-EXPORT Keys** and is a known MitM vulnerability caused by weak website encryption. It made it possible for attackers to backdoor in and spy on secured communications. You'll never guess who took advantage of that one!

There are also consumer products. Remote exec is probably one of the more popular ones out there. You can use this product to install applications silently, meaning that the user doesn't see an application being installed, executing scripts, copying, modifying, or deleting files. Maybe do a filter and say: *send me all DOCs*. I could even change the admin password or turn the machine off or on at any given time. Again, this product is designed for administrators to manage their environment, but if I install something such as this on your machine or get a client to install it, and have it report back to my server, I'll have total control of your box.

We've discussed how to maintain access and execute applications through several different tools and options, allowing us continued access to a system or network while remaining undetected. Next, we'll discuss hiding our tools.

Phase 4 – Maintaining access and hiding your tools

I know what you're thinking. There's no way he can come up with a joke for this one, right? So, when I'm talking about hiding your tools, what we're really getting into here is something I saw on one of those sarcastic t-shirts: *Shhhh…I'm hiding from stupid people!* That's what we're going to do here—hide our tools so that less intelligent people or those who are not security-minded will not be able to find them. Again, the last thing we want to do is go through all this effort to get our machine totally pwned and then lose it because we don't hide our software from users or IT experts.

Rootkits

When you find a rootkit in your environment, you're going to be terrified beyond the capacity for rational thought. You'll think, mother-puss-bucket!

> **Security Note**
> If you discover a system with a rootkit installed, you should never trust it. Don't *clean* it. Don't try to fix it. You need to reimage the system from scratch—operating system and apps, all new. Please don't make the mistake of trying to *save* the system.

Rootkits were first discovered by something that Sony tried to slip past everybody. This was back in 2005 when Sony started loading copy protection measures on about 22 million **compact discs (CDs)**. When you inserted the CD into a computer, the CD installed a piece of software that modified the operating system so that it would interfere if you tried to copy the CD. What was bad is this: 1) The rootkit couldn't be uninstalled; 2) It created additional vulnerabilities. And one of the programs that they utilized actually installed even if the user denied or refused its **end-user license agreement (EULA)**, and it phoned home and reported what the user's listening habits were. Now, this is back during the height of things such as Napster.

This was discovered by Mark Russinovich, the gentleman who created the Sysinternals software suite. He saw something going on with the CDs and he reported it. Nobody believed him, except for one small antivirus firm called **F-Secure**. F-Secure was one of the first companies that came out with one of the first rootkits and uninstallers.

So, why do we use rootkits? Well, they have two primary functions associated with them: remote control or a backdoor. As well as eavesdropping, rootkits allow an attacker to gain administrative control over a computer. This means that they can run any program, see what people are doing on the system, and even change the system's configuration.

There are different types of rootkits out there allowing for different functionality, but the biggest issue is these are extremely hard to remove. Rootkits are the mother of all infections if you want to think of it from a virus perspective. So, again, why are rootkits used? Well, we'll gain remote-control access and watch what's going on with the environment. If you're thinking "I just got my antivirus and it's doing just fine—it didn't detect it", you need to make sure your antivirus is always up to date, but there is something out there referred to as the polymorphism of rootkits. This technology makes rootkits extremely difficult to find because of what it allows a rootkit to do. It allows a rootkit to rewrite the core assembly code. So, now, suddenly, your antivirus, especially if it's signature-based, is useless.

The only way to find rootkits that use polymorphism would be to use technology that looks deep inside the operating system and compares it against a baseline of what a good operating system, or a healthy operating system, would be like.

There are several types of rootkits out there, as outlined here:

- **User-mode rootkit**: In user mode, the rootkit runs on the computer with administrative rights or privileges. This allows the rootkit to alter security, as well as hide processes, files, system drivers, and system services, and the rootkit stays installed by just simply copying the files to the computer's hard drive and automatically launching them every time the system boots. The downside, at least from the attacker's perspective, is that user mode is one of the only types that antivirus and anti-spyware applications can detect.

- **Kernel-mode rootkit**: What the attackers have done at this point is they know user-mode rootkits can be detected—so, how about if we just load the rootkit at the same level as the operating system? At this point, the operating system can't be trusted. One of the most famous kernel-mode rootkits was Da IOS Rootkit, which was focused on Cisco's **iPhone OS (iOS)** operating system. So, yes—you can get rootkits on network devices.

- **Hybrid rootkit**: This is the best of both worlds, where we can take some of the characteristics from a user-mode rootkit, being that it's easy to use and stable, along with the kernel-mode rootkit—meaning: I can hide this thing. This is one of the more popular rootkits out there today.

- **Firmware**: This type of rootkit is similar to a user-mode or a kernel-mode rootkit, but this rootkit actually hides in the firmware when the computer shuts down—so, when you restart the computer, the rootkit just reinstalls itself. When we say that it hides itself inside of firmware, it could be anything from a microprocessor code to a **Peripheral Component Interconnect (PCI)** expansion card firmware. And again, on every restart, the rootkit gets reinjected.

- **Virtual rootkit**: These are relatively new, and the most popular one I can think of is called Blue Pill, which is based on x86 virtualization. It was a POC that was presented in *Black Hat* back in 2006. The concept of Blue Pill was to trap a running instance of an operating system by simply starting a thin hypervisor and then virtualizing the rest of the machine underneath it. The previous operating system would remain, and any references to devices or files, or anything that dealt with hardware interrupts or requests for data, including system time, could be intercepted or faked by the new hypervisor.

  The gentleman who came up with this made a statement at *Black Hat* that he felt it would be 100% undetectable because the rootkit itself was virtualized. You might say: "Yes, but I still have an antivirus, and I keep it up to date." Well, it doesn't matter. Your antivirus might pick up the fact that you have a rootkit on your machine, and you can try to clean it off, but I want you to repeat after me, this is SuperDale rule number 385: "Any system that's been detected with a rootkit is no longer trusted." What that means is you're going to take it offline, format the hard drive, and reinstall. Do not—this is my personal feeling—continue using an operating system that has already been compromised because you don't know if it's firmware-based; cleaning it may clean the one instance, but as soon as you restart the machine, you're back to square one.

Now that we're here, let's look at some interesting rootkits.

Horse Pill

This rootkit was presented at *Black Hat* back in 2016 by a security engineer and member of the Red Team for Intel. Horse Pill was a POC Linux rootkit. That was really kind of interesting because it infected the internal RAM disk. Once there, it was put into a mount and a **persistent ID** (**PID**) namespace that allowed it to run covertly, including its storage. This also allowed it to run some network systems without the user knowing, such as a DNS tunnel.

Don't worry—I'm not going to just pick on Linux! Yes—we've got Windows too. There's one out there known as the GrayFish rootkit, which runs inside the Windows operating system. It is one of the most modern and sophisticated malwares implanted from a group that was called the **Equation Group** and was designed to provide an almost invisible presence using hidden storage, as well as malicious commands executed inside the Windows operating system. This was developed around 2013, but variations of it have been popping up all over the place. The reason it's so malicious is when the computer starts, GrayFish hijacks the operating system loading mechanisms by injecting its own code into the boot record. This basically allows it to control the launching of Windows at each stage, bypassing the Windows Secure Boot controls. Rootkits use stealthy storage, but GrayFish implemented its own encrypted virtual filesystem inside of the Windows registry.

If that's not emough to scare you, check this out. Hold on to your socks here. You ready? The Equation Group has released a module named `nls_933w.dll` that was the first of its kind that was designed to reprogram or reflash a computer's hard drive and its firmware with the malicious code. It has been found in drives from Seagate to Toshiba, Samsung, Western Digital, Micron, Nextdoor, IBM, and Hitachi. You may be saying: "Wow, whoever created this really thought this through." Yes—its origins are from some of the tools that my big brother—as I like to call the NSA—uses.

Alternate Data Streams

First, I need to make sure I have your attention. Next to passwords, this is my next biggest pet peeve. When it comes to **Alternate Data Streams** (**ADS**), there's something you need to understand. First, this is not a well-known feature. I'm surprised how many times I teach a security class and I mention ADS to people that have been in IT for years whose jaws drop as they say: "I didn't know that was something that could be done."

ADS has been around since NT 3.1. That's a long time ago, but it's still being used today. The reason this feature was first created was—thanks, Steve Jobs—so that Microsoft could be compatible with the Macintosh **Hierarchical File System** (**HFS**). Now, the Macintosh filesystem stores its data in two parts. There's a data fork and resource fork. The data fork is where we store the data itself about that file. The resource fork is what gives us additional information about a file. Because of these two forks, we're able to hide files extremely efficiently. So, this is one of those necessary evils. We want to be able to store additional data about a document, as well as the document itself.

Detecting rootkits

As far as detecting rootkits is concerned, it depends on the type of rootkit that is installed. It could be one of the following methods:

- **Integrity-based detection**: This can be regarded as a substitute to both signatures in a heuristic-based detection. What happens is the user will run a tool such as Tripwire or **Advanced Intrusion Detection Equipment (AIDE)** on a clean system. The tool then creates a baseline of a clean system and stores it in a database, and then we can use that database to compare existing workstations to see if there are any issues.

- **Signature-based detection**: This is like a fingerprint. It compares the characteristics of all the system processes, as well as the executable files with a database that's been created of known rootkit fingerprints—very similar to how most of our virus programs work.

- **Runtime execution path profiling**: This technique compares the runtime execution path of all the processes and the executable files. Normally, the rootkit adds new code near to the routine's execution path, which destabilizes it, and this runtime execution path profile picks it up.

- **Heuristic/behavior-based detection**: This works by identifying the deviations of the normal operating system behaviors and their patterns. The cool thing about these types of detection is that they are normally capable of identifying new, as well as previously unidentified, rootkits. They're able to do this because they can see a difference in what would be considered normal as far as the system pattern or its behaviors is concerned.

There are tons of tools out in the world that will help you detect rootkits, and that's fine and dandy, but a lot of times, attackers are coming up with new ways of bypassing or being undetected by this type of protection. So, it's sometimes best to check manually, and there are *two* different steps to do that.

The first and most common step is doing it through the filesystem by typing in d-i-r, which is short for directory; /s is to include subdirectories, followed by /b, which uses a bare format, meaning: I don't need any header information or summary; I just need the information itself. We will then type /a, which basically says: I want to include the following attributes. The attribute we're specifying here is h, which is hidden files. We would save that result, and then run a very similar command, except that you'll notice it's a little different on ah. Instead of ah, we do a-h. h means not—so, don't give me the hidden attributes. You would save those results and boot off a clean CD—it could be a Windows CD, an installation CD—and you get to Command Prompt and run the same commands again and save that output.

The second step is where we determine what the differences are.

We'll download a program called WinDiff by Microsoft and run that on the two sets of results to detect file-hiding ghostware. What we mean by that is files that aren't recognized while the system is on, which is what we did in the first two steps, versus files that are exposed or visible because we booted off the CD. Now, it should be noted that sometimes, you'll get some false positives, and you'll just need to track those down. This method doesn't detect stealth software that's hiding, for example, in the **basic input/output system** (**BIOS**) or in a bad disk sector or an alternate data stream, or even video card e-prompts. But it's something, right?

Steganography

Steganography, or—as we sometimes refer to it, **stega**—is the ability to take a document and hide it in plain sight. We do that by placing the document in—more commonly—a photo so that we can hide it behind or inside of other data. Unlike ADS, the size of the picture file—in this case, a photo—will increase in size. If I have a picture that's 1 **megabyte** (**MB**) in a file and a document that's 4 MB, the picture file becomes 5 MB in size. It hides inside of the other file by replacing the unused data bits with bits from the file you're trying to hide. It's extremely difficult to detect. In fact, some will say it's almost impossible to detect.

Steganography is broken into two classifications, technical and linguistic.

Technical steganography hides the message using a scientific method, whereas linguistic steganography hides the message inside of what they refer to as a carrier or some type of media that's used to transfer files back and forth or communicate. As far as the type of steganography that's accessible to us is concerned, we can hide files in an image. We can also use steganography to hide files in another document, very similar to what we saw with ADS.

Steganography can also be used to hide files inside of a folder, or the object representing the folder, and audio. Yes—I can hide a hidden message or file inside of an audio file. In fact, this is one of the things that's going on right now in fighting terrorism. A lot of terrorist organizations communicate with each other by hiding their messages inside audio and video-based files. You always hear on the news that a new video's been released by some terrorist organization and that the government is currently *reviewing* it. What they're doing here is going through and checking to see if there's anything hidden inside the video, as well as looking at the video in depth to find out if they can find out where it's coming from by looking at backgrounds and listening to background noises.

We can also hide our files inside of web-based applications or websites so that you must know exactly where to go within the website, either to a hidden image, a hidden URL, or just a hidden location on the page that would reveal information that is normally not visible.

We can also use it to hide information that we refer to as white space. We do this with a program called **Snow** that conceals the message, which is normally in an **American Standard Code for Information Interchange** (**ASCII**) format by pinning white space to the end of each line. Now, because the space and tabs are generally not visible in text viewers, the message is effectively hidden, and if you use built-in encryption, the message can even be read even if it's detected.

Steganography can also be used to hide files in emails. In fact, it's very similar to the web-based steganography types because most emails will support **HyperText Markup Language** (**HTML**). So, again, we can hide files or messages inside of emails.

We can also use it to hide files inside **digital versatile discs** (**DVDs**). So, again, I ask you this: Where did you get your last copy of the latest movie release? I could be hiding my tools, and when you run the movie or go to watch it, my tools inject.

Natural text-based is another type of steganography. These types of programs will convert information you're trying to transmit into a flow of text like a play. So, if somebody's looking at your text document, they'll be wondering: "What is this guy talking about? He's just talking about one day he went for a walk with his dog."

One of the more popular programs out there, Sams Big G PlayMaker, goes through and you hide your text within the play itself.

Another type of steganography is hidden operating system-based. This is where I inject my tool inside of some of your hidden operating system files and my tools execute anytime your operating system needs to use those files.

Now that we have been able to maintain access and hide our tools, let's discuss how we get out without leaving a trail and being detected by clearing logs and evidence we've been there.

Phase 5 – Covering your tracks – Clearing logs and evidence

So, why do we clear our tracks?

First, we want to remain obscure. We don't want somebody knowing that we've gotten into the system. Otherwise, all our hard work has gone to waste.

Second, we want to avoid tracebacks. This is where the victim hires a forensic expert to figure out exactly what happened. Back in the day when I had my own **internet service provider** (ISP) service, I had a customer who was complaining he wasn't getting the speeds he was paying for. Together with one of my friends, a white hat from Microsoft and author of several security and **integrated security system** (ISS) books, we saw something going on with this customer's antenna. We discovered the customer had plugged the internet connection directly into his company laptop without going through a router, and he got totally pwned. We found out the reason he wasn't getting the speeds is because somebody had uploaded movies on his laptop and was using his laptop as a parted FTP server. My friend was able to use some of the log files we were looking at to see the IP addresses of the connections coming in, and we were able to trace it back to an IP address in Germany. There wasn't much we could do about it at that point, which I guess really does sum up one of our biggest problems with the internet today: there is no sheriff in town. But that's what we want to avoid. We want to avoid tracebacks.

Third, we want to convince the victim or victims there is nothing is going on. "This machine has not been compromised; continue to do what you're doing." In fact, it's when machines start acting funny that people start getting their suspicions up, right? Now, we could also talk about the big issue for attackers not wanting to be detected as they don't want to go to jail.

Next, we'll look at a basic method of clearing our tracks, which would be the action of a good attacker, and then we'll look at what a great attacker might accomplish.

Basic method – Five things to do

A basic method is what a good attacker would accomplish or do while covering their tracks. They're going to do some basic things, and most of this will be detected very easily. This is what they'll do:

- **Clear browser history**: A basic method would be to clear any browser history on that machine relating to looking up information about the target, the vulnerabilities that are on the target, or if they're trying to upload a file or download a file from a website. If they've done any type of research, they're going to want to clear out the browser history.

- **Delete cookies**: There's also the issue of internal users not wanting the IT department or security professionals to know that they are looking up things about how to crack a hash on a Windows 7 box. They might also delete cookies. In the case of a website, cookies are designed to contain information about your preferences for that website. I'm always amazed that I have a lot of people that will come to me and say: "Can you help me clean up my computer?" and I'll be looking around only to notice their history and browser have been cleared out, but they forgot about the cookies. Well, it's all about the cookie. Cookies contain information about the sites they've visited, so this would be another entry that an attacker would want to delete.

- **Delete downloads**: You will want to delete any downloads that may have been done on this machine. Maybe as an attacker, I've downloaded a payload file that I made available on a website somewhere or an FTP site, so I would want to delete those.

- **Delete passwords**: I'd also want to clean out any password managers that may be on this machine. This would be more toward the aspect of an internal user who wants to make sure that nobody sees what their passwords are, but this would also possibly apply to an attacker.

- **Delete private data**: They'll also want to delete any private data that may be on the machine.

As an instructor, I go to different training centers, and most of them provide an instructor machine for me which I use while I'm teaching. While I'm using that machine, I may check my email, load up my Dropbox or my OneDrive, and on the very last day, I have a script I carry around with me now on a thumb drive I execute off. It goes through and clears out all that private data for me. You could say these would be some good guidelines to follow if you were ever in fear of somebody utilizing the same machine you've been using.

Advanced methods

Advanced methods are what great hackers do. This is about clearing out the logs. There are certain files on the system tracking everything happening on a machine and recording it inside of a text file. Now, you must be careful how this is done if you're clearing out the logs—you don't want to raise a flag about your activity. It can raise an obvious flag something has been messed with and removed. In fact, you'll see an event ID 1102, which is a *log was cleared* error.

The overall concept here with advanced methods is a great attacker is not going to just clear out the logs. They are going to use tools to help them do the following:

- Disable and turn off auditing so that the system is no longer looking at what they are doing. Simply open Command Prompt and use a built-in utility called Auditpol for audit policy. I want to set a category called Logon/logoff, and I'd like to change the success rate, so that any successful logins are disabled, as well as any failures. After disabling auditing, they then do their damage, try to hack the password, make modifications to files—whatever they need to do.

- Then, after they are done, they simply turn the auditing back on.

We have now covered the necessary steps to leave a system that's been hacked and some of the best ways to leave while covering our tracks.

Summary

In this chapter, we discussed the five phases of system hacking. In *Phase 1*, we covered how to gain access to the system. Once we understand the system and which services are running, we need to find out what the username and password are. We also discussed the various ways to crack passwords. *Phase 2* discussed escalating privileges. We can either escalate the privilege of an account we create or take an account that already exists. In *Phase 3*, we discussed how to maintain access by launching applications and tools that will allow you to continue your attack from inside the system and allow you to can get back in more easily. *Phase 4* discussed the various ways of hiding our tools. This allows us to hide information or anything we may want to use in our attack. *Phase 5* discussed covering our tracks and how we do that. It covered how to disable auditing, allowing you to accomplish the purposes of your hacking, and then how to enable auditing and get back out of the system undetected.

There are plenty of advantages to learning how to hack a system. You will be able to discover holes in your security, and if you know how to hack, you'll know how to better set up and protect yourself from other hackers, and you'll know the main issues involved in keeping your systems safe.

Next up, we get to hack humans, or what is called social engineering.

Questions

As we conclude, here is a list of questions for you to test your knowledge regarding this chapter's material. You will find the answers in the *Assessments* section of the *Appendix*:

1. Which filesystems are supported by **Alternate Data Streams (ADSes)**?

   A. VHD

   B. FAT32

   C. NTFS

   D. CDFS

2. What utility can be used to stop the auditing or logging of events?

   A. Auditpol

   B. ADS

   C. Regedit

   D. NTFS

3. An attacker adding higher privileges to their account (adding themselves to the administrators group) is called what?

   A. Trinity slide

   B. Vertical escalation

   C. Sideloading

   D. Pass the hash

4. Clark brings in a new keyboard to work and gives it to Lois; soon after, Lois's credentials are being used on other systems. What do you suspect is the cause?

   A. A keylogger

   B. Malware

   C. MFA attacks

   D. Ransomware

8
Social Engineering

There's no single security device that can guard against an attacker's use of social engineering techniques. Only through continuous training and educating employees on how to identify and respond to social engineering attempts can an attacker's chances of succeeding be reduced.

We will explore the many aspects of social engineering and the ways attackers use it to accomplish their purposes, as well as how to better identify and respond to and educate and protect ourselves and our organization from its purposes.

In this chapter, we will discuss the following:

- Understanding social engineering
- Attack-vulnerable behaviors
- What makes social engineering work?
- Social engineering's attack phases
- Social engineering methods
- Threats from within
- Threats to corporate networks from social media
- Identity theft
- Countermeasures

Before proceeding with this subject, let's review some of the basic concepts of social engineering.

Understanding social engineering

So, what is the definition of social engineering?

Social engineering is the skill of persuading others to give up sensitive information to use it for malicious purposes. By using social engineering to take advantage of people, attackers can breach an organization's sensitive information even with security policies in place. Employees are often unaware of security lapses and may unknowingly give out or divulge crucial information about the organization.

Examples are answering strangers' questions or responding to spam emails without realizing it.

Social engineering's most common victims

A social engineer's most powerful tool is the vulnerability of people. People generally trust others and find enjoyment in helping and assisting people. An attacker is skillful and will take advantage of a person who is helpful.

Let's discuss some of the most common targets of social engineering in an organization:

- **Receptionists and help-desk personnel**: Social engineers generally target service-desk or help-desk personnel by tricking them into divulging confidential information about the organization. To extract information, such as a phone number or password, the attacker first wins the trust of the individual with the information. On winning their trust, the attacker manipulates them to get valuable information. Receptionists and help-desk staff may readily share information if they feel they are doing so to help a customer.

- **Senior executives**: To gather essential information about an organization, attackers could approach senior executives from various departments, such as finance, HR, and CxOs.

- **Users and clients**: Attackers could pose as a tech support representative to approach users and clients of the target organization to obtain sensitive information.

- **Technical support executives**: Another target of social engineers is technical support executives. A social engineer may take the approach of contacting technical support executives to obtain sensitive information by pretending to be senior management, customers, vendors, or other figures.

- **System administrators**: A system administrator in an organization is responsible for maintaining the systems. Thus, they may have critical information, such as the type and version of the OS and admin passwords. This information enables an attacker to make a more planned and organized attack.

- **Vendors of the target organization**: Attackers may target the organization's vendors to obtain essential information that will aid in the execution of attacks.

To succeed, attackers take a special interest in developing social engineering skills and can be so proficient that victims might not even notice the fraud. Attackers are always looking for new ways to access information. They also ensure they know the organization's frontline contacts, such as security guards, receptionists, and helpdesk workers, to exploit people's vulnerabilities. People have conditioned themselves to not be overly suspicious, and they associate specific behaviors and appearances with known entities.

People are naturally cautious with strangers and identify certain behaviors and appearances. A man in a uniform carrying a stack of parcels for delivery could be mistaken for a delivery person. By tricking and using human vulnerabilities, attackers can get confidential information, authorization, and access data from people via social engineering tactics.

The effects of a social engineering attack on a company

Social engineering is a serious issue and can result in significant losses for a business.

The following are some of the effects of a social engineering attack on an organization:

- **Economic losses**: Competitors may employ social engineering tactics to obtain sensitive information and data from the target organization, such as development plans or marketing strategies, which could result in financial loss or strategic advantage.

- **Detriment to goodwill**: A company's perception of goodwill is critical for acquiring customers. By disclosing important organizational data, social engineering attempts may jeopardize such goodwill.

- **Loss of privacy**: Loss of privacy is a serious problem, particularly for large organizations. If an organization cannot maintain the privacy of its stakeholders or customers, people may lose trust in the company. As a result, people may stop doing business with them and they may suffer damage and losses.

- **Terrorism**: Terrorism and antisocial elements represent a threat to an organization's assets, including people and property. Terrorists may employ social engineering to create blueprints of their targets to infiltrate them.

- **Arbitration and lawsuits**: Lawsuits and arbitration generate negative publicity for a company and have a negative impact on its performance.

- **Closure – either temporary or permanent**: Social engineering attacks can lead to lawsuits and arbitration and can result in the temporary or permanent closure of a company and its operations.

Now that we have covered the basics of social engineering and how it impacts an organization, let's look at the types of approaches used to achieve this.

Attack-vulnerable behaviors

When we think about attack-vulnerable behaviors and what this means, we're talking about the natural, intrinsic feelings and responses of people. These can be exploited by an attacker using the following:

- **Authority**: The right to exercise power in an organization is referred to as authority. Attackers take advantage of this by posing as someone of authority in a target organization, such as a technician or an executive, to steal sensitive information.

- **Intimidation**: The use of bullying tactics to intimidate a victim into taking multiple actions is referred to as intimidation. It's frequently carried out by impersonating someone else and duping victims into divulging crucial information.

- **Social proof versus consensus**: People are frequently willing to like or do things other people enjoy or do, which is known as consensus.

  Attackers take advantage of this by building websites and posting fictitious customer testimonials regarding the benefits of certain items, such as anti-malware software (rogueware). As a result, when users search the internet for rogueware, they come across these websites and believe the fake testimonials. Furthermore, attackers may install malware alongside the malicious goods if people download it.

- **Scarcity**: Scarcity is frequently associated with social engineering. In a decision-making process, scarcity frequently entails instilling a sense of urgency. Because of the urgency, attackers might manipulate the decision-making process by controlling the information supplied to victims.

For example, if Apple announces a new product that quickly sells out, attackers can take advantage of the situation by sending phishing emails to the target customers, enticing them to buy the goods by clicking on a link supplied in the email. The users will be forwarded to a malicious website controlled by the attacker if they click on this link. As a result, the user may wind up disclosing account information or downloading harmful software, such as trojans.

- **Urgency**: Urgency is about acting right away. Attackers can take advantage of this by duping victims into doing something they don't want to do.

  Ransomware, for example, frequently employs the urgency principle, which forces the victim to take immediate action within a set timeframe. The victims notice a countdown meter running on their infected systems and realize that failing to make the required decision within the allotted time may result in the loss of critical data.

  Similarly, attackers can send phishing emails claiming that a specific product is on sale and that the consumer should click the *Buy Now* link to purchase it. A user is duped, and they've clicked on the link to act right away. As a result, they are routed to a malicious website, where users are forced to give personal information or download a virus file.

- **Familiarity or favoritism**: People are more inclined to buy things if they are advertised by a celebrity they respect. Familiarity or favoritism means people are more likely to be convinced to do something when they are asked by someone they like.

  People are more willing to allow someone to glance over their shoulder if they like or are familiar with them. If the person is disliked, the shoulder surfing attack is easily recognized and avoided. Similarly, if they like or are friendly with someone, they will typically allow them to tailgate them. In some circumstances, social engineers trick someone with charm and pleasant conversation to get a person to like them.

- **Trust**: Attackers frequently try to establish a trusting relationship with their targets. An attacker could, for example, call a victim and introduce themselves as a security expert. They may claim they work with XYZ firm and have spotted certain irregularities, such as the victim's machine sending out strange errors. The attacker establishes confidence by making use of the name of the company and their experience in the field of security. Once trust is established, the attacker instructs the victim with steps on how to proceed. The attacker then sends a malicious file in an email and urges the victim to open and download it. The attacker successfully installs malware on the victim's PC, infecting it and allowing the attacker to steal crucial information.

- **Greed**: Some people are naturally possessive and want to amass enormous sums of money through illicit means. By promising something for nothing (appealing to their greed), social engineers entice their targets to give information.

  An attacker may, for example, pose as a competitor and offer a substantial reward, to persuade the target staff to provide important information.

Next, let's discuss some of the factors that leave a business or organization open to being attacked.

Factors that predispose businesses to attacks

Companies are vulnerable to social engineering attacks due to a variety of circumstances, including the following:

- **Inadequate security education**: Employees may be unaware of the social engineering techniques employed by attackers to persuade them to provide sensitive information about the company. As a result, any organization's minimal responsibility is to educate its personnel about social engineering tactics and the hazards they pose to prevent social engineering attacks.

- **Inadequate security policies**: The foundation of security infrastructure is a security policy. It's a high-level document explaining security controls. Every potential security danger or weakness should be addressed with extreme caution. Password change policies, information sharing policies, access privileges, unique user identification, and centralized security are all desirable security measures to implement.

- **Unrestricted information access**: One of a company's most valuable assets is its database. Providing everyone access to such sensitive data or allowing limitless access to such sensitive data could lead to problems. As a result, businesses must guarantee that individuals who have access to sensitive data are properly trained and monitored.

- **Multiple locations**: Some companies' units are spread across the country, making it difficult to oversee the system. Furthermore, a configuration like this makes it easier for an attacker to gain access to the organization's sensitive data.

Next, we're going to discuss what makes social engineering work and be successful.

What makes social engineering work?

Social engineering, like other techniques, does not deal with network security; rather, it deals with psychological manipulation and exploitation of a human being to obtain desired information.

The following are some reasons social engineering is effective:

- Despite many security protocols, stopping social engineering is difficult since humans are fallible.
- There is no method guaranteeing total security against social engineering attacks.
- Detecting social engineering initiatives is difficult. The art and science of persuading others to reveal information is known as social engineering.
- This strategy is low-cost (or even free) and simple to apply.
- There is no unique hardware or software that can protect against social engineering attacks.

Next, we'll talk about the attack phases in which social engineering may occur.

Social engineering's attack phases

To carry out a successful social engineering attack, attackers perform the following steps:

1. **Target company research**

   An attacker acquires enough information to infiltrate the target organization's network before attacking it. One strategy that aids in knowledge extraction is social engineering. The attacker begins by gathering basic information about the target company, such as the nature of the business, its location, and the number of employees. The attacker engages in activities such as dumpster diving, browsing a company's website, and discovering employee information.

2. **Choose a target**

   The attacker selects a target for extracting sensitive information about the company after completing their research. Attackers frequently attempt to contact dissatisfied employees because they are often willing to share information about the target company and are easier to manipulate.

3. **Establish a relationship**

   Once the target has been identified, the attacker establishes a working relationship with that individual to complete their objective.

4. **Take advantage of the relationship**

   The attacker takes advantage of the relationship to obtain sensitive information about the company's accounts, finances, technologies in use, and future strategic plans.

An attacker may use several methods to carry out an attack. Let's talk about some of them next.

Social engineering methods

Attackers use a variety of social engineering methods to collect sensitive information from individuals or organizations that could be used to perpetrate fraud or other criminal acts.

This section will cover people-based, computer-based, and mobile-based social engineering approaches, all with examples to help you understand them better.

People-based social engineering

Human contact is a part of people-based social engineering. Pretending to be a real person, the attacker interacts with a target organization employee to obtain sensitive information, such as corporate strategies and networks, that will aid them in launching their attack. The attacker can simply access the server room by impersonating an IT support technician, for example.

An attacker can use the following methods to execute human-based social engineering.

Impersonation

Impersonation is a frequent people-based social engineering method in which the attacker poses as a legitimate or authorized individual. Attackers may carry out personal impersonation attacks or use a phone or another communication medium to deceive victims into divulging information.

The attacker could pose as a courier or delivery person, a janitor, a salesman, a customer, a technician, or a guest. By scanning terminals for passwords, searching for critical documents on employees' desks, rummaging through dumpsters, and other methods, the attacker acquires sensitive information. The attacker may even try to *shoulder surf* for sensitive information by listening in on private chats.

Impersonation techniques used in social engineering include the following:

- Pretending to be a genuine end user

- Acting as if you're important

- Assuming the role of a technical support agent

- Assuming the identity of an internal employee, a client, or a vendor

- Pretending to be a repairman

- Using vishing to impersonate a tech support agent

- Abusing the help desk's over-assistance

- Pretending to be someone with third-party permission

- Assuming the role of a respected authority

The human nature of trust, fear, and moral obligation are exploited by some impersonation methods used by attackers to gain sensitive information about the target company.

Pretending to be a genuine end user

An attacker may impersonate an employee and then use unethical means to acquire access to sensitive information. To gain sensitive information, they may use a bogus identity.

Another example is when an employee's *friend* requests they retrieve information that a bedridden employee reportedly requires. A well-known social interaction concept is that a favor begets a favor, even if the original *favor* is given without the recipient's request. This is referred to as **reciprocation**. Reciprocity is a common occurrence in business settings. One approach for social engineers to make use of this social trait is through impersonation.

Consider this case: "*Hi! I'm Paul, and I work in the finance department. I've forgotten my password. Is it possible to get it?*"

Acting as if you're important

Another behavioral trait favoring a social engineer is a person's tendency to not question authority. People regularly go out of their way to help people they believe are in positions of power. Impersonating a high-ranking figure, such as a vice president or director, might easily deceive an unprepared employee.

Attackers who take impersonation to the next level by impersonating a high-ranking employee add a layer of fear. In this case, where lower-level personnel may go out of their way to assist a higher authority, the reciprocation factor comes into play. For example, a help-desk staffer is less likely to refuse a request from a vice president who is pushed for time and requires critical information for a meeting.

If an employee refuses to reveal information, social engineers may use their position of power to intimidate them, including threatening to report their misconduct to their superiors. This strategy is now more important than ever.

Consider the following scenario: "*Hello there! I'm Kevin, the secretary to the CFO. I'm working on a deadline and have forgotten my system password. Are you able to assist me?*"

Assuming the role of a technical support agent

Another strategy involves an attacker impersonating a technical assistance agent, which is particularly effective when the target lacks technical knowledge. The attacker could pose as a hardware seller, a technician, or a computer vendor. During one demonstration at a hacking group, a speaker called Starbucks and asked whether their broadband connection was working properly. The confused staffer said that the problem was with the modem. Without providing any credentials, the hacker proceeded to have him read out the credit card number from the previous transaction. In a business setting, the attacker may require employees to provide their login information, including passwords, to fix a problem that does not exist.

Consider the following scenario: "*Sir, this is Mathew from X Company's technical assistance department. We suffered a system crash here last night, and we're looking for missing data. Could you tell me your username and password?*"

Assuming the identity of an internal employee, a client, or a vendor

An attacker usually wears office attire, or the same type of clothing others are wearing. They walk into a company's building while posing as a contractor, client, service technician, or another authorized individual. Then they go around unobserved looking for passwords trapped on terminals, extracting vital data from wastepaper bins and papers on desks, and gathering other data. Other social engineering techniques, such as shoulder surfing (observing users typing login credentials or other sensitive information) and eavesdropping (purposefully overhearing confidential conversations between employees) may be used by the attacker to gather sensitive information that could be used to launch an attack on the company.

Pretending to be a repairman

Generally, computer technicians, electricians, and telephone repairmen are trustworthy. Attackers could penetrate the organization by impersonating a technician or repair person. They'd go about their business as usual while searching for concealed passwords, crucial information on desks, information in garbage bins, and other relevant information; they may even place snooping equipment in secret spots. I've personally used this technique to walk out of an organization with full computer systems in hand.

Using vishing to impersonate a tech support agent

Vishing (also known as voice or VoIP phishing) is a type of impersonation scam in which the attacker employs **Voice over IP** (**VoiP**) technology to mislead people into disclosing sensitive financial and personal information. The attacker makes money off the information by impersonating someone and using caller ID spoofing. Vishing frequently includes prerecorded communications and instructions that appear to be from a real financial institution. The attacker uses vishing to deceive the victim into submitting bank account or credit card information over the phone for identity verification.

The attacker may send the victim a phony SMS or email message instructing them to call the financial institution for credit card or bank account verification; in some situations, the victim gets a phone call from the attacker. When the victim dials the phone number mentioned in the message of the attacker, they hear a recorded instruction requiring personal and financial data, such as name, date of birth, **Social Security Number** (**SSN**), bank account number, credit card information, or credentials such as usernames and passwords. The recorded message confirms that the victim's account has been verified when the victim submits the information.

Abusing the help desk's over-assistance

There's a reason why help desks are routinely targeted for social engineering attempts. Staff workers are trained to be helpful, and they frequently divulge critical information, such as passwords and network details, without first validating the caller's identity.

To be effective, the attacker must know the identities of employees as well as information about the person they are attempting to impersonate. Pretending to be a senior official, the attacker may call a company's help desk to extract important information.

For instance, a person might contact a company's customer service department and claim they can't remember their password. Their supervisor may fire them if they miss a deadline on a major advertising project.

The help desk employee pities the caller and promptly resets their password, unintentionally allowing the attacker access to the company network.

Pretending to be someone with third-party permission

Another common tactic employed by attackers is to pose as a person authorized by a senior-level leader in the organization to gather information on their behalf.

For example, if an attacker knows the identity of an employee at the target organization who is permitted to access the required information, they keep a close eye on them to gain access to the data they need in the absence of the employee in question. In this situation, the attacker can approach the help desk or other people and say the employee (authority figure) has asked for the information.

Even if there is doubt about the request's legitimacy, people tend to disregard it in favor of being helpful in the workplace. When someone mentions an important person and provides the necessary information, people tend to believe they are being truthful.

This method works well when the authority figure is on vacation or traveling and immediate verification is unavailable.

An example is as follows: "*Hello, my name is John, and I chatted with Mr. XYZ last week before he left. He's on vacation and indicated you'd be able to provide me with the information while he's away. Could you please assist me?*"

An attacker can employ vishing to impersonate a technical support staff member of the target organization's software vendor or contractor to obtain sensitive information, like the impersonation of a tech support agent described previously. The attacker may pose as a network technician and request the user ID and password for a computer to determine the issue. The user would submit the essential information, believing them to be a troubleshooter.

An example is as follows: (Attacker) "*Hello, my name is Mike, and I'm with tech support. The system and networks have been running slower than usual at your office, according to certain employees. Is this correct?*"

"*Yes, it's been a little slow recently,*" says the employee.

(Attacker) "*So, we've transferred you to a new server, and your service should now be significantly better. I can check your service if you provide me with your password. From now on, everything should be improved.*"

Assuming the role of a respected authority

Posing as a trustworthy authority figure is the most effective way of social engineering.

To collect sensitive information from the target, an attacker may pose as a fire marshal, superintendent, auditor, director, or another key individual over the phone or in person.

Some examples are as follows:

- *"I'm James, and I want to introduce myself. I'm with Jones Auditing, an external auditor. The company has asked us to conduct a surprise examination of your disaster recovery methods. Your team has 10 minutes to demonstrate how you would recover from a website crash."*

- *"Hello, my name is Ann, and I'm a sales representative from the Virginia office. I realize this is a last-minute request, but I have a group of prospective clients coming in and I've been attempting to persuade them to outsource their security training needs to us for months. They're only a few miles away, and I believe giving them a quick tour of our facilities will be enough to convince them to sign with us.*

  Yes, they're very interested in the security measures we've implemented. One of the reasons they're contemplating our firm is because their website was hacked a while back."

- *"Hi, I'm with Mountain AC/Heating Services. We got a call that the 4th floor is getting too hot, therefore I'll have to look into your HVAC system."*

  Using phrases with a professional ring to them, such as **HVAC (Heating, Ventilation, and Air Conditioning)**, may provide an intruder with just enough credibility to give them entry to the target secure resource.

Eavesdropping

Eavesdropping is when someone listens in on a discussion or reads other people's messages without their permission. It includes intercepting any type of communication, whether audio, video, or written, across channels such as phone lines, email, and instant messaging. Passwords, business plans, phone numbers, and addresses are among the sensitive data that can be obtained by an attacker.

Dumpster diving

Dumpster diving is rummaging through trash bins for sensitive personal or organizational information. Attackers look for user IDs, passwords, network diagrams, policy numbers, and other confidential information that can be extracted.

Attackers can find account numbers, calendars, bank statements, payroll information, source code, sales projections, access codes, phone lists, credit card numbers, and organizational charts. As a result, attackers could exploit this information to carry out a variety of malicious attacks. Ploys, such as impersonating a repair person, technician, cleaner, or other professional, are sometimes used by attackers to promote their dumpster diving efforts.

The following is information that can potentially be collected by going through garbage:

- **Phone lists**: A list of employees' names and phone numbers.

- **Organizational charts**: Describe the company's organization, physical infrastructure, server rooms, restricted areas and locations, and other information about the company.

- **Manuals on policy**: Make information about employees, system usage, and operations public.

- **Printouts, notes, faxes, and memos sent by email**: Reveal employees' personal information, passwords, contacts, internal working procedures, beneficial instructions, and other information.

- **Notes on events, calendars, and computer usage logs**: Information about users' log on and off times is revealed, allowing the attacker to choose the optimal time to launch their attack.

Reverse social engineering

Reverse social engineering is a challenging task because its execution necessitates a great deal of planning and skill. A perpetrator engages in reverse social engineering and plays the position of a knowledgeable professional so employees will seek information from them.

The social engineer will first create a problem by causing an incident, and then will portray themselves as the solution through general chat, enticing employees to make inquiries.

Here are some methods of reverse social engineering:

- **Sabotage**: After gaining access, the attacker will corrupt or make the workstation appear corrupted. Users seek assistance when they encounter a problem.

- **Marketing**: The attacker must promote and create awareness for a user to call them. The attacker can do this by leaving a business card or resource in the target's office with their contact information to solve the problem.

- **Support**: Even if the attacker has already obtained the desired information, they may continue assisting users to keep the victims unaware of the hacker's identity.

Piggybacking

Piggybacking usually entails entering a building or a secure area with the permission of an authorized individual. An attacker might, for example, request that an authorized individual unlock a security door, claiming that they have misplaced their ID badge. The authorized person will allow the attacker to pass through the door as a matter of courtesy.

Tailgating

Tailgating is when someone enters a building or a secured location without permission. It is the act of discretely following an authorized person through a protected entryway.

An attacker using a badge can try to gain access to a restricted area by closely following an authorized person through a keyed or locked access or entry door. They attempt to enter the restricted area while posing as an authorized individual.

This is another one of my personal favorites. One time I piggybacked into a building that may or may not have been a federal location, but that's a story for another time.

Theft by diversion

An attacker could use diversion theft to target delivery workers or transportation companies. The main goal of this strategy is to deceive a person in charge of making a delivery into sending the package to the incorrect location, causing the transaction to be disrupted. For instance, if the victim is a package delivery driver, they may be convinced to drive to a location different than the delivery site. The theft is made possible by subjecting the van driver to a series of social engineering techniques.

On the internet, social engineers can use diversion theft to persuade victims to transmit sensitive or confidential files to an unrelated individual who is not supposed to get them.

Honey trap

The honey trap is a tactic in which an attacker poses as an attractive person online and establishes a phony online relationship to collect confidential information. In this case, the victim is an insider who has access to sensitive information about the target company.

Baiting

Baiting is a strategy in which attackers entice end users to provide sensitive information, such as login credentials and other personal information, in exchange for valuable information. The end user's curiosity and greed are exploited. Attackers use this strategy by leaving a physical device holding malicious files, such as a USB flash drive, in places where people can easily find it, such as parking lots, elevators, and bathrooms. End users are duped into trusting and opening this physical device since it is tagged with a reputable company's logo. When the victim connects to the device and opens it, a malicious file is downloaded. It infects the system and allows the attacker to seize control.

An attacker might, for example, leave some bait in an elevator in the form of a USB drive labeled *Employee Salary Information 2019* and a valid company's logo. The victim picks up the device out of curiosity and opens it on their computer, where the bait is downloaded. When the bait is downloaded, malicious software is installed on the victim's computer, granting the attacker access.

Quid pro quo

The Latin term *quid pro quo* means *something for something*. Attackers use this approach to phone random numbers within a corporation, claiming to be from technical support. This is a baiting tactic in which attackers offer their services in return for personal information or login credentials from end users.

An attacker might, for example, collect random phone numbers from a target organization's personnel. They then begin dialing each number while impersonating the IT department.

The attacker ultimately locates someone who is experiencing a genuine technical problem and offers their assistance in resolving it. The attacker can then instruct the victim to follow specific steps and enter in certain commands to install and run malicious files containing malware designed to access sensitive data.

Elicitation

The practice of eliciting specific information is known as **elicitation**.

By engaging a victim in an ordinary conversation, you can get specific information from them. To take advantage of professional or social opportunities to communicate with people who have access to sensitive information, attackers must have good social skills. The goal of elicitation in social engineering is to extract useful information to acquire access to the target assets.

If an attacker's goal is to get the victim's login and password, but all they get out of the chat is stuff they enjoy, the attacker will have to focus more on the elicitation process to get the necessary information.

Let's talk about computer-based social engineering next and what it's about.

Computer-based social engineering

Attackers utilize harmful software, such as viruses, trojans, and spyware, as well as software applications, such as email and instant messaging, to undertake computer-based social engineering.

The following are some examples of computer-based social engineering attacks.

Pop-up windows

Popups persuade or force users to click a link that leads to a phony web page that requests personal information or downloads dangerous software, such as keyloggers, trojans, or spyware.

One way to get a user to click a button in a pop-up window is to warn them about a problem (for example, by showing a realistic OS or application error message) or to offer them more services. A window shows on the screen, urging the user to re-login or showing a warning of a host connection interruption and the necessity to re-authenticate the network connection. When a user follows these instructions, a malicious program is installed, which takes sensitive information from the target and sends it to the attacker's email address or a remote site. Trojans and viruses are used in this form of attack.

Hoax letters

A hoax is a message that warns recipients of a computer virus threat that does not exist. To expand its reach, it uses social engineering. Hoaxes usually do not result in physical harm or data loss, but they do result in a loss of productivity and the usage of an organization's precious network resources.

Chain letters

A chain letter is an email offering free goods, such as money or software, in exchange for the user forwarding the email to a certain number of people. Emotionally compelling stories, *get-rich-quick* pyramid scams, spiritual beliefs, and superstitious threats of bad luck are all common techniques utilized in chain letters. Chain letters depend on social engineering to be passed along.

Instant messaging

An attacker uses instant chat features to communicate with selected online users to obtain personal information, such as their date of birth or maiden name. They then use the information they've gathered to break into users' accounts.

Spam email

Spam consists of irrelevant, undesired, and unsolicited emails that are sent with the intent of collecting information that can be used for financial gain, such as SSNs and network information. Spam communications are sent to the target to obtain sensitive information, such as bank account numbers. Email attachments containing hidden and dangerous programs, such as viruses and trojans, may also be sent by attackers. By giving the attachment a large filename, social engineers try to hide the file extension.

Scareware

Scareware is a sort of malware that entices people to visit malware-infested websites or download or purchase potentially harmful software. Scareware is frequently encountered in popups informing users that their computer has been compromised with malware. These popups look to be from a reputable source, such as an antivirus business. Furthermore, these pop-up advertisements always convey a sense of urgency, instructing a victim to download the program as soon as possible to be free of the alleged infection.

Phishing

Phishing is a method of obtaining a user's personal or account information by sending an email or providing a link that falsely claims to be from a reputable site. The attacker registers a phony domain name, creates a spoof website, and then sends the URL to users via email. When a user clicks on the email link, they are taken to a bogus home page where they are enticed to share personal information, such as their address and credit card number.

Users' lack of awareness, being visually fooled, and failing to pay attention to security signs are all factors that contribute to the success of phishing schemes.

The following are the types of phishing methods used.

Spear phishing

Instead of sending out thousands of emails, some attackers utilize *spear phishing* to acquire sensitive data, such as financial information and trade secrets, by sending customized social engineering content to a single employee or a small group of employees in a business.

Phishing emails appear to come from a reputable source with a legitimate-looking website. The email also looks to be from someone in the recipient's workplace, usually someone in a senior position. The communication was sent by an attacker aiming to gather sensitive information about the receiver and their company; login credentials, credit card numbers, bank account numbers, passwords, confidential documents, financial information, and trade secrets are all examples of sensitive information. Because it looks to be from a trusted company source, spear phishing delivers a higher response rate than a standard phishing attempt.

Whaling

A whaling attack is a type of phishing attack that targets high-profile executives, such as CEOs, CFOs, politicians, and celebrities, who have complete access to highly confidential and valuable information. It's a social engineering trick in which the attacker convinces the victim to reveal critical corporate and personal information (such as bank account details, employee details, customer information, and credit card numbers). Whaling is different than phishing in that whaling is meticulously prepared, and it's focused on someone in executive leadership.

Pharming

Pharming is a social engineering technique in which an attacker installs malicious software on a victim's computer or server, which automatically redirects the victim's traffic to an attacker-controlled website when the victim types in any URL or domain name. The attacker steals personal information, such as passwords, banking information, and other data related to web-based services.

There are two ways to carry out a pharming attack:

- DNS cache poisoning:

    i.   The attacker performs DNS cache poisoning on the targeted DNS server.

    ii. The attacker modifies the IP address of the target website, `www.targetwebsite.com`, to a fake website `www.hackerwebsite.com`.

    iii. When the victim types the target website's URL into the address bar of their browser, a request is sent to the DNS server to acquire the target website's IP address.

    iv. The DNS server provides a forged IP address that has already been altered by the attacker.

    v.   The victim is then forwarded to the faked website.

- Host file modification:

    i.   Malicious code is sent as an email attachment by an attacker.

    ii. The code executes and alters local host files on the user's machine when the user clicks on the attachment.

    iii. When the victim types the URL of the target website into the address bar of their browser, the hacked host file instantly redirects the user's traffic to the hacker's bogus website.

Malware such as trojan horses and worms can also be used in pharming attacks.

Spimming

Spam over Instant Messaging (SPIM) takes advantage of instant messaging networks to disseminate spam. A spimmer is a spammer who sends spam via instant messenger. Spimmers typically acquire instant message IDs and send spam messages to them using bots (an application that performs automated activities via the network).

SPIM messages, like email spam, frequently include attachments or embedded hyperlinks that contain ads and viruses. When the user opens the attachment, they are routed to a malicious website that collects financial and personal information, such as login passwords, bank account information, and credit card information.

Tools for phishing

Attackers can employ phishing tools to create bogus login pages to steal usernames and passwords, send faked emails, and collect the victim's IP address and session cookies. The attacker can then use this information to impersonate a legitimate user and launch other attacks against the target organization:

- ShellPhish (`https://github.com/shellphish`)
- PhishX (`https://github.com/Userphish/PhishX`)
- BLACKEYE (`https://github.com/An0nUD4Y/blackeye`)
- evilginx (`https://github.com/kgretzky/evilginx`)
- Trape (`https://github.com/jofpin/trape`)
- Modlishka (`https://github.com/drk1wi/Modlishka`)

Let's discuss another aspect of social engineering, mobile-based.

Mobile-based social engineering

Mobile applications are used by attackers to conduct mobile-based social engineering.

Attackers deceive users by copying popular apps and creating harmful mobile apps with appealing features, which they then upload to the major app stores under the same name. Users download the dangerous program unwittingly, allowing the malware to infect their smartphone.

The following are some of the methods used by attackers to undertake mobile-based social engineering.

Creating and distributing malicious apps

In mobile-based social engineering, the attacker uses malicious mobile apps to carry out a social engineering attack. The attacker first produces the malicious program—for example, a game app—and then publishes it on major app stores under well-known brands. Unaware of the malicious program, a user will install it on their phone, assuming it to be legitimate. The device is infected with malware once the software is installed, which sends the user's credentials (usernames, passwords), contact information, and other information to the attacker.

Security applications that are repackaged

To accomplish mobile-based social engineering, attackers may send a false security application. In this attack, the attacker sends something bad to the victim's computer to infect it.

Next, they upload a malicious app to an app store. When the victim logs into their bank account, malware in the system displays a pop-up message instructing them to download an app to their phone to receive security messages. The victim believes they are getting a legitimate app when they download it from the attacker's app store. The attacker collects confidential information, such as the user's bank account login details (username and password), after which the bank sends the victim a second authentication by SMS. The attacker uses this information to gain access to the victim's bank account.

SMiShing

In **SMS Phishing** (**SMiShing**), the SMS text messaging system is used to lure users into taking instant action, such as downloading malware, visiting a malicious web page, or calling a fraudulent phone number. SMiShing messages are crafted to provoke instant action.

Consider Tracy, a software developer at a reputable firm. She receives an SMS supposedly from her bank's security department. It's an urgent request for Tracy to call the phone number mentioned in the SMS right away. Being concerned, she calls to check on her account, assuming the phone number to be a legitimate bank's customer service. Her credit or debit card number and password are requested in a recorded message. Since Tracy considers it to be a legitimate message, she shares her personal information.

A message may say the user has won money or been chosen at random as a lucky winner, and all they must do is pay a small price and disclose their email address, phone number, or other personal information.

Another important aspect of social engineering is threats that come from within an organization or business. Let's talk more about that next.

Threats from within

An insider is a trusted employee who has access to an organization's most valuable assets. An insider attack entails the use of privileged access to intentionally harm an organization's data or information systems. Insiders can easily circumvent security measures, tamper with valuable resources, and get access to sensitive data. Insider attacks could cost the organization a lot of money. They're also harmful because they're simple to launch and hard to detect.

Insider attacks are generally performed by the following:

- **Privileged users**: Insider attacks are typically carried out by the company's most trusted personnel, such as managers and system administrators, who have access to the company's proprietary data and are more likely to misuse it, either purposefully or unintentionally.

- **Employees who are disgruntled**: Attacks may originate from disgruntled employees or contract workers. Disgruntled employees who want to exact vengeance on the company gather information first and then wait for the ideal opportunity to compromise the company's resources.

- **Employees who have been terminated**: When an employee is terminated, they may take vital information about the company with them. After being fired, they access the company's data through backdoors, malware, or their previous credentials if they have not been disabled.

- **Employees who are prone to accidents**: This could be if an employee loses their mobile device by accident, sends an email to the wrong recipients, or leaves a system signed in with confidential data. Unintentional data disclosure can occur if you're not careful.

- **Third parties:** Remote employees, partners, dealers, and vendors are examples of third parties who often have access to information held by the company. However, their systems' security is a concern and could be a potential source of data leaks.

- **Undertrained employees:** Due to a lack of cybersecurity training, a trusted employee becomes an accidental insider. They don't follow security rules, procedures, guidelines, or best practices.

Reasons for insider attacks

Credit card firms, healthcare companies, network service providers, and financial and exchange service providers are all targets for insider attacks.

The following are a few reasons for these attacks:

- **Monetary gain:** Insider attacks are motivated by a desire for financial gain. The insider sells valuable company information to a competitor, steals a colleague's financial information for personal gain, or tampers with the company's or its employees' financial records.

- **Theft of confidential information:** By discovering a job opportunity, preparing someone to get through the interview, and having that person employed by the competition, a competitor might do damage to the target firm, steal crucial information, or even put them out of business.

- **Revenge:** It only takes one angry employee to seek vengeance for the company to be jeopardized. Attacks could come from disgruntled employees or contractors who have negative feelings about the organization.

- **Become a competitor in the future:** Current employees may intend to start their own rival firm, and by accessing the system with the company's confidential data, they may steal or alter the customer list.

- **Competitors bidding:** This is a feature that allows you to see what your competitors are doing. Even the most honest and trustworthy employees can be blackmailed or bribed into divulging the company's crucial information due to corporate espionage.

- **Public awareness:** An unhappy employee may desire to make a political or social statement, and in doing so, the company's confidential data is leaked or damaged.

Different kinds of insider threats

Insider threats can be divided into four categories:

- **Spiteful insider**: Insider threats might be perpetrated by angry or terminated employees that purposefully steal data or destroy company networks by inserting malware into the corporate network.

- **Careless insider**: Careless insiders are more prone to social engineering assaults since they are unaware of potential security concerns or just violate common security rules to satisfy workplace efficiency. Many insider attacks are the result of employees' disregard for security policies, procedures, and practices.

- **Expert insider**: Insiders who work in IT for a living are the most dangerous. They exploit their technical expertise to find flaws and vulnerabilities in the company's network and sell the company's proprietary information to competitors or black-market bidders.

- **Compromised insider**: This is an insider who has been compromised by an outsider. They have access to a company's essential assets or computing devices. This type of threat is more difficult to detect since the outsider poses as a genuine insider.

Why are insider attacks so successful?

Here are some reasons an insider attack is so effective:

- Insider attacks can go undiscovered for years and resolving them is costly.

- Insider assaults are simple to carry out.

- Insider attacks are difficult to prevent and can easily succeed.

- It's tough to tell the difference between damaging behavior and an employee's usual duties. It's difficult to tell whether an employee is acting maliciously.

- Even if harmful conduct has been uncovered, the employee may refuse to accept responsibility, claiming it was an error.

- Employees might easily cover their tracks by altering or deleting logs to conceal harmful behavior.

Let's understand this with the help of an example.

The Dissatisfied Employee

This individual tends to be introverted, cannot manage stress, is in conflict with management, is frustrated with their job or office politics, wants respect or a promotion, or may have been transferred or demoted or issued an employment termination notice. Employees who are dissatisfied with their jobs may sell company secrets and intellectual property to competitors for monetary gain, causing the company to suffer.

Disgruntled employees can use steganography applications to hide company secrets and then send the information to competitors via a work email account as an innocuous-looking communication, such as a photograph, image, or sound file. Because the attacker hides the stolen important information in a picture or image file, no one suspects them.

Insider threat behavioral signs

Insider threat behavioral indicators are things that are typically unusual for the individual and often contrast with their standard behavior and work activity. These atypical patterns need to be investigated further to determine whether they are malicious motives. A lack of employee awareness about security procedures is the most typical indicator of insider threat.

Insider dangers can be identified in a variety of behaviors:

- **Data breach warnings**: Alerts of unauthorized data gathering and transmission on the network could indicate a malware or insider attack. Insiders can also use paper, fax machines, hard drives, and portable or other computing devices.

- **Network logs that are missing or have been changed**: To escape detection, insiders attempt to get access to log files to delete, modify, and edit unauthorized access events, file transfer logs, and other information from systems and network devices. Attacks can be detected by log alteration, deletion, or access alerts.

- **Patterns of network usage**: Malicious activity can be detected by changes in the network patterns of network-specific protocols, packet sizes, sources and destinations, frequency of user application sessions, and bandwidth utilization.

- **Multiple failed login attempts**: By brute-forcing illegal systems or apps, an insider can get access. As a result, many failed efforts could signal an insider threat.

- **Temporal and behavioral changes**: Look for employee behavior changes over time, such as spending capacity, frequent travel, anger management concerns, regular quarrels with coworkers, and laziness. Some fraud indications might also be found when completing tasks.

- **Access at an unusual time and location**: Any inconsistency in an event's timeframe is suspicious and could suggest an insider danger, for instance, if activity is logged on employee systems while they are not present.

- **Critical data that is missing or has been changed**: Disgruntled employees can alter or delete important information to harm the company's reputation.

- **Downloading or copying sensitive data without authorization**: Insiders extract data from the perimeter of the organization using both authorized and malicious tools. Insiders can steal information via installing malware, trojans, and backdoors.

- **Different systems being logged by multiple user accounts**: Malicious activity may be indicated by unusual access times along with a change in the IP address of the system used to connect into the account.

- **Changes in revenue or expenditure over time**: Unexpected and inexplicable changes in an employee's financial situation indicate income derived from other sources. The company should conduct a financial audit to see whether the employee has been involved in any illegal actions.

- **Unauthorized physical asset access**: Employees accessing approved assets without verification, attempting to escalate their rights beyond their job requirements, or attempting to get physical access to assets are all examples of potential threats.

- **Employee productivity increases or decreases**: Employees that are unproductive, intimidating, or who have a sudden spike or reduction in their productivity can indicate questionable behavior if they disagree with intellectual property rights.

- **Working hours that are inconsistent, unusual business activities, and frequent or secret foreign trips**: Employees who engage in suspicious business activities, such as odd login times, odd office hours, unauthorized browsing and downloads, secret visits overseas, and meetings with representatives from other countries or organizations may pose a threat to the company.

- **Excessive behavior as a result of a potential mental health problem**: Some employees displaying unpredictable and excessive behavior, or a rapid change in behavior, could indicate a potential mental health problem. This increases the likelihood of them committing financial fraud, data theft, or physical theft.

- **Indications of vulnerability (drug or alcohol abuse, financial difficulties, gambling, and illegal activities)**: Employees who may be involved in drugs, gambling, alcohol abuse, or having relationship problems, may risk compromising the company's data for monetary gain. Organizations may need to keep a close eye on the activities of the employee on a frequent basis.

- **Complaints about a data breach of sensitive information**: Insider attacks might be identified by information or complaints about sensitive data exposures. Examine customer reviews and complaints for abnormalities, then analyze them to find the insider.

- **Abnormal system and user account access**: An insider threat could be indicated by a discrepancy between the systems assigned and the user accounts utilized to access the systems.

- **Use of social media in an irresponsible manner**: Insiders may try to harm the company by sharing irrelevant material on social media networks.

- **Attempt to enter restricted zones**: Employees with harmful intent may attempt to get access to restricted parts of the company to obtain sensitive data.

- **Social networking site impersonation**: Many people today use social networking sites to create online accounts, share information, and share materials such as photos, blog entries, and music clips. As a result, impersonating someone is relatively easy for an attacker. The victim is likely to trust the attacker and eventually divulge information that will assist the attacker in impersonating them and gaining access to the system.

Let's elaborate a bit more on the last point that we have discussed.

Impersonation on social networking sites

Because social networking sites, such as Facebook, Twitter, and LinkedIn, are so popular, attackers utilize them to impersonate people. An assailant can attack in two ways:

- By creating a false victim profile on a social networking platform

- By obtaining the victim's password or acquiring access to the victim's social media accounts in any other way

Because people post personal and professional information on social networking sites, such as name, address, cell phone number, date of birth, project details, job designation, company name, and location, attackers have a gold mine of information to work with. The more information people reveal on social networking sites, the more probable an attacker will be able to impersonate them and conduct attacks against them, their associates, or their company. They may also attempt to extract corporate data by joining the target organization's employee groups.

Organizational facts, professional details, contacts, connections, and personal details are among the types of information that attackers obtain through social networking sites, which they then use to carry out other types of social engineering assaults.

Facebook impersonation

Facebook is a popular social networking platform that brings people together. It's popular among friends who post comments and upload images, videos, and links. Attackers employ nicknames or aliases instead of real identities to spoof Facebook members. They create fictitious identities and try to add *friends* to access other people's profiles and obtain sensitive information.

Some methods taken by an attacker to persuade a victim to give sensitive information are as follows:

- Create a bogus Facebook user group called *Employees of Company XYZ*.

- Proceed to *friend* or invite actual employees to the bogus *Employees of Company XYZ* group using a fictitious identity.

- Users join the group and provide information, such as their date of birth, educational and professional backgrounds, or the names of their spouses.

- An attacker can compromise a secure facility by using the details of any one of the employees to obtain entry to the building.

Attackers can also make a false account and scan the information on various targets' profile pages on other social networking sites, such as LinkedIn and Twitter, to engage in spear phishing, impersonation, and identity theft.

Threats to corporate networks from social media

Private and corporate users should be aware of the following social and technical security threats before sharing data on a social networking site or expanding their channels, groups, or profiles:

- **Data theft**: Social networking sites are massive databases that are accessed by many people all over the world, increasing the danger of data exploitation.

- **Unintentional data leaks**: Employees may mistakenly share sensitive material about their firm on social networking sites in the absence of a robust policy that draws clear distinctions between personal and corporate information, which could aid an attacker in launching an attack on a target organization.

- **Focused attacks**: Attackers utilize information provided on social networking sites to perform targeted attacks on specific users or businesses.

- **Vulnerability in the network**: All social networking sites have weaknesses and problems, such as login issues and Java vulnerabilities, which attackers might take advantage of. As a result, confidential information relating to the target organization's network could be leaked.

- **Phishing and spam**: Employees who use work email IDs on social networking sites are likely to receive spam and become targets of phishing attacks, which could damage the company's network.

- **Modification of content**: Blogs, channels, groups, profiles, and other platforms can be faked or hacked in the absence of sufficient security measures and efforts to safeguard identity.

So, now that we understand some of the threats that we face, let's next talk about how attackers use the information they gather to steal someone's identity.

Identity theft

Many consumers today are victims of identity theft, so much so, that some state legislators in the United States have passed legislation prohibiting the use or disclosure of an person's SSN during the recruitment process. Identity theft is constantly mentioned in the news. Companies should be educated about identity theft so their own anti-fraud activities are not jeopardized.

Identity theft and identity fraud are terms used to refer to all types of crime in which someone wrongfully obtains and uses another person's personal data in some way that involves fraud or deception, typically for economic gain.

The Identity Theft and Assumption Deterrence Act of 1998, enforced by the Federal Trade Commission, makes the theft of personal information with the intent to commit an unlawful act a federal crime in the United States with penalties of up to 25 years' imprisonment and a maximum fine of $250,000.

Identity thieves steal the following types of personally identifiable information:

- Names
- Home and work locations
- Driver's license number
- SSNs
- Credit reports
- Phone numbers

- Birth dates
- Passport number
- Credit card information

The attacker steals people's identities to commit fraud, such as the following:

- Opening new credit card accounts in the user's name and not paying the bills
- Opening a new phone or wireless account in the user's name or charged to the user's current account
- Obtaining utility services, such as power, heating, or cable TV, using the victim's information
- Opening bank accounts to write phony checks using the victim's personal information
- Making electronic withdrawals from the victim's accounts via an ATM or debit card
- Obtaining loans the victim is responsible for
- Obtaining a driver's license, passport, or other formal ID card containing the victim's information
- Using the victim's name and SSN to receive their government benefits
- Impersonating an employee of a target organization to physically access its facility
- Taking over the victim's insurance policies
- Selling the victim's personal information
- Ordering goods online using a drop-site
- Hijacking email accounts
- Obtaining health services
- Submitting fraudulent tax returns
- Committing other crimes with the intention of providing the victim's name to the authorities during arrest, instead of their own

Let's look at the various forms of identity theft.

Different kinds of identity theft

Identity theft is on the rise, and thieves are continually devising new methods and tactics to obtain various types of target data.

Some of the methods by which attackers steal targets' identities to allow them to commit fraud and other criminal activities are as follows:

- **Child identity theft**: A minor's identity is stolen. This is an advantage since it may go undiscovered for an extended period of time. Identity thieves will use a child's SSN, along with a different date of birth, to apply for credit accounts, loans, and utility services, as well as renting a place to live and applying for government benefits, after the child is born. The attacker steals people's identities to commit fraud, such as opening new credit card accounts in the user's name and not paying the bills.

- **Criminal identity theft**: One of the most common and damaging types of identity theft is credit card fraud. To avoid being charged with a crime, a criminal assumes another person's identity. When they are apprehended or arrested, they reveal their false identity. The greatest approach to avoid identity theft from criminals is to keep all personal information private, which includes using safe internet practices and being wary of *shoulder surfers*.

- **Financial identity theft**: When a thief steals a victim's bank account or credit card information and uses it illegally, this is known as identity theft. They can use their stolen identity to max out a credit card and take money from the account, or open a bank account and take out loans and apply for new credit cards. Viruses, phishing assaults, and data breaches are used to gain the information needed to hack into the victim's account and steal their personal information.

- **Driver's license identity theft**: This is the simplest sort of identity theft because it just requires a little sophistication. A person's driver's license can be lost or stolen at any time. When a stolen driver's license falls into the wrong hands, the offender can sell it or use it to conduct traffic offenses that the victim is unaware of and fails to pay fines for, resulting in their license being suspended or revoked.

- **Identity theft insurance**: Insurance fraud is a serious problem. It has a strong link to medical identity theft. It can make it more difficult to pay medical costs, raising insurance premiums, and even making it more difficult to obtain future medical coverage.

- **Medical identity theft**: This can be the most hazardous type of identity theft, in which the perpetrator obtains medical supplies and claims health insurance or healthcare services using the victim's name or information without the victim's consent or knowledge. Erroneous entries in the victim's medical records are common because of medical identity theft. As a result of the frequent erroneous entries in the victim's medical records, doctors may make misleading diagnoses and make life-threatening judgments.

- **Taxpayer identity theft**: This occurs when a criminal obtains the victim's SSN to file false tax returns and receive false tax refunds. It makes it harder for the victim to obtain their lawful tax refunds, resulting in a financial loss. Phishing emails are one of the most common methods used by criminals to obtain information from their victims. Adopting safe internet practices is one way to protect yourself from identity theft.

- **Cloning and concealment of identity**: This category of identity theft includes all types of identity theft in which criminals seek to impersonate someone else to conceal their identity. Illegal immigrants, people fleeing from creditors, or people who simply wish to be *anonymous* could be the culprits.

- **False identity theft**: This is one of the most advanced sorts of identity theft, in which the criminal gets information from multiple victims to build a new identity. To begin, they steal an SSN and use it in conjunction with a false name, date of birth, address, and other information to create a new identity. The offender opens new accounts, loans, credit cards, phones, and other goods and services using this new identity.

- **Theft of social identity**: This is another common type of identity theft in which the perpetrator steals the victim's SSN to obtain various benefits, such as selling it to an undocumented person, defrauding the government by opening a new bank account, taking out loans, or applying for and receiving a new passport.

- **Theft of personal information from wallets, computers, laptops, cell phones, backup media, and other sources**: Physical theft is a widespread occurrence. Attackers steal personal electronics from hotels, clubs, restaurants, parks, beaches, and other public venues. They can extract valuable data from these sources if given enough time.

Identity theft warning signs

People don't recognize they've been the victim of identity theft until they start having unanticipated and unauthorized problems. As a result, it is critical that people are aware of the warning signals that their identities have been compromised.

Some of the indications of identity theft are as follows:

- Charges on your credit card you are unfamiliar with.
- Credit card, bank, and utility statements are no longer sent.
- Creditors contact you about an unidentified account in your name.

- You have a long list of traffic tickets on your record that you did not commit.

- You are billed for medical care or services that you have never received.

- There are multiple tax returns filed in your name.

- You are unable to access your own account and take out loans or utilize other services since you have been prohibited access.

- Due to stolen mail, you are not receiving your energy, gas, water, or other utility bills.

- Changes in your personal medical records reveal a condition you don't have.

- Receiving news that your personal information has been hacked or misused because of a data breach at a company where you work or have an account.

- A cash withdrawal from your bank account that you don't recall.

- Calls from debit or credit card fraud prevention offices informing you of questionable activity on your account.

- A denial of government benefits to you and your child because those benefits are already being received by another account that uses your child's SSN.

- Your medical insurance plan denies your legitimate medical claim since it had been previously submitted by someone else. Your medical records were tampered with, forcing you to exceed your benefit limit.

So, what can we do to protect ourselves and minimize our vulnerability to social engineering? Let's discuss that next.

Countermeasures

To get access to the targeted company's information resources, social engineers may exploit and use human behavior (such as politeness, excitement for work, laziness, or being naive). Social engineering attacks are difficult to detect since the victim may be unaware that they have been deceived. They're extremely like the other types of attacks used to get access to a company's sensitive data. To protect itself from social engineering attacks, a corporation must assess the danger of various types of attacks, calculate potential damages, and raise awareness among its staff.

Countermeasures against social engineering

Social engineering techniques are used by attackers to persuade people to give secret information about their businesses. They employ social engineering to commit fraud, identity theft, industrial espionage, and other nefarious activities. Organizations must build effective policies and processes to protect themselves from social engineering attacks; yet, simply developing them is not enough.

To be effective, a company should do the following:

- Communicate policies to employees and give appropriate education and training.

- Employees in high-risk occupations would benefit from specialized training to protect themselves from social engineering attacks.

- Obtain employee signatures on a declaration stating they are familiar with the company's policies.

- Define the ramifications of violating the policies.

User awareness, effective internal network controls, and security policies, procedures, and processes, are the major goals of social engineering defense methods.

Users can make the best security decisions with the support of official security rules and procedures. The following safeguards should be included.

Policies for passwords

Password rules that have the following guidelines aid with password security:

- Passwords should be changed on a frequent basis.

- Passwords that are easy to guess should be avoided; answers to social engineering questions such as "*Where were you born*?", "*What is the name of your pet*?", or "*What is your favorite movie*?" can be used to guess passwords.

- If a user's password guessing attempts fail more than a specific number of times, the user's account will be blocked.

- Make your passwords long (at least 6-8 characters) and complex (with a mix of alphanumeric and unusual characters).

- Don't give out your passwords to anyone.

Password security policies frequently contain recommendations for effective password management, such as the following:

- Do not share a computer account.

- Do not use the same password for multiple accounts.

- Don't save passwords on your computer or write them down on a piece of paper or a sticky note.

- Passwords should not be shared over the phone, by email, or SMS.

- Before leaving the computer, be sure it's locked or turned off.

Policies concerning physical security

The following areas are covered by physical security policies:

- Provide **identification cards** (**ID cards**), uniforms, and other access control measures to the organization's employees.

- Office security or personnel must escort visitors to designated visitor rooms or lounges.

- Restrict access to certain areas of an organization to prevent unauthorized users from compromising the security of sensitive data.

- Dispose of old documents that contain valuable information by using equipment such as paper shredders and burn bins as this prevents information gathering by attackers using techniques such as dumpster diving.

- Employ security personnel in an organization to protect people and property—supplement trained security personnel with alarm systems, surveillance cameras, and other equipment.

Planning for defense

To maximize effectiveness against social engineering attacks, we must be intentional and deliberate about having a strong plan in place:

- **Social engineering campaign**: To see how employees might react to real social engineering attacks, a business should run multiple social engineering exercises on a varied set of people using various tactics.

- **Gap analysis**: A gap analysis assesses the organization based on industry-leading practices, emerging threats, and mitigation methods, using information acquired from the social engineering campaign.

- **Remediation strategies**: Organizations establish a detailed remediation plan to minimize the vulnerabilities or loopholes discovered based on the results of the gap analysis evaluation. The plan is mostly educating and raising employee awareness based on their positions, as well as recognizing and managing any hazards to the company.

Discovering insider threats

Insiders are responsible for most data breaches, making them even more difficult to detect and prevent. Insiders are usually aware of the organization's security flaws, which they exploit. Insider threats can be used to steal confidential information, thus it's critical to handle them cautiously. They are difficult to stop and can result in significant financial losses and company disruptions.

The following are some ways of detecting insider threats.

Controls for insider threats

For security professionals, insider data risk adds another degree of complication. It necessitates the creation of security infrastructure that allows for effective monitoring of user permissions, access controls, and user actions.

Controls for deterrence

The security framework for the organization must include safeguards, follow employee and IT professional recommendations, establish a separation of roles, and assign privileges. The security risks to the organization's key assets are eliminated or minimized by these security policies.

Data Loss Prevention (**DLP**) is one of the deterrence controls that security professionals must have in place to prevent insider threats. **Identity and Access Management** (**IAM**) is another tool that is also available.

The following are some of the deterrent controls.

DLP tools:

- Symantec Data Loss Prevention (https://www.Symantec.com)
- SecureTrust Data Loss Prevention (https://Securetrust.com)
- Check Point Data Loss Prevention (https://www.checkpoint.com)

IAM tools:

- SailPoint IdentitylQ (`https://www.sailpoint.com`)
- RSA SecurlD Suite (`https://www.rsa.com`)
- Core Access Assurance Suite (`https://www.coresecurity.com`)

Countermeasures against insider threats

Insider hazards can be prevented or minimized by implementing the following safety measures:

- **Separation of duties and rotation of responsibilities**: To limit the amount of control or influence possessed by any one person, divide tasks among numerous employees. This helps to prevent fraud, abuse, and conflicts of interest, as well as the discovery of control failures (such as security bypassing and data theft). The rotation of responsibilities at random periods aids in the prevention of fraud and abuse of rights in an organization.

- **Least privileges**: Provide users with only the level of access they need to complete their assigned duties. This contributes to information security.

- **Controlled access**: Unauthorized users are prevented from accessing key assets and resources by access controls in various sectors of an organization.

- **Logging and auditing**: Perform logging and audits on a regular basis to ensure that corporate resources are not being misused.

- **Employee monitoring**: Use employee monitoring software that records all user sessions and allows security professionals to evaluate them.

- **Legal policies**: Enforce legal policies to prevent employees from abusing the company's resources or stealing critical information.

- **Archive vital data**: Keep a record of the organization's vital data in the form of archives that can be used as backup resources if necessary.

- **Employee cybersecurity training**: Educate employees on how to safeguard their credentials and the company's confidential information. They'll be able to spot social engineering attempts and respond appropriately with mitigations and reporting.

- **Employee background checks**: Conduct complete background checks on all potential employees before employing them, using Google and social networking sites, as well as consulting prior employers.

- **Periodic risk assessment**: Conduct a risk assessment on key assets on a regular basis to identify weaknesses and implement protective solutions against both internal and external threats.

- **Monitoring privileged users**: Privileged users should be monitored more closely, as these accounts can be exploited to install malicious malware or a logic bomb on the system or network.

- **Deactivation of credentials for terminated personnel**: Disable all access profiles for terminated employees. Immediately after termination, networks, systems, applications, and data are destroyed.

- **Periodic risk assessments**: Complete risk assessments on all the organization's essential assets, then establish and maintain a risk management strategy to protect those assets from insiders and outsiders.

- **Numerous layers of protection**: Use multiple layers of defense to prevent and defend important assets from insider attacks. To thwart such assaults, develop suitable remote access policies and procedures.

- **Physical security**: Create a competent security team to oversee the organization's physical security.

- **Surveillance**: Install video cameras to keep an eye on all your important assets. On all key servers, install and enable screen-capture software.

Countermeasures against identity theft

The following are several safeguards that, if implemented, will lessen the likelihood of identity theft:

- All documents holding confidential information should be secured or shredded.

- Make sure your name isn't on any marketers' hit lists.

- Review credit card statements on a regular basis.

- Never give your personal details over the phone.

- Empty your mailbox immediately to keep mail safe.

- Suspect and double-check all requests for personal information.

- Personal information should not be made public.

- Unless necessary, do not display account or contact numbers.

- Regularly monitor your internet financial activities.

- Never give away personal identifiers, such as your father's name, your pet's name, your place of residence, or your birth city, on social media platforms.

- On all online accounts, enable two-factor authentication.

- Never share or access critical information over public Wi-Fi.

- Install host security software on your computer, such as a firewall and antivirus.

The following are some additional anti-identity theft safeguards:

- Shred credit card offers and "convenience checks" that aren't needed.

- Use strong passwords for any bank accounts and don't save any financial information on the system.

- Keep your social security card, passport, license, and other valuable personal information concealed and protected.

- Check your phone and cell phone bills for calls you did not make.

- Read the privacy policies on websites.

- Before you click on a link in an email or instant chat, use caution.

Countermeasures against phishing

Here are some additional ways and tools to protect yourself from attacks.

Anti-phishing toolbars

Netcraft: `https://toolbar.netcraft.com`

The Netcraft anti-phishing community is a massive neighborhood watch program that empowers the most vigilant and knowledgeable members to protect everyone in the community against phishing assaults. The Netcraft toolbar helps keep users up to date and aware of security issues on the sites they visit on a regular basis and filters harmful sites. The toolbar has a lot of useful information about famous websites. This information will assist you in making an informed decision about the website's integrity.

PhishTank: `https://phishtank.com`

PhishTank is an online collaborative storehouse for phishing data and information. Developers and researchers can use an open API to integrate anti-phishing data into their programs.

Tools for social engineering

Social Engineering Toolkit (SET): `https://www.trustedsec.com`

SET is an open source, Python-based application for social engineering penetration testing. It's a general exploit that can be used to carry out advanced attacks against humans to breach a target and force them to disclose sensitive information. Email, online, and USB attacks are all classified as SET attacks based on the attack vector utilized to deceive humans. Human vulnerability is exploited by the toolkit, which takes advantage of people's trusting, scared, greedy, and helpful natures.

Using OhPhish to audit an organization's security for phishing attacks

The goal of initiating phishing campaigns against client employees is to examine employees' sensitivity to phishing attacks and to assist the client company in reducing the risks that result when employees fall prey to phishing attacks.

OhPhish: `https://ciso.eccouncil.org/phishing-solutions/`

OhPhish is a web-based tool for determining whether employees are vulnerable to social engineering attacks. It's a phishing simulation tool that gives businesses a platform to run phishing simulation campaigns on their staff. The platform records the responses and gives management information.

OhPhish may be used to check an organization's security for phishing attacks utilizing a variety of phishing techniques, such as enticing to click, credential harvesting, sending attachments, training, vishing, and smishing.

You have been given some great tools and insight into identifying and countering social engineering attacks. Having a plan and educating your employees is critical to raising awareness of all the different ways a social engineer can attack.

Summary

This chapter covered the fundamentals of social engineering as well as the many stages of a social engineering attack. It also covered a variety of people-based, computer-based, and mobile-based social engineering strategies. Insider threats, including the different kinds of insider threats, were explored here. We presented an outline of social networking site impersonation and also went over the many sorts of identity theft. The chapter concluded with a detailed explanation of numerous warning indicators to look for and actions to take to protect yourself from social engineering attacks, insider threats, and identity theft.

In the next chapter, we will be discussing the process of sniffing.

Questions

As we conclude, here is a list of questions for you to test your knowledge regarding this chapter's material. You will find the answers in the *Assessments* section of the *Appendix*:

1. The purpose of social engineering is _____.

    A. To create distrust with people

    B. To take advantage of human behavior

    C. Piggybacking

    D. Instant messaging

2. Phishing takes place using which of the following?

    A. Websites

    B. Email

    C. Piggybacking

    D. Instant messaging

3. How can you best avoid a social engineering attack?

    A. By hiring additional helpdesk/support staff

    B. To avoid scanning, install or upgrade a firewall

    C. Employee training

    D. An IDS logs review

4. Factors that can predispose a business to social engineering attacks are all of the following except for which one?

    A. Inadequate security policies

    B. Multiple locations

    C. Frequent, ongoing security education

    D. Unrestricted information access

Further reading

If you want to dive further down the *rabbit hole* with social engineering, I suggest you visit the Security Through Education website at `https://www.social-engineer.org/`, which is a great online resource for frameworks, podcasts, and other resources.

Section 2: A Plethora of Attack Vectors

In this section, you will learn about a plethora of attack vectors, including network-based, software-based, mobile devices, wireless networks, and IoT devices.

This part of the book comprises the following chapters:

- *Chapter 9, Malware and Other Digital Attacks*
- *Chapter 10, Sniffing and Evading IDS, Firewalls, and Honeypots*
- *Chapter 11, Hacking Wireless Networks*
- *Chapter 12, Hacking Mobile Platforms*

9
Malware and Other Digital Attacks

The difference between a threat and a treat is one letter. Malware is a treat depending on which side of the malware you're on. Malware is probably one of the biggest threats we have from a security perspective, for our networks in a professional capacity as well as our own private networks and devices.

As you read through this chapter, you will gain a greater understanding and awareness regarding what malware is, what it's designed to do, and the various methods of how malware infects a target.

In this chapter, we will cover the following main topics:

- So, what is malware?
- What is a Trojan?
- Viruses and worms
- **Denial of Service (DoS)** threats
- Session-hijacking threats
- Master list of countermeasures

One of the hardest struggles **information technology** (**IT**) people and end users deal with is the fact we've gotten so complacent and stuck in the mindset of networks that we don't care how they work.

Nathaniel Branden stated: "*The first step towards change is awareness. The second step is acceptance.*" This reminds me of *The Untouchables*, one of my favorite movies, starring Sean Connery and Kevin Costner.

Kevin plays Eliot Ness, one of the Untouchables, while Sean plays a street cop who's very much aware of the environment. On telling him he is going to go after Al Capone, Sean reveals to him all the stuff that's going on and then proceeds to ask: "*What are you willing to do about it?*" The question is, are we going to be complacent, or are we going to think a little bit differently here?

That's my goal for this chapter: to get us thinking differently.

So, what is malware?

Simply stated…it's a piece of software or computer program used to perform malicious actions or attacks on a target. Its name gives away what it does. Malware is a blend of two words: malicious and software. We have malware for computers, phones, tablets, and so on. The mobile industry is huge with malware right now. Once installed, attackers can potentially gain total control over your devices, or at least over the data on your devices.

Attackers can infect any computing device—including tablets and smartphones—with malware. Any person, company, or device is a target. The more computers and devices an attacker can infect, the more money they can make. In fact, they don't care who they infect—they just want to infect as many devices and people as possible. It's a numbers game. And guess what? It comes in various forms. Malware is just a categorization of security threats.

What's the purpose of malware?

The goals of malware include the following:

- Stealing data off your machine
- Access to customer lists
- Accounting data
- Harvesting usernames and passwords
- Deleting files

- Changing system settings
- Occupying space on your systems and encrypting it

If an attacker is not after you personally, they're after your resources and their access to others. Therefore, you have an obligation to make sure your machine is not compromised for the safety of others.

People who create, deploy, and benefit from malware can range from the whole scope of individuals who are just trying to hack their own internal network, to organized crime and government organizations. This is such a big business that people who create these sophisticated malware products are often dedicated to this purpose. It can end up growing like a snowball accumulating more and more snow as it rolls along. If I can get one piece of malware installed on any of your devices, I can use it to add additional pieces of malware.

This is so profitable that it has become a full-time job. And how do they make money off this? Once an attacker has developed and deployed their malware, they often sell the machines they've infected to other individuals or organizations. Those individuals start installing more pieces of malware, and that's where the snowball comes into play; eventually your machine ends up being a member of a botnet. This **botnet** is basically a mishmash of systems out there that are totally controlled by the attacker. The button can be remotely controlled, which cyber criminals then go and use for their purposes, and sometimes, they sell it to other cyber criminals. The reason we see such an influx of malware right now is that it is massively profitable.

You need a good understanding of how to speak **Trojan** (more about this in the next section) to survive. The people who create malware—and the attackers out there creating malware—use components that can help them achieve the goals they have in mind.

The basic components of malware include the following:

- **Crypter**—This software program conceals the existence of malware. Attackers and hackers use this software to elude antivirus from detecting it. It also protects the malware from undergoing reverse-engineering analysis.

- **Downloader**—This type of Trojan downloads other types of malware or even malicious code and files off the internet. Attackers install downloaders when they first gain access to the system.

- **Dropper**—If an attacker needs to install malware or some code on the system to make it run, a dropper will do this covertly. The dropper can contain unidentifiable malware code that's undetected by antivirus scanners. It's capable of downloading additional files as needed to execute the malware on the target system.

- **Exploit**—This part of the malware contains the code or sequence of commands needed to take advantage of your device. It's the code an attacker uses to breach the system securely or breach the system security. Based on the vulnerabilities an attacker might use, the exploits have different categories, including local exploits and remote exploits.

- **Injector**—This program injects the exploit or the code from the malware into the system. It's a way of hiding or preventing malware from being removed.

- **Malicious code**—This piece of code is malicious. It defines the basic functionality of malware and comprises the commands, resulting in the security breach itself. It can take the form of ActiveX controls, published content, Java applets, and browser plugins.

- **Obfuscators**—These are programs attackers use to conceal malware or malicious code using different techniques. It makes it a lot harder for security programs, antivirus programs, and professionals to find it and remove it.

- **Packer**—This software compresses the malware file and converts the code and data of the malware to an unreadable format, making it hard for your antivirus software to detect it.

- **Payload**—This is the file that is activated. It can be used for deleting your files, infecting the system, encrypting; it's basically the big bad boy.

Next, let's look at the different types of malware.

Types of malware

How does malware get in? Malware itself can be broken down into a couple of types, as outlined here:

- **Viruses**—These require human assistance. You must execute the file to get infected with a virus.

- **Worms**—These are automatic. They're called worms because they squirm throughout your network infrastructure and infect targets all on their own. They don't need any human interaction.

- **Backdoor**—This allows unauthorized user access by installing malicious code and exploiting system vulnerabilities. Allows continued access to an attacker.

- **Rootkit**—This is a malicious program or group of programs that installs and executes malicious code without being recognized by the end user.

- **Botnets**—Botnets are a group or network of electronic devices used for fraudulent and malicious cyberattacks. Bots are a tool used to automate large-scale group attacks such as data theft, malware distribution, and attacks on servers.

- **Ransomware**—This malicious software can limit, prevent, block access, or publish information. Usually, some type of ransom is demanded to allow user access again.

- **Spyware**—This allows an attacker to covertly gather information about user activity without being noticed. The data gathered could be used for malicious purposes by the attacker or a third-party attacker.

- **Adware**—Adware is unwanted or unsolicited advertisement-supported software installed on a computer. It generally shows up as pop-up ads while using a web browser.

Next, let's look at the life cycle of malware.

The life cycle of malware

As with any good little monster, there are phases or stages we go through within this life cycle, as outlined here:

- **Stage 1**—We create the malware. Anyone who has any type of programming knowledge can create a type of malware or worm. In fact, if you don't have that skill set, you can also use some cool things out there for script kiddies, such as a construction kit.

- **Stage 2**—Replicate the malware, meaning that we need to get it onto a target machine, plan how we will do that, and make sure it gets implemented.

- **Stage 3**—This is the discovery stage. When somebody discovers something is on their machine or is causing it to act a little different or funny, we refer to this as the detection stage.

- **Stage 4**—The resolution stage. This is typically done by the manufacturers of the antivirus products because they will try to create different types of defenses against the malware, and then of course they deploy those out.

- **Stage 5**—The purging stage is when we eliminate the malware itself, and then the whole process starts over. This is because one piece of malware will not necessarily last the test of time. We're always creating new and improved ones.

As far as the malware itself is concerned, once we get to *Stage 2* between replication discovery, we have two different phases.

Phase 1 – Infection phase

Several different things happen during this phase. The malware replicates and attaches itself to the targeted file or program we specified when we created it.

The malware needs to implement itself. It needs some way of implementing itself, so we have what's referred to as an event. For example, let's set it up so that the malware fires off when someone installs an application by infecting the startup files. Every time someone installs the program, the malware gets reinstalled. This is extremely prominent right now in the pirating world. You download pirated material; you may get a surprise!

We can also set up a startup setting that would modify certain sections of the registry, to make sure the malware activates every time it starts up.

Another thing we might implement, albeit a little old-school, is creating a **terminate-and-stay-ready** (**TSR**) program, which is basically where we hide the malware inside of memory, and it just executes or waits for a trigger, but waiting inside of **random-access memory** (**RAM**). In fact, there are some pieces of malware where you reboot the machine and they just get loaded right back into RAM again.

Phase 2 – Attack phase

The attack phase is where we see things such as corruption taking place. During the attack phase, the malware executes and does things to corrupt our files, such as deleting them completely, maybe going through and saying, *Find all JPEGs and whack them*, or *Find all COM files and delete those and anything you can do to make the system unstable*. I might have it alter the file contents or, better yet, I just change the file content, which could result in the system slowing down because the **operating system** (**OS**) doesn't understand how to handle the modified files. We can also execute tasks. This is in reference to having tasks performed that aren't related to the application at all. As you already know, the unexpected happening is a good indication you've got malware, meaning that the application did something it's not designed to do.

Phase 3 – Camouflage

This phase is where the malware will hide itself so that it can't be detected. In fact, some of the better malware has been written so that it doesn't execute until it has spread as thoroughly as it can, throughout the environment, host machine, or network, and then executes.

Next, we'll talk about how these pieces of malware get into the target systems.

How is malware injected into a target system?

There are several ways a piece of malware can get into your environment, as outlined here:

- **Untrusted sources for software**—This not only applies to desktop platforms but also mobile devices. Apple once announced as many as 4,000 apps were infected by the XcodeGhost malware product. When searching for a piece of software on your PC—for example, WinZip—do you go to `winzip.com` or just click on the first link, which may not be the actual vendor? Of course, when end users see a popup such as this, they always hit **Yes**—they never hit **No**. Why? Because they want the software.

- **Installation**—When installing a program, I always select **Custom install**. I never do a basic install. I'm always watching, and I never hit click, click, click, click. I take my time because many times, the application or the vendor is generating additional revenue by installing toolbars on your PC, which can lead to other malware infecting you.

- **Propagation**—Once you get one, I guarantee you're going to start getting more.

- **Email attachments**—Usually with malicious attachments.

- **Pirated software**—This would include not just the main software being pirated, but also *crackers* that claim (and some do work, while they inject malware) to turn trial software into full products.

- **Disabling security products or firewalls**—These actions will compromise any system's security.

- **Logic bomb**—This is a type of malware that gets triggered when the conditions for its operation are met. Logic bombs can be activated by events such as a particular date, time, or system count. For example, if an attacker corrupted your computer with a **remote access Trojan** (**RAT**) and you attempted to remove it, the RAT may be programmed to activate and delete your files at that moment or the next time you boot up.

- **Not updating or running antiviruses and malware**—Antiviruses don't get all the malware and all the malware don't get all the antiviruses. You need to use both. Not updating and running them is a huge detriment.

  You can ask yourself the following questions to help you assess this:

  - Does it have an icon associated with it or is it a process that's running? Look at the description. Any reputable process, when the developer creates it, will list a description with it.

- Does the application itself, or the process running, live inside of a Windows or user profile directory? It's important to know this because those directories are accessed by any user on the device.

- Are there any weird **Uniform Resource Locators** (**URLs**) in their strings—especially if somebody sends you a link? Be careful about the latest trend whereby people are creating shortcut links to websites.

- Also, look for any open **Transmission Control Protocol/Internet Protocol** (**TCP/IP**) endpoints where your machine is just listening on a port that you can't explain.

Now, let's talk about something really interesting—something that we see from nation-state organizations.

Advanced persistent threats

Advanced persistent threats, also referred to as **APTs**, should be a concern for any organization because they can damage not only resources but also your reputation.

What is an APT? Well, this is a type of network attack where the attacker gains access to your environment and then remains there for a long time without being detected. The term *advanced* is a representation of using technologies to exploit underlying vulnerabilities, the term *persistent* references the external **command-and-control** (**C2**) process that is continually pulling data and monitoring the victim's network, and *threat* signifies human involvement and coordination.

As I mentioned before, these types of attacks are extremely sophisticated. They involve well-planned and coordinated techniques, techniques that include things such as erasing evidence of our activities after we've done our evil tasks. The information that can be extrapolated by an attacker through an APT attack includes things such as classified documents, credentials for your users, personal information, network information, transaction information, credit card details, business strategies, and control system access.

Overall, the main objective is to try to obtain sensitive information, rather than destroying a network or sabotaging it. One of the best examples—and the most sophisticated piece of malware ever detected—was probably Stuxnet. This worm was used against Iran in 2010. Its complexity tells us that only a nation-state actor could have been involved with it.

Initially, this worm was introduced via infected **Universal Serial Bus** (**USB**) drives and contained three modules: a worm that executed the main payload, a link file that automatically executed the propagated worm copies, and a rootkit that hid all the malicious files. The worm itself went across the network, searching for the **Siemens Step7** software on computers controlling **programmable logic controllers**, or **PLCs**. Once it found target machines, the malware injected its rootkit into the PLC and the Step7 software, modified its code, and sent commands to the PLC while displaying normal operations. This was specifically targeted against the centrifuge for Iran's uranium-enrichment facilities. The malware forced the centrifuges to spin very fast for 15 minutes, and then returned them to normal speed. Within 5 months of the attack, the excessive speed changes caused the centrifuges to break, resulting in the loss of about 1,000 centrifuges. So, yes—pretty sneaky.

APTs have different characteristics, and these characteristics are the how, what, and why attackers design and plan their attacks. Let's have a look at this more closely:

- First, we have the objectives. The main objective of any of these types of attacks is to gather as much sensitive information by gaining access to an organization's network. But it shouldn't be limited to that—we could also include spying for political or strategic goals as well.

- There are also timelines, which refers to the time that is utilized by the attacker for looking at the target system for any vulnerabilities.

- Then there are the resources—the amount of knowledge, tools, and techniques that are going to be required to perform an attack. These types of attacks, again, are more sophisticated and are typically performed by highly skilled attackers, and when it comes to APTs, to have those levels of resources, it really does point us a lot to nation-state actors.

- There's also risk tolerance, which we define as the level up to which an attack remains undetected. This helps attackers to remain undetected on the network for extensive periods. There are also the skills and methods that are used by attackers to perform these types of attacks. This could include things such as social engineering techniques to gather information or even **open source intelligence** (**OSINT**) tools.

- We then have the actions. This is what makes them different from other types of cyberattacks. Again, our objective typically is to maintain our presence, so we've got to make sure that whatever actions we're taking don't get flagged.

- There's also the characteristic of attack points. This refers to the numerous attempts made to gain entry into a targeted network. To be successful in gaining initial access, we need to make sure (or, I should say, the attacker) to do a ton of research to again identify vulnerabilities.

- Then, there are the numbers involved in the attack. Remember we talked about botnets earlier? Well, in the case of a government agency, they're going to have their own botnet, and these host systems will be used as part of APT attacks against either organized crime or other nation states.

- Then, there's the knowledge source, which is defined as the gathering of information through online sources about specific threats.

- We then have multi-phases. This is one of the more important characteristics for APTs—that they follow multiple phases to execute an attack, and typically, those include reconnaissance, access, discovery, capture, and data exfiltration.

- We are tailored for vulnerabilities or to vulnerabilities. We want to make sure that the code we create, or the attacker creates is written and designed in such a way that the targets on the network have those specific vulnerabilities.

- And then, we have multiple entry points. What this means is an attacker, once they've made their initial connection or entry, they're going to create additional entry points so if one gets discovered, they can still get back in.

Now, when it comes to APTs, it's important to note that they are very similar to zero-day exploits because they are going to be made up of malware that hasn't been available or existed in the wild before. The issue with Stuxnet was that it accidentally got released into the wild, and that's how we found out about it. But typically, it's going to be able to bypass all your security mechanisms, your firewalls, your antivirus, your **intrusion prevention systems (IPSs)**, your **intrusion detection systems (IDSs)**, and email spam filters because it hasn't been used before.

APT attacks are usually impossible to detect, but unexpected user account activities or the presence of a backdoor Trojan, such as if we see even tons of data leaving the network or being transferred, might be a warning that you have an APT somewhere on your network.

Next, let's talk about Trojans.

What is a Trojan?

A **Trojan** is a type of malicious software disguised or included with a legitimate piece of software. It's hiding inside. The reason we hide it is that it's easy to install. The easiest way to get something done is to have the user do it for us. When it comes to Trojans, some people get this confused.

The Trojan horse gets its background from Greek mythology about the Trojan War, where the Greeks attacked the city of Troy. At the end of the war, the Greeks came up with a final plan of attack—they would build a giant hollow wooden horse (and for some strange reason, they were sacred to Trojans), and the hollow horse would be filled with soldiers. The Trojans brought the horse into the city and when they went to bed, the soldiers came out, including Brad Pitt, all glistening, and they ransacked the city. That's basically the same concept here. We're going to have a legitimate program, but our Trojan will contain some type of spyware, keylogger, a rootkit, or some other type of program we can use to get back in. We're going to have the victim bring the software onto their computer. Once executed, the Trojan can relay information or steal the data outright.

As far as the life cycle is concerned, the following steps occur:

1. We start off by creating the payload. This is the program we are going to design to do some specific things—for example, finding credit card numbers or personal information.

2. After creating this payload, we take our legitimate programs, such as Office, the latest version of Windows, an mp3, a movie, or an antivirus.

3. We inject the payload inside the legitimate program and put it out there via torrents, websites, or even a USB drop—dropping a USB thumb drive somewhere in the parking lot of a company or in the hallway of a company and waiting to see who plugs it in—or **Internet Relay Chat** (**IRC**) channels. This transmission method relies heavily on a social engineering concept, which is *I want something for nothing*—for example, if Microsoft just released the latest version of Office and you see it up on a torrent site, download, and install it. Why did somebody put that up on a torrent site?

4. After downloading it, you simply install the program. As you install the application, the Trojan gets the same permission as the user that's currently logged in. It can then start modifying itself. There are Trojans that morph themselves to make it harder to detect them. They transmit themselves and start infecting other nodes inside of your environment.

There are many different types of Trojans—let's discuss them next.

Types of Trojans

It's important to understand and know the different types of Trojans and how they are used.

Notification Trojans

There are several different types of notification Trojans. The whole purpose of a notification Trojan is to send the IP address of the target it has infected back to the attacker. We can do that at different times or in different aspects, depending on the type of notification Trojan you have installed. Here are some examples:

- **IRC Trojan**—This simply uses the IRC channels out there to communicate with the attacker.

- **PHP Hypertext Preprocessor (PHP) notification Trojan**—This Trojan sends its data by connecting to the PHP server the attacker owns or has pwned.

- **NetSend notification Trojan**—This basically sends information or commands to the targeted machine via the `NetSend` command.

- **Internet Chat Query (ICQ) notifications**—These are just different mechanisms or communication channels to talk with the attacker from the target that lets you know, "*Hey, I got installed*". Remember—the purpose of a Trojan is mass distribution. So, I'm just sitting here waiting via one of these channels for my payload to report back to me so that I can use the ICQ channels or through email.

Botnet Trojans

A botnet Trojan helps me combine multiple pwned systems together so that I can issue one command and control all the machines that have been infected with this Trojan simultaneously. One of the biggest targets for these types of Trojans would be educational, government, and military systems.

Another phrase you might hear when we talk about botnets is a zombie computer, which is simply a computer that's been infected with botnet Trojans. The attacker can bring these machines online at their whim to use them for things such as sending spam or launching a DoS attack against another company. The attacker, remotely with one command, can implement a DoS attack through their botnet. They could also use it for sending out mass mailings via spam, **Simple Mail Transfer Protocol (SMTP)**, or click fraud.

We could also use it for stealing product keys, login **identifiers (IDs)**, credit card numbers—all kinds of information. The reason why educational, government, and military systems are very popular for these types of Trojans is because of how many computers are in an educational environment, especially computer labs.

Proxy-server Trojans

A proxy-server Trojan starts proxying out for us once it gets loaded on our target, meaning the attacker can use the victim's machine or pass through it. We turn the victim's machine into a proxy server to make it possible for us to go after another target and get all the blame put on the first victim. It's like creating a proxy chain, and—believe it or not— there are thousands of machines out on the internet currently infected with proxy servers running as a hidden service on a machine without the end user or the enterprise admin knowing it.

FTP-server Trojans

If I can inject your system with this type of Trojan, I will install a **File Transfer Protocol (FTP)** server on your machine. Once it's been infected, the Trojan sends connection information back to the attacker almost like a notification, but we're simply going to use port 21 for that machine. And then, of course, at that point, the attacker will be given full access via the FTP protocol. They will also install additional malware to make it a little bit easier to get into the life cycle of a Trojan.

Again, the type of information an attacker can pull off a target machine would include things such as credit card information, confidential information, documents named password.docx, or email addresses, but as far as the connection is concerned, you'll just see an FTP service running.

Common Trojans

Let's review some common Trojans and what they can do.

VNC Trojan

A **Virtual Network Computing (VNC)** Trojan has two aspects to it, as outlined here:

- First, we simply infect your machine with a VNC Trojan, which fires up a VNC server daemon. After the attacker is notified the VNC server is up and running, they simply hook into it with a VNC viewer with the password. VNC is extremely popular—a lot of IT people use it for remote administration. And because it's so popular, it's classified as a utility, and therefore, it's unlikely your antivirus will pick it up as being any type of infection.

- Second, you can go on the internet and do a search for VNC software. If you've ever done that before, you know you'll get a plethora of cuckoo results. Obviously, not all of them are legitimate VNC products—most have been modified. There's RealVNC, TightVNC, and Chicken of the VNC, but the end user may not understand what they're doing, so as an attacker, I could create my own VNC, which basically has a built-in backdoor, and they just install it for me and, more than likely, with administrative privileges.

HTTP and HTTPS Trojans

Back in the old days, we used some pretty archaic technologies in order to gain access to resources—in particular, email. Back then, we had something—at least in the Microsoft world—called **Outlook Web Access (OWA)**, which simply used **HyperText Transfer Protocol (HTTP)** and **HTTP Secure (HTTPS)** to allow me to gain access to my email. Microsoft and some other companies have taken that technology and made it in a way we could create a tunnel. The issue we have here is most of these tunnels are created on port 80 or 443. Using those ports to create a tunnel, the security administrator or specialists will simply see standard HTTP traffic or web browsing traffic—they have no idea it's a tunnel.

Once we infect the target, a Trojan is executed on that target and spawns what we refer to as a child. The child program simply appears to be a target to the firewall, which then allows it to access the internet because it's going across ports 80 and 443. So, all the traffic technically gets converted to a Base64-type structure and given a value in a **Common Gateway Interface (CGI)** string. This way, the attacker's commands are hidden from the security professional and, in most cases, security appliances. With that, an attacker can use HTTP/HTTPS-based commands such as GET, so the GET command of the internal target is just the command prompt of the shell and the answer is an encoded ls command from the attacker.

As far as the administrator is concerned, when they open the connections to the attacker server and try to connect to it themselves in an attempt to track this thing down, the attacker just sees a broken web server because there's no token or password in the encoded CGI GET request. The kicker on this one is the programs are relatively small. In fact, there are some out there that are under 300 lines per file. These types of Trojans are not limited to PCs. Lately, they infect any device using a web browser or having access to the internet.

Command-shell Trojans

These are Trojans that install a server on the target machine, which in turn opens a port for the attacker to connect to. Once the attacker hits that client, they're given remote control of a command shell—hence the name *command shell*—on that target's machine. One of the most popular command-shell Trojans is Netcat. With Netcat, an attacker can open a full Telnet session into a shell on the target machine. They can create inbound and outbound connections using either TCP or **User Datagram Protocol** (**UDP**) and provide full **Domain Name Server** (**DNS**) forwarding and reverse checking so that they are able to transverse your environment.

To avoid raising any suspicions, we can implement slow motion. Here, we slow down the speed at which we send information back and forth. That way, it makes it harder for the security specialists to figure out what's going on—very similar to using **Paranoid** mode with Nmap. When using Nmap to scan, you can put it in paranoid mode to prevent it from being too noisy or loud on the network.

Document Trojans

When it comes to document Trojans, what we're doing is simply embedding our Trojan inside of the document. We then send the document to people via email: "*Dear Sir, Kindly find attached a new IRS form the government requires you to fill out to avoid being penalized.*" That sounded all official, didn't it? Believe it or not, a high percentage of people would click on that email attachment and of course, as an attacker, nothing is better than getting people to do my work for me. If it's a really cool, funny, or important document, they'll even forward the document for me.

Some of the biggest document Trojans out there right now exist in **Portable Document Format** (**PDF**) documents. Do me a favor—do not open PDF documents from people you don't know or from emails you are not expecting. I know this is a big list of things to remember not to do, which does interfere with our day-to-day productivity, but one of the bigger Trojans out there is the email-based Trojan. This bad boy fires off as soon as you open an email, and then it sends the commands via email back and forth to the Trojan. Those commands can include executing applications, searching for files, or opening files, as well as showing the attacker files on the victim's system.

Remote-access Trojans

Remote-access Trojans (**RATs**) are my favorite, and there are countless ones out there. The more famous ones are relatively old, such as Back Office, as well as NetBus.

Most of the RATs today are custom-made. In fact, recently, the latest RATs allow the attacker to turn on the victim's webcam. That's why I have a little cover I put over my webcam, just as a precautionary mechanism.

So, with a RAT, what we're doing is simply installing a small application on the target machine. This is known as the server side. The attacker hits that server from the outside to get remote access. From that point on, they can affect administrative controls, raise privileges, implement a keylogger, and so on. And there are several preconfigured RATs out there including DarkComet, Apocalypse, and Beast.

Backdoor Trojan

This is a program that can bypass most of the system authentication products you have in place, such as IDSs and firewalls. In these types of attacks, a black hat—a bad guy—uses a backdoor program to access the target system. The difference between this type of malware and other types of malware is that the installation of the backdoor is done without the user's knowledge. They don't recognize it's being done. This allows the attacker to perform all types of activities on the target, including transferring, modifying, and corrupting files, installing malicious software, rebooting the machine—all kinds of fun things. Backdoor Trojans are often used to group victim computers together to create a botnet or a zombie network, which can then be used against other targets.

So, what's the difference?

Now, you may be wondering, what's the difference between a RAT and a traditional backdoor? A RAT has a **user interface** (**UI**), but a backdoor doesn't. One RAT that will make your hair stand on the back of your neck is the Poison Ivy RAT kit. It consists of a **graphical UI** (**GUI**) and the backdoors are really small—like, 10 kilobytes in size. Good luck finding that! Once the backdoor is executed, it copies itself into the Windows folder or the Windows `system32` folder. As the creator of the backdoor, you get to choose where it'll copy the filename and the locations.

There are some variations of Poison Ivy that can copy themselves into **alternate data streams** (**ADS**). If you're not aware of these, read about system hacking and look at ADS.

You can also create a registry entry for the backdoor so that it starts up every time the computer is booted. The server, when it connects to the client, can use the address you defined when you created the server part. The communication between the server and the client is encrypted and compressed.

Poison Ivy can also be configured to inject itself into a browser process before making any type of connection that will bypass any firewall. I'm sure you're aware of how evil, bad, and wicked ransomware is. If you're not, you should be.

This type of Trojan can do several things, from encrypting files stored on your system hard drive to simply locking the system and tricking the user into thinking they need to pay. This is typically done through a web interface or a web page that pops up with no bars or anything and gives them a link they must go through and make a payment. It tells them their system has been encrypted, but it hasn't really. Payments are done with Bitcoin, making it hard to track down the attacker.

I know you can't take any more, but there's more. You thought your phone was safe? No. An attacker can trick victims into installing malicious applications, and when the victim downloads the malicious app, the Trojan then performs things such as getting your banking credentials and social networking credentials, encrypting your device, and so on.

Next, let's look at the motive behind executing these attacks.

Trojan creators' goals

So, what's the goal when it comes to what the Trojan creators are after? Initially, they are after an endgame, which includes any of the following or a combination of them.

Disabling the firewall

The first thing they may be after is to disable your firewall. Have you seen before where your firewall won't enable? Often, people will tell me they disable it anyway. Firewalls make it harder for us to configure things, but disabling it is being complacent.

Deleting the OS

Another endgame option would be to replace or delete OS files. If I can replace (with my Trojan) an OS file that does the exact same thing the OS file did—let's say, for example, Notepad—if I can replace it with my own version of Notepad or, better yet, an executable that's used all the time in the OS, every time you launch it, my Trojan would repopulate out, especially if you've deleted it. If I'm trying to be destructive, I might delete some very important OS files.

Opening a backdoor

Another goal might be to open a backdoor, create a Trojan, and put it on the internet, and somebody then launches it, effectively opening the back door. In many cases, it gets rid of all the issues of having to go do reconnaissance and footprinting.

Disabling the antivirus

Why do malware creators disable the antivirus? Because they don't want to be detected. And when I say disable both on the firewall and the antivirus, I mean you cannot enable it. In fact, one famous trick by attackers is taking the icon for the antivirus. When most antiviruses are disabled, you get a specific-looking icon. Remember to replace and delete OS files. How about if you just replace the disabled antivirus icon with one that looks like it's enabled?

Turning the target into a proxy

Another goal an attacker might use is to turn the target into a proxy so that they can issue attacks on other machines within your network. You would just think the machine was Dick Grayson's creating the traffic on your network and grabbing up stuff. I might even go down the road of adding you to my botnet. If you're not familiar with a botnet, do yourself a favor and do some googling. A botnet is an army of systems that I, as an attacker, have infiltrated and taken control of, and at a specific time and date, I can have all my botnet members do a specific command such as attack Citibank or send out spam email messages. And the real kicker is, I will do this late at night when you're asleep and your system is just sitting there.

Generating bogus traffic

The Trojan creator can generate bogus traffic on your network to create a DoS attack because sometimes, the motivation of the attacker is to cause disruption. Many times, that disruption is designed to create problems for that company. Other times, it could open vulnerabilities if I overload the system with too much traffic.

We could also use it to download and install additional spyware, malware, and adware. Think about all the toolbars out there you've seen. Every installation of a toolbar gives me the option to use a custom install, or a quick and easy install. Please—whatever you do, don't ever choose a quick install! Don't be lazy. Take the custom route so that you can see what's happening. If you do select the quick install, it could also say *Please install XYZ toolbar*, because the attacker probably gets an affiliation fee for every installation of the XYZ toolbar and all the traffic it generates. It's a money-making venture for the attacker. As an attacker, if I can get you to install additional spyware and malware, sometimes not even without your knowledge, I'll make more money.

Grabbing screenshots

Another goal is grabbing screenshots, especially when the target logs on to a financial website. As an attacker, I can get my Trojan to start recording video from your webcam, and no—there will be no flash because I will turn the light off so that you will not be able to tell. If you don't think that's dangerous, ask the *Miss Teen USA* who opened an email and clicked on the link she had been socially engineered to click on. The link installed a Blackshades application, and then the attacker proceeded to capture a video from her laptop of her during some personal moments. The attacker then tried to extort her with pictures captured of her for a nominal fee that, if paid, the attacker wouldn't reveal to the rest of the world.

The attacker ended up being her 19-year-old former classmate from high school. He was arrested and charged with multiple crimes, not only for extortion but taking control of someone else's computer remotely without their permission, which is a federal crime.

Stealing passwords and personal data

Stealing passwords, codes, financial data, and personal data is one of the things I would also do. In fact, if I were an attacker, I would use my Trojan to search your computer for any document named *password*, *passwords*, or *pwds*, because most IT people write down their passwords digitally. Attackers love it when IT people do that! An attacker will also look for documents that may be named *network layout* or spreadsheets named *user accounts* or *employee information*. I know you want to stop reading right now to rename all your files, right?

Targeting you for spamming

We could also use you as a target for spamming. If all else fails, I'm going to use your resources to send my Trojan to all your Outlook clients. Have you ever gotten an email from a friend that says, "*Hey, I found a cool link, click here*"? If you did click on the link, you got pwned.

Let's talk next about how a Trojan does what it does.

How Trojans communicate and hide

Let's take the hiding mechanism first. When you build a Trojan, we're going to attach it to a legitimate piece of software. So, technically, there are two different communication paths to a Trojan, as outlined here:

- The first one is an **overt channel**. Overt is something explicit, evident, or obvious. So, overt would be something such as the newest version of Office, or an mp3 file that everybody wants. An attacker must make the overt channel enticing for you to want to install it. And this is what happens with malware, and that's why there are so many pieces of malware out there.

- The second channel is the illegal side or the **covert channel**. It's the hidden path that is used to transfer data across the network. It's built into our payload. Most attackers will rely on the tunneling technique to make sure it's not visible to somebody monitoring the network. Maybe, as an attacker, I tunnel it across HTTP or HTTPS so that you can't see it—at least, anybody monitoring the network can't see it—because it gets encrypted. You may want to make sure you understand the differences between these two channels.

There are a plethora of ports used by different Trojans, and this is just a partial list. You'll notice that some of them utilize ports you would not suspect—for example, port 21 for BladeRunner. Typically, that's FTP port 80—the Executioner Trojan uses that one. What else runs on port 80? One of my favorites and very appropriately named—port 666. That's Satan's backdoor…

Again, this is a partial list—you need to be doing research and finding out the newest Trojans, which ports they're utilizing, and when you see traffic going across that port, you need to investigate. I know that's hard, especially in port 80. One of the things you will definitely want to do if you suspect a system is being infected by a Trojan is a fresh reboot of the system and see which ports are currently listening. There are actually different states for ports. When a port is in the listening state, it's there because the system put it in that state to listen or to wait to make a connection to another system.

Next, let's look at some of the symptoms of Trojan infection.

Symptoms of Trojan infection

How can you tell if you have a Trojan? Well, this is like asking: How do you know when you're getting sick? We get symptoms, right? When it comes to a Trojan, I say: "*Oh, this is way too late, you're already infected.*"

Disabled antivirus

If your antivirus is disabled and you can't enable it, there's a chance you have a Trojan infection. In fact, I've seen Trojans that have made it so that you can't do your updates through Microsoft updates, you can't launch Task Manager to see which processes are running, or you can't edit the host file. Every time you try to open Command Prompt, it shuts right back down.

Keys failing

You might also see things such as the *Ctrl + Alt + Del* keys failing to work altogether. Often, the user will just simply reset the PC and when you get to log in, the *Ctrl + Alt + Del* screen works there, but as soon as they get in, it stops working and they think there's something wrong with the software.

System restart and shutdown

Another thing that is likely to happen is that your system will just restart or shut down all by itself. If you have ever experienced that, you know the reason now.

Changing screensaver

The other common symptom is that your screensaver just arbitrarily changes. Maybe there's something displayed that you would never have chosen.

Disappearing taskbar

Your taskbar could also disappear on you. This can be caused by a Trojan, or possibly just me visiting you because I'm a wanted man at the local Sam's Club or Costco. When I get bored, my wife drags me off there to go shopping and I eat all the free samples, which, if you think about it, are nothing but social engineering. After I'm full on the free samples, I go over to the computer section and start playing around with some **Group Policy Object (GPO)** settings to take away the taskbar or **Start** button or find out what's going on with the system. One of my favorite things to do is making a print screen of the desktop, saving it as the background, and hiding all the icons, except for the Recycle Bin. There's probably a security photo of me in the employee break room that says, *Watch out for this guy!*

Screen orientation keeps changing

Another symptom of infection could be when you turn on the machine, the screen comes up and suddenly it starts flipping around or inverts.

Background changes

Sudden background changes are another symptom of Trojan infection. As you are working in your OS, everything could be working just fine, and suddenly, your background changes. It might be a photo of your cute little puppy, and you may think it's cute when it happens, but you need to find out why it happened.

Start button disappears

The disappearance of the **Start** button is another sign of Trojan infection. Imagine the frustration when you take away the **Start** button, taskbar, and disable the *Ctrl + Alt + Del* buttons. A good Trojan, even though some of these were initially designed for entertainment purposes, is one that you don't suspect is installed, so you don't necessarily see these things taking place. You might see the system rebooting because maybe I needed to reboot because of configuration changes I made.

Redirection

This symptom could include things such as your browser going somewhere other than what you've typed. For example, you type in `microsoft.com` only to end up on an inappropriate website. Again, the attacker just made money off you because they get paid for everybody who gets directed to that site.

DVD drive ejects

Another symptom is the DVD drive ejects randomly out of the blue, or you hear it spin up.

Documents printing

Documents might also start printing, and they will not be documents you sent to the printer.

Reversed mouse keys

Your mouse keys could also get reversed. An attacker could get people all confused with this one.

A lot of hard drive activity

A lot of hard drive activity is another telltale sign of infection. Look at your system when nobody's using it. Sometimes, we might see hard drive activity because the system is doing defragmentation, system maintenance, or backup. But knowing is half the battle. If there's a lot of activity with the hard drive or network and I'm just reading a Word document, I might be a little suspicious. Most of the maintenance tasks that OSs perform will wait until the system is not being used.

A lot of traffic

Another common symptom is that your **internet service provider** (**ISP**) calls you to say: *Listen, you've got a lot of traffic coming from your router.* This is something I had to deal with when I had my own ISP service. I had people get infected all the time, and I would see a ton of traffic coming out of their antenna that would start flooding our network and I had to shut off their antennas. I always thought it was interesting when I tried to contact them—I could never get ahold of them, but as soon as I disconnected their internet, within 2 minutes, people would call me.

Unknown credit card transactions

The mother of all symptoms is getting your credit card bill and there are some really weird and expensive purchases.

Next, let's talk about how we infect a target.

How to infect a target with a Trojan

There are three steps to create these little monsters, as follows:

- **Step 1**—We will need some type of toolkit to create them for us. There are many products we can use, including Kali Linux, which has a whole lot already built into it.

  There's a Trojan Horse construction kit out there, but you can just use some basic technologies that are built into the OS. For example, I can quickly create a script or a batch program that would do some damage—in the case here, delete a lot of important system files—and then use it along with my legitimate program. You can do it as you like, but the concept of this step is that you're creating damage you want to cause.

- **Step 2**—Create a dropper. Here, we basically take the monster we've created and tell it how to install itself utilizing the desired or legitimate program.

- **Step 3**—We are ready to take our monster and turn it into a cute little teddy bear. *"Go ahead, double-click on it—he won't hurt you!"* We will combine the two together by doing wrapping. This is software we use to combine the two programs together. There are a couple of programs out there you can utilize, including Petite, Graffiti, EliteWrap, and I'm sure you might have your favorites too.

The concept behind the wrapper is to be able to take those files and combine them. We can also combine multiple monsters together so that when somebody installs the latest antivirus, Office suite, or any other free software they downloaded from a pirated site, they're going to get multiple Trojans installed. By using some of these wrappers, they can do compression of the binary, making it possible for the Trojan to get in without being detected by most antivirus software. This is because most antivirus software is unable to detect the signatures of a file. And not executing programs will not work out either, because most of the time, the infection takes place via a socially engineered attack. For example, I will send you a file that contains adult material or a cool program such as a new screensaver.

More than likely, though, we see a lot of these Trojans being infected via email attachments because of actual files being attached, or links to files. I always tell people when they get an email that they should never click on links because it might look like the link is taking you to some type of cloud storage company such as Dropbox or OneDrive, but the code behind that link could be taking you to a different location.

Many times, we're being socially engineered, especially our end users. They get socially engineered all the time because of popups and usually, it's done in such a way that is designed to scare the end user or affect the greed factor. What's interesting with popups is whether you hit **Yes** or **No** or click anywhere on the pop-up window, you could inject the Trojan. In fact, there are really tricky ones where the pop-up ads look like a window that will show **Close**, **Minimize**, and **Maximize** buttons in the standard upper right-hand corner (or the left corner for Apple users) but guess what? I can make a web page look like that interface but those are not real buttons. If you click on it, the window will close but still go ahead and inject the Trojan.

With some of the more popular ones, a user would go to a malicious website or just get a piece of malware that would activate an interface that looks like some type of system application and looks like it's trying to protect us. Many times, it would give you false positives back, pretending it was helping you out when in fact they were just installing more Trojans and getting more information off your system.

The big one in 2015 was a product called **Crypto Blocker**. Whoever came up with it needs to be put in a maximum prison's padded room because it would encrypt your drives and data, including any mapped drive. We refer to this as extortionware because you had to pay them money to get the decryption key and, of course, the odds are they would drain your account. Or, we might use the fear technique: "*Oh, my computer's been locked. There's something wrong with my OS; I don't want to get in trouble. If I want to unlock it, I better pay $200. And I have 72 hours to take care of this, or else I'm going to be in trouble!*"

They could also say your IP address was used to visit websites containing pornography, child pornography, zoophilia, and child abuse—that your computer has those files on it. Sometimes, they would indicate you've been sending out spam messages to terrorists. This was a famous one for scaring people into paying for something when they weren't guilty of anything.

Just recently, emails have been going out saying: "*Hey, you can upgrade for free—just click here.*" The email looks like it's from Microsoft—it has their logo and their address on the bottom. All you need to do to upgrade for free is follow the attached installer and get started. Well, you will just get started giving up your data.

Let's discuss how Trojans get into systems next.

How do Trojans get into our systems?

Trojans will get into your system in several different ways.

Physical access

As an attacker, I can implement a Trojan via physical access. If I have my Trojan built into a thumb drive that I've dropped and somebody has picked up and plugged in, I'll have an auto-start in there that injects the Trojan. I could also inject it if somebody walks away from their system without logging off.

Email

Another way Trojans get into our systems is via email. You may be thinking, "*Well, I'm not going to open up an email from somebody I don't know.*" Okay—go back and think about what we've covered this whole time. As an attacker, I can very easily spoof. Let's say that Bruce Wayne sends Clark Kent emails all day long. If I've done my due diligence, I could simply create an email, make it look like it came from Bruce Wayne, and trick Clark into double-clicking on this file. It happens all the time. In fact, at least twice a month if not a week, I get emails from family members saying, "*I thought you'd be interested in this*", and there's a link, and that's all there is in the email.

Fake application

Another way into a system is via a fake application. So, you're out there looking for an application that helps you organize your garage. All you do is put in the dimensions of your garage or carport area, and it's supposed to help you organize it—at least, that's the promise. Well, the victim goes and downloads the program, and when they double-click on it to install it, they mark it as being trusted because they want the program so badly.

In fact, there's an interesting one I've seen out there many times. It mostly deals with an mp3 where kids go out and say, "*Hey, I'm looking for this hit song*", and they do a standard Google search that shows a site with that file, but they really don't have the file there. Attackers are extremely creative in how they lure someone into a trap. An attacker has taken popular search terms and leads people into thinking they have it on their site, but it's not. You would go to download the file and double-click on the mp3, only for the Trojan to execute. Sometimes, you might not see anything happen, or if they're nice, you'll get the song.

My favorite are programs that call themselves anti-Trojan software programs, yet they are in fact our Trojan. Make sure that you do your research on the programs you're installing.

Using torrents

You're in trouble if you watch videos from a torrent site thinking you got them for free. As I always say…nothing is free out there. More than likely, someone is using your greed to pwn you.

Freeware

There are some cool freeware products out there—for example, VNC. It's great, but make sure you download it from the right place because there are hundreds of sites out there that say: "*This is the website for VNC—this is where you download it.*"

Shrink-wrapped software

The software could have Trojans in it. More than likely, this is done by a disgruntled employee who's thinking: "*Man, I could totally pwn thousands of people because everybody wants a copy of this program.*" Large software companies have **quality assurance** (**QA**) mechanisms in place to stop that from happening, but that's not to say all software vendors take the same precautions.

Viruses

Many times, viruses will execute and install additional Trojans for us. In fact, there are times Trojans will help to install viruses. At this point, usually, most people think they need to go back and format their hard drive and start all over.

PDFs

Do yourself a favor—google `Trojans PDF documents` or just `PDF`. PDFs are horrendous right now because everybody puts up PDFs. You want a white paper? Yes— open that PDF and watch exploits from some of the PDF readers kick in, and somebody ends up getting into your system.

How Trojans avoid being picked up by antivirus

Trojans can evade antivirus. Now, I'm not telling you antivirus is your solution or your countermeasure. These are just ways to avoid being picked up by antivirus, and there are several different ways we can do this, such as these:

- Changing the checksum of the file itself because most antivirus programs will look at the checksum of known viruses and Trojans.

- Writing your own Trojan is another way you can avoid being picked up by an antivirus. That would technically make your Trojan a zero-day attack mechanism.

- Using a hex editor to make modifications will help hide your Trojan from antivirus software.

- You can also break the Trojan into multiple files because most antivirus programs are looking for specific files that represent the Trojan. By breaking it up, it would never be detected.

- We can also modify the syntax. A lot of antivirus programs are looking for specific syntaxes within the Trojans themselves and, of course, one of the best things to do— this goes back to writing your own Trojan—don't ever use Trojans that have already been identified by antivirus products. Always do a little bit of research.

Next, let's discuss viruses and worms.

Viruses and worms

So, what's the difference between a virus and a worm? Well, to look at these, we need to compare what they are designed to do. Some people say we're comparing apples with apples because these two are really close to each other. However, when it comes to a virus, you need to understand it's simply a piece of malware that's designed to execute. When it executes, it likes to associate or attach itself to a file or program.

Those files and programs could be almost any file or program, but as a virus creator, I want to make sure the virus executes every time the OS fires up. So, many times, the virus creator will make sure it replaces system files such that every time the OS boots up, we make sure the machine is infected.

We can also infect other types of files or programs. For example, I can make my virus attach itself to Word, but that virus would only become active once the application is launched.

One of the biggest differences between a virus and a worm is that, to execute, a virus requires some type of human interaction. Isn't that the case with a real virus? You don't get sick unless you meet somebody that has the virus. So, how do we get in contact? Typically, viruses are transmitted via downloads. I am a big proponent of not downloading programs, no matter how cool you think they may be or how bad you want them, unless they're coming from the manufacturer. This includes movies, music, books, games, and videos.

We can also get or transmit viruses via different types of drives. Today, most of this is done by USB drives. Remember the classic USB drop whereby we drop a USB drive in a parking lot or in a hallway and have someone plug it in? The victim might see a file in there named `TopSecretDon'tRun.doc`, and out of the same curiosity that killed the cat, they will execute from the USB drive, and they infect the machine.

A more productive way of transmitting viruses today is through email or social media. You just post things on social media sites that direct users to websites with malicious code injected into them. The email could also just include an attachment.

When it comes to worms, there are some very strong similarities to viruses. They will still want to attach themselves, but they'll copy themselves and replicate all on their own. They don't require any humans; they'll just execute by themselves. So, if one machine in your environment gets infected, it'll start working its way throughout your network environment. It does this through a vulnerability. It starts looking for vulnerabilities within your network. As far as transportation or transmission of worms is concerned, they still will enter the environment via the same techniques as viruses, but once inside, the worms—because they're all automated—use our standard file transport features to hook into multiple machines or all the machines within our network, sometimes even outside of our network.

One of the worst worms was SQL Slammer, which was created as a DoS attack and slowed down internet traffic. It attacked Microsoft SQL, both the server and the desktop engine database.

SQL Slammer infected 75,000 machines within 10 minutes. Now, I mentioned that SQL Slammer was a DoS attack and it slowed down the internet. The reason for this slowdown was that it caused routers to be flooded with traffic from the infected servers.

Normally, when a router gets a lot of traffic, the router is supposed to delay or temporarily stop network traffic. Instead, the routers crashed. When this happened, a neighboring router would notice these routers had stopped, and they would update their routing tables. So, the router started sending notices to other routers they knew about. Because these routing tables are being updated so fast, because so many nodes were being infected, it caused additional routers to fail because the bandwidth was being consumed by these routers trying to communicate with each other, trying to update the tables.

Now, this was so bad, stats show 300,000 cable modems in Portugal went out. South Korea basically went black—there was no cell phone or internet service for over 25 million people and 5 of the internet's 13 root name servers went down. Websites stopped responding, **automated teller machines (ATMs)** went down, and airline ticketing systems went down. For those of us in the **United States (US)**, this thing hit at 12:30 a.m. Eastern Time and, 30 minutes later, the number of slave servers doubled every 8.5 seconds.

This was a wake-up call to many, especially companies, and many started looking at security or at least protecting themselves with patches.

Types of viruses and worms

You can definitely say there is a plethora of viruses and worms. I often think of the phrase *"Daddy, make the bad man go away"* when I start to see all these things because they come at you from different angles, and they do different things.

Standard file virus

These viruses execute based on a file they've attached themselves to. There are tons of different types of file viruses out there currently. Typically, file viruses target files such as executables, or COMs. We can categorize them based on how they attack or attach themselves. For example, we have prepending file viruses, which write themselves to the beginning of the host file code. We also have appending ones, which I'm sure you can figure out. We also have overriding ones, which basically overwrite the host code with their own code, and inserting ones, which inject themselves inside gaps within the host file code.

Most of these types of viruses will target themselves specifically at OS files.

Cluster virus

A cluster virus doesn't change the targeted file or put any information inside the file. Instead, it just goes through and modifies the directory information, making the entry point to the virus code, instead of the actual program itself.

Boot sector viruses

Most OSs get divided into different areas referred to as sectors, which is where we store the programs for the OS. The most common is the **Master Boot Record** (**MBR**). How I envisioned the MBR is very similar to back in my day when I went to the library. If I wanted to find a book, I would go to this big, huge box that had all these drawers. Inside the drawers were index cards. If I wanted to find a book on **unidentified flying objects** (**UFOs**), all the books would be listed on each index card, which would provide me with titles to books about UFOs and a location. It could be found in *Section 104.5*, and you could go to *Section 104* and look for the book in the *.5* section. Well, that's like what the MBR does. It tracks everything on the hard drive—and if I can infect and destroy the boot sector, say goodbye to your data.

The DOS boot virus

The **DOS boot sector or record**, or the **DBR**, is executed whenever the OS is turned on or boots up. Again, this could be another place we could send an attack. Based on this, I could infect your boot sector with the virus codes. So, with the boot sector virus, we moved the MBR to a different location altogether and replaced it or retained it at the original location with our own virus code.

After the virus code is executed—because it was in the MBR—it passed on to where we moved the MBR to so that the OS would continue to launch, but the whole time, the OS was infected.

Polymorphic virus

This is a little scary, and you might see something about this type of virus in your future exam. Polymorphic viruses modify their code on their own to avoid detection. This morphing or mutation is executed by a polymorphic engine—also called a mutation or mutating engine. This engine is used to change the encryption module and the instruction sequence. So, it's always changing, which makes it harder for antivirus products to discover a zero-day-type virus.

Metamorphic viruses

These viruses rewrite themselves completely each time they infect a new file. So, talk about Skynet—these bad boys will reprogram themselves by taking their own code, translating them into a temporary representation, and then back to normal code. One of the most popular ones out there was Simile, which was written in an assembly language, and 90% of its code got rewritten every time it found a different machine, so there were a bazillion renditions of the Simile virus.

Zmist

Zmist used a technique called code integration, where the code inserted itself into other code, then regenerated the code and rebuilt the executable. Talk about a smart virus!

Cavity-based viruses

Also commonly referred to as file-overwriting viruses, cavity-based viruses were known as space fillers. The virus would take a document—assuming it was a Word document that was 1.5 **megabytes (MB)** in size— and overwrite the host file with consistent `null` statements. It would do this without increasing the length of the file, so the virus would then be able to technically install itself in unoccupied space without destroying any of the original code. Luckily, these types of viruses are very difficult to write, therefore we don't see them often.

Encryption viruses

You can pretty much guess what these bad boys do, right? With these, for each of the infected files that get hit, the virus is encrypted using a different combination of keys. And because they're encrypted, it's not possible for a virus scanner to directly detect the virus via the signature of the virus—because it's encrypted. Now, associated with these viruses is a decrypting module. So, even though you might find the decrypted module, you probably won't get ahold of the files that have been encrypted.

Camouflage

This is an old, tricky one. If you had a program called `word.exe`, a camouflage virus would make a copy of that executable, but give it a `.com` extension, and, of course, the file would be infected with the virus itself. Anybody who knows about Windows knows the order in which these files execute. If you have three files, all of them are called Batman— you have `batman.com`, `batman.exe`, `batman.bat`, or a batch file. If you were to go to a DOS prompt and type in `batman`, what executes? Well, if you're an old DOS dog like me, you'll know a COM would execute first, followed by the executable, and then batch files would be executed after that. So, by renaming the `word.exe` program or creating a copy of it and calling it `word.com`, if somebody were to type in `word`, the COM edition with the virus would automatically execute.

Shell viruses

This virus code forms a shell around the actual program code, making itself the original program and the host code a sub-routine.

Tunneling viruses

Sometimes, people refer to these as stealth viruses because they hide themselves from antivirus programs by hiding the original size of the file, or possibly creating a temporary place in a copy of itself in some other drive in the system. These viruses will hide the modifications they make. They take control of the system's function that reads and writes files and system sectors so that the antivirus can't identify them.

More and more files get created every day. Being aware of what's going on will help you defend yourself against these nasty little monsters.

Why a virus and signs you've got one

Why do people make viruses? Here are some possible reasons:

- **Financial gain**—If I can trick you into thinking your machine is broken and you have to pay me to get it fixed, that can be quite beneficial to me. Also, maybe I want to infect my competitors. There are several cases where people have gotten in trouble for attacking their competitors via viruses and digital means—which, by the way, is illegal.
- Research projects.
- Trying to figure out the ins and outs or whys of different viruses.

- **To play with people's minds**—One of my favorites is, *"Hey, that's a funny joke"*. It's not funny, but some people do think pranking people is humorous.

- Vandalism, especially when it comes to defacing or destroying content.

- **Political reasons**—One of the most notable examples of this was a worm, WANK, rumored to have been created by some attackers in Melbourne. Its political message, when you got infected, was the acronym **WANK**, which stood for **Worms Against Nuclear Killers**. This worm made its way around into some systems at the **National Aeronautics and Space Administration** (**NASA**) and the Department of Energy. In fact, the computers at NASA were infected just a couple of days before the shuttle launch that was to take the Galileo spacecraft up into orbit so that it could go and explore Jupiter and its moons.

Signs of infection

When a virus shows up, you need to know what some of the signs are. Here are some pointers:

- **Drive issues**—You might have a hard drive issue, or your hard drive may be flashing, even though nothing is running on the drive at the time and the system is not under a load.

- **Video issues**—You might experience video issues, either not seeing what you'd expect to see or even, possibly, the display looking strange.

- **Full memory**—Another symptom is the memory filling up completely so that the system slows way down in some cases, creating vulnerabilities or exploits.

- **Applications running slowly**—Applications running slowly when launched.

- **Strange filenames**—Filenames could turn strange. So, if you start seeing strange characters show up in the filename, you might be infected.

- **System freezes or locks up**—The system could also freeze or lock up.

So, how do viruses get spread or injected? We'll talk about that next.

Deployment of viruses

Deployment of viruses and worms is very similar to what we just saw with Trojans because they're just malware.

So, how do viruses and worms get around? They do it very easily, especially with so many different devices out there and with today's technology.

Downloads

People are sharing so much information that we see viruses and worms being deployed via downloads.

Email attachments

Email attachments and social networking links are probably the bigger ones right now.

Not updating the OS

These bad boys also get around when people fail to update their OS, applications, or antivirus. My favorite scenario, which I get at least once a year, comes via family members. They will bring their laptop to me and say: "*Hey, I bought this new laptop and it's starting to act kind of funny—I think I have a virus.*" My first question to them is: "*Besides the 30-day or 90-day evaluation of the antivirus product, have you paid for it so that you can continue to get updates, and when was the last time you downloaded the updates?*" Guess what? 9 times out of 10, they say: "*It's funny you should mention that…*", to which I say: "*It's also funny you should call me.*" This is a real issue for most. I know we see updates all the time for OSs, but the same thing applies to your applications.

Microsoft is great about updating its applications, but which other applications are you running? Are your custom applications being updated to protect them from possible vulnerabilities allowing these viruses to get in? You also need to watch your plugins.

One of the biggest issues I see happening today is we install an application on our smartphones or tablets, and we receive updates. Are you one of the handfuls of people who take time to review what the updates are going to update? Many times, it's getting more permission for your resources, contacts, and so on. The same thing happens with plugins for applications.

Compromised legitimate sites are one of the trickiest things today. If you don't know how they do that, I highly recommend doing a little research on hacking web servers because if I can hack your web server, I can make it inject the virus on your machine when you get online or hit my website. I can also do it via drive-by downloads. This happens when somebody visits a website, looks at an email message, or gets a pop-up window from a website that makes it look like an application. One of the most famous such instances is making it look as though your antivirus is scanning your hard drives, and by clicking on the window to dismiss the advertisement, we install the virus.

Spear phishing

Spear-phishing sites are another way to deploy. This is basically where an email or a website is purporting to be something it's not. For example, if I can DNS poison you so that you come to my version of a Citibank website, that would be a spear-phishing site. On here, I might ask you for things such as: "*Hey, you need to reset your password—please tell us what your current one is.*" You might also get an email from eBay or PayPal saying: "*Dear Sir, We need to verify you. Please verify your birth date.*"

Clickjacking

In what is known as a **UI redress attack (UIRA)**, the attacker uses multiple transparent layers on the image. You will think you're closing or minimizing the window, but you're clicking on **OK**. Your countermeasure for that one is, anytime you get a popup, never use the buttons to close or minimize, and if you can't or don't have the capability of closing it down via Task Manager, do yourself a favor—I know it's a long process—restart your machine. Leave it up and running, go to the **Start** button and restart the machine, and whatever you do, don't go back to that website.

Search engine optimization

If you're looking for WinZip, you'll first do a simple search for `winzip`. It's possible that the first selection in my Google search might not be the WinZip website. It could be an attacker who has made use of **search engine optimization** (**SEO**) to make sure their website appears before the legitimate site. If I download that version of WinZip, I'm in trouble. So, even though I want to grab a program quickly, I still need to be careful about where I'm getting the program from.

Is the virus real or fake, and does it even matter? Well, that really depends on your victim. Sometimes we might get an email message that reads: "*Hey, your computer is infected with a virus, and in turn, you have spread this virus to friends, family, and co-workers just by sending them an email. Please read this and pass this on to anyone that you've sent email since September 11.*" This was an actual email people received. It was referred to as the Baby New Year virus. It was totally fake, but obviously, what do they play on here? Well, when it comes to hoaxes, all the attacker is trying to do is to play on fear. In this case, the fear was surrounding September 11. That date has a significant influence on those of us who live in the US or even worldwide.

A fake virus is simply just that—fake. It's a bluff. It may try to get us to do something we normally wouldn't do. My favorite is when they tell you to send this out to everybody and make sure you include them in the header, or how some people just forward an email and leave everybody's email address in the header, including the attacker, who then gets a nice spam list. Sometimes, the fake virus warning message contains a virus as well.

To avoid this, check email headers and be suspicious if the email says it's from one person but the email address doesn't look right.

Sometimes, attackers do fake viruses to sell you something or a service. They can insinuate your antivirus isn't very good and get you to buy something very similar, which is a fake antivirus. As I mentioned earlier, the fake itself could have an attachment that has a virus. A good example is an email that went around saying: "*Hey, everybody gets Windows 10 for free. Click on this link to get your free copy.*"

What you can do to avoid falling for the fake is cross-checking. Don't believe it just because somebody says, "*Hey, this was on Oprah*" or "*This was on the Coca-Cola company's website*". Be careful if it's posted in a newsgroup if you're getting information from somebody you don't know or from an email address you are not sure about. It might also be a real issue, and maybe the government has said this virus needs to be killed. You need to check your hard drive to see if it's on there. However, if that type of information is going out, the governing body that issued the release will have it somewhere on their own website, so do a cross-check.

You can also look for websites supporting hoax viruses—they tell you all about them. As I mentioned before, be very careful about hoax or fake antivirus products or applications that promise to optimize your system for free. Nothing is ever free.

Next, we'll look at how we investigate what malware is doing.

Investigation of malware

So, how do we investigate or look at what malware is doing?

We start with a sheep dip. This system is set up to check the physical media, device drivers, and other files before the malware infects a machine to make sure you start off with an extremely clean environment. A great candidate for a sheep-dip computer would be a virtualized machine. In fact, some of the steps you go through to set up your lab environment are very similar to the steps you follow to configure a sheep-dip system.

Typically, this computer is used for nothing but a way of isolating and monitoring everything that's going on as you execute the piece of malware. You can do that with several different pieces of software, including antivirus software, some tools for monitoring registry entries, and even ports.

In an actual setup for a sheep dip, we start with the following:

1. Installing a type of virtualization on our host machine.

2. Quarantining the network so that anything we do on this machine won't affect our production environment.

3. Disabling any type of shared folder services going on or any service that might leak out from the virtual into the host environment, although most of the time, you are good to go if you quarantine the network.

4. Copying over the malware you've discovered. This can sometimes be a challenge because you may be wondering how to get the malware into the **virtual machine (VM)**. This depends on the virtualization you're dealing with. You can transfer files between the VM and the host machine and disconnect the host machine so that it no longer talks to the VM. Some virtualization technologies support the ability to map out to physical USB drives. That works if you have a thumb drive you've copied the malware profile over to.

    After that…start rubbing your hands together because it's about to get exciting.

Before launching it, use utilities that will help you track what's going on. There are several different pieces of software out there that can help you do your analysis of malware at different levels.

Types of analysis

There are two types of analysis: static and dynamic.

Static analysis

This is investigating an executable file without running or installing it. When it comes to static analysis, one of the techniques you can use is fingerprint analysis. This is the process of computing the hash value of the binary file to identify it to make sure it's the same file. So, we're going to compare an original file with what we suspect to be a piece of malware.

One of the more popular products out there to help you with this is HashMyFiles, a tool that has several functions to it, including the ability to create a fingerprint of a suspect file so that you can compare it.

It's important to consider the fact that almost all programs, whether malware or regular products, have file dependencies. When any software program needs dependencies, such as a built-in library from the OS to help perform a specific function such as copying or pasting, that's provided by the OS. The programs need to be able to work with these internal systems or files.

Being able to see which dependencies a particular file has is very important. A cool little product called Dependency Walker goes through and lists all the dependency modules of an executable file, and then builds a hierarchy or tree. It also records any outside calls for a particular file or program, and anything that might try to export out.

Dynamic analysis

This is where we look at the behavior of the malware as it's running on a monitored environment. When it comes to dynamic analysis, we will fire up the actual suspected file in a sandboxed environment because we want to protect ourselves.

We need to have a good system baseline of that system. Taking a snapshot of the virtualized machines will help us with that, but we should be able to capture the current state so that we have something to compare after the file is executed.

Another item is the host integrity monitor. This process looks at which changes have taken place across the system, not just within the app itself but the whole system. To cover all your bases, you'll probably want to make sure that you're monitoring ports, processes, and registry services.

When it comes to Windows service monitoring, attackers design malware so that they can install or run in the form of a service. As an attacker, I'll call that service something that you would never suspect—something that sounds technical. The goal here is for the attacker to run a service, and most of our services will run as a system account that has some good privileges on a particular machine.

You should also be keeping an eye out on things such as startup programs—that is, which programs get placed into the startup of the OS so that they launch every single time. Also, monitor your registry. This is important because you want to be notified of any changes a particular piece of malware or suspect file might have.

We also need to be checking event logs, system logs, and security logs of any application, and service logs will also be extremely helpful to you.

You might also want to compare string values. Luckily, there are several different products out there that can help with this. One of the more popular ones is Bintext, which allows you to extract text from any of your files, including the ability to define string values that may be in a binary file. This will help you find any files that have been wrapped inside of the executable.

You can also use a product such as **Ultimate Packer for Executables** (**UPX**). This is a free portable executable packer for several different platforms, including Linux, Windows, Windows **Embedded Compact** (**CE**), macOS, **Disk Operating System** (**DOS**), and FreeBSD. With it, you're able to decompress files without having to install a file. UPX is an open source product, so you don't have to worry about shelling out any money for it.

Another option to consider is software that will monitor your ports, checking to see which activity fires up when you execute your suspected file.

Other products you can use out there happen to be popular because they're less than a penny—for example, Wireshark. Microsoft has its own port monitoring software as well, and you've probably come across your own favorite version of this type of software.

Another option is Sysinternals, which has a fantastic suite of tools. One of my favorites is Process Explorer and Process Monitor, which allows you to see everything going on in real time—in both filesystems and registries. On the other hand, Process Explorer shows you all the processes that are currently executing.

You'll want to analyze your malware and debug some stuff. So, what we're looking for are the installation instructions and installation locations.

There are specific locations whereby if I can get my piece of malware inside of them (for example, the registry or some specific directories), I can make sure the application, or my piece of malware, will execute every single time.

One of my favorite programs to use when looking for stuff that's been installed is Autoruns. This is also done by Sysinternals. When debugging, you obviously don't want to install the malware just to see where it put the code in. Instead, I can use something such as IDA Pro, a product by a company called Hex-Rays, that has built into it a disassembler as well as a debugger system. It allows you to look at any software vulnerabilities as well as the interaction it will have when it installs. This is a neat little program used by most antivirus companies and anybody involved in security research.

I once came across an article that said the **National Security Agency (NSA)** was making everybody aware of the zero-day malware technologies being utilized, but it wouldn't reveal whether it was using them itself.

There are other resources that can help you out. There are several different companies that have online malware testing.

VirusTotal

This is one of the most popular ones. It allows you to take a file you suspect is corrupt and upload it to them, and they will check it to see if it has any type of suspicious programming associated with it. They also have the ability to check any questionable websites for you.

The issue here is this: when you look at a URL, you might not be willing to click on it, but the bigger issue is we have the latest trend—especially in the social networking side of things—of shortening URLs and putting links in. Be very careful about clicking on a shortcut URL, because it could take you to a site that is completely malicious.

Malware protection centers

A good example of a malware protection center is the **Microsoft Malware Protection Center** (**MMPC**), an anti-malware research and response center made up of seasoned malware protection researchers and engineers. They identify the latest and most harmful viruses and other malware and then provide tools to guard and protect against them.

There are several of these sites out there—just make sure they're legitimate sites because I've seen some sites that say they will help you scan, that all you need is to go to their site, and they'll tell you if your machine is infected or not. While they will deliver on this promise, they themselves are a website that's injecting malware on you.

Avast

Avast is another resource that you can utilize. It has its own online scanner as well.

When it comes to training end users, you need to make sure they completely understand that when we get links in an email, we don't assume that the link will go where it says it will. It may say www.microsoft.com, but the **HyperText Markup Language** (**HTML**) code on the backend might be taking you to youjustbeenhacked.com.

My general rule of thumb, even if I get an email from a friend—because people's email accounts can be compromised—if there's a URL listed in the email, I will highlight what's being shown to me visually, copy it, and then paste it inside of my browser because I can't guarantee that link.

It's been said, you cannot have too many tools…let's talk about some of them next.

Tools in our utility belt

As an IT security professional, you should be familiar with some of the following tools or—better yet—have them in your own little arsenal.

TCPView

This is very much like netstat but through an application. With TCPView, you can see everything going on all your connections being made via the network or the internet itself.

Autoruns

Autoruns shows everything going on with your machine at a particular time and breaks it down into different tabs of focus so that you can see everything that's currently running, the login information, what's starting up on login, and so on.

DriverView

This nifty tool is exactly what it sounds like. It's a program that shows you everything about the drivers you currently have loaded on your machine. You can go through and see different drivers. It tells you some of them that may be borderline. You'll want to make sure you understand every driver that has been installed on your machine.

System File Checker (SFC)

This nifty tool is built into all our Windows platforms. It's one of the cool tools out there because it scans your system for any corruption of Windows system files and restores the corrupted files. If they've been deleted, it will also restore them.

All we do is open Command Prompt. You'll need to make sure you've opened it with administrative-level privileges, which means you're going to right-click on it and select **Run as administrator**. From there, you just simply type in `sfc /?`. It will do a `/SCANNOW` operation, which goes through and checks and repairs any files if it's able to. You can do a `/VERIFYONLY` operation, which scans but doesn't do any type of repair. You can get specific if you're looking for a particular file you suspect is corrupt by doing a `/SCANFILE` or a `/VERIFYFILE` operation. You can see an illustration of this in the following screenshot:

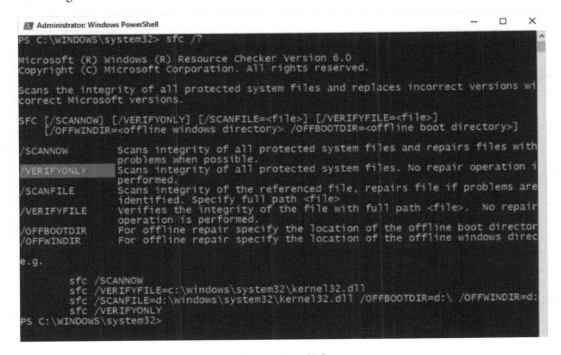

Figure 9.1 – SFC

As far as virus discovery methods are concerned, you need to know there's no single great solution out there. It's a combination of things.

Scanning

Scanning is basically having some type of antivirus solution installed on your systems to help protect them. I can't tell you which is the best antivirus to install because usually, that's all based on the timeframe. The best antivirus today can drop in position within 1 to 3 months.

I will throw a little plug in—I know Microsoft's forefront security solutions have up to five antivirus scanning engines for the Exchange servers, which is kind of cool. I wish we had more solutions that were that flexible. Unfortunately, that also slows things down, right? And you must remember these antivirus products are only able to find malware they're aware of.

Common sense

Now, there are also some commonsense items we need to make sure we teach our users, and that is dealing with email. Here's a golden rule for you: if it looks suspicious, then consider it suspicious. If you're not expecting an email from somebody and they send one to you out of the blue with weird subjects or "*Hey, check out this link*", or the header looks as though it's an email address of a relative or someone that you know, do me a favor— don't click on it.

In the background of what's happening during scanning, when a virus gets detected, the antivirus vendors are going to start to look at different ways they can identify this virus. They usually do this with a signature string. These strings are extracted from the virus and are added as a declaration of being infected to their antivirus database. So, as they scan your system, if the strings match, you'll be warned. One of the tricky things here is, when a malicious attacker writes a virus, they'll often try to create viruses just by modifying existing ones. That's why we always have variations of the same virus over and over. For example, MyDoom had several different variations.

Malicious attackers do this because the frequent changes throw scanners off as new signature strings are being generated. They not only rely on these signature strings, but the antivirus companies will use code analysis. This is typically the difference between a quick scan and a thorough scan. A quick scan is just looking at strings, while in-depth scans are typically looking a little bit deeper into your files to see if any of the code resembles what they've already discovered off these new pieces of malware.

Integrity checking

These types of products can verify the integrity of your systems. Some of them are built into our OSs, especially when it comes to the Windows platform. The OS checks to see if the core files or system files have been modified. If they have, it will consider them corrupt, and if so, it'll try to recover those for you. In your immediate future, you might see something about integrity-checking two different products. The first one is called TripWire. This is a company that makes a file-integrity and change-monitoring system designed for the enterprise level. TripWire monitors in real time and tells you where and when a file was modified and who or what did this. The second product for integrity checking is built into the OS by Microsoft and that is Sigverif, which simply helps to verify the integrity of critical files on your system.

Interception

This method utilizes interceptors. An interceptor simply maintains or looks at the requests that are made to the OS for network access, as well as some specific actions that help to identify threats that are being made to programs. If it sees one of these threats come up, the interceptor will typically have a popup to notify the user they're about to do something, or something is about to take place that makes a change. If you're from the Windows world, we refer to it as a **User Account Control** (**UAC**), which is a Windows feature everybody seems to disable because they don't understand that UAC is designed to protect us.

We have the same thing when it comes to both Linux and iOS when you get the prompts to enter in a root password, right? You can see that because there are different methods of discovery, this is a continual battle. Personally, I don't think there's a single best solution—I think it's always a combination of things. It's not always software-driven, although software does help us. To me, there's a lot of common sense that needs to be deployed.

Now let's take a look at some DoS threats.

DoS threats

DoS threats are among the most common threats faced by organizations. A DoS attack can be mounted against any organization, regardless of size or industry.

There are many different types of DoS attacks, but all have the same goal: to prevent legitimate users from accessing the organization's resources. Some of the most common types of DoS attacks include the following:

- **Flooding attacks**—In a flooding attack, the attacker sends a large number of requests to the organization's servers, overwhelming them and preventing legitimate users from accessing the resources they need.

- **SYN floods**—A **synchronize** (**SYN**) flood occurs when the attacker sends a large number of SYN packets to the organization's servers. Because the request is not complete, the servers are unable to send a SYN-ACK message, where **ACK** stands for **acknowledgment**. The servers become overwhelmed and legitimate users cannot access them.

- **Application layer assaults**—These attacks focus on specific applications or services that an organization uses. For example, there may be an attack against an organization's email server that prevents messages from being sent or received.

Any organization can be the target of a DoS attack, but some industries are more at risk than others. Healthcare organizations, for example, are often targeted because they hold sensitive data that can be used for identity theft or other malicious activities. Financial institutions are also frequently targeted in DoS attacks, as are government agencies and critical infrastructure providers.

Next, let's talk about DoS on steroids.

Distributed DoS (DDoS) attack

DDoS attacks, which are a type of DoS attack, are becoming increasingly common. A DDoS attack is when multiple systems are used to send overwhelming amounts of traffic to a target system, preventing it from functioning normally. Some of the most common types of DDoS attacks include the following:

- **UDP floods**—In a UDP flood attack, the attacker sends a large number of UDP packets to the target system. Because UDP is an unreliable protocol, there is no mechanism for the server to determine whether a request was sent. The target system becomes overwhelmed by UDP requests and cannot respond to legitimate users.

- **Internet Control Message Protocol (ICMP) floods**—In this type of attack, the attacker sends a large number of ICMP packets to the target. These packets spoof the source IP address so that it appears to be coming from the target system. As a result, the target system is overwhelmed with requests and cannot respond to legitimate users.

- **HTTP floods**—In an HTTP flood attack, the attacker sends a large number of HTTP requests to the target system. Because HTTP is a stateless protocol, there is no way for the server to determine whether a request has been sent before. The target system becomes overwhelmed and cannot respond to legitimate users.

DDoS attacks can be very difficult to defend against, especially if they are launched from multiple sources. Organizations should implement DDoS mitigation strategies to protect themselves from these types of attacks.

Botnets

One of the most common methods used to launch a DoS attack is using a botnet. A botnet is a collection of compromised devices that are controlled by the attacker. The attacker can then use these devices to launch a flood of requests at the organization's servers, overwhelming them and preventing legitimate users from accessing the resources they need.

Mitigation strategies

There are many ways to protect an organization from a DoS attack. The most important step is to have a good security posture, which includes having strong firewalls in place and ensuring that your systems are up to date. You should also regularly test your systems for vulnerabilities so that you can identify and fix any weaknesses before they can be exploited by an attacker.

It is also important to have a plan in place for responding to a DoS attack. This plan should include steps for identifying the source of the attack, stopping it, and restoring services to normal. Having a plan in place will help you to minimize the effects of an attack and ensure that your organization can return to normal operations as soon as possible.

There are several different mitigation strategies you can use to protect yourself from a DDoS attack. Some of these are listed here:

- **Use a DDoS protection provider**—A DDoS protection provider will monitor incoming traffic toward your server and filter out any malicious requests. This helps you to reduce the effects of an attack but does not prevent it entirely.

- **Implement network segmentation**—Segmenting your network will allow you to isolate each server so that attackers cannot target multiple systems at once. To limit the impact of an attack, try implementing micro-segmentation through software such as **Virtual Routers** (**vRouters**). This will allow you to separate your systems and protect yourself from a mass attack.

- **Implement application-layer protections**—The application layer is one of the most vulnerable parts of an architecture, but it can also be one of the easiest to protect against DDoS attacks. Software such as vArmour protects the application layer by providing an additional security layer for your servers.

- **Use DDoS detection tools**—There are many different network-based methods that can be used to detect a potential attack. These include mitigating DNS floods with **Berkeley Internet Name Domain** (**BIND**); Cisco IOS global rate limiting; and router **access control lists** (**ACLs**), blackhole routing, null routing, and source-based routing. You should also monitor your system logs for any signs of an attack.

Next, let's look at session hijacking.

Session-hijacking threats

Session-hijacking attacks are a type of attack in which an attacker diverts the session of a user to their machine. In this process, attackers try to capture users' packets and hijack their active sessions by cracking encryption codes or altering configurations. Sometimes, these attacks are conducted on a large scale for illegal activities that lead to economic gains, including credit card frauds and e-commerce scams. Attackers make use of easy-to-exploit and common vulnerabilities and attack victims where they are unprotected (open networks). However, session hijacking is more complex than other exploits because it depends on the attacker's ability to crack encryption codes.

Today, there are different types of session-hijacking attacks that are performed based on the level of access the attacker has to the network. The most common form of session hijacking is IP hijacking, where attackers divert traffic by acquiring the IP address of the victim and fooling the server into thinking that they are the original user. This can be done in several ways, such as **Address Resolution Protocol** (**ARP**) spoofing, DNS spoofing, or session splicing.

Some of the most common session hijacks are described next.

Cross-Site Scripting

In another type of attack called **Cross-Site Scripting (XSS)**, attackers inject malicious scripts into web pages viewed by the victim. When the user visits the infected page, the script is executed and the attacker gains access to the session. This type of attack is more common in public networks where users are not aware of the security risks involved.

Man-in-The-Middle attacks

Session hijacking can also be used to gain access to confidential information. In **Man-in-the-Middle (MitM)** attacks, the attacker intercepts all communication between the victim and the server and can see all data that is being exchanged. This allows the attacker to steal passwords, credit card numbers, or any other sensitive information.

Spoofing versus hijacking

You might be thinking that spoofing attacks are the same as hijacking. However, spoofing is different from session hijacking because, in spoofing, the attacker gains access to the place of the victim and gets the same privileges as the real user, such as accessing network resources or intercepting information sent by users. In session hijacking, attackers do not get such full access to resources, and they only get access to the sessions of users. This is why session hijacking is more dangerous than spoofing attacks.

Predicting session tokens

Many web servers create session IDs using algorithms that generate a unique token for each new session. This makes it difficult for attackers to hijack sessions, as they would not know the session ID unless they captured it during the initial login process. However, some servers do not implement such security measures and use easily guessable tokens or session IDs. In these cases, it is possible for the attacker to know the session token in advance and hijack user sessions.

The steps an attacker would use to predict a session token include the following:

1. Identifying the session management mechanism used by the server
2. Identifying the algorithm used to generate session tokens
3. Identifying weaknesses in the algorithm that could allow for the prediction of session tokens
4. Extracting a few session tokens and analyzing them to identify any patterns

5. Generating a list of possible token values based on the analysis of the extracted tokens

6. Trying out the possible token values to see if any of them matches the actual session token

7. Eventually, identifying the correct session token value that can be used to hijack user sessions

Man-in-the-Browser attacks

There are many security applications such as antivirus software, web filters, and **virtual private networks** (**VPNs**) that sit between the browser and server to protect user information. However, these security tools can be exploited by attackers through **Man-in-the-Browser** (**MitB**) attacks. This type of attack uses JavaScript code to manipulate the behavior of applications running on a client machine. When the user visits a malicious website, the script is executed by their browser and can perform any action controlled by the attacker. For example, it could send financial information to a different server.

Session-fixation attacks

Session-fixation attacks are similar to session hijacking because they allow attackers to steal user sessions. However, instead of manipulating the flow of data, attackers use this type of attack to create a new session for themselves and then trick users into using it.

In most cases, these types of attacks involve sending links or embedding links with session IDs in emails or instant messages. When the user clicks on the link, they are redirected to a website where their session is hijacked. Session-fixation attacks can also be used to exploit vulnerabilities in web applications.

Session ID spoofing

In session ID spoofing, attackers use fake session IDs to hijack user sessions. This type of attack is also known as a *phishing* attack because it tricks users into entering sensitive information on a website they believe is genuine. Attackers can create fake session IDs using tools that allow them to easily guess the underlying algorithm used by the application.

Attacking from public networks

In most cases, attackers use session-hijacking attacks from public networks such as the anonymous Tor network. They use tools such as Firesheep to sniff out session information on unsecured Wi-Fi networks and hijack user sessions with ease.

Other ways of hacking into accounts

Attackers also resort to other types of attacks, depending on the type of application they are targeting or their individual skills. For example, in pharming attacks, attackers use malicious DNS servers to redirect users to fake websites where they are asked to enter their login credentials. Once the user enters their information, it is sent to the attacker who can then log in and take over the account.

Preventing session hijacking

Session hijacking can be prevented by using strong authentication methods and by being aware of the security risks involved in using public networks. Users should also be careful when clicking on links or opening attachments in emails, especially if they don't know the sender.

Web application developers can also protect their applications from session-hijacking attacks by using strong authentication mechanisms and by verifying the authenticity of session tokens. They should also avoid using easily guessed session tokens or embedding them in URLs.

To protect yourself from session-hijacking attacks, you should always use strong passwords and install security patches as soon as they are available. You should also avoid using public networks to access your personal accounts.

Finally, you can reduce the risk of attacks by using a strong antivirus or internet security suite with features such as URL filtering, web filtering, keystroke encryption, data shredding, and a virtual keyboard.

I know, I've scared you a lot. Tell you what—let's now talk about some of the things we can do to protect ourselves from these monsters.

Master list of countermeasures

These are my own best practices that I've come up with based on my experience. Some of them have also been discussed in various publications.

There are three levels or different areas we need to make sure we're protecting, as follows:

- **Server level**—We have different products and solutions for our servers than we have for our desktop machines, laptops, or mobile devices. Please, please, please protect your mobile devices.

- **Desktop solutions level**—Just because you have protection in place at the server level doesn't mean that desktops don't need to be covered as well. Some people say: "*We have antivirus on our servers that scans everything.*" So, what happens when somebody plugs in a USB thumb drive they picked up in the parking lot? How is the server going to handle that? You should have desktop solutions as well as server solutions and vice versa because if you have stuff installed on your desktops, that doesn't mean your servers are completely safe.

- **Physical security level**—When it comes to ethical hacking, you need to understand attackers are not only looking for ways of getting into your environment, but even easier is getting into your environment by stealing your laptop, phone, or tablet. So, to guarantee physical security, we need to ensure we have things in place such as locked doors. I can't count the number of times I have seen a server sitting in an open room, or my favorite—the hallway closet in an office environment.

  Other obvious solutions for physical security is to control who has physical access to the office environment itself. And then there are different things you can do to solve that—for example, having a man trap: a man trap where one door locks behind you after you have walked through, and you can't open the next door until it has locked, or somebody has approved you. Therefore, it locks you inside of this area.

So, what's on my list of countermeasures? Let's discuss some of these solutions.

Antivirus

You need to make sure you have antivirus solutions for your desktop machines, mobile devices, and servers. You might have antivirus solutions for products. Many antivirus software solution providers or vendors don't just have the basics such as scanning desktops, servers, and all their files for viruses or malware—they might have a plugin specific to an application such as SQL, Exchange, or SharePoint, and how many people are running antivirus on your mobile devices?

Creating a security policy

The people in your company need to understand how to handle malware. Creating a policy will help ensure everyone tries to maintain security. It's not going to be just one policy; you will need a policy for antivirus to ensure everyone knows what to do if they think they have been infected. You will also need an email server policy that dictates how we plan on protecting the email server. You need email malware scanning policies to let people know when to scan, how often to scan, and who oversees updating those definitions.

You also need to come up with a policy on which file attachments people need to block. I know some companies who block not only the standard things—executables, batch programs, and so on—but also ZIP files, **screen saver files** (**SCRs**), or registration files. The policy needs to tell people what to do if they detect it. Should they quarantine it? Quarantine, then delete it after so many days? Or do we just whack it the first chance we get?

We also need a network exploit protection policy. This is the policy we use to inform people on how to handle remote users and mobile devices. For example, if I come in from the outside via VPN and I'm using my home PC, hopefully, you're going to limit me so that I don't have the same access to all the files on the network as I would have when at my office physically.

After creating these policies, you must make sure you share them and have training on them in your networked environment. In fact, I know my wife's company has them sign something to say they've read the policy because guess what? Doing certain things will get you an extended leave of absence.

Watching the download

When you go to install an application, you may be given some instructions on how to download and install it. I'm sure you've experienced this before...you'll go to download a piece of software and there's a big green button that says **Download** and you think that is the link to download the file you're looking for, but you're downloading something else.

The instructions for downloading on the website might also tell you to disable certain things. Sometimes, they'll be in these forums or blog sites, and they'll say: "*Hey, in order to install this, you've got to jump through these hoops—disable your antivirus because you might get a false positive.*" If you really want to have a good laugh, go look at some of these torrent sites and look at some of the comments that people make about installing. "*Hey, you know, my antivirus said there was a piece of malware in there*", and the author will say: "*Oh, no, that's just a false positive because of the hack that we used.*"

Updating your software

This is obvious, so most informed people religiously keep their software up to date. What about the OS? Most people say: "*You know, I wait until patches have been released for 30 or 60 days before implementing them.*" Well, guess what? That's 30 or 60 days that you're open to that vulnerability.

When it comes to Microsoft patches, you must install critical updates. They are not necessarily designed to do anything crippling to your environment—it's to patch a hole that's in your environment that Microsoft, Apple, or Linux is aware of. They're trying to help you, and critical updates get deployed immediately.

Updating applications

It's also important to make sure your applications are updated, whether it's the desktop-application or the server-application side of things. Server applications run on a server such as Exchange and SQL. Keep them up to date. And please, whatever you do, don't forget updates on your mobile devices.

Attachment issues

What do we mean by attachment issues? It's simple: try not to open attachments. I know we typically say: "*Our users just don't get it—can you believe they did this*?" Okay, I get it. But you know what? They're not as dumb as they used to be. Those of us who have been in this industry for 10 to 20 years remember our users as having been intelligence-challenged when it came to handling emails, but attackers are getting very tricky—they can trick anyone.

In fact, my wife recently got an email that said, "*Dear valued member, we've been receiving complaints of unauthorized usage of your USAA online banking system and due to concerns regarding safety integrity of your membership, we hereby issue this warning message*", and then they told her how to update her records. And how did they want her to update? Download and open the document they attached to the email and follow the instructions.

It looked like a document, but only if you don't finish the sentence out. In this email, they even copyrighted at the bottom and quoted things such as *Member FDIC*, which is how I knew it was spam. Of course, this was besides the fact we don't have a normal bank.

My wife's response was simple: "*We don't have a United Automobile account.*"

The other thing you want to do is ensure you block file attachments with more than one file type extension associated with them, such as `form.doc.txt` or `form.doc.bat`.

Legitimate source

Where is this coming from? Who is the source of this file? When I go to download a piece of software, I always make sure I go to the legitimate source. It's the same with drivers—I don't go to Billy Bob's download driver page to get my drivers. I got burned on that one once before.

Keeping informed

The one thing you want to do as a security expert or an ethical attacker is to stay current—daily, if not hourly in some cases. When a zero-day attack is announced, keep up to date with what's going on with it. This is obviously more than just scanning your environment.

Antivirus

This countermeasure speaks for itself. Your antivirus should be running daily.

Checking your media

Always check your media, which includes DVDs, CDs, as well as USB drives. Many people burn DVDs at home because they have documents and stuff they want to bring to work—documents, a collection of their favorite music, or a movie they would like to share with a colleague. The problem is their systems might be infected. You should have a policy about what is allowed to be brought in.

In fact, I am not a big fan of having optical drives in desktop systems just because of that issue. A friend who went to China came back with a DVD and handed it to me with a big smile: "*You're welcome.*" He thought it was all cool, but you should have seen the look on my face when I asked: "*What's this?*" "*Oh, I bought it for $15; it's every product Microsoft makes!*" It was pirated software and as I recall, it also had Symantec antivirus for *free*.

Watching your popups

Make sure your pop-up blocker in your web browser is turned on and remember: malware creators are getting quite creative with popups. They trick people by socially engineering them by making the popup look like something it's not. For example, it might look like antivirus but when you look at the border, you realize it's an **Internet Explorer** (**IE**) pop-up window without the URL bar. And because they're smart, they might make it an animated **Graphics Interchange Format** (**GIF**) file to make it look like it's scanning. No matter where you click, you will end up getting infected, even if you click the **Close** button. So, be very careful and vigilant about blocking popups.

Chat files

The reason this is important to check is because of the social networking environment where people are chatting back and forth. For example, Oswald Cobblepot, whom you just met on the internet, could say: "*Hey, I happen to like Batman too, do you want to see a really cool Batman screensaver? Let me send you a file.*"

Firewall and UAC

Who doesn't hate Microsoft firewall and the UAC? It is that annoying popup that asks: "*Are you sure you want to do this*?" I get it. As an administrator, I think: "*Of course I want to do it. I'm the one who typed in regedit.*"

Sometimes, we feel it's too much of a hassle to configure Windows Firewall. Well, guess what? Some of your attacks will not come from the outside—most are going to come from the inside. And believe it or not, the UAC is there to just remind you: "*Hey, you're about to make a change that is going to make a change to the system itself. Are you really sure you want to do this*?"

What's so funny is Microsoft gets hammered for this thing, yet what does Linux do? And Apple? Okay, full disclosure here. I have a laptop that I travel with for training purposes. I do turn the UAC off on it because I don't want to have to waste time by clicking **OK** when I'm doing presentations or demos. However, the UAC and firewall are enabled on all the servers at my house, my kids' machines, my wife's machine, and every other machine in my environment.

Again, you can turn your UAC and firewall off, but only if you know the consequences of that action. I'm using the word *consequences* because it worked with my kids—they always ran out of the room because that's the word we used instead of *grounding*. It's the same thing with users and for yourself—there are good consequences and bad consequences. Every choice you make has a consequence. Now, go to your room.

Summary

We first talked about what malware is and why it's created. It's critical we grasp the nature of malware because it's the number-one issue for us right now as far as security is concerned. We also talked about DoS threats, which can be devastating. We covered the dangers of session hijacking and how attackers try to predict and overtake a user's session to use their credentials to continue their attacks, and finally, we calmed your nerves by looking at countermeasures.

In the next chapter, we'll talk about sniffing and the different types of sniffing available to us. We'll also cover how sniffing can be used in an attack and how to protect ourselves from these attacks.

Questions

As we conclude, here is a list of questions for you to test your knowledge regarding this chapter's material. You will find the answers in the *Assessments* section of the *Appendix*:

1. To protect against Trojan attacks, how does Tripwire and other similar applications assist us?

   A. It's a file-integrity checking tool that detects and rejects malware designed for the kernel.

   B. It's an antivirus solution that quarantines and removes malware right away.

   C. It's a file integrity checker that alerts you when a system file is changed.

   D. It's an antivirus program that detects and removes viruses during a scan.

2. To continually pull data and monitor a network, what is typically used?

   A. Trojan

   B. APT

   C. A rootkit

   D. A virus

3. What component can be used to install malware on a target?

   A. Crypter

   B. Dropper

   C. Exploit

   D. Obfuscator

4. What is the name of a program that is concealed within another program?

   A. Multipart

   B. Ransomware

   C. Trojan

   D. Stealth

10
Sniffing and Evading IDS, Firewalls, and Honeypots

Sniffing is an old method with new technology. Back in the day—before smartphones—we had telephones. There was a method used to tap into the phone line and listen in on conversations. You could record traffic, as well as intercepting data going across the line.

This required you to select a target and then connect with a listening or recording device. This was typically achieved by unofficial or official channels—depending on the legality—as well as a direct line mechanism. You could also use radio wiretaps. The whole purpose here was to listen in on conversations or record data that was flowing.

An attacker can intercept and read any network packet containing plaintext information. This information could include usernames, passwords, personal codes, banking information, or anything else valuable to the attacker.

Packet sniffing has the same concept as wiretapping—just on a different platform. Instead of listening to audio, we're listening to ones and zeros. The attacker's goal is to look at all traffic and packets that go across your network.

By the end of this chapter, you should understand what a sniffing attack is and its role in extracting meaningful insights from the complex and large sets of data all around us.

We will cover the following topics in this chapter:

- What is sniffing?
- Types of sniffing
- Hardware versus software sniffing
- **Dynamic Host Configuration Protocol (DHCP)** assaults
- **Media access control (MAC)** attacks
- **Address Resolution Protocol (ARP)** poisoning
- **Domain Name System (DNS)** poisoning
- Detecting sniffing methods
- Evading **intrusion detection systems (IDSs)**
- Moving around firewalls
- Honeypots

What is sniffing?

Using sniffing tools, an attacker can monitor and capture packets passing through a network and spy on what is going on with internet activity.

Let's talk more specifically about what sniffing is and how to leverage it in an attack.

There are two types of wiretaps out there, as outlined here:

- **Active wiretapping** allows an attacker to manipulate and force themselves into the middle using a **Man-in-the-Middle (MITM)** attack, which allows the attacker to record and monitor traffic. As an active channel, it can allow the attacker to change the data flowing through or inject information. When it comes to ethical hacking, *active* means we're going to do something extremely aggressive by forcing a communication. You can see a depiction of a MITM attack in the following diagram:

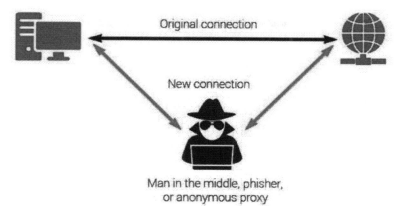

Figure 10.1 – MITM attack

- **Passive wiretapping** allows an attacker to eavesdrop or listen into conversations—nothing malicious; it's only for gathering information. We can use passive tapping to record that same information, but we're not manipulating anything or anyone.

Is this legal? Well, it depends on your environment, so you should always know the rules. Lawful interception or wiretapping is implemented by lawful authority via a warrant or if you have an agreement with a company and you're doing a penetration test with them.

Most of the time, these activities are extremely useful for things such as management, protection, and even monitoring infrastructure. Lawfulness is always determined by whether there is permission granted.

Lately, the big thing is terrorist activities being monitored around the world. We have government agencies sniffing or looking at the network passively for certain keywords or key traffic that flows through the internet, which could then raise flags if certain criteria are met.

There's a lot of debate as to whether governments should be involved in this kind of thing. I find it hard to debate because I see it as a *catch-22*. I understand the reason behind it, but I also like my privacy. Whatever you do, know the rules of your environment.

If you're thinking we have a switch network, well, trust me—I can get past that.

The concept here is that the attacker is going to try to look at information that passes through a segment by monitoring both hardware and software. Software will be our protocols, while hardware will be network devices.

If the attacker can compromise one of these devices, they can start monitoring all the information that's flowing through it. And what is the attacker looking for? Well, believe it or not, there are some applications that transmit passwords and usernames in cleartext. Guess what? Email is cleartext. And you'd be surprised how many times people send credit card information over email. If the web application is not locked down correctly, we may be transmitting in cleartext, and of course, any type of sensitive data will be a treasure chest for an attacker.

Sniffing dangers

So, how dangerous is this? Very dangerous because it's on your network—it's all there for them. And what can I see as I'm sniffing?

Well, I can see things such as this:

- DNS traffic
- A client machine requesting a DNS name resolution to a DNS server
- Email traffic
- **File Transfer Protocol (FTP)** passwords
- Web traffic
- Telnet passwords
- Router configuration
- Chat sessions

I'll also be able to see Telnet passwords if it's not properly locked down; unless you're using FTPS—the secured FTP—the password and username are going to go across as cleartext. I might also be able to pick up router configurations, as well as email traffic. And I'm not just talking about the emails themselves, but everything dealing with your email system. Exchange servers communicate with other Exchange servers, and all that traffic—if you don't lock it down—could expose quite a bit about your infrastructure. We all know that **HyperText Transfer Protocol (HTTP)** is cleartext, and as a matter of fact, there's a big push now to make everybody go **HTTP Secure (HTTPS)**. I agree. Most chat session environments can be sniffed, as well as **System Logging Protocol (syslog)** traffic.

Syslog can be used for system management and security auditing, as well as getting general information and looking at analysis and debugging messages. Now, think about that going across cleartext; not just software, but devices can have their own syslog files that are going to report back to a syslog endpoint. That can be printers, routers, and so on, and typically, these logs have information such as timestamps, hostnames, and even the **Internet Protocol** (**IP**) address of the device.

How is this done? Well, it's *à la mode*. See, I had the Big Mac earlier, and now I want some ice cream! What I mean by *à la mode* is this: you have a **network interface card** (**NIC**) that is hooked up to a switch, which is then hooked up to multiple systems that are out there. This is the standard network environment.

Typically, a network card operates by sending data from one location to another, and normally, a network card picks up all traffic it sees on the network and just simply disregards or dumps the packets that are not destined for its IP address, but it still sees it.

We can change the way the NIC is going to work by placing it into promiscuous mode. This causes the network card to pass all the traffic it sees to the **central processing unit** (**CPU**) rather than discarding the frames that are intended only for that NIC. In non-promiscuous mode, the network card does not have as much fun. No—the NIC receives a frame and will drop it unless the frame is addressed to that NIC's MAC address.

There are many **operating systems** (**OSs**) that require admin-level or superuser privileges to enable promiscuous mode, and normally, a network card only sees traffic that's on the same port, especially if it's in a switched environment.

I know I just mentioned something as ancient as the **video cassette recorder** (**VCR**), but that was the problem with the hub. It transmitted data through all the different ports. A lot of companies have moved to switched environments that are used to combat the use of promiscuous mode; if I did the same, I'd only be able to see data that was still destined for myself.

Next, let's talk about some options we can use when sniffing.

Types of sniffing

So, what are the different types of sniffing? Please don't say, "*It depends whether you're trying to figure out a scent or whether you have a cold.*" To us, sniffing is where we talk about the actual vectors available to us, and there are several different vectors we can look at.

Spoofing attacks

In this type of attack, the attacker pretends to be someone else by modifying or falsifying the information or data. By doing so, they can gain access to the resources or even steal personal information.

These types of attacks can be done in several different ways. The attacker can use an IP address that's associated with a victim, which would allow them to send out fraudulent emails or set up websites, try to get passwords or account information, and so on. There is no limit when it comes to spoofing attacks and what attackers can accomplish. You can even set up a fake access point for wireless connectivity and pretend to be legitimate users connecting through illegitimate connections.

DHCP starvation attack

In a starvation attack, we deplete the number of IP addresses by chewing up everything except the DHCP server. So, you've got your DHCP server and it's going to have a scope or multiple scopes representing different subnet ranges. In this case, we're going to go with `192.168.0.1`, all the way up to `254`. It's just simply a list or a database of IP addresses it can issue out to client machines. Now, as the network comes up, a client makes a request, and that information is passed through the switch, and then sent to the DHCP server to get their IP address. We'll talk more about this later in the chapter.

DHCP server attack

In this type of attack, the attacker will set up their own DHCP server. Matter of fact, as an attacker, I'll use these two techniques together. I'll set up a rogue DHCP server, do a starvation attack, and have everybody start getting their IP addresses from my rogue DHCP server. This will allow me to do fun things such as a **denial-of-service** (**DoS**) attack because now, they don't have a legitimate gateway where I could then implement DNS poisoning. We'll also talk more about this later in the chapter.

MAC flooding attack

You might think MAC flooding is what happens at an Apple store when Macs go on sale. To help you understand this better, let's figure out what a switch does. Now, a switch has a MAC table inside of it, and a MAC address is associated with network cards on nodes—or computers if you think of them that way—or printers. The switch keeps a list of the MAC addresses that are in each physical port on the switch, and this allows us to reduce broadcast traffic on our network. It also protects us from sniffing attacks.

With a typical MAC flood, the switch is fed a ton of Ethernet frames, and each frame contains different source MAC addresses sent by the attacker. The effects of this on the switch can vary depending on what the attacker is trying to accomplish. However, the big goal for most attackers is to force a legitimate MAC address out of the MAC table and inject a rogue MAC address to force traffic to go to a specific system they may be using for monitoring or for sniffing.

DNS poisoning

DNS poisoning is simply what it sounds like. It poisons the DNS entry, which resolves a name to an IP address. If I can tell you Citibank's IP address is my malicious website versus you going to Citibank's site, and I can inject that, I'm going to have a lot of fun with you. This is especially true if my malicious website looks just like Citibank's, including a username and login entry.

ARP poisoning

ARP poisoning is very similar to what we see with MAC flooding, but with ARP poisoning, we're going to try to associate the attacker's MAC address with the victim's address. This way, the traffic that is destined for the victim gets sent to the attacker instead.

Password sniffing

As the name suggests, password sniffing is the ability to sniff packets going across, looking for passwords that are being transmitted in cleartext or without any type of encryption. In cases where passwords are encrypted, the attacker can use a decryption algorithm to try to decrypt that password, and I'm guessing you know what's going to happen after that, right?

Switch-port stealing technique

This is extremely useful to sniff in a switched environment when ARP poisoning can't be done. It floods the **local area network** (**LAN**) with ARP packets. The destination MAC address of each stealing packet is the same as the attacker's, while the source MAC address is one of the victim's MAC addresses. By doing this to the switch, it steals the port from the victim.

What does this accomplish? All the packets destined for the victim's MAC address are received by the attacker, and when the attacker receives the packet of the stolen host, they stop the flooding process and perform an ARP request for the real destination of the packet. When they receive the ARP reply, they know that the victim has taken back their port, so the Ether cap can resend the packet to the destination as is. After that, we just loop that process over and over. It's quite tricky.

Hardware versus software sniffing

You may be thinking, how do we sniff? Well, we have both hardware and software solutions to deal with. I'm going to warn you ahead of time, the hardware side is not cheap. On the hardware side of things, we have protocol analyzers. These devices are designed to monitor network traffic. This would be the poor man's version:

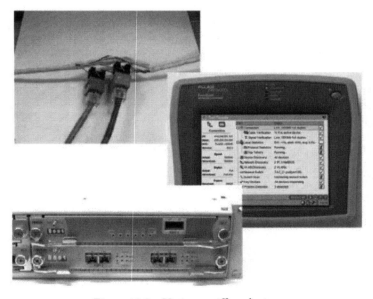

Figure 10.2 – Various sniffing devices

I had an opportunity to play around with one, the Fluke pictured in the middle and at the bottom in the preceding figure. It's such a fantastic little device. They're not only used to monitor but also analyze the data. With the Fluke, we can see how long the cable run is. If there were a break, we would see how far down the cable it was broken. You could also analyze the top protocols being used on the network. A multi-port testing system device such as the *N2XN5540A* would allow you to monitor and verify the performance of networks and devices.

Again, as mentioned earlier, not only can we analyze data, but we can also capture data and play it back later if we want to. The attacker can see the individual data bytes of each packet as it passes through the cable.

These devices are very expensive, and most run-of-the-mill attackers won't have that type of budget. The cheaper alternative is software. One of the more popular products out there is Wireshark, originally known as Ethereal. It is a cross-platform product that uses **Packet Capture** (or **PCAP**) as an **application programming interface (API)** that captures live network packet data to capture your packets. If you know me, you know I believe nothing is for free, but trust me—this product is completely free. It supports being able to look at data from Ethernet to the **Institute of Electrical and Electronics Engineers (IEEE)** *802.11 PPP*, as well as running from a **graphical user interface (GUI)** or a **command-line interface (CLI)**.

I had an opportunity to see Laura Chappell, the Wireshark expert, in a presentation, and she blew me away at how quickly she was able to recover passwords and look at the data. It's kind of where I got my start. This was back in the old days when *Novell* had a big market share of the networking world. That just tells you how old I am, right?

In your immediate future, you will see some questions concerning some of the filters for Wireshark, so I highly recommend you study up. You don't need to dive in too deep—just look at the basic ones out there. And there are other products out there such as OmniPeek, which has a nice little GUI.

There's also SoftPerfect's **Network Protocol Analyzer (NPA)**. Microsoft has its own product too: the Microsoft Network Monitor. If you saw it a long time ago, it's gotten a facelift, so you may want to look at it again.

And just to use my favorite word, there are a plethora of network sniffers out there that are used for the dark side. Some of them are extremely small—they can run off **Universal Serial Bus (USB)** drives, Raspberry Pis, and Cain and Abel, which happens to be one of my favorite ones because it's quick and dirty.

We also have AirSnort, which I'm sure you can figure out. There's one called Snort. AirSnort was Snort for Wi-Fi. Snort was extremely powerful. I used it with my **internet service provider (ISP)** service as well. It's so powerful—it sniffed the traffic, and if we saw DoS attacks coming in from a specific address, we had a Snort rule that executed off and automatically blocked that IP address at the router.

Now, not all of these are used for the dark side—I just want you to know there's a wide variety of products out there used for both good and evil, therefore bringing balance to the force. See how I got that one in?

Sniffing mobile apps

There may be situations where you may not have access to a laptop or you're just trying to be a little bit more discreet in your pen test, or the attacker's trying to be a little bit more discreet instead of walking around your environment with a laptop. That's okay. If you don't have one, there are mobile apps out there.

What I find interesting is, I looked on the Apple Store and I couldn't find anything that wasn't rated anything higher than one star, which is kind of weird. But then again, I'm not an Apple guy, so maybe you can find some of your own products out there for the Apple side.

On the Android side, though, there are a plethora of options, and that's one of the reasons I prefer Android. One of the most popular ones is Wicap 2, and it comes in two different versions. There's the demo version, which is just a demo of their product. It gets really good reviews and has a good following. However, it requires rooting of your phone.

This company also makes a full product, which is the one that really gets rave reviews. It comes at a price, but it's extremely popular as far as its ratings are concerned, and a lot of people have good things to say about it.

Another one is PCAP, and it's kind of scary. Not only does it work as a network sniffer, but it also includes **Secure Sockets Layer** (**SSL**) decryption, which it does through a MITM attack. It does not require root access, which could be why it's a little more popular as well, but the interface is very similar to what we see coming from Wireshark.

Once you learn one sniffing technique, you'll see similarities through the different product lines out there. Again, mobile apps are an option to go with when you're trying to sniff a network.

Next, let's take a deeper look into what DHCP assaults are.

DHCP assaults

DHCP Assaults sounds like a cool title for a movie, doesn't it? DHCP is such an integrated technology throughout our network infrastructure, it is an extreme target for an attacker to get to because we can control so many things when it comes to the use of this technology.

So, what is DHCP and what is it for? If you don't know what it is, I'll give you a quick overview of what it's designed to do.

DHCP is a specialized server role we install on a server. We do this because any computer that needs to connect to the network or gain access to resources, whether internal or external (such as the internet), needs some way of connecting, and we do that via IP addresses.

DHCP oversees assigning IP addresses to computers as they hit the network. It does that by creating a scope—basically, a database of IP addresses.

One of the main responsibilities of the DHCP server is to keep track of which computer has which IP address. This way, we don't get a lot of duplication going on.

DHCP is what we refer to as a client-server model, and being a protocol, it has its own set of messages it exchanges between the client and the server as they're trying to get an IP address. Once we assign an IP address to the client machine—workstations, printers, your cell phone, tablet, or other servers—there are certain servers we want to make sure are statically assigned an IP address. That would be, obviously, the DHCP server itself. You can't really get an IP address from yourself when you haven't even fired off yet, so the other thing we do, besides assigning IP addresses, is assign other **Transmission Control Protocol** (**TCP**)/IP settings.

Those settings would include things such as a DNS server. Where do I go to discover what *Yahoo.com* is equated to as far as an IP address? Or, where do I go to find out where the bat cave is located as far as an IP address is concerned?

Another type of setting we could assign would also be a default gateway, which is: how do I get out of this network? If I'd like to go to Yahoo, I've got a DNS server that tells me Yahoo is equal to this address, but how do I get there from here? That's what the default gateway is designed to do.

Now, granted—you could type these on individual computers if you would like, but imagine being an IT person in charge of 50 computers (which is actually a low number), and you must go type in the IP address, the DNS IP, the default gateway, and a subnet mask. Typing in that information over and over, even just 50 times, let alone thousands of times, could lead to a serious illness that's out there that I want to draw your attention to: fat fingers, which is something I have. I don't know how many times I've fat-fingered an IP address; I'll reverse it—instead of typing in 192, I'll type in 129, just because I'm going so fast and typing in that information over and over.

DHCP starvation attacks

DHCP starvation reminds me of the famous scene in *Oliver!* where the little boy goes up and says: *More, please.* And of course, the word *starvation* sounds so ominous. The concept is, you have your DHCP server and it's going to have a scope or multiple scopes that represent different subnet ranges. In this case, we're going to go with 192.168.0.1, all the way up to 254. It's simply a list or a database of IP addresses it can issue out to client machines.

As the network comes up, a client makes a request. That information is passed through the switch and then sent to the DHCP server to get their IP address. Along with that information comes information such as its default gateway, the DNS server, and how long the lease is going to be.

It's important to note that with a lease, the client itself will check when 50% of the **time to live** (**TTL**) of the lease has been expired back with the DHCP server to find out whether it's okay if it uses that IP address. This is all well and good in a normal environment, but enter our attacking machine, which basically goes and floods the network with DHCP requests or discovers and the DHCP server thinks it's different client machines requesting those IP addresses. In fact, the program is so sophisticated that it shows the different MAC addresses associated with those requests.

What ends up happening? The DHCP server thinks it's sent out all the different IP addresses and the scope is then depleted, meaning the client machine is then denied access to get an actual IP address, or it is starved.

There are several programs you can use to accomplish this type of attack. Two of the more famous ones are Gobbler and Yersinia.

Going rogue

When it comes to going rogue, what we're doing is making sure you understand the standard DHCP environment. What we end up doing is a starvation attack on that machine.

In a rogue attack, the attacker will introduce their own server that's going to issue out DHCP.

So, here, I have my client machines, and we've got our standard nifty little DHCP server that's legit for the network, hooked up with our switch:

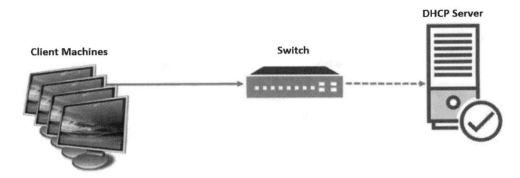

Figure 10.3 – Normal network with a DHCP server

Again, normally, they would send their DHCP discovers to the switch, which would then get approved by the DHCP server. However, when it comes to a rogue DHCP server attack, the attacker introduces a rogue DHCP server to the network.

To get the client machines to get their information from the rogue server, they simply must do the starvation attack against the DHCP server—the legitimate one. It goes offline, and then the requests automatically get redirected because the DHCP server is just looking for discovers, and it responds back to the client machines and issues them away from the settings that could compromise the box, as illustrated here:

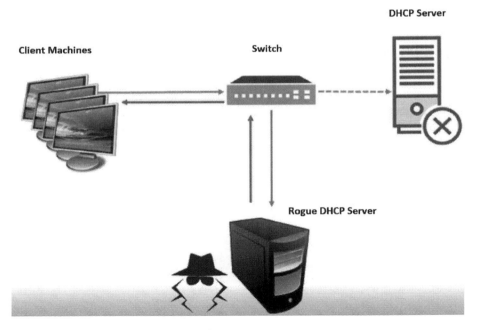

Figure 10.4 – Attack inserts a rogue DHCP server

For example, I could say your DNS is equal to my attacking DNS server, and in it, I have Citibank is equal to my malicious site that looks just like Citibank or eBay or PayPal or Amazon. I can totally control the environment. If you type in `Yahoo`, I could send you to Google.

The other result is all the traffic from the client will be sent to the attacker's IP address because I could also list it as the default gateway, which would then allow me to sniff the network. The client will simply assume everything is functioning correctly. I may be forwarding them from my rogue server out to the legitimate sites, but again, I'm going to have all the traffic pass through me.

Sometimes, we get a rogue server on the network nobody meant to get up there. We have a developer or somebody who's doing a test environment who fires up a DHCP server. Them placing this server on the network can interfere with the environment, and this type of attack is also extremely difficult to detect on the network unless you're taking some countermeasures.

Countermeasures

We'll start with stopping a DHCP starvation attack. Considering the attacking machine sends a DHCP discover request to the switch, one of the things we can do is implement port security, a feature of the switch designed to set the maximum number of MAC addresses per port.

If I know I only have five computers down this one line on this switch, I will want to set my port security to 5, which should prevent a starvation attack that would be implemented through that port.

On configuring port security, you will want to reference the manufacturer of your switch, but when we look at one of the most popular products out there, which would be Cisco, the port security is turned off by default. The switch itself must be a **level 2** (or **L2**), and when you need to enable port security, you simply type in `switchport port-security`, which activates port security.

You can also do things such as setting the maximum to 1, the maximum number of MAC addresses on a switch. You can also specify how many MAC addresses the switch can have on one interface at a time. The number could be anywhere from 1 to 6200 or so.

Something else we can do is set the action that's going to take place when a violation occurs on that interface. The default is to shut down the interface, effectively stopping any traffic from coming from the suspected system, but you can also use `switchport`. Port security violation is restricted, which just means it discards the traffic and sends a **Simple Network Management Protocol** (**SNMP**) message but keeps the port up and running.

We can also use the *protected* option on the switch, which discards all traffic, keeps the port up, but doesn't send an SNMP message. And of course, *shut down* does exactly what it says it's going to do.

Another option is setting the aging for port security. This would allow you to set the time, as well as the type for all secure addresses on the port or how long the port stays off. The aging time can go from 2 minutes to almost 1,500—the famous 1,440 minutes or 1,400 and 40 minutes. You can specify the type using `absolute` or `inactive`. For absolute aging, all the secured addresses on this port go out exactly after the minutes we specified and are removed from the secure address list. For inactive aging the secure addresses on this port go out only if there's no data traffic from the secured source for that specific amount of time.

To stop a rogue attack, we implement DHCP snooping, a feature that's going to be available on your switch. It stops ports from responding to DHCP offers. For example, if I had a DHCP server and it were connected physically to port 1, I would turn off snooping on ports 2 through 8.

What happens if an attacker manages to build up a DHCP server and puts it under the switch? They won't be able to get any responses or to respond to DHCP discover packets because it's only allowed to go down the ports your legitimate DHCP server is on.

Microsoft also did some interesting things—they started us up with Server 2008. If you had an **Active Directory** (**AD**) environment, you had to authorize the DHCP server in AD, which means it would come up. So, if you went and installed DHCP, that was one of the steps you had to do. If you didn't have the rights to do it, even though you had the role installed, it would never actually fire off.

This is great for the Microsoft world, but it doesn't stop somebody from firing up a Linux DHCP server, and that is where I would implement DHCP snooping on my switches.

Let's discuss MAC attacks next.

MAC attacks

If you are from the **United States** (**US**) and grew up around *McDonald's* back in the good old 1970s before it became the worldwide phenomenon it is now, you'll remember their interesting commercial with the phrase describing a Big Mac attack, which was two all-beef patties, special sauce, lettuce, cheese, onions, all on a sesame seed bun. However, we're not talking about food. MAC is short for **media access control**, and every single NIC we get has a MAC address.

Packets sent on Ethernet are always coming from a MAC address, and they're also sent to a MAC address. I know you're thinking: wasn't that the job of IP? Well, TCP/IP deals with MACs, but when we get down to it, it's the MAC address that is utilized for the transmission and receiving of packets. Each port, whether it's on a NIC or on a printer or a laptop, is going to be unique.

If the network adapter is receiving a packet, it's comparing the packet's destination MAC address to the adapter of this MAC address that's on its own card. If it matches, it then allows the packet to proceed. If it doesn't match, it just drops it.

The MAC address is typically a 12-digit number. As with an IP address, the MAC address also has a syntax to it, in the aspect the first 6 characters are what we refer to as the *prefix*. Those first 6 characters are uniquely assigned to different vendors. So, in those 12 digits, the first 6 are listed as a prefix, and the prefixes are assigned to specific vendors. As an example, there are several prefixes assigned to Linksys, so if I saw a prefix of a MAC address of 00:13:10 or 00:25:9C or 68:7f:74, I would know this was a Linksys device.

There's a MAC address out there that is unique. It is simply 12 Fs—that is, FF:FF:FF:FF:FF:FF. It is very similar to my report card in high school... It's a broadcast address and addresses every adapter in the network itself.

CAM

CAM is MAC spelled backward, but of course, that's not what it represents. **CAM** is short for a **content-addressable memory** table and every switching device it has inside of it. As packets pass through the switch, they include a destination and a source MAC address, meaning this is the destination I'm trying to get to and it's coming from this source.

As traffic passes through the switch, the CAM table simply tracks the MAC addresses' locations and specifies which port each MAC address is assigned to. So, in this case, you can see the switch knows I'm not going to read off the full MAC address here, I'll just do the last two letters, but you'll notice in the following diagram that FF is in the first port and the MAC address ending in TT is in the sixth port:

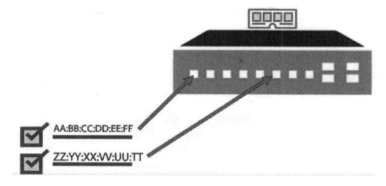

Figure 10.5 – CAM tables on a switch tracks MAC addresses

Now, when a packet goes through the switch, the switch does a broadcast using the FF:FF:FF:FF:FF:FF MAC address. It shoots out a Bulk API broadcast, trying to find the MAC address that ends with A1. When it reports back, it simply makes a notation in the CAM table, and that note is located on a given port. The CAM table is in the memory of the switch, so if you power off a switch or reboot a switch, the CAM table is cleared out. This feature of a switch, of learning where the different MACs are located, helps us in reducing broadcast traffic, as well as traffic destined for one computer not getting sent to the wrong port—at least, that's the goal.

It doesn't stop with a single switch because most networks have more than one switch. Here, I've got two switches, and of course, each one's going to have its own CAM:

Figure 10.6 – Each device will have its own CAM

In this case here, we're trying to find a destination ending in FF; you can see in *Figure 10.7* my destination MAC address and my source MAC address.

If in the actual network environment, the MAC address that's associated with FF is located on the second switch, that switch will know where that MAC address or that computer is located. However, this first router doesn't have any idea where that's located, and so if a computer is trying to send a packet or a piece of data to a machine on the secondary switch and it's located on the first switch, we must somehow resolve this.

Again, the first switch will have MAC addresses for systems that it's aware of, as well as the MAC address of the ports on the switch itself—in this case here, the uplink port:

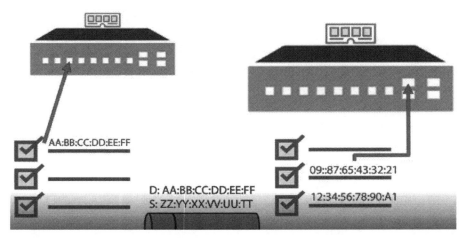

Figure 10.7 – CAMs track which port a MAC is on

Here, the uplink port is ending in `21`, and the switch is smart enough to know that this port is associated with the MAC address over here on the secondary switch in its uplink port:

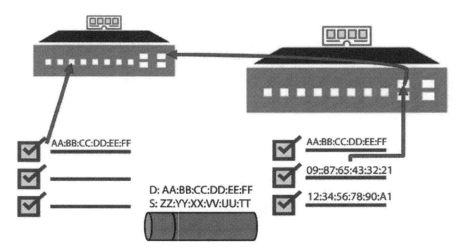

Figure 10.8 – Uplink ports know where to forward based on the CAM

As the first switch does a broadcast, the second switch responds and says, "*Hey, I know about that one, so just forward all the packets to me,*" and that's what happens.

The CAM table on this first switch says anytime you want to send something to FF, just forward it to 21, and then 21 will take care of it because it has the MAC address of that secondary switch. Now, did I clear up the water there or did I muddy it up?

This is also true with that secondary switch. It would be aware of the ports it's connected to back to switch 1, and this is how we have a fully switched networked environment. The whole process is quite efficient, which should tell you the government is not involved.

Flooding

Now that we understand how a switch works and how packets move across the network, our whole goal is to look at MAC attacks. Part of that attack is referred to as flooding.

You may be thinking it's cool the switch does all that, but as I said before, you can't sniff a network that is switched, and that is true unless you get the switch too full that it can't get any more notations of where MAC addresses are located. This kind of goes back to the old days of what different network devices do, and typically, as we move up the scale in our network device, we start off with a hub and a hub sends a broadcast out to every single port, then we move up to a switch. A switch will do what a hub does, but it does it on steroids, meaning it's going to start monitoring and directing traffic, which is what we saw with that CAM, and then you get into routing.

The overall concept is some switches go backward in time. If I have my switch and my CAM table, and I know where my different MACs are located on which port, a very common trick for an attacker to implement is to fire up their box. If I overload that switch with too many records for it to keep track of what's going on with which MAC, which we call flooding the switch, it does something interesting—it dumbs itself down and becomes a hub.

Every single packet will be broadcasted across all the ports. It's the default feature of most switches, especially consumer-rated switches because you don't want to lose connectivity.

As a side note, there are other ways you can sniff a network on a switch. Besides a MAC attack, there are actual ports on a switch, or a lot of managed switches referred to as **Switched Port Analyzers** (**SPANs**) or SPAN ports. These ports mirror and allow an attacker or a network administrator to monitor all traffic going across.

The MAC flooding method is extremely noisy on the network and very easily detected. However, it's only going to be detected by some of the more advanced switches out there, which is why it's always important to know about your inventory and what you've got running where (loading).

Countermeasures

When it comes to protecting yourself, you'll see a lot of repeats of what we've already talked about, and the reason we see this over and over is that it's all done at the network layer. There are some cool things you can use, such as Cisco's port security feature. You can use it to secure a port. So, if you assign a MAC address to the secure port, the port will only forward packets to the machine that's destined on that port.

What's cool about this technology is you can set up alerts to do that. For example, if something suspicious starts happening on the network, such as a MAC address of a machine trying to access a port that doesn't match an identifiable secure MAC address or any type of violations, we can be alerted of those things.

We also have the option of using an **authentication, authorization, and accounting (AAA)** server, which we often refer to as a RADIUS server.

These servers require computers and users to authenticate themselves and track what they're doing and where they're going automatically. Typically, this is done either by somebody logging in or possibly via a certificate. I had an AAA server with my ISP, and we did it for the accounting portion of it.

If you remember, back in the old days, you got charged for the time you were on the internet, right? As with the old *AOL* days. We didn't charge people; we wanted to be able to get a breakdown to our users saying, "*Hey, this is how much time you spent on the internet; this is how much data you've downloaded through our services*," and we were able to do that because we could match that up to the MAC address of their antennas and their routers.

We'll discuss ARP poisoning next.

ARP poisoning

ARP poisoning is a mechanism we can use during the sniffing process, and its capability is quite scary. The concept is… we're going to trick people into doing something or going to a place they don't intend to, and we do this at a computer level.

Growing up, my father would tell me: "*You can only trick people for so long, but until then, take advantage of the situation.*" Of course, he would say this in a light-hearted way—he didn't really believe this. It always seemed to him people were trying to do this to him. He was working for a movie theater chain and his job entailed going to different areas to find where managers and employees were stealing from the company. He always said people thought they could come up with a new way of finding "*a way around the system*" so that they wouldn't be detected, but technically, it was never a new way. It was just a new path using an old mechanism, and that old mechanism was just theft.

ARP takes us back to the old *Network+* days, possibly *A+* days, and if you're old enough, you'll remember the old *Networking Essentials* days. ARP is a protocol that has been around for some time. If you have gone through previous chapters, you'll remember we discussed network cards and how they had a MAC address associated with them. We also talked about how MAC addresses are the true way computers or nodes communicate with each other.

The computer needs to be able to resolve a MAC address to an IP address, which is very similar to what we refer to as name resolution. If you remember, we also mentioned in the other chapters that DNS gives us the ability to resolve a name such as *Yahoo.com* to an IP address.

Well, because computers or nodes are giving these physical addresses, ARP is what's responsible for resolving it to the IP address.

I know this totally blew your mind, and that's what ARP does for us. It's a protocol designed to map an internet IP address to a physical machine address. Typically, all of this is done via a table. Now, it's not a table such as a spreadsheet, but you can kind of think of it that way. We refer to it as an **ARP cache**, and because it's cached, it is information that is stored in memory.

Usually, the information does not stay in memory for a long time, which is kind of the downside to it. Besides, it's easily manipulated because when a packet is destined for a host machine on a particular LAN, it arrives at the gateway, which then asks ARP to find the physical host or MAC address that matches that IP address. If it doesn't have it in the cache, it does a broadcast if a node wants to update the switch or the router its MAC address has changed. This is kind of what we're going to do with an ARP poison: we'll trick the switch or the computer into thinking its ARP table is no longer valid.

ARP spoofing

ARP spoofing is another name for poisoning—we use the names interchangeably. This is all under the concept that the machine that sends the ARP request assumes the ARP reply comes from the correct machine, which we know in our case is not going to happen.

Some of you are now thinking: he's about to scare me again. No—it's time to put the big pants on and seek to understand what's happening here.

Here is what we can do to implement this type of attack. We send forged data—or, how I like to put it, forge our way. The attacker can create what we refer to as a malformed ARP reply containing the spoofed IP address and MAC address.

At this point, the target's machine blindly accepts the ARP entry into its ARP table. The attacker then overloads the switch, forcing the switch to go into a new mode, referred to as forwarding mode. They do this by sending a ton of ARP requests and reply packets to the switch.

After doing that, the attacker floods the target's ARP cache with the forged entries, which is what we refer to as spoofing or poisoning the target.

Spoofing or poisoning the target

Spoofing or poisoning the target looks like a complicated technique, but it's not that bad, because guess what? We have some really cool tools out there, including `dsniff`, which is actually a set of password-sniffing and network traffic-analyzing tools. And it has some other tools in there besides `dsniff`. There's `filesnarf`, `mailsnarf`, `messagesnarf`, and `arpspoof`—which simply allows us to poison a target.

Another tool out there is the Ettercap. It's also an open source security tool we can use for MITM attacks, and it does some protocol analysis as well as security auditing.

We also have Cain and Abel, which is a suite of tools we can use to do poisoning.

Again, you can use these tools for good, but remember: all tools can be used for evil.

How to poison the network via ARP

It's time to break out the brothers! I mean, install and try out Cain and Abel. Cain and Abel gets its name from a biblical story of two brothers, one that slays the other, therefore bad versus good. That's exactly what you see with this product. Sometimes, it's just referred to as Cain because it's mostly evil.

Now, raise your hand and say the oath that you will not do anything with some of these tools, and you will never tell law enforcement that *Dale told you it's okay to run this on a live network!* This tool can easily spoof and poison a device's ARP table and trick all the devices on the network to send their traffic through an attacker's system. You can see an overview of the tool's interface in the following screenshot:

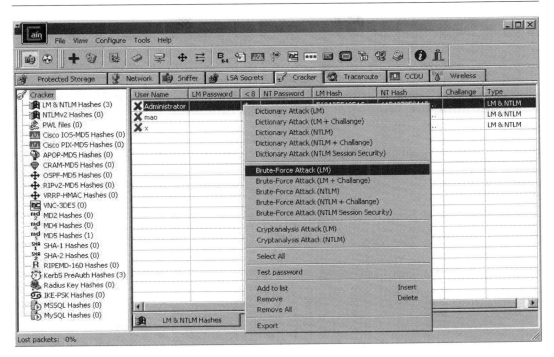

Figure 10.9 – Cain and Abel interface

Cain and Abel has some additional tools to it that can grab hash tables and crack the different passwords that may pass through, and the good thing is, it's not limited to capturing Microsoft passwords. It can capture some 802.11 captures, **Wi-Fi Protected Access-Pre-Shared Key** (**WPA-PSK**) hashes, Cisco IOS-**Message Digest 5** (**MD5**) hashes, and so on.

It's quite an interesting little program, and as I always say, knowing is half the battle. If you do a software inventory scan on your systems and see somebody running Cain and Abel, you will have a good idea of what they're doing with it.

IRDP attacks

Internet Control Message Protocol (ICMP) Router Discovery Protocol (**IRDP**) spoofing is an interesting routing protocol that allows a host to discover the IP address of active routers and get out to the internet. The routers must be on their own subnet. They do this by listening for router advertisements and solicitation messages on the network. When they discover those messages, they simply record who their router is and put that into their table.

An attacker can add a default routing entry to the system remotely by spoofing a router advertisement message and sending it directly to the victim. What's interesting is that IRDP doesn't require any authentication. The target host will prefer the default route defined by the attacker and update their table so that everything is passed through the router they have defined, even if they're using DHCP and a default router has been provided for them.

This is accomplished when the attacker goes and sets a preference level and a lifetime of the route at a very high level to make sure the target host will choose it as the preferred route. The downside of this one is that the protocol only looks for routers on its own subnet. The attacker must be on the subnet, but it can be done.

Using this type of spoofing allows the attacker to passively sniff the network and to implement a MITM attack, or even a DoS attack. So, yes—this one is not very good either.

Dangers of ARP attacks

So, what kinds of threats do ARP attacks create? ARP poisoning presents different threats.

Let's look at some of the different dangers and risks of ARP attacks, as follows:

- **DoS attack**: If you were to go through and link many IP addresses with a single MAC address of the target, it would be overloaded with a ton of traffic destined for different IP addresses.

- **Voice over IP (VoIP) conversations**: We can tap into these as well. If we were to do a port mirror, this would allow us to record VoIP conversations between the two systems.

- **MITM attack**: The attacker is going to stay right smack in the center between the target and the victim. Again, this is where the attacker's machine is going to be placed in between the two systems, or multiple systems, and intercept all the traffic that's going to pass through.

  I was teaching ethical hacking at a school district and a couple of people came from a different school district in Utah, including two gentlemen from the same school district—a boss and his sidekick who were good friends. They were staying in separate hotel rooms, so once the sidekick was back in his room after a lesson on sniffing and a demo, he jumped onto the Wi-Fi network, watched his boss log in to the **virtual private network** (**VPN**), and captured his VPN username and credentials. He then went over and showed him what he was able to do. I know what's running in your mind and, no—he didn't get fired.

Of course, he should have had permission to do that, but it was quite interesting. Both came in the next morning kind of perplexed and dumbfounded that this type of information can go across. Again, I'm very leery about what I do on Wi-Fi networks.

- **Session hijacking**: This can be done actively or passively. Basically, if you're being passive, you ride along in the session and get all the information. Being active makes it possible for you to bump that person off and take over the session they may have created with PayPal or their bank.

- **Data interception**: You can get IP address ranges, MAC addresses, computer names, and even **virtual LANs** (**VLANs**) connected to the switch.

- **Connection hijacking**: This is where the attacker manipulates the client's connection to take total control of their connection.

- **Data manipulation**: This is where the attacker decides to manipulate data. If we're able to be the go-between, the attacker can capture and modify packets, or even stop the flow of information between systems, which gets us back to that DoS issue. And, of course, we can also steal passwords.

- **A connection reset**: You know that ARP entries are stored inside of the cache for a specific period, even if the connection is not active, right? Well, if the host fails to initiate a connection, it should inform the ARP table it needs to delete that information. It stays in that cache to make resolution faster if it needs to talk to that same system.

When we do ARP poisoning, we're technically doing a connection reset so that it deletes that entry—at least, that's what Cain and Abel does. It can tell your Server 2008 R2 box that you need to delete the entry that's in there for the Windows 8 box, and when you do an ARP request, you're going to put it in a particular MAC address.

Countermeasures

There are many things that you can have in place to protect yourself from attacks. You just can't assume anything. One of the things you can do is implement **Dynamic ARP Inspection** (**DAI**). DAI is a feature with a lot of different switches and routers. It's a feature we're going to turn on for switches and routers as it looks at or intercepts all the ARP requests and responses that go across the network. Each of these intercepted packets is then verified with a valid MAC address, as well as a valid IP address they've been bound to. Any invalid ARP packages are just simply dropped.

DAI determines whether a packet is valid by looking at a trusted database that's created, and most of your switches and routers have this built in.

We can also take advantage of DHCP snooping. So, those IP addresses are assigned to a system (remember—IP addresses are assigned to machines when they come online), and the DHCP server records the MAC address that the IP address was assigned to. By combining these two features or technologies, we can create a more secure environment.

The long way of doing this is typing them all in by doing static ARP tables, but that's not something I'm really excited about doing.

Other software is out there, such as `arpwatch`, which is probably one of the more popular ones. It's a software tool that looks at ARP traffic on a network. It logs a pairing of IP addresses and MAC addresses, along with a timestamp of when it was paired up—when those two were paired up—and it will notify an administrator when someone is trying to spoof those paired IPs and MAC addresses.

Next, let's look at DNS poisoning.

DNS poisoning

DNS poisoning is one of my favorite subjects, just in the aspect of how effective it can be. You have nothing to fear... but an attacker with your DNS cache. DNS is simply there because humans are ill-advised and, in some cases, ill-equipped. It's hard for humans to remember a number. Can you imagine if you had to remember the IP address of a website instead of simply typing in a name? We associate and remember names better than we do numbers.

We're all familiar with the **Uniform Resource Locator** (**URL**) box where we type in the name of a website we'd like to go to. DNS oversees taking the name and converting it down to an IP address using tables. These tables can be distributed across multiple systems. Some of them are internal, while others are external names.

A DNS server typically hosts these databases. If the DNS server oversees looking at internal names and names of servers in your environment, that would be your internal DNS name server. For a DNS server in charge of looking at publicly available websites such as *Yahoo.com*, your DNS server is not authoritative for it; it's not in charge of it, so that would be referred to as an external DNS.

The overall concept is when we do DNS poisoning (spoofing), the attacker is simply going to try to get the user to think they're going to `gotham.com`, but they're going to be sent to a different IP address. You can type in the IP address instead of a DNS name in the URL bar and still get to the same place. Again, DNS is just there to make things convenient for us.

What happens is, a user hops onto their machine. Their computer has been configured to a specific method of DNS name resolution. The user then types in, I'd like to go to `gotham.com`, and the computer says: I need the IP address to go to `www.gotham.com`. This request gets forwarded to the user's local DNS server, and that local DNS server says: I'm part of `gotham.city`. I have nothing to do with `gotham.com`. I'm not in charge of it because I'm just inside their network. So, I'm going to forward this out, and we're going to forward this to a root server—our servers that are maintained by the internet and have their own records to point requests to the top-level domain.

The root server of the internet knows how to help resolve this whole namespace because `.com` servers have registered with it, so it tells (in this case) the local DNS server to contact the **Component Object Model (COM)** servers. COM servers are not aware of `www.gotham.com` but they are aware of `gotham.com`, so they have an entry because Gotham has registered their DNS name with—say—GoDaddy, and the local DNS server that would then contact the `gotham.com` DNS server.

We will then look for—in the case here—an entry for www, which just points to a folder located on a web server somewhere. The Gotham server would then say: I'm aware of www, and it's going to return that information to the local server. The local server will then send it back to the user's computer and say: Here is its IP address—go ahead and communicate with it.

Intranet poisoning

This is poisoning from within, and trust me, you need to be afraid. First, we know we have our switch on the network and we have our client machine. In this case, the client machine is making a request for an internal resource called `portal.gotham.com`. This request gets sent to the switch, and the switch then forwards it via the MAC address, an ARP resolution, to the local DNS server for Gotham. Gotham says: I'm authorized for it. Let me go find that server for you. It then finds the real web server and sends the information or IP address back to the client.

The problem we have here is when the black box comes into effect. An attacker sets up their machine and uses the ARP poisoning technique to look for the **identifier (ID)** of DNS requests from the internet. This infects the client machine, their target. Instead of going to the Gotham DNS server, the client goes to the attacker's black DNS server, which tells it the IP address—which is, in fact, their own fake website—that the attacker has set up.

If the attacker is good, they'll have a web page just like the real web server. It could be where people type in their credentials, and they're doing this on a fake server. Of course, if the attacker is good, they'll forward that credential back to the real web server after they type in their credentials. This way, the end user will have no idea they have been spoofed or poisoned.

The tools we use for this type of attack include `arpspoof`, a subcomponent of our DNS spoofing toolset, and of course, we've talked about Cain and Abel before.

Internet poisoning

Internet DNS poisoning is where we really have fun. This is your nightmare scenario because if I accomplish this, I'm going to have the whole network. And there are different ways we can accomplish an internet DNS poison attack.

There are a couple of things that are checked during normal name resolution. First, when you type in `www.gotham.com`, the first thing the computer does is check its cache to see whether it's been there before. The next thing the computer checks is a file on the local machine called the `hosts` file. Yes—it is plural, not singular, and there is no extension; it's not a `.txt` file, but you can edit it with a text file. If there's no entry there, the computer goes off and checks its IP address settings, most of which are assigned by DHCP. However, we can override those settings, and this could be done at the client level or at the server level if the target is a server.

Another mechanism used for DNS name resolution is the local DNS server. The concept—as a matter of fact, this happens with almost all DNS spoofing and/or poisoning attacks—is that the attacker is going to somehow get a piece of malware to modify one of these locations, so as the user gets infected, if the attacker's malware infects the `host` file, we'll put an entry in there that `Citibank.com` is equal to the IP address of their hacker's box. Alternatively, as I mentioned before, the attacker can modify the preferred DNS server, so it goes to their black hacker's box and, of course, the local DNS server.

Any of these targets, especially that local DNS server, is a high-value target because instead of just saying, "*I want one name going to a particular IP address,*" we can say "*I want all DNS resolution to come to me,*" and that's because instead of just affecting one DNS entry, we are actually directing all DNS traffic destined for the outside world: Citibank, PayPal, eBay, and so on.

Imagine what would happen if somebody got a hold of the DNS entries on your home router or your business router and says that PayPal is equal to this IP address. Everybody in the network would go to that fake site being controlled by the attacker.

Proxy server poisoning

Proxy server poisoning is a specific technique where the attacker can set up their own proxy server. A proxy server caches up websites or goes out in lieu of a user's request. So, we're going to have our victim's machine in the **Internet Explorer** (**IE**) browser settings, which is where we see this. You've seen this before, right? This interface says: use a proxy server for your LAN. It's not used for dial-up or VPN connections. This is telling your browser to go and use this IP address for DNS information. So, the attacker will send a piece of malware—hopefully, to change up these settings on the victim's machine, which would then force all DNS traffic from the victim to go to the hacker's proxy server. This would then allow them to sniff for information such as credit card information and redirect to the legit site.

You can make sure this is disabled, and there are many **group policy objects** (**GPOs**) out there or settings we can implement and push out to all of our client machines. One of them is to make sure this setting can't be changed. With Windows 10, there is a section for it. It's no longer a part of IE—it's part of the whole OS.

Poisoning the cache

If you remember how DNS operated, you saw how a client machine goes out to request the IP address of `Microsoft.com`. You know it's going to make a request for `xbox.microsoft.com` to the local DNS server. If it doesn't know anything about it, if it's the first time it's seeing this request, the first thing it does is to check its cache to see whether it's been there before from a previous request. It also checks to make sure it's not in charge of `Microsoft.com`. It's not, so it goes through the process of looking for a COM server. We hit a root server, a COM server, then the `Microsoft.com` server, and then finally, we get to `xbox.microsoft.com`, and that information gets sent back to the local DNS server.

The interesting thing is that cache memory has information in there for `Microsoft.com`, as well as for `xbox.microsoft.com` and a COM server, because the root servers kept redirecting it around. This is designed for faster name resolution. If somebody else comes online and requests to find `office.microsoft.com`, we don't want to have to repeat this whole process. Instead, the request hits the local DNS server, which then says: I haven't been to `office.microsoft.com`, but I do have an entry in here for `Microsoft.com`. It's still in my cache; I can make a connection directly to it and query the `Microsoft.com` server to find out where the IP address is for Office.

The problem is the cache is stored in memory on that machine and can be edited and updated at any time. An attacker can simply poison the cache on that server, not making modifications to the database itself or any host files, just the cache. And in doing so, they direct everybody to the wrong or fake site.

This is what drives me bonkers when it comes to malware. Many will get infected, and one of the worst things you could ever do is to be on a server and surf the internet to sites that may be malicious where you might get a piece of malware. An attacker who has gone through all the steps we've talked about will know where your DNS server is and can simply write up a script saying to always inject this domain name to this IP address, and just pop in that DNS cache and keep it refreshed.

So, after hearing this, do you still want to play with me, or do you want to take your ball and go home?

Detecting sniffing methods

There are different ways to detect sniffers on a network. Typically, a sniffer won't leave any type of trace because it doesn't transmit any data—it's only collecting data. So, knowing that, we need to look for devices or network interfaces on our network running in promiscuous mode.

Promiscuous mode simply means as packets go across the network, when they hit a computer, if that packet is not destined for that computer, the normal response is for it to ignore that packet altogether. If the packet goes out and reaches its destination, that computer holds the information or retains the packet. A NIC in promiscuous mode will see the packet, but instead of discarding it, it will add it to its tables or tracking mechanism.

In some cases, sniffers are easier to find because they may be running in active mode. If you remember, passive is just listening while active sniffing is injecting, as with Cain and Abel or dsniff.

When we have attackers who run those types of software programs on their machines, if you know what to look for, you might be able to find them. The big issue we have is with what we refer to as standalone sniffers or hardware-based sniffers, and this is because they neither transmit data traffic nor respond to some of the detection methods we'll be talking about here.

The upshot is most attackers don't like to spend money—they always run pirated software or free software because hardware-based sniffers are relatively expensive.

Various techniques to detect sniffing attacks

There are different ways we can detect sniffers on the network.

Detecting via a ping request

By sending a ping request to a suspected machine with its IP address and incorrect MAC address, the network adapter on a machine that's not in promiscuous mode or just a standard desktop machine will simply discard the packet. However, if we use the same method to a machine running in promiscuous mode, it will respond back; it doesn't reject the packet even though there's a different MAC address listed. So, at this point, I would know this device is running a sniffing program.

The ARP method

If you remember how ARP works, you'll know that ARP oversees remembering IP addresses to MAC addresses. Here, we simply use that mechanism to detect which machines are running in promiscuous mode.

The first thing we do is send out a non-broadcast ARP packet. This is simply an ARP request that has gone out, but instead of having a broadcast MAC address associated with it, we assign a MAC address to it. The machines will then record that information, for each of the nodes on the network. After we've done that, we then send out a ping message. This ping message needs to have an invalid MAC address.

Now, think about what's going to happen. The machines not running in promiscuous mode will simply respond back with an ARP request because they'll be thinking your MAC address was this, as packets come across to make a request to the new MAC address. The box that's running in promiscuous mode because it's absorbing packets is not really verifying; it just responds to the ping reply and we can pick that up on the network. Therefore, it identifies that machine as being a box that shouldn't be doing what it's doing.

Using DNS

If you remember, when we talked about Cain and Abel, one of the options you had was to resolve the IP address to a hostname, and a lot of sniffing programs do that for us automatically. Well, how does it do that? It does that via reverse DNS. Now, knowing that, you can simply look at which machines in your network are doing a bunch of reverse queries to your DNS server. Another way we can do this is by simply sending out an ICMP packet, which would be a ping, and ping a non-existing IP address, so that it goes out across the entire network.

Sniffing attacks countermeasures

Now, let's look at some of my top ways to help protect you from sniffing attacks, starting with the basic ones. Here we go:

- **Encryption**: This will be at the data level. We want to make sure we protect any confidential information we might have from being detected on the network.

- **Static MACs**: You can take advantage of gateways or your gateways on the network. This will help you, in as far as not being a victim of a MITM attack is concerned.

- **Set physical access level**: If you have ports throughout your network infrastructure that are not being utilized, make sure you disconnect them from your patch panels.

   I'll tell you a story real fast. I was working on a military base and talking about physical access and security with them. They told me they cut the wires behind the network jack as well as at the patch panel in case somebody plugged in the wrong patch panel, and the network wiring behind the physical jack in the room was totally cut. Curious, I asked, *"Okay, so what do you do when you need to hook that up?"* They said, *"Oh, we just, you know, re-splice it."* They had what looked like an extra 10 feet of cabling in the wall so that they could always be pulling it through. And then, of course, if they ever ran too short on cabling, they'd have to run whole new cable lines, which was kind of interesting. That was several years ago. Hopefully, by now, they have policies in place about patch panels.

- **Upgrade to IP version 6 (IPv6)**: Again, one of the biggest advantages for IPv6 is that **IP Security (IPsec)** is implemented, which means packets are encrypted as they're transmitted. Also, if your network device is supported, switch off network ID broadcasts.

- **Set static IP addresses and static ARP entries**: Do this on targeted machines to prevent attackers from adding spoof ARPed entries on the network.

   How about using HTTPS? There's a big movement today on the internet trying to make it possible for every connection we make to websites to use some type of secure layer or SSL connection. This would help protect our usernames and passwords when we're visiting different sites. However, there are other protocols that are considered more secure than the native protocol itself. Instead of FTP, we can use SFTP, VPNs, and IPsec.

   I have already mentioned SSL and TLS, and there's also a case to be made for **Pretty Good Privacy (PGP)** here, as well as **Secure/Multipurpose Internet Mail Extensions (S/MIME)**, and of course **Secure Shell (SSH)**. All these different protocols will make it extremely hard for a sniffer to pick up your information.

And we can't forget about that wireless stuff, right? We must make sure we're always using some type of encryption protocol such as WPA or WPA2. If not, go ahead and use **Wired Equivalent Privacy (WEP)** and let me know your **Service Set ID (SSID)**, I'd love to come visit you!

- **Direct MAC retrieval**: We do this from the NIC instead of getting it from the OS itself. For example, in Windows, we can say we want to change the MAC address; we're not physically changing it on the NIC—we're changing it inside of the OS itself to report back. By implementing this technology, getting the MAC directly from the NIC would help to prevent MAC address spoofing.

And you guessed it—there are several other tools out there we can use to detect whether any of our NICs on the network are operating in promiscuous mode.

Evading IDS

Hackers will attempt to bypass firewalls and **network IDSs (NIDSs)** when it comes to sniffing. NIDSs function by checking every packet that passes through the network, checking whether it's part of an established connection (such as a web page request) or whether it's trying to establish new network connections (such as someone trying to log in to your wireless router). It generates alerts when it spots any suspicious traffic, which is what an attacker wants to avoid.

Host-based IDS (HIDS)

HIDSs are installed on the host machine and monitor for processes that are attempting to gain unauthorized access or use of data. Again, they generate alerts when they spot anything suspicious.

HIDSs can be very effective with LANs, but most wireless connections do not require a login (such as Wi-Fi), so HIDSs are only applicable if you're on a network you trust.

IPS

An **intrusion prevention system (IPS)** is yet another solution. These are designed to check packets in real time, looking for any suspicious activity. They allow known good traffic through while dropping anything that appears to be malicious.

IPSs are different from firewalls and IDSs because they can stop an attack in progress instead of just trying to detect one after the fact. Another difference between IPSs and firewalls and IDSs is that an IPS will block all *bogon* traffic (any traffic it doesn't know about). If this kind of blocking occurs, the default response from the attacker will be to turn off whatever service they're using to launch attacks.

How do these different systems work? Well, the easier ones (firewalls and IDSs) will examine packets to determine whether they are allowed to pass or not. They use rules that define specific traffic characteristics, which you create when installing the software on your computer. Firewalls and IDSs are designed to prevent unauthorized network connections, whereas IPSs are designed to catch known bad traffic before it reaches its destination.

If you're using a wireless connection, IPSs are more effective than firewalls and IDSs because they detect known malicious traffic before the client machine can complete its network handshake. Firewalls and IDSs rely on rule-based detection methods, which means they must *learn* what bad traffic looks like first by intercepting some of it and inspecting the packets. That process can take anywhere from a few minutes to several hours.

Host-based IPS (HIPS)

An IDS monitors an individual system for suspicious activity, whereas an IPS looks for suspicious traffic targeting a particular network and attempts to block it.

An IPS can prevent 100% of attacks in specific environments, but the drawback is that if the source or target computer isn't running an IPS, there could be false positives—events that look like attacks but aren't really.

To bypass firewalls, hackers will try to exploit the security vulnerability of the network protocol that is being used. They can also use ICMP packets instead of using TCP packets because many network administrators trust ICMP traffic and do not bother to protect their networks from these packets. For IDSs, hackers can hide their attacks by modifying data in the packets they send out. In some cases, they will even change the source address as well. Hackers know that it is not possible for most IDSs to evaluate both the source address and data simultaneously.

There are several ways to bypass NIDSs and HIDSs, but one of the most popular is a technique known as ARP cache poisoning.

So, how do hackers evade IDSs?

Some attackers will send out packets with random data to evade IDSs. This is called *white noise* and makes it difficult for a device to determine whether an attack has happened.

Insertion attack

This is when the attacker inserts extra packets into the flow, such as fake TCP resets, to confuse the IDS. The IDS (being confused) accepts the packet an end system rejects. This allows the attacker to insert data into the IDS. This type of attack is normally only possible in less strict packet processing.

Evasion attack

This happens when the IDS can't determine what the traffic is doing. The IDS might think it's an attack, while it's legitimate packets in a stream. For example, if the IDS doesn't look at all parts of TCP connections but only looks at headers and payloads, then it'll most likely be fooled by the statement "*I'm an FTP session*" without having any idea how many packets it really consists of.

The IDS can't tell that those packets are spoofed and therefore sees no attacks and lets all packets through to the end system. When this happens, it's called a false negative, while false positives happen when an attacker sends out packets that look like normal traffic but the IDS decides it's an attack. False negatives are better than false positives because at least you can see attacks.

Insertion and evasion attacks are still possible if hackers use uncommon protocols or use old techniques that aren't really used anymore (such as FTP). On top of this, inserting data into the IDS is especially difficult because it will cause an overload for the IDS, which might drop packets.

DoS attack

If an attacker hits your IDS with a DoS attack, the attack could chew up all the resources of the IDS and therefore slow it down so much that it can't do its job. If this happens, the IDS won't be able to distinguish between real attacks and false alarms because it simply doesn't have enough processing power left to check every packet.

In some cases, the IDS is storing activity logs on a drive. If drive space runs out, it's game over. "*Why?*", you ask. Well, the IDS will no longer be able to store the actual actions/events that the attacker is doing. If the IDS can't see what's happening, it can't stop it.

Note that some IPSs can counter all these types of attacks (at least the basic ones). IPS devices are placed inline between the client and server so that they can detect and stop attacks.

Obfuscating

The technique is used to encode the data so the IDS can't see what's *inside* but the destination system can still decode the packet. An example of obfuscating is when the attacker encodes the binary data (0s and 1s) using **eXclusive OR** (**XOR**).

For example, let's say you've got a string of `10011100`, which in hexadecimal would be `E4`. An IPS could interpret this as code or other malicious stuff. An attacker could use an XOR encoder to turn that string into `4F`, which is much harder to detect.

A less-known trick is using subliminal channels. Hackers can encode data inside normal-looking packets (for example, the length of the packet might be slightly larger than it should be). This isn't really used much anymore since newer IDSs are aware of this trick.

Moving around firewalls

Firewalls come in several different flavors. Software- and hardware-based systems are designed to work with different network setups. If you are running a business, for example, your firewall unit will be entirely internal. This means that everything is locked down on one side of the computer's firewall, and everything outside of the network is locked down on the other side. Your firewall will also block all communication between users of your LAN. They do this by locking down your IP addresses so that only certain users can access certain sites based on the specific rules you have established.

Bastion host

These are designed to protect services on other machines and are often used to protect databases. Each time a request comes in, the bastion host checks whether it knows how to communicate with that service (and will allow that service to share back), then passes the request on.

Screened subnet (or demilitarized zone (DMZ))

These are used to protect internal networks with one or more bastion hosts that have access to the outside world. For example, a mail server is in a network. You can lock down specific IP addresses so that only your web server has access to the internet. This way, you know exactly which traffic is coming into your web server and can keep everything organized. A screened subnet is not designed to protect the machine itself.

Multi-homed firewall

These are typically systems with more than one interface and act as a router between networks. They are configured to manage traffic between the networks.

So, firewalls are used to protect our networks from external threats. They can be hardware- or software-based, and they come in different flavors, depending on how they are set up. Firewalls are generally placed in either a DMZ or screened subnet configuration. A bastion host can also help minimize an attack.

Software firewalls

These bad boys are typically installed onto desktops or servers via the OS and control traffic into and out of your network. They can be expensive and take up a fair amount of system resources, so they do not offer much protection for mobile or embedded devices.

Hardware firewalls

This is typically how we see firewalls configured. They're installed on hardware devices and typically run in an **application-specific integrated circuit (ASIC)** or **random-access memory (RAM)**. These types of firewalls are usually used with larger, more expensive devices.

Application proxy

An application proxy is kind of like a proxy server, but it's designed to allow traffic through for specific services only. Application proxies require fewer resources than full-blown proxy servers, and they come with the added advantage that the user does not need to configure their web browser settings or email client settings because those connections are filtered at the application proxy. Unfortunately, application proxies are only good for traffic that is related to specific applications. This means that if you want to use your web browser to watch YouTube videos, it's not going to work (not right away, at least).

Here is a summary of what you need to know: an IPS detects known bad traffic before the client starts its handshake but doesn't work for unknown threats because it will drop all anonymous traffic.

Firewalls and IDSs detect after the client has completed its handshake so that they can detect unknown threats, but it's not an instant process because the signature of the known bad traffic is needed to be effective.

A few techniques to evade firewalls

An easy way to evade a firewall is by using decoy packets. If you send out packets that look as though they belong together but don't do anything, the firewall doesn't know what it should be looking for. It'll just see a group of packets and accept them (because they look normal).

This is mostly used with encrypted protocols such as HTTPS. Because firewalls can't decrypt the packet, they only know that it's an encrypted stream and will simply let it pass through.

Another way to evade firewall detection is by fragmenting your packets. This is the default fragmentation type in the TCP protocol. If you split packets into smaller chunks, then it's much harder for a firewall to detect that something malicious is going on.

To defeat this technique, all firewalls must be configured to reassemble fragmented packets before processing them to avoid attacks such as session-splicing insertion.

If you want to make sure a firewall or IDS is configured properly, you can send out packets that aren't fragmented. If they're reassembled before being inspected, then you know it works!

The last method is source address rewriting, which basically means that the sender's address in a packet is rewritten to another value. This is mostly used by attackers who want to hide their true location. If you change the sender's address in the IP header, then routers and firewalls will send data back to that address.

To defeat this attack, all firewalls and IDSs must check the integrity of a packet by checking its hashes (in other words, make sure it hasn't been tampered with).

Using ICMP tunneling to bypass firewalls

ICMP is a protocol that's used for some nifty tricks. One of the neatest things it can do is help you bypass firewalls and IDSs. This is done by encoding your packets inside ICMP echo requests (or just ping packets).

If the firewall isn't configured to only pass through valid ICMP packets (most aren't), you can send your IP packets inside an ICMP echo request (ping) packet to an external host. The firewall will most likely let it pass since it looks like normal traffic (it's considered good because the destination address is the target system, not the attacker).

After bouncing through the firewall, another device on the trusted network (such as the DMZ) will send out an ICMP echo reply packet. The attacker can intercept this and extract their original data from the ICMP packet.

Honeypots

In addition to using scanners or IDSs, companies can also install honeypots on their networks to attract external people who just want to get in and break things. Honeypots give security managers and law enforcement an opportunity to get a close-up view of hacker methods and tools. Typically, after hackers enter honeypots through hacking techniques such as software bugs or vulnerabilities, their activities are carefully monitored until they access the systems that they really want or reveal other interesting information.

After falling into a honeypot, hackers find themselves in a special network that may be completely isolated from the company's own network or is set up to mimic certain important servers and services. Then, they can't connect to the usual ports of the usual services, and therefore cannot proceed with their work.

Detecting a honeypot

This is relatively easy. Just become friends with Winnie the Pooh. He'll tell you right away if there's a honeypot nearby. Come on—you knew a joke was coming your way!

Being able to identify and defeat honeypots without being detected is a basic task of a high-level hacker.

Honeypots will capture everything you do, so if you manage to get on a system without being detected it's pretty much game over.

First, the OS is usually outdated (so, unpatched), which means lots of software vulnerabilities can be exploited. Most honeypots are also running custom network services that aren't used anywhere else, which means that exploits can probably be found for those as well.

If you're on a honeypot and start doing some port scanning, the firewall will likely pick it up. This is because honeypots are usually placed in the DMZ where the internal network interfaces are exposed to internet scans.

A better way would be to think of all the things you shouldn't be able to do once inside a network. If you manage to do them, then it's likely that you're on a honeypot.

For example, scanning internal hosts from outside of an organization should never be possible because firewalls block these connections by default. If it does happen, then you must have found a way around the firewall. This would be a red flag, so keep your eyes peeled for more clues!

A quick and easy way to find out if you're on a honeypot is by simply SSHing into the system and checking its uptime. If it's less than 30 minutes, then that might be suspicious (systems usually run for months or years before being rebooted).

Honeypot tools

Yes—there are some tools out there that can help you. Send-Safe Honeypot Hunter (`send-safe.com`) is a great tool for the job.

It can fingerprint a honeypot system by sending it some specially crafted packets and checking how they're handled on the target machine. If you get an unusual response back, then that's your sign!

If you want to go all out, then use a tool such as Amun, which helps by performing checks on fingerprinted honeypot systems as well.

> **Note**
>
> Honeypots don't have to be connected to the internet; in fact, they can also be used as a defense against attackers who attempt to break into machines via the internet. In those cases, they would be called *honeynets* as opposed to just *honeypots*.

Summary

In this chapter, we have defined and introduced what sniffing is and how it can be used in an attack and to protect ourselves from an attack. We discussed the different types of sniffing available to us. We discussed how to leverage sniffing in our efforts to attack actively and passively. We also gave a quick refresher on DHCP and covered a lot of information on ARP. We talked about hardware versus software. We also covered the various types of assaults and attacks, such as DHCP assaults, MAC attacks, ARP poisoning, and DNS poisoning.

Up next, we'll dive into hacking wireless networks and devices.

Questions

As we conclude, here is a list of questions for you to test your knowledge regarding this chapter's material. You will find the answers in the *Assessments* section of the *Appendix*:

1. If an attacker is trying to see all the traffic traveling through a switch, which of the following protocols prevents them from seeing any sensitive data?

   A. FTP

   B. IMAP

   C. Telnet

   D. POP

   E. SMTP

   F. SSH

2. Which of the following methods can be used to collect data from a fully switched network or disable some of the switch's traffic isolation features? (Select two.)

   A. ARP spoofing

   B. Promiscuous mode

   C. DHCP starvation

   D. MAC flooding

3. In terms of sniffer discovery on a network, which of the following is true?

   A. Send ARP messages to all systems and wait for NOARP answers to find the sniffer.

   B. Ping all addresses and look for a lag in answers to find the sniffer.

   C. Finding the sniffer on the network is somewhat impossible.

   D. Configure the IDS to look for promiscuous NICs to find the sniffer.

4. Which of the following preventive measures against DHCP starvation attacks are the most effective? (Select two.)

   A. Configuring DHCP filters on a switch

   B. Blocking all UDP port 67 and port 68 traffic

   C. Enabling DHCP snooping on a switch

   D. Using port security on a switch

11
Hacking Wireless Networks

This is a topic I'm passionate about and have a vast background and experience with. In 2001, right after 9/11, I became unemployed. I live in a rural community in northern Utah, and we didn't have a high-speed internet service. I saw a need so decided to start up my own ISP service.

I rented space off the city water tower that can be seen for miles. Since there was no affordable high-speed internet, I decided to offer this service. So, I put two T1 lines into my garage and converted my garage from a standard garage to an office in a server room environment. I put an antenna on top of my roof, pointed it towards the water tower, and then put an array of antennas and **access points** (**APs**) on top of the water tower.

The company grew quite fast; it was one of the fastest-growing ISP services in the Mountain West area. We grew it to 600 customers; we got so busy that we ended up having to expand our service and we had to find another cell tower.

The thing about wireless is that a line of sight is critical for a strong signal. A lot of our customers couldn't get access to the internet because they didn't have a line of sight. In the case of the water tower in Syracuse, we put up several different sector-based antennas. We went and added tons of these as the company grew, including an omnidirectional antenna (we'll discuss why omnidirectional is technically not as powerful as sector-based antennas). As the company grew, we added that second tower and put in sector-based antennas as well. We were able to cover an 18 to 20 mile stretch of homes in this rapidly growing area.

After growing this company, I sold it because I saw the writing on the wall; we were finally getting Comcast, which at the time was Qwest, but I think is now CenturyLink. They're doing quite well because we have these new subdivisions popping up and the commercial ISPs can't get out there fast enough.

Kevin Mitnick, a famous hacker, says, *New security loopholes are constantly popping up because of wireless networking. The cat-and-mouse game between hackers and system administrators is still in full swing.* Just when you think it's safe to get back on the wireless network, we get another issue popping up. Hopefully, as you work your way through this chapter, you'll feel more prepared to deal with the rapidly growing wireless environment.

In this chapter we will cover the following topics:

- The wireless network and its types
- The right encryption can help
- A plethora of attack vectors
- Methodology of wireless hacking
- Hacking Bluetooth
- Countermeasures

Let's begin by discussing insights into the wireless world.

The wireless network and its types

The wireless environment is constantly evolving. As such, let's begin by defining some key terms you will need to know. You've probably heard some of these terms before, but let's review some of them and what the acronyms stand for.

Frequency hopping spread spectrum

Frequency hopping spread spectrum (**FHSS**) was invented by Hedy Lamarr. She was not only a famous Silver Screen actress but also very intelligent. In fact, she was an inventor. It's kind of funny to watch the documentary about her. She was so beautiful that a lot of men—you must think of the time when she was around—didn't take her seriously as far as some of her inventions were concerned.

FHSS was accomplished by manipulating radio frequencies at irregular intervals between transmissions and receptions, hence *hopping*.

Her invention also formed an unbreakable code because it was hopping around so nobody could listen in, meaning that classified messages could be transmitted without being intercepted. Typically, FHSS operates within the 900 MHz to 2.4 GHz range.

A variation of FHSS is called **adaptive frequency hopping** (**AFH**), which is also known as **Bluetooth**.

With any type of spread spectrum technology, if you have a lot of devices communicating on the exact same channel, that equals degradation of signal. So, what Hedy Lamarr did is create this technology that allows the channel or the transmission to jump between the different channels. You do this with a hop sequence.

It's extremely difficult for anybody to intercept this traffic. In fact, by looking at this information or looking at a frequency hopping environment with a spectrum analyzer, it just looks like interference. Obviously, the receiving and the sending antennas must be on the same hop count, so they know which channel they are hopping to and the next data packet transmission.

The problem with FHSS is its speed limitation. It is limited to 3 MB. I know you're thinking… *That's slow!* Well, I know, but back in my day, we offered high-speed internet up to 512 KB and people thought that was blazing fast. They paid me $69 a month for it. It was great. My slowest speed was about 128 KB, and I charged $19.99.

Direct sequence spread spectrum

Direct sequence spread spectrum (**DSSS**) is probably the most popular one. It has the same channels and the same frequencies, but you must select which channel both the sending and the receiving antennas are going to be on, and they stay there, which obviously makes it easier for someone to intercept traffic.

Because of how the channels overlay with each other, it can also create interference. You could also end up with interference from other wireless devices, such as cordless phones, microwaves, and even fluorescent lamps because they all cause interference.

With these channels, people ask how I select a channel that won't interfere with another channel? Well, believe it or not, there are three sweet spots. Channel 1 does not interfere with Channel 6, and it's the same between 6 and 11. There's a separation. Some people might think, *Well, five would be okay because 5 doesn't necessarily interfere with 1*. Well, technically, in the spectrum analyzer, that's not a clean separation.

Basic service set identifier

The **basic service set identifier** (**BSSID**) consists of the MAC address of the AP that has associated it with a **basic service set** (**BSS**). This is often confused with the **service set identifier** (**SSID**). Generally, users are unaware of the BSS to which they belong. When a user moves a device, the BSS used by the device could change because of a variation in the range covered by the AP, but this change may not affect the connectivity of the wireless device.

Now, the BSSID, as I mentioned before, deals with the MAC address of that device. What happens is that the BSS address gets incremented, and that is broadcasted and used for communication in the air. If you've got a wireless network that is broadcasting on multiple bandwidths, such as g, n, ac, or ax, it gets incremented again and again so it can be used for each one of those bands.

Even though you're connected to the same SSID that is supported by several APs, a device needs to know which AP to return its packets to.

If you use some type of packet capturing tool, you should be able to see the wireless MAC address floating around in the air, which should flag your *hacking senses* as an issue for wireless networks. You can also see the APs broadcast in the BSSIDs. This is probably more information than you really need to know; it's just information that is floating around in my head.

SSID

This is what everybody's familiar with when it comes to wireless, right? It's the network name; it can be up to 32 characters in length and it is attached to every single wireless packet that goes out onto the air. This is how you can have multiple APs transmitting data to different systems but dropping just as we see with a normal network environment. If the packet is not destined for that network, it gets dropped—it's the same concept, we just use this SSID because in the air, there's other information floating around, or maybe it's not information, just interference.

Global System for Mobile Communications

The **Global System for Mobile Communications (GSM)** is an open and digital cellular technology used for mobile communication. It uses four different frequency bandwidths: 850 MHz, 900 MHz, 1,800 MHz, and 1,900 MHz.

Hotspot

These are places where wireless networks are available for public use. Hotspots refer to areas with Wi-Fi availability, where users can enable Wi-Fi on their devices and connect to the internet.

Association

This simply refers to the process of connecting a wireless device to an AP.

MIMO-OFDM

This method affects the spectral efficiency of 4G and 5G wireless communication services. The use of MIMO-OFDM reduces interference and improves the reliability of the channel.

The disadvantages of Wi-Fi

Let's start with the negatives since they are the most significant concerns for us as wireless security experts. From a security perspective, the following are the biggest issues for us with Wi-Fi:

- **Upgrades**: One disadvantage is, obviously, upgrades. When they come out with a new speed, we're upgrading equipment like crazy, not only at the AP level but also on the devices. Then, we have to worry about whether they're backward compatible, and of course, backward compatibility always means that we have a security risk involved.

- **Interference**: Not interference from other APs, although that is a concern, but interference from other devices that have nothing to do with wireless networks. Electrical devices can interfere (for example, fluorescent lights, desk fans, and microwaves). Bluetooth devices can interfere, as can cordless phones and anything else that is kind of wireless itself, as well as anything that operates at the same signal level as your wireless devices.

- **Public access**: Isn't public access an advantage? Well, they want to make it seem that way because I can go down to McDonald's and jump onto the Wi-Fi. In fact, I happened to visit my local Walmart the other day and they had a sticker on the front door that said, *Free Wi-Fi at our store*. It seems like a good idea to most, but in my mind, I was thinking, *This is not good!*

You've probably heard this before, but I'll say it again. Please, do yourself a favor: if you see an AP that says, *Free Wi-Fi*, don't get on it! Most of the time, those are rogue APs, (*Figure 11.1*), or an attacker trying to get you to hook into their AP. Once you do it, the attacker becomes a man in the middle who can attack you. Isn't that nice of them to give you free Wi-Fi and all they get in exchange is your bank account details?

Figure 11.1 – A Wi-Fi Pineapple from Hak5, a rogue AP

Okay, now that I've most likely let you down and you don't want to use Wi-Fi anymore, let's get to the shiny side of things here.

The advantages of Wi-Fi

Here's a list of the advantages Wi-Fi has to offer:

- **Installation**: One of the biggest advantages is installation. Put a box up here and I've got access anywhere I want to go; I no longer rely on an Ethernet cable running through a wall or having to reroute cabling for somebody who wants to move their desk in the office. Or, if I buy the next building to expand our business, I don't have to worry about running cables across.

- **Easy connectivity**: Almost everybody knows how to hook into a Wi-Fi access point or network, but give somebody a crimping tool and some cable and watch the confused look on their face. It's very easy to add devices.

- **Mobility**: Being able to move around is one of my favorite advantages. As I said before, with installation, I don't have to worry about wanting to move from one room to another, especially in my home. If I want to go out on the back patio and just relax, I can take my laptop with me and sit wherever I want and still be connected.

Types of Wi-Fi networks

Types of Wi-Fi? Isn't it just all wireless? No, not really. Matter of fact, here's where we're going to play around with some terms because, today, we use terms such as APs. These are the different types of Wi-Fi:

- **Extension to networks**: The first type of Wi-Fi is the extension to networks. What this means initially is *APs*, which I have emphasized because whenever we say APs, we have this tendency to think of the little Cisco or Linksys, or the D-Link product, for example. We envision these devices as not only APs but also switches and routers. But you can purchase an AP designed to be a bridge to wireless folks, so they gain access to the wired network.

- **LAN networks**: Another type is to have extension networks designed to communicate with each other. We refer to these as LAN-to-LAN networks and often see this being done between buildings.

- **Multiple access point network**: This is where we have multiple APs representing the same BSSID. So, no matter where you go within the building or the environment, your traffic is directed back to the same network. To appropriately deploy these, you need to make sure the APs overlap each other as far as coverage is concerned. This makes it so the user can move around or roam between the two connections, never losing connectivity.

- **Cellular access networks**: This is where we use cellular service to provide access to the internet. Our phones become cellular hotspots and turn into full APs for us so when we're at the airport or out and about, we can turn on the hotspot access on our phone and connect a laptop, tablet, or another type of device to it.

Different Wi-Fi technologies

It all started with the 802.11 family, as explained here:

- **802.11 (Wi-Fi):** This standard applies to WLANs and uses FHSS or DSSS as the frequency-hopping spectrum. It was developed to operate on the 2.4 GHz ISM band and supported speeds of 1 Mbps – 2 Mbps. Compared to the speeds we have now, it would take longer to download files and cause challenges with group video calls, online gaming, and streaming.

- **802.11a:** This was the first standard to use the 5 GHz range, which allowed faster speeds (up to 54 Mbps) but was really limited by its range. It also was the first time we saw OFDM being used. We mostly saw these used in the business world as the devices weren't cheap.

- **802.11b:** This used only DSSS on the 2.4 GHz band and could achieve speeds of 11 Mbps. It was better at penetrating obstacles for a wider coverage area, but its downside was interference caused by other devices such as microwaves, cordless phones, and Bluetooth devices.

- **802.11g:** The developers took the best qualities of 802.11a and 802.11b to create the 802.11g standard. It supports a networking bandwidth up to 54 Mbps and operates under the 2.4 GHz band. The devices using this standard are only capable of tapping into the standard under which they operate, which means an 802.11b computer connected to an 802.11g AP can only go as fast as what the *b* standard allows. On the flip side, a *g* device connected to a *b* AP will only go as fast as what the AP offers.

- **802.11n:** Wireless-N was developed in 2009 to improve speed and reliability, and extend the range of wireless transmissions. It was the first standard to use **multiple-input, multiple-output (MIMO)** technology. MIMO products use a series of antennas to receive more data from one device at a time, which results in faster data transmissions. In addition, it was the first to allow the usage of two radio frequencies – 2.4 GHz and 5 GHz. The use of both frequencies makes the 802.11n standard compatible with 802.11a/b/g devices. With all its improved functionalities, 802.11n supported bandwidth speeds up to 600 Mbps and had a theoretical range of 230 ft indoors, which is a huge upgrade from the previous standards.

- **802.11ac**: The fifth generation of Wi-Fi was developed to reduce interference in the 2.4 GHz band; it was developed to operate under the 5 GHz band. Most of these devices are advertised as **dual-band** – but the real deal is that vendors incorporated Wireless-N technology to make ac products compatible with the 2.4 GHz band. It was also the first to use **downlink multi-user MIMO (DL MU-MIMO)**. It took Wireless-N MIMO technology one step further to increase data transmission even more. DL MU-MIMO allows wireless routers to transmit information to multiple devices at the same time, improving bandwidth speeds and reducing latency. With the help of Wireless-N technology, 802.11ac is compatible with 802.11a/b/g/n.

- **802.11ax (Wi-Fi 6)**: The new kid on the block. It's designed to deliver faster speeds, support more devices simultaneously, decrease latency, improve security, and increase bandwidth. To do so, it includes technologies such as OFDM, MU-MIMO, and 1024-QAM. With all of its improvements, it has a theoretical maximum speed of 14 Gbps. In addition, it operates on the 2.4 and 5 GHz bands, which hasn't been done since 802.11n. This allows it to be compatible with 802.11a/b/g/n/ac. In 2021, Wi-Fi 6 will have a subcategory known as **Wi-Fi 6E (Wi-Fi 6 Extended)**. The FCC has made the 6 GHz frequency available, thanks to Facebook and Google championing the release of another frequency to be opened for public use. Wi-Fi 6E devices will be able to operate on the 2.4, 5, and 6 GHz frequencies. As a result, compatible Wi-Fi devices will benefit from less congested frequency bands.

There are other 802.11 technologies out there, but these are the ones you should focus on.

Wi-Fi authentication modes

This has nothing to do with the type of encryption we're going to be utilizing. When IEEE released the 802.11 standards, they defined two different methods wireless devices could use to authenticate to a **wireless access point (WAP)** before actual network communication would take place:

- **Open System Authentication (OSA)**: For OSA to work, the SSID of the computer should match the SSID of the WAP. First, the computer or the device sends out a probe request looking to see whether there's an AP out there with that SSID. The AP then responds with a probe response. Next, the system, computer, or device sends a request for authentication. The AP generates an authentication code, usually random, and sends it back in an open system authentication response. At this point, the device accepts that authentication code and sends an association request. Then, the AP responds with an association response, and the system becomes a part of the network as long as the session continues and the computer remains within the range of the original APs.

- **Shared key**: To connect, a computer sends a request for authentication to an AP. A sequence of characters, called a **challenge text**, is generated by the AP. The computer then encrypts the challenge text with its **Wired Equivalent Privacy (WEP)** key and transmits the message back. The AP then decrypts the message and compares it to the result of the original challenge text. If there are no discrepancies, the AP sends an authentication code. The computer or the device is then able to hook into the network so long as the session stays open or if the device remains within range of the original AP. The shared key may look familiar to you because it's utilized primarily for WEP.

So, guess what? It's time to play wireless threats, and the top-dollar question is, *which authentication process is the least secure?* Is it OSA or shared key? If you selected OSA, you would be wrong. Shared key is the least secure mechanism. The reason behind this is because the shared key is shared, it's transmitted.

Even though OSA sounds like it's worse, we'll use other types of mechanisms to secure the network.

Chalking – ways to identify Wi-Fi networks

Here are some different ways we can identify Wi-Fi networks. To discover them, we can use one of the following methods:

- **Warwalking**: This is where we have a mobile device with us and we simply walk around a building, and it picks up APs and records information for us.

- **Warflying**: This is a relatively new concept and, with drones, it'll get even more popular. However, back in my day, they used model rockets, like the ones kids shoot and watch go up in the air. Well, some kids attached a WAP to one of them and shot it up. They picked up like a 15-mile range of WAPs as it went up and came back down.

- **Wardriving**: Wardriving, as the name suggests, is searching for wireless networks while in a moving vehicle.

So, after we've identified those networks, we want to make sure we can share this information. This is where **warchalking** came into play. Again, this may be a little bit of a deprecated technology or concept because of what we've done in the digital age; most of the stuff now is online. But it got its start back in 2002 by a gentleman by the name of Matt Jones, and it was inspired by the Great Depression and the homeless community.

When the homeless traveled, they communicated by leaving behind different marks that represented different things so other homeless travelers would know. For example, that it was okay to sleep someplace, that there was a doctor that would help them, or a policeman nearby who kept an eye out. They would make these marks these using chalk or coal to the Brotherhood. Well, guess what? It's still being utilized today, but with Wi-Fi networks; we use different symbols to identify them.

Let's start off by showing you what an open and closed node symbol would look like.

I bet you can't figure out which one's which (*Figure 11.2*):

Figure 11.2 – Open and closed nodes

Open means it's typically free, while closed means it's somehow locked down.

If it's locked down, we need to identify the encryption that's used. So, either it's a WEP encryption or a paid service. We typically list the speeds with the node identification at the bottom, and we would normally see the SSID above the representation of the node. If by chance they were doing any type of filtering, we would also use this symbol to identify that in this case here, it's a MAC filtered node.

What's funny is that whenever I teach this concept, people say, *Dale, I've never seen any of these symbols around.* Well, the problem is you haven't been looking for them.

Let me show you. So, what do you have here? You have an open node that's anywhere from 1 to 5 Mb, and its SSID is KYNANCE (*Figure 11.3*):

Figure 11.3 – Open node

Now, next time you run into some kids (especially my grandkids) with laptops or tablets, you might want to be careful or pay attention to what they're drawing (*Figure 11.4*):

Figure 11.4 – Kids with tablets

Antenna types

You may be familiar with only one or two of these, so, I want to make sure you understand them. It's amazing! After you study wireless, you'll start looking around as you drive, you'll start to see antennas that you never realized were there before, and they pop up in the strangest of places.

What you're trying to accomplish will determine the type of antenna you want to use.

Omnidirectional antenna

An omnidirectional antenna is a traditional one; everybody knows about it. You have seen something that looks just like these (*Figure 11.5*). The one on the left is a commercial-grade AP that we install on top of a mast, and the thick one on the right is what we usually see on the back of our AP.

Figure 11.5 – Omnidirectional antenna

Omnidirectional means the signal is transmitted 360 degrees and, by default, it's broadcasted out horizontally, meaning that our beam width starts at the antenna and moves in a horizontal direction (*Figure 11.6*):

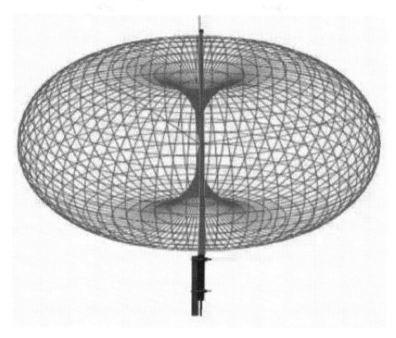

Figure 11.6 – Omnidirectional antenna 360°

We know the signal goes out in a 360-degree pattern. Instead, if I take that antenna and encase it with something highly reflective, that's where we get sector-based antennas. Most of the time, it's just sheet metal. That sheet metal takes the signal that hits it, reflects it, and pushes behind the signal that's already going in that other direction and amplifies (*Figure 11.7*). It's kind of a cool concept when you think about it—something so simple.

Figure 11.7 – Sheet metal amplification

Parabolic grid antenna

This is what a parabolic grid antenna looks like (*Figure 11.8*):

Figure 11.8 – Parabolic antenna

You may have seen these quite often. You have your transmitting element in the center and the grid portion is pushing as well as receiving, almost like a big satellite dish receiving the signal and focusing it back to that center arm.

These are also more powerful than omnidirectional antennas and they're typically used for long distances, such as 10 miles or more.

Yagi antenna

This is what a Yagi antenna looks like (*Figure 11.9*):

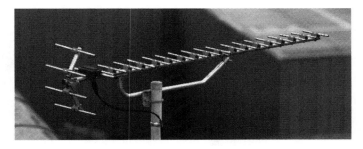

Figure 11.9 – Yagi antenna (by Tennen-Gas – own work, CC BY-SA 3.0)

This is used for extremely focused connectivity. With a parabolic antenna, you can be within a couple of degrees and pick up the signal, but with a Yagi antenna, you must be exactly on. Again, this type of antenna is for great distances.

Now that we understand more about wireless signals, let's discuss next how to encrypt those signals more securely.

The right encryption can help

Now that we've deployed our wireless environment, how do we make sure things are still secure? Well, once we've identified our weakness, we'll have strength, and that's when we get dangerous. It's so true because knowing is half the battle. Understanding where your weaknesses are helps to strengthen you.

WEP encryption

Believe it or not, WEP encryption is still heavily used. But, let's not even pretend here, **WEP** stands for **Wired Equivalent Privacy**, but it's not. That was the initial goal, and we'll discuss why they didn't achieve it when they implemented or had this ratified.

It was designed to protect us from digital eavesdropping and to help make sure our data was protected.

It also was there to help make sure we prevented anybody from getting on the network via Wi-Fi without being authorized to do so.

To prevent unauthorized access and eavesdropping, it uses a key. The key is the problem because it is used to encrypt the packets before transmission. However, this key is shared, making it kind of a nightmare for us.

So, what happened? First, when they came up with WEP, it was not reviewed by any academia or any type of public review for any type of input, nor were any cryptologists able to review this technology. Back in the day, they were so desperate to get some type of encryption, the result was like people threw things together hoping they would work. As I just mentioned, one of its biggest downfalls is the pre-shared key issue.

One of the reasons it wasn't strong was because of the issue they had with US restrictions on the export of various cryptography technologies. This led to manufacturers restricting their devices to only 64-bit encryption, but WEP only used a 40-bit key. When the restrictions were lifted, it was increased to 128-bit, but again, WEP ended up only using a 104-bit key size. And, even though they came out with 256-bit WEP encryption, which only uses a 232-bit key size, 128-bit remains one of those common implementations today.

The other issue is the fact that WEP used the RC4 algorithm for its encryption. The problem is that RC4 is designed for randomized keys to be encrypted, but WEP is not random at all. You create one shared key, and it's the same for everybody. The result is that WEP can be cracked if enough traffic can be intercepted.

I'm not here to say that WEP is totally useless; I would much rather use WEP than nothing at all. But please, if you're using it anywhere, turn it off. Or, if you're not going to turn it off, let me know the address of your AP. I think I'd like to come to visit you!

Wi-Fi Protected Access

Wi-Fi Protected Access (**WPA**) is like WEP all grown up, with its big boy pants on. Well, it has given us better protection than we experienced with WEP. It was formally adopted back in 2003, which was about a year before WEP was officially retired. So, it was designed to patch the issues we had with WEP.

The most common WPA configuration is using a WPA **pre-shared key** (**PSK**). These keys are 256 bits, which is much stronger than the 64-bit and 128-bit keys we saw with WEP.

One of the biggest changes in implementing WPA included a **message integrity check** (**MIC**). What we mean by that, in non-geek terms, is the ability to check to see if an attacker had captured or altered the packets as it was passing from the AP to the client.

We do that with the **Temporal Key Integrity Protocol** (**TKIP**). What's TKIP? Well, under TKIP, a client starts with a 128-bit temporal key that is then combined with the client's MAC address. Once the TKIP has been created, it wraps itself around WEP because that's all WPA is—fixing WEP—and then unique encryption keys are created for each wireless frame, creating a more secure network connection.

However, despite the improvement WPA gives us over WEP, the ghost of WEP still haunts WPA. The cool thing about WPA back in the day is it didn't require you to go off and buy new hardware. It was simply a firmware upgrade on the networking devices. But here's the downside to it: because it had to recycle certain elements used in WEP, it ended up creating exploits. In fact, today, WPA by itself is not considered secure, just like WEP.

WPA2

Then, along came our big brother, WPA2, which created much stronger protection for us.

WPA comes in two different types.

WPA-Personal

The first type of WPA is referred to as WPA-Personal. It uses a PSK, a 256-bit key for encryption, and the encryption is based on anywhere from 8 to 63 ASCII characters.

You have probably set up an AP before where you've gone through and created a passcode or a passphrase for your wireless network. Well, it's those characters that are used to help create that 256-bit key.

If you think you're safe because you are using WPA2, think again, because some of the same vulnerabilities that were the big hole in WPA armor exist with WPA2.

If on your Wi-Fi routers you're using **Wi-Fi Protected Setup** (**WPS**), it's that little button. All you must do is hit this button and you'll get your device to hook right up. WPS is burnt into the firmware, it doesn't change or rotate, and it's a code.

I could still try to break into your WPA2 network by using brute force attacks and it could take anywhere from several hours to a couple of days, maybe even a week. However, if I go after your WPS, this vulnerability can be hacked by some software called Reaver. I can crack that in anywhere from 2 to 14 hours depending on my system. So, if you can, try to disable WPS.

WPA2-Enterprise

This other *flavor* of WPA2 is referred to as WPA2-Enterprise. WPA2-Enterprise addresses the concerns regarding the distribution and management of those static passphrases. It's the control access on a per-account basis by tying into some type of authentication service. Those are typically handled by either the **Extensible Authentication Protocol** (**EAP**) or the **Remote Authentication Dial-In User Service** (**RADIUS**).

This mode requires credentials such as a user's name, a certificate, and maybe a one-time password. The authentication occurs between the station and this centralized authenticating server.

The AP or the wireless controller simply monitors the connection and directs the authentication packets to the authentication server. Typically, this is going to be a RADIUS box.

This is all based on the enterprise environment, using the **Advanced Encryption Standard** (**AES**) with the **Cipher Block Chaining MAC Protocol** (**CCMP**), which is extremely strong compared to **Rivest Cipher 4** (**RC4**).

WPA3

Let's take a look at advances that have been made in our newest WPA version. WPA3 has capabilities necessary to support various deployment sizes that range from large corporate network environments down to a simple home network.

It uses encryption algorithms such as AES and TKIP, which help to ensure cryptographic consistency, and it has enhanced network resilience by using **protected management frames** (**PMF**) to deliver a strong defense against eavesdropping and forging attacks. It rejects outdated legacy protocols. Some pretty cool stuff – and it's about time.

How it relates to WPA 2

First, WPA3's encryption/authentication security protocol is stronger and builds upon the security protocols in WP2. In this new version, there have been advancements that provide cutting-edge features to simplify Wi-Fi security. One of the reasons it's stronger is that it can be used to implement a layered security strategy that can protect all aspects of a Wi-Fi network. WPA2 was not able to protect users' passwords through the use of an offline dictionary attack if someone had enough time and processing power. Attackers would have to gain access to the password through a brute force attack by checking all possible combinations. In WPA3, passwords are encrypted through an improved key handshake protocol. The Dragonfly handshake/**Society of Automotive Engineers** (**SAE**) protocol is mandatory for WPA3 certification, and this reduces the risk of a dictionary attack.

It's important to note that the new authentication process requires devices to be in close physical proximity to the router, which means that your neighbor can't hack your wireless network if they aren't close to your house.

Just like WPA2, WPA3 also comes in two operation modes (Personal and Enterprise). If you have a device that doesn't support WPA3, the network will stay in WPA2 mode.

Weak initialization vectors

So, if things are encrypted, how do we break that encryption? Well, that's going to depend on the type of encryption you're using. When it comes to WEP, one of the biggest issues we have is the feeble **initialization vectors** (**IVs**) that are out there.

First is the fact that WEP uses RC4. While RC4 itself isn't weak, the problem is how WEP uses RC4. It utilizes it using a **key scheduling algorithm** (**KSA**) to create the IV and it is added to the base key.

Unfortunately, the first few bits are clear text, so it becomes very easy to predict what the IVs are going to be. Therefore, if I intercept enough traffic with WEP, I'll be able to figure out what your key is.

The other issue is the IVs are not explicit. They're reused over and over on your devices. So, if you get one key, you have everything. It's like *one ring to rule them all*.

Another weakness in the IV is the IV itself is appended to the beginning of the security key, which makes it vulnerable to **Fluher, Mantin, and Shamir** (**FMS**) attacks. It takes advantage of the weaknesses in the RC4 key scheduling algorithm to reconstruct the messages to determine what the key is, and we do this with simple scripts. It's so simple. In fact, a lot of the tools we use for hacking wireless networks, such as Aircrack-ng and AirSnort, can exploit this type of weakness.

Another weakness in the IV is the fact there's no way to detect that the message has been tampered with. There might be some other methods, such as check values, that can look at the message integrity, but they have their own drawbacks as well.

One of the most critical weaknesses is probably the use of short IVs. Basically, within a few hours of traffic—I can simulate the traffic to speed the timeframe up—the same IV will repeat itself. And, I can see those repeats using sniffing tools, capture the encrypted packets with the same key, and then use a tool such as Aircrack-ng or WEPCrack to decrypt the weak IV, which would then give me the base key. Again, the base key is the base key for everyone. So, knowing that these IVs exist, it's very easy to crack WEP.

Now, because WPA is basically a grownup version of WEP, it does make it a little bit tougher, but I can still brute force attack it if I'm able to capture enough packets.

The same applies to doing an offline attack. To implement this, we must be near the AP—only for a matter of seconds—to capture the WPA and the WPA2 authentication handshake. By capturing the right number of packets, we can then try to crack this offline.

The biggest advantage an attacker has is time. As an attacker, I don't have to sit there and be on your network consistently.

If you want to get tricky, we can do something called a de-authentication attack. With this, I'll find an active client and force them off or disconnect them from the AP. I'll then use some of my tools to capture the authentication packet when the client tries to reconnect to the AP, which normally happens within just a few seconds of it being disconnected. That authentication packet includes the **Pairwise Master Key** (**PMK**), which I can then brute force or dictionary attack to recover the WPA key. And, just like WEP, we can brute force the WPA keys.

Some of the tools we utilize for this process include Aircrack-ng, KisMAC, and Reaver, which grabs the WPS.

Security measures

Okay, it sounds like we should just never use Wi-Fi now. Well, no, that's not really what I'm saying, because we can do some things to defend ourselves against cracking on wireless.

Again, there is nothing that is completely secure but knowing what your risks are helps to make you stronger or safer. So, let's talk about how implementing some very basic things can beef up your security. Most people have the tendency of overlooking them, yet they can help you in securing your wireless network.

If you make the **passphrases** in WPA complicated, make them long as well. Get a passphrase with 20 characters, if not longer. Don't use real words that can be found in a dictionary.

Lastly, look at the client settings. Use WPA2 with AES and **cipher block chaining (CCM)** encryption only. Also, when it comes to the client settings for the validation server, make sure you use a specific server address.

Next, let's discuss threats from wireless technology.

A plethora of attack vectors

Wireless is a great technology. So, how do we evaluate the threats, or the possibility of threats, that we expose our networks to?

Let's look at some of the integrity attacks you could be a victim of. They can be summed up in several different categories.

Access control attacks

These types of attacks are designed to gain access to your network without your wireless security solutions detecting them or being able to bypass them altogether:

- **Wardriving** – This is basically driving around and using a device to search for the web beacons; these are little packets in the air that make it so your authorized devices know they're in range of your SSID. I personally use PassMark's WirelessMon, but other tools include Kismet, inSSIDer, and the classic NetStumbler.

- **Rogue APs** – We'll dive into this one a little later, but, for now, let's just describe them as unauthorized APs that a hacker brings into your environment.

- **MAC spoofing** – MAC spoofing occurs when an attacker searches a network for legitimate MAC addresses and then seeks to access and take control.

- **AP misconfiguration** – Yep, it's an AP that is configured incorrectly, either by the lack of knowledge or failing to configure something, for example, by using default settings.

- **Ad-Hoc connection** – This is again a way for an attacker to connect directly with your devices without an AP and then piggyback off your connection into your network, kind of like a NAT connection of sort.

- **Promiscuous mode client** – Attackers take advantage of the fact that your device will connect to the strongest signal, which could be their fake AP, and then forward your requests to the real AP; this is like an evil twin attack.

- **Client misconfiguration** – Remember the AP misconfiguration we just talked about? Same concept here, but on the client device instead.

- **Unauthorized connection** – These are unauthorized clients that connect to your APs. An attacker can gain access to your network through your APs if the security is weak.

Integrity attacks

Let's look at some of the integrity attacks you could be a victim of. They can be summed up in several different categories:

- **Data frame injection** – This is where we construct and send out forged wireless frames on the network.

- **WEP injection** – If you've been around wireless at all, you probably understand what this is. Basically, we construct and distribute forged WEP encryption keys.

- **Bit flipping attack** – This is where the attacker sniffs a frame on the wireless network. The attacker transmits the modified frame, and the AP accepts the modified frame, but when the destination receiver goes to decapsulate the frame, the checksum fails, and the receiver generates a predictable **Internet Control Message Protocol** (**ICMP**) error. The attacker simply sniffs the network LAN looking for the encryption error and, upon receiving the message of the error, the attacker can derive the keystream, which is the same thing we do with the IV replay attack.

- **Data replay** – This is where we simply capture the data frames and replay the frames later.

- **RADIUS replay** – This is where we capture the communication channel between the AP and the authentication server. Remember we talked about RADIUS servers? We can later replay that interaction to see if we can gain access.

- **Wireless network viruses** – Believe it or not, these are wireless network viruses. These aren't viruses that target computers and nodes; they target APs. One of the most popular ones is called Chameleon. When it attacks an AP, it doesn't affect how it works. Instead, it is able to collect and report the credentials of all other Wi-Fi users who are connected to it, and it can spread to other APs outside your wireless infrastructure. So yeah, your neighbor's AP could infect your AP.

Confidentiality attacks

These attacks are designed to intercept sensitive data. I told you it was going to get scary! These attacks include the following:

- **Eavesdropping** – This is where we're going to capture and look at traffic to see if we can obtain any type of potentially sensitive information.

- **Traffic analysis** – This can tell us quite a bit about the network infrastructure.

- **Cracking WEP** – This is another confidentiality attack. Just by capturing data, we can try to recover the WEP key using either brute force or an FMS cryptanalysis.

- **Evil twin AP** – This is probably the most notorious. Here, you basically pose as an authorized AP by using the same SSID, and hopefully, users hook into your AP mistakenly.

- **Honeypot AP** – This is simply where an AP SSID is set up to be the same as a legitimate AP.

- **Session hijacking** – This is very similar to what we see with the wired network, but it's where we manipulate the network, so the attacker's host appears to be the desired destination.

- **Masquerading** – Is this where we run around the office in a costume? No, this is where you pretend to be an authorized user to gain access to a system.

- **Man-in-the-middle attack** – This is simply a network, but instead of wires, we use wireless. If you're not familiar with the concept of man-in-the-middle, I recommend looking up the chapter on sniffing.

Availability attacks

These attacks include the following:

- **AP theft** – Yep, that will stop you and your users from having network access.

- **Disassociation attack** – This is another type of availability attack, and it is where we basically go and destroy the connection between the client and the AP and make the AP totally unavailable.

- **EAP failures** – In this case, we look at valid 802.1x EAP exchanges and then send the client a forged EAP failure message. Again, they would disassociate.

- **Beacon flooding** – Here, in order to take away the availability of the AP, the attacker generates hundreds or thousands of counterfeit 802.11 beacons and distributes them in the air, making it harder for the client to find a legitimate AP.

- **Denial-of-Service attack (DoS)** – If I send forged authentications or associations from random MACs, I'll end up doing an authorization flood, and you are going to have a very bad day!

- **Deauthentication flood** – This is where we flood clients instead of the AP with forged deauthentication or deassociation to disconnect them from the AP.

- **Routing attacks** – This is where we mess up the routing tables or even try to poison the routes and distribute that information throughout the network via the AP.

- **Authentication flood** – The attacker sends your AP so many fake authentication packets with random MAC that your AP's association table fills up, kind of like a MAC flood. Cool, huh?

- **ARP poisoning** – This is the same thing we do on the wired network. It's also one of our first steps in performing the man-in-the-middle attack.

- **Power saving attack** – APs will buffer all inbound data for a client that is in sleep mode until the client pulls the AP for its data when it wakes up. By spoofing the polling message on behalf of the client, an attacker can cause the AP to discard the client's packets while it is asleep, which basically causes a DoS.

- **TKIP MIC exploit** – This is basically where we, as an attacker, generate a bunch of TKIP data that exceeds the target's MIC error threshold. By exceeding that threshold, we shut down the AP.

Authentication attacks

The goal of authentication attacks is to steal the identities of Wi-Fi clients, their personal information, and their login credentials, so that the attackers can get into network resources without permission:

- **PSK cracking** – Using tools such as KisMAC or coWPAtty, we can recover WPA PSK data from the key handshake frames.

- **Lightweight EAP (LEAP) cracking** – Attackers can use dictionary attacks to recover user credentials from LEAP packets.

- **VPN cracking** – Tools such as Anger or THC-PPTP bruter can access users' credentials or IPSec **pre-shared keys (PSK)** via a brute-force attack.

- **Domain login cracking** – Here we can use a password cracking tool like John the Ripper to crack passwords and gain acces.

- **Key reinstallation attack** – Attackers prey on the four-way handshake of WPA2 to gain access.

- **Identity theft** – This is one of my favorites. It is where we capture users' identities from clear text 802.11x ID response packets.

- **Shared key guessing** – Remember WEP? Well, cracking WEP using the vendor default WEP key is a classic example of this one, or just outright cracking the WEP key.

- **Password assumption** – Here, the attacker captures identities; they continually attempt using 802.1X authentication to try to guess the user's password.

- **Application login theft** – This is another one of my favorites. It is where we capture users' credentials from cleartext application protocols. Most of us use the same password for the application as our login credentials, as well as to gain access to our wireless network. You didn't think about that one, did you?

Attacks on the APs

Let's look at some of the possible AP attacks:

- **Rogue AP attack** – A rogue AP is simply a device that isn't sanctioned by an administrator but is operating on the network.

  Sometimes, these rogue APs are deployed by employees who just want better reception. But from the attacker's perspective, they set up a rogue AP and place it near the target network. When the user turns their computer on, the rogue AP offers up a connection to the user's **wireless network interface controller** (**WNIC**).

  If the user connects to the rogue AP as the legitimate AP, it's going to try to authenticate itself, and therefore, the rogue AP picks up that whole communication channel.

- **Unauthorized association** – The attacker installs a soft AP, which is an AP program that runs via software and turns the laptop into an AP. Now, if successful, other machines might hook into that AP, and the attacker would be able to capture that information.

- **Honeypot AP attacks** – This is where the attacker creates an AP that has the same type of SSIDs as some of these retail locations, and because the signal may be stronger because I'm sitting next to you, you'll connect to me.

- **AP MAC spoofing** – I'm sure you can figure out what this is. We have our network infrastructure, we have our wireless systems running, and the attacker just simply comes in and spoofs the MAC address of an AP in the hope that somebody hooks up to them. Now, let's see, when would this also come into play? Let's say that you're on a transportation device that flies through the air, and they happen to provide wireless internet on your transportation device. Most of these are paid services and a legitimate user might log in with their laptop, and most of the access is controlled by MAC addresses, so the AP says, *Oh, yes, I allow this particular MAC address onto the network.*

  Somebody who may be curious—not saying I may or may not have done this before—but an attacker could simply duplicate the MAC address and be allowed access to the network. I know you're already thinking, *I'd better look to see if Dale's on my flight!*

Attacks on clients

These are simple, and we'll start off with the most basic:

- **DoS** – Under normal circumstances, we have our systems that are hooked up to our WAPs. To just totally mess up the network infrastructure, the attacker might send a deauthentication packet to the node, which basically shuts off its wireless—no longer associated with the AP. It's a simple attack.

- **Ad hoc attack** – A lot of devices, such as laptops, have both Wi-Fi and Ethernet cabling built into them. So, a user comes in and, for better communication on the network, they click into their RJ45 connection. *Ad hoc* means a one-to-one relationship, so the attacker simply comes in and creates an ad hoc connection to your laptop and then can pass through and gain access to the network. So, Super Dale rule number 583 reads, *Turn off your Wi-Fi if you're hooked in through Ethernet.*

- **Jamming** – Traffic jam? No. How about a paper jam? No. How about jamming with your favorite band? Yes, that's me with Collective Soul. However, the jamming we're talking about here is where we have a WAP, and we deny services. I sometimes wish I had a mobile jammer that I could turn on in the movie theater for those youngsters who talk on their phones or text during the movie. Yes, you can buy a device like this off the internet.

Jamming is extremely popular, especially when it comes to dealing with criminal activities. This is a jammer that does several frequencies including, not only cell but Wi-Fi, Bluetooth—everything (*Figure 11.10*):

Figure 11.10 – Using a Wi-Fi Pineapple as a jammer

Next, let's talk about the methods we use in wireless hacking.

Methodology of wireless hacking

Believe it or not, there is a methodology when it comes to hacking wireless networks.

Step 1: Wi-Fi discovery

This is the first step in the methodology of hacking wireless networks. We always look at this the same way we do with standard networks—that we need to first see what's going on around the environment itself. If you remember, one of the first steps is the process of footprinting or reconnaissance. All we're doing is looking around.

I like to refer to this process as a *looky-loo*. If you're not familiar with that term, I'll give you a description. In my state it just so happens if you're driving down the freeway and there's an accident on the other side and you can't see it, you're required to slow down and see if you can see what's going on, thereby slowing down traffic on the opposite side, which is nothing but totally frustrating and creates some road rage. We refer to those folks as looky-loos.

If you remember, when it comes to footprinting, this is simply where we're trying to locate and understand the network itself. We do that in a couple of different ways:

- **Passive method** – This is one of the ways you can use it. Passive is just sniffing the airwaves, seeing what's there. We're not hitting anybody or trying to connect with any AP, we're just looking at the airwaves themselves.

- **Active method** – This is obviously a little bit more intrusive. I could send out a probe request with an SSID to see if an AP responds.

Either way, to accomplish footprinting, you'll need a couple of things. You'll need applications, including desktop applications, and some of the newer ones based on mobile.

Some of the more common desktop applications include **Insider**, which is an open source, multi-platform Wi-Fi scanning software. It gives the attacker information such as the proper channeling of wireless networks, signal strength if the AP is filtered, and of course, we can export the Wi-Fi GPS data out to an XML file that we can then use inside Google Earth.

Another product out there is called **NetSurveyor**. This is a network discovery tool used to find WAPs in real time. It's a little bit more GUI as far as its interface is concerned, so it's a little prettier.

WiGLE.net is one of my favorites. It is an open platform and a website for collecting information about different wireless hotspots around the world. It started back in 2000, and by 2013, it had over 170 million recorded Wi-Fi networks in its database. Out of that 170 million, 105 million have GPS coordinates.

We also have Kismet. This is a layer 2 wireless network detector, sniffer, and IDS environment. There are probably more by now; it's like they're coming out daily.

Step 2: Wireless traffic analysis

After discovering our wireless networks, and using our GPS mapping to get their locations, the next step is doing wireless traffic analysis and determining any vulnerabilities that may be in the network. Tools such as PRTG Network Monitor (`https://www.paessler.com/howto-free-network-monitoring`) and Microsoft's Wi-Fi Analyzer and Scanner (`https://www.microsoft.com/en-us/p/wifi-analyzer-and-scanner/9nblggh5qk8q`) are great solutions, and there are also several tools available on the mobile apps stores.

We're going to do this in a couple of different ways. The first thing we'll do is look for vulnerabilities. This can be done just like we normally do on our wired networks. Again, our whole purpose is to determine an appropriate strategy for attacking the network.

The other thing you need to remember, and I've mentioned it a couple of times, is this is wireless, so traffic itself is just flowing through the air and it isn't serialized, which makes it extremely easy to sniff and analyze the packets.

Step 3: In-depth reconnaissance

The next step of the attack is doing a little bit more in-depth reconnaissance. We'll be looking for SSIDs, whether they're hidden or being broadcasted. We'll also look at APs—like how many there are, the encryption being utilized, as well as the authentication they're trying to use.

Why do we need to know how many APs they have? Well, two-fold. First, it gives us a layout of the network infrastructure itself. However, more importantly, I'm going to be looking to see if all the APs have been patched. Often, when companies have multiple APs, they may do firmware upgrades for one or two, but they may forget one, and that could be my door into their network.

There are more cool tools out there that will help us to determine all these reconnaissance requirements or issues. Those include things we've already seen including Wireshark; because packets are going through the network, Wireshark can sniff that out.

We also have some very specific products out there for wireless including AirMagnet, OmniPeek, and AirSnort.

Step 4: Launching the attack

Are you ready to start launching the attack? Well, for us to accomplish this, we can use probably one of the most powerful tools out there, Aircrack-ng. It's not just a simple application, it's a suite of applications designed to target the wireless environment. By suite, I mean, there are several different products inside the product. It's open source, and what's cool is it's free. It's done through the GNU General Public License.

As we said, Aircrack-ng is made up of several utilities. The ones you should be aware of for your exam would be the following:

- Aircrack-ng itself. This is the standard WEP, WPA, and WPA2-PSK cracking tool.

- We also have Aireplay-ng, designed to create traffic and fake authentication packets, as well as ARP request injections.

- There's also Easside-ng, a nifty little tool that allows you to communicate via WEP encryption with an AP without knowing the WEP key.

- Other tools include Airodump-ng, a utility used for packet capturing. It also can link in with a GPS receiver if you have one hooked up.

- I bet you can't guess what Airmon-ng does? Yep, we use it to enable the wireless NIC card to start monitoring the wireless interface and looking for different APs.

Now, you may never use some of these programs within the Aircrack-ng suite. I just want you to understand that, because it has so many utilities inside of it, you could say it's a sweet suite.

Step 5: Cracking the encryption

Once we have the SSID, the next thing we need to do is look at cracking the encryption. Now, as an attacker who may have gotten unauthorized access to the target network by doing things such as placing rogue APs, evil twins, and finding out what the hidden SSIDs are, the next step is to crack the security that's stopping us.

How we achieve this totally depends on the encryption that's being utilized, and there are many tools based on our requirements. We obviously know about Aircrack-ng and its suite of tools. On the macOS platform, we have something called KisMAC that is basically a playoff of Kismet, which is designed to run on a Linux environment.

We also know about Kali Linux, which has a plethora of tools. We've just talked about Aircrack-ng, but it has a ton of tools as far as wireless cracking is concerned.

It also has KillerBee, Blueport, BlueRanger, RedFang, and WiFiHoney – we could spend hours going over that information. And, of course, if you're on the Windows platform, good old Cain and Abel also can do some cracking for us.

Let's discuss Bluetooth next.

Hacking Bluetooth

Bluetooth is not normally something we would consider an attack vector, but it really is. It's a technology that allows for devices to share data over somewhat short distances. We're about to look at how Bluetooth works, the security mechanisms it has, the threats it provides or creates, and, of course, it can't be complete unless we talk about tools and attacks. Cheer up and let's get going!

I know by now your little brain is overloaded with tons of acronyms and terms, but you must make room for some new ones, especially when it comes to Bluetooth:

- **Bluejacking** – This is sending messages via Bluetooth from one device to another without the consent of the user. It's like spam. It's relatively harmless. The attacker can't access any information or intercept messages, but they can use Bluejacking as a way of social engineering a target to do something on the phone because a message told them to do it thinking it's an official thing. For example, *Turn on your Wi-Fi and hook into this access point*. It's annoying getting a ton of Bluejack messages.

- **Bluesmacking** – This is a DoS attack that causes a buffer overflow. It does it through a ping of death through ICMP packets being sent to the Bluetooth device.

- **Bluesnarfing** – Bluesnarfing is more dangerous than Bluejacking because it enables the hacker access to part of your data. The attacker uses customized software to request information from the device via Bluetooth push profile in this type of attack. The attack can be carried out in stealth mode against the device; however, this is unlikely due to the time required to determine the device's name.

- **Blueprinting** – Can you guess what it does? Hang on, I know you're thinking, *It has something to do with printers, right?* No. Blueprinting is simply a footprinting method. Now can you see the correlation between blueprinting and footprinting? This method allows the attacker to find out the model and make of the device they're going after.

- **Bluebugging** – This is when the attacker can gain remote access to the target Bluetooth-enabled device without the victim being aware of it, and it gives them full access to the 80 level commands of the device, meaning they would have read-write access to text messages and their phonebook or contacts. Bluebugging was developed after the onset of Bluejacking and Bluesnarfing. It's just on steroids.

You might want to make sure you have a couple of these terms at your fingertips for your immediate future, particularly, Bluesmacking, Bluejacking, and Bluesnarfing.

More about Bluetooth

Besides using frequency hopping as a security mechanism, remember both the master and slave must know the hop sequence; we have the PSK that's exchanged at pairing.

With Bluetooth, we have three different modes:

- **Discoverable mode** – This is the mode most people are used to. When you try to pair up a device, you make it discoverable, which means that it will respond to any inquiries that are made to that device. This mode should only be turned on while making the connection for the first time. Upon saving the connection, the two devices will remember each other and, therefore, the discoverable mode isn't necessary at a later point.

- **Limited mode** – This mode is exactly what it sounds like—only responding for a limited time. Most of our phones today, when we make them discoverable, have a timeout. My phone has 2 minutes before it becomes non-discoverable.

- **Non-discoverable mode** – This mode prevents the device from appearing on anybody's lists of available Bluetooth devices in the area. However, it's still available or visible to devices it has paired with previously.

There are two pairing modes that are available as well:

- **Non-pairing** – This is the first one and, just like the name sounds, the device itself rejects any pairing requests made by any device.
- **Pairing** – With this, the device accepts a pairing request upon receiving and establishing the connection with the pairing request device.

Eavesdropping and impersonation

What we mean by this is we allow an attacker to intercept or listen in or on communications between two or more devices. Now, here's where the frequency hopping comes into play; it makes it a little bit more difficult for us to listen in since it's hopping around. If I can figure out the frequency hopping algorithm you're using, or the hops sequence, I can simply listen in. In fact, to just circumvent the frequency hopping algorithm, all I have to do is use another Bluetooth listening device that's modified to listen to all frequencies. And I bet you'll guess that I got a tool for that, right? It turns the device into a sniffer for Bluetooth.

Person-in-the-middle attack

We need to be concerned about **person-in-the-middle (PITM)** attacks. *Whoa, wait, I thought it was a man-in-the-middle attack?* Well, it's basically the same thing, where the attacker who already has the link keys of the two Bluetooth devices can intercept the communication and initiate new communications to both devices posing as each other. With Bluetooth, there must be a master and a slave. Typically, your phone would be the master, your headset would be the slave, and that creates what they refer to as a *piconet*. Did I hear you say, *Oh, come on, Dale, you're making things up now*? Well, that's what we call it, it's an ad hoc network. By doing a person-in-the-middle attack, we end up creating two piconets since both devices are considered slaves and masters.

Countermeasures for Bluetooth

Now that we've talked about the big scary wireless, let's talk about countermeasures, shall we? By now, you know why we need to have countermeasures. I think the Dalai Lama summed it up best when he said, *Forgiveness doesn't mean forget what happened. If something is serious, and it's necessary to take countermeasures, you have to take countermeasures.* Such a wise statement.

The first thing you want to do includes obvious things such as not using default pins like 1234 or 1111 and making sure your Bluetooth devices are kept in the non-discoverable mode because if an attacker can't see it, they won't connect to it. Better yet, if you don't need it, turn it off. I only have my Bluetooth on when I feel like I'm in my safe zone, which is getting smaller and smaller all the time.

Also, check your paired devices to make sure there's nothing random suddenly showing up as a device that you've paired with, and don't accept any unexpected requests. If your device supports it, make sure you implement linking encryption on all connections.

The six layers of wire security

Every time I hear six layers, I always think of the *Six Degrees of Kevin Bacon* (`oracleofbacon.org`), and I'm sure if I start with APs within six layers, I'll be able to get to Kevin Bacon, but let's talk about wireless security here:

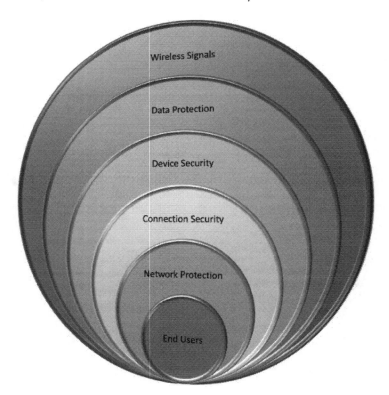

Figure 11.11 – The six layers of wireless security

Let's briefly discuss these layers:

- **First layer: Wireless signals**

  In wireless networks, the continuous monitoring and managing of the RF spectrum within your environment helps to identify threats and makes you aware of its capabilities. You may want to invest in something like an IDS system or even in a **wireless intrusion detection system (WIDS)**. Previously, I discussed how to limit the length of the transmission of your wireless network by using a reflector of some sort.

  I've also heard of users removing antennas from APs. Just because the antenna isn't physically attached, doesn't mean the AP doesn't continue to operate. It just gives it a stronger signal. If the signal is going too far, do yourself a favor: try taking the antenna off and looking at its transmission distance.

- **Second layer: Data protection**

  This is another layer within wireless security. Obviously, we've talked about the use of WPA2 and, yes, these encryption algorithms should help to protect your data during transmission. Again, it's not foolproof because of weaknesses and other subsystems.

- **Third layer: Device security**

  This is another layer, not only the physical layer of the device but also making sure that the device is up to date via patch management and scanning these devices for vulnerabilities. When I say scanning for vulnerabilities, I'm not necessarily saying hitting the device itself but doing research to see if there are any vulnerabilities that have been listed by the manufacturer or third parties.

- **Fourth layer: Connection security**

  Connection security per frame, or packet authentication, provides protection against man-in-the-middle attacks. It makes it almost impossible to accomplish. It does not allow the attacker to sniff data when two authorized users are communicating with each other. I would also look at centralizing the encryption method. Obviously, the centralization of this encryption, like a RADIUS server, requires additional security on the backend.

- **Fifth layer: Network protection**

  This means strong authentication ensures that only authorized users can access the network and its resources. When we say strong authentication, we're not only talking about the encryption and authentication mechanisms, but we're also talking about how long the passcodes or passphrases are. Weaknesses at that level make us extremely vulnerable.

- **Sixth layer: End users**

  I know it's hard to wrap your head around it, but believe it or not, if an attacker is able to associate with an AP, the personal firewalls installed on the end user's system on Wi-Fi networks can prevent attackers from gaining access to files.

Moving onto countermeasures next!

Countermeasures

Typically, this is where we have the most control as security professionals.

When it comes to wireless, do yourself a favor and change the default SSID. In fact, this might be a great opportunity to practice something I always talk about, and that is misdirection. For example, if I have a D-Link router, I know the default SSID is called D-Link. I'll switch it to Linksys or Tsunami, a different manufacturer, because when the attacker is wardriving through my neighborhood or a business environment and he sees D-Link, he'll throw D-Link attacks or vulnerabilities at that device, which obviously won't work.

Disable SSID broadcasting

Again, this will not stop an attacker, but that's not your job because that job is impossible. Your job is to slow them down. The attacker dared to be looking for a hidden SSID.

Disable remote login and wireless administration to the device

The last thing you want is for the attacker to be able to gain access to the device wirelessly. Let's make it a little bit harder for them. Make it so you have to be on the physical wired network to manage this device.

Enable MAC filtering

This is very similar to disabling the SSID broadcasting. It's not necessarily going to stop them, but it is going to slow them down. In fact, if I slow them down enough, I will hopefully discourage them

Update drivers on Wi-Fi devices

Make sure you update drivers on all the Wi-Fi devices. Again, I go back to how we are all so much aware of updating our applications, especially on our mobile devices, or we update our OS on the famous *Patch Tuesday* for Microsoft, right? But, I always ask people, *When was the last time you updated the firmware or the drivers on the Wi-Fi devices?* This should be done at a minimum of at least once a year; I would preferably see this on a task list, to be done every quarter.

Create a centralized authentication server

We've already talked about creating a centralized authentication server. Remember our RADIUS server? That's also going to require some best practices regarding locking it down.

Secure Wi-Fi devices

You may not have thought of this, but guess what? If you're not using it, turn it off, please. Just because you can be wireless doesn't mean you have to have it turned on.

Best practices for the SSID settings

Let's discuss some of the best practices when using SSID settings.

Change and hide the SSID

We've mentioned changing the default SSID and hiding it. This is also known as **SSID cloaking**. I once read an article on the internet that listed three reasons why hiding your wireless SSID was a bad idea. One of the three reasons was that hiding your wireless SSID tempts bad guys. Guess what? You're already tempting them by having a wireless network. We can also argue whether it's a waste of time because as we've seen, we can detect those, but that does require a different level of attacker.

Also, when you name your SSID, please, for the love of Pete, don't use anything identifiable such as the company name, address, or your last name, for example. At that point, you're just making things almost too easy.

Use a firewall or a packet filter

As far as layout is concerned, you should also make sure you place a firewall or a packet filter between the AP and the corporate network.

Encryption

Other encryption technologies we can use with wireless include, for example, IPsec for wireless, or setting up VPN tunnels between wireless users and APs—anything to slow the attacker down.

Now, I do need to probably give you a caveat here and that is, every time we add additional protections to our systems, we end up affecting performance, as well as creating some complexity. And as you probably know, anytime we hear the word *complexity*, we must associate it with the possibility of additional security holes being made. It takes a very vigilant IT security professional to keep up on all of this. But hey, that's what you're here for, right?

Summary

In this chapter, we discussed the various wireless network environments we experience. We shared insights into the evolution of wireless and wireless networking. We discussed the great advantages and some of the disadvantages of wireless networks. We shared insights into what makes wireless networks vulnerable to security issues and some countermeasures we can do to better protect ourselves from threats we face. We discussed the methodology of hacking wireless and Bluetooth devices.

In the next chapter, we will learn about hacking mobile platforms.

Questions

As we conclude, here is a list of questions for you to test your knowledge regarding this chapter's material. You will find the answers in the *Assessments* section of the *Appendix*:

1. Which of the following best describes a wireless hacking attack's *evil twin*?

    A. An attacker creates an access point for clients to connect to within a network range.

    B. Attackers create a system with the same MAC as a legitimate target.

    C. On a wireless network, an attacker sets up an authentication.

    D. An attacker logs in with the same username and password as a legitimate user.

2. A WEP-encrypted access point has been located by a team. To crack WEP, what is required to perform a fake authentication to the AP? (Select two.)

    A. The access point's MAC address

    B. The SSID

    C. A replay of an authentication packet that was captured

    D. The wireless access point's IP address

3. Which of the following statements about wireless security is correct?

    A. WPA2 is a superior encryption option to WEP.

    B. WEP is a superior encryption option to WPA2.

    C. The use of MAC filtering and cloaking the SSID eliminates the requirement for encryption.

    D. Increasing the SSID's length to its maximum improves the system's security.

4. Which wireless standard uses MIMO antenna technology to reach high data transmission speeds?

    A. 802.11g

    B. 802.11b

    C. 802.16

    D. 802.11n

12
Hacking Mobile Platforms

Today, when we see devices on mobile platforms come out, we have this tendency – hopefully, from the hacker's perspective – of thinking, "*What am I going to do now?*"

A favorite quote of mine comes from the great Star Wars character Master Yoda when he says, "*Size matters not. Look at me. Judge me by my size, do you?*" It's the same concept here with mobile devices. They're extremely small. Most of our smartphones are more powerful than the computer systems NASA used to get man on the moon in the 1970s. The rate at which mobile devices are coming out and the applications that are being supported on these devices is mind-boggling.

So, buckle up – I'm about to take you through several different aspects of the mobile platform from a hacker's perspective.

In this chapter, we will cover the following topics:

- Vulnerabilities in mobile environments
- OWASP's Top 10 risks for mobile devices
- Hacking Android
- Hacking iOS
- Mobile device management

Let's start by identifying the process and some keywords for attacking vulnerabilities or attack vectors in mobile devices.

Vulnerabilities in mobile environments

In addition to the vulnerabilities that we see in our network attacks, cloud attacks, and wireless attacks, there are more vulnerabilities or attack vectors associated with mobile devices than there are with standard desktop environments. Here are some of the other vulnerabilities that affect our mobile world:

- **Apps and app stores**: It's important to know where you're getting apps from because as an attacker, I'll take a popular application, recompile it with my malware, and try to redistribute it.

- **Viruses, worms, and rootkits**: The malware we deal with in the desktop environment is the same malware we will encounter in the mobile device environment.

- **Data storage**: Developers must carefully consider which data will be stored on the smartphone and how it will be secured. A mobile app should avoid storing sensitive information, such as passwords or credit card numbers, on the phone's local filesystem since that may allow an attacker to gain access after the device has been physically acquired.

  Storing any sensitive information on the local filesystem is not recommended but doing so in a SQLite database may be marginally better... if your security senses just tingled, it should be because of what we know about SQL and injection attacks. That's why I say marginally better.

- **Copying information**: If I get information via an email and I save it (since it came as an attachment) to my local **Secure Digital** (**SD**) card, and then I forward it to my Dropbox, I'll be exposing my system to attackers. You may want to consider encrypting your data storage so that if somebody pulls your SD card or gets hold of your device, they must type in a pin, just like when you turn a phone on from a cold boot.

- **Social engineering**: We covered this in *Chapter 8, Social Engineering*, but to reiterate, it's a non-technical method of getting people to do things they normally wouldn't do. We can use technology to socially engineer, but manipulation is always involved at the human level, not at the device level. From a mobile perspective, most social engineering happens via email, text messages, or multimedia messages.

You have probably been a victim of in-person social engineering – you just didn't know it. Social engineering also happens on social networking sites. Advertisement is also a way of implementing social engineering to get you to click on the link, like something, or hijack a Facebook account. Then, I can post to their friends saying, *"Hey, there's this new security issue out there, click on this link, I'm trying to help you out,"* and when they click on it, I infect them.

It's also being done via video chat. For example, when I installed Skype or Zoom to be able to do video conferencing, I received eight invitations within the first 3 minutes from strangers. Listen, I know I'm popular, but come on!

- **Short message service (SMS) environment**: There's a big increase in attacks in SMS environments, especially via SMS phishing, because most people don't know how devices are designed to work. We get messages from what looks like our banks or one we don't even have an account with. They include links that can very easily be links to a phone number that dials a different number from what's being displayed. When you click on it, they dial a different number or route you to a different phone number. Some links take you to a fake but identical website. They tell you, *"Hey, your account has been locked out, follow this link to learn more."*

- **Drive-by**: This is when an attacker delivers a piece of malware to a device when somebody browses a specific web page. A lot of times, a drive-by is software-created, or in web browsers. The software could be the operating system, Java, or any type of web plugin, but web browsers also create this big hole for us.

- **Older versions of operating systems on mobile devices**: It's hard for manufacturers to keep up with this. They struggle with updating the operating system. There are vulnerabilities in most operating systems and we're not talking about older legacy stuff. It could be a second-gen iPad on the network, a first-gen iPad, Samsung S3, or iPhone 4. The real challenge is if they are still allowing updates to fix holes in security.

- **Phishing**: This is done via fake emails. Sometimes, it's hard to realize that the link in an email is invalid or know if a website is fake. Of course, it's part of our social engineering environment. They get you to type in your username and password because of an email that says your Citibank credit card has been locked out and you need to log in. They then take you to a website that's not Citibank. Luckily, it is getting harder to accomplish phishing-type attacks because many companies have separate apps. People can confirm such information quickly.

- **Connections**: Is your device always connected to a cellular network, Wi-Fi network, Bluetooth, or the scary **Near Field Communication** (**NFC**)?

Now, let's look at what OWASP has specified as the top attack vectors for mobile.

OWASP's Top 10 risks for mobile devices

Open Web Application Security Project (OWASP) publishes the top 10 risks for mobile devices each year. The M stands for Mobile, and the list is pretty similar to the OWASP Top 10 web application risks that were finalized and published in 2016. Note that OWASP is a fantastic resource for you to follow and learn from (`https://owasp.org`). Let's take a closer look at these risks:

- **M1: Improper Platform Usage**: This category pertains to a violation of the platform's functionality or failure to use security features. This might be an Android intent, platform permissions, TouchID misuse, the keychain, or some other mobile system security feature that you don't utilize correctly.

- **M2: Insecure Data Storage**: There is a trade-off with supporting offline functionality. Developers must carefully consider which data will be stored on the mobile device and how it will be stored. A mobile app should avoid storing sensitive information on the local filesystem, if possible, as that could lead to an attacker gaining access after the physical acquisition of the device.

  Storing any sensitive information on the local filesystem is not recommended but doing so in a SQLite database may be marginally better.

- **M3: Insecure Communications**: Mobile apps should avoid using non-secured communication methods that could result in attackers sniffing or manipulating transmitted data. This includes HTTP, FTP, Telnet, WAP, and GPRS (if not over SSL). There are often cases where an HTTPS connection cannot be established due to certificate validation failures (for example, self-signed certificates). In this case, a developer may choose to accept the risk and disable HTTPS validation.

- **M4: Insecure Authentication**: Mobile apps should always implement secure authentication methods. This includes using OAuth 2.0 wherever possible, as well as implementing strong password/PIN policies to lock the device after a few failed attempts. An application that supports single sign-on should only do so with trusted sources that adhere to security best practices.

- **M5: Insufficient Cryptography**: Mobile apps should always use standard cryptographic algorithms and implementations. This includes using FIPS 140 validated cryptography for any operations that require strong cryptography. Weak cryptography increases the risk of a data breach, whether it's intentional or not.

- **M6: Insecure Authorization**: Insecure authorization exposes data, allows attackers to perform actions as authenticated users, and facilitates attacks such as Insecure Direct Object Reference.

- **M7: Client Code Quality**: Mobile app client code should never be trusted. Malicious mobile apps can easily exploit client-side vulnerabilities by modifying how the application functions using reflection, changing the flow of execution, injecting commands into the command stream, or even executing native machine code. Developers need to verify that mobile app clients are valid before accepting them. A mobile app scanner, such as Drozer, can be used to test for these vulnerabilities.

- **M8: Code Tampering**: Malicious mobile apps can leverage dynamic code loading to tamper with the original app. Several commercial and open source dynamic code loading frameworks are commonly used for legitimate purposes but also leave developers vulnerable to abuse.

- **M9: Reverse Engineering**: Mobile apps may be reverse-engineered using automated tools or manually by examining application binaries after being decompiled.

- **M10: Extraneous Functionality**: An attacker will download and inspect the mobile app in their environment. They'll look at the log files, configuration files, and perhaps the binary itself to see whether any hidden switches or test code was left behind by the developers. They will utilize these switches and covert functions on the backend system to execute an assault.

Now, let's talk about hacking Android.

Hacking Android

To begin, it's important to understand the bigger picture about what we're dealing with when it comes to hacking mobile platforms. So, let's start by understanding the Android security environment.

Android security

To understand any type of security, you need to know the architecture that lies underneath the platform, because it can show you where the holes are on that device.

Android security is layered like an onion. Let's look at each layer one by one.

Linux kernel layer

Like Windows, macOS, and others, Android has a Linux kernel as its first layer.

Android used it because it's stable – it has a proven driver set. The Linux kernel creates an interface between the hardware that may be installed on the device, be it the display, the camera on the device, USB ports, networking ports, the keypad on the screen, Bluetooth, Wi-Fi, sound, and the power features. All these devices are supported directly by the operating system via this layer of the architecture.

Libraries layer

This layer has some built-in libraries, including the following:

- **The Surface Manager**: This is simply there to compose the windows you see displayed on the screen.

- **Open Graphics Library (OpenGL) and Graphics Library Kit (GLKit)**: These oversee both 2D and 3D displays. What's cool about this infrastructure is that an application can switch from 2D to 3D almost seamlessly.

- **Media framework**: This allows you to play back and record multimedia (audio, video, or pictures) back on the display. For example, most of our codex is built into this framework, such as MP3. So, when you power on a brand-new phone, you can take a picture and look at it immediately. That's because it's in JPEG format. You can also download an MP3 file and listen to it immediately; you don't have to download and install any additional codex.

- **FreeType**: This component is there to render our fonts. You can change the fonts that are being displayed throughout the system, including their size and type. Some applications will also pull on this free type so that you can change the font within the application itself.

- **Open SSL**: This gives us security when we're communicating with other devices.

- **SQLite**: This is a database engine. However, it can create vulnerabilities on Android devices. The same type of vulnerabilities that we see in a standard **Structured Query Language (SQL)** database server can be implemented in some cases against these mobile devices.

- **WebKit**: This is an open browser. It's the same engine that Apple's Safari uses.

Next, let's talk about the runtime layer.

Runtime layer

At this layer, we have the core libraries and the Dalvik virtual machines. It is simply a runtime layer that includes a set of core Java libraries. This allows application programmers to build their apps using the standard Java programming language.

Here is a list of the most common runtime layers:

- **The Dalvik VM**: This is an open source software that was named after a fishing village in Iceland where the creator's ancestors hailed from. It's a virtual machine and it's been streamlined for mobile devices so that multiple virtual machines can be running to support multiple apps. In the Android world, we sandbox each of our apps. It has a low memory requirement, and it relies on the underlying OS for process isolation, memory management, and thread support.

- **Framework layer**: This is where we see the core applications that come with our device. For example, T-Mobile may load some default applications that are proprietary to their environment, such as TouchWiz, the interface they load on top of Android.

- **Activity manager**: This simply manages the life cycle of applications. This includes starting and running an application. It also manages a pause state if an application is paused because we switch out to a different app. There's a stop state if the application hasn't been used in a while, as well as a destroy state, which removes things out of the resources when the activity manager decides there's no more use for that activity.

- **Window manager**: This is what we see on the screen itself. So, there's a component that's managing that for us.

- **Package manager**: This keeps track of which applications we have installed when it comes to updates or how to uninstall a particular application.

- **Telephony manager**: This oversees managing your phone calls. If you've built an application in which when you click on a contact, you see their phone number, and when you click on it, you need to fire off and have it dial that phone number, the application is calling on the telephony manager.

- **Resource manager**: This manages the resources that your application may use.

- **Content providers**: This manages the data that's shared between applications, so we get that seamless feeling in the environment itself. For example, a couple of our default content providers include the call log, which provides our missed calls, call details, and the time of the calls. The address book or the user dictionary is also a content provider. As you start to type things in, the default user dictionary may not recognize the word, but you know that it's a correct word and you sometimes hit the check that says, "*This is the correct spelling.*" Another example would be when you install, say, Facebook – the Facebook wall is an activity. When you click on the photo button, you may pull up the content provider into the Photoshop gallery so that you can share photos via the Facebook application.

- **Location manager**: This is the framework that's used by your GPS and possibly your cell phone towers to determine where someone is located. For example, I can pull this up via an application and see where my kids are. They don't have to have GPS on – it triangulates through the cell towers.

- **The view system**: This is simply what it sounds like; the different views we have of applications and windows. It does a lot of communication through the windows manager.

- **Notification manager**: This application simply notifies us when we've missed a call or a text message.

Next, let's look at the apps layer.

Apps layer

This is where we see things such as the home screen or our contacts, the built-in applications, the phone, and the browser. As you add additional applications to your device, it adds them here at this level. It uses the framework, the libraries, and the runtime to interact with the devices to do what we want our device to do.

Now, let's look at **near-field communication** (**NFC**) attacks next.

NFC attacks

I love NFCs. As an attacker, I might be looking out for legitimate NFC tags. I may create a tag and place it on top of one on a sign in a mall or a grocery store or tear it off and replace it with mine. Usually, the user simply tags or taps to get information. I could then send them off to a website that has an exploit to a vulnerability in WebKit, such as 1759. Any user who scans the tag will end up with a rooted and compromised device.

Relay attack

All the attacker needs to execute a relay attack are two devices that act as a token and a reader. They create a connection via a proxy channel. This is typically Bluetooth, but it could also be Wi-Fi. This allows us to relay the information over a greater distance. The proxy reader is then used to communicate with the real token while the proxy token is placed near a real reader. The token assumes it's talking to the reader and responds accordingly. That response is then relayed back to the token proxy, which will transmit the information back to the reader.

Hacking techniques

Let's discuss some of the techniques as an ethical hacker you can gain access to devices, networks, and systems.

Rooting

When it comes to rooting, we escalate our privileges to gain root access to the device. Rooting allows you to make all kinds of customizations, including tweaking settings, loading custom OSs, and even improving performance. I root my devices so that I can get rid of bloatware that comes with most phones, but I do understand the risk that I take by doing so.

When it comes to applications, they are restricted by the security model so that an application can only access its own files, the external storage, or the external SD cards and only has access to resources and features that it requested during installation. By rooting, we're allowing certain applications to run as the root user. When this happens, the security model breaks down because we're bypassing the default permissions.

Not all applications will automatically use root-level access. Facebook, for instance, will still use the resources and information that it needs.

Rooting shouldn't be done by the weak-hearted or someone that doesn't understand what they're doing as you can *brick* a device or open you and your company to added risks.

Tools such as KingoRoot, TunesGo Root Android Tool, and One Click Root can be used to open things up a bit for you. Other options include rooting via the **Android Debug Bridge (ADB)** and tools such as Phonesploit.

Man-in-the-disk attack

When an attacker has physical access to a device and can install a harmful program on it, this attack can be performed. The app does not need to be downloaded via the official app store; malware may be installed in any way, including through a USB connection or over a wireless network. Once the app has been installed, it can exploit vulnerabilities in the Android operating system to gain access to sensitive data.

The Android OS consists of two types of storage: internal and external. In general, the internal storage for Android apps is sandboxed, whereas the external storage is intended to enable file sharing between applications, making it vulnerable to MITD assaults.

When a genuine program attempts to perform a typical upgrade, an attacker watches the data stored on the external storage and tries to modify, delete, or replace the application data by editing the source code of the upgrade. When the legitimate app update is successfully injected by malware, the user application downloads and executes the malicious code, allowing an attacker to install a fake app.

Speakerphone attack

Android applications may capture speakerphone traffic without any need for permission. Sniffing speakerphone voice conversations between remote mobile users is possible via the hardware-based motion sensor, known as the accelerometer, which attackers use to listen in on them. The accelerometer is a piece of hardware that is built into most smartphones and may be accessed by any app on the phone without requiring additional permissions. The motion sensor allows applications to monitor the device's physical movement based on changes in position and velocity. This built-in sensor may also capture speech reverberations because the speakerphone is on the same surface.

Tap 'n Ghost attack

There's a unique type of assault that may steal your PIN without you noticing it. The Tap 'n Ghost attack exploits NFC to obtain your PIN from your phone. Here's how it works: the attacker taps their phone against yours, and then quickly removes their phone before anything happens. This sends a signal to your phone that opens up a special page where you can enter your PIN. Since the page only appears for a split second, most people would not notice it. Even if you do notice it, you won't have time to enter your PIN before the attacker puts away their phone again.

This attack was demonstrated by security researchers at the Black Hat conference in Las Vegas. They showed how they could steal PINs from phones running Android. Then, not long after that, I got hit with this one at Defcon. Thank heavens I was using my burner phone so that I could take photos (this phone doesn't have any accounts or personal information associated with it – I just carry it to take photos at Black Hat and Defcon). So, I was standing to the side minding my own business, trying to put some books I had just bought into my backpack, when an individual came up to me and tried (poor attempt) to social engineer me by saying "What books did you buy?" As I turn to look at him, I felt my phone vibrate in my pocket. I stared at him, pulled out my phone, and he got real nervous. I said "hang on a second" and he turned and walked away real fast... my screen didn't show anything (that's how this hack works), but I was curious why my phone would have vibrated since it had no SIM card in it, the wireless was turned off, Bluetooth was off.... ahhhh, I forgot about the NFC feature! So, yeah, it's a good reminder to be careful when you're using your phone near other phones. And you know my mantra... if you don't use it, TURN IT OFF!

Next, let's talk about how we can lock down an Android device.

Locking down Android devices

When it comes to Android devices, there are a couple of things we need to look at. First, it's important to know about the wonder of app stores and how apps get onto their platforms.

The approval process for applications

This is going to be where Android suffers a tad because developers pay a one-time fee to upload their application to the Google Play Store and the application appears within an hour. However, Apple does statistical analysis to detect any improper usage of their API. This causes the application to take about a week to be approved.

Also, developers are required to pay a $99 developer fee, slightly raising the bar as far as entry into the App Store goes. Android supports installing apps from unknown sources. Can you see where the issue is just by that statement? We call this sideloading. What this means is a user can install an app from a third-party app store. And just because the app says it's signed doesn't necessarily mean it's signed, because Android doesn't care who signs the application. However, Apple only allows users to install iOS applications from its App Store. There's no sideloading natively, so the iOS kernel enforces this security mechanism by only executing signed code by an approved party.

When it comes to which one you should use, it's like choosing between driving a car and taking a flight. If I choose to drive, I risk getting into an accident or being affected by somebody else. A trip on a plane is much safer. Similarly, Apple's approach to its strict control gives the added benefit of a reduced target as far as malware is concerned – not that it's invulnerable. However, Google's approach allows more freedom but comes with more risks.

Other ways to secure Android devices

Here's a great list of items we can consider to help protect our Android devices. Note that these don't include looking at **Mobile Device Management** (**MDM**). We'll cover that in a second:

- Updates – not just the OS, but also the apps. Here's the real kicker – after a couple of years, you'll no longer have OS upgrade support from the manufacturer. Samsung just announced in 2022 that they would be expanding their OS support for new devices from 3 years to 4 years. After that time frame (or if you have an older device already), you're forced to upgrade.

- Add user information to your lock screen. My lock screen looks like this:

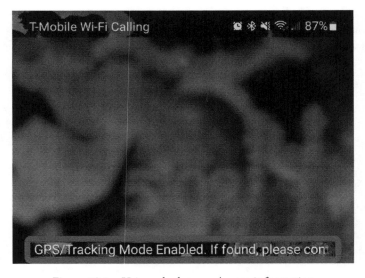

Figure 12.1 – Using a lock screen's user information

- Do I need to speak about anti-virus or malware protection?

- Use multiple accounts if your device is shared with others.

- Don't download .apk files from any source. Yes, this includes torrents!

- Encrypt your device using the necessary option in your settings feature.

- Read the permissions that an app wants on your device. No game should ever have access to your contacts or phone number.

- Turn off Wi-Fi when you're not using it… please!

- My favorite trick – uninstall apps you're not using. For example, when I'm not traveling, I do not need Uber, so I uninstall it. When I need it, I just reinstall it. This will also improve the performance of the device.

- Use a VPN when you're not on your network. My favorite statement is, "*Not your network? It may no longer be your device!*"

- Use a password manager.

- Enable two-factor authentication on any app that supports it.

Now, let's move on to the Apple side of things.

Hacking iOS

Now that we've covered hacking Android, let's discuss the process of hacking iOS and its products.

The Apple architecture

Apple is unique, but like Android, it has several different layers.

iPhone Operating System (iOS) is the platform Apple uses for iPhones, iPads, iPods, and other iDevices. It is an integrated system. Apple does not allow iOS to be implemented on non-Apple devices. iOS is simply an intermediary between the hardware and applications.

Applications are not supposed to try to access hardware directly. Instead, they go through several different layers of the architecture.

The core OS

The system level involves the kernel environment, the drivers, and low-level Unix interfaces of the operating system. iOS provides a set of interfaces for accessing many of the features of the operating systems. When folks create applications, those features are handled through the libSystem library. The interfaces are C-based, which gives us the ability to control things such as networking, BSD sockets, locale information, networking components, as well as filesystem access. It's also in charge of DNS services and Bonjour.

The Cocoa application

This is an important layer. It's the main layer that most developers deal with. It's responsible for the interface we see standardized throughout the Apple platform. It's also in charge of the text kit, which is what oversees the way the text is formatted – paragraphs, columns, and pages. It's also in charge of our push notification services. So, we can push text notifications or add a badge to our icon that says, "*You've got a notification, you have a new text message.*"

The media layer

This layer oversees several technologies that deal with media and what you see on the screen – the camera, audio, 2D, and 3D. It uses OpenGL and GLkit, which oversee both 2D and 3D rendering.

The core services layer

This layer has different features associated with it, such as the peer-to-peer services that your device uses to connect or initiate a connection to other devices that are nearby. This is mostly used in games.

iCloud storage

This feature allows you to write applications so that users' documents and data are pushed to the iCloud.

Other architecture layers exist to support iOS, but these are the main ones you need to be concerned about for your exam.

Now, let's discuss jailbreaking.

Jailbreaking

Jailbreaking is different from rooting. Jailbreaking can be compared to what Morpheus could do in The Matrix. He could bend the rules of The Matrix to overcome some restrictions. He could leap across tall buildings but could still be killed within The Matrix. Rooting is what Neo could do. He could not only bend those rules but break them.

What happens during jailbreaking?

When jailbreaking, we start by removing the restrictions that Apple has placed. Most people jailbreak their devices to be able to do things such as load applications that Apple doesn't necessarily want you to utilize. Apple does this for various reasons, including marketing issues such as blocking pop-up ads because some game manufacturers or developers make their money through advertisements.

We can accomplish this by loading up a custom kernel that has root access.

> **Note**
> Root access in iOS has a different definition from root access in Android. Once the user gives themselves this control, they're able to download applications and software that the app store doesn't want to allow.

It also allows for customization, such as adding themes or extensions that Apple doesn't support. It also lets you unlock the phone. This is how we were able to get AT&T versions of the iPhone to work on the T-Mobile network.

Jailbreaking allows you to use software Apple doesn't think you should have access to and one of the biggest ones is ad blockers.

Another cool feature is being able to untether Hey Siri. This means that normally, we say, "*Hey Siri*" and iOS picks that up for hands-free operation and voice commands, but it's typically restricted when you have your device plugged into a power outlet. Well, there's an app that allows you to recognize Siri when it's plugged in, or you want to get rid of some of the applications or interface elements. There's one out there called HideMe8, which allows you to hide apps, hide badges, get rid of certain elements, customize the date text, and change the lock screen.

Activator is another nifty item that's out there. It allows you to assign custom actions to gestures and button presses. So, if you wanted to launch Facebook, you could say whenever I do a three-finger swipe, launch Facebook. You could also say that if I short hold the home button, fire up the camera. You can get crazy with customizations. When it comes to dealing with WinterBoard, you can also change your toggle settings so that you can have a toggle for your VPN or personal hotspot. You can even bypass the tethering options so that regardless of whether your carrier allows you to tether or not, you can turn your device into a hotspot, and as far as your carrier is concerned, it's the iPhone or the iDevice that's requesting the data.

Remember, when jailbreaking, we are modifying the security of the device, so we must be careful. Do it if you know what you're doing. I would never jailbreak a device and hand it over to my in-laws or to a kid who doesn't understand what I've done to the device and why I did it.

Types of jailbreaking

There are different techniques for jailbreaking you can implement, as follows:

- **Untethered jailbreak**: This has the attribute that if a user turns the device off and then back on, the device starts up completely, and without the assistance of a computer, the kernel will be patched.

- **Tethered jailbreak**: Here, a computer is needed to turn the device on each time it's rebooted. If the device starts up on its own, it's no longer a patched kernel, and it gets stuck in that partially started state. By using a computer, the phone is essentially re-jailbroken each time it turns on, which sounds like a hassle.

- **Semi-tethered**: When a device boots, it will no longer have a patched kernel, so it won't be able to run any modified code, but it's still usable for normal functions, such as placing calls or texting. To use any features that require modified code to execute, the user must use a jailbreaking tool to start the device with a patched kernel.

Now, let's talk about the three types of jailbreaking.

The three types of jailbreaking

It's important to understand the three main ways you can jailbreak your device. We'll cover them in the following subsections.

The userland exploit

This is a piece of software that runs on the iOS device after the kernel has started. This exploit uses a loophole in the system application. It allows user-level access but does not allow iBoot-level access. These types of exploits cannot be tethered because nothing can cause a recovery mode loop. These types of exploits can and have been patched by Apple.

The iBoot exploit

The iBoot exploit allows for jailbreaking, user-level access, and iBoot-level access. It's an exploit that can be semi-tethered if the device has a new boot ROM. This exploit turns off code signing and runs a program that does all the work for us. This exploit can be patched with some firmware updates.

Boot ROM exploits

This exploit uses a loophole in the secure ROM, which is the first bootloader. It disables the signature checks, which can be used to load a patch or firmware. Firmware updates cannot patch these types of exploits. The boot ROM exploit allows user-level access and iBoot-level access. The only way for them to patch this is for Apple to update the hardware of the boot ROM.

Locking down the Apple platform

As far as locking down the Apple platform is concerned, when it comes to the jailbreaking device, even though you open a plethora of options that Apple doesn't necessarily want you to have access to, you just need to know what those ramifications can include because I can now gain access to the device remotely. Think of that from the attacker's perspective.

For me, the biggest issue is still at the physical level. If an attacker gets physical access to any device – Apple, Android, a PC, laptop, or server – we need to consider what risks come into play as we move around with these devices. We need to batten down the hatches:

- Passcode-lock your device. I know that's a *"duh Dale"* statement, but I needed to say it.

- Don't sideload apps.

- Disable JavaScript and add-ons from your web browser.

- Don't store sensitive data on any client-side databases.

- If you jailbreak, please change the default root password from "alpine."

- Configure Find My Phone to wipe if the device is lost or stolen.

- Update, update, update. This includes the OS, the apps, and any plugins.

- Disable iCloud services to stop sensitive enterprise data from being backed up to your cloud.

- Enable *Ask to Join Networks* so that you connect to rogue wireless networks.

- Enable Erase Data after 10 attempts.

- Turn off Siri. She doesn't need to be listening in and logging the things you talk about or what your company is talking about.

- While you're at it, turn off voice dial. Attackers can access your phone without entering your passcode if it's enabled and they have physical access to your device.

- Turn off some of the same protections we saw with Android. This includes turning off secure networks, two-factor authentication, encryption for the device, staying off public Wi-Fi, and stopping clicking on email links.

Now, let's explore MDM.

Mobile device management

MDM is a piece of software that monitors all your mobile devices, allowing us to deploy secure smartphones, tablets, desktops, and laptops.

MDM optimizes and automates the functionality and security of your devices throughout the enterprise in and out of the corporate network. We can control things such as allowing applications to be distributed where data is stored, how the device is configured, which patches to install, and how to handle the device that's been compromised. How about just shoot it, put it out of its misery?

MDMs work with frameworks and each device manufacturer has a framework that injects into the MDM. MDM usually has policies or features that mobile device administrators can control or enforce on these devices.

The combination of these policies and features forms the framework. Android, Blackberry, and Apple provide MDM frameworks to allow administrators and MDM vendors to simply link to their devices.

There are a bazillion different MDM software solutions out there, but these are the big boys:

- **AirWatch**: This is handled by the same people who developed VMware.

- **System Center Configuration Manager**: This is by Microsoft, and it supports the mobile Windows platform, Android, and iOS. It requires an additional component, Intune, a monthly subscription for you to be able to manage your devices when they're not inside of your network infrastructure. Intune acts as a proxy for you. It has a connection to the internet, your devices make a connection to it, and it relays it back to your system center configuration manager on the backend.

- **Spiceworks**: This is completely free and doesn't take up a lot of configuration or servers.

The overall concept here is to make sure you have some options when it comes to not only supporting organization-issued devices but also controlling **Bring Your Own Devices (BYODs)**. It's a fine line of controlling personal devices while protecting resources, but I get it, it's a cost-saving issue for most companies as well as an annoyance issue for employees having to carry two of the same devices. Oh, I could go off about BYODs and the reasons to not utilize them, but that would be another book in itself.

Now, let's talk about the importance of guidelines and some cool tools you can use.

Guidelines and cool tools

When it comes to guidelines, I can't think of a better phrase than Pirates of the Caribbean's Captain Barbosa's words, "*The code is more what you'd call "guidelines" than actual rules.*"

There are some good guidelines when it comes to mobile devices. Let's discuss some of them:

- **Apps**: One of the biggest issues I see out there right now with the mobile platform is that people load up too many apps.

- **Photos**: Try to be careful about automatically uploading photos to social networks. When I do presentations for communities, specifically for parents, I talk about how we're sharing way too much information. Sometimes, we don't even realize it. We post photos on Facebook without looking at the photo. What's in the background? Are you exposing your address or other personal or family information? Be careful not to put up too much information.

- **Control**: Can you maintain control of these devices? If you lose control of them, it's time to get them back in the office and reassociate.

- **Security assessment**: Do security assessments on the devices, the application, and its architecture.

- **Trusted applications**: Only install applications from trusted locations. I sideload all the time to make some useful applications available on my tablet.

- **Location**: Don't add any location-based features unless there's a component that supports the application. Don't load Google Maps if you don't need it. I know most Android devices come with those applications pre-installed but you also need to be careful of applications that want to look at your location. Only allow it if it's important.

- **Bluetooth**: Turn your Bluetooth off if you don't need it, especially while traveling. You'll get a little bit of extra battery life too.

- **Connecting to separate networks**: Don't connect to two networks at the same time, such as Wi-Fi and Bluetooth, as an attacker can use one network to pull information from the other.

- **Backup**: Do backups and check how often your devices are synchronizing, especially if they're synchronizing outside of your network.

- **Passwords**: Use strong passwords.

- **Idle timeout**: Set the idle timeout to automatically lock when the phone is not in use. My phone locks automatically when I hit the power button.

- **Lockout and wipe features**: Take advantage of the lockout and wipe features. If somebody types in my code incorrectly four times, my device gets wiped.

- **Jailbreaking and rooting**: A best practice by EC Council is to never allow rooted or jailbroken devices. However, I enjoy rooting my devices because when Stagefright came out for the Android, if I hadn't rooted my device, I would have waited until Samsung came out with a fix. However, because I run a custom ROM, it took the author of that ROM 2 days to come out with the patch and I was able to redeploy and be locked down.

- **Updates**: Keep all applications and the OS itself up to date. However, review the changes all the updates want to accomplish – don't hit **Apply all**; you could be lowering the security profile of your device because the application could sneak in a new game, for example, and the new patch gives them access to all your contacts.

- **Hardware encryption**: This is like encrypting the hard drive on a PC. If somebody steals your PC and they don't know the encryption key to type in when they boot up, they're not getting the data.

- **MDM**: Review your MDM policies. This comes down the road of change management because when you come up with these policies, you need to make sure there's complete agreement across departments on what is allowed and what's not allowed.

- **Emails**: Filter email forwarding barriers because most of our malware is coming across via email. Do we want those heading out to our devices? Some newer email servers make filtering easy. You can set a filter to only allow emails that are generated internally to be forwarded to mobile devices – don't forward emails from advertisers.

- **Browsers**: Harden up the browsers on these devices. This includes permission rules to ensure when somebody visits a page on these devices, they're not getting injected with some code that's going to jailbreak them or root them.

- **Signed applications**: Only use signed applications, meaning they've been signed by the app stores, or have been signed for internal use.

- **Erase data**: Set up to erase data to keep people from guessing passwords on the devices.

- **Auto-lock**: Ensure you have auto-locking turned on.

- **Backup location**: Make backups and locate them in a secure location.

- **Password**: Require a passcode. Studies show that people use patterns after the alphabet, giving attackers an easy time. They need a few guesses, starting with the initials.

- **Software maintenance**: Have a software maintenance plan in place. If there's an app you haven't used in 90 days, you probably don't need it.

- **Sandbox data and the app**: If you're a developer, sandbox data and the apps to avoid cross-infection.

- **Wi-Fi**: Always make sure someone must ask to join. Windows 10 allows devices to automatically join known Wi-Fi access points – not the ones you know but the ones Microsoft is aware of. That's risky.

- **Emails**: Don't allow emails to be cached. Even though you've deleted the email, it's still in the cache. If I get that device, I'll be able to read that information.

- **Data**: As a company, decide whether data can leave the environment. Do we allow people to send the payroll spreadsheet via email so that Bruce Wayne can open the spreadsheet on his device? Why not use the newer technologies, such as Share File Options, where I don't send you a copy of the file? Instead, I give you a URL link back to our SharePoint server or maybe back to a Dropbox location. That way, I don't have files leaving the environment.

- **Google**: When it comes to Android, watch what Google is backing up, what they're storing, what they're cashing, and all the data that they're collecting.

- **Notifications**: Turn off notifications on the lock screen so that someone must unlock it to see them.

- **Turn off autofill**: This is about convenience. The challenge with this is that if an attacker gets access to the computer, it becomes a liability as an attacker could easily get significant access to many things.

- **Users**: One of the best things you could ever do is train your users on how to use these devices, as well as what's acceptable and what's not acceptable. Make sure there are written policies in place so that they understand what the consequences are, and hold them to those consequences if they break them.

- **Timeout**: If users are getting in remotely, how long do you allow them to stay inactive before the session times out? It's annoying to keep typing in a username and password but don't cache domain passwords. That's as reckless as posting all your passwords on Facebook, Twitter, and Google Plus.

Okay, so who here is now thinking a little differently about mobile devices?

Summary

It's important to remember the shift we are experiencing as more and more is being done and transacted on mobile devices and less on desktops and laptops. Because of the mobility of these devices, we must prepare ourselves and how to best deal with the unique challenges and vulnerabilities that mobile platforms present to us. In this chapter, we provided an overview of how we can prepare to attack and protect ourselves on a mobile platform. We reviewed the key terms we must know when it comes to hacking mobile platforms. We also discussed hacking iOS, Android, and other mobile platforms before covering the importance of MDM.

In the next chapter, we will cover hacking web servers and web apps.

Questions

As we conclude, here is a list of questions for you to test your knowledge regarding this chapter's material. You will find the answers in the *Assessments* section of the *Appendix*:

1. What are the advantages of encrypting mobile devices?

    A. Data sent to websites is protected

    B. Malware protection

    C. Protection against gadgets that have been stolen

    D. Data security on lost or stolen devices

2. What does it mean to *jailbreak* a phone?

    A. Removing DRM from a system

    B. Getting rid of ransomware from a computer

    C. Removing a device from a network

    D. Taking control of a device by gaining root access

3. Which operating system is Android based on?

    A. Windows

    B. Linux

    C. OS X

    D. macOS

4. What is the impact of rooting a device on security?

    A. It improves it.

    B. It is hardened.

    C. It diminishes it.

    D. No change.

Section 3: Cloud, Apps, and IoT Attacks

This section covers how merging technology that delivers computing services, such as online business applications, online data storage, and webmail over the internet, is presenting a new vector that should be considered and reviewed.

This part of the book comprises the following chapters:

13
Hacking Web Servers and Web Apps

The purpose of hacking web servers and web apps is to search for and discover potential vulnerabilities. It helps us identify important upgrades that are needed for software, thus improving security and helping us recognize and respond to any malicious activity. Additionally, with so much being transacted online including shopping, banking, and communications, web apps give us an additional resource to gain access to a person's login credentials, private messages, and financial information.

In this chapter, we will cover the following topics:

- Why web servers create security issues
- Types of architectures
- Threats to both servers and applications
- The vulnerabilities of web APIs, web shells, and webhooks
- Detecting web server hacking attempts

Let's begin by discussing why web servers create security issues for us.

Why web servers create security issues

It's important to understand that web applications and servers are not inherently secure. The fact is that they were never designed to be secure – they were designed for functionality and to provide a service. The responsibility for making them safe rests with us, as system administrators, coders, and security professionals.

This is why attackers turn their attention to web servers and web application-level attacks – because a web server that hosts web applications is accessible from anywhere over the internet. This makes web servers an attractive target. Poorly configured web servers can create vulnerabilities in even the most carefully designed firewall systems. Attackers can exploit poorly configured web servers with known vulnerabilities to compromise the security of web applications. Furthermore, web servers with known vulnerabilities can harm the security of an organization, even if the web applications they host are secure.

Every open port on a web server is an entry point for a possible attack, especially if it hosts applications that use protocols such as HTTP and FTP. The operating system must protect the application from **Denial-of-Service** (**DOS**) attacks by ensuring that processes have sufficient resources to function properly. The real problem with these operating system security features is that they can be used against the application. Adding add-ons, plugins, and their configurations on top of the OS and its applications creates a perfect storm for attackers.

Before you start trying to hack a web server, it's important to understand how they work.

There are three main components to a web server:

- The web server software, which is what we want to attack.
- The website content/files, which need to be in a certain format for the web server to access and read them.
- The operating system itself.

Every web server essentially works the same way; it receives a request from a user and then tries to find the file they want. Then, it reads the file and sends it to the user so that they can see it.

Every web server has a piece of software behind it called an HTTP daemon/service/server. The name varies, depending on the server. Apache/httpd is a popular HTTP daemon for Linux-based servers, while **Internet Information Server** (**IIS**) is a popular one for Windows servers.

HTTP daemons essentially run in the background and receive requests from users on port 80 by default. So, every time you type `facebook.com` into your browser, your computer is sending a request to the Facebook web server to find out the files it needs to display for you to see the page.

The process of finding these files is called mapping URLs/domains to certain directories on the server, indexing, and so on. Then, when a user tries to access a file, it maps the filename onto the corresponding path that has been mapped to that URL.

These web servers also contain security features, such as limiting the amount of physical memory it can access for each process, preventing unauthorized code execution, and ensuring certain file types are not allowed to be executed.

Now, let's discuss the components of a web server.

Components of a web server

First, we have the **document root**. This directory is where all the web content/files are stored. For example, if you have an `images` directory inside your document root, all the images can be accessed from `http://wayne-technologies.net/images/`.

When a user requests a page using a URL, such as `wayne-technologies.net/`, it maps that URL onto the document root and then searches the folder for a file that matches that URL. This is called mapping URLs to files and folders. If it finds a match, it sends the contents of this file back to the user so that they can see it.

If no matching file is found, an index document such as the default page, or `index.php`, will be searched for and sent back if found.

If no index document is present, the server will typically return a 404 error to the user, saying that it can't find what they're looking for. A redirect may also be returned, telling them to look somewhere else for this file/content.

Second, we have the **server root**. This is the directory tree's top-level root directory, including the server's configuration and error, executable, and log files. It consists of the server's implementation code. Typically, the server root consists of four files. One file is dedicated to the server's implementation code, while the remaining three are subdirectories – that is, `conf`, `-logs`, and `-cgi-bin` – that contain configuration data, logs, and executables, respectively.

Third, there's the **virtual document tree**. In addition to the physical directory tree that stores content, a virtual document tree is maintained by HTTP daemon software. The purpose of the virtual tree is to map URLs onto files stored in the server's filesystem; for example, it may associate the `http://wayne-technologies.net/images` URL with an actual directory named `/var/www/images` on the server's filesystem.

Fourth, we have **virtual hosting**. This is where you may host multiple domains/websites on one web server. For example, you could have your main domain, `www.wayne-technologies.net`, and then to add another site, you would have to create a subdomain such as `blog.wayne-technologies.net` that points to the same document root directory to keep everything separate under one roof. Using this method, you could also host an unlimited number of sites on one web server. However, keep in mind that each subdomain will need unique passwords/credentials to prevent unauthorized access.

Fifth, we have the **web proxy**. A web proxy is a domain that acts as an intermediary between your computer and the website you are trying to access. When you type in an address, it goes through the proxy DNS server, which then forwards the request to your requested website's IP address. The response is sent back through the proxy server so that it cannot be traced back to you. Web proxies are used to help mask/hide your IP address, and anyone attempting to trace the request back to you will come up with a different IP.

Next, we will talk about the different types of architecture you may experience.

Types of architecture

Web server architecture is the overall layout of a web server. It gives an attacker an idea of how they can prepare for and deploy an attack. Let's discuss the most common web server architectures you may encounter.

IIS web server architecture

Let's take a look at the typical architecture of a web server and its applications, as shown in the following diagram. This is based on an open source architecture. As you can see, a lot of moving parts and components are involved in supporting an application. A web server is designed to host multiple sites on one system, which adds to the complexity. Did your *hacker red flag* just go up? It should have. Anytime we talk about complexity, it means more areas to make mistakes, overlook settings, or miss an attack vector:

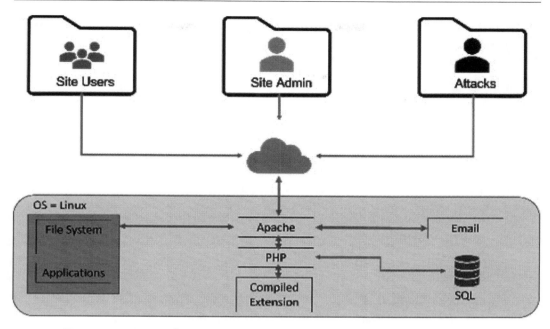

Figure 13.1 – A typical open source architecture for a web server and its applications

Open source web server architecture

The three most popular open source web servers are **Apache httpd**, **Nginx**, and **lighttpd**. Their principal components are as follows:

- Apache, which is designed to be a secure, efficient, and extensible server
- MySQL, which is ideal for storing data
- PHP, which is a widely used, general-purpose scripting language that is especially suited for web development and can interact with MySQL to retrieve and store data

Let's look into some of the challenges the Microsoft world gives us next.

Microsoft

Microsoft's **Internet Information System** (**IIS**) is the most widely used web server software in the world, boasting over 800 million downloads. IIS is flexible, secure, and easy to host using HTTP/HTTPS, FTP, RTSP, SMTP, and much more. Microsoft uses application pools, which are an extremely useful part of IIS. They allow the administrator to set different resource limits for applications running on port 80, or any other port you wish.

But why should you care about setting up user accounts and application pools? There are many reasons why an administrator may want to establish individual identities or set up application pools to run independent versions of the same website.

For instance, imagine that you run a very busy web server with two separate websites on it – one dedicated to your business and another that's a marketing site for a client's new product release. It would be ideal if each site ran under its credentials and had an application pool. The business website would require more processes, while the marketing site may need additional memory and processor speeds to handle large quantities of traffic. On a traditional server, these requirements would conflict and cause problems. With IIS and application pools, you can easily configure user accounts and resource allocations for each site with specifications without them affecting each other.

What about security?

Listen, I'm not trying to tell you that Microsoft's IIS is unhackable – far from it. Its history is quite sorted when it comes to being hacked, but it's come a long way.

Application pools for running websites have default settings that mimic the original Windows Server 2003 version of IIS. Unless the administrator changes it, there are no anonymous users (which is what hackers want), and no direct access to the webroot (we'll talk about this in a second). With application pools, you can set up an anonymous user with limited rights, or create another restricted account, as we mentioned previously for your marketing site. This way, if one website is breached, there's no chance that a hacker could get into the other one because they're running under completely different security settings… in theory. Again, there are a plethora of attack vectors out there that have Microsoft pretty busy patching IIS, but the same can be said about Linux and Apache.

Let's learn more about why web servers are compromised.

Why are web servers compromised?

The most common reasons for attackers to compromise a web server are as follows:

- Web servers are often used as attack launch points for attacking other applications.

- When an attacker compromises one system on the network, they can often use that system's access privileges to move around freely and gain access to additional systems that may host sensitive data. This is known as **privilege escalation**.

- Attackers are often able to use vulnerabilities in the web server's software to compromise the system because it's easy for developers to make mistakes when writing code, or they may leave backdoors and debug options open. Attackers can use these vulnerabilities and configuration errors to take control of a system.

Now, let's talk about adding web apps and how to do so more securely.

Adding web apps

Web applications are becoming more and more vulnerable to more sophisticated threats and attack vectors, which makes them less safe. In this section, we will teach you about web applications and attack vectors, and how to protect an organization's information from them. Web application hacking is a common method most attackers use to get into a system.

The best protection against web application hacking is to not have a vulnerable or insecure website. You can do this by evaluating the code and design practices before deploying your site.

A great example of why you need to secure code before deploying is what happened with Yahoo! Voices. The developers did not escape the input before inserting it into the database. As a result, a hacker was able to gain access to more than 450,000 unpublished articles on the website.

Now, let's look at some of the threats to web servers and applications.

Threats to both servers and applications

What types of attacks can be launched at these technologies? Well, first, let's start with web servers.

> **Note**
> You'll see some similarities in the attacks that are used to target both web servers and web applications as one can create a vector for the other.

Web server attacks

When it comes to the servers themselves, attackers can launch attacks against web servers using any of the following methods:

- **Denial of Service (DoS)**: By launching a DoS/DDoS assault on a web server, an attacker attempts to bring the service down or make it inaccessible to legitimate users. A DoS/DDoS assault on a web server is frequently directed at high-profile web servers, including bank servers, credit card payment gateways, and even root name servers.

- **Brute-force attacks**: Here, an attacker attempts to use combinations of usernames and passwords until one of them is found to be valid; these often result in a dictionary attack.

- **DNS server hijacking**: This occurs when an attacker hacks a DNS server and modifies its mapping settings to redirect users' requests to the attacker's rogue server. As a result, when a user enters a genuine URL into a browser, the settings redirect the user to the attacker's bogus site.

- **DNS amplification attacks**: For this attack, the attacker spoofs a DNS request from a target and sends it to another open DNS resolver. The targeted DNS server will now send a large DNS response to the forged IP address of the victim. This can result in a large number of data packets being sent to the victim's system and can overload and shut down the system.

- **Directory traversal**: This attack consists of an attacker obtaining access to a hidden directory on a web server, bypassing normal access restrictions, and exposing data that shouldn't be allowed to be accessed.

- **Man-in-the-middle**: This method is where an attacker intercepts communications between two systems without either of them knowing. The attacker intercepts the communication and can view or edit it before passing it back to the systems.

- **Phishing attacks**: This is an attack in which the attacker sets up a fake website to trick users into entering sensitive data, such as passwords and credit card information.

- **SQL injection**: This is a type of attack where an attacker attempts to access information from a database on a web server, which would normally be disallowed. However, if the web developer did not use parameterized queries when communicating with the database, it leaves the system vulnerable.

  Session initiation protocol (**SIP**) and **real-time protocol** (**RTP**) are used for communication by **Voice over Internet Protocol** (**VoIP**) systems and are also vulnerable to this attack.

- **HTTP response-splitting attack**: This is a web-based attack in which the attacker deceives the server by injecting new lines and arbitrary code into response headers. The attacker manipulates the input parameter and cleverly builds a request header that prompts the server to return two answers. By inserting header response data into the input field, the attacker makes a single request appear as two requests. Each request is then responded to by the web server. The attacker can provide malicious data to a vulnerable application, which then stores it in an HTTP response header.

- **Web cache poisoning attack**: This makes the intermediate web cache source less reliable because of web cache poisoning. In this attack, an attacker changes the cached content for a random URL that has malware on it. When requesting the required URL through the web cache, unaware users may mistakenly utilize the misidentified content rather than the genuine and secure material. The attacker causes the web server's cache to be purged of actual cache content and asks it to store a specially crafted request. As a result, all the users on the web server's cache will receive harmful content until the servers purge the web cache. Web cache poisoning attacks are possible if the web server and application have HTTP response-splitting flaws.

- **Secure shell (SSH) brute-force attack**: Attackers use the SSH protocol to make an encrypted SSH tunnel between two hosts so that they can send unencrypted data over an unprotected network. Most of the time, SSH runs on TCP port 22. Attackers will scan SSH servers using bots. Once the credentials have been discovered, attackers will use this powerful new host as a base station to target internal systems and/or scan for vulnerabilities on auxiliary servers.

- **Server-side request forgery (SSRF) attacks**: Attackers use SSRF flaws to send crafted requests to internal or backend servers through public web servers. These flaws come from the functions in an application being misused on public web servers. Internal servers are usually put in place by firewalls to keep unwanted traffic from getting into the network. SSRF flaws can allow attackers to send crafted requests from public web servers and connect to internal or backend servers directly.

Now, let's look at some common web server vulnerabilities.

Common web server vulnerabilities

Web servers may be configured with unnecessary features and services that create potential security holes. This could include files containing sensitive information, such as configuration files and scripts containing database names, user IDs, and passwords.

Some of the most common misconfigurations include the following:

- File and directory permissions that have been set up incorrectly or that allow unauthorized access to sensitive data

- Default usernames and passwords that haven't been updated from their default settings, allowing anyone who knows it to access the system without a password

- Unused services or accounts being enabled, which may have been left by mistake or by previous attackers

- Unnecessary features being enabled, which may have been installed for testing or development purposes and never removed after the site was put into production

- Poorly chosen passwords by administrators, allowing potential attackers to successfully guess administrative credentials, giving them unrestricted access to the web server itself

Authorization attacks

Here, the attacker finds a legitimate account with limited privileges, then logs in as that user, and gradually escalates privileges to access protected resources. Attackers then manipulate the HTTP requests to subvert the application authorization schemes by modifying input fields related to the user ID, username, access group, cost, filenames, file identifiers, and more.

HTTP request tampering

HTTP request tampering is when someone tampers with the information in a client request by changing the values within the URL to falsify data or steal user information. This can be used to fool users into providing sensitive information or to spoof entire pages, giving an attacker access to privileges that they would not normally have.

Most of the time, HTTP request tampering is used to change hidden values in a URL, such as HTTP_AUTHORIZATION, or cookies that have been sent to the server with the request. The most common types of attacks that are dealt with include **cross-site scripting (XSS)** or **man-in-the-middle (MITM)** attacks, in which the attacker is intercepting requests and sending different values in each request. When these are done correctly, the server will assume that the attacker has access to these values (to make things easier for users), when it's just the attacker talking.

Authorization attacks are very easy to prevent by using HTTPS and other security measures. HTTPS encrypts the data being transferred, which prevents MITM attacks from intercepting requests to change information. Authentication will always be present when you're using HTTPS, so XSS or cookie injection is nearly impossible with encryption. Authentication can also be used to prevent invalid token manipulation, as tokens are usually encrypted before being sent to the server.

The most important step to take is verifying the authenticity of all the requests that are sent from a user, which can be achieved by requiring authentication for sensitive pages and checking that all the other requests have valid tokens attached. This will stop any type of HTTP request tampering attacks before they begin.

Cookie parameter tampering

Cookie parameter tampering is when someone tampers with the information that's sent in a cookie from the client to the server by changing the values within a single cookie or multiple cookies. This can be used to fool users into providing sensitive data or to steal user information. Most of the time, this attack deals with manipulating session cookies, which are usually encrypted and unique for each user session. In most cases, the attacker is intercepting requests and sending different values in each request, specifically targeting the cookie that was used to access a protected service.

Burp Suite (`https://portswigger.net`) is a great tool to use to test your servers and apps for these types of attacks.

Next, let's look at the potential threats to web applications.

Web application attacks

Even if a web server has been set up securely or is protected by network security measures such as firewalls, a poorly written web application or the web server itself could give an attacker a way into the web server's security. An attacker can use many different types of attacks on web applications that aren't secure to get into the web server's security.

SQL injection attacks

SQL injection attacks occur when a developer does not properly validate their user input before passing it into a database. An attacker can inject SQL commands into the input and gain access to sensitive information on the server, such as usernames and passwords.

To avoid this flaw, developers should always escape their user input with special escaping methods so that the input cannot affect the query:

```
SELECT * FROM users WHERE UserID=2302 or 1=1
```

The `or 1=1` expression returns a value of TRUE, which can be used to get all the user IDs from the database. An attacker finds a flaw in a web application and uses it to get around normal security measures and get direct access to valuable data. When hackers try to do SQL injection attacks from things such as the web browser's address bar or form fields, queries, or searches, the hacker can get information that's not meant for them. Various commands can be used to modify data, delete massive amounts of data, or even create accounts within a web application.

To avoid SQL injection attacks, it is necessary to securely store web application data. The web application data should have correct character types to avoid SQL injection attacks. Also, SQL injection attacks can be prevented by using one of the most basic secure programming techniques – parameterized queries. However, they are still vulnerable to SQL injection attacks because folks don't use prepared statements. Prepared statements are the most secure way to prevent SQL injection attacks.

A prepared statement is an approach that helps prevent SQL injection attacks because it makes the web application explicitly indicate where user input goes in the statement. Many frameworks have adopted this method of preventing SQL injections, so developers don't have to worry about it.

However, there are still some web applications and developers that don't use prepared statements and can be vulnerable to SQL injection attacks, so be aware.

Other web application attacks

Let's look at some other types of web application attacks you can use:

- **DNS rebinding attacks**: This is when the hacker tries to fool the web browser's DNS system into looking up an IP address that is not correct. This forces your browser to bypass the firewall and gives the hacker access.

- **Cookie snooping**: These attacks occur when the hacker steals your authentication to a website by sniffing cookies. Cookies are often sent back and forth during HTTP requests, so they contain lots of important information about what someone has done on a website. If any of that information is sensitive (such as the session ID or user identification), then it can be used to log in to that website remotely.

- **Cookie tampering**: In this attack, the attacker manipulates cookies as they travel to a browser from a web server. In other words, an attacker can change the cookie's values before it reaches the user's browser. If the altered cookie has any unauthorized privileges associated with it, then the attacker gains those privileges when performing malicious tasks.

- **Obfuscation application**: Attackers are usually very careful and ensure they hide their attacks and stay out of the way. **Intrusion detection systems** (**IDSs**) keep an eye out for signs of well-known attacks, which forces attackers to come up with new ways to stay unnoticed. This type of attack involves the attacker encrypting the attack to look like something else.

- **Parameter/form tampering**: This is a type of malicious intrusion in which an attacker exploits web applications that include parameters to authenticate users. This includes form fields for user login names and passwords.

- **Cross-site scripting (XSS)**: This is a security flaw that's present in some web applications that allows attackers to gain unauthorized access to the victim's system. Attackers can exploit this vulnerability by injecting malicious scripts into HTML forms or by enticing the vulnerable site's visitors to click on an attacker-supplied link.

- **Session hijacking**: This is a type of attack in which an attacker steals another user's session ID and takes over their authenticated session. By taking control of the victim's browsing session, the attackers can gain access to the victim's account information without knowing their login credentials.

- **Unvalidated input attacks**: These are created so that an attacker can submit data to the frontend of a web application. The backend database can't handle this information, leading to unintended behavior within the application.

- **Directory traversal/command execution**: This is another web server attack where attackers exploit web servers that can't properly sanitize input. If the attack is successful, it allows attackers to read sensitive files, list directory contents, write files, and run arbitrary commands on the underlying system.

- **Denial of service attacks**: This is an attack in which a malicious party tries to make a machine or network resource unavailable for users. For example, they could try to send too many requests to a service, such as a web server. Attackers could also try to send malicious packets that will tie up resources or cause the system or application to fail.

- **SQL injection**: This is just like what we saw for web server attacks.

- **XSS attacks**: Here, the attacker tricks someone into viewing a page containing a malicious script. When the user accesses this URL, the browser renders the page containing the malicious scripts, which could send requests to other applications or embed malicious code in pages.

- **Buffer overflow attacks**: This attack occurs when an application tries to put more data into a buffer than it can hold. This causes the excess data to spill out, corrupting other data in the process. Buffer overflows are frequently exploited by attackers.

- **Source code disclosure**: This attack occurs when an attacker gains access to the source code or other information that could help them exploit vulnerabilities in the system. This threat occurs during product development, maintenance, and testing.

- **Cross-site request forgery attacks**: This attack forces an end user to execute unwanted actions on a web application that they're currently authenticated in. The most common example of this is forcing users to make purchases or transfer funds.

- **Command injection attacks**: This is an attack in which an attacker injects unauthorized commands into a command line that will run under the privileges of the user running them. If successful, attackers could gain access to operating system functions or download sensitive information.

- **Credential stuffing attacks**: Credential stuffing is the process of trying stolen credentials (usernames/passwords) on multiple websites. Most credential stuffing attacks are unsuccessful, but it can be worthwhile to monitor for this type of activity as users often use the same password on different sites. This could allow an attacker to gain access to other systems that were not part of the original attack.

Now, let's learn more about the vulnerabilities of web APIs, web shells, and webhooks.

The vulnerabilities of web APIs, web shells, and webhooks

It is important to understand and be familiar with the vulnerabilities of web APIs, web shells, and webhooks. Recognizing best practices will help you provide greater security.

Web APIs

One of the most important parts of a website is its web **application programming interface (API)**. The API takes data from a server and makes it compatible with another server. This way, other programs can read the information that would otherwise be difficult to access. With the help of an API, computer applications can perform actions on websites, such as posting comments. However, the API must be secure and not vulnerable to security concerns such as XSS.

Some of the most popular APIs are as follows:

- **SOAP API**: This is a standard that's used by Microsoft and uses the **Web Services Description Language (WSDL)**. WSDL is an XML language that contains information about how to communicate with a web server.

- **REST API**: REST stands for **Representational State Transfer**. This type of API is more of a software architectural style rather than an actual standard. It doesn't include WSDL but does use HTTP methods (GET, POST, and so on) to communicate with web servers.

- **XML-RPC:** This is like the SOAP API in that XML-RPC is an interface rather than a specification. It is created using HTTP requests with XML supplied as the data format.

- **JSON-PRC:** This is a modern web API standard that uses **JavaScript Object Notation (JSON)** for its data format and HTTP requests for communication.

Recent years have seen a huge rise in the use of web-based APIs to support different types of devices, such as mobile devices and IoT devices. APIs are often used by these devices to communicate with backend web servers. To make these web-based APIs easier for people to use, developers often cut corners on security. This makes online web services more vulnerable to attacks. Attackers use a variety of methods to find and exploit flaws in these APIs. The attackers who want to get into an API have to figure out what API technologies are used, what security standards are used, and where they can attack.

Now, let's discuss some API security best practices.

Best practices for API security

You should utilize the same strategies that work for web applications. In addition, you should set up a rate-limiting system to ensure an attacker can't make requests more frequently than legitimate users. You may also want to monitor your logs for requests from bots and scrapers as this could indicate attempts at gathering additional information on your application or website.

Here are some key points to help you out:

- Use HTTPS for encryption.
- Use IP-based whitelists to gain access to APIs.
- Monitor and review logs.
- Parameterize statements in SQL queries.
- Use quotas and throttling against your API.
- Limit the request body and length of your API.

It's also important to understand security standards. Let's discuss some of these standards next.

Web API security standards

APIs, like any other software, have security flaws. They adhere to standards such as OAuth and SSL but include numerous vulnerabilities that attackers can use. If any of these standards are configured incorrectly, hackers can exploit them. Often, the developers of web applications don't think about the consequences of using security flaws in their API. For example, they'll use session IDs to identify users and allow access to information on their website or server without realizing how easy it is for hackers to reroute fraudulent traffic through an authorized user's connection. Administrators must check for security standards such as SSL when they're testing their web applications for vulnerabilities. They should also review XSS and SQL injection attacks to prevent future attacks on that API.

Now, let's talk more about web shells and webhooks.

Web shells

A web shell is a backdoor on a website or server that allows attackers access via HTTP/ HTTPS. It can allow an attacker to upload and download files, execute system commands, modify server settings, view source code, and do other things. It's typically used to make the website or server more secure or easier to use by the administrators of that website or server. These types of shells are usually uploaded through vulnerabilities in the web application.

Preventing the installation of a web shell

An attacker can send a series of requests to install a web shell on the server. The payload for this attack would look something like http://kali:1337/index. php?install_shell=1&language=../../../../../etc/passwd%00.

To prevent this, make sure that the application has a strong input validation layer that is aware of the different types of above-the-fold input payloads. Note that this only prevents the installation of a web shell – it does not prevent an attacker from viewing any file on the system if they have been granted access to do so by another vulnerability.

The following is an example of preventing the installation of a web shell:

```
if (preg_match('/../../../../etc/passwd/', $_GET['install_
shell']) ) {
    // don't allow shell to be installed for this user }.
```

Webhooks

Webhooks provide a communication channel between two web APIs. This allows one API to receive notifications from another, so information can be exchanged without a direct connection. Webhooks are a little harder to detect because the source of the data isn't always clear unless it's a POST request or uses a similar type of identifier. These types of requests may bring attention to your web application if you're not expecting them or if you don't know what to do with them.

Many developers do not understand that webhooks require security, just like any other API endpoint: it is easy to make mistakes by doing what appears to be the right thing for a specific case, which can leave systems exposed to various attacks. These include MITM, replay, and arbitrary code execution attacks. The risk of attacks is higher when the webhooks are exposed to third parties, such as mobile applications or other outside services. It may be possible to blacklist certain IP addresses that appear to be performing these types of attacks, and implementing CAPTCHAs on your login pages will also help.

Detecting web server hacking attempts

There are several ways you can find out if your web server has been compromised.

The first way is to monitor the logs from the web server. A good practice is to have more than one log file, but it's even better if they're monitored and sent to a separate system so that if something happens on the current web server, the logs will still be available.

Another way to do this is to audit ports on the web server. Make sure that all the open ports are accounted for and do not return any strange responses.

You should also look at traffic between the web server and users. If you see abnormally large requests or file downloads, this could be an indication of hacking attempts.

Some other ways to protect your web servers/apps

The `machine.config` file specifies the resources that are available on the web server, including access to files, directories, and registry keys. Restrict access to these resources to prevent any kind of false file uploads and other dangerous requests.

You should also make sure all your other applications are up to date to ensure they're patched against any vulnerabilities that may have been found in them.

Next, secure any certificates that are used for your keys. This is the easiest way to protect your keys. If you don't need them, remove them. If possible, restrict the permission of user accounts on the server. This will keep an attacker from gaining local administrator access.

Also, look into implementing secure coding practices. If your web pages aren't built securely, then hackers will be able to exploit that weakness and gain access to the system.

Finally, install security patches for your operating system and other applications as soon as they become available. The longer you wait, the more opportunities your system will have to be compromised. Patch management is an important part of secure computing.

Now, let's look at web application security testing.

Web application security testing

Web application security testing is done to assess the performance and security of the apps you have in place. These types of tests should be scheduled regularly to ensure the app can handle a variety of different attacks.

Here are some tips on how to get started with your web application security testing:

- Identify what you hope to learn by conducting the tests.
- Identify which performance and security issues are the most important for your project.
- Create an attack plan before you start the testing process.
- Perform the tests you have planned out.
- Review the results of your testing and develop a plan for fixing any performance or security issues.
- Perform source code reviews.
- Evaluate the encoding schemes.

For more details on this topic, check out OWASP's *Testing Guide* at `https://owasp.org/www-project-web-security-testing-guide`.

At this point, I should mention that one of the best tools for testing the security of your web servers and their apps is Metasploit. Metasploit is an open source penetration testing software that allows users to find vulnerabilities in systems and networks and creates exploits for those vulnerabilities. This tool is a framework, which means that it is a platform that allows users to easily create custom tools and uses modules for different exploits.

Various things make Metasploit popular among the hacking community: it is free and has an immense library of user-generated scripts, modules, and modularization. You can also create modules.

Although the CEH exam doesn't cover a lot of information about the modules and plugins for Metasploit, I highly suggest that you learn about this awesome tool for your career. My recommendation would be *Metasploit 5.0 for Beginners – Second Edition*, from *Packt Publishing* (`https://www.packtpub.com/product/metasploit-5-0-for-beginners-second-edition/9781838982669`).

There are so many attack tricks and tips you should be aware of for the real world. A whole book could be written about web server/application hacking. However, our goal here was to cover the information you'll need to know for the exam.

Summary

In this chapter, we discussed ways you can hack web servers and web apps. This allows you to discover existing and potential vulnerabilities. Then, we discussed why web servers and web apps create security issues. We talked about some of the different types of architectures you may experience and looked at some of the threats the wireless world presents us with. After that, we covered some attacks you can use for web application attacks. We covered some of the specifics and vulnerabilities of web APIs, web shells, and webhooks. Finally, we discussed some of the ways we can detect web server hacking attempts and prevent or limit what attackers can do.

In the next chapter, we'll dive into hacking the **Internet of Things (IoT)** (or, as I like to say, Internet of THREATS) and **Operational Technology (OT)**.

Questions

As we conclude, here is a list of questions for you to test your knowledge regarding this chapter's material. You will find the answers in the *Assessments* section of the *Appendix*:

1. A web application is best described by which of the following?

    A. Code designed to be run client-side

    B. Database SQL code

    C. Web service targeting

    D. Code designed to be run server-side

2. What is used to store session information?

    A. A cookie

    B. A directory

    C. A snoop

    D. A file

3. The _____ scripting language is used on the client side.

    A. PHP

    B. JavaScript

    C. ASP.NET

    D. ASP

4. Which of the following is used to access content that is not located in a website's root directory?

    A. Directory traversal

    B. Brute force

    C. SQL injection

    D. Port scanning

14
Hacking IoT and OT

Wow, what a world we live in. The past few years have seen an explosion in devices connecting us to the internet. It's important to understand these **Internet of Things (IoT)** and **Operational Technology (OT)** devices, what they can do, and why security is so important to us with these devices. Seriously – we need to grasp this technology. Don't believe me? Ask the casino in Las Vegas that got hacked via a thermostat… on a fish tank! (`https://mashable.com/article/casino-smart-thermometer-hacked`)

In this chapter, we'll cover the following topics:

- Understanding IoT
- IoT hacking
- Methods used for IoT
- OT and methods used to hack it

So, let's start by understanding IoT.

Understanding IoT

You must be thinking – *Dale, Internet of Things, is it that big of a deal? I mean, isn't it just mostly in homes?* Well, it's in more places than you might think. What we're starting to see, and why it's such an issue for us, is that we're seeing it in things such as **Heating, Ventilation, and Air Conditioning** (**HVAC**) systems. The famous Target breach was all handled through an HVAC system. We're seeing it in fire and safety systems, lighting, and transport, and this could include office buildings, retail locations, education, hospitality, airports, and even stadiums.

We're seeing it emerge in the energy sector, such as windmills or turbines, batteries, generators, drills, and other energy-related machines that may be used to switch off electricity or slow it down. We also see it within the consumer and home sector. It just surprises me every day when I see a new device or appliance that has internet access. Again, whether it's gaming systems, alarm systems, speaker systems, or even lights or locks, chances are the device has access to the internet. I didn't even know this, but the dishwasher I purchased can contact the manufacturer for troubleshooting.

We're also seeing this phenomenon show up in the industrial sector. In mining, for example, you can use automation for resources, such as real-time asset tracking, predictive and preventative maintenance, and monitoring, which can detect excessive vibrations or temperature increases and forecast time to failure and what needs to be fixed. There are automation resources for agricultural and irrigation systems. I had an opportunity to work with a local city municipality where I live. We took the water that comes down the mountains and stored it, and we used it for what's called secondary water. It's stored, and then we distribute it throughout the communities and use that water to water our grass so that we're not using our drinking water to water our grass. All of this is controlled through automated valves. Automation helps us with cost-saving, and that's why it's so attractive.

We also have automation making its way inside the security and public safety sector – whether it be surveillance, tracking, or even emergency services. IoT is infiltrating quite fast, and of course, we're also seeing it pop up inside IT and network sectors, both at the public and enterprise levels.

An attacker that can access medical equipment could be a real issue for us. Let's look at an example. My wife happens to work for a large retail electronics store. They are partnering with several medical sector-based companies to provide monitoring for elderly people, either via a monitoring service or their adult children. Automation can provide real-time monitoring for bed pressure sensors, which would let me know if my dad may not be out of bed yet. This would help me figure out if he might be feeling ill. Being able to communicate directly with the elderly is important.

We're observing automation appear within medical implants as well, particularly in terms of modifying them. My son-in-law is about to have hearing surgery. The device they're going to be putting in his ear will allow him to link to baby alarms and smoke detectors so that he can hear them clearly or be notified that something's going on. So, if you weren't aware of all these sectors being affected by IoT, you can see that the landscape for attackers is growing almost daily to attack people – maybe even hourly at this point.

Let's talk more about how IoT works.

How does it all work?

You may be asking yourself – *how does IoT work?* Well, there are several different components that you need to be familiar with. Let's start with what's referred to as the sensing technology of those nifty little devices. Maybe it's a doorbell or a thermostat. It could even be a valve in an industrial environment that can be turned on or off.

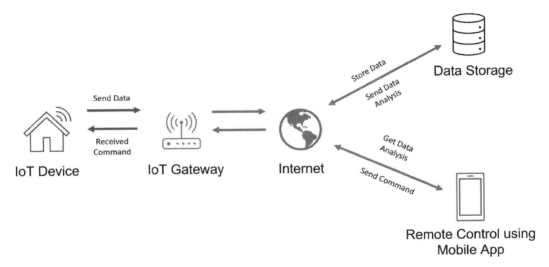

Figure 14.1 – Example of how IoT devices interoperate

These devices then interface with what is referred to as an **IoT gateway**. These gateways are used to bridge the gap between the IoT devices, as well as the interaction with the end user. Think of them as the middlemen with IoT.

Then, we have the **communication channel**, which is the internet. Through this communication channel, our gateways typically talk to what we refer to as either the data storage and/or a cloud server.

Here, the data is collected after it goes through the gateway and arrives at the cloud servers. That data is then stored and analyzed. Based on the application itself, that information can be sent to the end users' remote app, which could be on their smart device. So, from an attacker's perspective, you can see that there are a lot of different possibilities, as far as an *attack vector* is concerned, but we'll talk about that more later in this chapter.

Now, let's talk about the architecture of IoT.

The architecture of IoT

With IoT, there are different layers – or I should say, components – that are involved in the entire IoT environment. The architecture consists of several different layers, as shown in the following diagram:

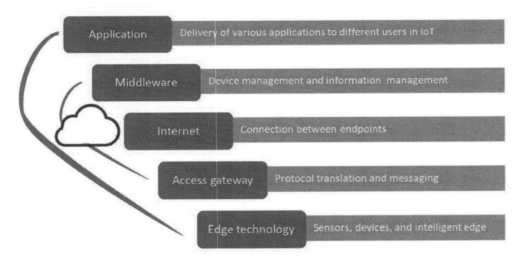

Figure 14.2 – The IoT architecture is made up of several layers

The first layer is referred to as the **edge technology layer**. This layer is where all the hardware parts, such as sensors, readers, software sensors, or the physical device itself, as well as **radio frequency identification** (**RFID**) tags, could be located. If you think of any of the devices we deploy, these would be at the edge technology layer. These devices are designed to collect information and they're going to send that information back to the cloud servers or the data storage locations.

The next layer is what we refer to as the **access gateway layer**. This is what bridges the connectivity between the providers on the backend side and our edge technology layer, or our devices.

Next, we have the **internet layer**, which is extremely important to us because it's how we communicate. Now, depending on the manufacturer, we can have two different endpoints, such as device-to device, device-to-gateway, or even device-to-cloud. This layer is what is utilized.

We also have what's referred to as the **middleware layer**, which is a two-way communication channel. This layer sits between the application layer and what we refer to as the **hardware layer**. Its main responsibility concerns data management, handling issues such as data analysis, data aggregation, data management, filtering devices, discovering devices, and even access control, where we can say who has access to these devices via the application.

Then, we have the **application layer**. This layer within IoT oversees making sure services are delivered to users from different areas geographically and in different departments, to ensure they have access to whatever it is that they need.

That wasn't too bad, was it?

Now, let's talk about the protocols and technology that IoT utilizes.

Protocols and technologies

Let's break these down into some different categories.

Short-range communication

Let's look at some of the short-range communication resources that are available to us.

Z-Wave

Z-Wave is a home automation standard. It allows us to manage things such as our air conditioners, HVAC systems, thermostats, and home theater rooms. We can control everything from door locks to speaker systems in this way.

ZigBee

This is another short-range communication protocol just like Z-Wave. Both these protocols can be considered mesh networks, but the advantage with ZigBee is that if a signal originates from a centralized hub, each device can act as a repeater.

There's an issue with how far the signals can go. With ZigBee, it's limited to about 40 feet. With Z-Wave, we can go up to about 330 feet in an outdoor environment while in an indoor space, it's typically about 100 feet. Now, ZigBee does have the advantage of theoretically connecting to around 65,000 devices, whereas Z-Wave is limited to a mere 232 devices. But one of the bigger downsides, at least for me, is that ZigBee uses the standard 2.4 GHz range, which a lot of our wireless devices are already utilizing, whereas Z-Wave uses the 908.42 MHz frequency. As far as communicating with their devices and controls is concerned, both use the **Advanced Encryption Standard** (**AES**) 128 encryption standard. It's a requirement to get certified by Z-Wave.

Wi-Fi

We know all about Wi-Fi, right? The most common standard for Wi-Fi is 802.11n, which gives us a speed of up to about 600 Mbps, with a signal of approximately 150 feet indoors and 300 feet outdoors if unobstructed.

Wi-Fi direct

This acts as peer-to-peer communication between devices. Here, one device acts as the access point, while the other one acts as the client.

Radio Frequency Identification (RFID)

RFID is extremely popular with those little tags that you see everywhere, where you can set your phone on the tag, and it'll look up the product that tag represents. On the attacking side, we love creating RFIDs that look like they're designed to do something, but they do something completely different. We're starting to see RFID tags being used in pets, as well as livestock, and even cars and pharmaceuticals.

Bluetooth smart or Bluetooth low energy (LE)

This is just Bluetooth technology, but it's designed to create a **Local Area Network** (**LAN**) or a personal network.

Light fidelity or Li-Fi

It sounds like Wi-Fi, right? It's very similar to Wi-Fi, but it does have two major differences. One is speed (at 224 Gbps), while the other is that it uses **Visible Light Communications** (**VLC**) (yeah, I know what some of you are thinking– *isn't that a media player?* All these acronyms we must keep track of), but basically, we're using light for communication.

Near-field communication (NFC)

This uses a magnetic field to communicate between two electronic devices. So, for example, when you purchase something with Apple Pay or any type of mobile payment method where you set your phone down, that typically uses NFC technology.

Quick response (QR) codes

QR codes are those square-looking barcodes most of us have seen. They allow you to store a little bit more information than regular barcodes, but both are going to contain information about the product itself or other products they may be attached to.

Now, let's talk about mid-range communication.

Midrange communications

Let's look at a couple of solutions we should all be aware of since they assist us with midrange communication.

HaLow

HaLow operates in frequency bands that are just below the 1 GHz range, which means it can transmit about twice as far as standard Wi-Fi, and it utilizes the 900 MHz band on the Wi-Fi channel. The 900 MHz band is unique because it handles going through walls or solid structures a little bit better. It doesn't require a true line of sight.

LTE-Advanced

This is a standard mobile communications frequency that's utilized. It provides an enhancement to the standard LTE, which means it gives us a higher capacity in terms of how fast data is transmitted, as well as how far it can be transmitted. This helps us as far as performance is concerned.

Long-range communication

Let's discuss some of the long-range communication resources we can use.

Low-powered wide-area networks (LPWANs)

As its name suggests, this is done through a low power, which is great, but it's been designed to provide a long-range communication channel between two endpoints.

Low-powered wide-area networks (LoRaWANs)

This is typically used in industrial machine-to-machine or secure two-way communication.

SigFox and Neul

SigFox and Neul are very similar to each other and are designed for devices that have very small battery lives. Both work below the 1 GHz bandh, but Neul leverages tiny slices of the TV white space spectrum to deliver highly scalable, high-coverage, low-power, and low-cost effective network switches.

Very Small Aperture Terminal (VSAT)

VSAT is another type of communication protocol that we use to transfer data. We typically see small satellite dishes being utilized for this type of communication

Cellular

Cellular is designed to give us high-quality data, but there's a cost associated with it – it's expensive and has high power consumption.

Now that we have covered the wireless side of things, let's look at the wired side.

Ethernet

Most of us should be familiar with Ethernet. It is used for connecting different devices to a wired LAN. It is the most common type of LAN.

Multimedia over Coax Alliance (MoCA)

We're not referring to the coffee here. This is a technology we can use with existing coax cabling to convert Ethernet signals to run across those coax cabling. Then, you have another converter on the other side that takes it off the coax and puts it back on the Ethernet. I've used a similar device to turn Ethernet into HDMI for longer HDMI runs.

Power-line communication (PLC)

Now, this is a cool one. It runs across our power lines in our home/offices! I know, right? This is where electrical wires are used as data transmission and power sources.

Next, let's discuss some of the available operating systems we can use for IoT.

Operating systems for IoT

In this section, we'll talk about the operating systems that IoT typically uses.

ARM Mbed

Yeah, you can tell it's short for embedded, and no, I didn't misspell it. This is one of the most used low-power device operating systems available. It's typically used in our wearable devices.

Zephyr

Zephyr is an operating system that's used in devices that are low in resources or constrained by resources, as well as low powered.

Ubuntu Core

Ubuntu is also known as Snappy, and we see this used in drones, as well as gateways. These can be found in IoT and robots.

Apache Mynewt

This is an operating system that's designed to run on devices utilizing low-energy Bluetooth protocols.

RIOT

We see this operating system on a lot of actuator boards, sensors, and even embedded systems. Typically, this operating system is extremely quiet, so it's a quiet riot. See what I did there? If you're not familiar, that's a famous 1980s rock, heavy metal band, so again, you can Google that one too, but don't *bang your head* over finding it. Okay? I won't give up my day job. I'll stick with this book.

Brillo

This is an operating system that's based on Android, and it's considered an embedded operating system. Again, we're going to use this on low-end devices, such as our thermostats.

Real-time operating systems (RTOSs)

These types of operating systems run extremely fast; we're talking milliseconds. The reason we need those types of operating systems is when we have a situation or a scenario where interaction must be spontaneous. For example, when your airbags deploy in your car, you can't wait multiple milliseconds for the bag to deploy to save your life.

Two of the most famous RTOSs include Nucleus and Integrity. The major differences between Nucleus and Integrity are that Nucleus features storage and database management, USB and networking, and multimedia support. It also has some advanced **Graphical User Interface (GUI)** capabilities, whereas Integrity is designed for more multi-core computers. RTOSs are typically used within military functions, such as the **Joint Strike Missile (JSM)**, which is being developed initially for the Royal Norwegian Airforce. Lockheed Martin is using it in conjunction with the F-35 fighter, where this operating system is running internally on a bomb bay door so that it can open instantaneously as missiles are being launched. Again, when the pilot pushes a button, it needs to happen then, not a couple of seconds from when they push the button.

Zephyr

We identified Zephyr as an operating system previously, but it's also a real-time operating system that can be used on all sorts of devices, whether it's a wearable device, an IoT router, or robotics.

Windows 10/11 IoT

Both Windows 10 and 11 IoT are editions of Windows that run on *headless* devices (that is, with no keyboard or mouse attached). It's designed to run without a display and offers integration for IoT devices, high security, and updates directly from Microsoft.

Amazon FreeRTOS

This RTOS is small. It's designed for microcontrollers that make small, low-power, edge devices easy to program, deploy, secure, and manage.

Next, let's discuss the challenges IoT presents to us.

The challenges that IoT presents

As you've seen so far, we've got some big issues when it comes to the different attack vectors that can be presented to an attacker regarding IoT. Here are some of the challenges that create a lot of vulnerabilities for us:

- One is the interoperability standards we have, or the lack thereof. There are so many products that come with IoT built into them that no one's following a real standard at this point. Some manufacturers aren't concerned about the security of their devices. Now, this is a problem because several of these manufacturers aren't looking at how their devices are used, especially when it comes to testing their **application programming interfaces** (**APIs**) or their inability to secure their devices. So, whether it's from the end user or a third party, a security hole is opened. For example, let's say that my SmartThings (`https://www.samsung.com/us/smartthings`) hub is interoperable with several different products, but to make that connection, it must issue an API. If that API is utilized and, for example, I've got wireless speakers in my house, if the product is flawed security-wise, an attacker could gain access to the Samsung Hub if they wanted to.

- We also have the issue of – believe it or not – clear text and open ports still being utilized. A lot of these devices are being sold without any encryption techniques being used to transmit data back and forth between either the device and the gateway or between the gateway and the cloud services. This can also happen with open ports because somebody may have forgotten to turn them off. We also have the issue of basic security and privacy issues not being followed. Again, a company that makes refrigerators may not have anybody on staff that's worried about security or privacy.

- We also have the issue of support being available for firmware and operating system updates. Sometimes, it can be difficult to update the firmware. Let's look at an example. I have a little computer on my bike, which I ride almost every day, and it tracks how far I've gone, my altitude, how much I'm climbing, my speed, my heart rate, and even my cadence. Well, this product shocked me quite a bit because I downloaded the application for it and after running the application for a couple of days, I started thinking about the firmware. Well, how do I update the firmware? After doing a little research, I found out that I had to download a separate application to update it, which I wasn't warned about, and I wasn't told that there was a separate app that I should download. Now, remember, we update the firmware in our operating system to patch holes or counter the vulnerabilities in a device, and in some cases, the manufacturer's updates could end up breaking some of the functionality of the device. So, in some cases, we have manufacturers who are refusing to allow firmware or operating system updates because it will stop things from working.

- Finally, we have storage issues. Nowadays, these devices are getting smaller and smaller as far as their physical size is concerned – for example, a water bottle that's going to remind me to drink water every day. There's not a lot of space there for a lot of hardware, so we're not going to have a lot of storage space. However, transmission by that device is virtually limitless, right? What this ends up doing is creating issues for us as far as data storage goes, as well as the management or protection we need to make sure we or manufacturers implement. You may have more data flowing across than you need at a particular time because there's no storage. We've got to get rid of it, right? Again, I'm speaking from the manufacturer's point of view. Yeah, can you believe this is happening? Default or weak credentials are still being used. In some cases, they're hardcoded. Often, the manufacturer doesn't even realize they're there. This is because they buy the operating system or the interface from a third party that they just want to implement within their product line.

So, as you can see, IoT adds some challenges we need to understand and be ready for. Now, let's talk about physical attacks.

Physical issues

Physical attacks on IoT devices include an attacker stealing the device from you, maybe modifying or tampering with it, counterfeiting it, or even injecting malicious code and then placing the device back within your network. That doesn't sound fun.

We also have insecure web interfaces. What we're finding is that a lot of these devices have web interfaces built into them. Any time we talk about a web interface, we know there's got to be a web server supporting it. If it hasn't been patched, it's just getting handled through clear text, or – better yet – it's not even secured, this type of challenge can lead to a vulnerability attack on the device itself.

It's a little computer, so can I do a buffer overflow? Absolutely. And since these devices are subject to buffer overflows, this means they're also subject to SQL injection or some type of an injection attack.

We also have development issues. What I mean by this is that we, as security professionals, have these devices coming into our network infrastructures. Sometimes, because of the complexity of these devices or how they operate, this adds to the complexity of the different policies we must deploy and implement. In some cases, I feel for the people that must create these policies because it's adding a completely new environment to what may be your already secure network, and now we've got IoT to worry about.

We also have an issue with vendor support. The device is only good so long as the vendor is there for you. In some cases, we see the vendors go out of business (especially after they've been breached). If you plan on bringing these devices into your infrastructure, the firmware and the operating systems must be upgradeable. This should be mandatory. If any company or vendor doesn't support you on that, you should look for a completely different solution because you're just asking for a door to be opened for you.

We also have regulatory and rights issues, and this is more of a *what can happen* issue. Because of all the interconnections of IoT devices, some security issues may come up where no legal law has been defined at this point. Let me give you an example. Let's go back to the example of the casino that was breached via the thermostat of a fish tank. So, who was at fault? Was it the thermostat manufacturer or was it the casino that hooked the IoT device to their internal network instead of a separated network? All these things are challenges for us, but hopefully, the field is going to clear up here soon.

Next, let's talk about the IoT hacking process.

IoT hacking

Let's talk about some of the vulnerabilities and some of the hurdles that IoT presents to us.

The first is what I term **data value**. This involves capturing data as IoT devices communicate with each other and with the cloud behind them or their cloud providers, which increases the risk because it makes IoT more obscure. Time after time, we're starting to see where the IoT environment is allowing attackers to access other devices, as well as networks they may be connected to. So, many companies deploy their IoT environments on their production network, which kind of makes me sad and sick inside.

Another issue is data aggregation. Again, we have a lot of devices here speaking with other resources that may be outside of our control.

There's also something that's referred to as sensor fusion, which is the ability to combine information from two completely disconnected sensing devices to create more complex information or a view of the environment the attacker is going after. Let me give you an example. In Boston, the city created an app that would identify potholes in the city's roads using mobile phones, accelerometers, and GPS data. This information was sent to the Public Works Department to help them find out where the worst potholes were. But if you think about it from an attacker's point of view, if I'm able to gain access to that environment, couldn't the attacker use this application or its information to possibly divert the city services away from the areas that need the most attention?

We also have the issue of integration. Now, you may be thinking, that's great – integration, right? We typically look at that as a positive thing. But when we start allowing these devices that aren't very secure onto our existing networks and integrate them into applications that we need to be developing internally, or even into other IoT apps, we should be a bit concerned.

This is a huge issue in that the healthcare industry is being inundated with hundreds and hundreds of different devices that are based on IoT environments. Imagine the complexity of thousands, if not hundreds of thousands, of these devices being deployed, and you need to make sure that a specific pump is given the right commands to update the dosage. We also need to make sure that only the physicians or the care practitioners have the authority to do so, and that nobody can hack it.

The culprits

First, it's going to be the application, right? The application can create problems by having no security updates allowing default passwords that are in place or even passwords or backdoors that can't be changed.

We also have the mobility issue and the fact that we have various communication channels. Are they encrypted? Are we using authentication? Do we lack the ability for proper storage security, even if someone's using an insecure API?

We also have the cloud. Again, maybe our authentication hasn't been set up correctly with their cloud providers, or maybe there's no encryption for storage or communication to the cloud. Then, there's the web interface for the application that's hosted on the cloud environment, and then we have the network itself. Are the services running that are supposed to be running, and have they been locked down and secured? Do we have any updates being pushed out to our devices either manually, automatically, or through a third-party application? Do you even have a firewall in place for your IoT environment? Again, the best practices here are to have your IoT environment on a completely segmented network, and just like any network, you need to make sure you have the same type of security devices in place. Remember, when we introduce the cloud, we're introducing a whole new infrastructure.

Device memory challenges

Let's talk about the massive attack surface, and when I mean massive, it is really big, folks – **device memory**. We're talking about how much space there is for the device to operate. Let's talk about some of the things that are possibly being stored in the device's memory.

Encryption keys? Yeah, absolutely. How about credentials from third-party vendors? Yup, and even the possibility of cleartext credentials being stored.

We also have ecosystem access controls; this means any of the components that are integrated within our IoT environment. Let's say we have trusts or different types of trusts between components. For example, Samsung, by default, with their SmartThings hub, automatically trust all their components – whether it's a water sensor, motion sensor, or location sensor – so these types of implicit type trusts can be a vulnerability for us. Also, there is the aspect of enrolling a device in your environment.

Let me give you an example. When I hooked up my Samsung SmartThings hub, I was shocked and amazed at how easily it worked – all I had to do was turn the motion sensors on and it automatically picked up several devices. So, not having any type of authentication taking place could allow for a malicious device to come on board.

Well, what do we do? We need to have some way of decommissioning those types of devices, such as clearing the data or even just resetting the device to the factory default to make sure there's nothing left in the device's memory or storage.

We also have a physical interface. The physical interface could include both a user **command-line interface (CLI)**, as well as an administrative CLI. Again, if we give an individual user access to the device and they have administrative rights on that device, that would be a great pivot point for me to get onto their network from an attacker's perspective, as well as the ability to go through a privileged escalation scenario. Does the device have a physical port, such as a USB port? Does it support universal Plug and Play? What happens when you plug in a Rubber Ducky? If you're not familiar with a Rubber Ducky, it's a USB thumb drive, but the system picks it up as a keyboard, which means I can type in all kinds of fun commands. When looking at IoT devices, one of the things you should look at is whether the vendors support a way of disabling these types of ports or different services that may be available on that device.

The other attack surface would be the web interface itself. Just like anything else, when there's a web interface involved, we've got issues that could occur, such as some type of an injection attack or a cross-site scripting attack, or even a cross-site request forgery attack. In some cases, I might be able to do some type of username or user account enumeration.

Now, let's talk about the various IoT attacks.

Types of IoT attacks

With all the various types of IoT that are out there, we need to be aware of some of the potential types of attacks that can occur with IoT devices.

DDoS attacks

This is where an attacker turns all your IoT devices into evil little devices that can perform DDoS attacks or make them a member of a bigger botnet.

Rolling code attacks

Most IoT devices operate on a rolling code. This is like the keyless entry system for your car or garage door opener, where you must press the buttons in the right order before it will open. The attacker forces you into pairing with their device by making you try lots of codes one after another until they find the right one that opens your door. Theoretically, it should be impossible because the attacker makes a device with a matching key fob and your controller doesn't allow more than one device with a particular key to operate in your area. But most devices don't make their rolling codes truly random.

BlueBorne attacks

BlueBorne is less of a specific IoT attack and more about IoT devices communicating using Bluetooth, which Android and Linux have supported by default since 2012. Android has had a patch available since September 2017 when this was made public knowledge. But as we've discussed, many products won't get patched, even when the manufacturer knows about it, because they can't afford to build another device at their price points. I think they should be illegal in most cases.

Sybil attacks

Imagine someone creating dozens of fake devices, such as baby monitors or lightbulbs, all with different MAC addresses. They use these fake devices to communicate with your real device and learn about your network. Then, they use the real identity of one device against you by taking over that device to discover things about your network.

Jamming attacks

This has nothing to do with toast, jam, and a knife. This is when someone broadcasts at the same frequency as your device and confuses it or causes it to not work at all.

Hacking a smart grid with a backdoor

This is where your electric company has a device on your home network that allows them to turn appliances on and off remotely. So, say that cybersecurity researchers found a backdoor in many of these devices that allowed them to turn your appliances on and off. Yeah, that wouldn't cause an issue at, say, a hospital, right?

SDR-based attacks

Software-defined radios (SDRs) present a new challenge for IoT infrastructures. SDR is the method with which radio-frequency hardware is controlled with software. This can be used for good or bad, depending on who it's being used by. SDRs are devices that can understand how to send and receive different frequencies within the radio spectrum. Attacks can be attempted at both the full-duplex (two-way communication) and half-duplex (one-way transmission) modes.

You can also use DNS rebinding to alter some DNS entries on the target's router or gateway and then talk to those devices through their web interface using the default password. Crazy huh?

Now, let's about the methods that are used for IoT.

Methods used for IoT

The methods attackers use will normally follow a certain methodology. These methods can be broken down into sections we'll discuss next. Let's take a look.

Reconnaissance

Most IoT devices are endpoints participating in an IP network. Network reconnaissance is the process of gathering information about these networks and systems. When we talk about IoT, this pertains to scanning for common vulnerabilities such as default passwords or hardcoded secret keys that may be publicly available. Most attackers will use specialized tools such as Metasploit or Shodan to find these targets. And depending on the type of network, a variety of tools can be used.

Shodan is crazy amazing as an information-gathering tool. This search engine can find all kinds of devices, including web servers, routers, printers, IP cameras, and more. It's common to find default passwords on devices such as **wireless access points (WAPs)** or IP cameras. All this information is valuable for the hacker to use later for exploitation (for example, taking advantage of a weak password).

As an example, to search on Shodan for webcams on a certain street, you must enter `webcamxp city:"GothamCity"` (or your target city), which would show you publicly visible webcams in your city. Want to find Google web servers? Type in `Server: gws" hostname:"google"`. Or do you want to see something scary? How about `password 1234`? Yep, this gives you a list of devices that are using a password of 1234. Crazy, huh?

If you want lots of information, head over to the FCC's website (The Federal Communications Commission in the United States) at `https://www.fcc.gov/oet/ea/fccid` (see *Figure 14.3* and *Figure 14.4*). This is an organization where all devices that are distributed or manufactured in the USA must register their devices. There's a plethora of intel here.

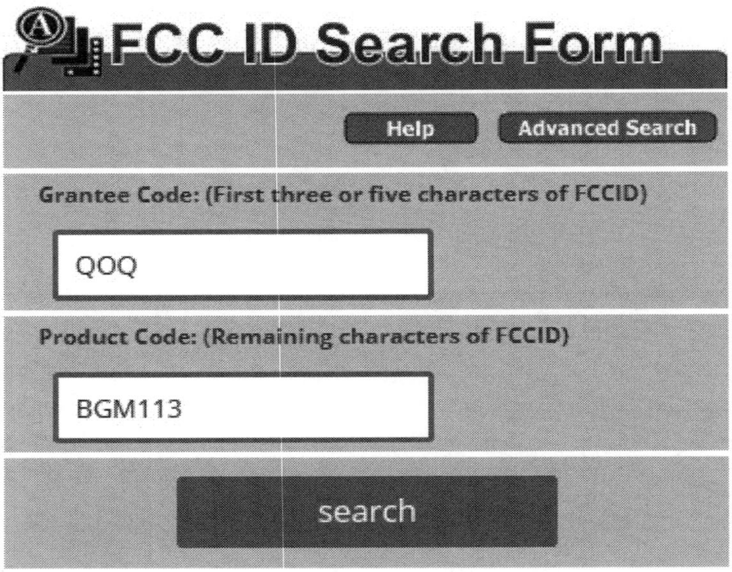

Figure 14.3 – FCC website

As shown in the following screenshot, it can provide a lot of great information:

BGM113 Blue Gecko *Bluetooth*® Smart Module Data Sheet

The Blue Gecko BGM113 is a Bluetooth® Smart Module targeted for Bluetooth Smart applications where small size, reliable RF, low-power consumption, and easy application development are key requirements. At +3 dBm TX power, BGM113 is ideal for applications requiring short and medium range Bluetooth Smart connectivity.

The BGM113 integrates all of the necessary elements required for a Bluetooth Smart application: Bluetooth radio, software stack, and GATT-based profiles, and it can also host end user applications, which means no external microcontroller is required in size, price or power constrained devices. The BGM113 Bluetooth Smart Module also has highly flexible hardware interfaces to connect to different peripherals or sensors.

BGM113 can be used in a wide variety of applications:

- IoT Sensors and End Devices
- Commercial and Retail
- Health and Wellness
- Industrial, Home and Building Automation
- Smart Phone, Tablet and PC Accessories

KEY FEATURES

- Bluetooth 4.1 Compliant (Bluetooth Smart)
- Software upgradable to Bluetooth 4.2
- Integrated antenna
- TX power: up to +3 dBm
- RX sensitivity: down to -93 dBm
- Range: up to 50 meters
- 32-bit ARM® Cortex®-M4 core at 38.4 MHz
- Flash memory: 256kB
- RAM: 32 kB
- Autonomous Hardware Crypto Accelerator and True Random Number Generator
- Integrated DC-DC Converter
- Onboard Bluetooth Smart stack

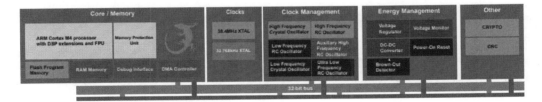

Figure 14.4 – Detailed PDF documents on an item from FCC

If you're looking for an actual application, check out MultiPing (https://www.multiping.com) or even IoTSeeker (https://github.com/rapid7/IoTSeeker), which will scan your devices and tell you whether they are still using the default passwords.

```
/Users/rapid7/freetools>perl iotScanner.pl 1.23.123.431,
1.23.123.443,1.23.123.453,1.23.123.457,1.23.123.459,1.23.123.461,1.
23.123.462,1.23.123.463,1.23.123.465,1.23.123.466,1.23.123.467,1.23
.123.469,1.23.123.472,1.23.123.473,1.23.123.475,1.23.123.477,1.23.1
23.479,1.23.123.480,1.23.123.481
device 1.23.123.431 is of type Stardot still has default passwd
device 1.23.123.443 is of type Arecont has changed passwd
device 1.23.123.453 is of type American Dynamics has changed passwd
device 1.23.123.457 is of type W-Box has changed passwd
device 1.23.123.459 is of type Arecont has changed passwd
device 1.23.123.461 is of type American Dynamics has changed passwd
device 1.23.123.462 is of type W-Box has changed passwd
device 1.23.123.463 is of type Arecont has changed passwd
device 1.23.123.465 is of type American Dynamics has changed passwd
device 1.23.123.466 is of type W-Box has changed passwd
device 1.23.123.467 is of type Arecont has changed passwd
device 1.23.123.469 is of type American Dynamics has changed passwd
device 1.23.123.472 is of type W-Box has changed passwd
device 1.23.123.473 is of type W-Box has changed passwd
device 1.23.123.475 is of type W-Box has changed passwd
device 1.23.123.477 is of type W-Box still has default passwd
device 1.23.123.479 is of type Arecont has changed passwd
device 1.23.123.480 is of type American Dynamics has changed passwd
device 1.23.123.481 is of type American Dynamics has default passwd
```

Figure 14.5 – Sample results after using an IoT seeker application

Another common approach that's used by attackers (in conjunction with network reconnaissance) is to try to tie together information that's been gathered from the device's web interface with what they know about Linux/Unix systems. Header meta-information in HTTP transactions, for example, often includes software version numbers and other clues that can reveal where vulnerabilities exist within implementations of common protocols.

Once attackers have some idea of how the IoT device operates internally, it's much easier for them to find vulnerabilities in its code. This is where scanning comes into play.

Vulnerability scanning

Once the attacker has found a list of potential targets, they will start vulnerability scanning. This entails using well-known exploits that may be available for public consumption that target specific vulnerabilities in the IoT device's software or firmware. Often, these exploits come from third-party research groups (Google Project Zero and others) who will identify and release security holes in all kinds of devices, or from vendors who may not disclose these types of vulnerabilities to their customers. Another great place to check out for vulnerability information is the **United States Computer Emergency Readiness Team** (**US-CERT**), as they often post advisories about recently identified flaws that may affect IoT devices.

Many of these vulnerabilities are based on known implementations, bugs, or design flaws within the protocol, which are necessary to understand before you can identify potential targets. This becomes easier as the list of protocols the device supports increases over time, as well as its ability to process what's being sent by an attacker.

Launching attacks

Once the attackers have identified a known vulnerability, they will begin penetration testing efforts by exploiting that specific vulnerability within the IoT device's particular operational environment. We can't stress enough how important conducting this type of activity in a lab environment is!

Gaining and maintaining remote access

This is where the IoT researcher (that's you!) will apply specific exploits against a particular vulnerability they have discovered. Then, the attacker can run a series of tests to determine whether a device has been successfully compromised and how it was done, as well as what user-level access is available after entering the system.

After remote access has been achieved, the attacker has several ways to infiltrate and exfiltrate data from an IoT device. This can include uploading and executing scripts on the IoT device to gain persistence, establishing a remote shell for later use, or even moving laterally within devices that are connected to compromise other devices on the network.

Once the attacker has gained access to the device, they employ various methods to maintain and extend access. Attackers remain hidden by deleting logs, upgrading firmware, and employing malicious applications such as backdoors, trojans, and other malware to stay on board. To exploit firmware, attackers utilize tools such as Firmware Mod Kit or Firmwalker, to name a few.

Speaking of firmware, firmware is a set of instructions that tells the hardware how to function. Firmware analysis is the process of examining the firmware of a target IoT device to identify its underlying flaws and risks. Attackers use firmware analysis to find passwords, API tokens, endpoints, vulnerable services running, backdoor accounts, and configuration files that are being used. With time and patience, attackers can reverse engineer the firmware and discover weaknesses and backdoors that present themselves as a means to maintain future access. Attackers don't always need to maintain all these capabilities; instead, they should be prepared for multiple contingencies by having other specialized tools at hand. For example, using malware such as Mirai or BASHLITE will maintain access for future use if or when the attackers wish to commandeer the device again.

Now, let's look at some ways in which we can protect our IoT devices.

Countermeasures to protect IoT devices

There is no one threat that we can correctly protect against since there are many different kinds, and each has a way of attacking and exploiting IoT devices. Combining everything would be too cumbersome and costly for most IoT users, but IoT device manufacturers are in a unique position to implement IoT security by design.

However, we have some steps we can take to protect the network. Let's take a look:

1. Disable any guest or demo accounts.
2. Utilize any *auto lockout* features for invalid login attempts.
3. Use strong authentication mechanisms.
4. Place your control systems and devices behind firewalls.
5. Isolate the IoT network away from your business network.
6. Protect IoT devices from physical access.
7. Disable Telnet.
8. Use end-to-end encryption and **public key infrastructure** (**PKI**).
9. Deploy IPS and IDS devices.
10. And you know this one – update, update, update.

Now, let's discuss operational technology.

OT and methods used to hack it

Operational technology (**OT**) is a term that's used to describe a variety of technologies that work together as an integrated or homogeneous system in today's modern society. Telecommunications, for example, makes extensive use of OT to move data from the electrical grid to the wheeling station. The same communications are also utilized for financial transactions between electrical consumers and producers. OT is a network of hardware and software that is used to monitor, manage, and control industrial process assets. It's critical to grasp the fundamental principles of OT before attempting to hack it.

The Purdue model

At this point, it's a great time to talk briefly about the Purdue model. The Purdue model is derived from the **Purdue Enterprise Reference Architecture** (**PERA**) model, which is widely used to describe the internal connections and dependencies of essential components in the ICS networks. It consists of three zones: the manufacturing zone (OT) and the enterprise zone (IT), which are separated by a **demilitarized zone** (**DMZ**).

The Purdue model can be used for analyzing, designing, and securing ICS networks. It can help identify potential security risks and vulnerabilities and provide guidance on how to mitigate them.

In this model, the manufacturing zone (OT) is the most critical part of the network as it includes all field devices that are responsible for process control and automation. The enterprise zone (IT) is less critical as it only provides data storage, connectivity, and other business functions. The DMZ is used to separate the manufacturing and enterprise zones, and it usually contains security devices such as firewalls and **intrusion detection systems** (**IDSs**).

We'll cover various OT topics in greater detail later in this chapter.

Let's start by answering the question, what is OT? OT, or an **industrial control system** (ICS), refers to a specialized system of computerized hardware and software that is dedicated to managing and monitoring physical equipment. ICSs, including **Supervisory Control and Data Acquisition** (SCADA), **Remote Terminal Units** (RTUs), **Programmable Logic Controllers** (PLCs), **Distributed Control Systems** (DCSs), and other specialized network systems that help monitor and manage industrial operations are part of this technology.

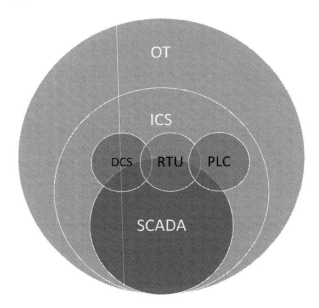

Figure 14.6 – The components of OT

Now, let's look at OT and the security challenges we must deal with.

OT and security – a dilemma

ICSs can monitor and control infrastructures such as electrical grids, oil pipelines, networks of elevated transit stations, and more, but these systems have a fundamental security disadvantage – they were built to monitor and control, not necessarily to protect.

This inaccuracy arises from the fact that OTs have limited access to information about what is going on inside complex infrastructures. For example, an OT control system for a manufacturing plant may provide information on the water levels in tanks, but it usually lacks access to information on water temperature or pH, which are critical parameters for the optimal operation of chemical processes.

Hacking OT – a threat to critical infrastructure

Contrary to popular belief, the systems that control infrastructures such as electrical grids, oil refineries, dams, and more are not secure. Since the sophistication of OT networks has increased, hackers have also had to increase their sophistication by learning more about the OTs they are targeting. The bad news is that it takes much less knowledge and skill to hack an OT system than, say, a traditional IT system.

The success of a hack is determined by two critical factors – the vulnerability of the targeted system and the ability of the hackers to exploit that weakness. In recent years, numerous vulnerabilities have been discovered in ICSs by security researchers who have published their findings at security conferences such as Black Hat, DEFCON, CanSecWest, and others. Some of these vulnerabilities have made it easy for experienced hackers to penetrate IT networks and control OT systems.

Should we combine IT and OT?

IT/OT integration can help a company's performance by reducing gaps between the two domains. The convergence of IT and OT is more than just about using technologies; it's also about personnel and processes. Traditional IT/OT teams are generally kept apart, with IT staff in one department and OT workers in another. For example, IT teams keep track of internal processes such as programming, system updates, and network security. OT teams, on the other hand, are responsible for ensuring that everything runs smoothly both internally and externally. Both IT/OT teams must be familiar with each other's operations and organizational structure. This does not imply that IT experts must be converted into field or plant personnel; it simply implies connecting them so that they may collaborate to enhance security, efficiency, quality, and productivity.

Challenges of OT risks

As I mentioned previously, most OT systems are still running on old versions of software and using antiquated hardware, making them susceptible to harmful exploits such as phishing, espionage, ransomware assaults, and other types of attacks. These sorts of assaults may be highly damaging to products and services.

To prevent these vulnerabilities from being exploited, here are some of the risks that OT presents to us:

- **Physical and environmental disasters**: This is one of the most well-known risks in the OT environment. An example would be a hurricane or tornado that can damage equipment and facilities.

- **Intentional attacks**: Acts of terrorism, sabotage, and espionage could result in considerable damage to both property and people.

- **Malicious programs such as viruses and malware**: These are some of the most common attacks that occur in OT environments. Viruses and malware can quickly spread, affecting various equipment throughout a plant.

- **Social engineering**: This entails the use of human-centric attack methods to gain access to OT systems. Examples include phishing or spammy emails being sent to employees who are tricked into giving up their passwords.

- **Network complexity**: OT systems use different technologies from IT, so there is a need for a clear separation of the network. However, additional entry points to networks can prove to be a security risk.

- **Lack of visibility**: OT networks are not monitored properly, so threats go undetected. This can lead to a cascading effect of threats that may affect many people and equipment.

- **Poor security management**: OT systems have weak security defenses, which makes them vulnerable to cyberattacks.

- **Outdated systems**: A lack of updates and patches can leave OT systems open to danger.

- **Convergence with IT**: As I mentioned earlier, convergence between IT and OT teams enables them to work together. However, this is not an easy task; it requires considerable effort for both sides to learn about each other's roles and how they can contribute to their respective domains.

- **Vulnerable protocols**: Protocol stacks are the foundation for all network traffic. Open and broken protocols can enable attackers to take control of OT systems.

- **Security by obscurity**: This refers to when manufacturers don't share knowledge about their products with others, including competitors. When this occurs, it becomes easier for hackers to find their way into these devices.

- **Lack of training**: OT personnel and teams do not get the relevant training to secure their systems. As a result, they put company equipment and data at risk.

- **Lack of security standards**: There are currently no security standards for OT devices; this means that every developer may implement their own defense mechanisms. Unfortunately, such measures often lack proper testing and validation, leaving vulnerabilities that can be exploited.

Next, we'll discuss ICSs.

Introduction to industrial control systems (ICSs)

ICSs are used to control industrial processes. They're computer systems that monitor and control the operations of equipment such as compressors, pumps, generators, motors, reactors, boilers, furnaces, ovens, turbines, conveyors, and more. These components are what make up an ICS environment:

- **Supervisory Control and Data Acquisition (SCADA)**: These are control systems that can monitor and control equipment via the ICS environment.

- **Distributed Control System (DCS)**: These are more advanced versions of SCADA that utilize distributed computing.

- **Programmable Logic Controller (PLC)**: These are small computers that work with discrete (discontinuous) signals. They can monitor and control equipment, process data, and more.

- **Human-Machine Interface (HMI)**: This is also known as a man-machine interface. It's used to obtain feedback from equipment, sensors, and more. If an HMI is being monitored by the ICS environment for any abnormalities or problems, it may send out alerts to other personnel via email, text message, and so on.

- **Business process control system (BPCS)**: These systems utilize specialized software and hardware that can monitor and control industrial processes. BPCSs may be used to run the entire ICS environment or just a single component of it, such as a PLC or DCS.

- **Safety Instrumented System (SIS)**: These are software programs that control the flow of (typically hazardous) materials in industrial processes. If they detect any issues, they can send out alerts to other personnel via email, text message, and more.

- **Industrial Explosive Device (IED)**: These are explosive devices that are used to deal with hazardous materials. They're usually part of the SIS's functionality.

Through the ICS environment, operators can monitor their equipment and processes anywhere in the world. However, this environment may be targeted by cyber attacks if it's not properly secured. It would be wise to practice good network security within such an environment because it controls important components that may pose a threat to people and property.

Let's discuss some of the different operation modes of ICS.

Operation modes of ICS

ICS systems can be configured to run in three different modes:

- **Open-loop**: In open-loop control, there is no feedback from the environment. Consider a temperature sensor placed in an oven. The oven's computer will turn on or off until it reaches the desired temperature that has been set by either a human operator or a program.

- **Closed-loop**: In closed-loop control, there is feedback from the environment. Now, let's take our oven scenario again. The temperature sensor will inform the computer to turn on or off accordingly until it reaches the desired set point.

- **Manual-moop**: In manual-loop control, there is feedback from the environment, but the control loop is under human supervision. This system won't turn on or off until a human operator intervenes in its operations.

Next, we'll discuss the potential risks and threats associated with ICS.

ICS risks and threats

Unfortunately, ICSs are vulnerable to cyber attacks. The following are several known risks and threats associated with ICS:

- ICS systems are susceptible to several network-related attacks (for example, network sniffing and spoofing). Attacks such as these can be launched to intercept sensitive information, modify data, and more.

- ICS systems are susceptible to malware attacks (for example, viruses and worms). Malware can cause physical damage to equipment and data loss, among other things. Merely looking at malware with the wrong type of equipment can cause it to go off.

- ICS systems are susceptible to ransomware attacks. These are malicious software programs that are used to encrypt ICS data until a ransom is paid in return for an encryption key.

- Attackers can use social engineering methods against personnel to gain access to ICS environments. For example, they can call up personnel pretending to be from a trusted company sending official-looking emails.

- ICS systems are susceptible to **Denial of Service** (**DOS**) attacks. These are used to cripple ICS environments by flooding computers with useless data designed to overwhelm their resources so that they're unable to perform their normal operations.

- ICS systems are susceptible to Trojan attacks. Trojans are used to gain backdoor access to computers. Like malware, they're capable of causing physical damage.

- ICS system components can be hacked to perform malicious acts. For example, a PLC or DCS could be hacked to cause process shutdowns or other issues within the ICS environment.

- ICS systems are susceptible to several client-side attacks (for example, cross-site scripting and cross-site request forgery). Attacks such as these can be launched against clients so hackers can gain access to the system using the victims' permission.

Now, let's look at port use when utilizing ICS/SCADA systems.

The ports that are used by ICS/SCADA systems

ICSs that are used in SCADA and other critical infrastructure systems typically use seven-port communications protocols to connect end devices:

- Port 80: HTTP (used for communications between ICS/SCADA clients and servers)

- Port 88: UDP (used for communications between ISC/SCADA components for status updates, device naming, and more)

- Port 21: FTP (used to transfer files between ICS/SCADA components)

- Port 25: SMTP (used for sending emails)

- Port 23: Telnet (used to connect to remote devices to configure them or check their status)

- Port 161: SNMP (used for network management and configuring devices over IP networks)

- Port 443: HTTPS (used for encrypted communications between ICS/SCADA components)

Now, let's discuss some of the attacks that ICS/SCADA may encounter.

Attacks on ICS/SCADA

ICS/SCADA has vulnerabilities regarding being attacked. Here are some of the potential attacks that may be used against ICS/SCADA:

- **HMI-based attacks**: HMI-based attacks target human-machine interfaces, which are used to view and manipulate data on ICS/SCADA systems. These types of attacks can be launched by gaining unauthorized access to the network or tricking operators into visiting spoofed websites that launch malware onto their computers.

- **Memory corruption**: A memory corruption attack is a hack that aims to corrupt the memory of an ICS/SCADA component so that it fails to perform as expected. These types of attacks can be launched by gaining unauthorized access to the network or intercepting communication between components to tamper with them.

- **Credential management**: These aim to gain access to an ICS/SCADA environment by using default passwords. This would also include the lack of encryption as data is in motion, which would reveal cleartext passwords and account names.

- **Code injection**: These types of attacks inject malicious code into ICS/SCADA software to cause technical issues, disrupt operations, or allow attackers to access the system. The vulnerabilities in this category include common code injections such as SQL, operating system, command, and some domain-specific injections. Gamma script, like many other domain-specific languages for HMIs, is vulnerable to code injection attacks.

Now, let's discuss some of the specifics of side-channel attacks.

Side-channel attacks

These types of attacks target the physical implementation of cryptosystems (for example, anything that processes cryptography). They exploit unintentional characteristics of the physical implementation that leak information about cryptographic keys or other sensitive data.

Power analysis can be used to derive information about cryptographic keys by observing details such as the amount of time it takes for computations to occur, or by measuring electromagnetic emanations from integrated circuits.

Timing analysis is another side-channel attack that's considered high-throughput, which allows attackers to perform it fast enough to be effective in most cases. Timing analysis can be used with ICS/SCADA systems because they typically run on embedded devices with RTOS. A loop approach is used by attackers to recover these passwords. They attempt one character at a time until they find the first one that works, and then they repeat for additional characters if the first was correct. If not, the loop ends. By monitoring how long it takes a device to complete one whole password authentication process, attackers can figure out how many characters that have been entered are correct.

How can you defend against OT hacking?

The best way to defend against OT hacking is with awareness and periodic audits, such as red-teaming exercises. Awareness can be achieved through regular training programs; audits should include testers who look for vulnerabilities in the network and digital filesystems of the devices. Such audits also consider what could happen if a system were hacked: how many devices could be impacted and how quickly would the business become aware of the threat?

Here is a list of some options to consider when you're trying to defend against OT hacking:

- To lower current risk exposure, conduct a risk assessment regularly.
- Use purpose-built sensors to discover the vulnerabilities in the network inactively.
- By combining threat intelligence with asset protection, you can detect threats and prioritize OT patches.
- Make sure your OT devices and software are always up to date.
- Unused ports and services should be disabled.
- For OT applications, use best security practices and secure coding.
- Continuously monitoring and detecting log data that's been generated by OT systems is required to discover real-time assaults.
- Raise security awareness among staff and provide them with up-to-date security measures.
- Use hashing to create strong and secure passwords and change the factory-preset passwords.
- Use two-factor authentication, VPNs, encryption, firewalls, and more to provide secure remote access through a variety of barriers.

So, as you can see, IoT has its challenges and those challenges will increase as more and more devices are brought into the world of IoT.

Summary

In this chapter, we discussed IoT and OT. In a time when so many products are being developed with some smart aspect to them, there is a challenge of balancing functionality with security. Unfortunately, the security aspect seems to be a second thought and that presents a new host of potential security vulnerabilities. We addressed what IoT is, some ways to hack IoT, and some methods attackers can use on IoT. Finally, we discussed the role OT also plays in the security challenges of IoT.

In the next chapter, we'll discuss cloud computing.

Questions

As we conclude, here is a list of questions for you to test your knowledge regarding this chapter's material. You will find the answers in the *Assessments* section of the *Appendix*:

1. Which of the following is responsible for message routing and identification in an IoT architecture?

    A. The middleware layer

    B. The edge technology layer

    C. The access gateway layer

    D. The internet layer

2. When is the Shodan search engine most likely to be employed in the IoT hacking methodology?

    A. Information gathering

    B. Vulnerability scanning

    C. Gaining access

    D. Launching attacks

3. Which of the following countermeasures are effective in preventing IoT hacking? (Select all that apply.)

    A. Enabling lockout features for excessive login attempts

    B. Disabling guest and demo accounts

    C. Enabling UPnP

    D. Disabling telnet

4. Of the tools listed, which is the best choice for quickly discovering the IP addresses of IoT devices on your network?

    A. MultiPing

    B. IoTInspector

    C. beSTORM

    D. Z-Wave Sniffer

15
Cloud Computing

Cloud computing is a new technology that allows you to access computer applications, data storage, and webmail over the internet. The use of cloud computing enables a decentralized workforce while lowering operational costs and offering data security. Many organizations nowadays are moving their data and infrastructure to the cloud due to these advantages. However, the cloud environment likewise contains several dangers and risks for businesses. Attackers are exploiting security flaws in the cloud software to gain unlawful access to valuable data that is kept there.

Cloud security is becoming increasingly important for both individuals and organizations. This chapter explains the various methods for attacking the cloud environment, which highlights underlying vulnerabilities. Understanding these assaults and vulnerabilities assists **Cloud Service Providers (CSPs)** as well as cloud consumers in developing secure cybersecurity measures to safeguard their cloud infrastructures. Remember, this chapter isn't designed to be *this is all you need to know about cloud technologies*, but rather how to protect them.

We'll cover the following topics in this chapter:

- Living on Cloud 9
- Attacking the cloud
- Tools and techniques of the attackers
- Best practices for securing the cloud

Let's first lay a foundation for the concepts of cloud computing.

Living on Cloud 9

Cloud computing is an on-demand delivery of IT capabilities, in which IT infrastructure and applications are provided to subscribers as metered services over networks. Examples of cloud solutions include Gmail, Facebook, Dropbox, and `salesforce.com`.

Cloud services are delivered using internet technologies, which can include public, private, or hybrid models. Let's look at these briefly next:

- **Public cloud services**: These are offered by providers such as Amazon, Google, and Microsoft. These services are available to the public and can be used by anyone who registers for an account. The provider manages the infrastructure and applications and makes them available on a pay-as-you-go basis.

- **Private cloud services**: These are offered by organizations such as IBM, Hewlett-Packard, and Rackspace. These services are used by the organization that owns them and are not available to the public. The provider manages the infrastructure and applications and makes them available on a pay-as-you-go basis.

- **Hybrid cloud services**: This is a combination of public and private cloud services. For example, an organization might use a public cloud service for email and a private cloud service for storage.

- **Multi-cloud services**: Multi-cloud is another one. It's a cloud environment made up of two or more clouds (private, public, or community) that remain unique entities and yet are linked to provide the benefits of various deployment methods. The company in this scenario makes some assets internally available and manages them, while other resources are external and handled by others. A great example of this is Microsoft's Azure or Zymr.

Let's discuss some of the different cloud computing models next.

Cloud computing models

To meet the different needs businesses have, there are a few cloud computing models used. Let's briefly discuss these next:

- **Software as a Service (SaaS)**: Saas is the most common model for delivering cloud services. With SaaS, the provider hosts the applications and makes them available to subscribers over the internet. The subscriber uses a web browser to access the applications and does not need to install any software.

  The application is available on a pay-as-you-go basis from the provider. SaaS is a great option for organizations that want to outsource their application hosting and don't want to worry about managing the infrastructure.

- **Platform as a Service (PaaS)**: PaaS is a model for delivering cloud services in which the provider hosts the infrastructure and makes it available to subscribers over the internet. A subscriber can access the application via a web browser. There is no need to install any software.

  The application is available from the supplier on a pay-as-you-go basis. PaaS is a wonderful alternative for companies who want to outsource their application hosting and don't want to deal with infrastructure management.

- **Infrastructure as a Service (IaaS)**: IaaS is also a model available to subscribers over the internet. A provider hosts the infrastructure and a subscriber uses a web browser to access the application. There is no need to install any software.

  This application is also available on a pay-as-you-go basis. IaaS is an excellent choice for companies who want to outsource their application hosting but don't want to deal with the infrastructure.

- **Identity-as-a-Service (IDaaS)**: Organizations subscribe to a cloud computing service that provides authentication services and is run by a third-party provider for identity and access management services. It's a SaaS product that provides **Single Sign-On (SSO)**, **Multi-Factor Authentication (MFA)**, **Identity Governance and Administration (IGA)**, access management, and intelligence gathering. These features allow customers to have more secure access to sensitive data both on and off-premises.

- **Security-as-a-Service (SECaaS)**: In this cloud computing model, security services are incorporated into company infrastructure in a cost-effective manner. It is based on SaaS and does not necessitate any physical hardware or equipment. As a result, it has significant cost savings over what organizations spend when they create their own security capabilities. It offers services such as penetration testing, authentication, intrusion detection, anti-malware protection, and security incident response.

- **Container-as-a-Service (CaaS)**: The cloud computing architecture behind it enables subscribers to utilize containers and clusters as a service. Through a web portal or an API, it offers virtualization of container engines, container management, applications, and clusters. Subscribers may use these tools to create rich, scalable containerized applications in the cloud or on-premises data centers. CaaS combines the features of IaaS and PaaS.

- **Function-as-a-Service (FaaS)**: The goal of this cloud computing service is to make it simpler to design, operate, and manage application features without the burden of having to build and maintain infrastructure (serverless architecture). This architecture is widely utilized in the creation of microservice applications. Consumers access on-demand features, which power off the supporting infrastructure and incur no costs when idle. IoT services, mobile and web applications, and batch-and-stream processing are just a few of the data processing services it offers.

Whew! I think that's all of them. Oh, I guess there is **Hacking-as-a-Service (HaaS)**. Although it's kind of a new concept, basically you pay hackers to phish for you or set up a **Distributed Denial of service (DDoS)** as a service and even just plain old *hire a hacker*. I know, crazy right?

Let's talk about the separation of responsibilities in cloud computing next.

Separation of responsibilities in cloud computing

Not all cloud computing models are the same. They differ in the way they distribute the responsibilities of delivering a cloud service.

The following three models illustrate how this distribution can take place:

- In a **provider-managed model**, the provider is responsible for everything from managing the applications to handling all customer support.

- In a **self-managed model**, the customer is responsible for managing the applications and for handling customer support.

- In a **hybrid model**, a combination of provider-managed and self-managed services is used.

Which model you choose depends on the needs of your organization.

Provider-managed services are a good option for organizations that want the provider to handle all the responsibilities, while self-managed services are a good option for organizations that want more control over their applications. If you're not sure which model is right for you, hybrid services are a good option because they offer the best of both worlds.

Next, we'll talk about how we deploy a cloud service.

Deployment models

Once you've decided on the type of cloud service you want, you need to decide on the deployment model.

The following four models are the most common ones:

- **Public cloud model**: The provider in this model is responsible for the development and constant maintenance of the public cloud and its IT resources since they make services such as apps, servers, and data storage available to the public over the internet. As a result, the provider is accountable for creating and maintaining these elements of the public cloud.

- **Private cloud model**: A private cloud, sometimes called an **internal** or **corporate** cloud, is a cloud infrastructure run by a single company and set inside the company's firewall. Organizations build private cloud infrastructures to maintain complete control of corporate data. This model utilizes software such as VMware, SAP, or Microsoft's System Center platform.

- **Community cloud model**: A community cloud is a type of private cloud that is shared by several organizations that have common interests, such as ensuring their data remains secure or sharing the cost of infrastructure.

- **Hybrid cloud model**: A hybrid cloud is a composition of two or more clouds (private, community, or public) that remain unique entities but are bound together by standardized or proprietary technology that enables data and application portability between them.

Organizations use hybrid clouds to extend the reach of their private clouds into the public cloud, to take advantage of the economies of scale available in public clouds, or to combine the strengths of two or more clouds. Which deployment model is right for you depends on your specific needs.

Let's talk about the use of container technology next.

Container technology

This emerging technology has been developed to specifically address the needs of cloud deployments. It addresses the issue of portability by encapsulating an application and all its dependencies into a self-sufficient package that can be run on any platform, in any environment.

Some of the features of containers include the following:

- They are portable, so they can be run on any platform or infrastructure.
- They are fast to deploy, so you can get your applications up and running quickly.
- They are lightweight, so they don't use a lot of system resources.
- They are secure because all the application's dependencies are included in the container, so you don't have to worry about security issues.
- They are easy to manage because you can track all the containers in your deployment and manage them as a group.

Container technology is still emerging, but it has already gained a lot of traction in the cloud computing world because of its many benefits. If you're looking for a way to make your cloud deployments more portable and efficient, you should consider using containers.

Let's discuss cloud storage architecture next.

Cloud storage architecture

Now that we have a basic understanding of how cloud-based systems work, let's look at the different components that make up a cloud storage system. There are three primary components: **frontend, middleware, and backend**.

The frontend layer is the part of the system that the end user interacts with. This might include a web interface or a mobile app. The frontend communicates with the middleware, which is responsible for managing the interaction between the frontend and the backend. The backend is the part of the system that stores the data.

The frontend and the backend might be in different data centers, and the middleware might be in a third data center. This configuration allows the system to scale by adding more frontends or backends.

Most cloud storage systems use a client/server architecture. The client is the part of the system that is installed on the user's computer. The server is the part of the system that stores the data.

The client/server architecture allows the system to scale by adding more clients or servers.

Let's talk next about some of the cloud storage services that are available to us.

Cloud storage services

Now that we have a basic understanding of cloud storage, let's look at some of the most popular cloud storage services.

- **Amazon S3** is a cloud storage service that allows you to store data in the cloud. The service is based on the **Amazon Web Services** (**AWS**) platform.

- **Azure Blob Storage** is a cloud storage service that allows you to store data in the cloud. The service is based on the Azure platform.

- **Google Cloud Storage** is a cloud storage service that allows you to store data in the cloud. The service is based on the **Google Cloud Platform** (**GCP**).

- **IBM Cloud Object Storage** is a cloud storage service that allows you to store data in the cloud. The service is based on the IBM Cloud platform.

Let's explore the **National Institute of Standards and Technology** (**NIST**) cloud deployment reference architecture next.

NIST cloud deployment reference architecture

Now that we have an understanding of cloud storage, let's look at the NIST cloud deployment reference architecture. The primary actors involved are the following:

- **Cloud consumer**: The individual or organization that contracts with the cloud service provider to use the cloud services for your organization.

- **Cloud service provider** (**CSP**): A cloud provider is a person or organization who purchases and manages the computing infrastructure required for offering services directly or via a cloud broker to interested clients via network access.

- **Cloud service broker**: The integration of cloud services is becoming too difficult for cloud consumers to manage and, as a result, they are turning to cloud brokers rather than CSPs. The **cloud broker** is a business that manages cloud services, including use, performance, and delivery, as well as the connection between CSPs and cloud consumers.

- **Cloud auditor**: An organization that is hired by the cloud consumer to assess, test, and report on cloud service providers and brokers, as well as the management and security of the cloud environment.

- **Cloud carrier**: The provider of transport services, such as bandwidth, for cloud-based systems.

Let's talk about a Docker next and how it's used in helping to facilitate the NIST architecture.

What's a Docker?

The acronym **Docker** stands for **digital container**. It's a software technology that lets containers be run on various platforms. To guarantee that apps function properly, all Docker dependencies are in the form of containers. Through OS-level virtualization, Docker provides a PaaS that delivers containerized software applications. This technology isolates apps from the infrastructure to speed up software delivery. The advantage of Docker is that it allows applications to run in any environment since they are packaged with their dependencies into a Docker container.

Microservices

Microservices are a software development technique that allows you to break your application down into smaller, more manageable pieces. Each microservice can be written in a different language and run on its own platform. This makes them easy to scale and manage, and it also gives you the flexibility to choose the best technology for each microservice. Microservices are perfect for cloud deployments because they make it easy to scale your application up or down as needed.

Understanding Kubernetes

Kubernetes is an open source system for managing containers at scale. It was developed by Google and is now maintained by the Cloud Native Computing Foundation. Kubernetes provides a platform for deploying, managing, and scaling containerized applications. It can be used on-premises or in the cloud, and it supports a wide variety of platforms, including Linux, Windows, and macOS.

Kubernetes is a powerful tool, and if you're using containers in your cloud deployments, you should learn how to use it. It can help you manage your containers more effectively and scale your applications up or down as needed.

Container security challenges

While containers offer a number of benefits, they also present some security challenges. Because containers include all the application's dependencies, they can be a target for hackers. You need to take steps to secure your containers and protect them from attack.

One way to secure your containers is to use authentication and authorization mechanisms. You can also use firewalls and other security measures to protect your containers from attack. It's also important to keep your container images up to date, so you can stay ahead of the latest security threat.

Serverless computing

Serverless computing is a new technology that allows you to run applications without having to worry about servers. With serverless computing, the server is abstracted away and all you need to worry about is the code. This makes it easy to deploy applications, and it also eliminates the need for server management.

Serverless applications are not entirely serverless; servers must be present, but they aren't visible to developers. In the service provider's cloud-hosted architecture, the application software executes on a third-party service provider's managed infrastructure. The cloud service provider is in charge of provisioning, scaling, load balancing, and securing the serverless infrastructure. The cloud service provider is also responsible for software and system patch management, as well as the underlying operating systems and applications and services.

Now that we have discussed how the cloud operates and what it does, let's talk about how we can attack the cloud next.

Attacking the cloud

The cloud has its security challenges as we're about to find out. Let's discuss some of the challenges we face when securing the cloud environment.

Cloud security

One of the biggest concerns with cloud computing is security. When your data is stored in the cloud, you need to be sure that it is safe and secure. Here's the secret about cloud security: it's just another network infrastructure that we might be including within our own networks. So, the exact same threats that we experience against our internal networks (including wireless) are the same threats we see with the cloud. Things such as injection attacks, authentication issues, data leakage, misconfiguration, coding issues, passwords, and web server/app weaknesses are just a few of them. However, I'd be failing you if I didn't at least talk about a couple of them, so here we go:

- Make sure you choose a reputable cloud provider with a good reputation for security.
- Use strong passwords and authentication methods.
- Encrypt your data.
- Avoid storing sensitive data in the cloud.
- Be aware of the cloud's vulnerabilities and how to protect against them.

The cloud is a great way to deploy your applications, and it offers several benefits, including flexibility, scalability, and convenience. But it's important to be aware of the security challenges involved in using the cloud and take steps to protect your data. With the right precautions, you can safely deploy your applications in the cloud and enjoy all the benefits it has to offer.

Let's now talk about some specific ways in which we can attack the cloud.

API vulnerabilities

If you want to hack cloud infrastructures, a good place to start is with API vulnerabilities. APIs are the backbone of many cloud-based services, and they often have more lax security than other parts of the infrastructure. By finding and exploiting vulnerabilities in APIs, attackers can gain access to sensitive data or disrupt service availability.

API vulnerabilities can be divided into two broad categories: those that allow access to sensitive data and those that allow attackers to cause a denial of service. API vulnerabilities that allow access to sensitive data include SQL injection flaws and **cross-site scripting** (**XSS**) flaws. API vulnerabilities that allow attackers to cause a denial of service include buffer overflow flaws and **cross-site request forgery** (**CSRF**) flaws.

Attackers can use various methods to locate API vulnerabilities, including data mining publicly available information, such as source code repositories and bug trackers. Attackers can also use automated tools to scan for known vulnerabilities in popular APIs.

Once an attacker has found a vulnerability in an API, they can exploit it in several ways. For example, they may use it to gain access to sensitive data or launch a denial-of-service attack.

To prevent attackers from exploiting API vulnerabilities, organizations should implement a comprehensive security program that includes both the static and dynamic testing of APIs. Static testing can help identify potential vulnerabilities, while dynamic testing can help verify that vulnerabilities have been properly fixed.

Organizations should also consider implementing rate-limiting and other controls to limit the impact of denial-of-service attacks. Organizations can help protect their cloud-based services from attack by taking these steps.

Service hijacking using social engineering

Yep, it's a "thing". The bad guys are getting craftier and more devious in their attacks. And unfortunately, social engineering is one of their favorite tools. An attacker steals the credentials of a CSP or a customer by phishing, pharming, social engineering, and exploiting software vulnerabilities in order to commit account or service takeover. The attacker obtains access to cloud computing services using the stolen credentials and jeopardizes data confidentiality, integrity, and availability. Attackers may attempt to reset passwords or IT personnel to access their cloud services to obtain passwords. Password guessing, keylogging malware, utilizing password-cracking approaches, and sending phishing emails are additional methods for obtaining passwords.

Side-channel attacks or cross-guest virtual machine (VM) breaches

Malicious insiders and attackers can use side-channel attacks to steal data or sensitive information from VMs. Cross-guest VM breaches are another way that attackers can do so. By compromising another guest's VM on the same physical server, attackers can steal data or sensitive information from other VMs on the same server.

Wrapping attacks

"This one's dedicated to all the hackers in the house!"

Even out settle scores quick,

Our disaster recovery requires even more disks,

Put your bytes up, prove it or you forfeit,

Got my C64 and we blew it into orbit"

– Dual-Core "All The Things" (https://www.youtube.com/watch?v=FoUWHfh733Y)

Oh, wrong kind of wrap. My bad.

In a wrapping attack, the adversary deception takes place during the translation of the **Simple Object Access Protocol (SOAP)** message in TLS. The intruder copies the message's body and transmits it to the server as though they were a legitimate user. The server verifies the authentication by comparing the signature value (which is also duplicated) to the original. An attacker can then break into the cloud and execute malicious code to disrupt the cloud servers' normal operation.

Man-in-the-Cloud (MITC)

An MITC attack is an attack in which the attacker controls or alters the cloud application's behavior. Attackers can use MITC attacks to bypass security controls, inject malicious code into applications, and steal data. They can also use MITC attacks to gain access to other users' accounts and conduct other malicious activities.

Cloud hopper attack

The cloud hopper attack is a sophisticated hacking campaign that targets organizations that use cloud-based services. Cloud hopper attacks are triggered at managed service providers (MSPs) and their customers. The goal of the attack is to steal data and intellectual property from these organizations. The cloud hopper attack uses a variety of techniques, including malware, phishing, and social engineering, to gain access to the organization's systems. Once they have access, the attackers steal data and intellectual property and then move on to other organizations.

Cloud cryptojacking

Cryptojacking is the unauthorized use of someone else's computer to mine cryptocurrency. Cryptocurrency mining is a process that uses computing power to solve complex mathematical problems in order to verify and record transactions on a blockchain. Cryptojacking is becoming a more common attack vector because it is easy to execute and does not require a lot of technical knowledge. Attackers can use cryptojacking to mine cryptocurrency on the victim's computer without their knowledge or consent. They can also use cryptojacking to mine cryptocurrency on the computer of an organization's employees. This can result in financial losses for the organization and decreased productivity for the employees.

Cloudborne malware

Cloudborne is a security vulnerability in a bare-metal cloud server that allows attackers to install a malicious backdoor into the firmware. The installed malware can remain even if the server is reassigned to new clients or organizations who utilize it as an IaaS. Physical servers are not confined to one client and can be moved from one client to another. Cloudborne malware is malware that is designed to infect cloud-based systems. Cloudborne malware can be used to steal data, sabotage systems, and spread ransomware. It can also be used to gain access to the organization's systems and steal data. Cloudborne malware is a growing threat because it is difficult to detect and can be used to target a wide range of organizations.

Gaining access by exploiting SSRF vulnerabilities

Server-Side Request Forgery (**SSRF**) is a vulnerability that allows an attacker to send requests from the server to external resources that the server should not be able to access.

One way an attacker can exploit an SSRF vulnerability is by sending a request to a cloud storage service, such as Azure Blob storage or Amazon **Simple Storage Service** (**S3**), and then reading the response from the service. This can be done by using the `fetch` API in JavaScript, or by using the `get has` command in Linux.

Once the attacker has access to the response from the cloud storage service, they can then download any files that are stored in the service.

Another way an attacker can exploit an SSRF vulnerability is by sending a request to a web server that is hosting a sensitive file, such as a configuration file or a database. The attacker can then download the contents of the file by using the `GET` command in Linux.

By exploiting an SSRF vulnerability, an attacker can gain access to sensitive files that are stored in the cloud, and they can also steal data from cloud-based applications.

Next, let's talk about container vulnerabilities.

Container vulnerabilities

Containers are a popular way to deploy applications in the cloud. They allow applications to be isolated from the underlying system and make it easy to move applications from one server to another. However, container vulnerabilities can allow attackers to gain access to the underlying system and steal data or install malware. Attackers can also use containers to hide their malicious activities from the organization's security tools. Containers are a popular target for attackers because they are easy to exploit and provide a lot of access to the underlying system.

The following are some of the more common vulnerabilities security professionals should be aware of:

- **Insecure container runtime configurations**: Containers can be insecure if the runtime configurations are not set up properly. Attackers can use these vulnerabilities to gain access to the underlying system and steal data or install malware.

- **Embedded malware**: Malware can be embedded in the application code that is run on the container. This malware can remain active even after the container is deleted or reassigned to another client.

- **Poor access control**: Containers typically have poor access control, which allows attackers to gain access to the underlying system and steal data or install malware.

- **Insufficient security controls**: Containers do not have the same security controls as the underlying system, which allows attackers to bypass security controls and steal data or install malware.

- **Leaky containers**: Containers can leak data to the underlying system, which can allow attackers to steal data or install malware.

- **Insecure data storage**: Container data can be insecurely stored on the underlying system, which can allow attackers to steal data or install malware.

Organizations should be aware of these vulnerabilities and take steps to mitigate them. Security professionals should also be aware of these vulnerabilities and take steps to protect their organizations from them.

Let's talk next about some of the specific tools and techniques that attackers use.

Tools and techniques of the attackers

To attack the cloud, a hacker will need tools to do so. Here, we will discuss some of the more common tools that are available.

The tools

A container image is a software package that includes an operating system, application, runtime, and other components. These containers are frequently reused throughout the industry and may include open source libraries with security concerns. These flaws endanger not only the security of each container but also that of the entire container engine. Tools such as Clair, Twistlock, and Trivy are great options for attacking containers.

Looking to find attack Kubernetes, also known as K8s? Most of the vulnerabilities we find are based on misconfiguration. Sysdig (`sysdig.com`) is a great tool to not only scan for vulnerabilities but also for validating container images.

Believe it or not, attackers use Google hacking techniques to identify Amazon Cloud storage services (called S3 buckets)! If you remember our Google hacks, we can use the `inurl` syntax to look for subdomains that are used by AWS.

For example:

```
inurl: s3.amazonaws.com
inurl: s3.amazonaws.com/ audio/
inurl: s3.amazonaws.com/video/
inurl: s3.amazonaws.com/backup/
```

```
inurl: s3.amazonaws.com/movie/
inurl: s3.amazonaws.com/image/
```

But if you want a more straightforward method, you can look at S3Scanner (`https://github.com/sa7mon/S3Scanner`) to identify open S3 buckets of cloud services, such as AWS, and retrieve their content for *evil* purposes.

Let's consider some additional tools and security risks these tools can assist us with next.

Enumerating AWS account IDs and roles

AWS accounts are identified by unique IDs that, if made public, might be used by attackers to target cloud services. These persistent identifiers are intended to be private, yet they are frequently exposed to the general public without the user's knowledge. Attackers can take advantage of this information leakage and use it for nefarious purposes. By analyzing AWS error messages, attackers can determine what **Identity and Access Management (IAM)** role names exist. The existence of a user is revealed in AWS Cloud services through the errors, which give information about the presence of a user. Users are usually permitted to take on numerous roles in AWS Cloud services. Every failure on the part of AWS results in information being revealed about the role's existence. If an AWS account is blocked after a certain number of tries, implementing a brute-force approach might be challenging but not impossible.

CloudGoat AWS

CloudGoat is a tool (`rhinosecuritylabs.com`) that allows you to test the security of your AWS account. The tool is based on the **Open Web Application Security Project (OWASP)** Top 10 security risks. Yep, OWASP has a list for cloud security.

The following are the top 10 security risks CloudGoat tests for:

1. **Injection**: The injection of unauthorized code into a web application.
2. **Broken authentication and session management**: Unsecured login credentials and session cookies.
3. **Cross-site scripting (XSS)**: Malicious code that is executed when a user visits a web page.
4. **Insecure direct object references**: Unauthorized access to sensitive data.
5. **Security misconfiguration**: Incorrectly configured security settings.
6. **Insufficient authorization and authentication**: Lack of proper authentication checks.
7. **Insufficient cryptography**: Weak cryptography algorithms and keys.

8. **Tampering with data**: Tampering with information to change its integrity.

9. **Cross-site request forgery (CSRF)**: Attackers trick a user into performing actions that they didn't intend to do.

10. **Information leakage and improper authorization**: Unauthorized access to data.

Other tools that can be used to analyze cloud services/deployments include:

- DockerScan

- GCPBucketBrute

- AWS pwn

And I'm sure there are hundreds more, but these are the ones you'll want to be aware of for your *immediate future*.

Let's consider some best practices for securing the cloud next.

Best practices for securing the cloud

The first thing that you can do to improve the security of your cloud-based systems is to enable SSL (Secure Socket Layer) and TLS (Transport Layer Security) encryption. This will help to protect your data from being intercepted by attackers.

You can also improve the security of your systems by using firewalls and an IDS (intrusion detection system) and an IPS (intrusion prevention system). These devices can help to protect your systems from being attacked by malicious traffic.

Here's a list of other things you can do:

- To protect your data, you should enforce the use of data encryption and access controls. This includes data that is in rest as well as in motion.

- Disaster recovery planning is another critical factor when securing your cloud-based systems. You should have a plan in place in case of a natural disaster or a security incident.

- Enforce SLAs to ensure your cloud provider meets the security requirements you have outlined.

- Utilize strong AAA (authentication, authorization, and auditing) controls. These controls can help to protect your systems from unauthorized access.

- Stop allowing user credential sharing with your employees. This will help to reduce the risk of a data breach.

- Isolate memory, storage, and network access. This can help to prevent attackers from gaining access to your systems.

- Understand your responsibility model for the cloud. This will help you to determine who is responsible for securing the cloud-based systems.

- Be aware of the risks associated with using cloud services. Educate your employees about these risks and take steps to mitigate them.

To secure your cloud-based systems, you need to establish and enforce cloud security policies. These policies should be based on the risk level of the data that is being stored in the cloud.

Some of the things that you should consider when creating your cloud security policies include:

- The type of data that is being stored in the cloud

- The level of security that is required for the data

- How the data is being accessed and used

- The authentication requirements for accessing the data

- The encryption requirements for the data

- The retention and disposal requirements for the data

- The incident response plan for responding to a data breach

- The disciplinary actions that will be taken against employees who violate the security policies

- The training requirements for employees who are accessing the data

You should also consider establishing a cloud security governance framework. This will help to ensure that your cloud security policies are being followed.

Double-check your compliance requirements

When you are storing data in the cloud, you need to make sure you are adhering to the relevant compliance requirements. These requirements vary from organization to organization, so you will need to consult with your legal department to make sure you comply.

Some of the standard compliance requirements that apply to cloud-based systems include:

- **The Health Insurance Portability and Accountability Act (HIPAA)**
- **The Sarbanes-Oxley Act (SOX)**
- **The Payment Card Industry Data Security Standard** (PCI DSS)
- **The Gramm-Leach-Bliley Act (GLBA)**

Finally, you should make sure that you regularly update the software and firmware on your devices. This will help to protect your systems from being exploited by known vulnerabilities.

By following these best practices, you can help improve your cloud-based systems' security.

Summary

In this chapter, we covered how cloud computing is a benefit, and also how it may be a challenge for us to secure. We discussed some ways in which the cloud is vulnerable to being attacked. We shared some of the tools and techniques attackers may use. And finally, we talked about some best practices to help you secure the cloud.

The important thing to remember is that many of the same weaknesses and attacks we see within the cloud are the same as what we've learned about on our normal networks and that they are just as much of a target for attackers.

In the next chapter, we'll talk about how the attackers look at cryptography and what we can do about it.

Questions

As we conclude, here is a list of questions for you to test your knowledge regarding this chapter's material. You will find the answers in the *Assessments* section of the *Appendix*:

1. All of the following can be configured in a cloud environment except which one?

    A. IaaS

    B. PaaS

    C. SaaS

    D. LaaS

2. What does a cloud-hosting SaaS environment provide?

    A. Development options

    B. Testing options

    C. Software hosting

    D. Improved security

3. Which of the following is separated by a cloud-based firewall?

    A. Hosts

    B. Networks

    C. ACL

    D. Permissions

4. How many kinds of cloud-hosting environments are there?

    A. Five

    B. Four

    C. Three

    D. Two

16
Using Cryptography

If you're new to **cryptography**, let's talk about its purpose. I'm going to try to make this easy to understand, because to some folks, cryptography can be overwhelming.

Cryptography is all about protecting data, usually in the form of messages or files. This can be done by taking data and transforming it into an unreadable format, often called **ciphertext**. The only way to transform the ciphertext back into readable data is with a **special key**, which only the sender and recipient of the message have access to. This process is called **encryption**, and it's the basis of how cryptography works.

When you're through with this chapter, my hope is that you'll come away with an added perspective and greater depth of understanding of the essential role cryptography plays in the guarding and protecting of information and digital communication.

Here is what we'll cover in this chapter:

- Understanding cryptography
- Standards and protocols
- Countermeasures for cryptography

Let's first discuss why cryptology is important to our security efforts.

Understanding cryptography

In this section, we'll discuss why cryptology is important and some of the best cryptology tools and resources available to us. Having knowledge of the proper tools and resources will be invaluable to you as a security professional. So, let's jump in and discuss what this is all about.

Why use cryptology?

So, what does cryptography bring to the table? Well, it brings **non-repudiation**. This means that whoever sent a message can't later deny having altered the document. For example, *"It wasn't me, Dale, I swear,"* to which I'll reply, *"No, it was you because it was encrypted with your key."*

Cryptography also brings **authentication** to the table. Sometimes we visit websites where it's important that we authenticate who we say we are, as well as obviously wanting to authenticate our credit card information, right? So, it's important to us, especially to those within our industry.

And, of course, **confidentiality** is another major factor as far as what cryptography can do for us. As far as confidentiality is concerned, we can only make certain resources available to authorized users. Now, as far as how this process works or how cryptography works, these are at a very plain or elementary level. The process goes like this.

We have **plaintext**; this is the text that is formatted and that we can read. Maybe it's a Word document, maybe it's an email, but it gets encrypted using an algorithm, such as the **Data Encryption Standard** (**DES**) or the **Advanced Encryption Standard** (**AES**), or even **Rivest—Shamir—Adleman** (**RSA**). After the encryption has been applied, we refer to that whole document as ciphertext. It's completely unreadable. This file is then transmitted, and on the opposite end, it just goes through the opposite process, right? The ciphertext uses the keys it's aware of to do decryption, and then it gives us the plaintext that the original sender or the resource wanted us to see.

Cryptography is an important part of keeping our information safe and secure and is used in a variety of different applications. Everything from our email to our financial information is protected by cryptography, and it's important to understand how it works.

See? I told you this would be easy.

Next, let's talk about the types of cryptography.

Types of cryptography

There's not a whole lot of talking to do on this subject because guess what? There are only two, symmetric and asymmetric:

- **Symmetric cryptography** is all about using the same key for both encryption and decryption. So, what we have are a sender and a recipient, and they're going to use the same key to encrypt the message they want to send back and forth. It's very fast, it's very efficient, but it also has a couple of major drawbacks:

    - The first is, if you lose that key, then you've lost all access to the information that's been encrypted.

    - And second, it's very difficult to manage large-scale deployments of symmetric cryptography.

- **Asymmetric cryptography** is just about as opposite of symmetric cryptography as you can get. Rather than using one key to do both encryption and decryption, it uses two keys, a public key and a private key:

    I.   The first key is the **public key** and it's a key anybody can have access to.

    II. The second key is the **private key**, and it's meant to be known only by the owner. It should never be given to anybody else. And, the great thing about this is that, if you use a public key to encrypt information, the only way to decrypt it is by using the corresponding private key. So, even if somebody were to intercept that message, they wouldn't be able to do anything with it because they don't have access to the private key.

The other great thing about asymmetric cryptography is that it doesn't require a secure initial exchange of keys like symmetric cryptography does. So, it's a little bit more secure in that sense. It's not perfect, but it's definitely more secure.

Asymmetric also utilizes **digital signatures**. Digital signatures are just a way to ensure the message has not been tampered with in transit. And, the way that this works is the sender of the message will use their private key to encrypt it, and they'll send both the message and their public key to the recipient. The recipient can then use the sender's public key to decrypt the message and then they can compare it to the original message to ensure it hasn't been tampered with.

Now, it does have some cons to it. It's a little bit slower than symmetric cryptography (we're talking about half an eyeblink versus a full eyeblink), and it also requires more bandwidth. But overall, it's a much more secure way to send information. Now, nothing is foolproof, right? If I've taught you anything through this series, it's that there's always a way. When it comes to asymmetric, it is susceptible to **man-in-the-middle (MITM)** attacks, as well as **brute-force attacks**. And, unfortunately, if the private key gets lost, then there's really no way to decrypt the information that's been encrypted with it.

Let's discuss some other keys next.

GAK

The **Government Access Key (GAK)** is a system proposed by the United States **National Security Agency (NSA)** to allow government access to encrypted communications. The key would be a mathematical value that would be used to decrypt messages. The existence of such a key would make it possible for the NSA to read encrypted communications, including those between citizens and businesses, as well as between different countries.

The problem with this system is that it would require a key that is incredibly complex and difficult to generate. And, of course, the NSA would need to keep this key completely secret. If the key were to get out, then anybody could use it to read encrypted communications. Has anyone seen the 1991 movie *Sneakers* starring Robert Redford? Talk about a movie that predicted the future of encryption! (*Homework assignment from Dale: watch this movie!*).

Another problem with GAK is that it would be very difficult to implement. Any change to the encryption algorithms used by businesses and governments would need to be approved by the NSA. This would give the NSA a lot of power, and it's not clear that they could be trusted with such power.

It's also worth noting the NSA is not the only government agency interested in reading encrypted communications. The United Kingdom's **Government Communications Headquarters (GCHQ)** has also expressed an interest in a system that would allow them to read encrypted communications.

Let's continue to talk further about another tool for encryption next called **ciphers**.

Learning about ciphers

What we're talking about when it comes to ciphers is an algorithm. You can think of it as a defined series of steps that have to be performed for the encryption and decryption process to occur. Once a message or data has been encrypted using a cipher, it is considered unreadable unless, of course, whoever's receiving the data or message knows the secret key that's required to decrypt it.

Now, believe it or not, ciphers are used everywhere, not just in our emails and our data itself, but we also use them in other communication technologies, such as cell phones. This is what makes our cell phone calls more secure.

Types of ciphers

Now, I know what you're thinking: *"Dale, is there only one cipher?"* No, there are several different types of ciphers. We can categorize them into two different types, either classical or modern. I know, it sounds like we're going to talk about art, but we're not.

Let's look at classical and modern ciphers.

Classical ciphers

Classical ciphers are those that were developed before the invention of the computer. They include classical ciphers such as the **Caesar cipher**, which is a simple **substitution cipher**, where each letter of the alphabet is replaced with another letter according to a defined pattern. *Figure 16.1* is an example of a Caesar cipher:

```
MY VOICE IS MY PASSWORD = DB XGOET OL DB HALLCGKR
```

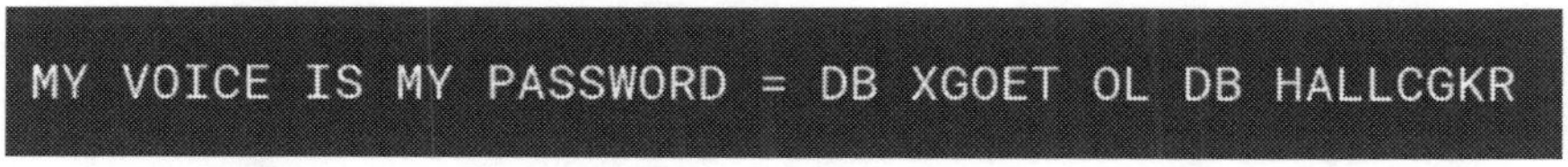

Figure 16.1 – Example of a Caesar cipher (a simple substitution of letters)

So, in this case here, **MY VOICE IS MY PASSWORD**, as you can see, gets translated to **DB XGOET OL DB HALLCGKR**. All we're doing is basically replacing the **M** with another letter, in this case, **D**. Notice how **DB** represents **MY** in both instances. This would help me to figure out how to decrypt this message, given enough time.

Another type of classical cipher is referred to as a **transposition**. In a transposition, you use what they refer to as a **key**. Now, depending on the transposition cipher that you're using, in this case, I'm showing you (in *Figure 16.2*) what they refer to as a **rail fence cipher**:

Figure 16.2 – Example of a rail fence cipher

In this case, the key is **3**, which means there are three spaces between characters. You see that **MY VOICE IS MY PASSWORD** is spelled out in this up-and-down method, and the spaces in between are kind of ignored completely. So, the first line ends up becoming just **MISAO** while the next line of code would be just simply **YOCIMPSWR**, and the third row would just simply equal **VEYSD**. Now, obviously, the recipient would have to know that the key is **3** to decrypt this.

Another type of transposition cipher is a **route cipher**. With the route cipher, we end up taking the same data or information we're trying to encrypt. In *Figure 16.3*, I'm going to use the text, **MY VOICE IS MY PASSWORD**, and I'm going to lay it out like this:

Figure 16.3 – Example of a route cipher

Can you see it all there? So, it lays the plaintext out in a grid pattern just like this, and, of course, the last two characters are just random characters. This type of cipher is determined based on the route.

Those are just some quick examples of classical ciphers.

Let's look at modern ciphers next.

Modern ciphers

You can see with the classical type how easy it would be to crack those types of ciphers. With modern ciphers, they're a little bit more difficult to try to crack manually. And typically, modern ciphers are there to provide authenticity, security, and integrity to the sender.

The types of modern ciphers you'll see are both symmetric and asymmetric. While I'm talking about it, there's a way to use both asymmetric and symmetric at the same time, but that might be going a little too deep here, so I'm just going to leave that up to you. If you want to do a little bit more research, you can look at that further.

There are also ciphers that are based on the input of data. We have what they refer to as a **block cipher**, and what we mean by *block* is the algorithm operates in groups of bits or a block of a fixed size. Most of the cryptography we see today, such as DES, AES, or even the **International Data Encryption Algorithm** (**IDEA**), are all using block-based ciphers. Now, if by chance, the block size of the data coming across is less than what is used by the cipher itself, there's some padding that helps to make sure it achieves the block size that's needed.

There are also **stream ciphers**. When it comes to a stream cipher, we're basically talking about a symmetric key cipher, where the plaintext digit is combined with a pseudorandom cipher digit stream, which we sometimes refer to as a **keystream**. In a stream cipher, each character is encrypted one at a time, and with it goes a corresponding digit of the keystream; this gives us a cyber-text digit stream.

Let's look at some other types of algorithms.

Using other algorithms

When it comes to different algorithms out there, the most common we will see are going to be **DES**, **triple DES** (**3DES**), **AES**, and **RC4**.

Let's discuss these next.

DES

This was created back in the 1970s by **IBM**. It utilizes a 64-bit block. On top of that, it only uses a 56-bit key for encryption and decryption, which is not that great. In fact, in 1999, this algorithm was cracked, especially considering the computing power we had back then was not very much. But, DES itself provided up to 72 quadrillion possible encryption keys, and we were able to crack it back in 1999. Now, because this was cracked, the US government got involved and helped. Now, obviously, to cover this vulnerability, which could be brute force-attacked very easily, we came up with triple DES, or some people might call it 3DES. The reason it's called 3DES is that it goes through and does the DES algorithm three times with three different keys.

Now, as far as how these keys are used, you have a couple of different options:

- The first option is all three of the keys are completely different or independent.

- The second option is using the **K1** and **K3** keys, but since they're both used for encryption, they are identical.

- And, there's a third option, which is where all three keys are the same, but that's not very secure.

The most secure would be the first option, which is where all three keys are independent.

AES

AES is kind of a fully grown adult compared to DES and 3DES. It utilizes a 128-bit block size, and its keys are 128, 192, or 256-bit in size. I bet you can't guess what they call each one of those, right? They're called **AES128**, **AES192**, and **AES256**. That was tricky, wasn't it? AES is a symmetric-key algorithm, created with the help of the **National Institute of Standards and Technology** (**NIST**). The government agencies use this for encrypting data that is considered unclassified.

RC4

Some folks call it **Ron Rivest**. Ron is the first name of the gentleman who helped create it, but the cipher is called Ron Rivest; it's **Rivest Cipher 4**. Now, this cipher is considered a variable key size symmetric keystream cipher. And, let's be honest, it's not that great because guess what? We use this in **Wired Equivalent Privacy** (**WEP**), which is the wireless security protocol that's been hacked very, very easily.

The reason why RC4 was vulnerable to different types of attacks was that it had what they refer to as a **biased output**. There is a rule that if the third byte in its original state is *0*, and if the second byte doesn't equal *2*, this means the second output byte is always *0*. Now, this may seem complicated, but trust me, once we see patterns like this, we're able to go through and reverse engineer the cipher and crack it. And, that's what happened to WEP.

Two other algorithms that we should be familiar with are **Blowfish** and **Twofish**.

Blowfish and Twofish

The Blowfish algorithm was developed back in 1993, and I know you're thinking, *"Dale, that's a long time ago."* But it's quite a strong symmetric block cipher that we still use today. It uses the same key to encrypt and decrypt. It utilizes a 64-bit block, and its key is a variable key anywhere from 32 to 448 bits. This protocol was designed to replace DES and triple DES.

Now, it may be surprising to know that a lot of people still enjoy using AES, and I guess there's nothing wrong with it, but you need to know that one of the advantages of Blowfish is its speed. It breaks things down into a 64-bit block as compared to AES, which, by using a 128-bit block, allows for faster encryption and decryption.

We also have something called Twofish. This encryption was created a few years after Blowfish. It was introduced to us back in 1998, and it's relatively close to the Blowfish cipher. That's why we have a similar name here, but it encrypts data with a 128-bit block just like AES. In fact, Twofish is very similar to AES because it supports a 256-bit block, as well as a 192 or 128 key size. And, just like Blowfish, it uses a single key.

Then, there's **Threefish**, which was developed in 2008 and is a part of the Skein algorithm. It is a 12-round Feistel network cipher with a block size of 128 bits and a key length of 256 bits. Threefish is very fast and very secure, with a high degree of resistance to attack.

Now, another reason why both these ciphers are extremely popular is that they haven't been patented. They're open-sourced. In fact, Twofish was the algorithm that was one of the top five finalists to replace DES for the US government but, unfortunately, it didn't win. *But I think it did win Ms. Congeniality. Now I'm just kidding.*

So, now that we've got the most popular algorithms out of the way, in the next section, we'll talk about standards and protocols.

Standards and protocols

Let's talk about some of the most common standards we see out there. In this section, we'll talk about more algorithms, hashes, ciphers, and other cryptographic mechanisms that will assist you in securing the data and communication you help protect.

DSA

This is a federal information processing standard for creating digital signatures. How this signature standard works is that it creates a 320-bit digital signature, but the signature is also accompanied by anything from 512- to 1024-bit security. It also utilizes our private and public key technology or process.

RSA

Hey, you know what? RSA are the initials of the creators. The *R* is from the same *Ron Rivest* from RC4, as well as from two other gentlemen. The *S* is after *Shamir,* and the *A* is after *Alderman.* All three of these gentlemen worked at the **Massachusetts Institute of Technology** (**MIT**). Rivest and Shamir worked as computer scientists and Alderman was a mathematician.

Now, RSA also uses a public key encryption system and uses two large prime numbers as its basis. We see RSA as a standard in a lot of our operating systems today: Microsoft, Apple, and Sun Microsystems, as well as being utilized in networking cards, smartcards, and even what we refer to as hardware-secured phones. Now, this may make your brain hurt a little bit, but let me give you a brief synopsis of how this works:

1. First, two large prime numbers are taken, and we're going to call them *A* and *B*. These two prime numbers and their product are determined by saying that *C* is equal to *A*B*, and *C* (in math, we'd see it this way: *C=AB*) and, therefore, *C* is referred to as the **modulus**.

2. RSA then chooses another number called *E* that is less than *C* and relatively prime to *(A-1)(B-1)*. What this does is it makes sure that *E* and *A-1 x B-1* have no common factors with each other except for the number *1*.

3. I know, it keeps getting better because then RSA chooses another number, *F*, and it does this so that *EF-1* is divisible by *A-1 x B-1*.

4. Now, some of you *algebra folks* are following right along. But wait, there's more. The values of *E* and *F* are referred to as the public and private exponents. In using those exponents, the public key is paired with *C* and *E* to create that public key, and the private key is created by pairing *C* and *F* together.

Now, the reason why this is extremely secure is that it's considered to be extremely difficult to obtain the private key from the public key. Now, obviously, if someone can factor *C* into *A* and *B*, then that person could decipher the private key, but the odds of somebody trying to get a hold of those two prime numbers that are taken at random are almost impossible. So, again, a lot more secure for us.

Hashes

I'm getting hungry. I think hash browns or just some good cabbage and hash are delicious. I've got to get food off my mind here!

When it comes to **hashes**, what we're trying to do is come up with a way to verify that a particular document hasn't changed. We want to know it's legitimate, that it has been signed, and no one has changed or tampered with it. Now, how we do this is we take the document, and we assign a **digital signature** associated with it. That signature is represented by a hexadecimal code. This code tells us the document and the default for this document; if it is equal to the hexadecimal code number, we know it's legit, it's been signed, and nobody has changed it. This also applies to an executable or an email. But, if somehow the document or the executable is changed, that hash value won't work, or it won't calculate out correctly.

Message digest

When we talk about cryptography, there's something that we need to keep in mind, and that is the **message digest**. The message digest is also referred to as a **hash value**. What it does is it takes a block of data and produces a unique fingerprint or hash value of that data. This is important because when we're talking about authentication, we're talking about making sure the data has not been altered in any way. And so, this allows us to look at the message and be able to say, *"Okay, this is exactly what was sent. It hasn't been changed in any way."*

Another hash method is referred to as **Secure Hash Algorithm 1 (SHA-1)** and was introduced in 1993 by the NSA. Now, its function is to take the input and produce a 160-bit hash value that is then turned into hexadecimal, which is about 40 characters long once it's converted. It's typically utilized with other protocols or security protocols, such as **Pretty Good Privacy (PGP)**, **Transport Layer Security (TLS)**, **Secure Shell (SSH)**, and **Secure Sockets Layer (SSL)**.

Now, I know what you may be thinking: *"Dale, why'd we start with 1? Where's the SHA-0?"* Well, **SHA-0** was 160-bit, but it was so bad it was pulled for a significant flaw. Well, they then obviously came out with **SHA-2**. Now, SHA-2 is extremely similar to SHA-1, but it does use 256-bit, but it is stronger and larger than SHA-1. And, what I mean by that is there are two different block sizes that it can use, either **SHA256**, which gives you a **32-bit word**, and **SHA256**, which, double it, **64-bit**, right? Guess what?

They then came out with **SHA-3**. It's unlike SHA-2, which was similar to SHA-1 (and SHA-1 was similar to SHA-0); SHA-3's only likeness is in its name. The reason behind it being a completely different beast is that it uses what's referred to as **sponge construction**. The data is absorbed, or the input is absorbed, and the output or the result is squeezed out. Now, during the absorption process, the message blocks themselves are XORed into initial bits of state or a subset. That subset is then transformed using a permutation function. So, yeah, it's a little bit tougher.

So, now that we've got our hands on these different types of ciphers, there are some ciphers that are designed for messages.

Ciphers designed for messages

We first start with **hash-based message authentication code** (**HMAC**). This algorithm includes the embedding of the hash functions, such as SHA-1 or the **message-digest algorithm** (**MD5**). Where its strength comes from is dependent upon the embedded hash function, key size, and the size of the hash output.

How HMAC operates is there are two different stages. Now, in those stages, there's a secret key that's created. There's one for an *innie* and one for an *outie*. I know, I just made a *belly button* joke. It's **inner** and **outer**, but the concept remains the same.

The first pass of the algorithm produces an internal hash derived from the message and the inner key. The second pass includes the final HMAC code derived from the inner hash result and the outer key. Now, HMAC itself doesn't encrypt the message, but instead, it takes the message whether it's encrypted or not, and it must be sent alongside the HMAC hash. This way, both parties can verify using the secret key that the message is coming from who it says it's coming from, or that its authenticity is correct.

Let's discuss another authentication mechanism next.

CHAP

The **Change Handshake Authentication Protocol** (**CHAP**) is an authentication mechanism we use via **Point to Point Protocol** (**PPP**) and a three-way handshake. CHAP provides a way to protect yourself against what we refer to as **replay attacks**. Now, the downside is that CHAP uses that shared key thing where both the client and the server must know the plaintext of the secret key. Now, the funny thing here is Microsoft came out with their own version of CHAP (called **MS-CHAP**) that doesn't require either the sender or the receiver to know the plaintext, and it doesn't transmit it, but it's also been hacked.

EAP

The **Extensible Authentication Protocol** (**EAP**) was originally designed for point-to-point communications. It is used as an alternative to CHAP, as well as the **Password Authentication Protocol** (**PAP**). I didn't talk about PAP because it's so outdated. EAP itself is more secure and supports different authentication mechanisms, such as using either one-time passwords, standard passwords, or smart tokens.

Let's talk about what **public key infrastructure** (**PKI**) is next.

PKI made simple

The PKI is asymmetric, which means we have a two-key technology to help make sure that information is encrypted and only decrypted by the appropriate parties. Remember, in symmetric, we only use one key that is shared between both parties. In this one here, we're going to have two keys, and you've heard me talk about public keys and private keys. Next, let's see what PKI consists of.

Your certificate

"Hey, Dale, you keep talking about this certificate. What is this so-called certificate?" So, a **certificate** is a way of identifying an organization, or even a user. Typically, certificates are based on what's referred to as an **X.509 standard**, and they typically contain fields such as when the certificate is valid, when it's expired, what algorithm is used for the encryption of the public key, and who issues the certificate.

In fact, let me show you something here real fast. So, here I am at the **Packt** website, and because we have an **HTTPS** connection, that means it's a secured connection.

Figure 16.4 – An HTTPS site will show a lock indicating a secure connection

I'm going to just hover over the lock here, and it tells me that I can view the site information or the certificate. So, I can come down and select to look at the certificate. It tells me it's currently valid without me having to drill into it, but let's go ahead and drill into it here. You can see here that it's created for the following purpose, to verify the identity of the remote computer and to provide your identity to the remote computer.

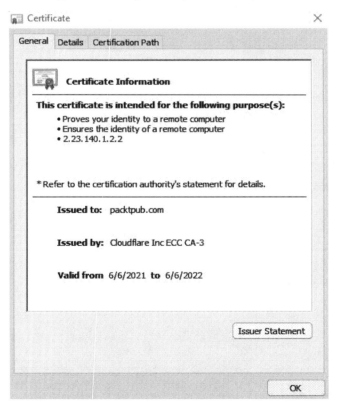

Figure 16.5 – The certificate shows the purpose and valid dates

This way, Packt can make sure they know who they're talking to. It shows who it was issued to. It tells us it was issued by **Cloudflare** on their **ECC CA-3** server. And, of course, the validity period here is anywhere from **6/6/2021** through **6/6/2022**. I can go into the **Details** tab for the certificate, and I can see all kinds of things here.

Figure 16.6 – The Details tab reveals more information

Again, I can see the issuer, which is **sha256**. I can see, again, the validity date, and the subject, which is basically, again, to who it applies. You can see that when they issued the certificate, you must fill out an application so they can issue it, and then they verify; in this case here, Cloudflare went through and verified that it was, in fact, Packt Publishing. This way, I can't create my own certificate for Packt and put it on the web and make people think that, hey, I'm Packt Publishing.

The public key, again, is **ECC (256 bits)**, and that's the key there. I can again scroll down and see information here about the subject alternative names, which, they've got their wildcard in here.

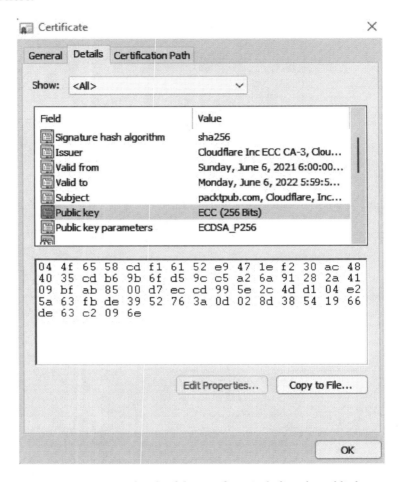

Figure 16.7 – More details of the certificate including the public key

So, everywhere that we go, we are interacting with certificates. Sometimes, you don't even realize it. Now, when it comes to certificates, there are two different types:

- There's a **signed certificate** where a CA signs it, a public CA, and issues the certificate. And, again, these certificates normally contain the public key and the identity of the owner of that key. The private key is kept secret by the CA.

- There are also **self-signed certificates**. This is where the identity of the certificate is signed by the same organization or the entity that identifies that it's certified. So, for example, if I wanted to create my own certificate within my organization, I'm going to have my own CA server, and I'm going to do a self-signed certificate from that server. We don't normally use self-signed certificates. In fact, you should never use a self-signed certificate in the wild, only within your own infrastructure.

See? I told you I'd make PKI easy to understand.

Let's talk about digital signatures now.

Digital signatures

It's designed to verify that a particular email or document came from a particular source. For example, if *Bruce Wayne* was sending an email to *Selina Kyle*, they both would have a public key and a private key.

Selina would take her private key and sign her email so that Bruce Wayne can make sure that it was from her. She uses that private key to sign the document, which isn't a physical signature, it's just a code that's attached to the email saying that it was from Selina. Again, anybody could try to fake this if they wanted. But, here's what happens. When the email gets sent over to Bruce, he grabs a copy of her public key. Remember that key? It's public and can go to anybody, and he uses that public key to run against the signature to verify that the email came from Selina. Again, what you must remember here is digital signatures do not in any way whatsoever encrypt. It's just to verify a document, an email, or even a file.

Up next, we'll talk about additional ways to secure our communications over a network.

SSL and TLS

SSL and TLS are both cryptographic protocols that can be used to secure communications over an insecure network such as the internet. SSL is the predecessor to TLS and is more commonly used today.

SSL and TLS use a combination of a symmetric key cipher and an asymmetric key cipher to encrypt communications. The symmetric key cipher is used to encrypt the data, and the asymmetric key cipher is used to exchange the keys. SSL and TLS also use digital certificates to authenticate entities and prevent MITM attacks.

When we look at TLS, it goes through a handshake process:

1. We're going to have our server that is encrypted or has the encrypted information, and then we have our client system. We know that we have public keys and private keys associated with that server or the data source itself.

2. What happens is the client sends another client a *Hello* message, along with a random value, and it tells the server the supported ciphers it can use.

3. The server responds by sending, *"Hey, how you doing? I'm a server."* It's called a server *Hello* message, along with the server's random value. The server also sends, *"Hey, I'm done saying hello to you."* Now, if the server has requested a certificate from the client, the client would then send one back.

4. The client then creates a random pre-master secret and encrypts it with the public key from the server's certificate, then sends that pre-master secret to the server, and here's what's interesting; once it's received, the server and the client will each generate a brand-new master secret and session key, which is based on the pre-master secret.

5. Once they've both done that, the client then sends a message that says, *"Hey, I'm going to change the cipher spec."* And that cipher spec is going to be based on the new session keys that we just generated, and we're going to use those for hashing, as well as encrypting. The client also sends a *"Yo, I'm done"* message or a **client finished message**. The server receives the updated cipher spec and switches over to a security state that will use a symmetric encryption using the session keys. The server also sends a *"Yo, I'm finished"* or a **server finished message**.

6. Now, both the client and the server have the new master secret, as well as the session keys; they'll both start using those session keys to exchange data back and forth over a secure channel.

    All the messages sent from the client to the server and from the server to the client are then encrypted. That's a lot, huh?

When it comes to using SSL and TLS, there are several different toolkits out there. The one I want to warn you about, it's probably one of the more popular but this is just more historical information, is one that's referred to as **OpenSSL**. Now, OpenSSL is like the Swiss army knife of cryptography, and because it's an open source resource, this makes it very attractive, right?

Now, there's one thing I need to warn you about and that is OpenSSL had a very big issue. It was something called **Heartbleed**, which was an extremely bad vulnerability. The Heartbleed vulnerability allowed anyone on the internet to read the memory of systems protected by the vulnerable versions of OpenSSL. Now, don't worry, it's been patched. Hint… you will want to know that in preparing to take the exam.

PGP

PGP is the understatement of the year. PGP gets its start all the way back in 1991. Now, the reason PGP is pretty good is we can use it for encrypting messages and files, as well as the digital signatures or signing documents, and, of course, deleting documents and even compression. In fact, PGP encryption uses a serial combination of hashing, then data compression, symmetric-key cryptography, and, finally, public-key cryptography. Each step uses several supported algorithms, and each of the public keys is bound to a username or an email address.

Let's look at how PGP happens and operates.

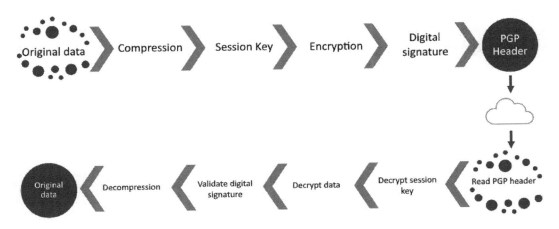

Figure 16.8 – PGP flow

1. When a user encrypts data with PGP, PGP compresses that data down. This compression helps to avoid some exploits that could be used to try to crack the cipher because the patterns in the plaintext have been compressed.

2. PGP then creates a random key that is a one-time-use-only, secret key, and it uses that key to encrypt the plaintext, which results in our ciphertext.

3. Once it's done encrypting, the random key is encrypted using the recipient's public key. That encrypted data is sent to the recipient. Obviously, the encryption operates in a reverse manner.

You may be thinking, *"But Dale, PGP is still good today. Isn't it?"* Yeah, it really is. In fact, the only way I'm aware they have been able to crack or attack PGP is by installing a piece of malware that would capture keystrokes so they could capture the passwords as they type them in. Now, at the time of writing this book, **Symantec** owns PGP, and they've renamed it. They call it the **Symantec Encryption Desktop**, and the server component is just referred to as the **Symantec Encryption Management Server**. But basically, it's still PGP.

So, now that we've got that down, let's finish up talking about countermeasures.

Countermeasures for cryptography

You know me, I don't want to leave you all panicking that all is lost! There are some countermeasures that we can take to mitigate the attacks that might come our way. Let's talk about some of these countermeasures.

EC-Council lists 12 countermeasures to use:

1. The first one is when it comes to accessing the cryptography keys, that access should only be given to users directly, as well as applications.

2. You should also make sure you have an **intrusion detection system** (**IDS**) that's been deployed, and you are monitoring the exchange and access of those keys, so you've got a log somewhere of what happened and when. This is just in case you must go back and take a look at those logs because something got compromised.

3. The other thing you're going to want to do is that if you plan on storing the encryption key on a system or on a drive, you need to use passphrases and passwords.

4. This next one's for you more advanced developers out there: under no circumstances should the keys be inside of the source code or inside of any binaries.

5. Now, when it comes to certificates for signing the transfer of private keys, it's a major no-no. We never, ever transfer private keys. We just say no, got it? I'll be a little happier now that you're agreeing with me.

6. When it comes to symmetric algorithms, you should make sure you use the maximum number of bits that you possibly can. You should be using at least 168 bits or 256 bits.

7. If you're going to implement encryption for symmetric key protocols, you've got to make sure that message authentication is performed.

8. As far as asymmetric algorithms are concerned, you need to use the largest sizes available, either 1536 or 2048. Just say 2048, please.

9. When it comes to your hash algorithms gain, use the highest bits possible, 168 or 256 bits, please!

10. When creating or implementing a cryptographic environment, please don't do anything homemade. I know some of you developers might be like, *"Well, I can do this a little bit better."* Trust me, don't! Use what would be considered an industry standard. Some people will try to create self-engineered crypto algorithms as well as functions, and inevitably they're going to leave some holes open for you.

11. I would also put a limit on the number of operations per second per key. This way, you don't have somebody trying to quickly brute force to try to discover what the key is.

12. And finally, the output of a hash or any hash function should have the largest bit length possible, so it makes it hard to decrypt.

Okay, see? That's how easy those 12 things are. And, this brings us to the end. So, as you can see, standards and protocols are essential for us when dealing with and protecting our data and communications. Understanding the tools and processes is necessary for you to be an effective IT security professional.

Summary

One of the major ways to protect your resources from attackers is to use encryption for data in motion or in waiting. Your job as a security professional isn't to stop attackers, that's impossible. Anything is hackable. Your job is to slow them down or discourage them, and cryptography definitely does this.

This brings us to the end of this book and the beginning of your journey in cybersecurity. As you study for the **CEH** exam, remember that it's not an easy task to accomplish. The test is designed to make sure you know your craft.

Keep in mind that if you haven't fully grasped all the concepts we've talked about in this book, review it again. Do your own research. Reach out to me via my social media channels. My passion and mission are to help everyone and every company stay safer while using technology. Please be sure to *tweet* me or post on LinkedIn when you pass your exam or that you've learned something from me. The comments I get from my students, viewers, and readers really do bring a smile to my face. And, do me a favor... Be safe!

Questions

As we conclude, here is a list of questions for you to test your knowledge regarding this chapter's material. You will find the answers in the *Assessments* section of the *Appendix*:

1. Which of the following terms does asymmetric encryption also go by?

    A.   A shared key

    B.   Hashing

    C.   A public key

    D.   Block

2. Which of the following is a mechanism for SSL?

    A.   Authenticating data

    B.   Securing stored data

    C.   Verifying data

    D.   Securing transmitted data

3. A common hashing protocol is which of the following?

    A.   RSA

    B.   MD5

    C.   DES

    D.   AES

4. _____ is another name for symmetric cryptography.

    A.   Shared key cryptography

    B.   Steganography

    C.   Public key cryptography

    D.   Hashing

17
CEH Exam Practice Questions

In this chapter, I have provided some questions to help you further prepare for the **Certified Ethical Hacker (CEH)** exam. These questions will help you prepare and test your knowledge of the necessary skills to be an effective **information technology (IT)** security professional and ethical hacker.

Exam questions

Please choose the best answer to the following questions. Some questions may have more than one possible answer, as indicated in the question:

1. When is it appropriate to test another person's system?

    A. If you've been given permission or have been invited to do so

    B. If you believe the system has been hacked

    C. When you've discovered a vulnerability in the system

    D. If you believe the system is valuable

2.   If you were using the Shodan web service, which device would you use?

    A.   Web servers

    B.   IoT

    C.   Mobile

    D.   Cloud storage servers

3.   Which type of scanning is a packet with all flags set?

    A.   SYN scan

    B.   TCP connect

    C.   Full open scan

    D.   XMAS scan

4.   Which of the following best describes enumeration?

    A.   User and machine name identification

    B.   Identifying the network's active systems

    C.   Password cracking

    D.   Router and firewall identification

5.   To find a vulnerability, an attacker sends probes and forged requests to a target. Which kind of scan is being performed?

    A.   Active

    B.   Passive

    C.   Flooding

    D.   MiTM

6.   Which hashing mechanism is disabled on newer versions of Windows?

    A.   NTLM

    B.   Kerberos

    C.   NTLMv2

    D.   LM

7.   All of the following can be used in social engineering except _____.

    A.   Mobile phones

    B.   Viruses

    C.   Instant messaging

    D.   Trojan horses

8.   Which of the following propagates without human interaction?

    A.   Trojan

    B.   Worm

    C.   MITM

    D.   Virus

9.   A switch port is connected to a target system (with a **media access control** (**MAC**) address of 12:34:56:AB:CD:EF). An attacker (with a MAC address of 78:91:00:ED:BC:A1) is connected to a different port on the same switch and is capturing packets. There are no port spanning or port security measures in effect. The target machine sends out two packets. The destination MAC address for message 1 is E1:22:BA:87:AC:12. Message 2's target MAC address is FF:FF:FF:FF:FF:FF. Which of the following claims about the communications being sent is correct?

    A.   The attacker will see neither message.

    B.   The attacker will see message 1.

    C.   The attacker will see message 2.

    D.   The attacker will see both messages.

10. Which of the following statements is correct? (Select all options that apply)

    A.   WPA2 encrypts with TKIP and the AES.

    B.   WEP employs RC4-based shared key encryption.

    C.   WEP employs TKIP's shared key encryption.

    D.   WPA2 employs RC4-based shared key encryption.

11. Which kind of access does rooting an Android device give you?

    A. Domain-level access

    B. Admin/root access with privileges

    C. Root access at the lowest level

    D. Root access at the highest level

12. Which kind of attack can be used to hijack an existing session?

    A. Session hijacking

    B. Cookie snooping

    C. Session sniffing

    D. Cookie hijacking

13. An attacker determines that a company's facility controls such as temperature monitors are somewhat insecure and manages to break into the system, enabling them to attack the local network remotely. Which of the following attacks would this be regarded as?

    A. Exploiting the HVAC

    B. BlueBorne attack

    C. DDoS attack

    D. Rolling code attack

14. Which of the following can be used to secure cloud-based data?

    A. SSL

    B. Harvesting

    C. Drive encryption

    D. Transport encryption

15. _____ is another name for symmetric cryptography.

    A. Steganography

    B. Hashing

    C. Shared key cryptography

    D. Public key cryptography

16. Regarding digital certificates, which of the following manages them?

    A.   Hub

    B.   CA

    C.   Key

    D.   Public key

17. What is the purpose of **Simple Object Access Protocol (SOAP)**?

    A.   Transports data

    B.   Makes it possible for applications to communicate with one another

    C.   Encrypts information

    D.   Wraps data

18. Which of the following technologies is the most widely used short-range communication in IoT devices?

    A.   RFID

    B.   LiFi

    C.   Zigbee

    D.   QR code

19. What is a method for storing session data?

    A.   Directory

    B.   Cookie

    C.   File

    D.   Snoop

20. Which of the following is the most accurate description of a web application?

    A.   Code that's intended to be run on a client

    B.   Targets web services

    C.   Code that's intended to be run on a server

    D.   SQL code for databases

564   CEH Exam Practice Questions

21. What is the purpose of rooting a device?

    A. Updates are removed from a system

    B. Removes a user's access

    C. Allows a user on a system to have root access

    D. Increases the device's security

22. SSID broadcasting has been disabled, MAC filtering has been activated, and wireless encryption has been implemented by Alan. He spots someone using an HP laptop, although the company only buys Dell computers. Alan decides that there are no rogue access points after reviewing access logs and site survey data, and all wireless connection attempts appear to be valid. With an HP laptop, how did the user gain access to the network?

    A. It doesn't matter whose laptop you use if the OUI is the same.

    B. Encryption has been brute-forced by the employee.

    C. An attack by an evil twin is underway.

    D. A legitimate MAC address has been faked by the employee.

23. You make the decision to intercept communications between two hosts. You start by broadcasting messages to Host A, indicating that your MAC address belongs to Host B. You send messages to Host B at the same time, indicating that your MAC address belongs to Host A. What exactly is going on here?

    A. ARP poisoning, which allows you to see all messages from both sides without interfering with their communications

    B. ARP poisoning, which allows you to view messages from Host A destined for any address

    C. ARP poisoning, which allows you to see messages from Host A to Host B and vice versa

    D. Failed ARP poisoning, which prevents you from seeing any traffic

    E. ARP poisoning, which allows you to see messages from Host B destined for any address

24. Which of the following is a legal and common mode of communication?

    A. Session hijacking

    B. Covert channel

    C.   Overt channel

    D.   Backdoor channel

25. The goal of social engineering is to _____.

    A.   Infect a system

    B.   Manipulate human behavior

    C.   Get a physical advantage

    D.   Create distrustful people

26. Phishing can be mitigated using _____.

    A.   Anti-malware

    B.   A spam filter

    C.   Education

    D.   Anti-virus

27. What benefit does NTLM provide versus what LM offers?

    A.   SSL

    B.   Performance

    C.   Mutual authentication

    D.   Security

28. When using a brute-force attack, how is it performed?

    A.   By trying all possible characters and combinations

    B.   By comparing hashes

    C.   By trying dictionary lists

    D.   By capturing hashes and trying those against a rainbow table

29. Which metric on a CVSS score covers elements that change over the course of a vulnerability's lifetime?

    A.   Follow the white rabbit

    B.   Base

    C.   Temporal

    D.   Environmental

30. To find hosts and vulnerabilities, which assessment type would you use?

    A. Automated

    B. Passive

    C. Active

    D. Distributed

31. Which of the following is a command-line tool used to look up a username from an SID?

    A. `UsertoSID`

    B. `PsGetSid`

    C. `GetAcct`

    D. `Userenum`

32. Which tool can be used to perform a DNS zone transfer on Windows?

    A. `NSlookup`

    B. `Whois`

    C. `DNSlookup`

    D. `Ipconfig`

33. Why would you be concerned about a system with ports `135` to `139` being open?

    A. The system is vulnerable to `null` sessions since SMB is enabled.

    B. Windows RPC is turned on, and the machine is vulnerable to remote Windows DCOM sessions.

    C. For *unauthenticated* connections, a secure FTP service is enabled.

    D. SMB is disabled, making the system vulnerable to `null` sessions.

34. Which tool is used to conduct passive reconnaissance?

    A. Host scanning

    B. A ping sweep

    C. WHOIS

    D. Traceroute

35. You stumble across a vulnerability on a network beyond the scope of the engagement while testing. What should you do?

   A.   Notify your company right away.

   B.   Determine the extent to which you can penetrate the network.

   C.   Analyze IDS logs to identify misconfigurations.

   D.   Return to your task and add the vulnerability to your discovery work.

36. Which kind of hacker's work is for the general good?

   A.   White hat

   B.   Black hat

   C.   Grey hat

   D.   Red hat

37. What is the correct command to run a 5-minute nmap SYN scan?

   A.   `nmap -sS -sneaky`

   B.   `nmap -ss -t5000`

   C.   `nmap -sS -paranoid`

   D.   `nmap -ss -fast`

38. What is an SNMP enumeration countermeasure?

   A.   Ports `135` and `139` shut down at the firewall.

   B.   Ports `80` and `443` shut down at the firewall.

   C.   Remove the SNMP agent from the device.

   D.   SNMP read-only security on the agent device is enabled.

39. SNMP is a protocol for controlling network infrastructure devices. What is the role of the read/write SNMP community?

   A.   Changing configuration information

   B.   Managing the SNMP management station

   C.   Viewing configuration information

   D.   Checking for problems on devices

40. Which assessment method is described as evaluating both client and server applications at the same time?

   A. Distributed

   B. Active

   C. Automated

   D. Passive

41. Which of the following would be considered an offline attack?

   A. Cracking

   B. Rainbow attack

   C. PtH

   D. Birthday attack

42. When targeting an individual, which influencing technique can be used?

   A. Training

   B. Means of dress or appearance

   C. Physical controls

   D. Technological controls

43. Which of the following steps in recovering from a malware infection is not recommended?

   A. Make a backup of your hard drive.

   B. Reinstall from the original installation media.

   C. Disconnect the computer from the network.

   D. Remove any system restore points that have been created.

44. In IPv6, which of the following is a loopback address?

   A. `fe80::/10`

   B. `::1`

   C. `fc00::/7`

   D. `fec0::/10`

45. To obtain access to the network, an attacker is attempting to crack the WEP code. They type `aireplay-ng -0 0 -a` after enabling monitor mode on `wlan0` and create a monitoring interface (`mon 0`) by typing `-c mon0` `0A:00:2B:15:22:AC 0A:00:2B:15:22:AC 0A:00:2B:15:22:AC`. What is the attacker's goal?

    A. To examine the answer to deauthentication packets that contain the WEP code, to obtain the WEP access code

    B. To determine the access point's BSSID

    C. To generate a lot of network traffic with deauthentication packets

    D. To determine the network's disguised SSID

46. What can a business do to protect itself against data loss if a phone is stolen? (Select all options that apply)

    A. Use passwords.

    B. Deploy patching.

    C. Perform a remote wipe.

    D. Use encryption.

47. A client-side scripting language is _____.

    A. ASP.NET

    B. PHP

    C. JavaScript

    D. ASP

48. A server-side scripting language is defined as which of the following?

    A. PHP

    B. JavaScript

    C. HTML

    D. SQL

49. Which of the following is used to access content that is not located in a website's root directory?

    A. Port scanning

    B. Brute force

C.   Directory traversal

D.   SQL injection

50.   Which of the following is a radio with advanced hardware and software that is used for IoT security testing?

A.   Fluke

B.   Alfa AWUS036NH

C.   Raspberry Pi

D.   HackRF One

51.   To set up a view list on their television, a homeowner uses an app on their phone. In this case, which IoT communication model is in use?

A.   Device-to-cloud

B.   Device-to-gateway

C.   Backend data sharing

D.   Device-to-device

52.   Which attack modifies data as it travels through the cloud?

A.   MITM

B.   Packet sniffing

C.   Port scanning

D.   Encryption

53.   What can changing a packet's checksum be used for?

A.   Sending URG

B.   Sending RST

C.   Evading NIDS

D.   Resetting a connection

54.   Which of the following is another name for asymmetric encryption?

A.   Public key

B.   Shared key

C.   Block

D.   Hash

55. Which of the following is the most accurate description of hashing?

    A. Non-reversible

    B. An algorithm

    C. A cryptosystem

    D. A cipher

56. Which kind of algorithm produces a message digest?

    A. Steganography

    B. Symmetric

    C. Asymmetric

    D. Hashing

57. What is the main goal of the DMCA?

    A. To provide guidance for security control systems

    B. To secure credit card processing transmission

    C. To prevent technology protections from being circumvented

    D. To develop a framework for *purpose limitations*

58. Which Act improves the accuracy and dependability of company disclosures, thereby protecting the public and investors?

    A. DPA

    B. DMCA

    C. GDPR

    D. SOX

59. Which form of social engineering attack can be classified as dumpster diving?

    A. Physical-based

    B. Paper-based

    C. Computer-based

    D. Human-based

60. Why is it not a good idea to scan using ICMP queries?

    A. Firewalls may prevent a response.

    B. The ICMP protocol is unreliable.

    C. The port may or may not be available at any given time.

    D. ICMP may not be running on the system.

61. TCP provides all but which of the following functions?

    A. In-order delivery

    B. Error detection

    C. Delivery acknowledgments

    D. Connectionless delivery

62. FTP uses which port number?

    A. 23

    B. 21

    C. 25

    D. 80

63. Which kind of assessment is described as determining the likelihood of network attacks?

    A. Credentialed

    B. Network-based

    C. Automated

    D. Host-based

64. An attacker uses what to return to a target system?

    A. Spyware

    B. Cracker

    C. Backdoor

    D. Service

65. Which file contains usernames and passwords in a domain environment?

    A. `ntds.dit`

    B. `SAM`

    C. `Passwd`

    D. `Shadow`

66. Abby receives an email claiming that her bank account has been compromised and that she needs to click a link and change her password for security purposes. Which type of attack is she being targeted with?

    A. Spam

    B. Phishing

    C. Vishing

    D. Whaling

67. To prevent potential social engineering attacks, which of the following options would help the most?

    A. Training

    B. Technology

    C. Physical controls

    D. Policies

68. Which virus kind is only executed when a specific condition is met?

    A. Multipartite

    B. Metamorphic

    C. Cavity

    D. Sparse infector

69. Bill's credit card statement shows some questionable charges. Which kind of attack has Bill been subjected to?

    A. Phishing

    B. Social engineering

    C. Bad luck

    D. Identity theft

70. A security camera captures a non-company employee trailing closely behind an employee as they approach the premises. Which kind of attack is going on?

    A. Walking

    B. Phishing

    C. Tailgating

    D. Gate running

71. Which of the following malware components is a piece of software that prevents malware from being reverse engineered or analyzed, making it difficult for security systems to detect?

    A. Dropper

    B. Payload

    C. Obfuscator

    D. Crypter

72. Which of the following could be a good way to protect yourself from ARP spoofing? (Select all options that apply)

    A. Set all NICs to promiscuous mode.

    B. Use ARPWALL.

    C. Use private VLANs.

    D. Use static ARP entries.

73. You have a Windows laptop and want to start sniffing. You download and install Wireshark, but soon realize that your NIC must be set to *promiscuous mode*. What gives you the ability to set your NIC to promiscuous mode?

    A. Installing `lmpcap`

    B. Installing `libPcap`

    C. Installing `winPcap`

    D. Installing `npcap`

74. Which of the following claims about TKIP is correct? (Select all options that apply)

    A.   WEP includes TKIP.

    B.   Every 10,000 packets, TKIP mandates a key change.

    C.   WPA includes TKIP.

    D.   TKIP prevents keys from changing during a session.

75. Which of the following statements about wireless network architecture is correct?

    A.   A BSSID is a service area supplied by a single access point.

    B.   An ESS is a service area supplied by a single AP.

    C.   An ESS is a service area offered by many APs functioning within the same network.

    D.   An ESSID is a service area supplied by numerous APs acting within the same network.

76. Which method would you use to install software that isn't available on Google Play?

    A.   Install sources that are not signed.

    B.   Install from an unidentified source.

    C.   Install from a service that isn't signed.

    D.   Install from unidentified sources.

77. Which technology can prevent session hijacking?

    A.   UDP

    B.   IPsec

    C.   IDS

    D.   TCP

78. Which of the following can prevent bad data from being entered into a form and being presented to an application?

    A.   Directory traversing

    B.   Input validation

    C.   Request filtering

    D.   Input scanning

79. A web server can be identified using _____.

    A. A banner grab

    B. Session hijacking

    C. Header analysis

    D. Traversal

80. The notion of DiD in the world of IT security refers to layering multiple controls on top of each other. Why would this be useful in defending against a session hijacking system?

    A. To improve logging capacity

    B. To satisfy auditors

    C. To give a superior defense

    D. To create interdependence between layers

81. Vehicles appear to be in numerous places at once in this VANET attack, generating traffic congestion and severely limiting data usage. Which of the following statements most accurately describes this attack?

    A. Rolling code

    B. Sybil

    C. BlueBorne

    D. Side-channel

82. Cloud technologies are used to accomplish which of the following?

    A. Increase management options

    B. Transfer legal responsibility of data to a third party

    C. Offload operations onto a third party

    D. Cut costs

83. Which kind of cloud service would host email and provide related security services?

    A. SaaS

    B. PaaS

    C. SSaS

    D. IaaS

84. Who is legally liable for data stored on the cloud?

    A. The CSP

    B. The client

    C. The IT department of the client

    D. The consumer

85. Why would someone not develop their own private cloud?

    A. To maintain universal access

    B. To offload technical support

    C. To increase availability

    D. To reduce costs

86. Which of the following services would be offered as a SaaS?

    A. Firewalls

    B. Email

    C. Applications

    D. AD

87. Which kind of algorithm produces a message digest?

    A. Steganography

    B. Symmetric

    C. Asymmetric

    D. Hashing

88. The owner of a public key keeps it in a _____ on their local computer.

    A. Private key

    B. Hash

    C. PKI system

    D. Smart card

89. Because of _____, symmetric key systems face key distribution issues.

    A. The type of data

    B. The number of keys

    C. Generation of key pairs

    D. The amount of data

90. Which of the following is the most accurate description of PGP?

    A. A symmetric algorithm

    B. A way of encrypting data in a reversible method

    C. A type of key

    D. A key escrow system

91. Which kind of cloud service might be used to create an application?

    A. BaaS

    B. PaaS

    C. SaaS

    D. IaaS

92. Which of the following would be a compelling incentive to migrate to a cloud-based environment?

    A. Reduced costs

    B. Improved performance

    C. Easier forensics

    D. Increased redundancy

93. To set permissions on content on a website, which of the following is used?

    A. HIDS

    B. ACE

    C. ALS

    D. ACL

94. On a web server or application, what could be utilized to monitor application problems and violations?

    A. NIDS

    B. HIDS

    C. HIPS

    D. Logs

95. Which of the following is a cookie security attribute?

    A. Encrypt

    B. Secure

    C. HttpOnly

    D. Domain

96. What does a POODLE assault aim for?

    A. TLS

    B. SSL

    C. AES

    D. VPN

97. What is the purpose of remote wipes?

    A. To reset a device to its factory settings

    B. To wipe a device's data completely

    C. To remove sensitive information from a remote system, such as contacts

    D. To place cookies and gadgets on your computer

98. You're looking at the physical configuration of a target's wireless network. On the site survey, you observe omnidirectional antenna access ports in the building's corners. Which of the following statements about this setup is correct? (Select all options that apply)

    A. The deployment of dipole antennas could increase the site's security.

    B. Sniffing from outside the building could make the place vulnerable.

    C. The usage of directional antennas may help to increase the site's security.

    D. Sniffing from outside the building does not pose a threat to the site.

99. You're attempting to deliver a payload to an internal target, but it's protected by an IDS. You're concerned about completing your assignment without arousing the attention of the IDS monitoring crew. Which of the following methods could be used? (Select two)

   A.   Session splicing

   B.   Overwhelming the network with bogus attacks

   C.   Session hijacking

   D.   Ensuring that traffic between you and the host is encrypted

100. Which malware evolves with each infection?

   A.   Cavity

   B.   Metamorphic

   C.   Polymorphic

   D.   Stealth

101. What benefits does a vulnerability scan aim to deliver to people who run it?

   A.   A process to expose vulnerabilities

   B.   An opportunity to find open ports

   C.   A means to diagram a network

   D.   A proxy attack

102. A proxy is used to _____ in social engineering.

   A.   Assist in scanning

   B.   Perform a scan

   C.   Keep an attacker's origin concealed

   D.   Automate the detection of vulnerabilities

103. Email campaigns known as _____ can be carried out using social engineering.

   A.   Splashing

   B.   Spamming

   C.   Phishing

   D.   Vishing

104. If you were trying to locate where the SAM database was stored, where would you locate it?

    A.   `C:\ProgramData\SAM`

    B.   `C:\Windows\System32\Config`

    C.   `C:\Windows\SAM`

    D.   `./root/shadow`

105. What is the term for hiding secret information within (or even on top of) a non-secret document or another medium to prevent detection?

    A.   Symbolic links

    B.   Rootkit

    C.   Steganography

    D.   Hidden attributes

106. If you use precomputed hashes to make an attack, what is the attack called?

    A.   Rainbow tables

    B.   PtH

    C.   NetBIOS

    D.   ADS

107. Which vulnerability assessment solution is said to be *installed in the resources of the organization*?

    A.   Product-based

    B.   Inference-based

    C.   Service-based

    D.   Tree-based

108. Which vulnerability assessment method is *provided by third parties*?

    A.   Service-based

    B.   Internal-based

    C.   Tree-based

    D.   External-based

109. Which kind of tool for assessment is used to focus on web servers and databases?

 A.   Host-based

 B.   Application layer-based

 C.   Scope-based

 D.   Depth-based

110. For SNMP to function, which ports does it use?

 A.   389 and 160

 B.   160 and 161

 C.   161 and 162

 D.   160 and 162

111. Which function is performed by SMTP?

 A.   File transfers

 B.   Monitoring network equipment

 C.   Sending email messages

 D.   Status information transmission

112. To view NetBIOS information, which command should you use?

 A.   nbtstat

 B.   netstat

 C.   nmap

 D.   telnet

113. A network's clocks are synchronized using _____.

 A.   FTP

 B.   NetBIOS

 C.   SAM

 D.   NTP

114. When using the nmap -sP command, what does it mean?

 A.   The most popular ports are scanned.

 B.   A port redirect attack is being simulated.

C.   A ping sweep is being used to scan.

D.   Private IP addresses are scanned.

115. If a target responds with an RST flag to a half-open scan, then...

A.   A Linux system is the target.

B.   A Windows system is the target.

C.   An open port is the target.

D.   A closed port is the target.

116. Which law mandates the use of a common national number by all providers, plans, and employees?

A.   The FISMA

B.   The HIPAA

C.   DPA

D.   GDPR

117. Which hacking step or phase follows reconnaissance?

A.   Maintaining access

B.   Gaining access

C.   Clearing tracks

D.   Scanning

118. Which kind of hacker is regarded as one who hacks without fear of legal repercussions?

A.   Suicide hacker

B.   Black hat

C.   Gray hat

D.   Script kiddie

119. Which form of attack was the 2021 SolarWinds attack, in which attackers were able to infect software that was then sold to customers?

A.   Insider

B.   Close-in

    C. Passive

    D. Active

    E. Distributed

120. Which answer best describes how Traceroute works?

    A. It determines the location of said router using a protocol that is refused by the gateway.

    B. It determines the number of hops from the sender to the router using the TTL value in an ICMP message.

    C. It sends a specially constructed IP packet to a router to find out how many hops there are between the sender and the destination network.

    D. It learns the name of a router and OS by sending an ICMP `destination unreachable` message.

121. Which are the four regional internet registries?

    A. APNIC, MOSTNIC, ARIN, RIPE NCC

    B. APNIC, LACNIC, ARIN, RIPE NCC

    C. APNIC, PICNIC, NANIC, ARIN

    D. APNIC, PICNIC, NANIC, RIPE NCC

122. It would be *what* kind of tool if an assessment tool is focused on OSs and apps?

    A. Application layer-based

    B. Host-based

    C. Depth-based

    D. Scope-based

123. Which type of scanner is used when the location and data from a scan are stored on a single system?

    A. Cluster-based

    B. Agent-based

    C. Network-based

    D. Proxy-based

124. Within your infrastructure, you install a new switch. What should be your initial step in securing this system?

    A.   Uplink port disabled

    B.   Broadcast storm protection enabled

    C.   Default password changed

    D.   Serial port disabled

125. You create a password based on an *Avengers* character. It has been discovered that your account has been hacked. Which kind of attack did you most likely face?

    A.   Rule-based

    B.   Brute-force

    C.   Syllable

    D.   Dictionary

126. The tendency of humans to behave in set patterns is known as _____.

    A.   Habits

    B.   Repetition

    C.   Piggybacking

    D.   Primacy

127. Using _____ when speaking with a victim can make an attack simpler.

    A.   Keywords

    B.   Eye contact

    C.   Threats

    D.   Jargon

128. Which tactic might an attacker employ to sway a victim?

    A.   Tailgating

    B.   Acting as tech support

    C.   Piggybacking

    D.   Name-dropping

129. The following Wireshark filter is used: `tcp.srcport == 80 &&ipc.src == 192.168.1.1`

    Which of the following statements about the capture filter is correct?

    A.   All traffic from `192.168.1.1` intended for port `80` will be displayed in the results.

    B.   All HTTP traffic to `192.168.1.1` will be displayed in the results.

    C.   All HTTP traffic from `192.168.1.1` will be displayed in the results.

    D.   Because of the incorrect syntax, no results will be displayed.

130. Lois tries to make a phone call on her cell phone, but it is unresponsive. She switches it off and on again after a few minutes of effort. The phone disconnects and becomes unresponsive again during her next call. Which Bluetooth attack is currently active?

    A.   Bluejacking

    B.   Bluesniffing

    C.   Bluesmacking

    D.   Bluesnarfing

131. Which of the following can be used to thwart a malware-delivered MITB attack?

    A.   Rooting a device

    B.   Anti-spyware

    C.   Anti-virus

    D.   Using Firefox

132. Which command would you use to get banner data from a website on port `80`?

    A.   `nc 192.168.10.27 -p -l 80`

    B.   `nc 192.168.10.27 80`

    C.   `nc 192.168.19.27 443`

    D.   `nc 192.168.10.27 -p 80`

133. How does a brute-force attack work?

    A.   Uses hashes as a comparison

    B.   Attempts all possible character combinations

    C.   Attempts words from the dictionary

    D.   Captures hashes

134. What is the Telnet command for retrieving header information from a web server?

    A.   `telnet < website name > -port:443`

    B.   `telnet < website name > 80`

    C.   `telnet < website name > 443`

    D.   `telnet < website name > -port:80`

135. What kind of information about a web application could be viewed using the Wayback Machine?

    A.   Where you can find job posts

    B.   Websites

    C.   Websites that have been archived

    D.   Websites' backup copies

136. What may be useful in preventing unauthorized personnel from viewing content on a web server?

    A.   Redirection

    B.   Encryption

    C.   Permissions

    D.   Firewalls

137. _____ is a popular attack against web servers and web applications.

    A.   Input validation

    B.   Banner grab

    C.   Buffer overflow

    D.   Buffer validations

138. In a cloud-based firewall, which port is normally open for HTTPS?

    A.   `110`

    B.   `25`

C. 80

D. 443

139. Which system is employed as a traffic bottleneck and may be offered as IaaS?

A. Bastion host

B. IDS

C. SNMP host

D. DMZ

140. At which layer of the OSI model do you think a cloud-based solution would work?

A. Layer 1

B. Layer 2

C. Layer 3

D. Layer 4

141. Which kind of firewall analyzes traffic and would be included in an IaaS solution?

A. Circuit-level

B. Packet filtering

C. Stateful inspection

D. NIDS

142. What may be used in place of a URL to get around some of the firewalls that protect cloud-based online applications?

A. Encryption

B. Stateful inspection

C. NIDS

D. IP address

143. In which phase of the Cyber Kill Chain methodology do attackers construct a path through which they can connect and send data back and forth?

A. **Command and control (C&C)**

B. Delivery

    C.   Weaponization

    D.   Actions on objectives

144. Which OS does SSL rely on?

    A.   AES

    B.   PKI

    C.   **Data Encryption Standard (DES)**

    D.   **Triple DES (3DES)**

145. Encryption and other procedures in IPsec take place at which layer of the OSI model?

    A.   Level 1

    B.   Level 2

    C.   Level 3

    D.   Level 4

146. What does the AH protocol perform in IPsec?

    A.   Encryption

    B.   Data security

    C.   Authentication services

    D.   Header security

147. When should SSL be used to secure data?

    A.   On a flash drive

    B.   On a hard drive

    C.   On Bluetooth

    D.   During transmission

148. IPsec employs which of the following?

    A.   PKI

    B.   SSL

    C.   AES

    D.   DES

Answer key

This answer key has been provided to help you confirm the answers to the test questions:

1. A – If you've been given permission or have been invited to do so
2. B – IoT
3. D – XMAS scan
4. A – User and machine name identification
5. A – Active
6. D – LM
7. B – Viruses
8. B – Worm
9. C – The attacker will see message 2
10. A; D – WPA2 encrypts with TKIP and AES; WEP employs RC4-based shared key encryption
11. B – Admin/root access with privileges
12. A – Session hijacking
13. A – Exploiting the HVAC
14. C – Drive encryption
15. C – Shared key cryptography
16. B – CA
17. B – Makes it possible for applications to communicate with one another
18. B – Li-Fi
19. B – Cookie
20. C – Code that's intended to be run on a server
21. C – Allows a user on a system to have root access
22. D – A legitimate MAC address has been faked by the employee
23. C – ARP poisoning to allow you to see messages from Host A to Host B and vice versa
24. C – Overt channel
25. B – Manipulate human behavior
26. B – A spam filter
27. D – Security

28. A – By trying all possible characters and combinations

29. C – Temporal

30. C – Active

31. B – `PsGetSid`

32. A – `NSlookup`

33. A – The system is vulnerable to `null` sessions since SMB is enabled

34. C – WHOIS

35. A – Notify your company right away

36. A – White hat

37. C – `nmap -sS -paranoid`

38. C – Remove the SNMP agent from the device

39. A – Changing the configuration information

40. A – Distributed

41. B – Rainbow attack

42. B – Means of dress or appearance

43. A – Make a backup of your hard drive

44. B – `::1`

45. C – To generate a lot of network traffic with deauthentication packets

46. A; C; D – Use passwords; Perform a remote wipe; Use encryption

47. C – JavaScript

48. A – PHP

49. C – Directory traversal

50. D – HackRF One

51. B – Device-to-gateway

52. A – MITM

53. C – Evading an NIDS

54. A – Public key

55. A – Non-reversible

56. D – Hashing

57. C – Prevent technology protections from being circumvented

58. D – SOX

59. D – Human-based
60. B – The ICMP protocol is unreliable
61. D – Connectionless delivery
62. B – `21`
63. B – Network-based
64. C – Backdoor
65. A – `ntds.dit`
66. B – Phishing
67. A – Training
68. D – Sparse infector
69. D – Identity theft
70. C – Tailgating
71. A – Dropper
72. B; C; D – Use ARPWALL; Use Private VLANs; Use static ARP entries
73. C – Installing `winPcap`
74. A – WEP includes TKIP
75. B; D – An ESS is a service area supplied by a single AP; An ESSID is a service area supplied by numerous APs acting within the same network
76. B – Install from an unidentified source
77. B – IPsec
78. B – Input validation
79. A – A banner grab
80. C – To give a superior defense
81. B – Sybil
82. A; C; D – Increase management options; Offload operations onto a third party; Cut costs
83. A – SaaS
84. B – The client
85. D – To reduce costs
86. B – Email
87. D – Hashing

88. C – PKI system

89. B – The number of keys

90. B – A way of encrypting data in a reversible method

91. B – PaaS

92. A; B; D – Reduced costs; Improved performance; Increased redundancy

93. D – ACL

94. D – Logs

95. B; C; D – Secure; HttpOnly; Domain

96. B – SSL

97. B – Wipe a device's data completely

98. A – The deployment of dipole antennas could increase the site's security

99. A; D – Session splicing; Ensuring that traffic between you and the host is encrypted

100. B – Metamorphic

101. A – A process to expose vulnerabilities

102. C – Keep an attacker's origin concealed

103. C – Phishing

104. B – `C:\Windows\System32\Config`

105. C – Steganography

106. A – Rainbow tables

107. A – Product-based

108. A – Service-based

109. B – Application layer-based

110. C – `161` and `162`

111. C – Sending email messages

112. A – `nbtstat`

113. D – NTP

114. C – A ping sweep is being used to scan

115. D – A closed port is the target

116. B – HIPAA

117. D – Scanning

118. A – Suicide hacker

119. E – Distributed

120. B – It determines the number of hops from the sender to the router using the TTL value in an ICMP message

121. B – APNIC, LACNIC, ARIN, RIPE NCC

122. D – Scope-based

123. B – Agent-based

124. C – Default password changed

125. D – Dictionary

126. A – Habits

127. A – Keywords

128. D – Name-dropping

129. C – All HTTP traffic from `192.168.1.1` will be displayed in the results

130. C; D – Bluesmacking; Bluesnarfing

131. C – Anti-virus

132. B – `nc 192.168.10.27 80`

133. B – Attempts all possible character combinations

134. B – `telnet < website name > 80`

135. C – Websites that have been archived

136. B – Encryption

137. C – Buffer overflow

138. D – `443`

139. A – Bastion host

140. C; D – Layer 3; Layer 4

141. C – Stateful inspection

142. D – IP address

143. A – C&C

144. B – PKI

145. C – Level 3

146. C – Authentication services

147. D – During transmission

148. A – PKI

I hope you feel more prepared for the CEH exam having now worked through all these questions. Review ones you may have missed and use them as a launching point to further study and understand the concepts being taught.

Assessments

In the following pages, we will review all the practice questions from each of the chapters in this book and provide the correct answers.

Chapter 1 – Understanding Ethical Hacking

1. A. – To detect security flaws before they are exploited by attackers
2. B. – Concealing activity
3. B. – A rootkit
4. E. – Passive

Chapter 2 – Introduction to Reconnaissance

1. D. – To avoid detection while gathering data on a target for potential vulnerabilities
2. A. – WHOIS
3. C. – Netcraft
4. B. – Scanning

Chapter 3 – Reconnaissance – a Deeper Dive

1. B. – Hostnames and IP addresses
2. A. – Investigating a target
3. C. – MX
4. C. – Competitive analysis

Chapter 4 – Scanning Networks

1. B. – Passive OS fingerprinting
2. D. – Port, network, and vulnerability
3. D. – Detecting services/applications that are listening
4. C. – Proxy chain

Chapter 5 – Enumeration

1. A. – User and machine name identification
2. D. – Sending email messages
3. C. – nbtstat
4. B. – NTP

Chapter 6 – Vulnerability Analysis

1. B. – Active scanning
2. C. – Active
3. C. – Product-based
4. D. – Agent-based

Chapter 7 – System Hacking

1. C. – NTFS
2. A. – Auditpol
3. B. – Vertical escalation
4. A. – A keylogger

Chapter 8 – Social Engineering

1. B. – To take advantage of human behavior
2. B. – Email
3. C. – Employee training
4. C. – Frequent, ongoing security education

Chapter 9 – Malware and Other Digital Attacks

1. C. – It's a file integrity checker that alerts you when a system file is changed.

2. B. – APT

3. B. – Dropper

4. C. – Trojan

Chapter 10 – Sniffing and Evading IDS, Firewalls, and Honeypots

1. F. – SSH

2. A. and D. – ARP spoofing and MAC flooding

3. C. – Finding the sniffer on the network is somewhat impossible.

4. C. and D. – Enabling DHCP snooping on a switch and using port security on a switch

Chapter 11 – Hacking Wireless Networks

1. A. – An attacker creates an access point for clients to connect to within a network range

2. A. and B. – The access point's MAC address and the SSID

3. A. – WPA2 is a superior encryption option to WEP

4. D. – 802.11n

Chapter 12 – Hacking Mobile Platforms

1. D. – Data security on lost or stolen devices

2. D. – Taking control of a device by gaining root access

3. D. – Linux

4. C. – It diminishes it.

Chapter 13 – Hacking Web Servers and Web Apps

1. D. – Code designed to be run server-side
2. A. – A cookie
3. B. – JavaScript
4. A. – Directory traversal

Chapter 14 – Hacking IoT and OT

1. C. – The access gateway layer
2. A. – Information gathering
3. A., B., and D. – Enabling lockout features for excessive login attempts, disabling guest and demo accounts, and disabling telnet
4. A. – MultiPing

Chapter 15 – Cloud Computing

1. D. – LaaS
2. C. – Software hosting
3. B. – Networks
4. B. – Four

Chapter 16 – Using Cryptography

1. C. – A public key
2. D. – Securing transmitted data
3. B. – MD5
4. A. – Shared key cryptography

Index

S

Packt.com

Subscribe to our online digital library for full access to over 7,000 books and videos, as well as industry leading tools to help you plan your personal development and advance your career. For more information, please visit our website.

Why subscribe?

- Spend less time learning and more time coding with practical eBooks and Videos from over 4,000 industry professionals
- Improve your learning with Skill Plans built especially for you
- Get a free eBook or video every month
- Fully searchable for easy access to vital information
- Copy and paste, print, and bookmark content

Did you know that Packt offers eBook versions of every book published, with PDF and ePub files available? You can upgrade to the eBook version at packt.com and as a print book customer, you are entitled to a discount on the eBook copy. Get in touch with us at customercare@packtpub.com for more details.

At www.packt.com, you can also read a collection of free technical articles, sign up for a range of free newsletters, and receive exclusive discounts and offers on Packt books and eBooks.

Other Books You May Enjoy

If you enjoyed this book, you may be interested in these other books by Packt:

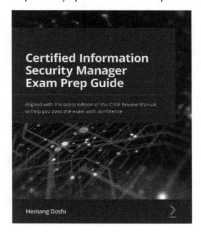

Certified Information Security Manager Exam Prep Guide

Hemangi Doshi

ISBN: 9781801074100

- Understand core exam objectives to pass the CISM exam with confidence
- Create and manage your organization's information security policies and procedures with ease
- Broaden your knowledge of the organization's security strategy designing
- Manage information risk to an acceptable level based on risk appetite in order to meet organizational goals and objectives
- Find out how to monitor and control incident management procedures
- Discover how to monitor activity relating to data classification and data access

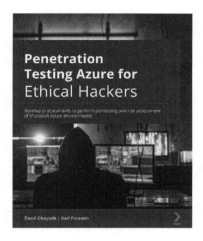

Penetration Testing Azure for Ethical Hackers

David Okeyode | Karl Fosaaen

ISBN: 9781839212932

- Identify how administrators misconfigure Azure services, leaving them open to exploitation
- Understand how to detect cloud infrastructure, service, and application misconfigurations
- Explore processes and techniques for exploiting common Azure security issues
- Use on-premises networks to pivot and escalate access within Azure
- Diagnose gaps and weaknesses in Azure security implementations
- Understand how attackers can escalate privileges in Azure AD

Packt is searching for authors like you

If you're interested in becoming an author for Packt, please visit `authors.packtpub.com` and apply today. We have worked with thousands of developers and tech professionals, just like you, to help them share their insight with the global tech community. You can make a general application, apply for a specific hot topic that we are recruiting an author for, or submit your own idea.

Share Your Thoughts

Now you've finished *Certified Ethical Hacker (CEH) v12 312-50 Exam Guide*, we'd love to hear your thoughts! Scan the QR code below to go straight to the Amazon review page for this book and share your feedback or leave a review on the site that you purchased it from.

https://packt.link/r/1801813094

Your review is important to us and the tech community and will help us make sure we're delivering excellent quality content.

Made in the USA
Middletown, DE
21 December 2023